Second Edition

Youth at Risk and Youth Justice

A Canadian Overview

John Winterdyk & Russell Smandych

OXFORD
UNIVERSITY PRESS

OXFORD
UNIVERSITY PRESS

Oxford University Press is a department of the University of Oxford.
It furthers the University's objective of excellence in research, scholarship,
and education by publishing worldwide. Oxford is a registered trade mark of
Oxford University Press in the UK and in certain other countries.

Published in Canada by
Oxford University Press
8 Sampson Mews, Suite 204,
Don Mills, Ontario M3C 0H5 Canada

www.oupcanada.com

Library and Archives Canada Cataloguing in Publication

Youth at risk and youth justice : a Canadian overview / edited
by John Winterdyk, Russell Smandych. — Second edition.

Includes bibliographical references and index.
ISBN 978-0-19-901821-5 (paperback)

1. Juvenile delinquency—Canada—Textbooks. 2. Juvenile
justice, Administration of—Canada—Textbooks. I. Smandych,
Russell Charles, author, editor II. Winterdyk, John,
author, editor

HV9108.Y67 2016   364.360971   C2015-908514-4

Cover image—Embassy of Imagination (www.embassyofimagination.com; embassyofimagination@gmail.com).
Chapter opening images—Chapter 1: Corepics VOF/Shutterstock; Chapter 2: alzay/iStockphoto; Chapter 3: Tannis Toohey/GetStock.com; Chapter 4: © Mark Harvey/Alamy Stock Photo; Chapter 5: arindambanerjee/Shutterstock; Chapter 6: 1000 Words/Shutterstock; Chapter 7: monkeybusinessimages/iStockphoto; Chapter 8: © Steve Atkins Photography/Alamy Stock Photo; Chapter 9: Rick Madonik/GetStock.com; Chapter 10: arindambanerjee/Shutterstock; Chapter 11: Photo taken by anthropologist, Kathleen Buddle on the film set of Ervin Chartrand's film "Sister" (2008, Working Sister Productions). The photo features actors Sterling Muskego and Travis M Boyko; Chapter 12: © Image Source/Alamy Stock Photo; Chapter 13: © Ethel Wolvovitz/Alamy Stock Photo; Chapter 14: defotoberg/Shutterstock; Chapter 15: © Kathy deWitt/Alamy Stock Photo; Chapter 16: THE CANADIAN PRESS/Nathan Denette.

Oxford University Press is committed to our environment.
Wherever possible, our books are printed on paper which comes from
responsible sources.

Printed and bound in Canada

2 3 4 — 19 18 17

Contents

Part I   History, Trends, and Legislation   1

Part II   Understanding Contemporary Youth Crime and Justice: Theories and Perspectives   119

Contributor Bios

Sibylle Artz is a professor in child and youth care at the University of Victoria. Her research focuses on youth aggression with an emphasis on girls' use of violence. She has undertaken numerous community-based collaborative research projects, including community-based violence prevention; a community-based approach for dealing with violent youth who are under the age of 12; collaborative work undertaken with service providers on developing girls' custody units; and a project that involved three Vancouver Island communities focused on developing a gender-sensitive community-needs assessment tool for supporting at-risk girls and young women. Dr Artz has also published more than 55 refereed articles and book chapters, written two books—*Feeling as a Way of Knowing* (1994) and *Sex, Power and the Violent School Girl* (1997)—and co-edited a third book, *Working Relationally with Girls* (2004), with Dr Marie Hoskins. In addition to her many other honours and awards, she was chosen, in 1998, as Academic of the Year by the Confederation of University Faculty Associations of British Columbia and received, in 2004, the Award of Distinction for Research from the McCreary Youth Foundation of Vancouver. Dr Artz is currently participating as the Canadian partner in an international research project on girls and aggression that involves six European countries and in research focusing on intimate partner violence.

Stephen W. Baron is a professor in the Department of Sociology at Queen's University. His research focuses primarily on homeless street youth and crime and substance abuse. He is concerned with how various criminological theories can be used to help us understand these forms of behaviour among the homeless street youth population. His work on these types of issues has appeared in a variety of academic journals, including *Criminology*, *Journal of Research in Crime and Delinquency*, *Justice Quarterly*, *Journal of Criminal Justice*, and *Deviant Behavior*.

Raymond R. Corrado is a professor in the School of Criminology at Simon Fraser University in Burnaby, BC, and the co-director of the British Columbia Centre for Social Responsibility. His main areas of research focus on developmental and life-course criminology, youth violence, Aboriginal youth in conflict with the law, youth justice, and mental health and law. He has published over 100 journal articles, book chapters, and government reports, and has co-authored seven books. He is currently a visiting fellow at Clare Hall College and the Institute of Criminology at Cambridge University and is in the Faculty of Law at the University of Bergen in Norway.

Louis-Georges Cournoyer is currently associate professor at the School of Criminology of the Université de Montréal. He has a PhD in psychology, has been a psychologist for 25 years, and has worked with various clientele, especially with high-risk young people and families at Centre jeunesse de Montréal—Institut universitaire (CJM-IU), with which he is now affiliated as a researcher. His research interests centre on the rehabilitation processes and effectiveness of treatments for youth offenders and drug addicts. He has conducted a major study with Jacques Dionne on the impact of the Montreal Youth Centre's intensive probation with treatment, which has since been acknowledged in Quebec as representing an important approach for rehabilitating youth offenders.

Jacques Dionne has been for 20 years an educator, psycho-educator, chief of unit, program director, and research and professional staff-training director of Boscoville 2000 in Montreal (an institution for youth offenders). He was full professor at the Université du Québec en Outaouais, associate professor at UQO, and researcher at l'Institut de recherche pour l'adaptation des jeunes du CJM-IU. Dr Dionne specializes in staff training, program development, and evaluation for youth offenders and adolescents in difficulty. Over the past 20 years, he has also been the leader of several international collaboration projects on rehabilitation, especially in Chile and Brazil.

Jordan Diplock is a research analyst with the Royal Canadian Mounted Police. He also teaches part time in the School of Criminology and Criminal Justice at the University of the Fraser Valley. He has co-authored numerous reports and articles relating to illicit drug production and use.

Sarah Gilliss is an instructor in the Police Foundations and Criminal Justice Programs in the Social Sciences Department of the New Brunswick Community College in Miramichi, New Brunswick. She has had experience on the front line as a youth worker and correctional officer working with youth in the youth criminal justice system. She is a facilitator for a national youth engagement project and is currently running weekly groups with the Youth Matters chapter inside the New Brunswick Youth Centre in collaboration with some of her students from the college.

Michèle Goyette is consulting director at l'Association des centres jeunesse du Québec (Youth Centers Association of Quebec) and has been director of specialized services for young offenders at Centre jeunesse de Montréal—Institut universitaire. She has worked for 35 years mainly as a criminologist or manager for young offenders' services. She participated in the development of different programs for young offenders and also collaborated with Quebec's major research partners, working on the provincial organization and orientation of services. A member of the board of directors of Quebec's Society for Criminology and of the Child Welfare League of Canada, she uses every possible platform in Quebec and Canada to promote the rehabilitation and social reintegration of young offenders.

Ross Green is a judge of the Provincial Court of Saskatchewan, sitting in Yorkton. Before his appointment to the bench in 2004, he practised criminal and family law with legal aid for many years. He was appointed as Queen's Counsel by the Saskatchewan Minister of Justice in 2001. He holds bachelor degrees in commerce and law from the University of Saskatchewan and an LLM degree from the University of Manitoba. He is also the author of *Justice in Aboriginal Communities: Sentencing Alternatives* (1998) and the co-author, with Kearney Healy, of *Tough on Kids: Rethinking Approaches to Youth Justice* (2003). His first book was nominated for a Saskatchewan Book Award in the first book category, and his second received the Saskatchewan Book Award for Scholarly Writing.

Hirsch Greenberg is the department head and practicum coordinator in the Department of Justice Studies, University of Regina. He has spent the past 41 years in Saskatchewan working for community-based organizations in Regina and File Hills (First Nations communities) in various roles: line staff, administrator, and volunteer. His research mostly engages community-based organizations and government projects dealing with homelessness, specialized courts, community policing, mental health, and substance abuse. He is the chair of the Collaborative Centre for Justice and Safety at the University of Regina. He is an active board member of the Regina Alternative Measures Program. He received the Regina YMCA Peace Medal in 2009 and was recognized by the Correctional Service of Canada in 2010 for his work in restorative justice. He has published chapters in a number of textbooks and is currently working on a full textbook on the "Hidden Face of Crisis Intervention." Hirsch has a BA in sociology and a master's in social work from the University of Regina.

Jana Grekul is associate professor of sociology and director of the (BA) criminology program at the University of Alberta. Her research interests include street and prison gangs, in particular Aboriginal gangs, and the study of punishment within the criminal justice system. Gender and the "doing of gender" in these environments is an important component of her research. Other research interests include pedagogy in the university classroom and, more recently, impaired driving and traffic safety culture. She teaches a variety of sociology and criminology courses and is co-author of *Sociology Matters*, *Sociology*, and *Criminology*.

Pierre Hamel worked as a lawyer for many years in the Litigation Department at the Centre jeunesse de Montréal–Institut Universitaire. Being a specialist in juvenile delinquency policy, he was responsible for the reference manual guiding the application of the Youth Criminal Justice Act for youth centres throughout Quebec. He also authored a 2009 book on the application of the YCJA in Quebec and was director of the Legal Department of the Association des centres jeunesse du Québec, from 2011 to 2013, where he played a key role in preserving the philosophy of the Quebec model of juvenile delinquency intervention. As of February 2013, he was nominated as judge of the Cour du Québec, chambre de la jeunesse (Provincial Court of Quebec, Youth Division).

Bryan Hogeveen is a professor and joined the Department of Sociology at the University of Alberta in 2002. He is co-author (along with his wife, Dr Joanne Minaker, MacEwan University) of *Youth, Crime and Society: Issues of Power and Justice* (2009). He has published widely on his academic interests, which include justice, violence, epistemology, youth crime, martial arts in/and society, continental philosophy, and the sociology of sport. He is the editor-in-chief of the international interdisciplinary journal *Societies* (http://www.mdpi.com/journal/societies). His Social Sciences and Humanities Research Council of Canada–funded research project examines the impact of governmental economic restructuring on the marginalized inner-city residents of Edmonton and Winnipeg. Dr Hogeveen has a forthcoming book with McGill-Queen's University Press titled *Cold Cities: Care and Control in the Inner City* (with Dr Andrew Woolford, University of Manitoba). He is the father of three incredible children, coaches hockey, and teaches Brazilian Jiu-Jitsu and submission grappling at the University of Alberta.

Bruce MacLaurin is an assistant professor at the Faculty of Social Work, University of Calgary, and a senior researcher at Wood's Homes. He has been a co-investigator on the three cycles of the Canadian Incidence Study of Reported Child Abuse and Neglect (CIS), as well as the principal investigator for provincial/territorial studies in British Columbia, Alberta, Saskatchewan, and Northwest Territories. In collaboration with Catherine Worthington and community agencies, he was a co-investigator on the Calgary Youth, Health and the Street Study funded by the Canadian Institutes of Health Research. His research and publishing has focused on child maltreatment, child welfare service delivery and outcomes, youth at risk, and street-involved youth. He has more than 15 years of front-line and management experience in non-profit children's services in Alberta and Ontario.

Chris McCormick is a professor and a co-founder of the Criminology and Criminal Justice Department at St Thomas University in Fredericton, New Brunswick. His research is in areas of cultural criminology, and he teaches courses on wrongful conviction, crime and media, and visual criminology. He has published in the areas of corporate crime, media studies, and criminological theory, and his most recent book is *Constructing Danger: The Mis/Representation of Crime in the News* (2010).

Susan McIntyre has approximately 30 years experience working with families and children in the treatment of juvenile justice arenas, which has allowed her to develop expertise in program management and development. She has a strong track record in identifying and meeting the needs of the organization and was responsible for the start-up of 30+ operations in the private and public sectors, guiding them from the concept stage through to full implementation and evaluation. Susan is recognized for her expertise on child sexual abuse and child sexual exploitation, and she is an international research and policy advisor. Susan is also the president of a retrospective research firm called the Hindsight Group, a leading-edge research and project management firm (see www.hindsightgroup.com).

Anne Miller is a credentialed evaluator through the Canadian Evaluation Society and an accredited social return on investment (SROI) practitioner and trainer through the Social Value Network International. She also holds a master's degree in public policy and public administration from Concordia University in Montreal. Overall, Anne has a passion for understanding impact and demonstrating value in the community sector. She has led numerous SROI analyses and program evaluations in fields such as crime prevention, young pregnancy, food security, healthy living, sexual exploitation, youth at risk, financial literacy, and homelessness/housing. She is also passionate about good research. She has contributed to research around emerging policies and has helped agencies create a sound basis in research and best practice for their programming. Anne runs her own consulting company called Constellation Consulting Group (see www.constellationconsulting.ca).

Joanne C. Minaker is a sociologist, qualitative researcher, and mother of three. She is an associate professor at MacEwan University in Edmonton, Alberta. Her interests focus on care, human connection, and social justice. An emphasis on knowledge for social transformation resonates deeply and underscores her scholarly, creative, and pedagogical work, which includes the book *Youth, Crime and Society: Issues of Power and Justice* (2009), co-authored with Bryan Hogeveen, a

2013 TEDx Talk, Just Care, where she spoke about the transformative power of caring (http://tedxtalks.ted.com/video/Just-care-Joanne-Minaker-at-TED), and numerous articles that identify the processes through which marginalized women and criminalized youth are excluded, silenced, and dehumanized. She is currently engaged in a research project about Care and Marginalized Young Mothering. In 2013, Joanne founded Cared Humanity, a care-based education resource and community dedicated to supporting individuals and groups in the fundamental human work of self-care and practising care for others. She blogs about her adventures in care at caredhumanity.com.

Brenda Morrison is co-chair of the Safe Schools and Communities Special Interest Group of the American Education Research Association and a member of the Scientific Committee of the International Observatory of Violence in Schools. She has presented papers at UNESCO, in Paris, and for the House of Lords in London and chaired many panels on restorative justice and schools for the World Congress of Criminology as well as for a number of other associations. She is a research partner with PREVNet (Promoting Relationships and Eliminating Violence Network) within Canada's Networks of Centres of Excellence. In British Columbia, she is a member of the Working Group for Social Responsibility and Collaborative Learning in Education. In her home community, she is an active board member for the North Shore Restorative Justice Society.

Rhonda Nelson received her PhD in educational psychology exploring the potential for change in self-perception as a learner among youth in their period of post-involvement with criminal behaviour. She accomplished this while serving as the director of education for the Paul Dojack Youth Centre, a custody facility. An educator, she has focused on educational programming and supports for children and youth at risk in learning and life throughout the previous roles she has held within school divisions and government. As a sessional instructor for the University of Regina, Rhonda taught both educational psychology and core education courses to pre-service teachers. She is currently the executive director of the Starbright Children's Development Centre (Central Okanagan Child Development Association), a non-profit agency that provides early intervention for children with developmental special needs from birth to school entry.

Colleen Pawlychka is a doctoral student at Simon Fraser University, School of Criminology. She teaches as a sessional instructor in the areas of restorative justice, corrections, the Canadian criminal justice system, and the sociology of crime and deviance. Her current research interests include the impact of psychological trauma on the brain and behaviour and its role in the generation of anti-social and criminal behaviour, and she has conducted research in the areas of presentation and implementation of restorative justice practices and implementation of RJ on youth justice committees. She is a facilitator and co-facilitator of experiential workshops in conflict resolution and RJ, and a participant in RJ circles in a BC federal institution. Colleen graduated from the University of Winnipeg with an interdisciplinary BA, Honours, degree focusing on restorative justice, and from the University of Manitoba with a master's degree in sociology.

Adrienne M.F. Peters is a sessional instructor in the School of Criminology and Criminal Justice and a research assistant at the Centre for Public Safety and Criminal Justice Research at the University of the Fraser Valley in Abbotsford, British Columbia. Her doctoral research, completed at Simon Fraser University, focused on the offending and risk assessment outcomes for severely mentally disordered, serious-violent, and/or gang-involved young offenders assigned to specialized probation caseloads. Adrienne's research interests include serious and violent youth offending; mental health and its association with delinquency; young offender treatment, programming, and rehabilitation; and the Youth Criminal Justice Act and young offender policy. She has presented at conferences and co-authored publications in each of these areas. Adrienne acts as the research director for the Study on Specialized Community Case Management of Young Offenders and has served as a research assistant on a number of other research projects.

Darryl Plecas is professor emeritus and former RCMP research chair and director of the Centre for Public Safety and Criminal Justice Research at the University of the

Fraser Valley. He is the author or co-author of more than 200 articles and research reports addressing a wide range of criminal justice issues, including numerous recent works dealing with drug production, trafficking, and use. He has an active interest in drug prevention and treatment, and was a member of the board of directors for the Canadian Centre on Substance Abuse from 2006 through to 2013. He received his BA and MA from Simon Fraser University and his EdD from the University of British Columbia.

Susan A. Reid is a professor of criminology and criminal justice at St Thomas University in Fredericton, New Brunswick. She is also the director of the Centre for Research on Youth at Risk, which is the eastern hub of the Students Commission of Canada/Centre of Excellence for Youth Engagement at St Thomas. Her research interests include youth justice, youth at risk, youth voice, and youth engagement. She has been actively involved in promoting adult–youth research partnerships and being an adult ally to youth through the New Brunswick Network Youth Matters. She has written a number of publications on youth justice and in 2014 was inducted into the New Brunswick Crime Prevention Hall of Fame for her community outreach and service.

Lorinda Stoneman is a doctoral candidate in the School of Child and Youth Care at the University of Victoria and is engaged in research and writing on youth justice policy, specifically diversion and other community-based responses to youth offending. She received her master's degree in criminology from Simon Fraser University in 2008, and the intersections between the disciplines of criminology and child and youth care form a key area of interest for her. Other interests range from qualitative and community-based research methods to criminological and post-structural theory, with publications on topics such as crime prevention and historical perspectives on youth justice policy. In addition to her academic work, since 2012 Lorinda has been employed as a research and policy analyst for the BC Ministry of Justice.

Mark Totten is a professor of criminal justice at the Humber Institute of Technology and Advanced Learning and the president of Mark Totten & Associates Inc. He has worked with groups across Canada in the areas of gangs, mental health, violence, and corrections for many years. Over the past decade he has evaluated large-scale gang projects and has partnered with Aboriginal bands in northern communities focused on ending cycles of violence. As a certified social worker, Mark has extensive experience counselling dangerous and violent offenders. He has authored four books and over 60 academic articles and government reports. *Nasty, Brutish and Short: The Lives of Gang Members in Canada* was published in 2012 and *Gang Life: Ten of the Toughest Tell Their Stories* was released in Spring 2014. His latest book, *The Construction of Women and Girls in Gangs in Canada*, is to be released in 2016. He is a frequent media commentator and keynote speaker at provincial and national conferences.

Ronda Trumper is a psychologist working in private practice in Calgary, Alberta. For the past 25 years, she has worked as a clinical consultant and trainer for addictions treatment and prevention programs, focusing on youth and families who are experiencing substance abuse issues. She has written resources for the province of Alberta on substance abuse prevention and community engagement topics as well as contributing to a UN resource on supporting youth-led initiatives. She has been a session instructor in the child- and youth-care department at Mount Royal University and continues to conduct training workshops for professionals around the province. She has a BA in child and youth care and an MA in educational psychology from the University of Victoria.

Catherine (Cathy) Worthington is an associate professor at the School of Public Health and Social Policy, University of Victoria. She has a background in health services research, social work, and public health, and conducts research on community health and social services, particularly those for underserved populations. She has conducted research in collaboration with AIDS service organizations, people living with HIV, street-involved youth, Aboriginal organizations, and African immigrant communities for studies that contribute to HIV prevention and care services. She was the principal investigator on the CIHR-funded Calgary Youth, Health and the Street Study. Her current work focuses on HIV and housing, employment, training and mentoring, and community-engaged research methods.

Preface

We are extremely pleased to have been able to edit this second edition of this book, and again we hope that you will not only enjoy reading it but also learn and be inspired to inquire further. As co-editors, we have both taught courses on young offenders and youth justice as well as published nationally and internationally on the general subject of youth crime. In addition to lending our own knowledge and experience to this book, we have assembled a list of contributors who are all well-established experts in their chapter themes. This brings a richness and an elevated level of comprehensiveness to the book that we could not have matched otherwise. As a result, the readers are the beneficiaries of the collaborative effort that has allowed us to prepare this textbook.

Despite its long history, the study of youth crime and youth justice remains one of the most intriguing and invigorating, yet enigmatic, areas within criminology and criminal justice. For example, whether locally, provincially, or nationally (and even internationally), criminologists and social scientists in general have been intrigued by the challenges of youth crime and its prevention and control. At a more fundamental level, everyone reading this book has at one time or another likely wondered why young people commit delinquent or criminal acts and what we can, or should, do about it. While this book does not profess to provide answers to all the questions, the book does explore a wide range of topics and issues that will provide the reader with a thorough understanding of the richness and complexity of youth crime, youth at risk, and youth justice.

In an effort to provide an appropriate overview of youth crime and justice, we have intentionally attempted to avoid endorsing any particular ideological agenda. However, we have asked the chapter authors to be reflective and, where appropriate, critical about the topics or subjects they have covered. The editors feel that by introducing students not only to the history of youth justice but also to a variety of theoretical perspectives and a range of topical issues (e.g., gangs, substance abuse) that are framed in an informative but also reflective manner, students will learn to reflect critically on the various chapter topics and form their own observations and conclusions about the different issues being covered.

Given this perspective, we solicited chapters for this book with several key goals in mind. First, we wanted to ensure that the book was comprehensive in its coverage, substantial in content, and yet reader friendly so as to encourage students to not only read but be challenged by the questions offered and intrigued by the additional sources identified. Although the book is divided into four main parts, each with its own introduction, the sections and chapters do not need to be followed in sequence, nor do they necessarily all need to be covered. Yet, collectively, they serve to provide a solid foundation for almost any undergraduate-level Canadian course on youth at risk, young offenders, and the workings of the youth justice system.

Second, we were eager to include pedagogical materials and features that are intended not only to enliven student understanding of the topic but also to stimulate further questioning, further reading, and possibly a desire to take more advanced or specialized courses on one or more of the chapter themes. The questions for review and critical thinking, the suggested readings, and the key terms (and glossary) combine to make the book student friendly and to serve as a primary text at the undergraduate level. Where appropriate, chapters also include information textboxes, tables, and figures that are intended to enrich the chapter content without detracting from the main message.

A third goal we had in mind was to ensure topical coverage. Each chapter devotes attention to a specific topic that is seen as fundamental to understanding the complexity of youth crime and youth justice. In addition, we wanted to include important topics that were timely but not commonly addressed in as much detail in other undergraduate textbooks. For example, the chapters on street-involved youth (Chapter 13), adolescent male prostitution (Chapter 14), the Quebec approach to youth justice (Chapter 15), and the coverage of restorative justice (Chapter 16) have received little to no attention in textbooks with a similar focus. Yet we also wanted to ensure that the core themes typically introduced in youth crime and justice courses were covered as well—as is the case with all the other chapters, which range from a historical overview of youth justice in Canada (Chapter 1) to an examination of current youth justice legislation (Chapters 3 and 4), to young female offenders (Chapter 7), youth gangs (Chapter 12) and substance abuse (Chapter 10), and Aboriginal youth in conflict with the law (Chapter 11).

Organization of the Book

As indicated above, the textbook is organized into four parts. "Part I: History, Trends, and Legislation" presents four chapters that collectively serve to provide a foundation for a better understanding of the development of legislative and policy approaches taken in Canada over the last century to define, measure, and deal with at-risk, delinquent, and criminal youth. Part I includes chapters aimed at accounting for historical and contemporary trends in delinquency and youth justice legislation (Chapter 1), understanding how we measure and use different data sources to describe and explain contemporary youth crime (Chapter 2), describing the current Youth Criminal Justice Act (YCJA) and some of its effects (Chapter 3), and examining the youth criminal justice system "in action," using the system operating in British Columbia as a specific example (Chapter 4). The chapters follow a similar format so as to facilitate reading about, reflecting critically upon, and understanding these important topics.

"Part II: Understanding Contemporary Youth Crime and Justice: Theories and Perspectives" shifts attention to examination of the different ways a student can try to develop a broad understanding of youth crime and justice in today's society. Chapter 5 offers an evocative discussion as to why we need to maintain a separate justice system in which young persons' needs are recognized and supported. The authors also place the examination of Canada's youth justice system within an international context by referring to the United Nations (UN) Convention of the Rights of the Child, and they argue for changes in youth justice that give young people a voice in decisions that affect their well-being. Chapter 6 turns to a critical examination of the role of the media in creating public knowledge and awareness of youth crime and youth justice, while the subsequent chapters focus more on the various theoretical approaches that have been developed to explain juvenile delinquency and youth crime. Because the behaviour of females is often influenced by different factors than those that influence the behaviour of young males, Chapter 7 focuses on young female offending behaviour, while the remaining two chapters in Part II focus on new theoretical perspectives on youth crime (Chapter 8) and the need for a critical criminological perspective on youth and crime that pays attention to issues of power and justice (Chapter 9).

Inevitably when we think of young offenders, we tend to categorize their behaviour as either that of offenders or that of victims. And within each category, we then attempt to refine our labelling based on the behaviour(s) the youth are engaged in. In "Part III: At-Risk and Criminalized Youth in Canada: Selected Types and Problems," we focus on five areas that in addition to being topical also serve to reflect the complexity of young persons' behaviour. For example, in Chapter 10 we cover the age-old problem of drug use/abuse among youth to see what, if anything, has changed and how well it is working. Chapter 11 focuses on a dark period in the history of Canada that persists even today—the overrepresentation of Aboriginal youth in the youth criminal justice system. Also included in this section is a chapter on the topical issue of youth gangs (Chapter 12). Chapter 13 covers the unfortunate plight of homeless youth, who, while commonly seen as victims of social and personal circumstances, often turn to crime to survive. In an era when awareness and resources have never been so plentiful, the question of whether or not we really care takes centre stage. Part III concludes with a chapter on adolescent male prostitutes (Chapter 14).

After reading all, or parts, of this section of the book, students will have a deeper appreciation of the diversity of what constitutes youth crime as well as for the complexity of trying to address the problem. For example, it is clear that while young people may engage in anti-social and illegal activity, such behaviour is not always a matter of choice. To this end we might reflect on the chapters in Parts I and II and ask, again, if we are "doing the right thing."

What lies ahead for the administration of youth justice in Canada remains unclear. Notwithstanding, in Part IV on "Keeping Kids out of the System: Exploring Progressive Approaches to Youth Crime and Justice," we will see that a number of different initiatives are being utilized with varying degrees of success and controversy. Collectively, Chapters 15 and 16 speak to public policy and legislative issues that show promise in the possible refinement (or overhauling) of the youth justice system. Specifically, Chapter 15 provides an overview of the multidisciplinary assessment and intervention approach as used in Quebec, while Chapter 16 explores the history and feasibility of restorative justice.

Finally, to paraphrase the esteemed 1970s psychiatrist Karl Menninger, who once said that society gets the youth crime it deserves, it may be argued that if we fail to understand youth crime and respond with poorly informed evidence, then we cannot blame anyone but ourselves for the current state of affairs. As is reflected throughout this textbook, over the past century we have seen a considerable transformation of youth justice policy and practices, from the introduction of the Juvenile Delinquents Act in 1908 and the Young Offenders Act (YOA) in 1984, to the implementation of the Youth Criminal Justice Act in 2003. During this history we have shifted from a welfare model, which emphasized a social work approach that focused on diagnosing the problem and providing treatment under the premise of *parens patriae*—the state knows best—toward a justice model with the YOA in which due process and accountability were emphasized but in measured ways (see Chapter 3). Arguably, the YCJA, with its revised objectives, is reflective of what Reid and Reitsma-Street (1984) referred to as a "community change model" or "modified justice model" that attempts to strike a balance between crime control and providing rehabilitative and restorative options for young offenders.

We realize that in spite of our efforts to prepare a textbook that would span the spectrum of course curriculums that focus on youth crime and youth justice, we may have come up short in some areas. We debated long and hard about including more content, but in part because of practical constraints, we had to make informed decisions about what to include and what not to. These decisions were in part guided by the helpful feedback from the various anonymous reviewers whom we would like to acknowledge and thank, but in the end we are responsible for the final product. Along the way, should you have any constructive feedback, we would welcome hearing from you because we are always receptive to trying to improve the approach we have taken in our attempt to contribute to an understanding of youth risk and youth justice in Canada.

References

Reid, S.A., and Reitsma-Street, M. (1984). Assumptions and implications of new Canadian legislation for young offenders. *Canadian Criminology Forum,* 7: 1–19.

Acknowledgements

Although I did not know it at the time, my 30+-year involvement with writing and editing books on young offenders and juvenile justice dates back to the late 1970s when I agreed to run a wilderness adventure program in Ontario for an eager and creative probation officer by the name of Rick Mazur (we are still dear friends to this day). My experience over those two years eventually drew me back to school, intent on learning more about young offenders and youth at risk. And while much has transpired since the days of ACTION (Accepting Challenge Through Interaction with Others and Nature), my interest in young offenders and youth justice remains steadfast.

In the preparation of this new edition, little has changed. Co-editing this collection of original articles requires considerable teamwork and dedication by all involved. Although the process never seems to get any easier, it has also been a joyous experience to witness how well so many different ideas, agendas, and personalities can come together with dedication to a common cause. Therefore, for my part, I again would like to express my deepest appreciation to all the contributors who were kind enough to prepare their chapters and who graciously worked with us as we finalized their submission for the book. Without their contribution, the book would never have been published.

I remain deeply appreciative of having Russell Smandych join me as co-editor again. Our friendship dates back to our days as students at Simon Fraser University, and it has been a genuine pleasure and honour to work with him again on this edition of the book. I look forward to working on future editions with him.

I would also be remiss if I did not thank my students, who diplomatically endured being subjected to portions of the new material and who regularly offered constructive feedback. It is for you that this book has been written and edited with the hope that it will inspire you to want to make a difference for our youth, especially those youths who are at risk in society today.

Finally, but most definitely not least of all, is my partner in life and happiness, Rosemary Buck. While she will likely continue to question the sanity of my academic dedication, I am truly blessed to have a partner who has stood by me and been my confidante and best friend over the past few decades. And to our two sons, who, now as young men, still wonder at times why I do not take my own advice when it comes to understanding them, I say, thanks, guys, for being who you are.

— John Winterdyk

I am appreciative of having again had the opportunity to work with John Winterdyk, my long-time friend and fellow graduate student from our years at Simon Fraser University. Unlike John, however, my interest in youth crime and justice has been more recent, starting, rather ironically, in the middle of the 1990s, during the peak of the moral panic over youth crime that soon led to the introduction of the YCJA, which appeared at the time to symbolize a further shift toward the "adulteration" of young offenders—that is, the move toward treating young people more like adults in the criminal justice system. I began to ask questions like "What is happening to youth in the criminal justice system?" and "How did we get to where we are today?" The lack of adequate answers to these questions led me to try to answer them myself and share what I learned with my students. Along the way, I have incurred many professional and personal debts: first, to the many other youth justice researchers who inspired and provided a foundation for my own work; and second, to my friends and family who supported me along the way. The most important of these are my partner, Kathryn, and our children, Timothy, Amelia, and Alissa, who survived my years of learning how to be a parent and are now, quite amazingly, all carving out their own interesting educational paths and adult careers. I would also again like to thank the many friends and colleagues who have been a huge help to me in my career and personal life, including my colleagues Elizabeth Comack, Rod Kueneman, and Rick Linden, and my reliable home-province (of Saskatchewan) contact, Ross Green, who continues to keep me humble by reminding me where I came from.

—Russell Smandych

To the staff at Oxford—words cannot express our gratitude. A special thanks goes to David Stover, former president of Oxford University Press Canada, who embraced the initial project and encouraged us to follow through with it after incurring a number of stumbling blocks; to Amy Gordon, our developmental editor, who adeptly helped to get this project on track and keep us all within a reasonable time frame; and to Mark Thompson, acquisitions editor, who skilfully helped to guide the project along and to keep us within the time constraints. A special thanks to Judith Turnbull, who provided invaluable copy editing.

Finally, the caveat that so often appears at the end of acknowledgement sections and remains true in this edition: any shortcomings within this text still remain ours alone. Just as we must learn to have compassion for each other rather than sympathy, we hope you will see the intent in this edition and provide feedback so that the book can continue to evolve to serve its readers even better.

John Winterdyk
Department of Economics, Justice, and Policy Studies
Mount Royal University
Calgary, Alberta

Russell Smandych
Department of Sociology
University of Manitoba
Winnipeg, Manitoba

About the Editors

John Winterdyk is the former director of the Centre of Criminology and Justice Research at Mount Royal University. He is also an adjunct professor at St Thomas University in Fredericton, New Brunswick, at the University of Regina, as well as at the Polytechnic of Namibia in Windhoek, Namibia. John has held three visiting positions at the Max Planck Institute in Freiburg, Germany. He has published extensively in the areas of youth justice, human trafficking, international criminal justice, and criminological theory. To date he has authored/edited some 28+ textbooks and is currently finalizing a new textbook on criminology in Canada (OUP), editing a textbook on crime prevention (Taylor & Francis Group) as well as preparing a new book on Canadian pioneers in criminology and criminal justice (with Rock's Mills Press) while juggling several research projects and riding his bike.

Russell Smandych is a professor of sociology and criminology in the Department of Sociology at the University of Manitoba. His current research and teaching interests include global criminology and criminal justice, comparative legal history, and comparative youth justice. He is the editor and co-editor of nine books and has published widely in leading Canadian and international journals in the fields of legal history and criminology. He has held honorary appointments as a distinguished visiting professor and scholar at universities in Canada, Ireland, Australia, New Zealand, and England, and in 2010 he was awarded the University of Manitoba, Faculty of Arts Award in Internationalization for his work in promoting student awareness of international culture, perspectives, and issues through his teaching and research.

Contributors

Russell Smandych—University of Manitoba

John A. Winterdyk—Mount Royal University

Ross Green—Provincial Court of Saskatchewan

Adrienne M.F. Peters—University of the Fraser Valley

Raymond R. Corrado—Simon Fraser University

Susan A. Reid—St Thomas University

Sarah Gilliss—New Brunswick Community College

Chris McCormick—St Thomas University

Lorinda Stoneman—University of Victoria

Sibylle Artz—University of Victoria

Stephen W. Baron—Queen's University

Bryan Hogeveen—University of Alberta

Joanne C. Minaker—Grant MacEwan University

Jordan Diplock—University of the Fraser Valley

Darryl Plecas—University of the Fraser Valley

Ronda Trumper—Trumper Psychology

Jana Grekul—University of Alberta

Hirsch Greenberg—University of Regina

Rhonda Nelson—Starbright Children's Development Centre

Mark Totten—Humber College

Bruce MacLaurin—University of Calgary

Catherine Worthington—University of Victoria

Susan McIntyre—The Hindsight Group

Anne Miller—Constellation Consulting

Louis-Georges Cournoyer—Université de Montréal

Jacques Dionne—Université du Québec

Michèle Goyette—Centre jeunesse de Montréal–Institut universitaire

Pierre Hamel—Cour du Québec, chambre de la jeunesse

Brenda Morrison—Simon Fraser University

Colleen Pawlychka—Simon Fraser University

Part I
History, Trends, and Legislation

In order to understand current problems and issues surrounding youth at risk and the operation of the Canadian youth justice system, there are several steps we must first take: (1) develop a knowledge of youth justice history; (2) learn how we go about acquiring information about youth crime and youth justice; and (3) determine the objectives and purposes of youth justice legislation. The specific historical and comparative questions we need to address include the following:

- Why do we have a youth justice system in Canada?

- How did that system develop?

- How well is it working across the country and in comparison to youth justice systems in other countries?

We also need to attempt to answer questions about how, over time, criminologists and governments have attempted to assess trends in "juvenile delinquency" and "youth crime" and respond to them in various ways.

One of the most common ways with which Western countries have responded to juvenile delinquency and youth crime since the late nineteenth century has been to enact and implement legislation to treat and punish at-risk youth and young offenders. Since the beginning of the twentieth century, the Canadian federal government has followed this pattern by putting into place three succeeding legislative regimes: the Juvenile Delinquents Act (JDA) (1908); the Young Offenders Act (YOA) (1984); and the Youth Criminal Justice Act (YCJA) (2002). Collectively, the chapters in Part I help us to better appreciate how the approach taken in Canada to define, measure, and deal with at-risk and criminalized youth has developed over the past century and evolved into its current form.

In Chapter 1, Russell Smandych adopts a critical historical and comparative approach to explain the development of Canada's youth justice system. He argues that in order to answer the question of why we have a youth justice system, one has to start by developing a knowledge of the factors that contributed to the creation of the early juvenile justice systems in Canada and the United States, beginning in the late nineteenth century. Similarly, in order to understand current developments occurring in the Canadian youth justice system—including the apparent trend toward a more punitive approach to dealing with youth crime—one needs to take into account comparable cross-national developments that also may be influencing these changes. In addition to emphasizing the need for a broader comparative perspective, Smandych closely examines historical literature on the development of early juvenile courts in the United States and Canada. In doing so, he points to a variety of different accounts of reform in the youth justice system, including, most notably, Thomas

Bernard's perspective on the cyclical nature of changes in juvenile justice. Smandych argues that although Bernard's cyclical theory of juvenile justice reform does not provide a specific explanation of the reasons underlying historical changes in Canada's youth justice legislation, the theory nonetheless provides a relevant perspective on youth-justice-system reform that can be applied to Canada. In particular, Smandych notes that Bernard's theory provides a useful starting point for explaining the ostensibly cyclical nature of the legislative shift from the JDA to the YOA and the YCJA.

In addition to understanding the social, political, and legislative context of youth justice, one must also have a clear understanding of how "youth crime" is defined and measured in Canada. The study of youth crime and/or delinquency poses many of the same challenges as the study of crime in general. For example, just as more general concepts and definitions of crime have changed over time, the concept of youth crime has only in recent years come to be used by governments, criminologists, and the media in most of the Commonwealth countries, including Canada, England and Wales, New Zealand, and Australia. On the other hand, the earlier popular concepts of "juvenile delinquency" and "juvenile crime" continue to be more commonly used in other countries such as the United States. While at first glance this might appear to be an unimportant difference, these various concepts also imply different views about the level of culpability and responsibility that the legal system should attribute to young people who break the law, with juvenile "delinquency" implying less culpability than youth "crime." In Chapter 2, John Winterdyk provides an overview of the concepts and data-collection methods that criminologists have developed to study what we now commonly refer to in Canada as youth crime. Importantly, this discussion illustrates that one of the main purposes of governments' measuring and recording juvenile delinquency and youth crime has been to provide justification for the state to control "the problem." Consequently, as Winterdyk carefully outlines, one must develop a thorough understanding of the strengths and weaknesses of the major data-collection methods used to study and develop and/or inform government policy on the perceived contemporary problem of youth crime.

In Chapter 3, Judge Ross Green offers a systematic overview of key provisions of the YCJA. In doing so, he outlines similarities and differences between the YCJA and the earlier YOA, and highlights how the new legislation is now being interpreted by the courts and how it is being formally implemented. Green examines the policy objectives underlying the YCJA and how these objectives are reflected in the Act's provisions, the youth court process through which the Act is enforced, the rights and obligations of young people and parents under the Act, and issues surrounding the use of discretion in determining the most appropriate measures for dealing with young persons who may be charged with criminal offences. Judge Green's chapter is important for the perspective it provides on how judges who work on a day-to-day basis in the Canadian youth justice system are interpreting the YCJA and attempting to apply it—both in the best interests of young people and in the better protection of society from crime. The chapter is also valuable for the information it provides on some of the challenges judges face in applying the legislation, including issues surrounding the sentencing of Aboriginal young people and the problem of finding adequate ways of dealing with young people who suffer from developmental challenges (such as fetal alcohol spectrum disorder) and mental health issues.

In Chapter 4, Adrienne Peters and Raymond Corrado provide an overview of how the Canadian youth justice system works in action on a day-to-day basis in different Canadian provinces, territories, and municipalities. This includes, first, describing how young offenders are dealt with at various stages of the youth justice process—from first contact with the police to court appearances—and, in the case of convicted young offenders, the way in which they experience community and custody-based correctional sanctions. In addition, the authors address key current challenges and issues faced by professionals working in the youth justice system, including net-widening, police racial profiling, the changing scope of the work of probation officers, the increasing use of risk assessment tools in youth courts and corrections, and the challenges of dealing with young offenders who suffer from mental disorders. Overall, the authors observe that despite some of the controversies created by the original enactment and more recent amendment of the YCJA, for the most part the Act has been successfully implemented across the country and has resulted in a reduced number of young offenders being formally involved in the justice system. Consequently, they conclude that for youth justice workers and professionals to continue to make progress in developing effective responses to youth crime, it is important that they embrace the principles and goals of the YCJA at each stage of a young person's contact with the justice system.

From "Misguided Children" to "Criminal Youth": Exploring Historical and Contemporary Trends in Canadian Youth Justice

Russell Smandych

Overview

This chapter offers a historical and comparative perspective on the development of juvenile justice legislation in Canada and other Western countries from the late nineteenth to the early twenty-first century. Particular attention is given to accounting for the development of early juvenile justice systems in the United States and Canada in the late nineteenth century and the more recent contemporary shift—referred to by some as the punitive turn in youth justice—that now appears to be occurring in a number of Western countries. The primary purpose of this chapter is to develop an understanding of the importance of historical and comparative research in helping to explain contemporary trends in youth justice in Canada.

Key Objectives

After reading this chapter, you should be able to:

* Explain how "deviant" and "dependent" children were typically dealt with in Western countries prior to the invention of juvenile courts.

* Understand the factors that led to the creation of early delinquency legislation and juvenile courts in the nineteenth and early twentieth centuries.

* Identify factors linked to changes in early juvenile delinquency and to more recent youth criminal justice legislation in Canada.

* Understand the role of historical and comparative research in helping to explain contemporary trends in youth justice in Canada.

Introduction

In the past century Canada has seen the introduction of three different legislative regimes for administering juvenile justice: the Juvenile Delinquents Act (JDA) of 1908, the Young Offenders Act (YOA) of 1984, and the Youth Criminal Justice Act (YCJA) of 2002. In the course of this legislative history, Canada has followed a pattern of legislative change that appears similar to that of many other Western countries, including Britain, Australia, and the United States. In each of these jurisdictions, the 1980s and 1990s witnessed an earlier, predominately child welfare model of juvenile justice eroded and replaced with more legalistic, and arguably more punitive, due process and crime-control models of juvenile justice procedure (Bernard and Kurlychek 2010; Hutchinson, Parada, and Smandych 2008). As a result of these changes, specialized justice systems designed for "juvenile" or "young" offenders, but sharing some of the characteristic features of adult criminal justice systems, remain largely in place in many Western countries today.

These historical developments around legislation and models of juvenile justice have also been accompanied in some countries by changes in the terminology used to refer to young people who are caught up in the criminal justice system. Most notable among these is the shift in language that has occurred, from considering such young people as "misguided children" or "juvenile delinquents" who have committed acts of **juvenile delinquency** that are best dealt with in **juvenile courts**, to viewing them as "criminal youth" whose alleged anti-social and criminal acts are best dealt with through more formal **youth criminal justice systems**. Stating this somewhat differently, Bryan Hogeveen and Joanne Minaker (Minaker and Hogeveen 2009, pp. 12–18) have argued that in Western countries like Canada discussions of how society should deal with troubled and/or troubling youth have oscillated over time between the two competing discourses: first, the discourse of the **reformable young offender**, which prevailed for much of the nineteenth and twentieth centuries and proposed that troubled youth "required intervention and could be rehabilitated," and second, that of the **punishable young offender**, which has been prominent in debates since the 1990s and proposes that "troubling" youth require "punishment first and foremost, leaving reform and rehabilitative interventions as

juvenile delinquency
The legal term that came into popular use in the nineteenth century to describe violations of the law by persons who had not reached the legal age of adulthood.

juvenile courts
Specialized courts first created in the late nineteenth century to apply juvenile justice laws in the care of dependent and delinquent children.

youth criminal justice systems
A term often used today as a substitute for *juvenile courts*. Critical criminologists argue that it signifies a shift toward treating young offenders more like adult offenders.

reformable young offender
A term coined by Bryan Hogeveen (2005) to describe the discursive construction of some young offenders as "troubled" and therefore needing intervention in the hope they can be rehabilitated.

punishable young offender
A term coined by Bryan Hogeveen (2005) to describe the discursive construction of some young offenders as "troublesome" and therefore requiring punishment in order to make them accountable for their criminal acts.

secondary measures." Indeed, criminologists such as Minaker and Hogeveen argue that recent decades have witnessed a "punitive turn" in youth justice in Canada that parallels similar trends in both the adult and juvenile (or youth) justice systems of a number of other Western countries (Muncie and Goldson 2006). On the other hand, other prominent Canadian criminologists disagree with this **punitive turn thesis** and contend that there is very little evidence to support the claim that Canada's more recent approach to dealing with young people in conflict with the law (under the Youth Criminal Justice Act) is any more punitive in practice than it was in earlier decades (when the JDA and YOA were in effect) (Bala, Carrington, and Roberts 2009; Doob and Sprott 2006).

punitive turn thesis
The argument that in recent decades the criminal justice systems of many Western countries have become more punishment oriented, with longer prison sentences and higher rates of incarceration.

One of the aims of the current chapter is to evaluate the merit of competing views on historical and contemporary developments in Canadian youth justice, including the origins of Canada's early juvenile delinquency legislation and the alleged punitive turn in youth criminal justice since the 1990s. As we will see, this task is complicated because attempts to account for changes in Canadian youth justice must also take into consideration the way in which Canadian developments have often been tied to and influenced by similar changes in other countries. Indeed, a key argument made in this chapter is that the nature and direction of historical and contemporary trends in Canadian youth justice cannot be adequately understood without taking into account the connected experiences of other countries. The essential questions addressed in this chapter are as follows:

- Where did our modern (Western) juvenile or youth justice systems come from, and why did they come about when they did?

- What are the key changes that have occurred in juvenile justice administration over the course of the twentieth and early twenty-first centuries, and to what extent have Canadian developments been influenced by developments in other countries?

The essential point we will learn is that while there are many commonalities that link the historical development and current state of juvenile systems across various Western countries, there are also important historical, cultural, and political differences that make Canada's current approach to youth justice unique. In turn, as we will attempt to show, understanding these commonalities and differences can help us better appreciate how the Canadian public and Canadian youth justice law- and policy-makers can more fruitfully undertake the complicated task of improving the way we deal with the recurrently perceived problems of juvenile delinquency and youth crime.

The Development of Modern Juvenile Justice Systems

From "Little Adults" to "Misguided Children": The Changing Role and Status of Children in Western Society

In order to understand why young people are viewed the way they are by the criminal justice system today, we must begin by exploring the meaning of childhood and how this meaning has changed over time (Empey 1982). Of all of the historians who have written on the topic, criminologists have been most influenced by the work of Philippe Ariès. In his provocative book *Centuries of Childhood: A Social History of Family Life*, Ariès (1962) undertook a detailed historical study of the treatment of children in Western Europe from the Middle Ages to the nineteenth century, and in doing so, he was the first social historian to propose an argument explaining how children were viewed and treated by adults in earlier times and how these views and practices changed over the centuries.

Ariès argued that the modern concept of childhood was "discovered" in Western Europe in the seventeenth century. According to Ariès, prior to this time few distinctions were made between individuals on the basis of age, and young people were fully integrated into the mainstream of social life. This integration was evident, for example, in children's wearing essentially the same clothes as adults from a very early age. Ariès also pointed out that prior to the seventeenth century most of the education received by young people took the form of apprenticeships that involved learning a trade or profession through working daily, for many years, in the company of adults. For Ariès, evidence like this showed that the concept of childhood, as we know it today, did not exist in Western Europe in the Middle Ages. He also claimed that the very high infant mortality rate at the time discouraged parents from wanting to invest emotionally in their children.

That many more children died prematurely in the Middle Ages than in later periods is a well-known demographic fact (Shahar 1990). However, Ariès argued that despite the high mortality rate and the lack of emotional investment they received from parents, children living prior to the seventeenth century were probably happier than they were in later periods. According to Ariès, because pre-seventeenth-century Western European society was not preoccupied with raising the young and severely restricting their lives, conditions for children were relatively good. Indeed, he claimed that much of the status ambiguity and intergenerational conflict that now exist because of the way children are treated in modern Western society did not exist before the "discovery" of childhood in the seventeenth century. Indeed, he argues that "[r]ather than repressing, judging, or attempting to protect children with a special set of moral rules, adults shared all aspects of existence with them. The years of littlehood, as a consequence, were sociable and happy" (Empey 1982, p. 33).

Over the years a number of criminologists have drawn on Ariès's research to try to explain the reasons for the "invention" of juvenile delinquency and the juvenile court. Most notable among these is Lamar Empey, who, in his influential textbook *American Delinquency: Its Meaning and Construction* (1982), relies mostly on Ariès to provide support for the argument that "[i]t was not until Europe began to awaken from the intellectual hibernation and social stagnation of the Middle Ages that a handful of moral philosophers began to question the customary treatment of children" and that "[o]ver a period of the next two or three centuries, age-old tendencies either to ignore or to exploit them were replaced with an ardent concern for their moral welfare." Simultaneously, over this period "parental care for children became a sacred duty; the school gradually replaced the apprenticeship system as the second most important child-raising institution; and childhood became a transitional period in which protection from, rather than indulgence in, adult activities became the rule." According to Empey,

Out of this process grew the modern concept of childhood stressing the idea that children have value in their own right and that because of their sweetness and simplicity they require a careful preparation for the harshness and sinfulness of an adult world [and] [f]urthermore, it was only after childhood became a special status in the life cycle that the concept of a special court for juveniles began to develop. (Empey 1982, p. 8)

The work of juvenile justice historians who have drawn on Ariès's thesis has been criticized for creating an oversimplified account of the invention of juvenile delinquency and the juvenile court. In particular, it has been pointed out that these authors have ignored the work of later historians of childhood and the family, including Pollock (1983), Shahar (1990), and Gottlieb (1993), among others (Spagnoli 1981; Wilson 1984), whose studies raise serious concerns about the validity of Ariès's thesis on a number of grounds (Smandych 2001). The most damaging of these concerns is the apparent manner in which Ariès allowed his personal religious and ideological beliefs about the role of parents in child rearing and the need to maintain traditional conservative family values to bias his historical analysis (Spagnoli 1981).

Box 1.1	Youth Justice in Action

Is It Harder Raising Children Today Than in the Past?

In her study *The Family in the Western World from the Black Death to the Industrial Age*, Gottlieb provides many examples that illustrate how ambiguous the category of "youth" was in Western countries prior to the nineteenth century. Gottlieb (1993, pp. 156–7) notes that prior to the nineteenth century "[y]oung people were subject to full parental authority as long as they were under the parental roof, and the father's legal authority usually continued after they left home." In addition, regardless of how old they were, "[i]t was next to impossible for single people to be considered adults." With the exception of young men in Catholic countries who entered the celibate clergy, adulthood did not begin for males until they were married. Gottlieb (1993, p. 157) further notes that, not entirely unlike today, "[t]he adulthood of women was an even more ambiguous matter," since "[t]he only grown women who could function as full legal adults were widows in certain localities and under certain circumstances." In her discussion of the ambiguity of youth in pre-industrial Western society, Gottlieb makes another statement that probably sounds

quite familiar to many parents of today's Canadian youth, who are usually under the age of 30 but are sometimes even older:

> Since most people did not marry until their middle or late twenties, it is plain that a sizeable chunk of the population drifted in a no-man's land between childhood and adulthood, the ill-defined territory called "youth." It was generally assumed that by fourteen, or at the latest sixteen, nobody could any longer be considered a little child. On the other hand, before being established in the religious life or as the head of a household, a male over sixteen was necessarily a dependent of some sort. . . . Youth of both sexes constituted a large mobile population that formed only temporary attachments to households. Some journeymen and maid-servants spent years moving about before they finally settled into marriage, the only conceivable end to youth. (Gottlieb 1993, pp. 157–8)

Source: Smandych 2001, p. 9.

In addition, historians like Beatrice Gottlieb (1993) show that it is misleading to talk about the "discovery of childhood" as having occurred at a specific point in time, since both historically and in more recent times adults have displayed a great deal of ambiguity in their thinking about the definition and treatment of children and youth. The currency of this continuing dilemma of parenting is captured well in Box 1.1 in the discussion and quote from Gottlieb's (1993) study.

The lesson that stands out from studies like Gottlieb's is that parents have always found raising children to be a complicated and difficult task. The literature also points to the persuasiveness of the argument that while changing adult sensibilities about childhood in seventeenth-century Europe may have had some influence on thinking about the need for a different way of dealing with juvenile delinquency, many other local, national, and more broadly international influences need to be taken into account. The following section describes and offers a critical analysis of the various explanations that juvenile justice historians have developed to account for the creation of late nineteenth- and early twentieth-century delinquency legislation and juvenile courts in the United States, in selected European countries, in Britain, and in Anglo white-settler colonies, including Canada. However, before turning to this comparative historical discussion, it is relevant to note some important common facts about the how juvenile delinquents were dealt with in the legal systems of Western countries before the creation of specialized delinquency legislation and juvenile courts. As well, the following section describes some common features of how juvenile delinquents were dealt with after early child welfare–model delinquency legislation came into force.

Precursors to the Creation of Delinquency Legislation and Juvenile Courts

The term *juvenile delinquency* was first used in the eighteenth century, primarily as a legal term to describe "violations of the law by persons below the community's legal age of adulthood" (Graebner 1994, p. 379). By the late nineteenth century, however, the term was in widespread use and new juvenile justice systems had begun to be put into place in order to deal with the special needs of perceived delinquent and dependent children. Although, as we will see in this chapter, it is clear that a transformation in the way young people were dealt with by the criminal justice system did occur in the nineteenth century, one must be careful not to exaggerate the extent of this transformation. In particular, it is not true that prior to the development of juvenile courts young offenders were dealt with in exactly the same way as adult offenders. Historians who have examined the operation of English-based criminal courts in common-law countries prior to the mid-nineteenth century have shown that the severity of the criminal law was often mitigated by sympathetic juries and paternalistic judges who showed mercy toward those accused of serious crimes (see Beattie 1986; Langbein 1992). Evidence also shows that young people who were accused of crimes that made them liable to the same punishment as adults were usually shown an even greater degree of mercy than adults who came before the courts (Carrigan 1998). It is also significant that under English common law, persons below the age of seven years could not be convicted of committing an offence, while "youths between the ages of seven and fourteen were subject to the doctrine of ***doli incapax***, which involved a presumption of incapacity that could be contested by the Crown" (Griffiths and Verdun-Jones 1994, p. 597).

Common Features of Early Child Welfare–Model Delinquency Legislation

Before examining the development of delinquency legislation and juvenile courts in specific countries, it is also important to highlight a number of common features shared by juvenile justice systems. Although the timing of their establishment varied between jurisdictions, three common features came to characterize the operation of all newly invented juvenile courts and the laws that provided for their establishment.

First, the laws commonly recognized that there were three distinct age-graded levels of criminal accountability:

- no criminal accountability for youth under a certain legislatively determined age (for example, under 10 years old);

- limited criminal accountability for youth who were subject to the jurisdiction of the legislation because they fell within a certain legislatively determined age range (for example, 10 to 15 years old); and

- full criminal accountability for youth above a certain age (for example, 16 years old). In other words, all late nineteenth- and early twentieth-century juvenile delinquency legislation came to be formally premised on the concept of **diminished criminal responsibility** for so-called juvenile delinquents.

A second general feature, related to both legislation and the operation of early juvenile courts was that they were based on the principle of ***parens patriae***—the idea that the state had a duty to intervene in the lives of children and assume the role of a substitute parent for those who were found to be either "delinquent" or "dependent."

A third feature of the delinquency legislation enacted in many jurisdictions—including the United States, France, Belgium, England and Wales, Australia, and Canada—was the extent to which it reflected the common belief that juvenile delinquents should be viewed as "misguided children" and treated with "friendly helpfulness" (Hogeveen 2001). Most commonly, the state made this operational in juvenile courts by giving judges wide discretionary power to deal with juvenile delinquents as they saw fit and by appointing probation officers to give individual attention to the cases of young people who were brought before the court. Indeed, throughout Western countries where new juvenile justice systems were created in the late nineteenth and early twentieth centuries, probation officers came to assume a key role in the development and operation of those systems. While these were important common features of the way early delinquency legislation and juvenile courts were in theory supposed to operate (as we will see in the following discussion), across all of the jurisdictions where they came into being the development of juvenile courts was also uneven and, in some cases, took many decades to evolve from inception to more uniform practical implementation.

The Invention of the Juvenile Court in the United States

A great deal has been written in the past and continues to be written today about "the invention of the juvenile court" in the United States (Bernard and Kurlychek 2010; Colomy and Kretzmann 1995; Getis 2000; Platt 1969; Redding, Goldstein, and Heilburn 2005; Tanenhaus 2004). One reason for this is that the United States, and more specifically the state of Illinois, was arguably the first jurisdiction where a juvenile justice system was created based explicitly on a child welfare model. Another reason for the attention US criminologists and juvenile justice historians have given to the topic may be that in the 1980s and 1990s the juvenile justice system in the US came under increasing and constant attack from critics, many of whom argued for replacing the existing child welfare–oriented system with a more punitive one based on reforms, including the more frequent waiver of juvenile cases to adult court and the use of tougher "more adult-like" sentences for juvenile offenders (Feld and Bishop 2013; Thorson 1999). Some of the recent accounts of the original juvenile court movement in the US have clearly been written with knowledge of and concern about these contemporary trends, and they express misgivings about the punitive turn in juvenile justice in the US that characterized developments in the 1980s and 1990s. It is obviously not possible in this chapter to extensively review the wealth of literature on the early development of the juvenile court systems in the US. However, it is important to develop an understanding of the evidence and arguments advanced by specific key authors, both for what they have to tell us about the invention of the juvenile court in the US and for what their studies reveal about the shortcomings of existing historical writing on the topic. Significantly, one of these weaknesses is the lack of attention most US historians have given to cross-national connections that linked late nineteenth-century juvenile justice reform movements in the US and other countries.

Much of the US historiography on the juvenile court has focused on histories of the circumstances and events that surrounded the creation of the first state-wide juvenile court system in Illinois in 1899, and its evolution, which began with the establishment of the Cook County Juvenile Court in Chicago. The first criminologist to undertake a detailed study of the origin and operation of the famous Chicago Juvenile Court was Anthony Platt, in his (also soon to be acclaimed) book on *The Child Savers: The Invention of Delinquency* (1969). Platt argued that the Illinois juvenile justice system and the Chicago juvenile court came about as a result of the child-saving movement that emerged in Chicago and many other US cities in the late nineteenth century. This movement was led mainly by conservative, middle-class social reformers. More specifically, Platt portrayed the child-saving movement in the United States as a middle-class, Anglo-Saxon, Protestant movement dedicated mainly to attempting to control the moral behaviour of lower-class families and immigrants, who were perceived to pose a threat to moral values as well as to the economic interests of the more "respectable" middle class. In his study, Platt shows that rather than being the product of an outpouring of genuine humanitarian concern for "saving children" from lives of poverty and parental neglect—which often contributed to dependency and delinquency (as earlier historical accounts claimed)—the child-saving movement was an ideologically conservative movement that was influenced in particular by ideas associated with "social Darwinism and European [criminological] positivism" (Platt 1969, p. 13). According to Platt (1969, p. 19),

[t]he child-saving movement, like all moral crusades, reaffirmed ideal values and stressed the positive capacities of traditional institutions. The child savers' ideology was an amalgam of convictions and aspirations. From the medical profession, they borrowed the imagery of pathology, infection, immunization, and treatment; from the tenets of social Darwinism, they derived their pessimistic views about the intractability of human nature and the innate moral defects of the lower classes; [and] finally, their ideas about the biological and environmental origins of crime can be attributed to the positivist tradition in European criminology and anti-urban sentiments associated with the Protestant, rural ethic.

In essence, according to Platt's analysis, racism and class discrimination were the most important factors that led to the enactment of juvenile delinquency statutes and the establishment of juvenile courts throughout the United States. He notes that in the years following the enactment of the Juvenile Court Act of Illinois, the Act came to be used "as a model statute by other states and countries," such that "[b]y 1917 juvenile court legislation had been passed in all but three states and by 1932 there were over 600 independent juvenile courts throughout the United States" (Platt 1969, p. 10). While Platt does not extend his critical analysis in any way to take into account simultaneous developments occurring in Canada, it is notable that his interpretation, which he advanced even more explicitly in later writing (Platt 1974), was later criticized by Canadian juvenile justice historians Hagan and Leon (1977, 1980) for its inability to explain the factors surrounding the emergence of the child-saving movement and the juvenile court in Canada. As we will also see a little later, in their early comparative historical research, Hagan and Leon (1977, p. 240) did draw attention to the "cross-fertilization of ideas that occurred between Canada and the United States in the juvenile justice context."

A second and quite different account of the invention of the juvenile court in the United States is given by David Rothman (1980) in his book on *Conscience and Convenience: The Asylum and Its Alternatives in Progressive America*. Whereas Platt (1969, 1974) stresses the importance of examining changes in the social structure and economy of American society to explain changes in juvenile justice, Rothman examines the power of the ideas and rhetoric of social reformers involved in the late nineteenth-century child-saving movement. In particular, Rothman links the efforts of child-saving reformers and "the invention of the juvenile court" to a much broader range of social reform movements that emerged in the United States toward the end of the nineteenth century. Specifically, he shows that reform innovations in the areas of child welfare and juvenile justice were linked to more sweeping changes that were also occurring in the adult criminal justice system and in the mental health system in the US. According to Rothman (1980, p. 43), the "Progressive era" in American history (which continued through the first two decades of the twentieth century) "marked a major divide in attitudes and practices toward the deviant, creating new ideas and procedures to combat crime, delinquency, and mental illness." The emergence of these new sensibilities regarding the methods to be employed in treating deviant individuals was reflected in the Progressive era in the dramatic rise of alternatives to, and innovations in, institutional confinement. In the same period that "Americans enacted probation, parole, and indeterminate sentences for adult offenders," measures were taken to establish "juvenile courts for delinquents" and "outpatient clinics for the mentally ill." In each of the areas of criminal justice, mental health, and child welfare, Rothman points to the growing occupational and professional status of reformers and to the increasing extent to which they relied on social-scientific knowledge about the causes and treatment of deviant behaviour to justify the introduction of new methods of treatment and control.

According to Rothman (1980, pp. 207–11), the person who perhaps best epitomized the social-scientific approach that came to underpin the Progressive-era juvenile court movement was psychologist G. Stanley Hall, "who made the first systematic studies of childhood in the United States." Hall introduced the term **adolescence** to describe the critical period of human development when people move through a distinct stage in which they progress, both biologically and emotionally, from being a child to being an adult. Hall's extensive two-volume book *Adolescence*, published in 1904, sold over 25,000 copies, which did much to cement his reputation as the leading American child psychologist of the period (Comacchio 2010; Hall 1904). Rothman notes the profound influence that Hall's ideas on adolescence and delinquency had on educated Americans, from women who belonged to the National Congress of Mothers (the forerunner of the Parent-Teacher Association), to criminologists, social workers, and advocates of the juvenile court. Significantly, Hall identified several causes of delinquency, which, although mostly environmental, included everything from "heredity, bad antenatal conditions, bad homes, unhealthful infancy and childhood," to "extremes of wealth and poverty" and "overcrowded slums with their promiscuity and squalor" (Hall 1904; cited in Rothman 1908, p. 210). Hall also strongly advocated a juvenile court system in which juveniles had to be treated completely apart from adults.

According to Rothman, two of the juvenile court advocates who perhaps did more than any others to promote Hall's ideas on the causes and prevention of delinquency were Richard Tuthill, the first judge appointed to the Chicago Juvenile Court, who was persuaded that the delinquent's faults were "due not to hereditary taint, but to bad environment," and Ben Lindsey, who presided as judge in the first juvenile court in Denver, Colorado, and became a proverbial "one-man traveling road show" in the cause of promoting the juvenile court movement throughout the United States (Rothman 1980, pp. 211, 215). Significantly, the original age of jurisdiction for both the Chicago Juvenile Court and the Denver Juvenile Court was under 16 for any child, but within five years Illinois extended the age of jurisdiction upward "to include boys under the age of seventeen and any female child under the age of eighteen" (Dohrn 2002, p. 271). While offering important insights into the broader reform process that influenced the establishment of delinquency legislation and juvenile courts in the United States—particularly regarding the undeniable power of the social-scientifically informed ideas and rhetoric of child-saving reformers—Rothman can also be criticized for ignoring the cross-fertilization of ideas on juvenile justice that occurred between the United States and other countries, as we will see later in this chapter when we turn to look at the overlapping and interconnected experiences of other countries, including Canada.

More recently, Tanenhaus (2004) has published a richly detailed study of the origin and early development of the Chicago Juvenile Court that moves beyond the work

adolescence
A term popularized by child development expert G. Stanley Hall to refer to the stage of life during which a person progresses, both biologically and emotionally, from being a child to being an adult.

of Rothman and other American juvenile justice historians by focusing more attention on "the actual working of juvenile courts in the early twentieth century." In doing so, Tanenhaus (pp. 164–5) shows that rather than being born in an "institutionally intact" or fully complete form, the Chicago Juvenile Court took several decades of "trial and error" innovations to evolve into the model child welfare court that it was, rather inaccurately, reputed to represent from its beginning in 1899. Like Rothman and other earlier US juvenile justice historians, however, Tanenhaus (pp. xxiv–xxv) only gives passing attention to noting that the Chicago Juvenile Court soon became "a model . . . for policy makers in European, South American, and Asian nations" and that many of the "child savers" from other countries "looked to this American creation to learn how to divert children from the criminal justice system and to handle their cases in a less punitive fashion."

Another significant observation made by Tanenhaus (2004, p. 165) is that "child savers in the early twentieth century struggled with many of the same issues that twenty-first-century policy-makers must address." This observation about long-term historical continuity in the fundamental issues faced by youth justice policy-makers is consistent with Bernard's (1992) argument about the cyclical nature of juvenile justice reform, which he originally proposed to explain the late nineteenth-century juvenile court movement in the United States and which has been more recently extended to account for late twentieth- and early twenty-first-century reforms in US juvenile justice (Bernard and Kurlychek 2010). Unlike other juvenile justice historians, Bernard develops a general, theoretically based argument about the recurrent nature of cycles of juvenile justice reform to explain major shifts in juvenile justice law and procedure over time. In his initial study of the invention of the juvenile court in the nineteenth century, Bernard explains the establishment of the Chicago Juvenile Court in 1899, arguing that it represented yet another example of how adults commonly tend to respond to growing perceptions that juvenile crime is on the increase. According to Bernard's cyclical theory of juvenile justice reform, a movement toward reform

> begins at a time when justice officials and the general public are convinced that juvenile crime is at an exceptionally high level, and there are many harsh punishments but few lenient treatments for juvenile offenders. In this situation, justice officials often are forced to choose between harshly punishing juvenile offenders and doing nothing at all. As a consequence, many minor offenders are let off scot-free because lenient treatments are not available and because justice officials believe that the harsh punishments will make the minor offenders worse. (Bernard and Kurlychek 2010, p. 3; see also Figure 1.1)

To account for the invention of the juvenile court, Bernard documents this cyclical pattern of juvenile reform by comparing the circumstances that surrounded the creation of the Chicago Juvenile Court in 1899 with earlier reform movements that also led to the introduction of a more lenient approach to dealing with juvenile delinquents. In particular, he shows how the introduction of a more lenient justice system for juveniles in Chicago in 1899 was preceded 75 years earlier by a similar attempt, in New York, to create "Houses of Refuge" for the care and confinement of dependent and delinquent children.

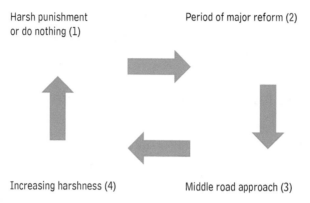

FIGURE 1.1 Cycles of Juvenile Justice Reform

1. Juvenile crime is thought to be unusually high. There are many harsh punishments and few lenient punishments. Officials often are forced to choose between harshly punishing juvenile offenders and doing nothing at all.
2. Juvenile crime is thought to be unusually high and is blamed on the "forced choice": that is, both harshly punishing and doing nothing at all are thought to increase juvenile crime.
3. A major reform introduces lenient treatments for juvenile offenders. This creates a middle ground between harshly punishing and doing nothing at all.
4. Juvenile crime is thought to be unusually high and is blamed on the lenient punishments. Harsh punishments gradually expand and lenient treatments gradually contract.

Source: Adapted from Bernard 1992, p. 4; and Bernard and Kurlychek 2010, p. 4.

In a manner analogous to the Chicago Juvenile Court, the establishment of the New York House of Refuge by the Society for the Reformation of Juvenile Delinquents in 1825 was aimed at introducing a less punitive alternative for juvenile offenders who otherwise might be sentenced to an adult penitentiary. Prior to the establishment of the New York House of Refuge, however, what occurred more often was that juries who were disturbed over the harshness of current punishment practices simply acquitted youth who were accused of crimes that could have led to their being jailed in an adult penitentiary. Given the choice of continuing to do nothing at all or working to introduce a more middle-of-the-road approach, supporters of the New York House of Refuge chose the latter approach. According to Bernard (1992, p. 99), this cycle was repeated in the late nineteenth century, at which time similar perceptions of "high juvenile crime rates were accompanied by a firm belief that these could be lowered by the proper policy response"—namely, the middle-of-the-road approach promised by the juvenile court. According to Bernard,

> The juvenile court, as a reform, was designed to provide leniency for those who would have been harshly punished by being sent to Chicago's jails and poorhouses, and to do something for juveniles for whom nothing would have been done by the adult criminal justice system. That is, it was designed to provide a middle ground between punishing harshly and doing nothing at all. In terms of "criminal justice thermodynamics," the juvenile court reduced the severity of the penalty to increase the frequency of its application.

As we will see in the following sections of this chapter, Bernard's cyclical theory of juvenile justice reform, alongside Tanenhaus's observation that many of the issues faced by early twentieth-century juvenile justice reformers are the same as those that policy-makers struggle with today, provides useful insights to keep in mind when examining both historical and contemporary trends in juvenile or youth justice.

Paths of Juvenile Justice Reform in Other Western Countries

The cross-fertilization of ideas on juvenile justice reform pointed to in some of the works of US and Canadian researchers is an important but largely overlooked aspect of juvenile justice history. Among US researchers, it invariably takes the form of noting how the US juvenile court model, rather than being interconnected with and perhaps recipro-cally influenced by ideas on juvenile delinquency and juvenile justice reform in other countries, influenced developments in other countries. Part of our interest in this chapter is with learning about the broad range of factors associated with the creation of early delinquency legislation and juvenile courts in the nineteenth and early twentieth centur-ies. As such, we will explore what researchers have documented about the origin and outcome of juvenile justice reform movements that emerged in other Western countries during the same period and about how these different paths of juvenile justice reform may have been interconnected.

In an article written in the year of "the centennial of the Chicago Juvenile Court," Jean Trépanier (1999), the leading French-Canadian criminologist and juvenile justice histor-ian, reflected on the operation of juvenile courts in North America and other, mainly European, countries over the century. While Trépanier recognizes that the Chicago Juvenile Court undeniably served as the model that was later followed in a number of other countries, he also points out that "the diversity that characterises the history and evolution of juvenile courts in Western societies" makes it important to examine the coinciding but also sometimes noticeably different paths of development that were fol-lowed elsewhere (ibid., p. 303).

One of the commonalities Trépanier points to is the gradual separation of juveniles and adults in court proceedings and institutions of confinement. For example, in France, Penal Codes enacted in 1791 and 1810 instituted a different court process for children under 16, while in the United States similar laws separating minors' trials from adults' were passed in 1874 in Massachusetts and 1892 in New York State. Also, in the same year that New York State passed its legislation, a new Criminal Code of Canada was enacted that "provided for the possibility of private trials for children" (Trépanier 1999, p. 310). Along the same lines, in Canada as far back as 1857 two statutes were passed in the Province of Canada: one that provided for "more expeditious trials" for young persons (An Act for the More Speedy Trial and Punishment of Young Persons) and another that created separate "reforma-tory prisons" for young offenders (An Act for Establishing Prisons for Young Persons). Similarly, in the United States, the House of Refuge movement started in the 1820s, mark-ing the beginning of the gradual removal of children from adult prisons. This movement coincided closely with a parallel reform movement in Britain that between 1840 and 1900 led to the wide-scale transfer of young offenders from adult prisons to variously titled youth "reform prisons," "reform schools," and "industrial schools" (Trépanier 1999, p. 310; Minaker and Hogeveen 2009). This pattern of gradual separation of juveniles from adults in court proceedings and institutions of confinement occurred in many other Western countries during the nineteenth century, as shown in a summary form in Table 1.1. What this comparative historical data clearly show is that there was an international dynamic in nineteenth-century juvenile justice reform that most likely involved an extensive cross-fertilization of reform ideas between various countries (see also Shore 2003; Vanstone 2008). However, while this pattern occurred across many jurisdictions, the specific ages of young people who came under the jurisdiction of new juvenile justice systems varied between different Western countries and sometimes even between different provinces and states within a country. For example, similar to the cases of states like Illinois and Colorado in the United States, with the enactment of the **Juvenile Delinquents Act** (JDA) in Canada in 1908, individual provinces were allowed to set their own maximum age of jurisdiction of the JDA at anywhere between 15 and 17 years old, while different age categories could also be selected for males and females. This was the case in Alberta, where the maximum age of jurisdiction was 15 for boys and 17 for girls (Hackler 1978).

Although all Western countries eventually established separate criminal court processes and institutions for dealing with juvenile offenders, the specific nature and timing of these developments varied considerably and, in some jurisdictions, occurred only quite gradually over the course of the first half of the twentieth century (Shore 2003). One

Juvenile Delinquents Act (JDA)
Canada's first juvenile delinquency legislation enacted in 1908 and in force until 1984.

Table 1.1	Juvenile Justice Reforms in Selected Western Countries	
Country or State	**Date of Earliest Delinquency Legislation and/or Functioning Juvenile Court**	**Date of Earliest Separate Juvenile Houses of Refuge, Prisons, Reformatories, and Industrial Schools**
Australia (by state)[1]	1895 to 1918	Most states, from 1863 to 1874
Belgium[2]	1912	1847
Canada[3]	1908	1858 (Quebec); 1859 (Ontario)
England and Wales[4]	1908	1838
France[5]	1912	1830
Germany[6]	1923	1833
Netherlands[7]	1922	1857
New Zealand[8]	1906	1867
Sweden[9]	1902	1838
United States[10]	1899	1825

Data Sources:
1. Cunneen and White 2007, pp. 5, 8–9, 14; O'Connor and Cameron 2002, p. 211; Trépanier 1999, p. 310.
2. Shore 2003, p. 117; Trépanier 1999, pp. 304, 312; Trépanier and Tulkens 1993.
3. Minaker and Hogeveen 2009, p. 48; Trépanier 1999, pp. 307, 310.
4. Corrado and Turnbull 1992, p. 78; Cunneen and White 2007, pp. 8–9; Morgan and Newburn 2007, p. 1024; Shore 2003, pp. 113, 117; Trépanier 1999, pp. 304, 313–14.
5. Blatier 1999, p. 241; Shore 2003, p. 112; Trépanier 1999, pp. 304, 310, 316.
6. Albrecht 2004, p. 443; Crofts 2002, p. 107; Trépanier 1999, pp. 304, 316.
7. Shore 2003, p. 117; Trépanier 1999, pp. 304, 316.
8. Morris 2004, pp. 247–8.
9. Janson 2004, p. 394; Shore 2003, p. 113.
10. Trépanier 1999, pp. 306, 310.

example of this is England and Wales, where the early juvenile courts provided for under the Children Act of 1908 were simply "special sittings of magistrates' courts . . . [that] were empowered to act in criminal, begging, and vagrancy cases, though they remained, in essence, criminal courts" (Morgan and Newburn 2007, p. 1024). Or, as Henri Giller (1999, p. 395) explains in more detail, in England and Wales the original juvenile court "was primarily a court with modified procedural arrangements which, in part, recognised the immaturity of youth," and it was not until 25 years later, with the passing of the Children and Young Person Acts of 1932 and 1933, that the court was formally allowed to make "the welfare of the child a particular (although [still] not overriding) consideration when determining what was an appropriate disposition for an offence." Similarly, Cunneen and White (2007, p. 15) have noted that although created as separate courts, early juvenile courts in Australia were "not as different from the adult courts" as they were in the US.

On the other hand, France was a country that patterned its juvenile justice system explicitly on the Chicago Juvenile Court model. This was apparently in large part through the influence of Edouard Julhiet, the son of a French Appeal Court judge, who lived in the United States from 1902 to 1906, where he learned about the Illinois system and returned to France to advocate for the establishment of a similar system (Vanstone 2008, p. 742). This was also the case for Germany, where "the youth court movement" that led to the enactment of the country's first Youth Court Law in 1923 "relied heavily on the thinking of the North American child-saving movement and on North American experiences with juvenile courts" (Albrecht 2002, p. 174).

From these comparative examples, we can more adequately appreciate the diversity that characterized the history and evolution of juvenile courts and also how the development of the juvenile court in Canada was influenced by ideas and practices that already existed in other countries.

Paths to Reform in Canada and the Origins of the JDA of 1908

While the history of the origin of the juvenile court model has not been seriously contested, a few claims have been made that the Chicago Juvenile Court was not the first. Some have claimed that South Australia "introduced the first juvenile court in the world" through state legislation enacted in 1895 (O'Connor and Cameron 2002, p. 212; Cunneen and White 2007). It has also been claimed that the state of Colorado established a juvenile court by way of enacting an education law that came into effect earlier in 1899 than the Juvenile Court Act of Illinois (Hagan and Leon 1977, p. 239). In addition, in the Canadian context, it was also claimed early on by none other than J.J. Kelso, one of the key lobbyists for the enactment of the Canadian JDA of 1908, that it was he who actually did more than anyone else to create the modern juvenile court. Although Kelso's claim was eventually effectively repudiated by his critics, the fact that he could make this claim and create the debate he did with his contemporaries shows a great deal about how Canada's JDA came into being.

J.J. Kelso was a "young, passionate and crusading Toronto newspaper reporter" who became a key leader in the child-saving movement in Ontario in the 1880s (Davis-Barron 2009, p. 31). Kelso later recalled that as a young reporter in Toronto, he witnessed first-hand the miserable conditions experienced by poor and neglected street children and pledged "to devote his life to 'plead for these little ones' who perished by the wayside 'in a land abounding in Christian activities'" (cited in Sutherland 1976, p. 112). Kelso figured prominently among the "new breed of child-savers" that emerged in Ontario and elsewhere in the 1880s, and along with them, he argued for an expansion of "the definition of needy children to include those who suffered from parental neglect or cruelty" while also promoting "the idea of foster homes as the most efficient, humane, and economical approach to child-welfare" (Bullen 1991, p. 136). In 1887, at the age of 22, Kelso "founded the Toronto Humane society, a voluntary organization dedicated to the protection of women, children, and animals," and by the following year he had successfully lobbied for the enactment of new Ontario legislation entitled An Act for the Protection and Reformation of Neglected Children, which, among other significant changes, empowered local municipalities to appoint commissioners "to conduct trials of juvenile offenders apparently under the age of sixteen" while also providing that all defendants under the age of 21 "be tried apart from other offenders, 'as far as practicable.'" In the same year, "he founded a charitable society known as the Fresh Air Fund for the purpose of providing poor city children with summer excursions," and in 1891, he founded and became the first voluntary president of the Toronto Children's Aid Society. In 1893, Kelso was recognized for his child welfare and juvenile justice reform efforts by being appointed Ontario's first superintendent of neglected and dependent children, a position created under a new child welfare act (entitled An Act for the Prevention of Cruelty to, and Better Protection of Children, commonly called "The Children's Act"), which Kelso himself had lobbied the provincial government to enact. This position, which Kelso occupied for the next 41 years, gave him the power to oversee directly the implementation of the Children's Act of 1893 as well as to lobby for additional child-centred social reforms (Bullen 1991, pp. 138–45).

Kelso was also in a good position to lobby the federal government to enact legislation that would enshrine Ontario's approach to dealing with dependent and delinquent children, and he began to do this with the help of Ottawa lawyer and president of the Ottawa Children's Aid Society W.L. Scott. Kelso and Scott worked together to campaign for the enactment of federal delinquency legislation. In the course of this effort, they both took every opportunity to strengthen support for their campaign from constituencies like the police, judges, and federal politicians in Ottawa. Toward this end, Kelso and Scott both corresponded with and travelled to the US to meet with juvenile justice reform experts, and through their efforts prominent American juvenile court proponents were invited to Ottawa "to address Senators and Members of the House of Commons regarding the benefits of a juvenile justice system for Canada" (Davis-Barron 2009, p. 36). Among their many cross-border connections, two of the most notable were Kelso's long-time acquaintance and correspondence with Judge Harvey B. Hurd, who drafted the Illinois legislation, and Judge Ben Lindsey of Denver, whom he met while travelling to conferences in the US. Significantly, however, historian Neil Sutherland claims that "Canadians . . . turned neither to Chicago or Denver but to Philadelphia for the model for their first systematic effort to put the notion [of a juvenile court] into practice." This stemmed from an event in May 1906. W.L. Scott, as president of the Ottawa Children's Aid Society (CAS), and his paid secretary, John Keane, attended an annual meeting of the National Conference of Charities and Correction in Philadelphia, where they learned about the system of juvenile probation used in that city; they subsequently returned to Ottawa to persuade the executive committee of the Ottawa CAS to adopt the same system. Later that year, Scott and his influential father, Senator R.W. Scott, invited Mrs Hannah Kent Schoff, chairperson of the Philadelphia Court Committee, to come to Ottawa to "address a special meeting of senators and members of Parliament" on the benefits of creating a juvenile court system like the one in Philadelphia (Sutherland 1976, pp. 119–21). Scott also shortly afterward hosted Judge Ben Lindsey in Ottawa to address members of Parliament on the benefits of enacting legislation for creating a specialized juvenile court (Hogeveen 2001).

It is true that historians commonly recognize that it was W.L. Scott who drafted the JDA and, with his father's help, lobbied most vigorously for the passage of the legislation first through the Canadian Senate and then through the House of Commons. However, in later years Kelso claimed that the juvenile court movement started neither in Chicago nor in Philadelphia but in Ontario, beginning with the effort he undertook in 1888 to lobby for the enactment of An Act for the Protection and Reformation of Neglected Children, which provided for separate trials for juveniles. Moreover, Kelso claimed that he had influenced the creation of the Chicago Juvenile Court by corresponding with "officials in Chicago" and attending three conferences there in 1893, where he advocated his "Children's Court ideas as one of the chief solutions of juvenile crime" (cited in Hagan and Leon 1980, p. 240). In 1933, in response to lingering stories about the role Kelso claimed for himself in the creation of the JDA, Scott wrote a letter in which he disputed Kelso's story with his own claim that it was he who had drafted the original legislation, taking into account mainly the juvenile court acts of Illinois and Colorado (Hagan and Leon 1980). In the end, however, it would be misleading to give credit for the origin of Canada's modern juvenile justice system solely to the humanitarian conscience and power of the ideas and rhetoric of social reformers like Kelso and Scott, as Rothman (1980) analogously did in the US context. In addition, we must take into account a number of other factors, including earlier precursors to the juvenile court, the changing social and economic climate of the last half of the nineteenth century, the gradual rise of the social welfare state in many countries, and other international influences such as the cross-fertilization of ideas about juvenile justice reform (for a more detailed discussion of these factors, see Minaker and Hogeveen 2009).

The JDA nonetheless represented a fundamental shift in the way juvenile justice was administered in Canada. In addition to making the supervision of juvenile offenders in the community a central feature by way of probation, the Act cast a wide net in defining the types of delinquent and dependent children who would henceforth come under the jurisdiction of the legislation. Specifically, the JDA originally defined a juvenile delinquent as "any child who violates any provision of *The Criminal Code* . . . , or of any Dominion or provincial statute, or of any by-law or ordinance of any municipality, for which violation punishment of a fine or imprisonment may be awarded; or, who is liable by reason of any other act to be committed to an industrial school or juvenile reformatory under the provisions of any Dominion or provincial statute." A 1924 revision to the Act further broadened the definition of *juvenile delinquent* to include any child "who is guilty of sexual immorality or any similar form of vice" (cited in Davis-Barron 2009, p. 41). This broadened definition of delinquent youth led to the creation of what later came to be referred to as **status offences**, or offences that a youth could be found guilty of simply because he or

status offences
Behaviours that are considered delinquent or criminal only because the person who engages in the behaviour is not yet an adult. Examples include truancy (e.g., skipping school), underage drinking, and promiscuous sexual behaviour.

she was underage. These included offences like "the consumption of alcohol, truancy, running away from home, refusal to obey parents, having delinquent friends, and the use of profanity" (Tanner 2010, p. 31). In many provinces children were committed to industrial or training schools for such offences or for being found guilty of either "unmanageability" or "incorrigibility" (Bala 1997). The doctrine of *parens patriae* embodied in the JDA also gave juvenile court judges and corrections officials the discretion to sentence children to **indeterminate sentences** of incarceration, which meant that they would not be released until "they were no longer a threat to the public . . . or until they reached the age of 21" (Minaker and Hogeveen 2009, p. 59). As a general rule, the JDA exerted jurisdiction over children ranging from 7 to 15 years of age. However, the Act also allowed for considerable variation between provinces; each province was allowed to decide the cut-off age, above 15, at which point a trial involving a young person would be held in adult court. In most provinces the age was set at 16 years, while in Manitoba and Quebec it was set at 18 years, and as noted previously, in Alberta these age cut-offs were also made gender specific (Hackler 1978). As in the case of the juvenile courts established in other countries, the child welfare orientation of the JDA was also reflected in the informal nature of proceedings in juvenile courts, where judges, many of whom had no legal training themselves, sought to give hopefully wise advice to "misguided children," and where lawyers were discouraged from appearing in order "that 'unnecessary technicalities' would not interfere with or delay the treatment considered to be in the child's best interests" (Bala 1997, p. 44).

When the JDA came into effect, juvenile courts and probation services, as in other countries, developed unevenly across Canada, and it was well into the twentieth century before many rural and remote areas had a functioning juvenile justice system. This, along with the differences in the cut-off age for juvenile offenders, not surprisingly contributed to a great deal of inter-provincial and regional variation in the application of the legislation (Hogeveen 2001; Myers 1999; Sangster 2002; Sutherland 1976; Woloschuk 2009).

Yet even before the JDA became more evenly implemented across the country, its operation began to be criticized on a number of grounds. By the 1960s and 1970s, the move toward juvenile justice reform in Canada, again noticeably influenced by parallel developments in the United States, was well under way (Minaker and Hogeveen 2009). When the **Young Offenders Act (YOA)** was finally introduced in 1984 to replace the JDA, many criminologists and youth justice policy-makers viewed it as a long-overdue reform that finally brought in needed "due process" rights and safeguards for young offenders, which included most importantly a guaranteed right to obtain and instruct legal counsel (Bala 1997; Leschied, Jaffe, and Willis 1991). At the same time, however, critics of the new legislation viewed it as representing an unfortunate shift away from the child welfare–based child-saving approach of the JDA toward a more justice- and crime-control-based child-blaming approach, in which priority would be given to holding young offenders accountable for their criminal behaviour (Havemann 1986, 1992).

The relatively short 15-year life of the YOA was marked with controversy from the outset, and the Act underwent a number of significant amendments before it was finally replaced with the **Youth Criminal Justice Act (YCJA)** in 2003 (see, generally, Bala 1997; Doob and Sprott 2006; Hogeveen and Smandych 2001). In the remaining part of this chapter, more attention is given to more recent contemporary trends in youth justice and,

indeterminate sentences
Sentences of incarceration that have no fixed expiration date, which means that a person can be held in custody until he or she is deemed by correctional officials either to be rehabilitated or to no longer pose a threat to society.

Young Offenders Act (YOA)
The federal legislation that replaced the Juvenile Delinquents Act from 1984 to 2003.

Youth Criminal Justice Act (YCJA)
The federal legislation enacted in 2002 to replace the Young Offenders Act and which came into effect on 1 April 2003.

in particular, to the question of whether in recent years Canadians have taken a more punitive approach to dealing with young criminals.

Contemporary Trends in Youth Justice Law and Practice in Canada

With the enactment of the YCJA in 2002 and its formal implementation on 1 April 2003, Canada entered into a new era in the administration of juvenile or youth justice. As in the years following the enactment of the JDA and the YOA, youth justice professionals from across Canada—including police, lawyers and judges, and youth corrections personnel—have now taken up the task of attempting to interpret and apply the legal principles underlying the YCJA (Bala and Anand 2009; Tustin and Lutes 2013). Meanwhile, criminologists and government policy analysts are continuing to assess how in fact the YCJA has been implemented in practice across the country and what the outcomes of its application have been to date (cf. Alain, Reid, and Corrado 2016; Bala, Carrington, and Roberts 2009; Corrado, Kuehn, and Margaritescu 2014; Doob and Sprott 2006; Peterson-Badali and Broeking 2009; Sprott 2012). In addition to this burgeoning research literature, a number of the authors of later chapters of this book also make insightful contributions to our knowledge of the implementation and effects of the YCJA. See, in particular, Chapters 2, 3, and 4. These chapters include important details about the YCJA and should thus be read along with the current chapter, which is concerned more with highlighting the role of historical and comparative research in helping to explain contemporary trends in youth justice in Canada.

The Origins of the YCJA and the Punitive Turn Debate

Like its predecessors, the JDA and the YOA, the enactment of the YCJA was clearly part of a broad international shift away from a child welfare model of juvenile justice toward more legalistic and ostensibly punitive justice and crime-control models. However, in many countries this shift was not solely away from what were perceived as lenient juvenile crime prevention and response strategies and toward harsher ways of punishing wayward youth (Bernard 1992; Muncie 2008). This appears to be particularly the case in Canada. When it was enacted in 2002, for instance, the YCJA contained sections that provided for the harsher, adult-like punishment of violent young offenders while restricting the use of custody sentences for youth convicted of non-violent crimes. The Act also introduced a wide range of formal and informal extrajudicial measures for diverting first-time and less serious young offenders out of the youth justice system. Such measures included police warnings, cautions, and community-based conferences (for details, see Chapter 3). In effect, these measures made Canada's new youth criminal justice system, at least formally on paper, a **bifurcated youth justice system**—"wherein petty and non-serious offenders would be handled through community-based and diversionary programs while serious and violent offenders would be subject to more carceral and punitive interventions" (Minaker and Hogeveen 2009, pp. 78–9).

One of the issues currently being debated by Canadian criminologists is the degree to which the implementation of the YCJA has resulted in a shift toward more use of "carceral and

bifurcated youth justice system
Literally, a two-pronged justice system, meaning that it provides avenues for diverting first-time and less serious young offenders out of the system while at the same time making possible more punitive forms of punishment for more serious offenders.

punitive interventions" in the youth justice system and less use of "community-based and diversionary programs," which are generally perceived to be more lenient. It is not my purpose in this chapter to try to resolve this debate but, rather, to show that a better understanding of the factors that led to the creation of the YCJA and the punitive turn debate itself can be obtained by placing both of these in their respective historical and comparative contexts.

In a study published just prior to the enactment of the YCJA in 2002, Hogeveen and Smandych (2001) located the immediate origins of the YCJA in the political discourse surrounding the perceived crises in youth crime in Canada in the 1990s. To carry out this research, they drew on the approach of other criminologists and historians who had earlier attempted to explain the origins of the JDA and the YOA by analyzing parliamentary debates and media reports (e.g., Havemann 1986; Trépanier 1991). From their study of parliamentary debates and media reports of the period, they found that the dominant view expressed in the speeches of most federal politicians at the time and in newspapers reports on youth justice reform was that the YOA was too lenient on youth offenders and unable to effectively address what was perceived to be a growing crisis of youth crime. While Hogeveen and Smandych did not attempt to predict how young offenders would be dealt with under the YCJA in the future, they did argue, in line with what would later come to be referred to as the "punitive turn thesis," that the wording of the legislation appeared to mark a significant shift away from referring to deviant youth officially as either "juvenile delinquents" or "young offenders," signifying their reduced responsibility and toward viewing them as "young criminals" and making them "appear much closer to adult criminals" (2001, p. 166).

In two subsequent separately authored studies, Hogeveen (2005) and Smandych (2006) develop arguments that more directly address the issue of the alleged punitive turn in youth justice. In these studies, they offer similar skeptical views of the YCJA's ability to facilitate the promotion of community-based extrajudicial ways of dealing with young offenders. They also point to the continuing potential for the YCJA, and its possible perceived failures, to be used to justify more punitive responses to various types of broadly defined "youth violent crime" and "serious violent offenders" (Tanner 2010). Both authors also point out that the growing demand in Canada in the 1990s for tougher legislation to deal with criminal youth paralleled contemporary trends in other countries, such as the United States and Britain, toward "the further dismantling of traditional 'child-welfare' juvenile court procedures" (Smandych 2006, p. 23) and the introduction of new legislation aimed at getting tough on juvenile crime (Hogeveen 2005, p. 77).

In recent years other critics, including criminologists, lawyers, and the leaders of youth-serving and youth advocacy organizations, have added their voices to the growing concern with the **adulteration** of youth justice policy and practice under the YCJA (Justice for Children and Youth 2011; Smandych et al. 2016). A focal issue that prompted some of this criticism was the introduction of the Conservative federal government's omnibus Bill C-10 in the fall of 2012, which, along with "toughing up" on many aspects of the adult criminal justice system in Canada, introduced a number of measures aimed at treating young people accused of crimes more like adult offenders (Canada 2012). One of these measures has been to enable youth justice court judges to consider "specific deterrence" and "denunciation" as valid principles in sentencing convicted youth. While traditionally allowed as principles that judges could consider in sentencing adult offenders, prior to the passage of Bill C-10 neither of these principles was allowed to be used in sentencing youth because of provisions

adulteration
The dismantling of a distinct system of criminal justice for youth and the re-merging with systems of justice for adults.

of the YCJA and judicial case precedents that embodied the view that the lack of maturity and full legal culpability on the part of most youth made the general use of these sentencing principles in youth cases inappropriate (Tustin and Lutes 2013, pp. 85–7). Another concern raised by critics of Bill C-10, is the manner in which it substantially broadens the definition of "a violent offence." Prior to Bill C-10, the YCJA and related court decisions reaffirmed that a violent offence in a youth case excluded pure property offences and only referred to "an offence in the commission of which a young person causes, attempts to cause, or threatens to cause bodily harm" (also see Chapter 3). However, since the addition of Bill C-10 amendments to the YCJA, the definition of such an offence now includes any "offence in the commission of which a young person endangers the life or safety of another person by creating a substantial likelihood of causing bodily harm." Critics are concerned that these amendments introduced in Bill C-10 have the potential of opening the door for judges to sentence more young offenders to custody than has previously been the case.

While it is still relatively too short a time since the introduction and amendment of the YCJA to offer "any definitive statements about its impact on the administration of juvenile justice in Canada" (Tanner 2010, p. 250), other criminologists have argued that available youth court processing and sentencing data show that there has been no real increase in the punitiveness of the Canadian youth criminal justice system in recent years (Bala, Carrington, and Roberts 2009; Doob and Sprott 2006). Anthony Doob and Jane Sprott (2006, p. 224), in a critique of Hogeveen's (2005) study, also make the historically based claim that the intention of the government of Canada when it introduced the YCJA was not to create tougher legislation but simply to make it appear that it was doing so in order to deflect the criticism from political opposition parties that it was too soft on youth crime. According to Doob and Sprott, by formally creating a bifurcated youth justice system, federal government legislative drafters had quite astutely "crafted a law" that offered more opportunities than had existed before to "reduce the level of punitiveness" of the youth criminal justice system (2006, p. 224). Whether or not this was actually the case, it is difficult to predict the direction in which the administration of juvenile justice in Canada will move in the future (Mann 2011). One reason for this, as we have begun to learn in this chapter, is that we must consider contemporary trends in Canadian youth justice within the context of comparable juvenile justice developments in other countries (see Bateman 2012; Bernard and Kurlychek 2010; Dillard 2013; Feld and Bishop 2013; Champion 2013; Muncie 2008).

In addition, in order to arrive at more definitive conclusions about whether the Canadian youth justice system is taking a punitive turn, we need to also take into account whether trends in the punishment of youth are moving in a similar or different direction than punishment trends in the adult criminal justice system (Hamilton 2014; Loader 2010; Meyer and O'Malley 2005; Moore and Hannah-Moffat 2005; Snacken 2010). At present, perhaps the most accurate observation that can be made is the one offered by Julian Tanner (2010, p. 250), who states, "It remains to be seen how the Youth Criminal Justice Act will be judged by members of the voting public, especially victims' rights organizations, who are inclined to view all juvenile justice legislation as being too lenient. It seems unlikely that the popular appeal of 'get tough' approaches to young offenders will ever completely go away." In this respect, Tanner's observation very much complements Bernard's cyclical theory of juvenile justice reform, which, as we have seen, highlights the perennial policy-choice dilemma in youth justice between choosing harsh punishments or doing nothing at all.

Summary

This chapter has stressed the value of historical and comparative research in understanding contemporary trends in Canadian youth justice. It has shown that Canada's current approach to dealing with young people who come into conflict with the law evolved over many centuries and involved many significant turning points along the way. One of these was the gradual shift that occurred in adult sensibilities about childhood—or what Ariès argued amounted to "the discovery of childhood"; over time, adults changed from viewing young people as little adults from a very early stage in life to viewing and treating them as innocent and vulnerable children who needed to be nurtured and protected for a more extended period of time. By the late nineteenth century this extended period of "growing up," or the transitional years from childhood to adulthood, came to be referred to as adolescence. Social-scientific knowledge about this newly defined stage in life in turn had a noticeable influence on the thinking of social reformers about the causes of juvenile delinquency and the value of having a separate juvenile court for dealing with troubled youth, who now were perceived mainly as either dependent, neglected, or misguided and therefore mostly in need of friendly helpfulness.

Historical research, however, shows that many other factors were in operation that help to account for the enactment of the JDA in 1908, such as earlier precursors to the juvenile court, the changing social and economic climate of the last half of the nineteenth century, the gradual rise of the social welfare state in many countries, and the international cross-fertilization of ideas about juvenile justice reform. In its description of the essential research findings on the origins of the YCJA and the debate over the alleged recent punitive turn in Canadian youth justice, this chapter highlights the value of historical and comparative research to an understanding of more recent, and possibly future, trends in the Canadian youth criminal justice system.

Key Terms

adolescence
adulteration
bifurcated youth justice system
diminished criminal responsibility
doli incapax
indeterminate sentences
juvenile courts
juvenile delinquency
Juvenile Delinquents Act (JDA)

parens patriae
punishable young offender
punitive turn thesis
reformable young offender
status offences
Young Offenders Act (YOA)
Youth Criminal Justice Act (YCJA)
youth criminal justice systems

Review Questions

1. What can we learn from studying the history of childhood that is relevant to understanding the development and operation of modern juvenile justice systems?

2. What were the major factors that contributed to the development of specialized youth justice systems in Western countries, including Canada in the late nineteenth and early twentieth centuries?

3. How important were humanitarian conscience and the rhetoric of social reformers in the development of early juvenile delinquency legislation and juvenile courts in the US and Canada?

4. What is Bernard's cyclical theory of juvenile justice reform, and how might it be used to explain reforms in Canadian youth justice legislation, such as the introduction of the JDA (in 1908) and the YCJA (in 2002)?

Critical Thinking Questions

1. Is it harder to raise children today than in the past? Why?

2. Do we really need a specialized youth justice system in Canada? Why or why not?

3. Has there been a punitive turn in youth justice in Canada? What types of data could you use to try to answer this question?

4. If you were given the power to make changes in the Canadian youth criminal justice system, would you want the system to be more lenient or more punitive? Why?

References

Alain, M., Reid, S., and Corrado, R. (Eds). (2016). *Implementing and Working with the Youth Criminal Justice Act across Canada*. Toronto: University of Toronto Press.

Albrecht, H.-J. (2002). Juvenile crime and juvenile law in the Federal Republic of Germany. In J. Winterdyk (Ed.), *Juvenile justice systems: International perspectives* (2nd ed.), (pp. 171–206). Toronto: CSPI.

Albrecht, H.-J. (2004). Youth justice in Germany. In M. Tonry and A. Doob (Eds), *Youth crime and youth justice: Comparative and cross-national perspectives* (pp. 443–93). Chicago: Chicago University Press.

Ariès, P. (1962). *Centuries of childhood: A social history of family life*. New York: Vintage Books.

Bala, N. (1997). *Young offenders law*. Toronto: Irwin.

Bala, N., and Anand, S. (2009). *Youth criminal justice law*. Toronto: Irwin.

Bala, N., Carrington, P., and Roberts, J. (2009). Evaluating the Youth Criminal Justice Act after five years: A qualified success. *Canadian Journal of Criminology and Criminal Justice*, 51(2): 131–67.

Bateman, T. (2012). Who pulled the plug? Towards an explanation of the fall in child imprisonment in England and Wales. *Youth Justice*, 12(1): 36–52.

Beattie, J. (1986). *Crime and the courts in England 1600–1800*. Princeton: Princeton University Press.

Bernard, T.J. (1992). *The cycle of juvenile justice*. New York: Oxford University Press.

Bernard, T.J., and Kurlychek, M. (2010). *The cycle of juvenile justice* (2nd ed.). New York: Oxford University Press.

Blatier, C. (1999). Juvenile justice in France. *British Journal of Criminology*, 39(2): 240–52.

Bullen, J. (1991). J.J. Kelso and the "new" child-savers: The genesis of the children's aid movement in Ontario. In R. Smandych, G. Dodds, and A. Esau (Eds), *Dimensions of childhood: Essays in the history of children and youth in Canada* (pp. 135–58). Winnipeg: University of Manitoba, Legal Research Institute.

Carrigan, D.O. (1998). *Juvenile delinquency in Canada: A history*. Toronto: Irwin.

Champion, D.J. (2013). *The juvenile justice system: Delinquency, processing, and the law*. Upper Saddle River, NJ: Pearson.

Colomy, P., and Kretzmann, M. (1995). Projects and institution building: Judge Ben B. Lindsey and the juvenile court movement. *Social Problems*, 42(2): 191–215.

Comacchio, C. (2010). Lost in modernity: "Maladjustment" and the "modern youth problem," English Canada, 1920–50. In M. Gleason, T. Myers, L. Paris, and V. Strong-Boag (Eds), *Lost kids: Vulnerable children and youth in twentieth-century Canada and the United States* (pp. 53–71). Vancouver: University of British Columbia Press.

Corrado, R., Kuehn, S., and Margaritescu, I. (2014). Policy issues regarding the over-representation of incarcerated Aboriginal young offenders in a Canadian context. *Youth Justice* 14(1): 40–62.

Corrado, R., and Turnbull, S. (1992). A comparative examination of the modified justice model in the United Kingdom and the United States. In R. Corrado, N. Bala, R. Linden, and M. Le Blanc (Eds), *Juvenile justice in Canada: A theoretical and analytical assessment* (pp. 75–136). Toronto: Butterworths.

Crofts, T. (2002). *The criminal responsibility of children and young persons: A comparison of English and German law*. Aldershot, UK: Ashgate.

Cunneen, C., and White, R. (2007). *Juvenile justice: Youth and crime in Australia* (3rd ed.). Melbourne: Oxford University Press.

Davis-Barron, S. (2009). *Canadian youth and the criminal law*. Markham, ON: LexisNexis Canada.

Dillard, D. (2013). Limited disproportionate minority contact discourse may explain limited progress in reducing minority over-representation in the US juvenile justice system. *Youth Justice*, 13(3): 207–17.

Dohrn, B. (2002). The school, the child, and the court. In M.K. Rosenheim, F.E. Zimring, D.S. Tanenhaus, and B. Dohrn (Eds), *A century of juvenile justice* (pp. 267–309). Chicago: University of Chicago Press.

Doob, A.N., and Sprott, J. (2006). Punishing youth crime in Canada: The blind men and the elephant. *Punishment and Society*, 8(2): 223–33.

Empey, L. (1982). *American delinquency: Its meaning and construction*. Chicago: Dorsey Press.

Feld, B.C., and Bishop, D. (2013). Juvenile justice. In M. Tonry (Ed.), *Oxford handbook of crime and criminal justice* (pp. 627–59). Oxford: Oxford University Press.

Getis, V. (2000). *The juvenile court and the progressives*. Urbana: University of Illinois Press.

Giller, H. (1999). From center stage to spear carrier: The repositioning of the English juvenile court. *European Journal on Criminal Policy and Research*, 7(3): 395–403.

Gottlieb, B. (1993). *The family in the Western world from the Black Death to the Industrial Age*. New York: Oxford University Press.

Graebner, W. (1994). Juvenile delinquency. In P. Stearns (Ed.), *Encyclopedia of social history* (pp. 379–81). New York: Garland Publishing.

Griffiths, C., and Verdun-Jones, S. (1994). *Canadian criminal justice*. Toronto: Harcourt Brace.

Hackler, J. (1978). *The prevention of youthful crime: The great stumble forward*. Toronto: Methuen.

Hagan, J., and Leon, J. (1977). Rediscovering delinquency: Social history, political ideology, and the sociology of law. *American Sociological Review*, 42(August): 587–98.

Hagan, J., and Leon, J. (1980). The rehabilitation of law: A social-historical comparison of probation in Canada and the United States. *Canadian Journal of Sociology/Cahiers Canadiens de Sociologie*, 5(3): 235–51.

Hall, G.S. (1904). *Adolescence: Its relation to physiology, anthropology, sociology, sex, crime, religion, and education*. New York: D. Appleton.

Hamilton, C. (2014). Reconceptualizing penality: Towards a multidimensional measure of punitiveness. *British Journal of Criminology*, 54(2): 321–43.

Havemann, P. (1986). From child saving to child blaming: The political economy of the Young Offenders Act 1908–1984. In S. Brickery and E. Comack (Eds), *The social basis of law* (p. 225). Toronto: Garamond.

Havemann, P. (1992). Crisis justice for youth: Making the Young Offenders Act and the discourse of penality. In D. Currie and B. MacLean (Eds), *Rethinking the administration of justice* (pp. 86–112). Halifax: Fernwood.

Hogeveen, B. (2001). "Winning deviant youth over by friendly helpfulness": Transformations in the legal governance of deviant children, 1857–1908. In R. Smandych (Ed.), *Youth justice: History, legislation, and reform* (pp. 43–63). Toronto: Harcourt.

Hogeveen, B. (2005). "If we are tough on crime, if we punish crime, then people get the message": Constructing and governing the punishable young offender in Canada during the late 1990s. *Punishment and Society*, 7(1): 73–89.

Hogeveen, B., and Smandych, R. (2001). Origins of the newly proposed Canadian Youth Criminal Justice Act: Political discourse and the perceived crisis in youth crime in the 1990s. In R. Smandych (Ed.), *Youth justice: History, legislation, and reform* (pp. 144–68). Toronto: Harcourt.

Hutchinson, T., Parada, G., and Smandych, R. (2008). "Show me a bad kid and I'll show you a lousy parent": Making parents responsible for youth crime in Australian and Canadian contexts. *Australasian Canadian Studies*, 26(2): 40–86.

Janson, C.-G. (2004). Youth justice in Sweden. In M. Tonry and A. Doob (Eds), *Youth crime and youth justice: Comparative and cross-national perspectives* (pp. 391–441). Chicago: Chicago University Press.

Justice for Children and Youth. (2011). Justice for Children and Youth's submission on Bill C-10: Youth Criminal Justice Act amendments. Submitted to the House of Commons Committee on Justice and Human Rights, 6 November 2011.

Langbein, J. (1992). *The London hanged: Crime and civil society in the eighteenth century*. Cambridge: Cambridge University Press.

Leschied, A., Jaffe, P., and Willis, W. (Eds). (1991). *The Young Offenders Act: A revolution in Canadian juvenile justice*. Toronto: University of Toronto Press.

Loader, I. (2010). For penal moderation: Notes toward a public philosophy of punishment. *Theoretical Criminology*, 14(3): 349–67.

Mann, R. (2011). A specialized criminal justice system for Canadian youth: Critical overview of historical and contemporary developments in law and procedures governing youth offending. In K. Kramer (Ed.), *Criminology: Critical Canadian perspectives* (pp. 57–77). Toronto: Pearson.

Meyer, J., and O'Malley, P. (2005). Missing the punitive turn? Canadian criminal justice, "balance," and penal modernism. In J. Pratt, D. Brown, M. Brown, S. Hallsworth, and W. Morrison (Eds), *The new punitiveness: Trends, theories, perspectives* (pp. 201–17). Cullompton, UK: Willan Publishing.

Minaker, J., and Hogeveen, B. (2009). *Youth, crime, and society: Issues of power and justice*. Toronto: Pearson.

Moore, D., and Hannah-Moffat, K. (2005). The liberal veil: Revisiting Canadian penality. In J. Pratt, D. Brown, M. Brown, S. Hallsworth, and W. Morrison (Eds), *The new punitiveness: Trends, theories, perspectives* (pp. 85–100). Cullompton, UK: Willan Publishing.

Morgan, R., and Newburn, T. (2007). Youth justice. In R. Reiner (Ed.), *Oxford handbook of criminology* (pp. 1024–60). Oxford: Oxford University Press.

Morris, A. (2004). Youth justice in New Zealand. In M. Tonry and A. Doob (Eds), *Youth crime and youth justice: Comparative and cross-national perspectives* (pp. 243–92). Chicago: Chicago University Press.

Muncie, J. (2005). The globalisation of crime control—The case of youth and juvenile justice: Neo-liberalism, policy convergence and international conventions. *Theoretical Criminology*, 9(1): 35–64.

Muncie, J. (2008). The "punitive turn" in juvenile justice: Cultures of control and rights compliance in Western Europe and the USA. *Youth Justice*, 8(2): 107–21.

Muncie, J., and Goldson, B. (Eds). (2006). *Comparative youth justice: Critical issues*. London: Sage.

Myers, T. (1999). The voluntary delinquent: Parents, daughters, and the Montreal juvenile delinquents' court in 1918. *Canadian Historical Review*, 80(2): 242–68.

O'Connor, I., and Cameron, M. (2002). Juvenile justice in Australia. In A. Graycar and P. Grabosky (Eds), *Cambridge handbook of Australian criminology* (pp. 211–34). Sydney: Cambridge University Press.

Peterson-Badali, M., and Broeking, J. (2009). Parents' involvement in the youth justice system: A view from the trenches. *Canadian Journal of Criminology and Criminal Justice*, 51(2): 255–70.

Platt, A.M. (1969). *The child savers: The invention of delinquency*. Chicago: University of Chicago Press.

Platt, A.M. (1974). The triumph of benevolence: The origins of the juvenile justice system in the United States. In R. Quinney (Ed.), *Criminal justice in America* (pp. 356–89). Boston: Little, Brown.

Pollock, L. (1983). *Forgotten children, parent–child relations from 1500 to 1900*. Cambridge: Cambridge University Press.

Redding, R., Goldstein, N.S., and Heilbrun, K. (2005). Juvenile delinquency: Past and present. In K. Heilbrun, N.S. Goldstein, and R. Redding (Eds), *Juvenile delinquency: Prevention, assessment, and intervention* (pp. 3–18). New York: Oxford University Press.

Rothman, D.J. (1980). *Conscience and convenience: The asylum and its alternatives in progressive America*. Boston: Little, Brown.

Sangster, J. (2002). "She is hostile to our ways": First Nations girls sentenced to the Ontario Training School for Girls, 1933–1960. *Law and History Review, 20*(1): 59–96.

Shahar, S. (1990). *Childhood in the Middle Ages*. London: Routledge.

Shore, H. (2003). "Inventing" the juvenile delinquent in nineteenth century Europe. In C. Emsley and G. Dunstall (Eds), *Comparative crime histories* (pp. 110–23). Cullompton, UK: Willan Publishing.

Smandych, R. (1991). Tory paternalism and the politics of penal reform in Upper Canada, 1830–1834: A "neo-revisionist" account of the Kingston Penitentiary. *Criminal Justice History: An International Annual, 12*: 57–83.

Smandych, R. (2001). Accounting for changes in Canadian youth justice: From the invention to the disappearance of childhood. In R. Smandych (Ed.), *Youth justice: History, legislation, and reform* (pp. 1–23). Toronto: Harcourt.

Smandych, R. (2006). Canada: Repenalisation and young offenders' rights. In J. Muncie and B. Goldson (Eds), *Comparative youth justice: Critical issues* (pp. 19–33). London: Sage.

Smandych, R., Dyck, M., La Berge, C., and Koffman, J. (2016). Youth justice in Manitoba: Developments and issues under the YCJA. In M. Alain, S. Reid, and R. Corrado (Eds), *Implementing and working with the Youth Criminal Justice Act across Canada*. Toronto: University of Toronto Press.

Snacken, S. (2010). Resisting punitiveness in Europe? *Theoretical Criminology, 14*(3): 273–92.

Spagnoli, P.G. (1981). Philippe Aries: Historian of the family. *Journal of Family History, 6*: 434–41.

Sprott, J. (2012). The persistence of *status offences* in the youth justice system. *Canadian Journal of Criminology and Criminal Justice, 54*(3): 309–32.

Sutherland, N. (1976). *Children in English-Canadian society: Framing the twentieth-century consensus*. Toronto: University of Toronto Press.

Tanenhaus, D.S. (2004). *Juvenile justice in the making*. New York: Oxford University Press.

Tanner, J. (2010). *Teenage troubles: Youth and deviance in Canada*. Toronto: Oxford University Press.

Thorson, A.M. (1999). From *parens patriae* to crime control: A comparison of the history and effectiveness of the juvenile justice systems in the United States and Canada. *Arizona Journal of International and Comparative Law, 16*(3): 845–71.

Trépanier, J. (1991). The origins of the Juvenile Delinquents Act of 1908: Controlling delinquency through seeking its causes and through youth protection. In R. Smandych, G. Dodds, and A. Esau (Eds), *Dimensions of childhood: Essays in the history of children and youth in Canada* (pp. 205–32). Winnipeg: University of Manitoba, Legal Research Institute.

Trépanier, J. (1999). Juvenile courts after 100 years: Past and present orientations. *European Journal on Criminal Policy and Research, 7*(3): 303–27.

Trépanier, J., and Tulkens, F. (1993). Juvenile justice in Belgium and Canada at the beginning of the century: Two models or one? *International Journal of Children's Rights, 1*: 189–211.

Tustin, L., and Lutes, R. (2013). *A guide to the Youth Criminal Justice Act*. Markham, ON: LexisNexis.

Vanstone, M. (2008). The international origins and initial development of probation. *British Journal of Criminology, 48*: 735–55.

Wilson, S. (1984). The myth of motherhood a myth: The historical view of European child-rearing. *Social History, 9*: 181–98.

Woloschuk, C. (2009). Protecting and policing children: The origins and nature of juvenile justice in Winnipeg. In E.W. Jones and G. Friesen (Eds), *Prairie metropolis: New essays on Winnipeg social history* (pp. 63–81). Winnipeg: University of Manitoba Press.

Measuring Youth Crime in Canada: An Elusive Challenge

John A. Winterdyk

Overview

This chapter provides an overview of the official and unofficial facts about youth crime in Canada. To provide a contextual framework, a brief historical description of the social and historical influences on youth crime will serve to help us understand how and why we measure youth crime today. The chapter then reviews the types of data and information that can be gleaned from official data sources as well as from unofficial data sources (for example, self-report and victimization surveys). A review of various youth crime characteristics and trends will be presented along with an examination of some provincial variations. The findings are discussed within the context of describing some of the key trends and patterns of youth crime.

Key Objectives

After reading this chapter, you should be able to:

- Understand the importance of social and historical influences on the evolution of youth justice and the measuring of youth crime in Canada.

- Understand how we define youth crime.

- Recognize that measuring and recording youth crime is influenced by varying formal social control mechanisms.

- Describe some of the key facts and trends of youth crime over the past several decades.

- Understand the strengths and weaknesses of official statistics in relation to self-report and victimization data.

- Critically reflect on what the three measurement methods tell us about youth crime, as well as what they do not tell us.

Introduction

> Juvenile delinquency is a complex, multi-faceted issue. In order to devise effective prevention and intervention strategies for youth at risk, it is important to understand the context in which this behaviour occurs.
>
> (A statistical snapshot . . . 2012)

As a social scientist who has been studying youth crime since the early 1970s, I am regularly asked by the media to explain the apparent nature and extent of youth crime locally and at times internationally. Given that some 23 per cent of Canada's population is under the age of 20 (A statistical snapshot . . . 2014), it would seem fair to ask: How serious and how common is it? Is the legislation too lenient? Who is committing these criminal and/or deviant acts and why do they do it? Unfortunately, researchers are seldom able to provide definitive answers to these questions, and unless the media seek out informed opinions, the presentation of youth crime in the media and through political debate is not always based on empirical reality but on what Schissel (2006, p. 72) describes as "constructed versions that serve political and moral purposes." Nevertheless, Brantingham and Brantingham (1984, p. 41) have pointed out the ongoing motivation for investigating youth crime: "[C]ounting crime seems to satisfy some fundamental urge to know the dimensions of our misery, as if knowing by itself makes things better."

To better understand, explain, and ultimately predict youth crime, we need to draw from a variety of sources of measurement, each of which has strengths and weaknesses. In this chapter, we begin by examining the major factors that have contributed to the historical emergence of youth crime and youth justice. Next, we draw on two separate sources of measurement that describe the nature and extent of delinquency and youth

dark figure of crime
Refers to incidents of crime
or delinquency that go
undetected or unreported by
the police.

youth at risk
Refers to young people who
are "at risk" of offending or
being victimized because of
various social, family, and/or
personal factors.

crime: (1) official accounts of social control (e.g., police, courts, and corrections) and (2) unofficial sources. Self-report and victimization surveys allow researchers to determine the nature and extent of unrecorded delinquency, the so-called **dark figure of crime**, and compare the results with official accounts of delinquency. Before we review the evidence from these different methods, however, we must first appreciate the complexity of the terms *youth crime* and **youth at risk**.

Although delinquency and youth crime can be, and have been, defined in a number of different ways by sociologists (see Siegel and Welsch 2013) and psychologists (see Bartol and Bartol 2014), we will briefly review the legal definition as it is largely used in the measurement of youth crime.

Defining Youth Crime

Delinquency and *juvenile delinquency* were terms used in the 1908 Juvenile Delinquents Act (JDA) to describe "any child who violates any provision of the Criminal Code or any federal or provincial statute" (s. 2.1). With the passing of the Young Offenders Act (YOA) in 1984, the terms were replaced with the less pejorative phrase *young person* (s. 2.1), which continues to be used (also s. 2.1) under the Youth Criminal Justice Act (YCJA) (2003). A young person who commits an offence is referred to as a "young offender," and when formally acknowledged and counted, the offence becomes a "youth crime" even though it violates the same laws as those that apply to an adult. The shift in terminology, while perhaps appearing subtle, has also had an impact on how we measure youth crime today. For example, Bartol and Bartol (2014, p. 29) note that *juvenile delinquency* was "an imprecise, nebulous, social, clinical and legal label for a wide variety of law- and norm-violating behaviour." The term *young offender*, by contrast, refers only to behaviours against the Criminal Code. Hence, it is important to understand how youth crime is defined and how its meaning has changed over time.

Legal Definition

Historically, criminologists have tended to focus on the legal rather than on the psychological or sociological definitions of youth crime. The YCJA (s. 2) defines a young person as "a person who is or, in the absence of evidence to the contrary, appears to be twelve years old, or older, but less than eighteen years old and, if the context requires, includes a person who is charged under the Act with having committed an offence while he or she was a young person or who is found guilty of an offence under this Act." Should the young person meet these conditions, their act then constitutes a "youth crime."

Although the JDA definition of *juvenile delinquency* (s. 291) was intended to support the concept of family and to build an informal system of social control (Fetherston 2005), the YCJA places a greater emphasis on a legalistic approach under which young offenders are held legally responsible for their actions (see Chapter 3).

Limitations in Assuming a Purely Legal Definition

Although clearly restrictive from a social science perspective, notwithstanding the technical offence of administrative-type transgressions (e.g., breach of conditions), the legal definition of youth crime focuses primarily on predatory (e.g., break-and-enter, robbery) and aggressive (e.g., assault, homicide) behaviour that is deemed punishable by law (Winterdyk forthcoming). As the legal definition only enables us to describe the problem, there are a number of limitations to its use:

- *Theoretical insight.* The legal definition does not take into account victimless crimes, and because of the vague meaning of youth crime, the definition limits the scope of theoretical insight.

- *Demographic.* Changes in the age distribution, particularly for high-risk (15- to 24-year-old) offender groups, can influence crime rates.

- *Case filtration and dismissal.* Depending on the nature of the deviance, cases of youth crime are often eliminated because they are perceived as lacking sufficient gravity or are deemed unlikely to result in a conviction owing to insufficient evidence. Local police policies and procedures may also affect recording rates.

- *Policy and administration variation.* How the YCJA is interpreted varies among, and even within, provinces and territories (see Prevost 2011 and Chapter 3 in this volume). Similarly, the policies of police departments that report these crimes are likely to vary with the level of public pressure, police administration, and available personnel.

- *Method of gathering statistics.* The data used to track youth crime trends, cleared crime, and patterns of youth crime are derived from different administrative sources: police records, judicial records, and correctional records. Although these findings are published annually by Statistics Canada, the resulting statistics can be misleading because the enumeration of youth crime gives us a measure of the political success (or failure) of our crime-control policies and Statistics Canada does not enumerate all crimes. For example, historically Statistics Canada enumerates only those offences made known to the police, court, and/or corrections. In other words, whoever gathers the data can have an (unintended) agenda that goes beyond the published data (see Huff 1954).

- *Reporting rates.* The extent to which youth crime is reported often depends on the public's willingness to report youth crime, as well as on varying social and economic factors (see Charron 2009). Reporting rates are intimately related to society's attitudes toward law enforcement, the perceived gravity of the offence, and society's level of punitiveness. Reporting rates are therefore connected to what Wheeler, Bonacich, Cramer, and Zola (1968) refer to as the "cultural climate."

- *Public perception.* At any given time, society's perception of youth crime can profoundly affect the legal implementation of the youth justice legislation. Referring to various national polls (e.g., Environics and the National Gallup Poll) a public safety report notes that while Canadians in general support the YCJA, they feel the legislation is not punitive enough (Public perception of crime . . . 2010). As discussed in Chapter 6, numerous researchers point to the influence of the media and the lack of public education about the Act as the impetus for this change in attitude (also see Barak 2012). Therefore, obtaining a realistic picture of the extent of youth crime can be difficult.

- *Technologies.* Changes in technology create new opportunities for complex crimes to emerge and go undetected (e.g., cyber- and Internet-based crimes). Until the crime is recognized and defined, it is not legally a crime.

As we will discuss later in this chapter, the answer to whether youth crime has increased or decreased and whether public fear is justified is subject to continuous debate. This chapter attempts to shed light on what is happening by examining both official and unofficial sources of data on youthful offending behaviour.

Measuring Delinquency: A Historical Overview

Juvenile delinquency is a social construction and a normative term that has evolved over time and has created certain dilemmas for the youth justice system. Until recently, most interpretations of youth crime have lacked a sense of history. Yet, to understand the nature and extent of youth crime today, we need to become familiar with how law-violating young people have become a concern and focus of attention. As philosopher George Santayana (1905) has said, "[T]hose who cannot remember the past are condemned to repeat it."

For illustrative purposes, the history of youth crime trends in Canada can be divided into three periods: pre-Confederation, state intervention, and the twentieth century. The overview will serve to show how and why we created the term *delinquency* and how and why we started to count delinquent acts.

Delinquency Trends: Pre-Confederation to the Nineteenth Century

Given the frontier spirit of the Canadian pioneers during the early seventeenth century, children were allowed considerable freedom, which resulted in crime and hooliganism. Carrigan (1998) notes that children were, indeed, involved in petty theft, brawling, and vandalism, and young girls, in prostitution, as they were swept up in the violence that permeated the fur trade. J.G. Moylan, inspector of penitentiaries in New France at this time, claimed that "immigrant children greatly added to the criminal ranks and that their immigration should be stopped" (cited in Carrigan 1998, pp. 82–83).

Youth crime during the seventeenth century was also most likely caused by the uncontrolled growth of New France. Many young families were enticed to come to the New World with promises of land, prosperity, and opportunity. However, many of these families soon broke up because of too extreme economic and physical hardships (Carrigan 1991). This disintegration of families ultimately resulted in numerous young people being abandoned, neglected, and/or abused. It was this lack of supervision that led to crime and subsequently drew official attention by social service–type agencies (Carrigan 1998).

Until 1876, when the Dominion Bureau of Statistics (now Statistics Canada) began to record official statistics in Canada, accounts of juvenile delinquency were obtainable only through limited newspaper sources that were often based on first-hand observational reports. As a result, the delinquency problem in pre-Confederation Canada cannot be accurately quantified. However, some information is available. On the basis of the first annual report of the Board of Inspectors of Asylums and Prisons in 1860, Carrigan (1998) concludes that of 11,268 incarcerations, 6 per cent were young offenders under the age of 16 of which only 23.2 per cent were female. Between 1869 and 1889, the rate of juvenile incarceration fluctuated between 23.2 and 31.6 per cent of all offences. And as we will see shortly, the delinquency problem at the end of the nineteenth century in many ways resembles the trends we are experiencing at the beginning of the twenty-first century. Now, as then, boys continue to be disproportionately represented in the youth justice system, most crimes are property related, most delinquencies occur in urban centres (see below), and familial problems are often associated with youth crime. Being the product of parental neglect and/or maltreatment is still seen as one of the more common characteristics, or risk factors, among young offenders (see Hoge and Andrews 2010).

Table 2.1 provides an overview of juvenile convictions for indictable (i.e., serious) offences between 1885 and 1889 in the existing provinces and territory. As noted above, during this time period significantly more young males than young females were convicted. Males accounted for over 90 per cent of all convictions. However, what is not clear is to what extent the official data reflect reporting and/or recording bias.

Table 2.1	Youth Crime Convictions for Indictable Offences by Province, 1885–1889			
	Under 16 Years		**16–20 Years**	
Provinces	**Male**	**Female**	**Male**	**Female**
Ontario	5,687	242	6,550	580
Quebec	2,516	200	3,095	256
Nova Scotia	367	14	446	42
New Brunswick	181	4	218	16
Manitoba	209	7	311	22
British Columbia	174	1	192	19
Prince Edward Island	81	1	57	9
Northwest Territories	21	0	94	4
Totals	9,236	469	10,963	948

Source: Based on "Youth Crime Convictions for Indictable Offences by Provinces, 1885–1889," from Carrigan 1998, p. 93.

State Intervention: The First Step in Defining and Officially Counting Delinquency

American sociologist Anthony Platt (1977), in the postscript to his acclaimed book *The Child Savers*, suggests that the dramatic increase in youth crime throughout the 1870s can be attributed, in large part, to the deterioration in economic conditions in North America. He notes that, at that time, more than a half-million young persons were neither in school nor employed. By the late nineteenth century the social support networks that had typically characterized rural or agrarian communities were in the process of deteriorating. Urbanization and industrialization were changing the ways in which people lived. Children were less and less supervised, and as a result, they became more criminally active, particularly in the growing cities.

As the nature and extent of delinquency grew, it was believed, especially among the dominant middle and upper social classes, that the problem could be solved by state intervention. Universal public education was the first step the state took to help alleviate growing delinquency. In 1871 Ontario made school attendance compulsory for 7- to 12-year-olds for four months a year. Several industrial schools (also referred to as residential schools)[1] for boys and girls were also established across the country (Carrigan 1991). The impetus for this came primarily from the middle-class "child savers," who believed that the root causes of delinquent behaviour rested in a child's environment, especially the family. By keeping count of children's delinquent behaviour, it was then possible to measure the impact of the state's efforts.

The state intervention philosophy marked a new era in youth crime, and the need to record and measure delinquent activity was also reflected in early twentieth-century law. The JDA was intended to support young offenders within the context of the family as a social unit. It also sought to build an informal system of social control as opposed to a formal system. As discussed in Chapter 1, J.J. Kelso (1864–1935) was instrumental (along with W.L. Scott) in establishing the first Ontario juvenile court system.

Youth Crime Trends: The Twentieth Century

The early twentieth century marked a new era in youth crime because of "the introduction of juvenile courts and a generally more efficient system of responding to juvenile crime" (Carrigan 1991, p. 228). For example, between 1911 and the early 1940s, the rate of conviction for youth between the ages of 10 and 15 rose from 172 to 423 per 100,000. This represents more than a 200 per cent increase as compared to just over 30 per cent growth in the population of youth aged 10 to 15 years (Carrigan 1998).

Although the increase was dramatic, most of the offences committed during the early twentieth century were petty property-related offences, and the increase was a reflection of the shift in formal attention to young offenders. The fluctuation in property crime (a high of 36 per 100,000 in 1930 to a low of 24 per 100,000 in 1945), it has been suggested, coincided with the changing social and demographic climate and to some extent with the increasing desire for the state to exercise social control. DeMause (1988, p. 52) refers to this period (circa nineteenth century to mid-twentieth century) as the "socialization mode," during which youth were given extra attention by their parents and society. Fathers, in particular, began to invest more time and effort in training/raising their children.

The youth crime rate slowly dropped from 1940 onward, until 1955 when the youth crime rate was just under 300 per 100,000. DeMause (1988, p. 54) refers to this stage as the "helping mode," during which there was an explosion of faddish techniques for child rearing and discipline. Children were brought up to feel "unconditionally loved."

This phase appears to have been short-lived, however, as delinquency rates began to climb again. The increase has been attributed, in part, to improved social and economic conditions as the country emerged from the hardships of World War II. By 1966, the delinquency rate had climbed to 459 per 100,000, as North American society experienced a social and cultural revolution. Families in which both parents worked had become more common, the influence of the mass media was everywhere, and there was a general erosion of values. According to Carrigan (1998), these social changes, among others, prompted calls for the revision of the JDA. A special committee report in 1965, entitled "Juvenile Delinquency in Canada," stated that the increase in juvenile crime had become "alarming" and that it could be expected to continue to increase (ibid., p. 159).

Comparing these numbers to those of the 1980s and 1990s is revealing. By 1989, the youth crime rate was 5.5 times that of the 1960s (i.e., 2568 per 100,000). During the same year, young offenders between the ages of 12 and 17 represented 22 per cent of all persons charged with Criminal Code offences (CCJS 1992a). Then, in 1991, the overall youth crime rate began to decline for the second time in the twentieth century. However, as we discuss below, this decline does not pertain to all offences.

Further State Intervention: Solutions for a Changing Society

As described within a different context in Chapter 3 in this volume, by the early 1980s there was a growing sentiment that new laws were needed to address the growing problem of youth crime even though there was no unanimous agreement that the increase was even due to the JDA (see Tanner 2010). Nevertheless, this socio-political-motivated need resulted in the introduction of the YOA of 1984. During its 20-year tenure, the YOA underwent numerous reforms and received considerable criticism for not being able to fulfill its objectives of reducing youth crime and/or providing the appropriate response to the needs of young offenders (see Bala, Carrington, and Roberts 2012). The YOA was eventually replaced with the YCJA in 2003. Since the purpose of this chapter is not to examine the relative impact of the YCJA on youth crime (see instead Chapters 3 and 4), this chapter will focus on presenting some of the facts about youth crime in Canada as obtained through **official** and **unofficial data** sources.

Characteristics of Today's Young Offenders— The Official Picture

. . . 37% of youth reported having engaged in one or more delinquent behaviours in their lifetime, either acts of violence, acts against property or the sale of drugs.

(A statistical snapshot . . . 2012, p. 5)

official data
The Canadian Centre for Justice Statistics, a branch of Statistics Canada, collects offender and offence data from the police, courts, and corrections for administrative purposes. The centre produces regular reports that are readily available to the public.

unofficial data
Refers to data that are collected and usually published by private or independent researchers or research facilities. The primary data-collection techniques are self-report surveys and victimization surveys. Unofficial data are often used to enhance official data.

As was suggested at the outset of this chapter, fuelled mostly by the mass media (see Chapter 6), the public has historically had a rather pejorative image of the extent, gravity, and nature of youth crime (see Brooks and Schissel 2008). Although the media is bound by a code of ethical reporting, it is the sensational reporting of negative-related youth crime that triggers cautionary attitudes toward youth and ultimately a *moral panic*. There is little question that youth crime is damaging not only to our youth but also to our communities. Therefore, it is important to know the facts before recommending responses to youth crime.

The term *official data* refers to the records of youth whose illegal activities have come to the attention (i.e., reported to or discovered by) of the various social control agencies (i.e., law enforcement, youth courts, and youth corrections). Agencies in each of the provinces and territories are expected to provide Statistics Canada with their data, which are then compiled and aggregated and made available through standardized publications and/or posted on the Statistics Canada website (see http://www5.statcan.gc.ca/olc-cel/olc.action?objId=85-002-X&objType=2&lang=en&limit=0 to access *Juristat* publications). Not all data received are presented or published; however, if specific data have been collected, they can be purchased from Statistics Canada. Therefore, only youth with a public record are official young offenders as opposed to those who commit an infraction but do not become part of the official record (i.e., the dark figure of crime) because they remain unknown to officials.

While the accuracy of official statistics has been the subject of much debate (Brantingham and Brantingham 1984), these statistics remain the most consistent source of measurement for youth offending and are readily available through the Canadian Centre for Justice Statistics (CCJS) at Statistics Canada in Ottawa. In terms of youth crime, CCJS expresses crime data in three ways: (1) the number of youth charged; (2) the rate of youth charged per 100,000 youth ages 12 to 17; and (3) the percentage of change in total youth rate between the reporting year and previous year. Within this context, the offences reported are limited to "132 Criminal Code offence categories and several drug and trafficking offences" (Creechan 1995, p. 99). This chapter will provide an overview of some of the information that can be gleaned from various official sources.

Demographic Facts of Young Offenders

Gender

As already mentioned, ever since Canada started collecting official data on young offenders, such statistics have shown that young males tend to commit more reported crimes than females do. According to a 2012/13 Statistics Canada report that draws its data from the Integrated Criminal Court Survey, almost 72 per cent of youth court cases involved accused males while 21 per cent involved a female accused[2] (Boyce, Cotter, and Perreault 2014; Dauvergne 2013). This pattern shows a slight shift in the gender balance since the early twenty-first century when the percentage of young males involved in youth crime was around 80 per cent and of young females around 20 per cent. Also, since the introduction of the YCJA in 2003, the youth court data reveal that those cases completed tend to be older young persons and that male involvement in crime increases with age, while female involvement peaks at around 15 years of age (see Brennan 2012 and Moyer 2005). Males are more likely to be accused of sexual assault (92 per cent), drug possession (85 per cent), attempted murder (82 per cent), and weapons offences (82 per cent) while the highest representation of females involved prostitution (44 per cent), common assault (36 per cent), and fraud (35 per cent)[3] (Milligan 2010).

However, it is still unclear whether the increase in violent crimes among young persons and the difference in rates and frequency between young males and females can be attributed to changes in reporting patterns, media sensationalism, the "crime funnel" effect, the alleged growth of "girl gangs" (see Chapters 7 and 12), the use of extrajudicial measures in formal processing, and/or young females becoming more like their male counterparts. For example, some researchers have been paying more attention to crimes committed by both young males and young females, and they are relying on different sources of data (i.e., police versus court administrative records) to clarify the apparent trends. But the fact remains that males have always committed, and continue to commit, most of the youth crimes. Official measurement of youth crime is also unable to tell us what role the various risk and protective factors in society play in helping to explain the gender differences in offending patterns. However, Chapters 7 and 8 offer an overview of different theories that might help to explain such differences.

Age

Next to gender, age is one of the most important determinants that researchers focus on to explain youth crime trends and patterns (see, generally, Blumstein 1995). As illustrated in Figure 2.1, the rate of persons accused of crimes steadily increases from age 12 to 17, the peak age, and then begins to decline for all offence types. Is this due to social, psychological, and/or biological factors or a possible interaction of the consequences of formal legislation? Official data are unable to provide any direct answers.

According to various official reports by the CCJS, the age-related pattern of being accused of an offence has remained fairly consistent since the early 1990s. What is perhaps more revealing is the type of offences different age groups engage in. For example,

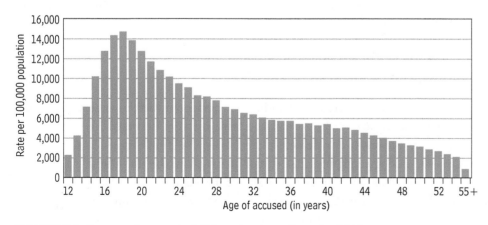

FIGURE 2.1 Persons Accused of Crime, by Age, Canada, 2010

Source: A Statistical Snapshot of Youth at Risk and Youth Offending in Canada, 2012. http://www.publicsafety.gc.ca/cnt/rsrcs/pblctns/ststclsnpsht-yth/ssyr-eng.pdf. Reproduced with the permission of the Minister of Public Safety and Emergency Preparedness Canada, 2015.

those who are younger are more likely to engage in property-related crimes (approximately 45 per cent of all of their offences versus about 37 per cent among 17-year-olds). Older youth, on the other hand, are proportionately more likely to commit **administrative offences** (e.g., charges not generally considered to be criminal, such as failure to appear in court and failure to comply with **disposition**—the two most common guilty findings [Sanders 2000]), than are 12- or 13-year-olds (e.g., 12 per cent versus 4 per cent, respectively).[4] What is perhaps noteworthy from the official data on the cases completed in youth court by age is that 12- and 13-year-olds are proportionately more frequently charged with "crimes against the person" than are 16- and 17-year-olds (i.e., 41 per cent and 36 per cent versus 24 per cent and 23 per cent, respectively). Again, although the official data do not offer any explanation, Doob and Cesaroni (2004) have suggested that, proportionately, young persons engage in more anti-social behaviour because they are less organized and more spontaneous than their older peers. If so, what effect, if any, is the YCJA having on the different age groups?

As pointed out, one of the advantages of using official data is they allow us to examine trends and patterns over a period of time. According to CCJS data, even though 16- to 17-year-olds still commit proportionately more offences than those youth ages 12–15 (see Dauvergne 2013, p. 3), since the 1990s young people appear to have been getting involved in delinquent activities at an earlier age than ever before. For example, 2001/02 data reveal that in spite of the introduction of alternative measures programs, the proportion of youth court caseloads dealing with 12- and 13-year-olds still increased from 10 per cent in 1992/93 to 11 per cent in 2001/02, while for 16- and 17-year-olds, the proportion increased from 52 per cent to 54 per cent during the same years (Thomas 2003). While the increase was perhaps an artefact of the way data were collected as well as police charging practices, there did appear to be a slight increase during the two time periods. For the recording period of 2008/09, the percentage of youth court cases for youth ages 12 to 15 increased slightly to 41 per cent, while for 16- and 17-year-olds the proportion of cases continued to drop, from 63.4 per cent in 2009 (Milligan 2010) to 57 per cent in 2010 (A snapshot . . . 2012) (see Figure 2.2). The trend may also be explained, in part, by one of the objectives of the YCJA—to use police diversion and extrajudicial measures as well as the host of new programs and/or resources being made available under the YCJA.

Measuring Youth Violent and Non-violent Crime

Violent Crime

In the mid-1990s there were two opposing viewpoints on whether youth violent crime had been increasing in Canada. Corrado and Markwart (1994) claimed that violent crime among young persons had increased, while Carrington (1995) argued that the violent incident rate among young persons had not increased. In the late 1990s, Gabor (1999) suggested that while youth crime may not have increased dramatically, the level of seriousness had. A few years later, in 2004, Sally Spencer, executive director for the group Youth Assisting Youth in Toronto, reinforced Gabor's observation when she stated that "the severity of what is happening is definitely on the rise" (Violent Crime in Canada 2008). However, if we take into consideration the youth **Crime Severity Index (CSI)**, which was

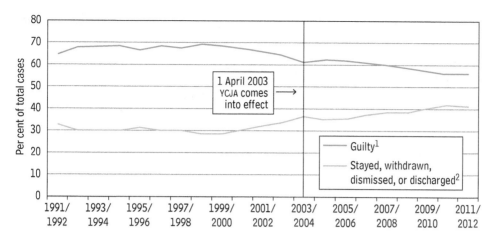

FIGURE 2.2 Cases Completed in Youth Courts by Gender and Age Group of Accused, Canada, 1991/1992 to 2011/2012

1. Guilty findings include guilty of the offence, of an included offence, of an attempt of the offence, or of an attempt of an included offence. This category also includes cases where an absolute or conditional discharge has been imposed.
2. Includes stays, withdrawals, dismissals, and discharges at preliminary inquiry as well as court referrals to alternative or extrajudicial measures and restorative justice programs.

Note: A case is one or more charges against an accused person or company that were processed by the courts at the same time and received a final decision.

Source: Dauvergne 2013, Chart 5, p. 6.

introduced in 2009, we get a slightly different official picture. Instead of simply relying on measures of police-reported crime, the CSI measures the seriousness of crime reported to the police. The CSI scores for all crimes declined steadily between 2003 and 2013. In 2013 the CSI was 39 per cent lower than in 2003 (Boyce, Cotter, and Perreault 2014). The same trend holds for youth crime between 2003 and 2013, when the index scores dropped from 92 to 65 in 2013. Specifically, the youth violent CSI remained relatively stable between 2003 and 2009 (around 95),[5] when it began to drop (in 2013 it was 70.0)—a 13 per cent

Box 2.1   Youth Justice in Action

Youth Crime and Risk Assessment Questions to Ponder

Until fairly recently, risk assessment of youth at risk was not a common practice. In 2009, a team of Saskatchewan researchers conducted a meta-analysis of three popular forensic instruments of risk assessment (i.e., Level of Service Inventory [YLS/CMI, LSI-SK], Psychopathy Checklist [PCL-YV], and Structured Assessment of Violence Risk for Youth [SAVRY]) for young offenders. They analyzed the predictive accuracy for general, non-violent, violent, and sexual recidivism for the three instruments and found that all three were significant in the prediction of general, non-violent, and violent recidivism (Oliver, Stockdale, and Wormith 2009).

Critical Thinking Question

To what extent might such instruments serve to enhance clinical service provision with youth clientele?

drop. Meanwhile, the non-violent crime index score has dropped 19 per cent over the decade. The report shows that between 2003 and 2013 the overall CSI score and the violent and non-violent CSI scores showed a slow but continuous decline (see Brennan 2013; Boyce, Cotter, and Perreault 2014). This would appear to bode well for any moral panic that may still be lingering among Canadians. But the facts may not be that simple. For example, in 2013 University of Toronto criminologist Anthony Doob suggested that "governments and police like to take credit when crime statistics improve, but more often than not, such numbers point to broad long-term trends rather than the effect of specific policies" (Statsna 2013).

While the overall violent crime rate has stabilized in recent years and the CSI has continued to drop since the mid-1990s, if we look at certain types of violent crimes, we see that the characteristics of violent crime suggest a different story. For example, Beattie and Cotter (2010) observe that youth homicide rates were the highest they had been in 30 years with the greatest increase and number of incidents occurring in Manitoba. Conversely, between 2010/11 and 2011/12 robbery declined 7.4 per cent and major assaults dropped 14.7 per cent, but homicide rose 2.2 per cent—but this only represented an increase from 45 to 46 homicides (Dauvergne 2013). However, since the absolute numbers were comparatively low, they did not have a comparable impact on the violent crime rate or the CSI (see Figure 2.3).

Official sources also reveal that regionally, in 2012–13, British Columbia had the lowest rate of violent youth crimes (i.e., 50.3), while (outside of the Yukon, Nunavut, and the NWT) Saskatchewan continued to have the highest CSI (i.e., 169.9) (Boyce, Cotter, and Perreault 2014). In the majority of violent offence cases for 2012, the principal charge is assault (Level 1), with a rate of 481 per 100,000—but down from 502 in 2011. Uttering threats is a distant third behind Level 1 and 2 assaults, at 202, while the rate for attempted murder and murder cases in 2011–12 was 2 per 100,000—accounting for less than 1 per cent of police-reported crimes (see Perreault 2013). The regional variations speak to a host of different economic, demographic make-up, cultural, social, availability of supporting

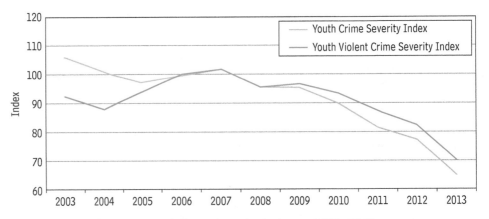

FIGURE 2.3 Police-Reported Crime Severity Indexes, 2003–2013

Note: The base index was set at 100 for 2006 for Canada.

Source: Boyce, Cotter, and Perreault 2014, p. 22.

resources, and political factors across the country, as well as potential variations in public fear about youth crime that prompted more reporting. And while it has been suggested that such variations are reflective of the punitive nature of official legislation, the trends cannot be explained solely by the introduction of the YOA or the YCJA. As Dauvergne (2013) and Perreault (2013) both observe, there is considerable variability between the provincial and territorial jurisdictions in how the YCJA is applied.

Prince Edward Island, for example, had the highest proportion of guilty pleas (21 per cent), while Manitoba has the lowest proportion of guilty pleas (9 per cent) in 2012. The national average was 15 per cent (Dauvergne 2013). Outside of the Yukon and the two territories, Saskatchewan had the highest youth crime rate among youth in 2012 at 11,513 per 100,000, while Ontario had the lowest rate at 4016, with the national rate being 5588. The same pattern held true for both violent and property-related crimes (Perreault 2013).

While official violent crime data are interesting, they do not provide insight into the richer social science interests and issues. For example, to what extent are the rates of different crimes, as well as the seriousness of the crimes, related to the growth of youth gangs (see Chapter 12), an escalation in the use/accessibility of weapons, an apparent increase in female violence (see Chapter 7), or perhaps social and/or cultural diversity in a province/territory, etc.

Non-violent Crime

Non-violent crimes have been declining since the early 1990s (well before former prime minister Stephen Harper started to introduce his "tough on crime" policies), and in 2013 the police-reported crime rate for property crime stood at 3148 per 100,000—down 3 per cent over 2012 (the largest drop in over a decade) (Boyce, Cotter, and Perrault 2014). Yet these crimes still account for the greatest proportion of all youth crime, followed by crimes against the person, offences against the administration of justice, and other Criminal Code offences (see Figure 2.4). As reported by Dauvergne (2013), the drop in property crime can be explained by a notable decline in the rate for frauds and break-ins, as well as a drop in

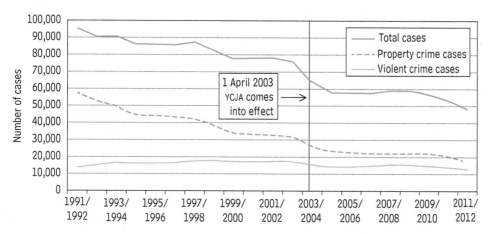

FIGURE 2.4 Youth Accused of Police-Reported Crime, Canada, 1991/1992 to 2011/2012

Source: Boyce, Cotter, and Perreault 2015, Table 8a.

the incident rate of possession of stolen property. As noted above, proportionately, those charged with property crimes tend to fall within the 12- to 13-year-old age spectrum and are mostly young males. In spite of the declining rates in youth crime, the federal Conservative government, as indicated in its passage of Bill C-10 in 2012, appeared determined to revamp the YCJA and shift the focus away from rehabilitation toward specific deterrence and retribution (Dauvergne 2013; see also Chapter 3).

Again, as is evidenced with any of the characteristics regarding the nature and extent of youth crime, there is considerable variation across the country as well as among the different crime categories. For example, while property/non-violent crimes have been going down, certain types of illicit drug offences and drug possession have been going up. Between 1996 and 2006, cocaine charges went up 135 per cent, while "other" drug offences went up 156 per cent over the same period. Only heroin-related offences dropped (i.e., 56 per cent) between 1996 and 2006, but they increased 156 per cent from 2005 to 2006 (Youth crimes reported to police for selected Criminal Code offences 2009). In 2011–12, the number of cases of drug possession went up 6.8 per cent (Dauvergne 2013; also, see Chapter 10).

In summary, while it is encouraging that the overall youth crime rates continue to drop, it is perhaps more disconcerting that violent crime has not followed the same trend. Future researchers should endeavour to better understand and predict such behaviour so as to better identify relevant risk and protective factors. In addition, we need to be careful when examining crime trends over any period of time because, for various reasons, some provinces do not report in certain years. In addition, depending on the official source, the numbers are only a valid representation of the youth criminal activity known to the police, the courts, or youth corrections. Hence such data are a more realistic indicator of youth justice involvement than of youth crime. And yet we typically rely on such information to construct our "reality" of youth crime.

Youth Court–Related Facts

Court Dispositions

Contrary to public opinion (also see Chapter 6), data from the CCJS show that throughout the 1990s there was a shift toward finding more young offenders guilty and imposing harsher sentencing practices for young offenders. However, since 2004, the trend appears to be moving in a less punitive direction. When examined in more detail (see below), the patterns and trends, however, have not been consistent and are subject to interpretation. For example, between 1992/93 and 1996/97 the percentage of those youth who were found guilty of a crime and were placed on probation increased from 48 to 66 per cent and then peaked at 70 per cent by 2002/03 before steadily declining to 57 per cent by 2011/12 (Dauvergne 2013) (see Figure 2.5). Yet, again, there remained considerable geographic variation in the use of probation. In 2008/09, for example, Prince Edward Island had the highest percentage of youth being placed on probation (over 78 per cent) and Saskatchewan had one of the lowest percentages (43 per cent) (Milligan 2010). Keep in mind, however, that official statistics provide no insight into why the variation exists or how the length of probation is determined.

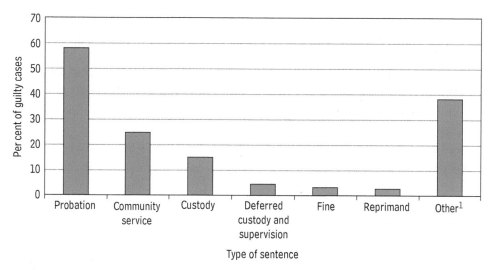

FIGURE 2.5 Guilty Cases Completed in Youth Court, by Type of Sentence, Canada, 2011/2012

1. Other sentence include conditional sentences, intensive support and supervision, attend a non-residential program, absolute discharge, restitution, prohibition, seizure, forfeiture, compensation, pay purchaser, essays, apologies, counselling programs, and conditional discharge.

Source: Dauvergne 2013, p. 7.

As regularly reflected in the media, Canadians tend to believe we are too lenient when it comes to holding young offenders accountable for their crimes (see Box 2.2). Officially, there would appear to be mixed evidence to support such an opinion. In 1986/87, just over 6 per cent of young offenders were placed in secure custody, while in 1997/98, this portion had jumped to 16 per cent and peaked at 26.9 per cent in 2003/04 (Thomas 2005). However, consistent with the objectives of the YCJA, since 2003/04 fewer youth are being placed in secure custody (see Chapter 3 for further discussion).

Box 2.2 Youth Justice in Action

Can We Learn Something from the Norwegians?

There are at least six different juvenile justice models that can be used to characterize juvenile justice systems around the world (see Winterdyk 2015, p. 6). All the models can be traced back to the welfare paternalistic model of the late 1800s and the justice model that emphasizes ideas of judicial rights and accountability for crimes, but today's models are more complex owing to a variety of factors. Canada has what has been described as a modified justice model, and like other countries with a (modified) justice model, it tends to have higher delinquency rates and higher rates of custody (ibid.). By contrast, Norway, and to a slightly lesser extent its Scandinavian neighbours, uses a "Nordic" welfare model and has markedly lower offending rates and virtually no juveniles in custody.

Critical Thinking Question

Consider engaging in other cross-cultural comparisons to explore whether there may be other ideas that Canada could consider to help further curb youth offending rates.

Additional evidence would also appear to be reflected in the decline in the number of youth court cases: between 1991/92 and 2002/03 the number of youth court cases declined by 19.8 per cent (CCJS 1992a; Thomas 2005, p. 14). Perhaps what is more telling is that since the introduction of the YOA and then the YCJA, the incarceration rate has steadily dropped from 2003/04 to 2013/14 (from approximately 110 per 10,000 to 63) (Youth correctional statistics . . . 2013; also see Table 2.2). This steady decline is largely attributed to the increased use of diversion and other extrajudicial measures as well as to the fact that, under the YCJA, youth custody sentences have often been followed by a period of probation to ensure some form of supervision on reintegration into the community (see Table 2.2).

Since the early 1990s and into the "new" millennium, there has been an apparent shift toward greater accountability of young offenders engaged in serious offences. For example, the percentage of youth who received secure custody and supervision orders or sentences of less than one month increased steadily, from 6 per cent in 1986/87 to 30 per cent in 1995/96, and then to 49 per cent in 2003/04 (Thomas 2005). However, after 2008/09 custody and supervision dropped dramatically to around 12 per cent in 2011/12, but they again showed considerable variation across the country (Dauvergne 2013). Excluding

Table 2.2	Percentage of Youth Cases Sentenced to Custody in Canada: 2002/2003 to 2011/2012							
Province/Territory	2002/ 2003	2003/ 2004	2004/ 2005	2005/ 2006	2006/ 2007	2007/ 2008	2008/ 2009	2011/* 2012
				Percentage				
Canada	26.9	21.9	21.1	18.4	16.6	15.9	15.4	15.0
Newfoundland and Labrador	38.5	21.3	23.5	20.3	18.0	12.0	15.6	12.0
Prince Edward Island	39.5	19.7	16.0	17.3	18.7	15.8	19.4	21.0
Nova Scotia	32.8	14.7	13.3	11.5	13.7	12.1	11.0	13.5
New Brunswick	25.8	23.2	20.9	16.1	16.5	13.5	12.2	10.5
Quebec	21.2	15.9	15.3	12.5	11.2	11.3	12.0	10.2
Ontario	28.1	27.5	26.3	23.8	20.9	21.7	20.3	21.0
Manitoba	26.0	15.9	15.7	8.6	7.9	6.7	6.2	8.5
Saskatchewan	30.9	26.1	21.2	18.0	16.7	14.8	16.3	14.7
Alberta	19.3	12.9	13.3	12.4	12.5	11.1	10.5	13.0
British Columbia	31.6	22.1	21.5	21.6	18.6	16.7	15.6	16.5
Yukon	46.9	27.3	25.0	44.1	31.8	34.1	41.2	10.0
Northwest Territories[1]	39.2	19.1	15.6	20.1	20.3	17.3	17.3	12.2
Nunavut	24.7	21.3	23.2	22.2	18.8	9.7	14.6	6.0

1. From 2004/05 to 2008/09, for the Northwest Territories, the number of custody orders has been under-reported and the number of probation orders has been over-reported by unknown amounts owing to clerical procedures. The majority of custody orders were captured as probation.

* Approximate.

Sources: Milligan 2010 (Summer—from Table 8); and Dauvergne 2013 (from Chart 8).

Nunavut, the percentage of those placed in sentenced custody ranged from a low of around 8.5 per cent in Manitoba to a high of 21 per cent in Ontario (Dauvergne 2013).

For the fiscal year 2011/12, the number of youth placed in any type of custody was the lowest it had been since 1994. In addition to fewer youth being placed in custody, they were also serving shorter sentences than a decade ago. Although some 15 per cent of those case convictions received secure custody, the median length of sentences in secure custody declined from 94 days in 1992/93 to 39 days in 2011/12 (Dauvergne 2013). However, it is perhaps worth noting that the median length of sentence for serious crimes has become much longer. For example, in 2011/12 it was, for homicide, 730 days, for attempted murder 240 days, and for sexual assault 176 days. Arguably, this variation is consistent with the intent of section 3.1 (a)(1) of the YCJA.

One of the stated objectives of the YCJA was to ensure that justice would be administered more quickly; however, increasingly we hear about delays in our youth justice system. The concern would appear to be somewhat justified. As reflected in Figure 2.6, since the early 1990s the court case completion time remained fairly steady until the introduction of the YCJA, when there was a dramatic spike in the length of time it took to complete a court case.

Again, as with other trends and patterns across the country, there is considerable variation (see Dauverge 2013, p. 13). And although the provinces and territories are responsible for administering the YCJA, such variations raise concerns about the fairness, efficiency, and effectiveness of youth justice. For example, how is it that four provinces and the Yukon exceed the national median length of days for completing a case?

After the introduction of the YCJA, the median number of days to complete youth court cases rose steadily to the point that for 2008/09 the median elapsed time to process a case in youth court was 119 days, but as noted above, by 2011/12 the median number

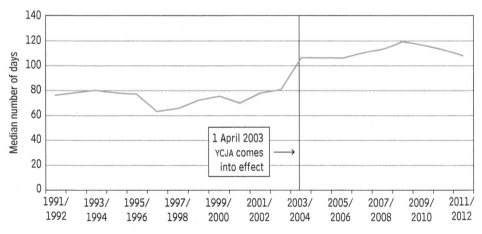

FIGURE 2.6 Median Length of Cases Completed in Youth Court, Canada, 1991/1992 to 2011/2012

Note: The median represents the mid-point of the number of days taken to complete a case, from the first to last court appearance. A case is one or more charges against an accused person or company that were processed by the courts at the same time and received a final decision.

Source: Dauvergne 2013, Chart 10.

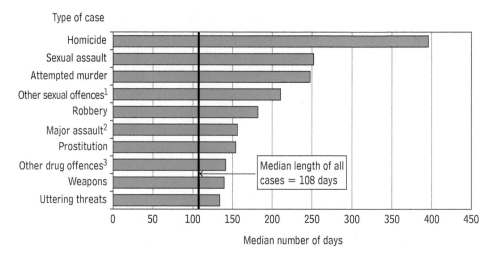

FIGURE 2.7 Median Number of Days to Complete Youth Court, Canada, 2011/2012

1. Includes, for example, sexual interference, invitation to sexual touching, child pornography, luring a child via a computer, and sexual exploitation.
2. Includes assault with a weapon (level 2) and aggravated assault (level 3).
3. Includes drug trafficking, exportation and importation, and production.

Source: Dauvergne 2013, Chart 11.

of days had dropped to 108 days. Yet, this is still almost a month longer than in the year prior to the enactment of the YCJA (see Figure 2.7).

The increase in case processing time that occurred with the introduction of the YCJA may, in part, be due to the fact that the courts are hearing lengthier cases as a result of less serious cases being diverted from the court process (e.g., extrajudicial measures) (Milligan 2010). This, however, is consistent with the principles and objectives of the YCJA (see Chapter 3). Nevertheless, official statistics provide less insight into the complex set of factors that can contribute to case processing delays (e.g., resources and workload, jurisdiction size, case characteristics such as offence type and severity, various procedural factors).

Transfers to Adult Court—Adult Sentencing

Under the JDA and during the first few years of the YOA, their respective juvenile justice models have been described as a "tug of war" between *welfare* (i.e., informality, indeterminate sentencing, and a focus on individuals' needs and rehabilitation) and *modified justice* (i.e., due process informality, determinate sentences, and sanctioning of behaviour and provision of treatment) (Winterdyk 2015). As a result, transfers to adult court were relatively infrequent until the early 1990s when amendments to section 16 of the YOA were introduced to facilitate transfers because of Parliament's concern about the public perception that the YOA was too lenient. The amendments were limited to the most serious offence cases involving youth between the ages of 16 and 17 (unless otherwise ruled by the court).

Between 1986/87 and 1989/90, the number of transfers to adult court dropped from around 80 to approximately 25; however, after the amendments were introduced, the number of transfers increased to a high of 85 cases in 1994. At that point, critics argued that youth incarceration was being overused. In fact, Canada, at one point, had the highest youth incarceration rate in the world—even higher than that in the United States. Various scholars began to point out that the transfer process was unfair, too complex, and contributed to lengthy delays (see Thomas 2003).

The current legislation no longer provides for the transfer of youth to adult court as the focus of the YCJA had shifted toward *rehabilitation* and re-entry into society (i.e., s. 3.1(a)(ii)).

Even though the YCJA no longer includes specific provisions for adult transfer as a measure of denunciation, in 2010, Conservative Justice Minister Rob Nicholson introduced Bill C-4, dubbed **Sebastien's Law**, which now allows young offenders who have committed serious, violent acts, or who are serious repeat offenders, to be detained during pre-trial detention and for the courts to consider publishing the names of some young criminals, such as sex offenders (Perreault 2013). This controversial bill was introduced even though the Crime Severity Index score for young offenders had been declining since 2001. However, one might still want to question the rationale behind Bill C-10, also referred to as the Omnibus Bill, and whether it actually fulfills or meets its adopted name of "Safe Streets and Communities Act."

Recidivism

It has been suggested that the success, or failure, of punishment can be measured by **recidivism**, or the rate at which convicted individuals reoffend. However, as reflected in a report by Correctional Service of Canada, the concept is not that straightforward. For example, what is called "recidivism" may also actually refer to return to custody on technical violations and/or new offences (FORUM on Correctional Research 2009). For the purpose of this section, we will rely on the general definition of an individual's reoffending.

Recidivism data on young offenders in Canada are not regularly recorded. Given the limitations of official information in such cases, official recidivism should perhaps be viewed as "a measure of political success . . . how well (or poorly) our crime control policies are working" (Brantingham and Brantingham 1984, p. 41).

Notwithstanding this cautionary comment, official data tell us that in the early 1990s about 18.6 per cent of young offenders who appeared in court had five or more prior convictions (Moyer 1992). The same report notes that approximately 46 per cent of those charged in youth court had one or more prior convictions since 1984. By the late 1990s, official youth court statistics for 1998/99 showed that nearly 42 per cent of cases with convictions involved repeat offenders (Carriere 2000). Furthermore, the older a youth gets, the more likely it becomes that he or she has had prior charges. And as with other youth crime facts presented in this chapter, for recidivism data there are also regional variations. For example, if we use data obtained from the Manitoba corrections branch, the reoffending rate for those young offenders who had been incarcerated is a staggering 100 per cent (Morris 2010).

Finally, one of the most comprehensive Canadian studies whose data should provide considerable insight into the criminal careers of young persons is the work being undertaken by Carrington, Matarazzo, and Souza (2005). They are involved in the first quasi-national Canadian study of the criminal careers of a birth cohort; it uses linked data from the Youth Court Study and Adult Criminal Court Survey for youths born in 1979/80. Their preliminary data from six provinces tends to parallel the recidivism results presented above, but in

Sebastien's Law
In 2010 the federal government introduced Bill C-4 as a measure to get tough on repeat young offenders. The bill was subsequently amended to become part of the Omnibus Crime Bill, passed in 2012. Section 3(1)(a) of the YCJA was subsequently slightly amended to read "protect the public," which encompasses the spirit of Sebastien's Law. The namesake of the law is 19-year-old Sebastien Lacasse, who was beaten and stabbed to death at a 2004 house party in Quebec by a 17-year-old. The incident prompted the courts to consider adult sentences for youth 14 or older found guilty of serious crimes like murder and aggravated assault.

recidivism
Repetition of criminal and/or delinquent behaviour. Recidivism can be measured through official sources or through self-report surveys.

the future the richness of their data set should provide a deeper understanding of criminal career trends as well as evidence-based insight into how to better address youth crime.

Before we examine the unofficial measures of youth crime, we should reiterate that a number of real and artificial pitfalls affect the accuracy of official data. Furthermore, official data reflect the action (or inaction) of social control agencies (e.g., police) rather than the real numbers and features of delinquent behaviour. Nevertheless, if we view the data longitudinally, for the most part the observations remain relatively consistent. As long as we remain sensitive to some of the pitfalls surrounding the use of official data, these data can provide insight into how official agencies have/have not responded to youth crime over the years.

Measures of Youth Crime: The Unofficial Picture

We will now highlight some of the facts about youth crime based on self-report studies and victimization surveys. These are referred to as *unofficial* sources of data because criminal justice agencies are not required by law to collect this information. Instead, academics and research centres usually compile such data.

Self-Report Surveys

self-report (SR) survey
A social-science questionnaire survey designed to ask respondents to report on their involvement in criminal or delinquent activities.

West (1984, p. 86) suggests that **self-report (SR) surveys** and related scales were developed during the 1940s and 1950s because "police and court statistics were too hopelessly biased." Although self-report studies have become more popular and are proving to be useful in helping to uncover the "dark figure" (i.e., unreported or unrecorded crimes) for certain offences, they are not without their limitations. Some of the more common limitations to conducting self-report studies with youth include young people's literacy level and ability to comprehend questions, their short-term versus long-term memory, the extent to which they are willing to give information voluntarily, and the fact that respondents may exaggerate their answers in order to conform—or may even telescope their answers by admitting to something that took place before the actual reference period.

Research methodology texts are quick to point out that, despite the preceding problems with self-report surveys, a great deal of progress has been made in improving the validity and reliability of this method, to the point that SR surveys have gained acceptance as a valid measure of young offenders. Over the years, various studies have repeatedly shown that most youth engage in acts that would have qualified as an offence had these youths been caught. In fact, offending among young persons is far more prevalent than official data or the media report (Le Blanc and Tremblay 1988). Over 80 per cent of youth surveyed admitted to at least one delinquent act while less than 3 per cent of these acts had been detected by the police. However, one of the first Canadian SR studies to be conducted on young offenders in the 1960s revealed that while offending was common among young people, the nature of offending among middle-class youth was less serious than among lower-class youth (Vaz 1966). Nevertheless, as West (1984) observed in Canada, (1) there is little SR evidence to suggest that youth crime has increased over the years, and (2) the difference between the amount of delinquent activity that males and females engage in is not as dramatic as official data would lead us to believe. For example,

West (1984, p. 88) reported the male to female offending ratio to be about 5:1, whereas official statistics indicate that the ratio is between 5:1 and 10:1. In a slightly more recent study, Simourd and Andrews (1996) found the ratio to be 3:1, male to female.

The most recent results from the last National Longitudinal Survey of Children and Youth (NLSCY), which has collected data every two years since 1994, show that about 38 per cent of young persons engaged in a repeated offence in the previous year, of which almost 70 per cent involved "minor" offences (The correlates . . . 2010). However, the NLSCY includes only youth between the ages of 11 and 13 and asks only very general questions about the nature and extent of victimization (see Sprott, Doob, and Jenkins 2001). As of 2014, no further results or updates on the NLSCY have been available.

In addition to examining issues around unreported delinquent behaviour, researchers could also begin to probe specific offence variations, compare demographic relationships, do comparative studies with other countries, and conduct follow-up surveys. Some of these concerns are already being addressed internationally in several ongoing studies involving researchers at the University of Southern California and the Dutch Research and Documentation Centre (see Junger-Tas, Marshall, and Ribeaud 2003; and Junger-Tas 2010). The research involves the largest self-report study of young people in the world: the International Self Reported Delinquency Survey (ISRD), which starting in 2013 marked the beginning of the third international sweep involving up to 50 countries. During the second round of this survey, some 30 countries were included. In 2006 Canada participated for the first time with its International Youth Survey, which was limited to the city of Toronto. Among other findings, the study reported that second-generation immigrant youth remained at higher risk of reporting delinquent acts than their native-born counterparts (Self-report delinquency . . . 2009; also see Sprott and Doob 2010).

In summary, while the use of self-report surveys has increased, the methodologies and designs used have not been consistent, hence limiting interpretation, comparison, and extrapolation. However, such surveys do serve to provide qualified insight that is not always captured by official statistics.

Victimization and Victimization Surveys

Although society and the media tend to focus on the offences committed by young people, we must remember that young people are also the victims of a great deal of violence, not only from members of their own age group but also from adults. **Victimization survey** data indicate that young people are more likely to be victims of crimes than are adults (Ogrodnik 2010). In fact, several years ago an international report observed that even though 190 countries—including Canada—had signed the United Nations Convention on the Rights of the Child, victimization of children was on the rise (Chin 1998). The report also observed that young people were at greater risk of being victims of assault, sexual assault, and robbery than those over the age of 24 (AuCoin 2005).

In the early 1990s, based on information from 13 major police departments across the country, it was demonstrated that nearly one-quarter of all violent crime victims were teenagers (CCJS 1992b). More recent data reveal that most of these victims were males and that children under 12 years of age were most often the victims of common assault, or

victimization survey
A social-science questionnaire survey designed to measure the experiences of respondents as victims of crime(s).

sexual assault, and youth between the ages of 15 and 17 were at the greatest risk of being victims of a violent crime (Ogrodnik 2010).

A review of other Canadian research suggests that victimization rates have continued to increase since 2000. This appears to be the case in such areas as bullying and street youth (see Chapter 13) and in particular among Aboriginal youth (see Chapter 11). For example, Brzozowski, Taylor-Butts, and Johnson (2006) note that Aboriginal youth are three times more likely to be victimized than non-Aboriginal youth. Furthermore, the initial results from the 2009 General Social Survey (GSS) indicated that young people (i.e., those ages 15 to 24) were almost 15 times more likely to have been a victim of a violent crime than seniors 65 and older (Perreault and Brennan 2010). Unfortunately, the GSS only collects data on victimization of persons 15 years of age or older.

One of the most ambitious Canadian victimization studies, the Canadian Urban Victimization Survey (CUVS), which began in 1983 and was repeated every few years, involved seven major cities and included more than 61,000 interviews. The 2004/05 cycle of the survey included 25,000 participants. However, because only youths 15 years of age and older were interviewed for this survey, the results were somewhat limited in terms of adolescents. Using data from the CUVS, Sacco and Johnson (1990) found that

- young persons (composing a 15–24 age group) were the most victimized age group (37 per cent versus 24 per cent for all age groups);

- the age group of 15–24 had the highest incidence of repeat victimization (16 per cent had been victimized two or more times) compared with all other age groups;

- contrary to popular opinion, the difference between males and females in the percentage of victimization was not all that large (18 per cent for males and 14 per cent for females, aged 15–24); and

- the group ages 15–24 consistently had higher rates of victimization for personal theft, violent incidents, robbery, sexual assault, and common assault.

In 1999, Paetsch and Bertrand conducted a victimization survey of young persons in Calgary. Their results were generally similar to those reported by Sacco and Johnson (1990), but they focused more specifically on the relative influence of school. Several of their key findings included the following:

- Overall, males were more likely than females to report they were victimized, but the difference was in type: victimization was greater among those young persons who attended school than those who did not.

- The strongest predictors of victimization were type of peer group, weak family relations, and socializing more with youth of similar age than with adults.

- Difficulties in school (e.g., suspension, dropping out, and negative attitude toward school) correlated with higher likelihood of being victimized.

- Students with psychological challenges were more likely to be victims than those not expressing psychological problems.

Over the years, there have been at least three major *Juristat* reports that have examined children and youth as victims of violent crime. Given the dates of publication, they allow for some general comparisons. When 1996 data (Fitzgerald 1997) is compared to that of 2003 (AuCoin 2005), young females are more often the victims of assault crimes than young males are. More specifically, young females are more likely to be the victims of sexual assault than are young males, and their victimization is more likely to be at the hands of friends and/or acquaintances than at the hands of strangers. Conversely, in terms of physical assault, young males are more likely to be victims than are their female counterparts. However, just as with sexual assault offences, the perpetrators tend to be friends and acquaintances. A more recent *Juristat* report prepared by Ogrodnik (2010) and drawing upon victimization data from the GSS points out that about 80 per cent of "youth aged 15–17 who had been victimized did not report the incident to police" (p. 1). The report indicated that violence against children and youth was highest in Saskatchewan (2136 per 100,000) and lowest in Prince Edward Island (894 per 100,000).

In one of the largest victimization studies of its kind, Tanner and Wortley (2002) found that more than half of the 3400 high school students in Toronto and 400 local street youth surveyed failed to report to an adult that they had been victimized. With the recent concerns surrounding bullying, hazing, and media-profiled cases, the implications of this "code of silence" are alarming; not only is the dark figure for young victims quite large but there are no clear provisions in the Criminal Code to address the problem. As Tanner and Wortley note, there is no easy solution to the problem of such victimizations. We must educate our youth that it is okay to report such incidents.

Notwithstanding the previous observation, the overall trends of victimization among young persons sharply contrast with what one might be led to believe from most media reports. For example, Mathews (1996) cites research that found that the first time many victimized teens receive attention is when they come in contact with the legal system because of an offence they have committed. This finding suggests that prior victimization may be a key risk factor for criminal activity and that we need to look more carefully at the causes underlying youth crime and determine whether accountability and punishment are more important than treatment, counselling, or other forms of support. The underlying assumption is that it is more cost effective and cost efficient to invest and prevent crime from happening than to wait to respond to it (see, for example, Keeping communities safe . . . 2011).

As we will see in Part III, a notable number of these victimized youth end up turning to a life of drugs, joining gangs, becoming involved in prostitution, and/or following a general path of self-destruction—including suicide (see Coloroso 2004; Navaneelan 2012; Wasserman, Cheng, and Jiang 2005). Consequently, one can ask, do these facts lend support to our need not only to understand the risk factors that lead to victimization but also to learn more about the protective factors that might help to build resiliency among such youth?

Before concluding this section, we should briefly address the relationship between young offenders and young victims of crime. Some academics have argued that these may be artificial categories (see Fagan, Piper, and Cheng 1989), based on the general observation that victims of crime and abused youth are the most likely to become offenders (abusers) themselves. These assertions, however, tend to rely on single disciplinary and theoretical perspectives. For example, why don't all victims become offenders? Why do some non-victims become offenders? Supporters of victim–offender causality typically subscribe to the influence of the nurture assumption, which asserts that anything that goes wrong in our lives can be attributed to our upbringing (see Harris 2006). Thanks, in large part, to improved research strategies, we can explore the relationship between biological traits and a host of social and psychological factors, as well as how they might more accurately explain the similarities and the differences between young offenders and young victims. As Ezzat Fattah (1991), a Canadian pioneer of victimology, has noted, this will require a new theoretical orientation (see Giannini and Rossi 2009).

Finally, although the quality of victimization and self-report studies has improved over the years, they are by no means perfect. The true nature and facts about youth crime will always remain somewhat elusive. After all, youth crime, as something separate from adult crime, has existed ever since the term *delinquency* was coined; and, as reflected above, the trend and patterns have not changed significantly over the years. However, as we continue to examine the strengths and weaknesses of data collection, we will better be able to confirm or reject existing theoretical formulations and to develop new ones that have a more practical application in controlling and preventing youth crime. In an effort to more accurately uncover the dark figure of crime, researchers can and often do rely on a process that is referred to as **triangulation**. The term refers to the process of using different sources of data to help provide a richer factual accounting of the facts being examined.

triangulation
A research methods technique that involves using more than one source of criminological data to assess the validity of what is being observed. For example, this technique can include combining official crime data with self-report data to obtain a clearer picture of crime or delinquency facts.

Summary

This chapter offers a broad overview of three major sources of information on youth crime in Canada from the pre-Confederation era to the present day. We can make a number of observations about these trends. Although there have been periods of increases, since 1991 (and based largely on official statistics) there appears to have been a marked decline in official youth crime. However, the picture is not absolutely clear because of the nature and quality (i.e., reliability and validity) of our data sources, changes in legislation, shifts in demographics, and so on. The one exception to the declining crime rates among young persons has been violent crimes. This has been particularly evident since the beginning of the new millennium. The overall drop in the severity of youth crime is largely due to declines in property-related crimes. Furthermore, although somewhat controversial, what is perhaps more alarming is the apparent fact that young persons are not only engaging in more serious youth crime but are also becoming active criminals at an earlier age. As well, recidivism rates have steadily risen over the years, the courts have become backlogged, and the public has become increasingly dissatisfied with the judicial system's ability to control the problem. These challenges, in part, explain why we saw a number of major changes to the former YOA, which was eventually replaced by the YCJA, as well as a move toward alternative solutions, such as restorative justice initiatives, alternative measures programs, and a range of outreach programs (see Chapter 16 for further discussion).

Furthermore, considering that we continue to allocate considerable resources to the attempt to control/manage youth crime with marginal returns, it is even timelier that we refine our crime measurement techniques before we make assumptions about how best to respond to youth crime. Unless we have more reliable and valid data, we risk making poorly informed policy decisions.

Finally, as much as it has become fashionable to focus on identifying and responding to risk factors and on supporting the protective factors and/or helping to build resiliency in our youth (see Howell 2009; Simich and Andermann 2014), we need to have our facts straight first. While it is relatively easy to identify risk and protective factors associated with youth offending, it is a different matter when it comes to applying and implementing protective factors in intervention. In the meantime, while each measurement method provides useful information, no one technique is better than the other, and until we are able to improve the quality of how we measure youth crime, the dark figure of crime will remain somewhat elusive for most crimes. Therefore, we are limited to speaking in generalities, and as stated at the beginning of this chapter, there is no clear answer to the question: How serious is youth crime? Hence, as informative and interesting as the data from measuring youth crime might be, the quality of the data still remains relatively imprecise and relying on it to predict future youth crime trends and patterns remains speculative. Yet, on a positive note, being aware of this fact will hopefully encourage young scholars such as you to embrace and tackle the issue.

Key Terms

administrative offences
Crime Severity Index (CSI)
dark figure of crime
disposition
official data
recidivism

Sebastien's Law
self-report (SR) survey
triangulation
unofficial data
victimization survey
youth at risk

Review Questions

1. Identify some of the major factors that appear to have led to increased state intervention in the lives of young persons.
2. Identify several advantages and disadvantages of relying on official statistics to provide a picture of youth crime issues.
3. How can self-report studies and victimization surveys be used to better understand youth crime?
4. Review and discuss how violent crime has changed over the years. What explanations can you offer? Try to substantiate your explanations with evidence.
5. What types of youth crime activities appear to be most problematic for Canadians today? Explain your answer and offer a possible creative and constructive solution.

Critical Thinking Questions

1. Review and discuss how violent crime has changed since the early 1990s. What explanations can you offer? Try to substantiate your explanations with evidence.

2. Why is it considered useful to practise triangulation when describing youth crime trends?

3. Throughout this chapter, we have looked at youth crime trends. Based on the information presented, what do you predict for the future? What, if anything, should we as a society focus on in regard to youth crime? Are there particular problem-related areas that might require extra attention?

4. There have been a number of notable changes in the trends and patterns of youth crime and youth court cases since the enactment of the YCJA. In light of the changes in the trends and patterns since the YCJA came into force, does the Act appear to be fulfilling its objective in addressing youth crime? What, if any, might be some of the long-term benefits or challenges?

5. This chapter has presented a number of cautionary comments about the reliability and validity of youth crime data. Do you agree? If so, how might we begin to improve the collection of such information?

Endnotes

1. For an overview of industrial schools in Canada, see Milloy 1999.
2. For the other 7 per cent, gender was not recorded.
3. Note that the police index crime category of "other" offences only includes Criminal Code charges, while in court statistics the "other" category also includes administrative charges. These charges only came into effect after the introduction of the YOA.
4. The overall youth violent crime rate was, however, 11 per cent higher in 2009 than in 1999.
5. See http://laws-lois.justice.gc.ca/eng/annualstatutes/2012_1/page-1.html for further detail on the Safe Streets and Communities Act.

References

A statistical snapshot of youth at risk and youth offending in Canada. (2012). Ottawa: Public Safety Canada. Retrieved 7 July 2014 from http://www.publicsafety.gc.ca/cnt/rsrcs/pblctns/ststclsnpsht-yth/index-eng.aspx

AuCoin, K. (2005). Children and youth as victims of violent crime. *Juristat*, 25(1). Statistics Canada Catalogue no. 85-002-XIE.

Bala, N., Carrington, P., and Roberts, J. (2012). Implementing youth justice reform: Effects of the Youth Criminal Justice Act. In J. Winterdyk and R. Smandych (Eds), *Youth at risk and youth justice: A Canadian overview* (pp. 80–104). Don Mills, ON: Oxford University Press.

Barak, G. (2012). Mass media and the social construction of crime: A critique and implications for the future. In W. DeKeseredy and M. Dragiewicz (Eds), *Handbook of critical criminology*. New York: Routledge.

Bartol, C.R., and Bartol, A. (2012). *Criminal behavior: A psychological approach* (10th ed.). Englewood Cliffs, NJ: Prentice-Hall.

Beattie, S., and Cotter, A. (Fall 2010). Homicide in Canada, 2009. *Juristat*. Statistics Canada Catalogue no. 85-002-XIE. Ottawa. Retrieved 15 July 2015 from http://www.statcan.gc.ca/pub/85-002-x/2010003/article/11352-eng.htm

Blumstein, A. (1995). Youth violence, guns and the illicit drug industry. *Journal of Criminal Law and Criminology*, 86(1): 10.

Boyce, J., Cotter, A., and Perreault, S. (2014). Police-reported crime statistics in Canada, 2013. Ottawa: Statistics Canada. Retrieved from http://www.statcan.gc.ca/pub/85-002-x/2014001/article/14040-eng.htm?fpv=2693

Brantingham, P.J., and Brantingham, P.L. (1984). *Patterns in crime.* New York: Macmillan.

Brennan, S. (2012). Youth court statistics in Canada: 2010/2011. Ottawa: Statistics Canada. Retrieved from http://www.statcan.gc.ca/pub/85-002-x/2012001/article/11645-eng.htm

Brennan, S. (2013). Police reported crime statistics in Canada, 2011. Statistics Canada Catalogue no. 85-002-XIE. Ottawa.

Brooks, C., and Schissel, B. (Eds). (2008). *Marginality and condemnation* (2nd ed.). Halifax: Brunswick Books (formerly Fernwood Books).

Brzozowski, J-A., Taylor-Butts, A., and Johnson, S. (2006). Victimization and offending among the Aboriginal population in Canada. *Juristat*, 26(3). Statistics Canada Catalogue no. 85-002-XIE. Ottawa.

Carriere, D. (2000). Youth court statistics, 1989/90 highlights. *Juristat*, 21(2). Statistics Canada Catalogue no. 85-002-XIE. Ottawa.

Carrigan, D.O. (1991). *Crime and punishment in Canada: A history.* Toronto: McClelland & Stewart.

Carrigan, D.O. (1998). *Juvenile delinquency in Canada: A history.* Toronto: McClelland & Stewart.

Carrington, P. (1995). Has violent crime increased? Commenting on Corrado and Markwart. *Canadian J. of Criminology*, 37: 61–73.

Carrington, P.J., Matarazzo, A., and deSouza, P. (2005). *Court careers of a Canadian birth cohort.* Ottawa: Statistics Canada.

CCJS (Canadian Centre for Justice Statistics). (1992a). Sentencing in youth court, 1986–87 to 1990–91. *Juristat Service Bulletin*, 12(16).

CCJS (Canadian Centre for Justice Statistics). (1992b). Teenage victims of violent crime. *Juristat Service Bulletin*, 12(6).

Charron, M. (2009). Neighbourhood characteristics and the distribution of police-reported crime in the city of Toronto. *Crime and Justice Research Series*. Statistics Canada Catalogue no. 85-561-MEI-No. 18. Retrieved 16 April 2014 from http://www.statcan.gc.ca/pub/85-561-m/85-561-m2009018-eng.htm

Chin, E. (1998, September). Child victimization on the rise. *Crime and Justice International*, p. 13.

Coloroso, B. (2004). *The bully, the bullied, and the bystander: From preschool to high school—how parents and teachers can help break the cycle of violence.* New York: HarperCollins.

Corrado, R., and Markwart, A. (1994). The need to reform the YOA in response to violent young offenders: Confusion, reality or myth? *Canadian Journal of Criminology*, 36: 343–78.

Correlates of delinquency: A look at gender differences. (2009). Retrieved 2 October 2010 from http://www.csc-scc.gc.ca/text/pblct/forum/e061/e061g-eng.shtml

Creechan, J. (1995). How much delinquency is there? In J. Creechan and R. Silverman (Eds), *Canadian delinquency.* Scarborough, ON: Prentice Hall Canada.

Dauvergne, M. (2013). Youth court statistics in Canada, 2011/2012. Ottawa: Statistics Canada. Retrieved 2 October 2014 from http://www.statcan.gc.ca/pub/85-002-x/2013001/article/11803-eng.htm?fpv=2693

DeMause, L. (Ed.). (1988). *The history of childhood.* New York: Peter Bedrick.

Doob, A., and Cesaroni, C. (2004). *Responding to youth crime in Canada.* Toronto: University of Toronto Press.

Fagan, J., Piper, E., and Cheng, Y.-T. (1989). Contributions of victimization to delinquency in inner cities. *Journal of Criminal Law and Criminology*, 78: 586–613.

Fattah, E. (1991). *Understanding criminal victimization.* Scarborough, ON: Prentice Hall.

Fetherston, D. (2005). The law and young offenders. In J. Winterdyk (Ed.), *Issues and perspectives on young offenders in Canada* (3rd ed.). Toronto: Nelson.

Fitzgerald, R. (1997). Assault against children and youth in the family, 1996. *Juristat*, (17)11. Statistics Canada Catalogue no. 85-002-XIE. Ottawa.

FORUM on correctional research. (2009). Retrieved 6 October 2010 from http://www.csc-scc.gc.ca/text/pblct/forum/e053/e053h-eng.shtml

Gabor, T. (1999). Trends in youth crime: Some evidence pointing to increases in the severity and volume on the part of young people. *Canadian Journal of Criminology, 41*(3): 385–92.

Giannini, A.M., and Rossi, C. (Eds). (2009). *Victim's care: A handbook.* Milano, Italy: Echo Communications.

Harris, J.R. (2006). *No two alike.* New York: W.W. Norton and Co.

Hoge, R.D., and Andrews, D.A. (2010). *Evaluation for risk of violence in juveniles.* New York: Oxford University Press.

Howell, J.C. (2009). *Preventing and reducing juvenile delinquency: A comprehensive framework* (2nd ed.). Thousand Oaks, CA: Sage.

Huff, D. (1954). *How to lie with statistics.* New York: W.W. Norton and Co.

Junger-Tas, J. (2010). The significance of the International Self-report Delinquency Study (ISRD). *European Journal on Criminal Policy and Research, 16*(2): 71–87.

Junger-Tas, J., Marshall, I., and Ribeaud, D. (2003). *Delinquency in an international perspective: The International Self-report Delinquency Study (ISRD).* New York: Kugler.

Junger-Tas, J., Marshall, I.H., and Ribeaud, D. (2010). The significance of the International Self-report Delinquency Study. *European Journal of Criminal Policy and Research, 16*(2): 71–87.

Keeping communities safe: Three year progress report 2008–2011. Edmonton: Government of Alberta. Retrieved 17 July 2015 from https://justice.alberta.ca/programs_services/safe/Documents/ThreeYearProgressReport-2008-2011.pdf

Le Blanc, M., and Tremblay, R.E. (1988). Homeostasis: Social change plus modifications in the basic personality of adolescents equal stability of hidden delinquency. *International Journal of Adolescence and Youth, 1*(3): 269–91.

Mathews, F. (1996, March). *The invisible boy.* Ottawa: National Clearing House of Family Violence, Health Canada.

Milligan, S. (2010, Summer). Youth court statistics, 2008/2009. Statistics Canada Catalogue no. 85-002-XIE. Ottawa. Retrieved 15 July 2015 from http://www.statcan.gc.ca/pub/85-002-x/2010002/article/11294-eng.htm

Milloy, J.S. (1999). *A national crime: The Canadian government and the residential school system, 1879 to 1986.* Winnipeg: University of Manitoba Press.

Morris, J. (2010, 10 March). Criminal recidivism rates in Canada. Retrieved 6 October 2010 from http://www.employeescreen.com/iqblog/criminal-recidivism-rates-in-canada/

Moyer, S. (2005). A comparison of case processing under the Young Offenders Act and the first six months of the Youth Criminal Justice Act. Department of Justice Canada.

Navaneelan, T. (2012). Suicide rate: An overview. Ottawa: Statistics Canada. Retrieved from http://www.statcan.gc.ca/pub/82-624-x/2012001/article/11696-eng.htm

Ogrodnik, L. (2010). Child and youth victims of police-reported violent crime, 2008. *Canadian Centre for Justice Statistics Profile Series*, no. 23. Statistics Canada Catalogue no. 85F0033M.

Oliver, M.E., Stockdale, K.C., and Wormith, J.S. (2009). Risk assessment with young offenders: A meta-analysis of three assessment measures. *Criminal Justice and Behavior, 36*: 329–53.

Paetsch, J.J., and Bertrand, L.D. (1999 Summer). Victimization and delinquency among Canadian youth. *Adolescence, 34*(134): 351–67.

Perreault, S. (2013). Police-reported crime statistics in Canada, 2012. Statistics Canada Catalogue no. 85-002-XIE. Ottawa. Retrieved 16 July 2015 from http://www.statcan.gc.ca/pub/85-002-x/2013001/article/11854-eng.pdf

Perreault, S., and Brennan, S. (2010). Criminal victimization in Canada, 2009. Retrieved 30 November 2011 from http://www.statcan.gc.ca/pub/85-002-x/85-002-x2010002-eng.htm

Platt, A.M. (1977). *The child savers* (2nd ed.). Chicago: University of Chicago Press.

Prevost, A. (2011). *Empirical exploration of the importation, deprivation and integrated models concerning types of aggression in youth custody.* Unpublished PhD thesis. Burnaby, BC: Simon Fraser University, School of Criminology.

Public perception of crime and justice in Canada: A review of opinion polls. Retrieved 2 October 2010 from http://www.justice.gc.ca/eng/pi/rs/rep-rap/2001/rr01_1/p6.html

Sacco, V.F., and Johnson, H. (1990, March). Patterns of criminal victimization in Canada. Catalogue no. 11-612E, no. 2. Ottawa: Statistics Canada.

Sanders, T. (2000). Sentencing of young offenders in Canada, 1998/99. *Juristat, 20*(7). Ottawa: Canadian Centre for Justice Statistics.

Santayana, G. (1905). *The life of reason*. London: Constable.

Schissel, B. (1997). *Blaming children*. Halifax: Fernwood.

Schissel, B. (2006). *Blaming children* (2nd ed.). Halifax: Fernwood.

Self-report delinquency of immigrant youth: Toronto 2006. (2009). Statistics Canada Catalogue no. 81-004-X. Ottawa. Retrieved 2 October 2010 from http://www.statcan.gc.ca/pub/81-004-x/2008005/article/10799-eng.htm

Siegel, L., and Welsch, B. (2013). *Juvenile delinquency: The core* (5th ed.). Belmont, CA: Wadsworth.

Simich, L., and Andermann, L. (Eds). (2014). *Refuge and resilience*. New York: Springer.

Simourd, L., and Andrews, D. (1996). Correlates of delinquency: A look at gender. In R. Silverman, J. Teevan, and V. Sacco (Eds), *Crime in Canadian society*. Toronto: Harcourt Brace and Co.

Sprott, J.B., and Doob, A.N. (2010). Gender treatment: Girls and treatment order in Bail Court. *Canadian Journal of Criminology and Criminal Justice*, 52(4): 427–41.

Sprott, J.B., Doob, A.N.M., and Jenkins, J.M. (2001). Problem behaviour and delinquency in children and youth. *Juristat 21*(4). Statistics Canada Catalogue no. 85-002-XIE. Ottawa

Statsna, K. (2013, 26 July). What's behind Canada's improving crime stats? CBC News online. Retrieved 06 July 2014 from http://www.cbc.ca/news/canada/what-s-behind-canada-s-improving-crime-stats-1.1315377

Tanner, J. (2010). *Teenage troubles: Youth and deviance in Canada* (3rd ed.). Toronto: Oxford University Press.

Tanner, J., and Wortley, S. (2002). *Toronto youth crime and victimization survey: Overview report*. Toronto: University of Toronto, Centre of Criminology.

The correlates of self-reported delinquency: An analysis of the national longitudinal survey of children and youth. (2010). Retrieved 1 October 2010 from http://www.justice.gc.ca/eng/pi/rs/rep-rap/2003/rr03_yj2-rr03_jj2/p3.html#sec3_1

Thomas, J. (2003). Youth court statistics, 2001/02. *Juristat*, 23(3). Statistics Canada Catalogue no. 85-002-XIE. Ottawa.

Thomas, J. (2005). Youth court statistics, 2003/04. *Juristat*, 25(4). Statistics Canada Catalogue no. 85-002-XIE. Ottawa.

Vaz, E. (1966). Middle-class adolescents: Self-reported delinquency and youth culture activities. *Canadian Review of Sociology and Anthropology*, 2: 52–70.

Violent crime in Canada (2008). Retrieved 18 April 2011 from http://www.thefreeradical.ca/Violent_crime_in_Canada_fact_sheet.pdf

West, G. (1984). *Young offenders and the state: A Canadian perspective on youth crime*. Toronto: Butterworths.

Wheeler, S., Bonacich, E., Cramer, R., and Zola, J.K. (1968). Agents of delinquency control. In S. Wheeler (Ed.), *Controlling delinquents*. New York: John Wiley and Sons.

Winterdyk, J. (Ed.). (2015). *International juvenile justice: Models, trends and patterns*. Boca Raton, FL: CRC Press.

Winterdyk, J. (Forthcoming). *Canadian criminology*. Toronto: Oxford University Press.

Youth correctional statistics in Canada, 2013/2014. (2013). *Juristat*. Statistics Canada Catalogue no. 85-002-XIE. Ottawa.

Youth crimes reported to police for selected Criminal Code offences. (2009). Retrieved 10 October 2010 from http://www.statcan.gc.ca/daily-quotidien/080516/t080516a-eng.htm

Youth Criminal Justice Act: Changing the law on young criminals. (2003, 23 June). Retrieved 20 December 2010 from http://www.cbc.ca/news/background/crime/ycja.html

Understanding the Youth Criminal Justice Act

Ross Green

3

Overview

This chapter offers an overview of key aspects of the Youth Criminal Justice Act (YCJA), which was enacted by the Parliament of Canada in 2002 and implemented in 2003. It focuses in particular on explaining policy objectives underlying the YCJA and how these objectives are reflected in the Act's provisions, the youth court process through which the Act is enforced, the rights and obligations of young people and parents under the Act, and issues surrounding the use of discretion in determining the most appropriate measures for dealing with young persons who may be charged with criminal offences and made subject to provisions of the Act.[1]

Key Objectives

After reading this chapter, you should be able to:

- Explain the historical context leading to the passage of the YCJA.

- Explain the policy objectives underlying the YCJA and how these objectives are reflected in the Act's provisions.

- Explain the youth justice and youth court process through which the Act is enforced.

- Explain the sentencing provisions in the YCJA.

- Summarize the rights and obligations of young people and parents under the Act.

- Discuss the interrelation or distinction between criminal procedures and other social measures made in the Act.

- Discuss why the mental health of young people, and in particular the presence of fetal alcohol spectrum disorder (FASD), is an important consideration in youth court.

Introduction

The Youth Criminal Justice Act (YCJA) came into force in 2003, replacing the Young Offenders Act (YOA). The YCJA is a complex statute that is significantly longer than the YOA, spanning 165 substantive sections in comparison to 70 sections in the YOA. As a result, the following discussion of the YCJA is not intended to be a comprehensive analysis of all aspects of this Act but, rather, an outline of its important features.

Historical Context Leading to the Passage of the Youth Criminal Justice Act (YCJA)

Youth justice legislation has existed in Canada since passage of the Juvenile Delinquents Act (JDA) in 1908. Prior to that statute, no separate treatment of young people occurred within the criminal justice system. "Historically, children were tried alongside adults, upon reaching the age of seven, the common law age of criminal responsibility" (Lane 1995, p. 6). Development of a distinct court for youthful offenders became largely a development of the twentieth century.

The JDA, which allowed a court to find a youth between 7 and 16 years of age to be a "juvenile delinquent," represented what has been called a paternalistic view to youth justice. By imposing a *parens patriae* philosophy, the youth court came to stand in the role of parent for youths thought to be misguided and the product of improper upbringing in their family life. Youths charged under the JDA were not considered to be criminals but, potentially, could be found delinquent "for actions for which adults could receive no punishment, most notably truancy, running away, and sexual promiscuity" (Lane 1995, p. 27). Little emphasis was placed on due process, such as the right to legal representation. Rules of evidence were relaxed. The JDA allowed an enormous discretion to the youth court respecting both the process followed in court and the resulting sentences for young people.

The JDA was replaced by the Young Offenders Act (YOA) in 1984. The YOA heralded a new focus on making young offenders accountable for their crimes, while at the same time affording them due process protection, such as the right to legal representation, the right to consult a parent, lawyer, or other person before giving a statement, and the right to the least interference with their freedom as was "consistent with the protection of society, having regard to the needs of young persons and the interests of their families" (YOA, s. 3(1)(f)). In comparison to the JDA, the YOA brought the treatment of young offenders more into line with the process and system faced by adult offenders.

After the JDA was replaced by the YOA, dramatic increases in the number of young people in custody were experienced across Canada (Quigley 1994). As well, despite the intended goals of youth accountability and due process protection, the YOA came to be widely criticized for not holding young offenders accountable and hence not being "tough enough" to make a difference. These criticisms reflected a perception that repeat and violent offenders were being over-protected, often at the expense of innocent law-abiding victims (Hogeveen and Smandych 2001). It was within this context that the federal government developed and passed a new youth statute, the Youth Criminal Justice Act.

Policy Objectives Underlying the YCJA

The content and structure of the YCJA reflect key policy objectives held by the federal government of the day. Minister of Justice Anne McLellan, in introducing the YCJA for second reading in the House of Commons, said that this Act was intended to reduce the unacceptably high level of incarceration under the YOA and that the YCJA was drafted so as to ensure that the most serious interventions in the youth justice system should be reserved for the most serious crimes, thereby reducing the overreliance on custody. McLellan further said that, in contrast to the YOA, the YCJA reserves custody primarily for violent offenders and serious repeat offenders. At the same time, the government's view was that the youth justice system was being overburdened by minor offences that could be better dealt with outside of court. McLellan said experience in Canada and elsewhere had shown that out-of-court measures could provide effective responses to youth crime (Davis-Barron 2009, p. 65).

This suggested a trade-off: the youth justice system would be able to better deal with more serious offences and offenders if fewer resources—especially court resources—were spent on less serious offences and offenders. As McLellan said, "The proposed youth criminal justice act is intended to enable the courts to focus on serious youth crimes by increasing the use of effective and timely non-court responses to less serious offences."

Richard Barnhorst, a lawyer with the federal Department of Justice and a drafter of the Act, summarized the main components of the philosophy underlying the Act as including the following:

- *Restraint*, encompassing both sentencing and the decision of whether to use the formal court process in the first place.

- *Accountability*, with a focus on holding youth accountable for their actions by imposing meaningful consequences that will promote the rehabilitation and reintegration of the youth into society.

- *Proportionality*, meaning that consequences imposed on young people be proportionate to the seriousness of the offence and the youth's degree of responsibility.

- *Protection of the public*, which the system can contribute to through holding youths accountable in a fair and proportionate manner while acknowledging that "there are many factors outside the youth justice system that can have as much effect, or greater effect, on public protection than the activities of the youth justice system."

- *Rehabilitation and addressing needs*, ensuring that the "seriousness of the offence sets the degree of intervention, and efforts to address the rehabilitative needs of youths fit within the proportionate response."

- *Structured discretion*, reflecting Parliament's view that officials in the youth justice system be given more legislative direction on how to exercise their discretion in a way that is consistent with the Act's objectives. (Barnhorst 2004, pp. 233–5)

The YCJA is divided into a preamble (containing definitions and a declaration of principle) and nine parts, the most significant of which deal with extrajudicial measures (handling offending behaviour outside of court), the organization of the youth criminal justice system, judicial measures (procedures and processes to be followed in **youth justice court**), the sentencing of young people, procedures governing youth custody sentences and supervision following release, and rules governing the publication of names.

The preamble of this Act states that members of society share a responsibility to address the developmental challenges and the needs of young people and to guide them into adulthood. At its core, the YCJA establishes a separate legal and sentencing regime for young people. The Supreme Court of Canada, in *R. v. B. (D.)*, said that this was because "young people are entitled to a **presumption** of diminished moral blameworthiness or culpability flowing from the fact that, because of their age, they have heightened vulnerability, less maturity and a reduced capacity for moral judgment."

A frequently heard criticism of the statement of principles in the YOA was that it contained "a number of potentially conflicting, inconsistent, and un-prioritised principles" (Anand 1999, p. 251). Although the declaration of principle in section 3 of the YCJA contains more guidance than did its counterpart in the YOA, these general principles still retain the often-conflicting goals of accountability, on the one hand, and rehabilitation,

youth justice court
The court in which young people charged with an offence created by Parliament, usually under the Criminal Code or the Controlled Drugs and Substances Act, appear in order to enter a plea and then to have their trial or be sentenced.

presumption
A rule of law that permits a court to assume something is true until such time as there is evidence that disproves (rebuts) the presumption.

on the other. To some extent, these ambiguities are addressed in three other areas of the YCJA, which now sets the principles and objectives of extrajudicial measures (in sections 4 and 5), the purpose and principles of sentencing (in s. 38), and the purpose and principles of custody and supervision (in s. 85).

The YCJA establishes procedures for young people that, in most respects, are simpler than the procedures for adults under the Criminal Code. A **young person**, defined as being between 12 and 17 years of age, must appear before and be tried in a youth court. For the vast majority of youth charged under the Act, that will mean appearing before a youth court judge who also acts as a provincial court judge for adults. For a small number of serious offences, a young person can elect to be tried in a Superior Court of Justice. These include offences for which the Crown has given notice that an adult sentence is being sought for a youth who has reached 14 years of age or for the offences of first- or second-degree murder for a youth who has not yet reached 14 years (s. 67(1)).

In what the government described as a "bifurcated" approach, the YCJA, at a number of junctures, makes a distinction between the treatment of youths who commit violent offences and those who commit less serious, and non-violent, offences (Minaker and Hogeveen 2009, p. 78). Regarding sentencing, the prerequisites to custody are set out in section 39, making it clear that committing an offence of violence automatically makes custody a possible sentence for a youth. Further, the sentence of a deferred custody and supervision order (DCSO), which is served in the community and not in a custodial facility, is not available where the youth commits or attempts to cause "serious bodily harm."

Extrajudicial Measures: Dealing with Less Serious Offences and Less Experienced Young Offenders outside of Court

A key issue in the youth justice system is whether young offenders without any significant involvement can be diverted from youth court and instead dealt with by so-called **extrajudicial measures**, which were called "alternative measures" under the YOA. The YOA contained only a general statement of principle (in s. 3) that, where not inconsistent with protection of the public, police or prosecutors should consider either taking no measures (e.g., doing nothing) or taking measures other than judicial proceedings (e.g., informal police warnings). In the YCJA, the declaration of principles respecting extrajudicial measures is much broader. Section 4 of the YCJA states that extrajudicial measures are

- often the most appropriate and effective way to address youth crime;

- able to allow for effective and timely interventions focussed on correcting offending behaviour;

- presumed to be adequate to hold a young person accountable for his or her offending behaviour if the young person has committed a non-violent offence and has not previously been convicted of an offence; and

young person
A youth 12 to 17 years of age who can be charged under the YCJA with having committed an offence.

extrajudicial measures
Under the YCJA, measures other than judicial proceedings (i.e., youth court) that are used to deal with a young person alleged to have committed an offence (including extrajudicial sanctions).

- [to be] used if they are adequate to hold a young person accountable for his or her offending behaviour, and if the use of extrajudicial measures is consistent with the principles set out in this section, nothing in this Act precludes their use in respect of a young person who: (i) has previously been dealt with by the use of extrajudicial measures, or (ii) has previously been found guilty of an offence.

In addition, section 5 states that extrajudicial measures should be designed to:

- provide an effective and timely response to offending behaviour outside the bounds of judicial measures;

- encourage young persons to acknowledge and repair the harm caused to the victim and the community;

- encourage families of young persons—including extended families where appropriate—and the community to become involved in the design and implementation of those measures;

- provide an opportunity for victims to participate in decisions related to the measures selected and to receive reparation; and

- respect the rights and freedoms of young persons and be proportionate to the seriousness of the offence.

While alternative-measure programs were the only alternative to court proceedings defined in the YOA, the YCJA formally sets out a number of alternatives other than laying charges. The range and prominence of front-end options in the YCJA parallel similar developments in New Zealand and England (Green and Healy 2003). More specifically, similar to legislation in these countries, section 6(1) of the YCJA compels a police officer, faced with a young person alleged to have committed an offence and before "starting judicial proceedings or taking any other measures" under the Act, to consider the following: (1) taking no further action; (2) warning the young person; or (3) with the consent of the young person, referring the young person to a program or agency in the community that may assist the young person in ways that help him or her not to commit further offences. Although these options were previously within the discretion of police officers under the YOA, the formalization of these alternatives in the YCJA lends priority to considering approaches other than proceeding to youth court. Another front-end option contained in the YCJA is *the caution*. Specifically, section 7 of the Act provides that the attorney general of each province may establish a program authorizing the police or prosecutors "to administer cautions to young persons instead of starting judicial proceedings."

Greater consideration of front-end options in the Canadian youth justice system came as a result of the reality that, in 2000, less serious offences made up over 40 per cent of youth court cases. Such offences included theft under $5000, possession of stolen property, and failure to appear and failure to comply with a disposition (i.e., breach of probation) (Minaker and Hogeveen 2009, p. 103). Keeping less serious and first-time offenders out of the court system leaves more of the system's scarce resources available to deal with more serious offences.

Rights and Obligations of Young People and Parents under the YCJA

Procedural Protection for Young People

Section 3(1)(b)(iii) of the YCJA provides that the criminal justice system for young people must emphasize "enhanced procedural protections to ensure that young persons are treated fairly and that their rights, including their rights to privacy, are protected." In 2005, in *R. v. R.W.C.*, Justice Fish of the Supreme Court of Canada stated that "in keeping with its international obligations, Parliament has sought as well to extend to young offenders enhanced procedural protections, and to interfere with their personal freedom and privacy as little as possible." In recognition of the range of procedural protections afforded to Canadian young people, the preamble of the YCJA states that

> WHEREAS Canada is a party to the United Nations Convention on the Rights of the Child and recognizes that young persons have rights and freedoms, including those stated in the *Canadian Charter of Rights and Freedoms* and the *Canadian Bill of Rights*, and have special guarantees of their rights and freedoms . . . .

For the purposes of this discussion, the key sources of procedural protections for young people come from the Canadian Constitution, specifically the Canadian Charter of Rights and Freedoms, and from additional protections set out in the YCJA. A discussion of the procedural protections for young people found under the Charter is an enormous endeavour that goes far beyond the scope of this chapter (see Davis-Barron 2009, Ch. 6). The most important protections for youth under the Charter can be summarized as follows:

- *Section 7* provides that "[e]veryone has the right to life, liberty and security of the person and the right not to be deprived thereof except in accordance with the principles of fundamental justice." These rights have been held to encompass the right of a young person to remain silent during the police investigation and the trial, the right to full disclosure from the Crown of the case against the young person, and the right to make full answer and defence in response to a charge.

- *Section 8* provides the right to be secure against unreasonable search and seizure.

- *Section 9* provides the right not to be arbitrarily detained or imprisoned.

- *Section 10* provides the right, on arrest or detention, to be informed promptly of the reasons for being taken into police custody and the right to retain and instruct a lawyer and to be told of this right.

- *Section 11(b)* provides the right to be tried within a reasonable time.

- *Section 11(d)* provides the right to be presumed innocent.

- *Section 12* provides the right not to be subjected to any cruel and unusual treatment or punishment.

In addition to, and at times as an adjunct to, the rights provided for young people under the Charter, the YCJA sets out a series of rights that protect the interests of young people charged under the Act. These include the following:

- The presumption that extrajudicial measures will be adequate to hold a young person accountable for his or her offending behaviour if the young person has committed a non-violent offence and has not previously been found guilty of an offence (in s. 4(c)).

- The right, upon arrest, detention, or otherwise being ordered to appear on a charge in youth court, to have a parent or guardian notified about the young person's status before the court (s. 26) and, further, the qualified right to have his or her parent or guardian attend court (as a judge under s. 27 can order such attendance if deemed to be in the best interests of the young person).

- The right to be represented by a lawyer, and the right to be advised of this by the judge at various stages during the proceeding (s. 25(3)). If the young person is not able to obtain a lawyer, the judge can appoint one (s. 25(6)), who, where the interests of parent and child differ, can be a separate lawyer from the parent's counsel (s. 25(8)).

- The right, on first appearance in court, to have the charge read aloud and to receive an explanation of the right of the young person to be represented by a lawyer (s. 32(1)). If the youth does not understand the charge, the judge is obligated to enter a not-guilty plea (s. 32(4)). If the youth is unrepresented and does not understand the charge, the right to plead guilty or not guilty, or the possibility of an adult sentence (if applicable), the judge shall appoint a lawyer to assist the young person (s. 32(3)).

- The right not to be detained in custody prior to being sentenced as a substitute for appropriate child-protection, mental health, or other social measures (s. 29(1)).

- The right not to be denied bail (kept in custody pending completion of the charge[s]) unless the prosecutor shows this is necessary to (1) ensure the young person comes back to court on the charge(s); (2) protect the public; and/or (3) maintain confidence in the administration of justice (ss. 29(2) and (3)).

- If denied bail by a justice of the peace (as opposed to a youth court judge), to have that decision reviewed—in effect to have another bail hearing—before a youth court judge (s. 33). This provision is utilized most often in Ontario, where many initial bail hearings for young people are done before a justice of the peace.

- The qualified right to be held in custody separate from adults, including while on remand (s. 84 and s. 30(3)).

Another key protection for young people charged under the Act is a restriction on the admissibility of statements given by the young person to a person in authority, such as a police officer. The YOA (s. 56) contained a series of requirements to be met before a young person's statement could be admitted as evidence in a court proceeding. These requirements have been repeated in s. 146 of the YCJA and prevent admission of such statements unless the statement is voluntary and the person to whom the statement is made has explained a number of factors. These include the young person's right to silence; that any statement may be used against them; their right to consult a lawyer, parent, or other adult; and the right to have the person consulted present during the statement. Any waiver of these rights by a young person must be formally recorded and signed by the young person.

In 1990, in *R. v. J. (J.T.)*, the Supreme Court of Canada ruled that a statement that did not comply with the strict requirements of section 56 of the YOA was inadmissible. Apparently in response to this interpretation, the YCJA now allows a youth court, under section 146(6), to admit a statement into evidence despite a technical irregularity if satisfied that "the admission of the statement would not bring into disrepute the principle that young persons are entitled to enhanced procedural protection to ensure that they are treated fairly and their rights are protected." Further, under section 146(5), a court can accept as valid a waiver of rights not made in strict compliance with the Act as long as the court is satisfied that the young person was informed of his or her rights and voluntarily waived those rights.

Parents under the YCJA

parent
Includes any person who is under a legal duty to provide for a young person or any person who has the custody or control of a young person.

The preamble to the YCJA specifically mentions **parents** as participants in attempts to (1) reduce crime by addressing its underlying causes; (2) respond to the needs of young persons; and (3) provide guidance and support to those at risk of committing crimes. Under specific provisions of the Act, parents are given both rights and responsibilities. The rights include the following:

- The right to receive notice from the police when their child is arrested or detained or otherwise summoned to court (s. 26)

- The right to be advised of the sanction when their child is dealt with by way of an extrajudicial sanction (s. 11)

- The right to receive a copy of any document their child is entitled to receive if that youth is the subject of a mental health proceeding under Part XX.1 of the Criminal Code, such as a psychiatric remand (s. 141(2))

- The right to request that their child, if subject to a custody sentence, be brought before the youth court to review the youth's sentence, subject to minimum time limitations and to grounds for the review set out in the Act (ss. 94(3) and (6))

And following are the responsibilities:

- To attend court with their child if so ordered by the youth court judge (s. 27(1)) and, if they fail without reasonable excuse to do so, to be subject to a warrant compelling their attendance or to be punished for contempt of court (s. 27(4) and (5))

- The legal responsibility of complying with any condition placed on that parent by a judge when a youth is released to that parent as a responsible person (s. 31(3)) and potentially to being charged under s. 139(1) for a breach of that condition

Outside of the power to set reasonable conditions on a parent to whom a child is released or the power to order a parent to attend court, a judge has no power under the YCJA to order a parent to follow any course of conduct or programming. That stands in contrast to the situation in England and some US states where a youth court can order a parent to take part in counselling to help in the understanding of adolescent development and to improve parenting skills (Bala and Anand 2012, p. 159). It also stands in contrast to Canadian child-protection proceedings, where, under provincial child-protection legislation, a court could, in appropriate circumstances and when deemed to be in the best interests of the child, order a parent to take specific programming. Nor is there any provision in the YCJA to make parents financially liable to victims for crimes committed by their children. However, some provincial governments—in particular Manitoba, Ontario, and British Columbia—have passed legislation that "imposes limited civil liability to victims by parents of young offenders" (ibid., p. 161).

Despite the laudable goals of parental involvement in the youth court system, one study concludes that parents are often not involved in ways that are effective and meaningful because of (1) conflict between the parent and the youth and (2) conflict between the competing parental roles of socializing their child while at the same time promoting their interests in an adversarial court system (Peterson-Badali and Broeking 2010, p. 2).

Sentencing under the YCJA

A substantial part of the YCJA deals with sentencing young people. As a result, this section discusses the following:

- Sentencing principles set out in the Act

- Variety of sentences available

- Limitations on custody

- Provisions regarding the sentencing of Aboriginal young people

- Circumstances under which a youth can be sentenced as an adult

- Provisions for the community supervision and reintegration of young people

Sentencing Principles

In 2006, in *R. v. P. (B.W.)*, the Supreme Court noted that the sentencing principles in the YCJA "have been characterized as 'the most systematic attempt in Canadian history to structure judicial discretion regarding the sentencing of juveniles.'" Whereas the YOA contained no separate statement of purpose guiding the sentencing of young offenders, the YCJA states, in s. 38(1), that the purpose of sentencing is to "hold a young person accountable for an offence through the imposition of just sanctions that have meaningful consequences for the young person and that promote his or her rehabilitation and reintegration into society, thereby contributing to the long-term protection of the public."

Major changes were made to the Criminal Code sentencing provisions (for adults) in 1996. These amendments included a set of broad-ranging, competing, and at times contradictory sentencing principles. The YCJA has now adopted this approach, with a detailed set of sentencing principles contained in s. 38(2). These require that

- the sentence must not result in a punishment that is greater than the punishment that would be appropriate for an adult who has been convicted of the same offence committed in similar circumstances;

- the sentence must be similar to the sentences imposed in the region on similar young persons found guilty of the same offence committed in similar circumstances;

- the sentence must be proportionate to the seriousness of the offence and the degree of responsibility of the young person for that offence;

- all available sanctions other than custody that are reasonable in the circumstances should be considered for all young persons, with particular attention to the circumstances of Aboriginal young persons; and, subject to the principle of proportionality, the sentence must
  (a) be the least restrictive sentence that is capable of achieving the overall purpose of sentencing in s. 38(1),
  (b) be the one that is most likely to rehabilitate the young person and reintegrate him or her into society, and
  (c) promote a sense of responsibility in the young person, and an acknowledgment of the harm done to victims and the community.

Under section 38(3) of the YCJA, the youth court, in determining a sentence, shall consider

- the degree of participation by the young person in the commission of the offence;

- the harm done to victims and whether it was intentional or reasonably foreseeable;

- any reparation made by the young person to the victim or the community;

- the time spent in detention by the young person as a result of the offence;

- the previous findings of guilt of the young person; and

- any other aggravating and mitigating circumstances related to the young person or the offence that are relevant to the purpose and principles set out in this section.

As well, under section 39(6), the judge must, before imposing a custodial sentence, consider a pre-sentence report and any sentencing proposal made by the young person or his or her counsel, unless the judge, with the consent of the prosecutor and the young person, dispenses with the report if satisfied that the report is not necessary. Under section 40 of the Act, the written pre-sentence report will include

(a) the results of an interview with the young person and, where possible, with the parents of the young person and the extended family;

(b) the results of an interview with the victim;

(c) any information that is applicable to the case, including:
  - the age, maturity, character, behaviour and attitude of the young person and his or her willingness to make amends,
  - any plans put forward by the young person to change his or her conduct or to participate in activities or improve himself or herself,
  - any history of previous findings of guilt or participation in extrajudicial measures respecting the young person,
  - the availability and appropriateness of community services and facilities for young persons and the willingness of the young person to avail himself or herself of those services or facilities,
  - the relationship between the young person and the young person's parents and the degree of control and influence of the parents over the young person, and
  - the school attendance and performance record and the employment record of the young person.

(d) any information that may assist the court in determining under subsection 39(2) whether there is an alternative to custody; and

(e) any information that the provincial director considers relevant, including any recommendation that the provincial director considers appropriate.

As a result of the 2012 amendments to the YCJA, two principles of sentencing that are now contained in the YCJA (but were not previously) are specific deterrence (deterring the youth in question and others from this form of conduct) and denunciation of the behaviour. That amendment is significant because in 2006, in *R. v. P. (B.W.); R. v. N. (V.N.)*, Justice Charron of the Supreme Court concluded that Parliament's omission of the word *deterrence* was deliberate, and as a result, this principle was not incorporated into the YCJA's sentencing regime.

These amendments were controversial when proposed in 2010 by the then Conservative minority government. The Canadian Bar Association (CBA) set out the following concern:

This proposed amendment appears to respond to a previous SCC decision in *R. v. P. (B.W.); R. v. N. (B.V.)* to make youth court sentences more onerous. However, this represents a radical departure from the stated goals of the YCJA as discussed in the Court's decision in *D.B.*, for example. In the *P. (B.W.)* case, the SCC states that omitting "deterrence" is not a mere oversight but rather an intentional recognition of the fact that it is a controversial theory. There is little evidence that general deterrence is an effective sentencing principle . . . indeed, it has been criticized in both judicial and academic spheres. It is unlikely that it is in any way effective for young persons, considering their diminished capacities.

The wording of the current YCJA recognizes this. Studies show that the principle of "deterrence" primarily affects one group—judges. Including deterrence in the sentencing principles would suggest to judges that they should impose longer, harsher sentences. But for immature offenders unable to anticipate or appreciate consequences in the same way that adults do, it is particularly troubling that this principle would be grafted onto an otherwise progressive sentencing regime. This amendment would offer judges considering the imposition of a jail sentence a "peg to hang their coat on," but would go against other sections of the Act that clarify that jail should be avoided, and used only as a "last resort." Those sections are based on sound social science that shows imposing jail time is generally *not an effective deterrent* as against a young person, which has been proven conclusively over the last seven years. (CBA 2010, p. 7; footnotes omitted)

Whether the inclusion of specific deterrence and denunciation as sentencing principles will significantly change the sentencing decisions of judges in cases that come before them in the long run remains to be seen, given the recency of this amendment. However, Professor Nicholas Bala, a widely respected commentator on youth justice in Canada, commented that while the addition of "specific deterrence" and "denunciation" as principles of youth sentencing may result in harsher sentences for youth who have endangered public safety or who have committed repeat offences, the changes to the youth bail provisions in the YCJA may well result in fewer youth in custody (Bala 2015). Regardless of how judges decide to interpret the new amendments to the YCJA introduced in Bill C-10, it is likely that their decisions will result in more legal debate and public controversy, given the varied viewpoints Canadians appear to hold on how youth should be dealt with in the courts.

Variety of Sentences

Section 42 of the YCJA sets out the potential sentences for young persons. Like the YOA, the YCJA allows a youth court judge to grant a conditional or absolute discharge; to fine the young person; to order the young person to pay restitution to victims of his or her crime; to order the young person to do either personal service for a victim or community service hours; to make an order of prohibition, forfeiture, or seizure against the young person as authorized under any act of Parliament; or to place the young person on probation for up to two years. Section 51 further allows the judge to make a firearms prohibition against the young person for up to two years.

The YCJA, however, provides additional sanctions. A youth court judge can reprimand a young person—that is, make an oral statement condemning the youth's behaviour. Subject to agreement by the provincial director, a youth may now be ordered into an **intensive support and supervision program** or may be ordered—assuming the young person is a suitable candidate and that such programming would not interfere with his or her work or education—to attend a non-residential program approved by the provincial director over a period not exceeding six months. For a young person convicted of an offence that is not a serious violent offence, the court can make a **deferred custody and supervision order** that is for a specified period not exceeding six months.

intensive support and supervision program (ISSP)
In the YCJA, a community-based sentence that provides more supervision than a probation order and, in provinces where such programs exist, can provide young offenders with access to programs that are appropriate to their specific needs (e.g., mental health needs).

deferred custody and supervision order (DCSO)
In the YCJA, a community-based alternative to a custodial sentence under which the young person will serve his or her sentence in the community under a set of strict conditions. If these conditions are not followed, the young person may be sent to custody to serve the balance of that sentence.

The intensive rehabilitation custody and supervision order (as per ss. 42(2)(r) and 42(7)) provides an option to other available youth sentences, or to an adult sentence, for a youth convicted either of first- or second-degree murder, attempted murder, manslaughter, or aggravated sexual assault or of an offence in which the youth caused or attempted to cause serious bodily harm and for which an adult is liable to imprisonment for more than two years when that youth has been previously convicted twice for such an offence. Such an order may be made for the same duration as a normal custody and supervision order if

- this youth is suffering from a mental illness or disorder, a psychological disorder, or an emotional disturbance;

- a plan of treatment and intensive supervision has been developed for the young person, and there are reasonable grounds to believe that the plan might reduce the risk of the young person repeating the offence or committing a serious violent offence; and

- the provincial director has determined that an intensive rehabilitative custody and supervision program is available and that the young person's participation in the program is appropriate.

The YOA provided two levels of custody for young persons: open and secure. The appropriate level was to be determined at sentencing by the judge. The YCJA, in section 85, also requires each province to establish two levels of custody, "distinguished by the degree of restraint." According to that section, the decision as to level of custody is to be made by the provincial director, not by the judge. However, section 88 allows each province, rather than to adopt this new process of determining custody levels, to retain the YOA's process of letting the judge determine whether open or secure custody is to be imposed on a young person. While it appears to have been Parliament's intent to allow the provincial director the discretion to make this decision, the reality is that all provinces and territories chose to retain the previous system (Tustin and Lutes 2005, p. 132).

As a result, youth court judges continue to make this decision, based on the criteria established previously by section 24.1 of the YOA. In deciding between open custody and secure custody, the judge must consider the following factors:

(a) that a young person should be placed in a level of custody involving the least degree of containment and restraint, having regard to:
  (i) the seriousness of the offence in respect of which the young person was committed to custody and the circumstances in which that offence was committed,
  (ii) the needs and circumstances of the young person, including proximity to family, school, employment and support services,
  (iii) the safety of other young persons in custody, and
  (iv) the interests of society;

(b)   that the level of custody should allow for the best possible match of pro-
      grams to the young person's needs and behaviour, having regard to the
      findings of any assessment in respect of the young person;

(c)   the likelihood of escape if the young person is placed in open custody; and

(d)   the recommendations, if any, of the youth court or the provincial director,
      as the case may be.

The total length of a custody and supervision order under the YCJA shall not exceed
two years, or if the young person is found guilty of an offence for which the punishment
provided by the Criminal Code or any other Act of Parliament is imprisonment for life, it
shall not exceed three years from the date the order comes into force. These maximums
are the same as those that were contained in the YOA. Likewise, the maximum sentences
for first- and second-degree murder remain unchanged under the YCJA: ten years for first-
degree murder and seven years for second-degree murder (with each sentence including a
period of conditional supervision).

Limitations on Custody

Despite calls for a more punitive response toward young offenders in the debate leading
up to passage of the YCJA, the Act contains language that suggests limiting the scope of
custody for young offenders. As noted earlier in this chapter, this change in policy came
about because of concern with the overuse of custody. Writing in 1999, in *R. v. J.K.E.*,
Chief Judge Lilles of the Yukon Territorial Court recounted the high rates of youth incarceration in Canada in comparison to other countries:

> Adults are incarcerated at a rate of 130 inmates per 100,000 population in
> Canada, less than the rate in the United States. Yet Canada incarcerates young
> people under the age of 18 at a much higher rate than adults, 447 per 100,000.
> Moreover, this is considerably higher than the corresponding youth incarcera-
> tion rate of 311 per 100,000 for the United States, 86 per 100,000 for Scotland
> and 69 per 100,000 for England and Wales. . . . Further, more than one-half are
> incarcerated for property and process offences rather than for offences involving
> personal injury. (ibid., para. 60)

As an apparent response to these alarming rates, section 39(1) states that a youth
court shall not sentence an offender to custody unless that young person

(a)   has committed a violent offence;

(b)   has failed to comply with noncustodial sentences;

(c)   [has committed an indictable offence for which an adult could be jailed for
      over two years while possessing a history indicating a pattern of criminal-
      ity; or]

(d) in exceptional cases, has committed an indictable offence, the aggravating circumstances of which are such that the imposition of a noncustodial sentence would be inconsistent with the purpose and principles set out in s. 38.

Not surprisingly, the issue of when a young person can receive a sentence of custody has resulted in much debate. While litigation over section 39(1) is certain to continue and evolve, to date the following has been determined:

- *Under section 39(1)(a)*, the 2012 amendments to the YCJA broadened the definition of "violent offence" to now constitute "(a) an offence committed by a young person that includes as an element the causing of bodily harm; (b) an attempt or a threat to commit an offence referred to in paragraph (a); (c) an offence in the commission of which a young person endangers the life or safety of another person by creating a substantial likelihood of causing bodily harm." This would, therefore, include an offence where a young person did not intend to cause but in fact did cause bodily harm.

- *Under section 39(1)(b)*, the young person must have failed to comply with two separate non-custodial sentences (Davis-Barron 2009, p. 369).

- *Under section 39(1)(c)*, the only findings of guilt that the judge can consider in deciding whether a pattern of criminality exists are the convictions entered as of the date of the offence for which the young person is being sentenced. Further, the Crown must generally present evidence of at least three prior findings of guilt, although findings need not relate to similar or to indictable offences (*R. v. S.A.C.* [2008] S.C.J. No. 48 (S.C.C.)). However, it is significant that Bill C-10 redefined this pattern of offending as comprising either extrajudicial sanctions or findings of guilt under the YCJA.

- *Under section 39(1)(d)*, "exceptional circumstances" refer to cases where the circumstances of the offence are so extreme that only a sentence of custody would reflect societal values; hence, the application of this provision is limited to the clearest of cases where a custodial disposition is the only one that can be justified (*R. v. R.E.W.* (2006), 79 O.R. (3d) 1 (Ont. C.A.)) (see Davis-Barron 2009, pp. 357–83).

The wording of section 39(1) makes clear Parliament's attempt to restrict significantly the number of young people who can be incarcerated for property or other non-violent offences. Yet even if the restrictions in section 39(1)(a) to (c) (above) apply, section 39(2) of the Act further restricts the applicability of a custody sentence by requiring the youth court judge, before imposing custody, to consider "all alternatives to custody raised at the sentencing hearing that are reasonable in the circumstances" and to determine that there is no alternative to custody that is consistent with principles of sentencing set out in the Act. As well, sections 39(4) and (5) of the Act state that the previous imposition of a particular non-custodial sentence on a young person does not preclude a youth justice court from imposing the same or any other non-custodial sentence for another offence and that custody should not be used as a substitute for appropriate child-protection, mental health, or other social measures.

Provisions Regarding the Sentencing of Aboriginal Young People

One of the final amendments to the YCJA before final passage in the House of Commons was made to the principles of sentencing as they relate to Aboriginal young people. Section 38(2)(d) provides that "all available sanctions other than custody that are reasonable in the circumstances should be considered for all young persons, with particular attention to the circumstances of Aboriginal young persons." Section 50 of the Act makes the similar sentencing principle for adult offenders in the Criminal Code to be the only adult sentencing principle applicable to young people.

In 1999, in *R. v. Gladue*, the Supreme Court of Canada interpreted section 718.2(e) of the Criminal Code, which requires sentencing judges to consider a similar provision for adult Aboriginal offenders. In *Gladue*, Justices Cory and Iacobucci interpreted this subsection as a "direction to sentencing judges to undertake the process of sentencing Aboriginal offenders differently, in order to endeavour to achieve a truly fit and proper sentence in the particular case." The Court considered the "circumstances of Aboriginal offenders" within the context of what was described as the "tragic history of the treatment of Aboriginal peoples within the Canadian criminal justice system."

Trial courts were directed to pay particular attention to so-called systemic and background factors that may have played a part in bringing an Aboriginal offender before the court. These factors were said to include the effects of poverty, substance abuse, a lack of or the irrelevance of education, and community breakdown. In addition to these factors, however, the Supreme Court outlined the following:

> . . . it must be recognized that the circumstances of Aboriginal offenders differ from those of the majority because many Aboriginal people are victims of systemic and direct discrimination, many suffer the legacy of dislocation, and many are substantially affected by poor social and economic conditions. Moreover, as has been emphasized repeatedly in studies and commission reports, Aboriginal offenders are, as a result of these unique systemic and background factors, more adversely affected by incarceration and less likely to be "rehabilitated" thereby, because the internment milieu is often culturally inappropriate and regrettably discrimination towards them is so often rampant in penal institutions. (*R. v. Gladue*, para. 68)

As a result, the court urged judges to seek alternatives to jailing Aboriginal offenders in appropriate circumstances, given their overrepresentation in the prisons of Canada. The search for alternative sentences was to utilize, wherever possible, restorative principles of justice, including healing and rehabilitation and restoration of the relationship between the offender, victim, and community.

The *Gladue* decision was held to apply to young persons under the YOA, despite there being no mention of the circumstances of Aboriginal young people in that Act (see *R. v. J.K.E.*, 1999). The specific reference to paying "particular attention to the circumstances of Aboriginal young people" in section 38(2)(d) makes the *Gladue* decision directly applicable to the sentencing of Aboriginal young people under the YCJA (see *R. v. T.D.P.*, 2004).

The complexity of the issue of overrepresentation of Aboriginal young people in the youth justice system cannot be overstated. The Manitoba Aboriginal Justice Implementation Commission stated that the roots of such overrepresentation are not "found only in the justice system, but in the broader social setting, and will require concerted action from all three levels of government in Canada." The commission also said this:

> Aboriginal people who are at risk of becoming involved in crime often face multiple problems: racism, domestic violence, community violence, poor access to health care and education, inadequate housing and limited employment options. These problems generate hostility, stress and demoralization, and can lead to criminal behaviour. (Chartrand and Whitecloud 2001, p. 135)

The commission suggested a crime prevention approach that would address all these issues in a coordinated fashion.

Despite the goal of reducing the number of Aboriginal young people in custody, recent statistics suggest that the number of Aboriginal youth in custody has actually increased, rather than decreased, since the implementation of the YCJA. In 2011/12, Aboriginal youth represented 7 per cent of the youth population in nine reporting provinces and territories. However, the proportion of Aboriginal youth admissions to remand during 2011/12 was nearly five times their representation in the youth population and had increased from 24 per cent in 2008/09 to 34.2 per cent in 2011/12 (Porter and Calverley 2011, p. 20; Perreault 2014, Table 2). In addition, the proportion of Aboriginal youth in sentenced custody was more than six times their representation in the youth population, having increased from 36 per cent of youth in sentenced custody in 2008/09 to 45 per cent in 2011/12 (Calverley, Cotter, and Halla 2010, pp. 5, 29; Perreault 2014, Table 2).

The current situation of Aboriginal youth in Canada's youth custody facilities is best summarized by a research study published in 2014:

> There is a consensus among Canadian researchers that the YCJA and related provincial/territorial laws and policies have been effective in reducing the absolute number of young offenders given prison sentences including Aboriginal young offenders; yet the latter's historical over-representation in youth custody has not changed despite the Act's emphasis on alternative and culturally specific sentences for these young people. This continued disproportionality suggests that additional strategies need to be considered. (Corrado, Kuehn, and Margaritescu 2014, p. 56)

Circumstances under Which a Youth Is to Be Sentenced as an Adult

The YOA provided for the transfer of a youth charged under the Act to adult court and hence permitted a youth to be tried as an adult. The YCJA provides that a youth can only be tried in youth court, regardless of the charge, but that in some circumstance a youth can be sentenced as an adult.

A major feature of the YCJA, when put into force, was the definition of so-called presumptive offences—those for which there was a presumption, unless rebutted by the youth, that a youth convicted of such an offence would be sentenced as an adult. These offences, which apply only to a youth who has reached 14 years of age, were defined in section 2 to include murder, attempted murder, manslaughter, and aggravated sexual assault or, in the alternative, a serious violent offence where the youth has twice before committed such an offence. This presumption, however, was determined to be unconstitutional—as a violation of section 7 of the Charter—by the Supreme Court in 2008 in *R. v. D.B.* As a result, while it is still possible for a youth to receive an adult sentence—for an offence for which an adult would be liable to imprisonment for more than two years and which is alleged to have been committed after the youth attained the age of 14 years—the onus is on the Crown to show why an adult sentence would be appropriate for the youth. However, since the enactment of Bill C-10, the Act now includes a related provision requiring the Crown to consider whether a youth should be sentenced as an adult for a serious violent offence committed after the youth reached the age of 14 years.

Provisions for Community Supervision and Reintegration

Section 83 of the YCJA states the purpose of the youth custody and supervision system to be twofold: (1) to carry out sentences imposed by courts through the safe, fair, and humane custody and supervision of young persons; and (2) to assist young persons to be rehabilitated and reintegrated into the community as law-abiding citizens by providing effective programs to young persons in custody and while under supervision in the community. The principles to be used in achieving that purpose, in addition to the general principles in section 3 of the Act, are said to include the following:

- That the least restrictive measures consistent with the protection of the public and of personnel working with young persons and of young persons be used,

- That young persons sentenced to custody retain the rights of other young persons, except the rights that are necessarily removed or restricted as a consequence of a sentence under the YCJA or another act of Parliament,

- That the youth custody and supervision system facilitate the involvement of the families of young persons and members of the public, and

- That custody and supervision decisions be made in a forthright, fair, and timely manner, and that young persons have access to an effective review procedure.

While a youth court previously had discretion as to whether or not to place a young person on probation in addition to or as an alternative to custody, the YCJA now provides that any custody sentence be followed by a supervision order, which is usually one-half as long as the period of custody and contains conditions defined in section 97. The supervision order—similar to conditional supervision, which formed the latter part of a sentence for murder under the YOA—brings the process of youth custody and release closer to that set out in the Criminal Code and to the associated correctional legislation for adults.

An adult offender receives remission or "good time" usually equal to one-half of the time actually served in jail. After two-thirds of the total sentence, such offenders are to be released on mandatory supervision unless the authorities apply, in limited cases, to have them held in prison until their warrant-of-expiry date, the so-called gating or detention-hearing process. In the case of a young person sentenced to custody for a serious crime of violence—including murder, manslaughter, or aggravated sexual assault—the attorney general can apply under section 104 of the YCJA (and similar to the gating provision for adults) to revoke the community supervision part of the sentence. Such an application can be granted where there are reasonable grounds to believe that the young person is likely to commit an offence causing death or serious bodily harm before the end of his or her sentence.

Multidisciplinary Approaches to Youth Justice and Crime Prevention

There is often an interrelation between the supports available to a young person from their family and community, or the lack of these, and the presence of that young person in youth court. In many cases, that interrelation can best be described as a breakdown. Many police officers, lawyers, youth workers, and judges encounter, daily, youth who they believe would be more appropriately dealt with by child-protection or mental health workers, rather than by being processed through the criminal justice system. This has led some commentators to suggest that the criminal justice system has become our society's default system, taking in all those youth that fall between the cracks of other systems and resources (Green and Healy 2003, pp. 70–83).

The YOA, in section 24(1.1)(a), provided that custody should "not be used as a substitute for appropriate child protection, health or other social measures." Similarly, the YCJA now provides in section 29(1) that a young person shall not be detained in custody prior to sentence "as a substitute for appropriate child protection, mental health or other social measures" and in section 39(5) that custody shall not be used "as a substitute for appropriate child protection, mental health or other social measures." The YCJA, in section 35, further provides that "a youth justice court may, at any stage of proceedings against a young person, refer the young person to a child welfare agency for assessment to determine whether the young person is in need of child welfare services."

While the YCJA clearly evidences an intent that criminal sanctions are not to be used where other social measures would be appropriate, at the same time the drafters of this legislation also foresaw the need for multidisciplinary and wide-ranging approaches to youth justice. In its preamble, the YCJA contains a statement that "communities, families, parents and others concerned with the development of young persons should, through multi-disciplinary approaches, take reasonable steps to prevent youth crime by addressing its underlying causes, to respond to the needs of young persons, and to provide guidance and support to those at risk of committing crimes." These multidisciplinary approaches necessitate co-operation among a broad spectrum of people and organizations, including employees working in various services and agencies and other groups and individuals within each community. This approach suggests putting an emphasis on a co-operative view of justice. In a society where public sector cutbacks have at times become a reality, there is an obvious need to pool resources in attempting to address the causes and effects of crime and, as a result, to provide for safer communities.

The goal of multidisciplinary co-operation within the justice system has, however, proven to be a challenge at times. The extent to which the system has remained aloof from the rest of society, in contrast to many other institutions, was questioned by Chief Judge Stuart of the Yukon Territorial Court in 2002, in *R. v. M.N.J.*:

> How can a system remain so robust when no one can make the case it is suc-ceeding and everyone can agree it should be doing much better on almost every front? When the evidence for changing to a holistic, co-ordinated, value-based approach is so overwhelming, how can the justice system remain a jungle of complex, disjointed interactions that preserve numerous self-serving fiefdoms, all with different values, different objectives? When the pub-lic has not merely challenged, but penetrated and participated directly in the shaping of other public processes (Education, Health, Environment, Labour Relations, etc.), how has the justice system managed to keep the public at its outer gates, misinformed and ineffective in changing our arcane processes? We have achieved, often despite our best intentions to be otherwise, a level of excellence in maintaining the status quo, despite constant external pressures to change. (at para. 129)

As a signal that those employed within the justice system must now be open to new partnerships with other agencies and community members, the general principles of the YCJA (i.e., s. 3(1)C)(iii)) state that measures taken against young persons who commit offences should, "where appropriate, involve the parents, the extended family, the com-munity and social or other agencies in the young person's rehabilitation and reintegration." This provision represents a recognition of the complexity of today's society and hence of the need to pool and focus the efforts of people and organizations in providing both servi-ces and supports to young people and an increased sense of safety at the local level.

Although there is much to be said about how inter-agency and multidisciplinary approaches to justice can help youth already caught up in the justice system, another sig-nificant aspect of this form of co-operation lies in the area of crime prevention—that is, helping young people stay out of court in the first place. In recognition of the importance of this goal and of the interrelationship between the causes of crime and crime preven-tion, the YCJA (s. 3(1)(a)(i)) holds, as a key principle of interpretation, that the youth crim-inal justice system is meant to "prevent crime by addressing the circumstances underlying a young person's offending behaviour."

Furthermore, education is a key part of crime prevention. As an example of this, the Manitoba Aboriginal Justice Implementation Commission recognized the interconnected-ness of young people, their families, and their communities, and stated that "there is clear evidence that money spent on early years' education decreases the likelihood of a young person's coming into conflict with the law" (Chartrand and Whitecloud 2001, p. 137).

Conferencing under the YCJA

The YCJA promotes the involvement of a broad cross-section of people and organizations in assisting young people within the youth justice system in general and within youth court in particular. Under the community **conferencing** provisions of this Act (in s. 19), a "youth justice court judge, the provincial director, a police officer, a justice of the peace, a prosecutor or a youth worker may convene or cause to be convened a conference for the purpose of making a decision required to be made under this Act." These conferences can involve the participation of a variety of people who previously would not have had their voices heard in youth court or elsewhere in the youth justice system.

conferencing
A collaborative and non-conventional approach to decision-making in youth court.

The most frequent use of conferencing has been in considering whether a youth is to be released pending completion of a charge (i.e., during the bail stage) or in considering a fit sentence for a young person. Although these conferences may focus on a variety of purposes and results, some of which are not necessarily restorative in nature, this section does provide considerable latitude for the use of restorative practices at different stages of the youth justice process. In a Canadian context, this provision represents a formalization of the conferencing processes that a number of courts have already employed through the use of sentencing circles in Aboriginal communities (see Green 1998, Ch. 5).

There are many potential benefits of conferencing. One is allowing voices other than judges, lawyers, and police to enter the youth justice dialogue. In the context of court organization and circle sentencing, Judge Barry Stuart of the Yukon Territorial Court—a pioneer in bringing restorative processes to Canadian courts—explained the need to look outside of status quo court procedures and processes in seeking new approaches to justice and new alternatives for the participation of offenders, victims, and community members:

> For centuries, the basic organization of the court has not changed. Nothing has been done to encourage meaningful participation by the accused, the victim or by the community. . . . If the objective of the sentencing process is now to enhance sentencing options, to afford greater concern to the impact on victims, to shift focus from punishment to rehabilitation, and to meaningfully engage communities in sharing responsibility for sentencing decisions, it may be advantageous for the justice system to consider how court procedures and the physical arrangements within court-rooms militate against these new objectives. (See *R. v. Moses*, 1992.)

Under section 18 of the YCJA, youth justice committees can also act as a conference. These committees—which can be appointed by the federal government or the relevant provincial government—are organizations that can play a part in promoting community-wide consultation and co-operation on youth justice matters. The Act (s. 18(2)(iii) and (iv)) provides that the functions of youth justice committees include "ensuring that community support is available to the young person by arranging for the use of services from within the community, and enlisting members of the community to provide short-term mentoring and supervision" and "when the young person is also being dealt with by a child protection agency or a community group, helping to co-ordinate the interaction of the agency or group with the youth criminal justice system."

Mental Health Issues as a Consideration in Youth Court

The first preamble to the YCJA provides that "members of society share a responsibility to address the developmental challenges and the needs of young persons and to guide them into adulthood." Key to addressing these developmental challenges and needs is an understanding of the mental health issues faced by young people who come before the court. Section 34 of the YCJA provides that a judge may, at any stage of proceedings against a young person, require that the young person be assessed by a qualified person who is required to report the results in writing to the court. These assessments may be completed in conjunction with a pre-sentence report (PSR) prepared by a youth worker. Such an assessment can be ordered if the judge believes a medical, psychological, or psychiatric report regarding the young person is necessary for a purpose such as considering a bail application or passing sentence, and if one of the following applies:

(i)   The court has reasonable grounds to believe that the young person may be suffering from a physical or mental illness or disorder, a psychological disorder, an emotional disturbance, a learning disability, or a mental disability.

(ii) The young person's history indicates a pattern of repeated findings of guilt under this Act or the Young Offenders Act.

(iii) The young person is alleged to have committed a serious violent offence.

Box 3.1   Youth Justice in Action

Mental Health Programming in the Youth Justice System

While there is not a lot of research in this area in general, the prevalence of mental health concerns among young offenders—serving both custodial and community sentences—has led some researchers to call for more and better mental health programming in the youth justice system. A study from Victoria, Australia, published in 2014, shows a high prevalence of substance dependence, poor mental health, and risky sexual behaviour in both youth serving custody sentences and those serving in the community. The study concluded that there was a "compelling case for scaling up health services for young offenders in custody and in the community, and for routinely monitoring the health of young offenders serving custodial and community orders" (Kinner et al. 2014, p. 521).

Similarly, in Canada, a study of 300 male and female young offenders serving in-custody sentences in British Columbia found that overall rates of mental disorder for male youths were 91.9 per cent and 100 per cent for female youths (Gretton and Clift 2011). In Saskatchewan, a study by researchers at the Royal University Hospital, in which 95 adult inmates at the Regional Psychiatric Centre were interviewed, found that there were high rates of attention deficit hyperactivity disorder (ADHD) among the inmates, many with the condition in childhood, and that this disorder had not been diagnosed or treated prior to incarceration. That study concluded that ADHD is "highly prevalent in the criminal justice system and is associated with greater drug use and criminal offences" (Mela et al. 2014).

Critical Thinking Question

In your opinion, what steps need to be taken to improve mental health services for young offenders?

Fetal Alcohol Spectrum Disorder (FASD)

Among the many mental health issues that appear in youth court, neurological damage and cognitive impairment resulting from prenatal exposure to alcohol has become a significant focus of youth court judges, lawyers, youth court workers, and others employed within the youth justice system. In addition to prenatal exposure to alcohol, a diagnosis of fetal alcohol syndrome (FAS) requires evidence of a delay in growth, a distinctive pattern of facial features, and a central nervous system (or brain) dysfunction (Conry and Fast 2000). Fetal alcohol effect (FAE) refers to those young people who have suffered prenatal exposure to alcohol and who meet some but not all of the formal criteria for FAS (Boland et al. 1998). Experts in this field stress that FAE "is not a 'milder' form of FAS, and people with FAE have the same risk of developmental and behavioural disabilities as those with FAS" (Conry and Fast 2000, p. 1). The range of cognitive disabilities stemming from prenatal consumption of alcohol has come to be known as **fetal alcohol spectrum disorder (FASD)**.

fetal alcohol spectrum disorder (FASD)
The range of cognitive disabilities that are caused by prenatal consumption of alcohol by a youth's mother.

The neurological damage resulting from prenatal alcohol consumption is permanent and irreversible, and the effects of FASD are wide-ranging and profound. The inability of young people suffering from FASD to connect unacceptable behaviour with consequences is of paramount concern. In 2001, in *R. v. W. (D.)*, Judge Mary Ellen Turpel-Lafond of the Provincial Court of Saskatchewan stated this:

> The prenatal brain damage which causes FAS leaves its victims with neuro-developmental abnormalities such as diminished IQ, fine and gross motor delays, learning disabilities relating to language dysfunction, verbal learning and memory deficits, and behaviour effects such as impulsivity and a failure to learn from mistakes.

Information gained through assessments ordered under section 34 or otherwise provided by a youth worker within a pre-sentence or bail report is important to the court as the dangers of incarcerating individuals suffering from FASD cannot be overstated. These include the following:

- A significant risk of being victimized while in custody

- A difficulty in comprehending and following institutional rules, often leading to an inaccurate labelling of such youth as resistant and defiant

- A significant risk of negative influence through association with criminal peer models (Conry and Fast 2000)

To show how concerns over the treatment of youth with FASD continue to be at the forefront of the youth justice system, the Canadian Bar Association passed a resolution in 2010 urging all levels of government to allocate additional resources for alternatives to the current practice of criminalizing individuals with FASD; to develop policies designed to assist and enhance the lives of those with FASD; and to prevent persistent overrepresentation of FASD-affected individuals in the criminal justice system. The resolution also urged the federal government to amend criminal sentencing laws to accommodate the disability of those with FASD.

The Public's Right to Know v. Young People's Right to Privacy

Youth courts in Canada, in many respects, function like adult courts. Members of the public are free to attend the court proceeding, at all stages, subject to a few exceptions. The power of a youth court to exclude any person from the court is set out in section 132: in effect when the judge considers the presence of the person in question to be unnecessary to the proceeding and is further of the opinion that (1) information to be heard in court would seriously injure or prejudice the young person, a youthful witness, or a youthful victim; or (2) excluding any or all members of the public from the courtroom would be in the interest of public morals, the maintenance of order, or the proper administration of justice. This is broader than, but still similar to, the power of an adult court judge to exclude the public.

There is, however, a key difference between youth and adult court respecting public access to the proceeding—and that involves the publication of the names of young persons who appear in youth court. This difference has led to much public debate. At the root of that debate stands a conflict between the right to privacy of young people charged or convicted under the Act, on the one hand, and "the public's historic right to know who stands accused in the criminal court rooms of the nation," on the other hand (Davis-Barron 2009, p. 433, and, in general, Ch. 9).

Subject to a few exceptions, the YCJA (in s. 110(1)) prohibits publication of the name of a young person or any other information that would identify the young person as being dealt with under the Act. Further, regarding youth victims or youth witnesses in youth court, section 111(1) prohibits the publication of any information that would identify the youth as a victim or witness.

One of the exceptions to non-publication of names in the Act (s. 110(2) (a)) allows for the publication of the name of a young person sentenced as an adult. This provision follows a similar one in the YOA that allowed for the publication of the names of young persons transferred to adult court. In addition, the YCJA provides in section 75(3) that the onus of dispensing with the ban for these offences is on the prosecution. The Act (s. 75(1)) also includes a provision requiring the youth court to consider allowing the publication of the name of a young person convicted of a violent offence and receiving a youth sentence.

The Preamble of the YCJA states that information about youth justice, youth crime, and the effectiveness of measures taken to address youth crime should be publicly available. However, it appears that both the substantive provisions of the Act and judicial interpretation of this issue favour protecting the right to privacy of young people over the public's right to know the name of young people charged or convicted under the Act. As an example, Justice Binnie of the Supreme Court of Canada, in *R. v. F.N.* (146 C.C.C.(3d)1), stated that "[s]tigmatization or premature 'labelling' of a young offender still in his or her formative years is well understood as a problem in the juvenile justice system" and that a "young person once stigmatized as a lawbreaker may, unless given help and redirection, render the stigma a self-fulfilling prophecy." Further, Justice Abella of the Supreme Court in *R. v. D.B.* ([2008]2 S.C.R., par 41) stated that international youth protocols and prevailing judicial comment in Canada recognized "that lifting a ban on publication makes the young person vulnerable to greater psychological and social stress" and, as a result, that the sentence for such a youth is rendered "significantly more severe" (paras. 85–87).

Some Effects of the YCJA on At-Risk and Chargeable Youth

So far, we have examined information on the history, legislative provisions, case law, and prominent current issues tied to the administration of the YCJA. However, it is also important to introduce available data on some of the effects the implementation of the YCJA has had to date on at-risk youth and young offenders. One way of doing this is by examining national and regional/provincial statistical trend data on how cases involving young persons as alleged offenders are dealt with by police and in the courts. Data of this type show that while, overall across Canada, the number of youth court cases began to decline in the early 1990s, a more substantial downward trend began to occur after the enactment of the YCJA in 2002 (see Figure 2.4 in Chapter 2). Although this downward trend is accounted for mainly by the decline in the number of property crime cases, it is also significant that, contrary to popular public perceptions, the number of violent crime cases completed in youth court remained relatively unchanged until after the enactment of the YCJA, when it also began to decline slightly. Notably as well, more recent data indicate a continued decline in the number of cases completed in youth court in every province, with the exception of Manitoba, where both the number of youth court cases and the use of custody have witnessed an anomalous increase in recent years (Brennan 2012, p. 5; Munch 2012, p. 3; Smandych et al. 2016; also see Chapter 2 in this book).

One of the reasons for the decline in the number of cases completed in youth court is that since the enactment of the YCJA, in most provinces, proportionately fewer youth are being charged with criminal offences. For example, in 2010, the police recorded nearly 153,000 youth accused of a crime. These accused youth, each formally defined as a **chargeable young person**, included both "those who were charged (or recommended for charging) by police and those who were dealt with by means other than the formal laying of a charge." Those "not charged" included "youth diverted from the formal criminal justice system through the use of warnings, cautions and referrals to community programs" (Brennan and Dauvergne 2011, p. 18). Although prior to the enactment of the YCJA youth charged by the police regularly outnumbered those who were diverted from court, as the data displayed in Figure 3.1 show, beginning in 2003 this trend reversed and since then more chargeable youth have been diverted than formally charged.

Another possible measure of the effect the YCJA is having on the processing of youth through the criminal justice system is data on the use of youth custody, which includes both **remand custody** and **sentenced custody**. In addition to providing overall aggregate national reported information on the use of youth custody, these data highlight the existence of regional (provincial and territorial) variation in the manner in which specific provisions of the YCJA are being applied across Canada. Just as fewer youth today are being charged with criminal offences, proportionately more convicted youth are being given a **community-based sentence**, while in most provinces fewer are being placed in sentenced

chargeable young person
A young person who has been identified by police as an offender and against whom a charge could be laid.

remand custody
The practice of holding a person in a custodial facility before or during his or her court appearance(s); also known as pre-trial detention.

sentenced custody
Being held in a custodial facility as a result of a court sentence (as opposed to *remand custody*).

community-based sentence
A sentence that is served in the community (and, therefore, not in a custodial facility); also known as a *non-custodial sentence*.

custody. At the same time, data show that in recent years the number of youth being held in remand custody has increased proportionately to the extent that in some provinces the average daily count of youth in "remand" now exceeds the number of youth serving a **custodial sentence**. For example, in 2010/11, in 16 per cent of guilty youth cases, the offender was sentenced to custody, compared with 29 per cent of cases in 2000/01 (Brennan 2012, p. 5). On the other hand, following the implementation of the YCJA in 2003, the proportion of youth held in remand custody began to increase proportionately relative to custody sentences and in particular provinces (see Table 2.2 in Chapter 2). Within a few years the number of youth held in remand began to exceed the number of youth placed in sentenced custody (Porter and Calverley 2011, pp. 5, 17–18; see Figure 3.2 and Figure 2.5 in Ch. 2).

As mentioned earlier, shifts in the use of courts and custody have varied from province to province since the enactment of the YCJA. For example, between 2005/06 and

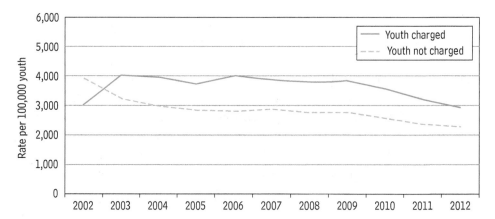

FIGURE 3.1 Youth Accused of Crime, by Clearance Status, Canada, 2002 to 2012

Note: Youth not charged includes youth diverted from the formal criminal justice system through the use of warnings, cautions, and referrals to community programs.

Source: Perreault 2013, p. 22.

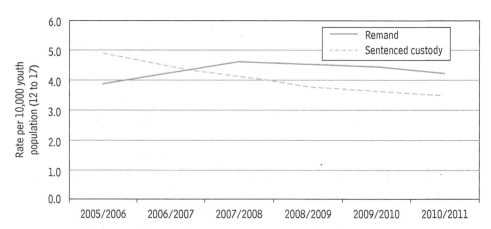

FIGURE 3.2 Average Counts of Youth in Remand and Sentenced Custody, Canada, 2005/2006 to 2010/2011

Note: Excludes data from Quebec.

Source: Munch 2012, p. 9.

2010/11 the largest drop in youth incarceration rates (including remand and sentenced custody) was reported in Newfoundland and Labrador, where it dropped 58 per cent, in contrast to Manitoba, where during the same period it increased 38 per cent. In addition while in 2010/11 "youth in remand outnumbered those in sentenced custody for the fourth year in a row," Manitoba reported "the highest rate of remand, at almost 5 times the overall rate" (Munch 2012, p. 3).

As we see from these data, while many factors may affect the level of youth crime and the number of youth charged, there is little doubt that the implementation of the YCJA played a significant part in reducing the overall number of youth charged, the number appearing in court, and the number being sent into custody. However, these trends have been uneven across the country and in some instances have shown substantial interprovincial variation.

Summary

The YCJA was intended to reduce the overreliance on custody and to reserve custody for the most serious crimes and young offenders. It was also intended to enable youth courts to focus on more serious youth crimes by increasing the use of effective and timely non-court responses—called extrajudicial measures—for less serious (and often non-violent) offences and for less experienced offenders. Other policy objectives addressed in the Act are holding young people accountable for their transgressions, ensuring a proportionate response to the wrongdoing, protecting the public, rehabilitating young people, and allowing for a structured discretion in decision-making under the Act.

The YCJA contains a distinct legal and sentencing regime for young people, separate and apart from that for adults under the Criminal Code. The Act provides enhanced procedural protections for young people charged under the Act and, at the same time, establishes both procedural rights and responsibilities for their parents. The Act also restricts the publication of the names of young people charged under the Act, with a few exceptions that include public access to the name of a youth who is sentenced as an adult.

Unlike the YOA before it, the YCJA now has a separate statement on the purpose and principles of sentencing. This includes a provision that all available sanctions other than custody that are reasonable in the circumstances be considered for all young people, with particular attention to the circumstances of Aboriginal young people (the so-called *Gladue* clause for Aboriginal young people). The possible sentences under the Act include a discharge, a reprimand, a restitution order, a fine, a deferred custody and supervision order, open or closed custody, an intensive support and supervision program order, and an intensive custody and supervision order.

Because of the goal of reducing the use of custody, a custodial sentence can only be a possibility if the youth has (1) committed a violent offence; (2) failed to comply with non-custodial sentences; (3) committed an indictable offence for which an adult could be jailed for over two years while possessing a history indicating a pattern of criminality; or (4) in exceptional cases, committed an indictable offence, the aggravating circumstances of which are such that the imposition of a non-custodial sentence would be inconsistent with the purpose and principles of sentencing in the Act.

The YCJA draws a distinction between criminal procedures or sanctions, on the one hand, and other interventions (i.e., child-protection, mental health, or other social measures), on the other. Custody is not to be used as a substitute for these later social interventions either pending sentence or as a sentence in itself. The YCJA further allows a judge, at any stage of the proceedings, to refer a young person to a child welfare agency for assessment to determine whether the young person is in need of child welfare services. While the Act draws a distinction between criminal and non-criminal interventions, the YCJA nevertheless encourages multidisciplinary approaches to youth justice, seeking to encourage the coordination of resources to support a young person and the co-operation of various players within the justice and youth court system.

Conferencing is a non-conventional approach to decision-making recognized in the YCJA. In particular, conferencing can be used when a youth court judge is considering whether to release a young person on bail or considering a fit sentence for a youth. Conferences may be restorative in nature and involve a cross-section of participants who would not normally be heard from in youth court.

The mental health of young people is a key consideration for judges in youth court. The YCJA provides a means to obtain a professional assessment of a range of mental health challenges a young person may have. Of particular concern is fetal alcohol spectrum disorder. A young person with FASD suffers from multiple deficits, including difficulties in cognition and an inability to learn from his or her mistakes, and is generally at a greater risk than other youth of being victimized.

Key Terms

chargeable young person
community-based sentence
conferencing
custodial sentence
deferred custody and supervision
    order (DCSO)
extrajudicial measures
fetal alcohol spectrum disorder (FASD)

intensive support and supervision
    program (ISSP)
parent
presumption
remand custody
sentenced custody
young person
youth justice court

Review Questions

1. What were the policy issues and concerns that the federal government sought to address through passage of the YCJA?
2. What are the procedural protections for young people under the YCJA?
3. What are the issues that arise in the sentencing of a young person under this Act?
4. What are the factors a youth court should consider in dealing with a young person diagnosed with fetal alcohol spectrum disorder?

Critical Thinking Questions

1. Are the YCJA's overriding sentencing goals of accountability, on the one hand, and rehabilitation, on the other, conflicting?

2. Should there be a separate justice system for young people? If so, why?

3. Can you give some examples of how custody could be used as a substitute for appropriate child-protection measures, health measures, or other social measures?

4. What are the benefits of a youth court using a conference as opposed to the conventional court proceeding?

Endnote

1. Portions of this chapter are taken or adapted from *Tough on Kids: Rethinking Approaches to Youth Justice* (Purich Publishing, 2003), with the consent of Purich Publishing and my co-author, Kearney Healy.

References

Anand, S.S. (1999). The good, the bad, and the unaltered: An analysis of Bill C-68, the Youth Criminal Justice Act. *Canadian Criminal Law Review*, 4: 249–70.

Bala, N. (2015). Changing professional culture and reducing use of courts and custody for youth: The Youth Criminal Justice Act and Bill C-10. *Saskatchewan Law Review* 78: 127–80.

Bala, N., and Anand, S. (2012). *Youth criminal justice law* (3rd ed.). Toronto: Irwin.

Bala, N., Carrington, P., and Roberts, J. (2009). Evaluating the Youth Criminal Justice Act after five years: A qualified success. *Canadian Journal of Criminology and Criminal Justice*, 51(2): 131–67.

Barnhorst, R. (2004). The Youth Criminal Justice Act: New directions and implementation issues. *Canadian Journal of Criminology and Criminal Justice*, 46(3): 231–50.

Boland, F., Burrill, R., Duwyn, M., and Karp, J. (1998). Fetal alcohol syndrome: Implications for correctional service (unpublished, July 1998).

Brennan, S. (2012). *Youth court statistics in Canada: 2010/2011.* Ottawa: Statistics Canada. http://www.statcan.gc.ca/pub/85-002-x/2012001/article/11645-eng.htm

Brennan, S., and Dauvergne, M. (2011). Police-reported crime statistics in Canada, 2010. *Juristat* (July): 1–39. http://www.statcan.gc.ca/pub/85-002-x/2012001/ article/11692-eng.pdf

Calverley, D., Cotter, A., and Halla, E. (2010). Youth Custody and Community Services in Canada, 2008–2009. *Juristat* (April): 1–29. http://www.statcan.gc.ca/pub/85-002-x/2010001/article/11147-eng.pdf

Canadian Bar Association. (2010). *Submission on Bill C-4 Youth Criminal Justice Act amendments.* Ottawa: Canadian Bar Association, National Criminal Justice Section. Block quote reprinted with permission of the Canadian Bar Association.

Chartrand, P., and Whitecloud, W. (2001). *Aboriginal Implementation Commission: Final report and recommendations.* Winnipeg: Statutory Publications Office.

Conry, J., and Fast, D. (2000). *Fetal alcohol syndrome and the justice system.* Vancouver: Law Foundation of British Columbia.

Corrado, R., Kuehn, S., and Margaritescu, I. (2014). Policy issues regarding the over-representation of incarcerated Aboriginal young offenders in a Canadian context. *Youth Justice*, 12(1): 40–62.

Davis-Barron, S. (2009). *Canadian youth and the criminal law.* Markham, ON: LexisNexis Canada.

Green, R., and Healey, K. (2003). *Tough on kids: Rethinking approaches to youth justice.* Saskatoon: Purich Publishing.

Gretton, H., and Clift, R. (2011). The mental health needs of incarcerated youth in British Columbia Canada. *International Journal of Law and Psychiatry*, 34: 109–15.

Hogeveen, B., and Smandych, R. (2001). Origins of the newly proposed Canadian Youth Criminal Justice Act: Political discourse and the perceived crisis in youth crime in the 1990s. In R. Smandych (Ed.), *Youth justice: History, legislation, and reform* (pp. 144–68). Toronto: Harcourt.

Kinner, S., Degenhardt, L., Coffey, C., Sawyer, Hearps, S., and Patton, G. (2014). Complex health needs in the youth justice system: A survey of community-based and custodial offenders. *Journal of Adolescent Health, 54*: 521–26.

Lane, K. (1995). *The philosophy of the Young Offenders Act and its impact on the formal legal education and practice of advocates for youth.* LLM thesis, University of Alberta.

Mela, M., et al. (2014). Adult attention deficit hyperactivity disorder in a secure forensic treatment facility: Implications of self-reported prevalence (unpublished, n.p.).

Minaker, J., and Hogeveen, B. (2009). *Youth, crime, and society: Issues of power and justice.* Toronto: Pearson.

Munch, C. (2012). Youth correctional statistics in Canada, 2010/2011. *Juristat* (October): 1–22. http://www.statcan.gc.ca/pub/85-002-x/2012001/article/11716-eng.pdf

Perreault, S. (2013). Police-reported crime statistics in Canada, 2012. *Juristat*, online. http://www.statcan.gc.ca/pub/85-002-x/2013001/article/11854-eng.htm

Perreault, S. (2014). Admissions to youth correctional services in Canada, 2011/2012. *Juristat*, online. http://www.statcan.gc.ca/pub/85-002-x/2014001/article/11917-eng.htm#a3

Peterson-Badali, M., and Broeking, J. (2010). Parents' involvement in the youth justice system: Rhetoric and reality. *Canadian Journal of Criminology and Criminal Justice, 52*(1): 1–27.

Porter, L., and Calverley, D. (2011). Trends in the use of remand in Canada. *Juristat* (May): 1–28. http://www.statcan.gc.ca/pub/85-002-x/2011001/article/11440-eng.pdf

Quigley, T. (1994). Some issues in sentencing Aboriginal offenders. In D. Gosse, J. Youngblood Henderson, and R. Carter (Eds), *Continuing Poundmaker's and Riel's Quest* (pp. 267–300). Saskatoon: Purich Publishing.

Smandych, R., Dyck, M., La Berge, C., and Koffman, J. (2016). Youth justice in Manitoba: Developments and issues under the YCJA. In M. Alain, S. Reid, and R. Corrado (Eds), *Implementing and working with the Youth Criminal Justice Act across Canada.* Toronto: University of Toronto Press.

Statistics Canada. (2013). *The Daily*, Thursday, 13 June. http://www.statcan.gc.ca/daily-quotidien/130613/dq130613-eng.pdf

Tustin, L., and Lutes, R. (2005). *A guide to the Youth Criminal Justice Act.* Toronto: Lexis-Nexus Butterworths.

Cases Cited

[1990] 2 S.C.R. 755, 79 C.R. (3d) 219, 59 C.C.C (3d) 1.

[1992] *R. v. Moses* (1992), 71 C.C.C. (3d) 347 (Yuk. Ter. Ct.), 355-356.

[1999] Y.J. No. 119 (Yukon Ter. Ct.).

[1999] 1 S.C.R. 688.

146 C.C.C. (3d) 1.

[1999] *R. v. J.K.E.*, [1999] Y.J. No. 119 (Yukon Youth Ct.).

[2000] S.J. No. 373 (QL) (Sask. Youth Ct.).

[2001] S.J. No. 70 (QL) (Sask. Yth. Ct.) at para. 25.

[2002] Y.J. No. 49 (Yukon Territorial Court).

[2004] *R. v. T.D.P.*, [2004] 3 C.N.L.R. 318 (Sask. Youth Ct.).

[2005] 201 C.C.C. (3d) 321 (S.C.C.).

[2006] 38 C.R. (6th) 1 (S.C.C.).

[2006] 1 S.C.R. 941, para. 23.

[2008] 2 S.C.R. 3, para. 41.

[2008] S.C.J. No. 25.

The Youth Justice System in Action

Adrienne M.F. Peters and Raymond R. Corrado

4

Overview

This chapter provides an overview of how the Canadian youth justice system works in action on a day-to-day basis in different parts of the country. It roughly follows the young offender through various stages of the youth justice process, from first contact with the police, to court appearances, and, in the case of convicted young offenders, into community and custody-based correctional sanctions. In turn, the chapter also addresses key current challenges and issues faced by professionals working in the youth justice system, including net widening, police racial profiling, the changing scope of the work of probation officers, the challenges of dealing with young offenders with mental disorders, and the increasing and somewhat controversial use of risk assessment and management tools in youth courts and corrections.

Key Objectives

After reading this chapter, you should be able to:

- Understand the different processes undertaken by the police with young offenders and at-risk youth.
- Outline the overarching procedures followed when a young person becomes formally involved in the youth criminal justice system.
- Comprehend how restorative justice–based principles are integrated in portions of the current Canadian youth justice legislation.
- Explain the more recent approaches utilized across Canada to manage and address the needs of young offenders with mental health issues.
- Differentiate between screening and risk assessment tools utilized for young offenders in both community and custodial settings.
- Summarize the experiences of young offenders supervised in community settings and in custodial settings in Canada.
- Discuss the considerations for young offenders once they have completed any imposed disposition(s).

Introduction

As a federal document, the Youth Criminal Justice Act (YCJA), in theory, should be applied in a similar way to young offender cases across Canada. Despite its introduction as a progression from the former Young Offenders Act (YOA), the YCJA continues to present challenges related to how it would be applied owing to the conflicting principles and justice models that were inherent in it, as well as the diversity that exists in the provinces and territories of Canada. Young offenders, therefore, are processed differently through the Canadian youth criminal justice system at various stages. These differences are not only provincially and territorially based but also municipally based, as a result of variability in the availability of community-based supports and resources.

Although multiple agencies are involved in the processing of young offenders, formally and informally, in recent years the requisite services have been working to enhance their collaborations to provide a fair, meaningful, and holistic response to youth offending. This experience begins with encounters with the police, then moves to community-based services or the courts, the latter of which comprises the involvement of youth defence and Crown lawyers and judges, and possibly goes on to include correctional/custodial or community probation services. Involved at various points in this process may also be youth justice advocates, youth centre counsellors, youth delegates, youth workers, community program coordinators, and service providers, Aboriginal representatives, and mental health professionals. This chapter outlines each stage of this process and the unique approaches of different provinces, territories, and municipalities.

Police

In Canada, the entrance of young offenders into the youth justice system begins with their initial contact with the police. From 2012 to 2013, there was a 16 per cent decline in the rate of young persons accused of a Criminal Code offence. More specifically, approximately 22,000 fewer youth were accused of such violations in 2013 than in 2012 (Boyce, Cotter, and Perreault 2014). Furthermore, this represented a 40 per cent reduction over the decade since the implementation of the YCJA. Nevertheless, when these interactions do occur, the behaviour necessitates a certain level of response. This can range from an informal warning to a formal charging (or, in British Columbia, a request to the Crown to charge) of the young person with a criminal offence.

As noted in Chapter 3, children who are under the age of 12 cannot be held criminally responsible for their actions under the YCJA, and thus other non-criminal justice community agencies are tasked with developing an appropriate response to address the child's behaviour and prevent the continuation of such behavioural patterns in the future. While the police may be involved in this process at the earliest stages, this involvement terminates fairly quickly given the youth justice system's goal of refraining from stigmatizing and labelling children as delinquent or criminal. The goal at this stage is to talk to the young people about the behaviour and explain to them the consequences of their conduct (see Box 4.1). If deemed necessary, the police may choose some type of non-legal response to the behaviour.

Box 4.1   Youth Justice in Action

Responding to Children under 12 Years of Age Who Commit Crimes in Canada

Unfortunately, there have been a few isolated Canadian cases in which a child was responsible for the most serious type of offence under the Criminal Code—murder. For example, in the late summer of 2013, a six-year-old boy living on the Kahkewistahaw First Nation community in Saskatchewan was killed near a recreation centre by another child who was under the age of 12 (CBC News 2013). The boy suspected of committing this crime, who was not publicly named, had had previous contacts with the police as a result of incidents of violent behaviour and had also come to the attention of a child welfare agency. Following the incident, the agency had him undergo a series of assessments to help in the development of an appropriate case plan and an appropriate response for this young person. Since these types of cases are exceedingly uncommon in Canada, however, there are limited options available. The response in this case, in consideration of the child's age, was continued involvement with child welfare services. According to Nicholas Bala (2013):

Although provincial child welfare law deals with serious cases of offending behaviour by children under twelve, it has significant limitations. Institutional priorities and legal constraints restrict the willingness and ability of these agencies to respond to offending behaviour, unless it has already become extremely serious. This can result in a missed opportunity for earlier, potentially more effective intervention while waiting for a child to turn twelve and be brought into the youth justice system. (par. 8)

Critical Thinking Question

Should the child welfare systems across Canada develop strategies and policies specific to cases that involve more serious/violent offences committed by children under the age of 12?

In contrast to adult offenders, when criminal offences are committed by young offenders, the police assume a greater responsibility in responding to this delinquency. The YCJA outlines clear objectives related to extrajudicial measures (EJM) and encourages police to divert young people away from the formal youth justice system whenever possible. The current Act has ultimately led to the greatest successes in achieving its diversionary objective.

Looking more closely, one sees that of those youth who were accused of a Criminal Code violation in 2013 in Canada, 55 per cent were dealt with outside of the formal criminal justice system through extrajudicial measures, compared to 45 per cent of youth who were formally charged by police (Boyce, Cotter, and Perreault 2014). Although EJMs are applied country-wide, this **discretion**-based response is exercised the most in the provinces of Quebec and British Columbia (Brennan 2012). Still, for first-time young offenders or youth who have committed minor offences in any province, police are expected to rely on **pre-charge diversion** through EJM, in which the police can decide whether to take no further action and offer the youth an informal caution (this is not documented by the police) or to make a formal warning to the young person or make a referral to a community-based agency. For the last option, a number of community programs have been developed and have received funding since the enactment of the YCJA so that police officers can develop relationships with these groups and make suitable referrals for young people.

When the police respond to a call involving a more serious offence and/or repeat young offender, the options available to them become more formalized and may include arresting and holding the young person in custody or charging the young person and releasing him or her into the custody of their parents/legal guardians. In the most serious cases, the young people can be held in youth custody/detention as they await processing in the youth court system. Such cases require a **bail** hearing to occur within 24 hours of this arrest. During the judicial process, it may be determined that certain youth would benefit from a more formal diversionary measure in the form of a court-ordered extrajudicial sanction (EJS). Under the former YOA, in which diversionary measures were first introduced, police were more likely to utilize this type of post-charge diversion as opposed to the YCJA's emphasis on pre-charge diversion (Greene 2011). Even after the implementation of the YCJA, some provinces, such as Ontario, continued to employ post-charge diversionary practices regularly (Bala and Anand 2009). This is often explained by the lack of consistent research into the efficacy of diversion programs, as well as by concerns over the provision of young people's rights.

Research has demonstrated that police officers take a number of factors into consideration when determining whether or not a young person would be suitable for and benefit from extralegal measures. A young person's criminal history and the seriousness of the offence are commonly the most important factors that guide the police's decision-making in this regard (Doob and Chan 1982; McAra and McVie 2007). The more recent research in this area has also found that police are more likely to charge male youth and those who had greater social disadvantage. Because youth who are involved in less serious offences are believed to have the greatest probability of successfully completing assigned programming and the lowest probability of reoffending (e.g., Forgays 2008; LeGalbo and Callahan 2001), they are the most likely to be diverted by police.

discretion
The latitude assigned to police officers and other professionals in the Canadian youth criminal justice system to decide how best to respond to a young person's delinquent or criminal behaviour before laying a formal charge.

pre-charge diversion
The diverting of young offenders from the formal youth criminal justice system before they are charged with an offence by the police under the Criminal Code.

bail
Also referred to as *judicial interim release*. Occurs when a young person has been formally charged by the police but has been determined by the courts to be eligible for release from custody while the youth awaits his/her next court appearance. During this release, the young person will be held by a specific set of conditions.

Across Canada, some police officers have expressed concern regarding the rehabilitative and deterrent effectiveness of diversionary practices. While this issue has been debated in the existing empirical research (see Greene 2011), other officers value the expanded autonomy bestowed upon them through their decision-making powers and ability to rely on their personal experiences with youth in determining the best way to proceed and assist the young person. Although the actual outcomes of this approach require further research, this option has become a pronounced approach to first-time and minor young offenders and has been successful in dealing with some of these delinquent youth.

As discussed earlier, under section 10 of the YCJA, more formal EJS may be considered during the formal trial process after the police charge the young person with an offence. These sanctions are utilized in cases involving young offenders who have been determined to be appropriate candidates for a less severe sanction that can simultaneously maintain the public's best interests. To receive this type of sanction, the youth must consent to the sanction and accept responsibility for the related offence. One concern, however, associated with the formal regulating of diversionary practices through the introduction of EJM and EJS is known as **net widening**. Net widening may occur as a result of a rise in the number of EJMs utilized that surpasses the decline in the number of youth charged or as a result of the usage of more cautions and community-programming referrals rather than no further action taken or no informal warnings offered (Carrington and Schulenberg 2005). Amendments to the YCJA introduced in Bill C-10 in 2012 now require that records be kept related to youth's EJM histories so that patterns of delinquency and police contacts can be observed. If this amendment is implemented in practice, police officers will be engaging in increased paperwork, and another possible inadvertent outcome may be more net widening in the youth justice system.

On a more positive note, police officers today are more educated on youth justice issues than they once were owing to the expansion of criminology and the criminal justice programs and courses that are currently offered. Subsequent to the adoption of the YCJA, police officers have also developed closer relationships with the courts and prosecutors, thereby improving their knowledge of many procedural aspects of the youth court process and of how they fit into this process (Alain and Hamel 2015; Corrado, Gronsdahl, and Markwart 2015).

net widening
A process whereby, in the attempt to divert individuals away from the criminal justice system, certain policies result instead in a greater number of individuals being formally processed.

Racial and Social Profiling

Although police education and co-operation with other agencies have certainly contributed to the enhancement of police responses to young offenders, despite these promising developments, the police and youth justice system still need to achieve considerable progress in relation to their response to Aboriginal and minority youth. This is dramatically reflected in Box 4.2, which describes the outcome of the tragic case of Neil Stonechild, an Aboriginal youth who was the victim of alleged **racial profiling** by police in Saskatoon, Saskatchewan.

Racial profiling continues to be a contentious issue in discussions on policing practices. Data collected from a Toronto high school in the early 2000s revealed that black youth were more likely to be stopped and questioned by the police and also more likely to

racial profiling
The increased surveillance of certain racial groups or culturally distinct neighbourhoods by the police that cannot be explained by such groups' actual increased involvement in criminal activities.

Box 4.2   Youth Justice in Action

The Death of Neil Stonechild and the Outcome of the Stonechild Commission

In 1990, a 17-year-old youth from Saskatoon by the name of Neil Stonechild was taken into police custody by two police officers from the Saskatoon Police Service and then driven to the outskirts of the city where he was left outside in a field in −28°C weather. He consequently died of hypothermia. The main finding highlighted in the Stonechild Commission Inquiry (supported by the Commission on First Nations and Métis Peoples and Justice Reform) was that there were problematic relations between the police and First Nations people in Saskatchewan (Wright 2004). Included in the resulting reform goals was the reduction of the criminalization, victimization, and, ultimately, incarceration of First Nations people. In relation to young people, the main focus of the recommendations was to strengthen family supports and community development and to rely on alternatives to formal sanctions for youth under the YCJA (Savarese 2015).

In response to the tragic Stonechild case (and associated 2006 commission report), the police in Saskatchewan expanded training on cultural diversity and modified the complaint process. In addition, the Saskatoon Police Service initiated ongoing efforts to recruit and hire First Nations members to their police force (Government of Canada 2006), and as of 2012, it had managed to increase the proportion (approximately 11 per cent) of Aboriginal members in the service; it is also continuing to increase the number of Aboriginal police officers through working with the Saskatchewan Police Aboriginal Recruiting Committee (Government of Canada 2011). According to Saskatoon Police Chief Clive Weighill (as cited by Fischer 2014), the Saskatoon Police Service has met all of the recommendations that were made in the Neil Stonechild inquiry (see Wright 2004).

Critical Thinking Question

Despite the progress that has been made in diversifying police departments, there are invariably opportunities to improve. What could police agencies and other criminal justice branches do to further promote the recruitment of individuals from diverse cultures and backgrounds?

be caught engaging in delinquent and/or criminal behaviours than were Caucasian youth, Asian youth, and South Asian youth, in that order (Wortley and Tanner 2003). Further analysis indicated that when the researchers controlled for a series of deviant and criminal behaviours, as well as for social class, important racial differences in police practices could not be explained by actual increases in such activities. So, even though social profiling may also occur in situations where certain individuals or neighbourhoods are targeted owing to their social status and disadvantage (including homelessness), these researchers concluded that racial profiling specifically was occurring with respect to black youth in Toronto (Wortley and Tanner 2005).

Despite the earlier research findings, many police agencies maintain that racial profiling is not a negative strategy employed by their organizations based on actual stereotypes or prejudices against certain groups, but that it instead is a technique used to guide police decision-making (Satzewich and Shaffir 2009). After years of debate on this issue, the police in Toronto have implemented new procedures as a part of their street-check approach; these include providing individuals who have been stopped by the police with a check receipt, which serves as an attempt to avoid the repeated over-targeting of certain individuals and/or ethnic groups in the city (see Kempa 2012; Rankin 2012).

Court

Following the initial contact that young offenders have with the police, the next step in the formal judicial process for youth is court. Young offenders reach the court stage of the judicial process if they are formally charged by the police with a Criminal Code offence, at which point they may be either charged and released or placed in youth detention. In the first scenario, youth are released on what is known as judicial interim release or bail. During this release into the community, youth are required to abide by the court's set conditions or risk being placed in custody. In the latter scenario, a youth can be held in custody awaiting a bail hearing. If the youth is not released at the first appearance before the justice of the peace, there is a second opportunity for him or her to be released during a show-cause hearing. For the continued **pre-trial detention** (also known as **remand custody**) of the youth, the court must show that there is concern related to the young person's appearance in court for the next court appearance and that detention in custody would be necessary to ensure this or that the youth should be detained for the purpose of protecting the public (see Figure 4.1).

There are some restrictions on the use of pre-trial detention. For example, a young person cannot be detained "as a substitute for appropriate child protection, mental health or other social measures" (s. 29(1)) or in cases where the young person could not receive a custodial sentence if found guilty of the offence (s. 29(2)). When youth are released into the community preceding their trial, they are assigned a series of conditions that may prohibit the use of substances and contact with certain individuals, delineate a curfew, and/or order the youth to have regular appointments with a youth probation officer. In some cases, the judge may include an order requiring a money deposit or a **bail surety** to ensure that the youth returns to court on the established date. The youth may also be placed in the care of a responsible person as an alternative to custody and/or if there are potential concerns in returning the young person to his or her home. Finally, the request to be released on bail may be denied and the youth will be returned to youth custody until the next court appearance.

As outlined above, before the enactment of the Safe Streets and Communities Act (SSCA) in 2012, the courts had to look to the Criminal Code when using pre-trial detention for young offenders; however, this information is now clearly outlined in the YCJA. The new guidelines state that a young person charged with a serious offence or who has a history that shows a pattern of outstanding charges or findings of guilt meets the criteria to be detained in a youth custody facility prior to his or her trial. The previous presumption was that pre-trial detention be reserved for youth who could be sentenced to custody in the case of a guilty finding for the respective offence, but this stipulation has since been removed. As an extension of this, another amendment to the SSCA is the modified definition of serious offences. A *serious offence* constitutes any indictable offence for which an adult could receive the maximum punishment of imprisonment for five years or more; included in this definition are violent offences, more serious property offences, and offences that, in their commission, may endanger the safety of the public.

Beyond the determination of bail for a detained young person, the primary first step in the youth court process is an arraignment, where youth either plead guilty or not guilty to

pre-trial detention/ remand custody
The detention of a young person who has been charged with a Criminal Code offence in a youth custody facility as the youth awaits his or her trial/next court date.

bail surety
A promise made by someone connected to the youth to pay the court money if the young person, who was released on bail, fails to return to court on the subsequent court date.

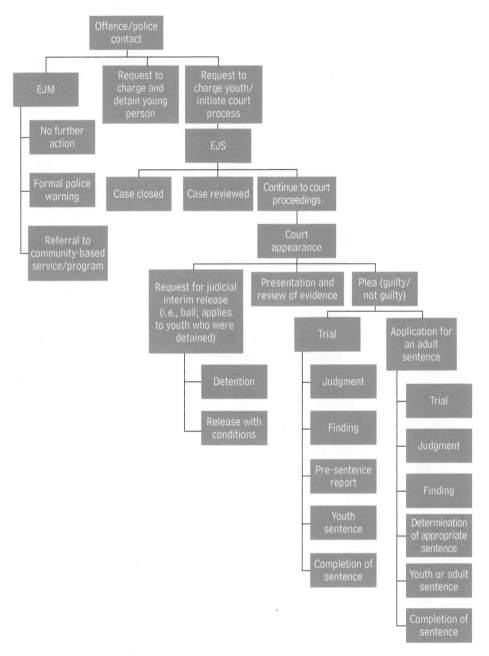

FIGURE 4.1 The Fundamental Legal/Judicial Process for Young Offenders

Source: Based on Gouvernement du Québec, Justice Québec 2009, *The Youth Criminal Justice Act*: The legal procedure.

the charges brought against them. If the offender pleads guilty to the charges, an appropriate sentence for the young person is determined. If a youth pleads not guilty, however, the case will proceed to trial and a date for this will be set. Under the YCJA, a young person is tried only by a youth court judge, except in more serious cases in which young offenders have three trial options. When a young person has pled or been found guilty of a crime to which the Crown is seeking an adult sentence, the youth is being sentenced as an adult, or when the youth has been charged with murder, the young person may elect to have either a youth justice court judge without a jury and without a **preliminary inquiry**; a trial by judge, without a jury, following a preliminary hearing; or a trial by judge and jury following a preliminary inquiry (s. 67(2)). In some cases, the attorney general may be granted permission to override the young person's request and call for a trial by judge and jury for the youth. Preliminary hearings in youth court proceed in the same way they do in adult court.

Before a youth case proceeds to trial and if a young person has pled guilty to an offence, the Crown will determine whether an EJS may be more appropriate than proceeding with a court trial and a more serious sanction. If this option is not deemed appropriate, a trial will proceed. When youth cases result in a guilty plea or finding, under section 32 of the YCJA youth probation officers are called upon by the courts to assist in the determination of an appropriate sentence through the provision of a **pre-sentence report**. This report details the young person's familial, educational/vocational, social, extracurricular, physical and mental health, and criminal history, as well as additional information on the youth's case, offence, and feelings of remorse. The results of psychological, psychiatric, and educational assessments may also be provided to present a complete and accurate portrayal of the young person (see Chapter 15 for a discussion of how Quebec handles such matters and Figure 4.1).

Under the YCJA, the publication of young offenders' names is prohibited. In cases that involve vulnerable youth victims, the victims' names may also be protected from publication. Members of the public can nevertheless attend youth court cases. Amendments made to the YCJA as a result of the SSCA have given judges the discretion to lift a publication ban in cases where a young offender receives a youth sentence for a violent offence, the objective being to protect the public against any risk that the youth poses. With regard to the new *violent offence* definition, this now embraces a number of offences, including causing, attempting, or threatening to cause bodily harm to another person and endangering the life or safety of another person.

In recent years the majority of cases that have come before youth courts have been disposed of by way of guilty pleas. For example, of the youth court cases completed in 2011/12, just over half (57 per cent) resulted in a guilty plea or finding of guilt, with the highest percentage of guilty verdicts occurring in New Brunswick (just under 80 per cent) and the lowest in Ontario (50 per cent) (Dauvergne 2013). One explanation for this finding was based on the fact that some provinces (i.e., New Brunswick, Quebec, and BC) exercise pre-charge screening. Moyer (2005) also found that guilty verdicts are more common in youth court cases that involve youth who are being charged with multiple offences. The other most common outcomes for youth court cases were the staying, withdrawing, dismissing, or discharging of cases (which result in the stopping—temporary or permanent—of the proceedings) owing to insufficient evidence or a referral to extrajudicial measures or the successful completion of an extrajudicial sanction; this occurred in 42 per cent of youth court cases in 2011/12. In the final two outcomes, 1 per cent of completed youth cases resulted in an acquittal (where the youth was found not guilty), and less than 1 per cent of cases led to an alternative finding (e.g., the youth was found not criminally responsible or determined unfit to stand trial based on his or her mental health) (Dauvergne 2013).

In 2011/12, the time needed to complete a youth court case in Canada dropped, continuing a three-year trend, with the median time needed being 108 days. The longest court case completion time was found in Manitoba (140 days) and the shortest was in

preliminary inquiry
Occurs before the case proceeds to trial and is a hearing in which the judge can determine if there is sufficient evidence to proceed to trial.

pre-sentence report
Report prepared by a probation officer or youth centre councillor in Quebec; these written documents present the youth court with detailed information on the young person.

Prince Edward Island (29 days). Despite the overall expediting of youth court cases, this has not held true in all provinces. For example, in British Columbia, youth court judges also act as provincial court judges, and the increase in workload because of these cases has negated the impact of the reduction in youth-related cases (Corrado et al. 2015).

Crown Counsel

Beyond the above-mentioned roles that Crown counsel may assume during the youth court process, the Crown may also adopt even greater responsibilities in certain Canadian provinces. In some provinces, police officers are not permitted to make the determination of whether or not a young person should be formally charged or whether the youth can be diverted from the formal system (Corrado et al. 2015); this is the responsibility of the prosecutors, also known as Crown counsel, to whom the police file a "Report to Crown Counsel." The prosecutor is then tasked with reviewing the report in order to make a decision regarding the "likelihood of conviction" (which should be deemed "substantial") as well as assess the safety of the public and what is "in the public interest." When Crown counsel decides to utilize EJM, the youth case is referred either to a youth probation officer, who would conduct an **extrajudicial sanctions** inquiry, or to the identified appropriate community-based program. In more serious offending cases and/or with repeat young offenders, these would typically result in the filing of a formal Crown report in which the Crown makes a final determination (ibid.).

extrajudicial sanctions
Under the YCJA, relatively formal diversion programs that have been authorized by the provincial authorities.

Defence Lawyers

The YOA introduced youth's right to representation by a lawyer, which has continued under the YCJA. Legal counsel for a young person can be a representative from Legal Aid, a private lawyer, a duty counsel, or a lawyer who has been appointed by the courts. This last option may be necessary for youth who are not able to obtain their own lawyer or who are refused Legal Aid (Doob and Cesaroni 2004). Defence lawyers assist youth in understanding the legal process and, most importantly, their own rights. Under the YCJA, youth defence lawyers have had to familiarize themselves with a series of additional sentencing options that were added for young offenders convicted of an offence in Canada, including both custody- and community-based **dispositions**, such as intensive support and supervision program (ISSP) orders, deferred custody and supervision orders (DCSOs), and the intensive rehabilitative custody and supervision (IRCS) program.

disposition
For young offenders, this is the equivalent of sentencing for adults. Under the YCJA, a disposition should in theory be more rehabilitative and/or restorative than retributive.

Parents/Guardians

Young offenders' parents/guardians also assume responsibilities under the YCJA. These range from their right to be notified that their child has been arrested, to supervising their child during any community sentences, to supporting their child throughout the court process and assisting them in their rehabilitation (see Chapter 3). Beyond the young person's right to legal counsel, they additionally have the right to have their parent(s) or legal guardian present during police questioning. Unfortunately, research from Ontario has found that parents experience barriers to accessing the youth justice system and court proceedings; as a result of their single-parent, low-socioeconomic status, many parents, typically mothers, are not able to make it to the police station when their child is arrested or attend any scheduled court hearings (Broeking and Peterson-Badali 2010).

Sentencing

While the sentencing principles underlying the YCJA and the variety of sentences handed out by judges have already been discussed in Chapter 3, it is important to devote additional attention to some of the developments and issues surrounding sentencing practices in provincial youth justice courts across the country.

There are several factors to be taken into account in discussing the sentencing of young offenders in Canada. One of these is that there are a number of provincial differences in the sentencing of young people. For example, while provinces like Saskatchewan rely considerably on extrajudicial sanctions, especially for Aboriginal offenders, even before the YCJA (Savarese 2015), Ontario has made, and continues to make, the greatest use of youth custody in Canada (see Chapter 2).

At the court stage, a somewhat comparable outcome for youth of the diversion utilized by the police is a reprimand, or admonishment, by the youth court judge in which the judge gives a very stern warning to the young person; such a sentence is commonly utilized for minor, first-time offenders and does not include any criminal sanctions. The YCJA offers additional non-sanctioned sentencing options: an absolute discharge or a conditional discharge. In each of these cases, the young person has been found guilty of a minor offence, and it is usually his or her first offence. In the case of an absolute discharge, the judge decides that the offence was not so serious as to warrant the registering of the conviction, and in consideration of the best interests of the young person, as well as the interest of the public, no further actions are taken. Alternatively, in the case of a conditional discharge, the judge assigns a series of conditions to the youth, which she or he has to follow in the community. If the young person successfully completes this sentence without breaching her or his conditions in the elected time frame, the conditional discharge will become an absolute discharge. On the other hand, if the youth does not successfully abide by the conditions set by the court, the young person will be returned to court where she or he may receive a harsher sentence.

The Role of Youth Probation Officers

Given that most convicted youth will receive some type of community-based sentence, it is important to examine how changes in sentencing practices affect the work of probation officers. Under the YCJA, probation is the most commonly applied sanction for youth convicted of a Criminal Code offence (Brennan 2012; see Chapter 2). It should also be noted, however, that youth probation officer caseloads have experienced sizeable reductions in youth cases requiring supervision. Such caseloads in British Columbia, for example, in 2011/12 fell from 30 or more young offenders per youth probation officer to an average of 18 (Corrado et al. 2015).

Although the maximum possible probation sentence is a period of two years (YCJA 2002), the average youth probation sentence in Canada in 2011/12 was one year (Dauvergne 2013). As noted in Chapter 2, probation is a popular sentencing option because it provides the court system with a sentence that is viewed as fair and meaningful, one that holds the youth accountable but also offers an alternative to the more punitive custodial sentence.

Under the supervision of a youth probation officer/youth delegate, the young person is expected to abide by a series of court-ordered conditions. These conditions always include keeping the peace and being of good behaviour, as well as appearing in court whenever required; they may also include living in a specified location and/or with specified individuals, abiding by a curfew, attending school and/or specialized programs, obtaining employment, abstaining from alcohol and drugs, and regularly reporting to a probation officer. Youth who fail to comply with the probation order assigned to them are often charged with a breach of probation that can eventually result in a custodial sentence (Bala, Carrington, and Roberts 2009).

Probation officers also play an important role in administering other community-based sentences, including ISSP orders, which share many characteristics with youth probation orders (i.e., the initial meeting with a YPO and the two stipulated conditions). The main distinction is that an ISSP order permits an increased level of monitoring, supervision, and support of the youth, often provided with the assistance of a youth probation officer and a specially assigned ISSP worker.

As well, probation officers play a role in court decision-making, where they act as the communication bridge between the courts, corrections, the young person's family, and the young person involved in the youth criminal justice system. While youth court judges do not maintain ongoing contact with custodial facilities, youth probation officers do engage in contacts and communication with the court system (by attending court and through pre-sentence reports) and with corrections (by being involved in case management and release planning).

Probation officers/youth delegates are also responsible for supervising young offenders in the community during their time on bail or during the completion of other community-based sentences. As part of their responsibilities, they collect and present critical information to the courts in pre-disposition, pre-sentence, post-disposition, and *Gladue* reports. YPOs balance an enforcement and rehabilitative role by monitoring the youths' compliance with their court order(s), completing screening and risk assessments of the youth, and referring them to appropriate evidence-guided programming and services in the community, while also completing the necessary casework in preparation for trials, sentencing, and custodial releases (Marroney, Quinn, Kinney, and Hufford 2010; Skeem and Manchak 2008). YPOs also retain the responsibility of preparing release and transition plans for when youth return to the community after a period of time in custody (Corrado et al. 2015).

In some cases, probation conditions are more severe than those received in custody (e.g., some youth have received such restrictive conditions that they are essentially incapable of meeting them). This results in the young person's return to youth court for a reconsideration of a custodial sentence (Alain and Hamel 2015). It is, therefore, the responsibility of the courts to ensure that they balance the goals and principles of the youth sentence they employ.

Despite some of the intricacies of the YCJA (Trépanier 2004), overall YPOs appear to have successfully adapted to it and have been applying its outlined principles, sanctions, and practices (Kuehn and Corrado 2011). In recent years, other changes have affected the role played by probation officers, including the creation of specialized youth probation caseloads to respond to the unique needs of some young offenders in the community—for example, those with severe mental health or substance abuse problems, serious/violent patterns of offending, and a conviction for sexually based offences.

Custody-Based Sentences

Exceptions to community-based sanctions under the YCJA occur in those cases where a young person has committed a more serious and/or violent offence or the youth has a pattern of repeated offending. A broad body of research literature has shown that custody can be **criminogenic** for offenders (e.g., Cullen, Jonson, and Nagin 2011), especially so in the case of low-risk offenders. For this reason and based on the rehabilitative and reintegrative goals of the YCJA, a custodial sentence is only imposed on a young offender in a select set of circumstances. According to the provisions outlined in section 39 of the Act (discussed in more detail in Chapter 3), custodial sentences can only be imposed for serious violent offences after all other reasonable alternatives and their likely success for the youth have been considered. As also discussed in Chapter 3, as a result of the Safe Streets and Communities Act, the YCJA's definition of serious offences and violent offences has been expanded. The extension of this definition to now include a greater range of crimes and the SSCA's inclusion of denunciation and deterrence as youth sentencing principles have presented a potential opportunity for the youth justice system to increasingly rely on more severe custodial sentences for convicted young offenders.

criminogenic
Situations or environments that cause or exacerbate criminal behaviours. These can even include institutions or programs that have been designed to reduce such behaviours.

In 2011/12, the youth courts imposed custodial sentences in 15 per cent of youth court cases in which there was a guilty verdict (Dauvergne 2013; see Chapter 2 for further details). This represented a 24 per cent to 29 per cent decline since the 1990s and early 2000s. To examine the bigger picture, in total in 2010/11, 90 per cent of justice system–involved youth received some type of community supervision (mainly probation) compared to the 10 per cent of youth who were in custody (Munch 2012). In addition, youth custody sentences were typically incredibly short; in 2011/2012, 74 per cent were three months or less (Dauvergne 2013). It will be interesting to see if there are any changes in the use of various youth sentences, particularly custody, after the SSCA has been fully adopted.

Sentence Lengths

In addition to outlining the principles of youth sentencing and the available options, the YCJA establishes the maximum sentence length that a young person can receive, alone or in combination with any of the detailed sentences, as detailed in section 42, subsections 14, 15, and 16. For a youth case in which the young person has been charged with one offence, the young person may receive a sentence, or a combination of sentences, that cannot exceed two years. In the case where a young person has committed multiple offences, excluding murder, the sentence, or combination of sentences, cannot exceed three years in length. For first-degree murder (including cases in which the young person is simultaneously being sentenced for other offences committed), the combined sentence length cannot exceed 10 years and for second-degree murder, the sentence cannot exceed 7 years. There are, additionally, some rare cases where a young person will commit another offence or a series of offences during the time she or he is serving another sentence. In these situations, the sentence length may be longer than the previously stated maximums. Although it is incredibly uncommon, a young person may be given a life sentence, such as when a youth 16 or 17 years of age has committed murder and has been sentenced as an adult. Parole eligibility is reached after the youth has served 10 years of her or his life sentence.

While the YCJA applies to youth aged 12 to 17, some young offenders do not reach the sentencing stage of the judicial processing until she or he has already turned 18 years old. If the young person is age 18 or older during this process and the sentence imposed is less than two years, the youth may be placed in provincial custody. If the sentence imposed is more than two years, however, the youth may be placed in a federal facility. If a young person turns 20 years of age while in custody, she or he is typically moved to an adult facility to serve the remainder of the sentence. If a young person is sentenced as an adult but is under the age of 18, the YCJA amendments made by the Safe Streets and Communities Act stipulate that the young person cannot be placed in an adult prison or penitentiary; this is true as well for youth under 18 years of age who receive a youth sentence.

Adult Sentences

Despite the fact that adult sentences are typically reserved for cases involving the most high-risk youth who have committed murder or another very serious/violent crime (Corrado et al. 2015), the Safe Streets and Communities Act has amended the previous provisions related to this. The YCJA outlined that adult sentences were only to be considered in cases involving young people 14 years of age or older and in cases where the courts believed that a youth sentence was not sufficient in length to serve the function of holding the youth accountable. Under the now repealed section 62 of the Act, youth who were found guilty of what was formerly known as a presumptive offence could be considered for an adult sentence. Presumptive offences included first-degree murder, second-degree murder, manslaughter, attempted murder, aggravated sexual assault, or a serious/violent offence with two previous guilty findings of a serious/violent offence. The new provisions of the amended Act set out that an adult sentence must be considered for a young person if certain criteria are met. The attorney general may

> make an application to the youth justice court for an order that a young person is liable to an adult sentence if the young person is or has been found guilty of an offence for which an adult is liable to imprisonment for a term of more than two

years and that was committed after the young person attained the age of 14 years. (YCJA 2002: s. 64(1))

If the attorney general has determined that, based on the above criteria, an adult sentence would be appropriate but he or she makes the decision not to make an application, "the Attorney General shall advise the youth justice court before the young person enters a plea or with leave of the court before the commencement of the trial" (YCJA 2002: s. 64(1.1)). In effect, these revisions now direct the Crown to consider a request for an adult sentence for a youth, and if it chooses not to pursue this sentence, it is expected to notify the court of this decision. A final comment on the use of adult sentences for young offenders is that the onus is on the Crown to demonstrate to the court the appropriateness of an adult sentence.

Additional considerations that the youth court must consider in the sentencing of young offenders under the Act are the young person's role in the commission of the offence, the harm done to the victim(s), the reparation (if any) to the victim or the community made by the young person, the time the young person spent in detention (if any) in connection to the offence, the nature and number of previous findings of guilt (if any), and any other relevant aggravating (e.g., gang involvement, lack of remorse, offence planning) and mitigating circumstances (e.g., mental health, lower age) in connection to the youth or the offence (s. 38(3)(a–f); Roberts and Bala, 2003).

Youth Corrections: Treatment Regimes in Open- and Closed-Custody Facilities

Youth who are sentenced to serve a custodial sanction in a youth custody centre may be placed in either open or closed custody, which is determined by the youth court during sentencing based on the severity of the offence and the needs of the young person. The safety of other youth in custody may be considered as well depending on the youth's behaviours in the community and during previous custodial placements. Youth may also be placed in a secure isolation unit (i.e., solitary confinement or segregation) for a brief period of time during their incarceration if they have been engaging in behaviour that suggests there is a risk of their becoming aggressive and causing serious harm to another person, to themselves, or to the property, and that this behaviour cannot be suppressed by alternative means (Office of the Auditor General of Ontario 2012). Young offenders also receive daily behavioural ratings from correctional staff that can be used to determine what time they are to be in their cell at night. Since the number of female young offenders who require detention is too small to necessitate a separate facility, there are distinct units for female young offenders in which their accommodations are detached from the male offenders' areas.

During a period of incarceration, all young offenders have access to a range of programming options that can assist in the development of pro-social attitudes and behaviours, such as educational/vocational training, life skills programs, recreational programs, substance abuse programs, individual and group counselling, anger management programming, cultural and religious programs, and culinary activities. There are also more specialized programs offered to youth who have mental health conditions and/or who have committed a sexual and/or violent offence (Corrado et al. 2015). Educational and substance abuse programs—the most commonly delivered programs in youth detention centres—offer promising educational, as well as offending, outcomes once youth are released from custody (Young, Dembo, and Henderson 2007; also, see Chapter 10). The most successful substance abuse programs are those that are long in duration rather than high in intensity (Lipsey and Wilson 1998) and that address substance abuse as well as co-morbid mental health disorders (Teplin et al. 2006). Research has also highlighted the success of violent offender treatment programming comprising cognitive-behavioural therapy and anger management strategies (see Serin, Gobeil, and Preston 2009). Youth who completed such programs experienced reductions in violent and non-violent recidivism (Gretton et al. 2007).

Restorative Justice

Although not explicitly stated in the YCJA, there are practices utilized within the youth criminal justice system that reflect restorative justice ideas (see Chapter 16). These include diversionary measures and youth justice conferences. Similar to the restorative justice framework, these provisions often require the young person to admit guilt (Wemmers and Cyr 2005), and they can also include victims in the related processes. As stated explicitly in the Act's sentencing principles, a youth justice sentence should "promote a sense of responsibility in the young person, and an acknowledgement of the harm done to victims and the community" (YCJA 2002: s. 38(2)(e)(iii)). The Act therefore encourages reparation and restorative-based sentences.

As noted in Chapter 16, restorative justice programs exist all across Canada and can be especially beneficial to Aboriginal young offenders. These programs can ensure that the YCJA's proportionality principle is not disregarded, and some of these approaches can be partly punitive, including, for example, family group conferencing that is conducted outside the formal court system and convenes the offender, the victim, their families, community representatives, and a mediator (Anand 2003).

Restorative measures may be utilized at various stages of the youth's criminal justice proceedings. Irrespective of whether they are used before or after sentencing, the young person's failure to complete the restorative justice arrangement made can result in the youth's return to court for more formal sanctioning. If a young person successfully participates in and completes a restorative-based program or reparation process, however, the youth court will view this as a **mitigating factor** in their case (Roberts 2003).

Youth Justice Committees and Advocates

In relation to extrajudicial measures, section 18 of the YCJA defines the role of youth justice committees (YJCs). These committees comprise volunteer citizens from the community who are delegated with the task of assisting in administering the Act and/or

mitigating factors
Information presented to the courts in relation to the facts of the case and the accused that may result in a lesser charge or sentence if he or she is found guilty. Conversely, aggravating factors are facts presented to the court surrounding the offence or the offender's circumstances that may aggravate or increase the severity of the offence.

determining suitable programs for low-risk youth involved in the youth criminal justice system. YJCs operate in every province and territory (Calgary Youth Justice Society 2014). These committees work collaboratively with members of the criminal justice system and community organizations to promote the successful rehabilitation and reintegration of young offenders, typically with regard to extrajudicial measures. In many provinces and territories, there is a particular emphasis on Aboriginal youth (Hann & Associates 2003). Youth justice advocates can be pivotal to restorative justice approaches, assisting in the bringing together of the victim and the offender and facilitating communication between these two sides.

There are variations in the role of these youth justice advocates from province to province and between the territories. In Manitoba and the Northwest Territories, for example, these committees receive information from Crown counsel for the purpose of making decisions related to youth programming. In British Columbia and Ontario, YJCs participate in extrajudicial measures and also act as citizen advisors. In Nova Scotia, the police and Crown counsel, rather than youth justice advocates, are relied upon to determine which youth are referred to extrajudicial measures; however, these advocates then deliver the restorative justice and community service programs (Calgary Youth Justice Society 2014). According to the YCJA, YJCs may also partake in discussions with the federal and provincial governments, advising them on the compliance of young people's rights and protection and on youth criminal justice policies and procedures (Department of Justice Canada 2013).

Challenges in Dealing with Youth Mental Health Issues in Youth Courts and Corrections

As in the case of youth courts (Chapter 3), professionals working in youth corrections face immense challenges in attempting to develop more effective ways of dealing with young offenders suffering from mental health problems. While these challenges are too many and too complicated to cover in detail in a single chapter, in the following sections we attempt to highlight some of the most significant issues being addressed today.

Young Offenders with Mental Health Disorders

A significant proportion of young offenders in our youth justice system (approximately 50 to 90 per cent) have been diagnosed with or display symptoms of a mental health condition (Gretton and Clift 2011; Penner, Roesch, and Viljoen 2011; Fazel, Doll, and Långström 2008).

These high numbers may be explained, at least in part, by the fact that youth with mental health disorders fail to engage in delinquent behaviours discreetly and thus have a greater likelihood of being detected, and/or by their inability to understand the detrimental implications—for society and themselves—of their behaviours (Pozzulo, Bennell, and Forth 2009). The specific set of conditions and disorders that young offenders typically present with at higher levels than young people in the general population include anxiety, depression, aggression, and low self-control (Grisso 2008; Kramer and Zimmermann 2008; Sedlak 2009). As well, youth who have been diagnosed with attention deficit hyperactivity disorder (ADHD), conduct disorder, or attachment disorder are more likely to become involved in delinquency and the criminal justice system (Katner 2006; Odgers, Burnette, Chauhan, Moretti, and Reppucci 2005). Beyond these numbers, many youth involved in the criminal justice system also have co-morbid mental health conditions, meaning that they meet the criteria for two or more disorders (Abram, Teplin, McClelland, and Dulcan 2003; Gretton and Clift 2011).

In light of these alarming numbers, the YCJA has established protocol for responding to youth who may have a diagnosable mental impediment that should be weighed as a mitigating factor in the youth court. Section 34(1) of the Act states that if a young person and the prosecutor consent, "a youth justice court may, at any stage of proceedings against a young person, by order require that the young person be assessed by a qualified person who is required to report the results in writing to the court." Furthermore, lawyers and judges are required to request assessments if there are reasonable grounds that any mental health disorder(s) appear to be present, if there is a history of repeated convictions for the young person, and/or if the youth "is alleged to have committed a serious violent offence" (YCJA 2002: s. 34(1)(b)(iii)). Subsequent to this, the court can impose appropriate programming and treatment recommendations.

Psychiatric reports are an important part of this process. During the completion of a psychiatric assessment by a youth forensic psychologist, a young person may be held in remand custody; however, this cannot continue longer than 30 days and can only be used when the courts deem it necessary and/or a qualified person believes it could assist in the completion of the assessment and the youth consents to this. The completion of court-ordered psychiatric assessments for youth can take considerable time in some cases, and in many provinces and jurisdictions wait-lists can be approximately six to eight weeks for psychological assessments and three months for psychiatric assessments (St John, as cited by the Canadian Mental Health Association Ontario 2005).

Issues Related to Mental Incapacity and Fitness to Stand Trial

Another challenge in the management of young offenders with a mental illness in the youth justice system is determining the impact that their mental health had on the commission of the offence and their ability to participate fully in the court process given their mental status. The courts must therefore assess whether young people's mental illness (1) prevented their appreciation of their actions and (2) will prevent them from comprehending and actively participating in the criminal proceedings against them. In relation to these issues, comparable to the process with adult offenders, a small number of young offenders may be found **not criminally responsible on account of a mental disorder (NCRMD)** or **unfit to stand trial (UST)**. Very few youth court cases result in a finding of NCRMD or UST, as the standards to meet each of these are very high and must be determined by a psychiatrist during a psychiatric assessment.

Fitness to Stand Trial

Individuals are determined to be unfit to stand trial in situations when the accused is "unable on account of mental disorder to conduct a defence at any stage of proceedings

not criminally responsible on account of a mental disorder (NCRMD)
Based on the Criminal Code's definition, a mental disorder is viewed as a "disease of the mind." For an individual to be found NCRMD, there must be a mental abnormality (not caused by voluntary intoxication, temporary mental conditions, or uncontrollable urges) causing significant impairment to preclude the individual's understanding of their behaviour.

unfit to stand trial (UST)
When an individual is not fully capable of instructing counsel or understanding the nature and consequences of their trial.

before a verdict is rendered or to instruct counsel to do so, and, in particular, unable on account of mental disorder to: (a) understand the nature or object of the proceedings, (b) understand the possible consequences of the proceedings, or (c) communicate with counsel" (Criminal Code 1985: s. 2). When a young person is found unfit, there follows a 90-day period after which the courts can reassess this status to determine whether the individual is now fit. If there is insufficient evidence to support the re-prosecuting of the young person, the result is a case acquittal. If the accused youth is found to be fit, however, the trial will proceed.

Not Criminally Responsible on Account of Mental Disorder (NCRMD)

Regardless of the presentation of fitness to stand trial, the NCRMD defence may be raised. The assessment to determine this is carried out if the issue of severe mental disorder at the time of the offence has been presented by the Crown prosecutor once the court has found the accused guilty of the offence or if the accused individual has him- or herself raised the issue. The NCRMD criteria are that the act was "committed or an omission [was] made while suffering from a mental disorder that rendered the person incapable of appreciating the nature and quality of the act or omission or of knowing that it was wrong" (Criminal Code 1985: s. 16(1)). This is, therefore, a distinct finding compared to the court's use of guilty/not guilty verdicts. The court has three possible options after a person has been found NCRMD. The types of dispositions available to the courts include detention in a psychiatric hospital, a conditional discharge, or an absolute discharge. These outcomes, except for an absolute discharge, are reviewed by a review board to ensure that the disposition was appropriate, and the board may impose an alternative disposition. These reviews occur within 90 days. An individual who receives an in-hospital disposition cannot be mandated to accept treatment while there, unless it has been determined necessary to his or her maintaining good health, in which case the disposition falls under the mental health acts that are provincially/territorially administered.

In cases where there are apparent mental health problems but the young person is found fit to stand trial and criminally responsible, the presence of any conditions is taken into consideration during youth court sentencing. More specifically, the YCJA created the intensive rehabilitative custody and supervision (IRCS) order, which is a specific youth sentencing option offered in cases where young people have committed a serious violent offence and also suffer from mental, psychological, or emotional disorders/disturbances. The government has allocated a proportion of youth justice funding to each province and territory to provide specific assistance and resourcing for these young people during their time in custody and in the community to ensure that an individualized case management and treatment plan is developed to support such cases. Despite the promising potential impact of these sentences, IRCS orders are seldom used (Evaluation Division 2010). This may be the result of fewer serious violent youth cases coming before the courts. This sanction also necessitates a special court review process to assess the suitability of the young person for such a sanction and requires the Crown and youth court to support this measure, which may deter the courts from imposing it more often.

The Potential for Specialized Youth Mental Health Courts

Research has indicated that specialized services aimed at diverting mentally disordered youth from further court involvement and custodial sentences are effectively working in some jurisdictions. In Ontario, several specialized youth mental health courts have been developed to support criminally involved and mentally disordered youth. The first youth mental health court in Canada opened in Ottawa in 2008 (Campbell 2015). Since that time, the program has increased from 13 mental health court sites to 45 sites. The primary objective of these courts is to better facilitate a collaborative approach to managing the needs of this specific group of young offenders. Young people may be referred to these courts if they are within the age restrictions of the YCJA (i.e., 12 to 17 years old) and are at risk of receiving formal police charges, have already been charged by the police, or have been found UST or NCRMD. Furthermore, the case must be deemed low risk. Through this program, the Crown, a court worker, the defence counsel, a youth team case manager, probation officers, addiction workers, and other committed community partners work together to review the youth's related assessments and reports and use this information to guide the treatment plan for the young person. A psychiatrist and the youth's parent(s)/guardians are also involved in this process. To participate in this program, youth have to admit guilt and accept their responsibility in committing the related act. Upon determination of the sentence, the Crown remains involved in the monitoring of the young individual's progress.

Research has not been conducted on the outcomes of these courts in Canada. However, there have been suggestions from those involved that courts have been able to reduce recidivism for many of the youth in the program. The program has also led to faster processing, as intended, and a more community-based diversion sentence (CanWest MediaWorks Publications 2008).

The Use of Risk Assessment Tools in Youth Courts and Corrections

screening tools
Instruments used to identify at-risk youth and assist in their referrals to appropriate programs and services.

risk assessment tools
Instruments used to assess the multitude of risk and protective factors that have been and/or are present in young people's lives that can influence the likelihood of recidivism. Youth are rated as low, medium, or high risk and individualized interventions are developed based on these risk assessment outcomes.

Because of the extreme high-risk and/or mental health profiles of some youth involved in the criminal justice system, youth courts, community-based services, and youth centres rely on both screening and risk assessment tools to guide the way youth are responded to at various stages of the system. **Screening tools** can be differentiated from **risk assessment tools** in that the former are utilized to identify youth who may be at risk or who possess certain risk factors associated with specific needs areas, and should therefore be used to make appropriate service, programming, and treatment referrals. Risk assessment tools, however, assess the young person as being low, medium, or high risk to recidivate based on a set of indicators that typically include, but are not limited to, familial measures, educational/vocational measures, substance use measures, peer measures, and attitudinal measures. These tools compose an important part of effectively managing young offenders in the criminal justice system. Based on the empirical support for the effectiveness of these instruments, both community probation offices and correctional services employ risk assessment tools in the management of young offenders.

The foundation for the use of risk assessment lies in Andrews, Bonta, and Hoge's (1990) risk-needs-responsivity (RNR) model. This model outlines three key principles. The first is the *risk principle*, which states that risk assessments should begin by identifying an offender's risk level and identifying services that can target the(se) risk(s). Next, the *needs principle* directs that assessments be used to establish the risk factors that contribute to a person's offending behaviour, as well as the protective factors that may help the young person's rehabilitation. Finally, the *responsivity principle* includes an assessment of the offender's likely receptivity to any treatment based on the offender's learning style, in addition to her or his strengths and abilities.

Several youth screening and assessment tools have been developed, and while there are too many to discuss in depth here, it is worthwhile to take note of a few of the instruments that are most commonly used in Canada among at-risk youth and young offender populations. One instrument that has been developed and is employed in community and custodial youth justice settings in Ontario and Alberta is the Youth Assessment and Screening Instrument (YASI), which assesses youth's risk, needs, and protective factors (Andrews et al. 1990). More specifically, the instrument was designed for at-risk youth ages 12 to 18 with no specification based on gender; a version has more recently been developed to be used specifically with girls. The tool collects information on youth's **static risk factors**, such as age, gender, ethnicity, and prior criminal history, and **dynamic risk factors**, which include substance use, antisocial peers, and gang involvement (Savignac 2010). Preliminary research has found that the YASI is an effective tool to assess young offenders risk level (Geck 2012).

Another commonly employed instrument that provides both a screening and risk assessment tool is the Youth Level of Service/Case Management Inventory (YLS/CMI). Developed in Canada, this tool is currently being used in Nova Scotia, Newfoundland and Labrador, Prince Edward Island, and the Yukon for youth ages 12 to 17 (Savignac 2010). As is the case with the YASI, individuals working in the criminal justice system utilize the YLS/CMI to assess young offenders' specific set of needs and their risk of recidivism and then rely on this information to create more tailored interventions and case management plans. Research on the reliability of the YLS/CMI supports its use in predicting future reoffending risks (McGrath and Thompson 2012) for both male and female young offenders (Andrews et al. 2012); it has also produced improved accuracy in predicting offending and violent offending compared to other risk assessment tools (Viljoen, Elkovitch, Scalora, and Ullman 2009) and in guiding the development of youth interventions (Hoge 2005).

A final standardized risk and needs assessment instrument that is used, for example, in British Columbia and the Yukon is the Structured Assessment of Violence Risk in Youth (SAVRY). The SAVRY is intended for young offenders 12 to 18 years old who have been incarcerated or who require a more in-depth assessment of their risk for violence (Savignac 2010). The SAVRY has been successful in predicting violent and non-violent recidivism (Vincent, Guy, Gershenson, and McCabe 2012). Furthermore, the SAVRY has been moderately successful in influencing youth probation outcomes (e.g., Catchpole and Gretton 2003; Childs et al. 2013; Olver, Stockdale, and Wormith 2009).

static risk factors
Risk factors that are unchangeable; they include those traits that may contribute to an offender's offending and recidivism and cannot be altered through rehabilitation programming.

dynamic risk factors
Risk factors that are changeable; they are factors that may also contribute to criminal behaviour but can be modified through targeted interventions and/or treatment.

Issues with Relying on Risk Assessment Tools

Some issues have been identified and raised by academics and criminal justice professionals related to the suitability of standardized risk assessment tools for specific types of young offenders, more specifically special or minority groups such as girls and Aboriginal young offenders. Moreover, the standardization of these instruments is based on comparisons to non-criminal samples that may not necessarily be representative of the young people involved in our legal system, such as girls and minority or Aboriginal young offenders (Kempf-Leonard 2007), the latter group being disproportionately overrepresented in the criminal justice system.

Issues Related to Youth Records

A young person's involvement in the criminal justice system will result in the creation of different types of records, including youth justice court records, police records, government records, and records classified in an "other" category, such as those that were created by community agencies during extrajudicial measures. Furthermore, the imposition of an adult sentence for a young person results in an adult record. Although, under section 119(2) of the YCJA, youth records are active, accessible, and disclosable to criminal justice staff and professionals during the **access period**, based on the rehabilitative principles of the YCJA, after a set period of time following the completion of the youth sentence, the youth's records are sealed and/or destroyed and cannot be used to supplement information collected concerning future adult offending and court involvement or to be held against the offender.

     The destruction of youth records occurs at various times following a young person's guilty verdict or the completion of the sentence, and it depends on the type of sanction imposed. These are presented in Table 4.1. Once the access period has passed and a youth's record has been closed, police, court, and corrections files, as well as the information contained in them, cannot de disclosed.

     The destruction of youth records is important in protecting the identification and rights of young people under the YCJA; still, these records may remain open after the young person has reached the age of 18. They may also prevent the young person from entering some education programs, accessing certain employment opportunities, or obtaining volunteer positions, and they inhibit the young person's entry into countries outside of Canada (Department of Justice Canada 2013).

Summary

A young person's movement through the youth criminal justice system can vary depending on the youth's circumstances and offence(s) and on which province/territory he or she is charged. Nevertheless, the standard procedures followed at each stage of the process have been presented in this chapter, beginning with the youth's first contact with

access period
The designated time frame during which a young person's youth record is active or disclosable and can be shared among relevant individuals attached to the young person as outlined in the YCJA (e.g., the youth, his/her parents, defence counsel, Crown counsel, detention centre, or correctional facility director).

How Offence Is Dealt with/Type of Offence	How Long before Record Will Be Sealed or Destroyed? (Access Period)
Youth is acquitted (other than verdict of not criminally responsible on account of mental disorder)	Two (2) months after the time allowed to file an appeal or, if an appeal is filed, three (3) months after all proceedings related to the appeal are completed
Charge is dismissed or withdrawn	After two (2) months
Youth is found guilty and given a reprimand	After two (2) months
Charge is stayed	After one (1) year, if no further court proceedings have been taken
Extrajudicial sanction is imposed	Two (2) years after the young person has consented to the extrajudicial sanction
Youth is found guilty and given an absolute discharge	One (1) year after the young person has been found guilty
Youth is found guilty and given a conditional discharge	Three (3) years after the young person has been found guilty
Youth is found guilty and sentenced for summary conviction offence	Three (3) years after the sentence has been completed (any subsequent offence will result in an extension)
Youth is found guilty and sentenced for indictable offence	Five (5) years after the sentence has been completed (any subsequent offence will result in an extension)
Murder, manslaughter, attempted murder, or aggravated sexual assault	Record may be retained indefinitely
Certain scheduled offences	Record will be retained for an additional five (5) years
Youth is found guilty and receives an adult sentence	Record is treated as an adult record, and the rules applicable to adult records apply
Person is convicted of an offence committed after he or she turns 18, while the access period for their youth offence is still open	Record for the youth offence will be treated as an adult record, and the rules applicable to adult records apply

Table 4.1 Destruction of Youth Criminal Records

Source: Youth Records factsheet, http://www.justice.gc.ca/eng/cj-jp/yj-jj/tools-outils/sheets-feuillets/pdf/recor-dossi.pdf, Entire table. Department of Justice Canada, 2013. Reproduced with the permission of the Department of Justice Canada, 2015.

the police. This encounter can then lead either to a diversionary response or to a formal charging and continuation into the formal youth justice system. At this stage, the youth will attend court and will receive an extrajudicial sanction or a stern warning from the judge; be found not guilty, not criminally responsible by reason of mental disorder, or unfit to stand trial; or be sentenced to one or a combination of the more formal options. While a young person's record does not typically remain accessible indefinitely, it can present challenges for future employment and travel.

In consideration of the unique characteristics of each young person who comes into contact with the police and the legal system, the flexibility offered through the current youth justice legislation does provide a greater range of options to be considered in our response to young offenders.

Key Terms

access period	pre-charge diversion
bail	preliminary inquiry
bail surety	pre-sentence report
criminogenic	pre-trial detention/remand custody
discretion	racial profiling
disposition	risk assessment tools
dynamic risk factors	screening tools
extra-judicialanctions	static risk factors
mitigating factor	unfit to stand trial (UST)
net widening	
not criminally responsible on account of mental disorder (NCRMD)	

Review Questions

1. Describe the process that a first-time offender might face when apprehended for a non-violent offence by police.

2. What is one identified limitation of the process utilized by police officers in British Columbia to determine whether a young person should be diverted away from the youth criminal justice system or be formally charged with a criminal offence?

3. How and under what circumstances are young offenders in Canada determined to be unfit to stand trial and NCRMD?

4. What is the longest time that a person's youth record can remain open and under what circumstances? Are criminal justice staff allowed to share or rely on any of this information after this time?

Critical Thinking Questions

1. How would a more evenly applied approach to responses and sanctions for youth across Canada be advantageous and disadvantageous to young offenders?

2. How could specialized probation caseloads ultimately help and potentially hinder young offenders' rehabilitation?

3. What could be the potential benefits and hindrances to relying on restorative-based sanctions for young offenders? Should the police and youth courts rely on these approaches more (or less) than they do now?

4. Should the youth criminal justice system avoid the use of custody for first-time/less serious young offenders but continue to impose such a sanction on the most serious/repeat young offenders?

5. What would be the implications to the young person and the justice system of keeping a young person's youth record active indefinitely?

References

Abram, K.M., Teplin, L.A., McClelland, G.M., and Dulcan, M.K. (2003). Comorbid psychiatric disorders in youth in juvenile detention. *Archives of General Psychiatry, 60*: 1097–108. doi:10.1001/archpsyc.60.11.1097

Alain, M., and Hamel, S. (2015). The situation in Quebec: "Vive la différence"? In A. Alain, R. Corrado, and S. Reid (Eds), *Implementing and working with the Youth Criminal Justice Act across Canada*. Toronto: University of Toronto Press.

Anand, S. (2003). Crafting youth sentences: The roles of rehabilitation, proportionality, restraint, restorative justice, and race under the Youth Criminal Justice Act. *Alberta Law Review, 40*(4): 943–63.

Andrews, D.A., Bonta, J., and Hoge, R.D. (1990). Classification for effective rehabilitation: Rediscovering psychology. *Criminal Justice and Behavior, 17*: 19–52.

Andrews, D.A., Guzzo, L., Raynor, P., Rowe, R.C., Rettinger, L.J., Brews, A., et al. (2012). Are the major risk/need factors predictive of both female and male reoffending? A test with the eight domains of the Level of Service/Case Management Inventory. *International Journal of Offender Therapy and Comparative Criminology, 56*: 113–33. doi:10.1177/0306624X10395716

Bala, N. (2013, 5 September). When a child kills in Canada, there's no sense of justice. *Globe and Mail*. Retrieved from http://www.theglobeandmail.com/globe-debate/when-a-child-kills-in-canada-theres-no-sense-of-justice/article14119129/

Bala, N., and Anand, S. (2009). *Youth criminal justice law* (2nd ed.). Toronto: Irwin Law.

Bala, N., Carrington, P., and Roberts, J. (2009). Evaluating the Youth Criminal Justice Act after five years: A qualified success. *Canadian Journal of Criminology and Criminal Justice, 51*: 131–67. doi:10.1353/ccj.0.0050

Boyce, J., Cotter, A., and Perreault, S. (2014). Police-reported crime statistics in Canada, 2013. *Juristat, 34*(1). Statistics Canada Catalogue No. 85-002-X. Retrieved 5 November 2014 from http://www.statcan.gc.ca/pub/85-002-x/2014001/article/14040-eng.pdf

Brennan, S. (2012). Youth court statistics in Canada, 2010/2011. *Juristat, 32*(1). Statistics Canada Catalogue No. 85-002-X. Retrieved 10 September 2014 from http://www.statcan.gc.ca/pub/85-002-x/2012001/article/11645-eng.pdf

Broeking, J., and Peterson-Badali, M. (2010). The extent and nature of parents' involvement in Canadian youth justice proceedings. *Youth Justice, 10*: 40–55. doi:10.1177/1473225409356759

Calgary Youth Justice Society. (2014). *Section 3: Youth justice committees*. Retrieved from http://calgaryyouthjustice.ca/programs/youth-justice-committees/information/for-volunteers/e-learning-course-1/section-3/

Campbell, K.M. (2015). Youth criminal justice law in Ontario. In A. Alain, R.R. Corrado, and S. Reid (Eds), *Implementing and working with the Youth Criminal Justice Act across Canada*. Toronto: University of Toronto Press.

Canadian Mental Health Association Ontario. (2005). *Network: Youth justice*. Retrieved from http://ontario.cmha.ca/network/youth-justice/

CanWest MediaWorks Publications. (2008, 13 November). Mental health court proves a huge success. *Ottawa Citizen*. Retrieved 10 November 2014 from http://www.canada.com/ottawacitizen/news/story.html?id=d343a2d3-a48f-4836-8298-0c149767ae05

Carrington, P.J., and Schulenberg, J.L. (2005). *The impact of the Youth Criminal Justice Act on police charging practices with young persons: A preliminary statistical assessment*. Ottawa: Department of Justice Canada. Retrieved from http://www.justice.gc.ca/eng/rp-pr/cj-jp/yj-jj/pdf/prelimin.pdf

Catchpole, R.E.H., and Gretton, H.M. (2003). The predictive validity of risk assessment with violent young offenders: A 1-year examination of criminal outcome. *Criminal Justice and Behavior*, 30: 688–708.

CBC News. (2013, 3 September). *Child under 12 acted alone in beating death of boy, 6, RCMP say.* Retrieved from http://www.cbc.ca/news/canada/saskatchewan/child-under-12-acted-alone-in-beating-death-of-boy-6-rcmp-say-1.1400513

Childs, K.K., Ryals, J., Frick, P.J., Lawing, K., Phillippi, S.W., and Deprato, D.K. (2013). Examining the validity of the Structured Assessment of Violence Risk in Youth (SAVRY) for predicting probation outcomes among adjudicated juvenile offenders. *Behavioral Sciences and the Law*, 31: 256–70.

Corrado, R.R., Gronsdahl, K., and Markwart, A. (2015). Youth justice system and approaches in British Columbia. In A. Alain, R.R. Corrado, and S. Reid (Eds), *Implementing and working with the Youth Criminal Justice Act across Canada: A view from the ground*. Toronto: University of Toronto Press.

Cullen, F.T., Jonson, C.L., and Nagin, D.S. (2011). Prisons do not reduce recidivism: The high cost of ignoring science. *The Prison Journal*, 91: 48S–65S.

Dauvergne, M. (2013). Youth court statistics in Canada, 2011/2012. *Juristat*, 33(1). Statistics Canada Catalogue No. 85-002-X. Retrieved 6 August 2013 from http://www.statcan.gc.ca/pub/85-002-x/2013001/article/11803-eng.pdf

Department of Justice Canada. (2013). *Youth records*. Ottawa: Author. Retrieved from http://www.justice.gc.ca/eng/cj-jp/yj-jj/tools-outils/sheets-feuillets/pdf/recor-dossi.pdf.

Doob, A., and Cesaroni, C. (2004). *Responding to youth crime in Canada*. Toronto: University of Toronto Press.

Doob, A.N., and Chan, J. (1982). Factors affecting police decisions to take juveniles to court. *Canadian Journal of Criminology*, 24: 25–37.

Evaluation Division, Office of Strategic Planning and Performance Management. (2010). *The Youth Justice Initiative funding components evaluation: Final report*. Ottawa: Department of Justice Canada. Retrieved from http://www.justice.gc.ca/eng/rp-pr/cp-pm/eval/rep-rap/11/yjifc-vfijj/yjifc-vfijj.pdf

Fazel, S., Doll, H., and Långström, N. (2008). Mental disorders among adolescents in juvenile detention and correctional facilities: A systematic review and metaregression analysis of 25 surveys. *Journal of the American Academy of Child & Adolescent Psychiatry*, 47: 1010–19.

Fischer, J. (2014, 24 October). Ten years later: The Neil Stonechild inquiry's affect on Saskatoon. *CTV News Saskatoon*. Retrieved from http://saskatoon.ctvnews.ca/ten-years-later-the-neil-stonechild-inquiry-s-affect-on-saskatoon-1.2070628#ixzz3L9XdffSw

Forgays, D.K. (2008). Three years of teen court offender outcomes. *Adolescence*, 43: 473–84.

Geck, C.M.R. (2012). *The Youth Screening Instrument: A psychometric evaluation with Canadian male youthful offenders*. Master's thesis, Carleton University, Ottawa.

Government of Canada. (2006). *International Convention on the Elimination of All Forms of Racial Discrimination, Seventeenth and Eighteenth Reports of Canada*. Gatineau, QC: Human Rights Program, Department of Canadian Heritage. Retrieved from http://publications.gc.ca/collections/Collection/CH37-4-10-2005E.pdf

Government of Canada. (2011). *International Convention on the Elimination of All Forms of Racial Discrimination, Nineteenth and Twentieth Reports of Canada*. Gatineau, QC: Human Rights Program, Department of Canadian Heritage. Retrieved from http://www.canadianheritage.gc.ca/DAMAssetPub/DAM-drtPrs-humRts/STAGING/texte-text/19-20_1362690863117_eng.pdf?WT.contentAuthority=3.1

Greene, C.T. (2011). *Creating consensus: An exploration of two pre-charge diversion programs in Canada*. Doctoral dissertation. Retrieved from University of Toronto, Open Access Theses and Dissertations.

Gretton, H.M., Arabsky, S., Rajlic, G., Clift, R.J.W., Catchpole, R., and Buchanan, T. (2007). *Violent Offender Treatment Program (VOTP): Outcome evaluation executive summary*. Burnaby, BC: Youth Forensic Psychiatric Services.

Gretton, H.M., and Clift, R.J. (2011). The mental health needs of incarcerated youth in British Columbia, Canada. *International Journal of Law and Psychiatry*, 34: 109–15. doi:10.1016/j.ijlp.2011.02.004

Grisso, T. (2008). Adolescent offenders with mental disorders. *Juvenile Justice, 18*: 143–64.

Hann & Associates. (2003). *A national survey of youth justice committees in Canada* (RR03YJ-7e). Ottawa: Department of Justice Canada. Retrieved from http://www.justice.gc.ca/eng/rp-pr/cj-jp/yj-jj/rr03_yj7-rr03_jj7/rr03_yj7.pdf

Hoge, R.D. (2005). Youth level of service/Case management inventory. In T. Grisso, G. Vincent, and D. Seagrave (Eds), *Mental health screening and assessment in juvenile justice* (pp. 283–94). New York: Guildford Press.

Gouvernement du Québec. (2009). *The Youth Criminal Justice Act: The legal procedure.* Justice Québec, Québec City. Retrieved from http://www.justice.gouv.qc.ca/english/publications/generale/projud-a.htm#sans

Katner, D.R. (2006). The mental health paradigm and the MacArthur Study: Emerging issues challenging the competence of juveniles in delinquency systems. *American Journal of Law & Medicine, 32*: 503–83.

Kempa, M. (2013, 28 June). Police street checks promote community safety? Prove it. *National Post.* Retrieved from http://fullcomment.nationalpost.com/2013/06/28/michael-kempa-police-street-checkspromote-community-safety-prove-it/

Kempf-Leonard, K. (2007). Disproportionate minority contact after nearly 20 years of reform efforts. *Youth Violence and Juvenile Justice, 5*: 71–87.

Kramer, U., and Zimmermann, G. (2008). Fear and anxiety as the basis of adolescent externalizing and internalizing behaviors: A case study. *International Journal of Offender Therapy and Comparative Criminology, 53*: 113–20.

Kuehn, S., and Corrado, R.R. (2011). Youth probation officers' interpretation and implementation of the Youth Criminal Justice Act: A case study of youth justice in Canada. *International Journal of Comparative and Applied Criminal Justice, 35*: 221–41.

LeGalbo, A.P., and Callahan, C.M. (2001). An evaluation of a teen court as a juvenile crime diversion program. *Juvenile and Family Court Journal, 52*(2): 1–11.

Lipsey, M.W., and Wilson, D.B. (1998). Effective intervention for serious juvenile offenders: A synthesis of research. In R. Loeber and D.P. Farrington (Eds), *Serious & violent juvenile offenders: Risk factors and successful interventions* (pp. 313–45). Thousand Oaks, CA: Sage.

McAra, L., and McVie, S. (2007). Youth justice? The impact of system contact on patterns of desistence from offending. *European Journal of Criminology, 4*: 315–45.

McGrath, A., and Thompson, A.P. (2012). The relative predictive validity of the static and dynamic domain scores in risk-need assessment of juvenile offenders. *Criminal Justice and Behavior, 39*: 250–63. doi:10.1177/0093854811431917

Marroney, G.A., Quinn, T., Kinney, E., and Hufford, S. (2010). *Colorado probation and evidence-based practices: A systemic view of the past, present & future of EBP in Colorado Probation: Progress report.* Denver: Colorado Division of Probation Services.

Moyer, S. (2005). *A comparison of case processing under the Young Offenders Act and the first six months of the Youth Criminal Justice Act.* Ottawa: Department of Justice Canada. Retrieved from http://www.justice.gc.ca/eng/rp-pr/cj-jp/yj-jj/pdf/compar.pdf

Munch, C. (2012). Youth correctional statistics in Canada, 2010/2011. *Juristat, 32*(1). Statistics Canada Catalogue No. 85-002-X. Retrieved 16 October 2013 from http://www.statcan.gc.ca/pub/85-002-x/2012001/article/11716-eng.pdf

Odgers, C.L., Burnette, M.L., Chauhan, P., Moretti, M.M., and Reppucci, D. (2005). Misdiagnosing the problem: Mental health profiles of incarcerated juveniles. *Canadian Child and Adolescent Psychiatry Review, 14*: 26–9.

Office of the Auditor General of Ontario. (2012). *2012 annual report of the Office of the Auditor General of Ontario: Youth justice services program.* Toronto: Author. Retrieved from http://www.auditor.on.ca/en/reports_en/en12/2012ar_en.pdf

Olver, M.E., Stockdale, K.C., and Wormith, J.S. (2009). Risk assessment with young offenders: A meta-analysis of three assessment measures. *Criminal Justice and Behavior, 36*: 329–53.

Penner, E.K., Roesch, R., and Viljoen, J.L. (2011). Young offenders in custody: An international comparison of mental health services. *International Journal of Forensic Mental Health, 10*: 215–32.

Pozzulo, J., Bennell, C., and Forth, A. (2009). *Forensic psychology* (2nd ed.). Toronto: Pearson Education.

Rankin, J. (2012, 22 March). Known to police: No need for review of Toronto police contacts with "racialized" youth, act now, says watchdog group. *The Star*. Retrieved from http://www.thestar.com/news/gta/2012/03/22/known_to_police_no_need_for_review_of_toronto_police_contacts_with_racialized_youth_act_now_says_watchdog_group.html

Roberts, J.V. (2003). Sentencing juvenile offenders in Canada: An analysis of recent reform legislation. *Journal of Contemporary Criminal Justice, 19*: 413–34. doi:10.1177/1043986203259124

Roberts, J.V., and Bala, N. (2003). Understanding sentencing under the Youth Criminal Justice Act. *Alberta Law Review, 41*(2): 395–423.

Satzewich, V., and Shaffir, W. (2009). Racism versus professionalism: Claims and counter-claims about racial profiling. *Canadian Journal of Criminology and Criminal Justice, 51*: 199–226.

Savarese, J.L. (2015). Moving forward & standing still: Assessing restorative based justice in Saskatchewan after the Youth Criminal Justice Act. In A. Alain, R. Corrado, and S. Reid (Eds), *Implementing and working with the Youth Criminal Justice Act across Canada*. Toronto: University of Toronto Press.

Savignac, J. (2010). *Tools to identify and assess the risk of offending among youth*. Ottawa: National Crime Prevention Centre, Public Safety Canada. Retrieved from http://www.publicsafety.gc.ca/cnt/rsrcs/pblctns/tls-dntf-rsk-rprt/tls-dntf-rsk-rprt-eng.pdf

Sedlak, A.J. (2009). Surveying youths in custody. *Corrections Today, 71*: 92–4.

Serin, R.C., Gobeil, R., and Preston, D.L. (2009). Evaluation of the persistently violent offender treatment program. *International Journal of Offender Therapy and Comparative Criminology, 53*: 57–73.

Skeem, J.L., and Manchak, S. (2008). Back to the future: From Klockars' model of effective supervision to evidence-based practice in probation. *Journal of Offender Rehabilitation, 47*: 220–47. doi:10.1080/10509670802134069

Teplin, L.A., Abram, K.M., McClelland, G.M., Mericle, A.A., Dulcan, M.K., and Washburn, J.J. (2006). *Psychiatric disorders of youth in detention*. Washington: Office of Juvenile Justice and Delinquency Prevention, Office of Justice Programs, U.S. Department of Justice.

Trépanier, J. (2004). What did Quebec not want? Opposition to the adoption of the Youth Criminal Justice Act in Quebec. *Canadian Journal of Criminology and Criminal Justice, 46*: 273–96.

Viljoen, J.L., Elkovitch, N., Scalora, M.J., and Ullman, D. (2009). Assessment of reoffense risk in adolescents who have committed sexual offenses: Predictive validity of the ERASOR, PCL:YV, YLS/CMI, and Static-99. *Criminal Justice and Behavior, 36*: 981–1000. doi:10.1177/0093854809340991

Vincent, G.M., Guy, L.S., Gershenson, B.G., and McCabe, P. (2012). Does risk assessment make a difference? Results of implementing the SAVRY in juvenile probation. *Behavioral Sciences and the Law, 30*: 384–405. doi:10.1002/bsl.2014

Wemmers, J., and Cyr, K. (2005). Can mediation be therapeutic for crime victims? An evaluation of victims' experiences in mediation with young offenders. *Canadian Journal of Criminology and Criminal Justice, 47*: 527–44.

Wortley, S., and Tanner, J. (2003). Data, denials, and confusion: The racial profiling debate in Toronto. *Canadian Journal of Criminology and Criminal Justice, 45*: 367–89.

Wortley, S., and Tanner, J. (2005). Inflammatory rhetoric? Baseless accusations? A response to Gabor's critique of racial profiling research in Canada. *Canadian Journal of Criminology and Criminal Justice, 47*: 581–609.

Wright, D.H. (Honourable Justice). (2004). *Report of the Commission of Inquiry into Matters Relating to the Death of Neil Stonechild*. Retrieved from http://www.justice.gov.sk.ca/stonechild/finalreport/Stonechild.pdf

Young, D.W., Dembo, R., and Henderson, C.E. (2007). A national survey of substance abuse treatment for juvenile offenders. *Journal of Substance Abuse Treatment, 32*: 255–66.

Statutes Cited

Criminal Code, RSC 1985, c. C-46.
Safe Streets and Communities Act, S.C. 2012, c. 1.
Youth Criminal Justice Act, S.C. 2002, c. 1.

Part II

Understanding Contemporary Youth Crime and Justice: Theories and Perspectives

There are many different ways one can approach attempting to develop an understanding of youth crime and justice in today's society. What most people believe about youth crime and youth justice is likely based on a variety of sources (e.g., mass media, authority, tradition, personal experience, and common sense) that are not necessarily scientifically based yet serve to inform us about social issues. While these methods might serve us well personally, they risk the problems of overgeneralization and selective observation and, therefore, have been viewed with skepticism by most criminologists, who, depending on their training, prefer instead to rely on a wide range of disciplinary and theoretical perspectives. In this part, we present five chapters that collectively highlight and contrast the different approaches that have been taken in society and among criminologists to try to understand youth crime and justice today.

In Chapter 5, Susan Reid and Sarah Gilliss offer a perspective on the importance of maintaining a separate system of youth justice while at the same time giving youth themselves more of a voice in youth justice policy and practice. Referring to national legislation and the United Nations Convention on the Rights of the Child, the authors present a strong case for why we need to oppose the trend toward treating youth more like adults in the criminal justice system. In addition, they examine the key challenges faced in attempting to address the needs of youth at risk and young persons who are already caught up in the criminal justice system. Based on this examination, they argue that there is no one ideal way of trying to address the needs of youth at risk and young offenders. This is especially the case, given that many of these youth display different patterns of highly complex emotional, personal, physical, and social needs. In light of this, they conclude that what is needed most is an approach based on principles of effective youth crime prevention and correctional treatment that can be used to direct programs at youth at risk and young offenders who can benefit most from crime prevention and correctional interventions. According to Reid and Gilliss, the key to developing such programs is for adults to work as partners with young people in a supportive manner that provides young people with a chance for meaningful participation and a voice in developing youth-focused policy both within and outside of the criminal justice system.

Most people have no training in criminology or direct experience with the youth justice system and learn what they know about these topics from the media, including both traditional print and electronic media, such as newspapers and television, and more recent media like the Internet. In Chapter 6, Chris McCormick provides a thoughtful analysis of the role of the media in producing knowledge about youth crime and justice. He contrasts this with other ways of learning about reported and unreported youth crime, including official statistics and self-report studies. McCormick critically argues that while most people, including criminologists, tend to privilege "one way of knowing youth crime over the other," it is more useful and valuable to look at a variety of information sources, including the media, statistics, and self-report studies, as complementary but different ways of making sense of youth crime. McCormick's chapter is particularly unique in that it critiques the work of criminologists and media sociologists who tend to either ignore or discount the important role played by the media in contributing to the public debate over crime and justice issues generally and over youth crime and justice more specifically. In essence, McCormick points out that the media provide a crucial public arena in which youth crime and the justice system are debated and that, as such, the media contribute to a different way of understanding youth crime and justice than that offered through the more narrow study of official crime statistics or self-report studies.

Other ways that criminologists have attempted to learn more about youth crime and justice are, first, through carrying out research with the aim of developing formal, testable theories of juvenile delinquency and youth crime, and, second, through developing critical theoretical insights on the operation of youth justice agencies and practices. In Chapter 7, Lorinda Stoneman and Sibylle Artz combine these approaches by providing an overview of traditional and contemporary theories of female crime, along with a critical analysis of the failure of the Canadian youth justice system to address adequately the needs of girls who come into conflict with the law. Stoneman and Artz cover the wide variety of theories that have been used to try to explain female crime and delinquency, ranging from early biological and more recent biopsychosocial theories focused on the individual, to more sociologically based strain, control, and gender role theories. The authors also discuss promising directions that are now being taken to more adequately theorize the causes of female crime and delinquency and to more effectively intervene in the lives of girls who are at risk of becoming involved in crime. Particular attention is given to developing an "intersectional" approach for guiding interventions that addresses the unique circumstances faced by girls and their complex and varied pathways toward delinquent behaviour and involvement in the criminal justice system. According to Stoneman and Artz, one of the reasons for the continuing failure of social agencies and the youth justice system to adequately address the needs of at-risk and "delinquent" girls has been the lack of sensitivity to the manner in which variables like age, gender, race, class, ethnicity, and sexuality intersect in shaping the life circumstances and behaviour of individuals. In addition, the authors suggest that the failure of even well-intended social agencies and youth justice workers to develop an awareness of these types of complex "demographic intersections" leads to piecemeal and typically overly punitive approaches to dealing with female youth crime.

In Chapter 8, Stephen Baron examines a number of more recent theoretical perspectives that have been offered to help explain and understand youth crime. Particular attention is given to recent sociologically based control, strain, and coercion theories that have attempted to improve on the earlier theories discussed by Stoneman and Artz in Chapter 7. While some of these new perspectives, like Gottfredson and Hirschi's general theory of crime, build on specific earlier theories, others, like Sampson and Laub's age-graded theory and Tittle's control balance theory, attempt to bring together or integrate a number of the previously examined perspectives to create new explanations of criminal behaviour. Baron provides a systematic examination of the main causal factors identified by each theory, the key research studies that have been carried out to test the amount of empirical support for each theory, and the extent to which these theories complement or conflict with one another. Baron's review of these recent theoretical perspectives on youth crime shows the variety of ways in which positivist-oriented criminologists, who believe in the need for scientifically rigorous theory formulation and testing, have approached the topic. Baron concludes that to successfully understand youth crime, we must identify and include ideas from a range of complementary theoretical perspectives that help to better explain the causal process of youth crime, thus allowing for a more complex and nuanced understanding of how youth crime emerges and evolves.

In Chapter 9, Bryan Hogeveen and Joanne Minaker contribute to the discussion by offering a series of insights on youth crime and the operation of the youth justice system from the perspective of critical criminology. Hogeveen and Minaker argue that while mainstream positivist criminology has tended to focus attention on the "causes, consequences, and control of youth crime," critical criminology attempts to unmask the structural inequalities that marginalize young people and thereby contribute to their behaviours being criminalized and dealt with through various agencies of governmental control, including the youth justice system. For example, critical criminologists have begun to show how social inequalities linked to age, class, race, and gender work to "structure the life chances of the marginalized other—Aboriginal youth, the poor, and racial minorities—and translate into overrepresentation in the contemporary youth justice system." Consequently, rather than thinking of youth crime as freely chosen behaviour on the part of youth that can therefore be simply deterred through the threat of punishment, critical criminologists like Hogeveen and Minaker link the criminalization of youth to "systemic conditions of marginalization, exclusion, and social inequality" and advocate forms of "social justice praxis" that are "dedicated to making meaningful changes to improve the life chances of young people." In their chapter, Hogeveen and Minaker offer an engaging introduction to key concepts, theories, and practical experiences that are informing the efforts now being undertaken by critical criminologists in promoting justice for Canadian youth.

Key Challenges in Hearing the Voice of Youth in the Youth Justice System

Susan A. Reid and Sarah Gilliss

5

Overview

This chapter analyzes the ongoing debate about maintaining a separate system of youth justice versus promoting the "adulteration" of youth by treating them as adult criminals. First, it focuses attention on the articles within the United Nations (UN) Convention on the Rights of the Child that point to the importance of giving youth a voice in decisions that affect them. Second, it provides an overview of some innovative youth-led program initiatives inside youth custodial institutions that reflect these principles. In light of recent Canadian cases and research on crime prevention programs, the chapter offers a discussion of what works with youth at risk and youth with highly complex needs. The chapter considers the importance of the needs of the young person as well as the relationships that develop between youth and the adults responsible for their care, rehabilitation, and reintegration.

Key Objectives

After reading this chapter, you should be able to:

* Understand the difference between what works and what does not work for youth-at-risk programming.
* Understand the principles behind a separate system of justice for youth.
* Understand the challenges faced by youth with complex needs in the youth criminal justice system.
* Understand the importance of recognizing the articles of the UN Convention on the Rights of the Child in hearing the voice of youth in all matters.
* Consider how young persons in conflict with the law may contribute to their own rehabilitation and reintegration through supportive adult–youth relationships.

Introduction

The chapters that make up this volume draw attention to the myriad issues that are involved in the implementation of youth justice in Canada. This chapter is intended to draw attention to the positive developments in the juvenile justice policy field as well as to some of the challenges that are still ahead as we continue to draw on our research and evidence of the most appropriate means of intervening in the lives of troubled youth. In particular, this chapter focuses on the inclusion of the voice of young people in decisions that affect them.

The Legal Regulation of Childhood and Adolescence

The law that regulates criminal conduct for children and youth is based on a binary system, where the state focuses on the protection of children until such time as they cross the threshold, known as the *age of majority*, to adulthood. Prior to the age of majority, children and youth receive the protection of the state in the form of restrictions on their freedom and investment in their development with the intent that such policies will pay dividends in terms of the promotion of competent adults as productive members of society. While there is variation in the upper age jurisdiction of the youth court throughout the world, the age of majority assumes that the individual in question has reached a period in their development wherein they can be seen as fully autonomous individuals who are responsible for their actions (see Winterdyk 2015). The problem with this binary system, which focuses only on *immature children* and *competent adults*, is that there is no opportunity to include the evolving capacities of children as they mature during their adolescent years. However, adolescents' capacity for self-regulation in situations that are emotionally charged is considerably less than that of adults. Similarly, young people's capacity for future-oriented decision-making is also less than that of their adult counterparts. Youth are more sensitive to peer pressure and immediate incentives than adults, and this has a dramatic impact on their likelihood of engaging in high-risk behaviours (Skeem, Scott, and Mulvey 2014).

Where there have been changes to the age of consent, these policies have been put in place to allow for changing capacities of young people based on the notion that social welfare and the welfare of the young person can both benefit through such a reclassification. One example is related to the age of consent for a minor vis-à-vis medical treatment. If the age of consent is lowered, there is a benefit to the young person and to the larger community in the form of reduced health costs associated with pregnancy, sexually transmitted disease, and other social welfare costs. In the case of **youth justice**, however, the rationale for lowering the age is not focused on the promotion of the welfare of youth. Rather, treating a youth like an adult for the purposes of criminal responsibility is more a reflection of societal values as reflected in the adage "adult crime equals adult time." Moreover, a number of juvenile justice statutes undermine the principle of confidentiality in youth justice proceedings by increasing the number of opportunities to share information about the youth defendant with criminal justice, education, and social service agencies, and the media. This punitive stance has been underscored by such repressive policies as zero tolerance, curfews, and naming and shaming rituals.

The **best interests of the child** doctrine, which is a key principle of the UN Declaration on the Rights of the Child (UNCRC), appear to be in direct opposition to an increasing trend toward the **adulteration** of youth crime throughout the world. Internationally, there are now provisions in juvenile criminal statutes that provide for the transfer of youth who commit criminal offences to the adult system, either for adjudication or for punishment. Research evidence is clear, however, that increased criminal justice processing of youth runs counter to the reduction of youth crime. Further, imposing adult penalties and including young people in adult prisons have led to serious problems for young people, as evidenced in New Brunswick with the case of Ashley Smith (see Box 5.1 below).

The Codification of a Separate System of Youth Justice in Canada

In 1985, the UN Standard Minimum Rules for the Administration of Youth Justice, known as the Beijing Rules, recognized the special needs of young people and the promotion of diversion from court proceedings. Further, these standards underscored the principle that custody should be used as a last resort for children and that all proceedings against young people should be anonymous in order to protect children from lifelong stigma and **labelling**. The UNCRC expanded on these rules and was proclaimed in 1989. The UNCRC has been ratified in more than 190 countries and reiterates that children have a right to be protected from degrading and cruel punishment and to receive special treatment in the justice system. Further, it states that children below a minimum age shall be presumed to lack the capacity to infringe the penal law.

The UNCRC states in Article 3 that "[i]n all actions concerning children and the courts of law, the best interests of the child shall be a primary consideration." Article 40 requires

youth justice
A separate and distinct criminal justice system that explicitly meets the unique needs of young people.

best interests of the child
When the interests of a young person are paramount in decision-making regarding his or her experience in the criminal justice system.

adulteration
The dismantling of a distinct system of criminal justice for youth and the re-merging with systems of justice for adults.

labelling
The stigmatization of a young person as deviant.

| Box 5.1 | Youth Justice in Action |

Ashley Smith

Ashley Smith, a 19-year-old woman from Moncton, New Brunswick, died on 19 October 2007 while in federal custody at Ontario's Grand Valley Institution. Ashley had spent three years in and out of the New Brunswick Youth Centre (NBYC), which is the only **secure custody** institution in the province. During those three years, Ashley spent two-thirds of her time in segregation—that is, in solitary confinement in an 8-by-10 cell for more or less 23 hours a day, with lights on 24 hours a day. Ashley's trouble with the law began in March 2002, at the age of 14, with offences related to public disturbances, trespass or violence (harassing telephone calls to unknown persons, assaulting strangers on the streets, and insulting passengers and drivers on public transportation). Ashley was referred by the province's Youth Treatment Program team for a 34-day assessment at a six-bed residential program, the Pierre Caissie Centre, in Moncton. The psychiatrist ruled out depression but added "narcissistic personality traits" to an addendum to the report. The psychiatric assessment stated under the category of "diagnostic impressions" that Ashley suffered from "learning disorder, ADHD, borderline personality disorder." The assessment recommended that her parents receive counselling sessions on how to deal with an "oppositional defiant youth" and that everyone work together in dealing with Ashley's behaviour. While she was at the assessment centre, her behaviour escalated and the police were called twice for her assaults on staff. She was remanded to NBYC for one month where she incurred a number of institutional charges for not following orders and threatening self-harm. In less than three months, Ashley was in and out of the NBYC five times. She would be released on community supervision and then either breach her conditions or commit a new offence, which would send her back to remand at the youth jail. She spent approximately three years in the youth jail and during that time there were hundreds of institutional charges, 50 criminal charges, and over 150 self-harm incidents.

With the promise of more gender-specific programming and therapeutic mental health treatment offered through the Correctional Services of Canada, the provincial director made an application under section 92 of the YCJA to transfer Ashley to the adult system. During the one year she was housed in the federal system, she spent all of her time in administrative segregation and was transferred 17 times between three federal penitentiaries, two treatment facilities, two external hospitals, and one provincial correctional facility in four different provinces. The coroner's report revealed that Ashley died as a result of asphyxiation: she did place a ligature around her neck, but she did not intend to die.

After Smith's death, Bernard Richard, the New Brunswick provincial ombudsman and child and youth advocate, launched an investigation into her death at the urging of Smith's mother. Richard released *The Ashley Smith Report* in 2008, which put forth 25 recommendations to "revamp" the youth criminal justice system in order to take full advantage of the provisions of the Youth Criminal Justice Act. Richard argued that "youth who commit *punishable acts* but who are not, themselves, forcibly *punishable*" (Child and Youth Advocate 2008b, p. 8) should not be held in closed-custody facilities. Ashley, he concluded, fell under this category.

A high-profile coroner's inquest returned a verdict on this case on 19 December 2013 ruling that Ashley's death was a homicide. The report provided over 100 recommendations detailing the need for a careful overhaul of the correctional system and its treatment of female young adult offenders, the treatment protocols for inmates presenting with mental health challenges, and clearer guidelines for administration and training (Reid 2013a).

Critical Thinking Question

Article 40 of the UN Convention on the Rights of the Child requires that children who have violated the penal law be treated in a manner consistent with the child's age and with the desirability of promoting the child's reintegration and his or her taking up a constructive role in society. Was this article followed in the case of Ashley Smith?

---

secure custody
A form of custody under the YCJA whereby youth are removed from a community and confined to an institution.

reintegration
The introduction of the young person back into the community after a custodial sentence as a productive member of society.

that children who have violated the penal law be treated in a manner consistent with the child's age and the desirability of promoting the child's **reintegration** and his or her taking up a constructive role in society. The UN Convention further underscores socio-educational interventions and diversion from criminal proceedings and extrajudicial solutions. It recommends deprivation of liberty only as a last resort when dealing with young people who offend.

The UNCRC has laudable objectives in its principles and articles, and it is the most ratified of all human rights instruments, but it is also perhaps the most violated of the human rights treaties. Breaching the provisions of the UNCRC does not lead to any formal sanction. Canada's international obligations to all children who have committed offences support a presumption that young offenders are not to be treated like adults. However, Canada has continually violated the spirit of the UNCRC by insisting on a reservation under Article 34 with respect to the rule about housing adults and youth in separate facilities (Winterdyk 2015).

Although Canada has had a formal system of youth justice that has been separate and apart from the adult justice system since the proclamation of the Juvenile Delinquents Act (JDA) in 1908, it was not until the Youth Criminal Justice Act (YCJA) expressly stated in section 3(1)(b) that "the criminal justice system for young persons must be separate from that of adults," that Canada was explicit in its law that there were two distinct systems of justice. Prior to this time, Canada did not expressly adhere to the UNCRC, even though Canada had ratified it in 1991.

Diverting Children from a Life of Crime: Sustaining the Original Purpose of a Separate System of Youth Justice

If we consider the origins of the juvenile justice system in North America, at the turn of the century the "child savers," as they were known, attempted to divert young people from the harshness of the adult system (see Chapter 1). The years that followed the enactment of the Juvenile Delinquents Act of 1908 have been replete with arguments for policy changes that centre on the culpability of children as criminals (see Chapters 1 and 3).

The JDA was marked by a singular approach focusing on social welfare concerns with a strong emphasis on the "best interests" doctrine of child welfare and protection hearings. As more attention was drawn to the inequities of justice that were being meted out in the youth court, there was a call for more procedural safeguards. Equally, adults began to question whether or not the "discipline" of the youth court was sufficient to provide the community with protection from the sometimes heinous acts of young people. This "care" versus "control" argument has been the mainstay of the controversy surrounding the most suitable way to handle youth in conflict with the law since the mid-1960s and the release of a pivotal discussion document, *Juvenile Delinquency in Canada* (Canada 1965).

While the successor of the JDA heralded a change in youth justice with the elimination of social welfare concerns under the YOA, there were still a number of provisions within the legislation that recommended that alternatives to the court system—albeit a mitigated accountability court system—were to be preferred for first-time, minor offenders. The implementation of the YOA, with its contrary goals of **rehabilitation** and the protection of society, led to an increased use of the youth court and to an even greater use of **custodial sanctions**

rehabilitation
A fundamental concept of the Youth Criminal Justice Act that holds that a young person can be reformed or changed as a result of appropriate treatment programs.

custodial sanctions
Under the Youth Criminal Justice Act, the sentencing of a young person to custody.

than had been experienced under the former legislation. As Tustin and Lutes (2008, p. 2) point out, "Instead of promoting the use of diversionary programs to keep young people out of custody, the introduction of the YOA increased the use of custody to the point where Canada had the highest rate of youth incarceration in the western world."

In 1997, a federal/provincial/territorial task force was established by the then ministers responsible for justice to complete a review of the former legislation, the YOA, to assist and complement the work of the then Standing Committee on Justice and Legal Affairs in their efforts to improve the youth justice system. The group determined at that time that there were six broad priority areas to be addressed, with *diversion* being seen as an important part (Canada 1996). In 1998, the Department of Justice released its *Strategy for the Renewal of Youth Justice*, which underscored the need for "crime prevention" and "meaningful consequences" for youth who came in conflict with the law. Between 1998 and 2002, the YCJA was introduced and reintroduced with a series of amendments to be proclaimed in April 2003.

Across Canada, the YCJA has had the effect of reducing the number of young people who have been sentenced to custody. The focus is on alternatives to the formal system while reserving the youth court for the small number of serious and persistent offenders. In 2012, with increasing calls for the protection of the public from this small number of serious offenders, a series of amendments were passed under the Safe Streets and Communities Act, which clarified the definition of serious violent offences and provided for the imposition of adult sentences in such cases (see Chapter 3). While a number of the amendments were aimed at strengthening the youth court system with a singular view of crime control and public safety, the essence of the legislation still retains a focus on the diversion of the majority of young people in conflict with the law out of the formal criminal justice system. Early prevention and intervention through school networks, through communities, and with the assistance of families helps to avoid stigma and labelling and may be the most suitable alternative for the majority of young people who offend. Keeping youth in their community allows for a "holistic intervention approach" focused on identifying individual, family, and community risks and strengths and treating them comprehensively (Sullivan, Veysey, Hamilton, and Grillo 2007).

There will always be, however, a small number of young people who are persistent offenders and who require a range of multidisciplinary assistance set within a clear path over a fairly substantial period of time. Arguably, we make our biggest mistake when we provide intensive treatments to our low-risk offenders and set them off on a trajectory of net widening and further entrenchment within the system.

The YCJA is based on research that shows that incarcerating young people can do more harm than good and that our most successful interventions should involve less criminal justice processing for the majority of offenders who present as low-risk, low-need offenders. Petrosino, Turpin-Petrosino, and Guckenburg (2010) in their meta-analysis of 29 studies that assessed the impact of juvenile justice system processing of 7300 juvenile offenders over a 35-year period concluded that not only does formal processing of juveniles appear not to control crime, it actually seems to increase it on all measures studied. A meta-analysis of diversion programs conducted by Wilson and Hoge (2013) found that those programs that were primarily police caution programs were most effective in reducing recidivism for low-risk offenders compared to programs that provided some form of intervention. They report that "low risk youth referred to caution programs were 2.44 times less likely to reoffend," while the same low risk youth that were referred to an intervention program were only "1.49 times less likely to reoffend."

For these reasons, the YCJA places increased emphasis on extrajudicial measures to respond appropriately to youth while keeping them out of the justice system and on non-custodial sentences for those youth who are formally charged and found guilty. Custodial sentences are seen as a measure of last resort for the highest-risk offenders.

Challenges Faced by Youth with Highly Complex Needs

In the fall of 2004, a high-speed police chase involving a young offender in a stolen vehicle led to the tragic death of Theresa McEvoy when the car she was driving was struck by a vehicle driven by the fleeing youth. Given the prior youth record of the young person and the fact that he had been released on judicial interim release two days prior to the fatal incident, the Nova Scotia government called for a public inquiry and appointed a retired justice of the Nova Scotia Supreme Court, Hon. D. Merlin Nunn, as the commissioner. The Nunn Commission resulted in a 381-page report that provided a series of 34 recommendations with respect to youth justice administration and accountability, youth crime legislation, and the prevention of youth crime.

The first recommendation was that there should be additional training and adequate funding for assessment and early intervention in the education system for children and youth with learning disabilities and other mental and psychological disabilities that may increase the likelihood of their coming into conflict with the law (Nunn 2005). This recommendation was based on research presented to the commission that found that approximately 80 per cent of repeat young offenders were living with disabilities, including mental health disabilities (ibid., p. 269).

In Canada, statistics indicate that only one in five children who need mental health services receives them and the majority of young adults living with mental illness report that their problems began in childhood (CMHA 2014). Indeed, research has shown that young offenders experience high levels of mental health issues (Kapp, Petr, Robbins, and Choi 2013), and despite these high levels, they are not having their treatment needs met (Whitted, Delavega, and Lennon-Dearing 2013; Liebenberg and Ungar 2014). A study of 152 youth who were involved with either the youth justice system or the mental health system found that youth who were referred from the mental health sector accessed significantly higher rates of service not only from health care and mental health but also through school support structures than their youth justice counterparts (Liebenberg and Ungar 2014). Further, according to the study, a lack of engagement with treatment service providers has always been problematic for young offenders. This lack of service is particularly disconcerting in that youth who have been diagnosed with multiple mental health disorders are more likely to offend than those without such challenges and have a higher likelihood of recidivism (Hoeve, McReynolds, and Wasserman 2013; Espinosa, Sorensen, and Lopez 2013).

In 2002, the state of Texas implemented a Special Needs Diversionary Program (SNDP) for youth sentenced to formal probation who presented with a minor offence and diagnosed mental disorders. Evans-Cuellar, McReynolds, and Wasserman (2006) compared 148 youth who were referred to the program over a one-year period with a group of youth who met the eligibility criteria but were placed on a waiting list for the program. The most common mental disorder for the combined sample was substance abuse disorder (38.8 per cent), disruptive disorder (38.1 per cent), anxiety disorder (32.1 per cent), and affective disorder (18.4 per cent). The results indicated that more than half of the youth with mental disorders were re-arrested within one year. However, the individuals who were enrolled in SNDP had lower probabilities of re-arrest (0.86) than their peers who were not enrolled (1.54). Over a one-year period, the researchers found 63 fewer arrests occurred per 100 youth served. In terms of responding to the complex needs of young people, this research provided evidence of not only the need for additional services given the large number of youth who were placed on the waiting list for services, but also the impact of providing targeted mental health treatment for youth with mental health challenges.

Programs applying the theory of *therapeutic jurisprudence* have been developed that attempt to respond to youth with complex needs (Winick 2003). The main goal of therapeutic jurisprudence is to bring together the law with a variety of therapeutic techniques while still allowing other values, such as justice and due process, to be fully respected. Mental health courts, drug courts, and other "problem-solving" courts have been created in an attempt to combine the goals of justice and the therapeutic needs of the accused (Madell, Thom, and McKenna 2013). Mental health courts and mental health diversion programs are designed to be treatment-oriented and are based on the assumption that for certain types of individuals, problem-solving responses are more appropriate than punishment (Wexler 2000; Madell et al. 2013). The intent of such specialized services is to improve coordination across justice and social service agencies, improve efficiency, increase predictability of the court proceedings, and ultimately improve the quality of justice (Gilbert, Grimm, and Parnham 2001). Skowyra and Powell (2006) argue that many youth with significant mental health issues are in the justice system for relatively minor offences and are placed in jail by default. The provision of diversion for youth with mental health needs not only provides more effective and appropriate treatment but also facilitates the further development of community-based mental health services. Further, reviews of the research on such programs has pointed to the improvement in working relationships of cross-systems groups, an expedited court processing of youth into appropriate services, and a greater likelihood of encouraging family participation in treatment plans (Wiener et al. 2010).

Skowyra and Cocozza (2007), in their *Blueprint for Change*, outline a "comprehensive model for the identification and treatment of youth with mental health needs in contact with the youth justice system." They have set out the following underlying principles:

Guiding Principles:

1. Youth should not have to enter the juvenile justice system solely in order to access mental health services or because of their mental illness.
2. Whenever possible and when matters of public safety allow, youth with mental health needs should be diverted from the juvenile justice system into evidence-based treatment in a community setting.

3. If diversion out of the juvenile justice system is not possible, youth should be placed in the least restrictive setting possible, with access to evidence-based treatment.

4. Information collected as part of a pre-adjudicatory mental health screen should not be used in any way that might jeopardize the legal interests of youth as defendants.

5. All mental health services provided to youth in contact with the juvenile justice system should respond to issues of gender, ethnicity, race, age, sexual orientation, socio-economic status, and faith.

6. Mental health services should meet the developmental realities of youth. Children and adolescents are not simply little adults.

7. Whenever possible, families and/or caregivers should be partners in the development of treatment decisions and plans made for their children.

8. Multiple systems bear responsibility for these youth. While at different times, a single agency may have primary responsibility, these youth are the community's responsibility, and all responses developed for these youth should be collaborative in nature, reflecting the input and involvement of the mental health, juvenile justice and other systems.

9. Services and strategies aimed at improving the identification and treatment of youth with mental health needs in the juvenile justice system should be routinely evaluated to determine their effectiveness in meeting desired goals and outcomes. (p. 11)

Based on these principles, consider the case of Ashley Smith and ask yourself what might have been put in place at the early stages of her involvement in the youth justice system to alter the course of events that led to her death in an adult penitentiary (see Box 5.1).

While a disproportionate number of young people within the criminal justice system have mental health challenges, this does not mean that mental illness "causes" criminal behaviours that result in incarceration. While psychological conditions are related to the poor functioning of those who struggle with mental illness in the community, the main predictors of criminal behaviour and violence are a criminal history, anti-social personality, anti-social cognitions, and anti-social peers. Individuals with mental illness and those who do not suffer from mental illness may equally possess these risk factors (Skeem, Manchak, and Peterson 2011). This will be taken up in the next section following a discussion of the programs that do not seem to work to reduce offender recidivism.

What Does *Not* Work?

The evaluation process determining whether a particular prevention program works at all, let alone works well, is difficult because many factors contribute to criminal behaviour. One leading scholar in the field has suggested that, in designing our policies and programs for youth who find themselves within the youth justice system, we should, above all, "do no harm" (Layton-MacKenzie 2013, p. 1). Since the mid-late 1990s, programs have been designed that focus on restricting the activities of convicted offenders so that they would not be able to continue their criminal activities. Incapacitation can be achieved through close monitoring of an individual through intensive supervision, electronic monitoring, and incarceration. Other programs were created with a clear focus on deterrence whereby the punishments were seen as so onerous that the individual would not want to continue this kind of behaviour in the future. Examples of such programs include shock incarceration or boot camps. Similarly, some programs have been developed for young offenders with the premise that they can be deterred from serious crime by being subjected to a "scared-straight" program; for example, they could be frightened by a tour through a maximum-security prison and the chance to talk to inmates serving long sentences.

The research evidence shows that programs that increase the severity of punishment do not reduce recidivism (MacKenzie 2006; Lipsey and Cullen 2007). In fact, aversive sanctions and supervision programs may increase future criminal behaviour as has been shown in studies of scared-straight programs (Petrosino, Turpin-Petrosino, and Buehler 2003; Guerra and Williams 2012) and boot camps (Cullen, Blevins, Trager, and Gendreau 2005; Meade and Steiner 2010). The failure of programs that focus on punishment without producing a rehabilitative benefit have been referred to in the profession by Latessa, Cullen, and Gendreau (2002) as "correctional quackery."

What Works? Addressing Risk Factors

It has become almost common knowledge that in order to understand youth offending, one must look at a range of factors, broadly grouped as individual factors, family factors, school factors, and community factors. Research to date suggests that individual characteristics include such things as impulsivity, anti-social attitudes, continued contact with anti-social peers, and alcohol and other drug abuse (see Chapter 10). Family factors include such things as parenting styles, inconsistent and harsh discipline, parental criminality, and poor parental supervision. Truancy, poor academic performance, a lack of school engagement, and aggressive behaviour at school have been shown to relate to youth offending. Finally, disorganized communities, the availability of drugs and alcohol, and a lack of amenities such as access to sports, leisure, and other activities are factors that contribute to a lack of belonging and an increased risk for youth crime. It is not uncommon that youth will have multiple **risk factors**, and the cumulative risk factors sometimes make it difficult to untangle the effects of individual risk factors (Loeber and Farrington 1998). The more problems a youth has, the more difficult it becomes to address his or her needs. To do so, it is important to first identify potential sources of problem behaviour and then address these problems with a package of services aimed at the individual's needs.

risk factors
Factors that may cause a young person to be more likely to offend. These factors can be individual, environmental, etc.

Individual characteristics such as impulsivity, low empathy, poor internalized norms, and attitudes supporting offending may indeed be factors that foster anti-social behaviour, but they are often long-term problems and not easily changed. However, some factors are situational and short term and may be amenable to intervention; these include boredom, frustration, alcohol, or drug misuse, status with peers, and the perceived costs and benefits of offending (Farrington 1996). Andrews refers to such intermediate factors as **criminogenic** needs, which, if targeted appropriately, can result in effective outcomes

criminogenic
Producing or tending to produce crime or criminals.

(Andrews and Bonta 2010). Such needs when tied to effective outcomes include the following:

- Changing anti-social attitudes and feelings through cognitive-behavioural programming

- Reducing the number and opportunities for anti-social peer associations

- Fostering and promoting family affection, communication, monitoring, and supervision

- Increasing self-control, self-management, and problem-solving skills

- Finding and maintaining positive social role models

- Ensuring that the offender is able to recognize "risky" situations and has concrete and well-rehearsed plans for dealing with those types of situations and circumstances

- Confronting and working toward changing the personal and circumstantial barriers that are in the way of effective outcomes

However, when considering the effectiveness of any program, it is essential that we look at the unpredictability of even evidenced-based programs as a "one-size-fits-all" solution. The same structured program may work in different ways in different circumstances, and sometimes it will not work at all.

How to Make "What Works" Common Practice

Lösel (2011) suggests that the literature on "what works" has progressed to include ways to make these principles work in routine practice and effective program delivery. Elements include the program design, the curriculum and content, the context of delivery of the program, and the characteristics of the individuals involved in the program. Effective programs appear to have the following characteristics:

- They are designed to target crime-related characteristics that can be changed (dynamic factors) and that are predictive of future criminal activities.

- Individuals must spend sufficient time considering the changes desired.

- They are implemented in a way that is appropriate for the participant's age and stage of development and that uses methods based on social learning or cognitive-behavioural theories of change that emphasize positive reinforcement and provide contingencies for social behaviour.

- They are delivered by well-trained staff who are knowledgeable and skilled.

- The most intensive programs are delivered to those at the highest risk of reoffending and are individualized as much as possible.

The risk-need-responsivity (RNR) model (Andrews and Bonta 2010) suggests that programs should be delivered in a manner that addresses the specific risk level of the offender, targets his or her specific criminogenic need, and takes into account the unique learning styles and capabilities of those involved in the program. Koehler, Lösel, Akoensi, and Humphreys (2013) report that when there is full adherence to the RNR principles, there is an average reduction in young offender recidivism of 30 per cent. The implementation of a strong program based on the principles of effective correctional treatment seems to show the most promise to date. Hoge, Guerra, and Boxer (2008, p. 119) suggest that through greater collaboration and partnerships between researchers and juvenile justice practitioners, research may be able to determine which program elements are essential and which components can be implemented with greater flexibility (see Box 5.2).

Youth Engagement, Adult–Youth Partnerships and the Promise of Resiliency

While the research literature is clear that risk can be reduced when the principles of effective intervention are followed, "therapeutic pessimism" abounds with respect to dealing with high-risk youth because the process of treating them is often difficult (Skeem et al. 2014, p. 723). Some of the risk factors that contribute to their offending, such as negative attitudes, non-compliance, and disruptive behaviour, often make these youth difficult clients to work with. In a meta-analysis of 114 studies of attrition from treatment, those offenders who were most likely to benefit from the treatment intervention owing to their high-risk and high-needs profile, were the least likely to complete it (Olver, Stockdale, and Wormith 2011).

Criminal behaviour in young people cannot simply be tackled as an episode of individual criminality disassociated from the social context or from the available child welfare, education and health, social, and recreational provisions (Whyte 2005, p. 9). The social context is just as important as the individual personal and skill development outcomes are because "social circumstances and relationships with others are both the object of the intervention and the medium through which change can be achieved" (Farrall 2002, p. 21). We know from the **resiliency** literature, for example, that not all young people exposed to multiple risk factors become offenders, nor do all young people who offend grow up in low socio-economic classes (Ungar 2004; Steinberg, Blatt-Eisengart, and Cauffman 2006). Resilience is fostered through the adult–youth relationships present in the milieu in which the young offender is being treated. As Ungar (2013) has argued, resilience might best be defined as the young person's ability to navigate toward resources while the institution provides the necessary resources and possible relationships for the young person. In the context of high risk, relationships with supportive adults are crucial in mitigating the toxic effects on youth of incarceration. Unless a youth is empowered to make some choice about engaging with the programs and resources, however, the likelihood of resilience is dramatically weakened.

In a study of 497 high-risk children and youth who were multiple-service users, Ungar (2013) found that it was not the quantity of the services that the youth received, but rather the quality of the relationships between a single service provider and the young person that was predictive of positive outcomes for the youth. Adult–youth relationships that attended to the needs of young people, that engaged their voices through the

resiliency
The ability of children and youth to develop positive self-esteem and self-efficacy despite facing crisis, challenges, or adversity.

Box 5.2   Youth Justice in Action

Quantum Opportunities Program: Connecting Youth at Risk of School Failure to Their Communities

In 1998, the Quantum Opportunities Program (QOP) was listed as a model program through Blueprints for Violence Prevention and has been supported by others since that time (US Surgeon General 2001; Schirm et al. 2003; Mihalic and Aultman-Bettridge 2004; National Crime Prevention Centre 2008). Taggart (1995) reported a 70 per cent reduction in arrests for the youth in QOP by the time of expected high school graduation.

QOP is a long-term, multi-component intervention program that aims to reduce dropout rates, pregnancy, and delinquency among disadvantaged high school students by directly addressing low academic achievement, problematic life choices such as drug or alcohol abuse, and anti-social, aggressive, or violent behaviour. The program targets students entering Grade 9 who come from low-income families, and it supports them for the full four years that they are in high school. The research literature has shown consistently that both academic failure and school dropout are risk factors highly correlated with criminal activity.

evidence-based principles
Principles based on a foundation of reliable research.

protective factors
Circumstances and experiences that buffer young people's involvement in behaviours that would be damaging to themselves and to others.

The interventions of the program fall into three general components: (1) educational activities, (2) developmental activities, and (3) service activities. The program requires that the students complete 250 hours of activity per year in each of these components, for a total annual participation of 750 hours and a total of 3000 hours of participation over the project's four-year duration. An important element of the QOP is the reinforcement of desired behaviour through a system of motivational incentives that allows the project to recognize effort, progress, and achievement on the part of the youth involved. As youth achieve certain intermittent milestones (e.g., completing 250 hours of annual activity in a particular component of their contract), they will be offered incentive opportunities, such as field trips to cultural or social events in the community, and attendance at or enrolment in sports or recreational events/activities.

One of the essential ingredients of this program is the continued involvement of the QOP counsellors in the lives of the young people, regardless of whether or not these youth have been removed from the formal school system through expulsion, illness, incarceration, or simply relocation. The slogan, "once in Quantum, always in Quantum" ensures that youth may continue in the program despite the hurdles they may face.

Over four years, the QOP was funded in New Brunswick and Ontario by the John Howard Society through the National Crime Prevention Centre. The John Howard Society applies specific operational principles and criteria to all its programs: all programs must be **evidence-based**; there must be sufficient resources and facilities for effective program development and implementation; and only trained and qualified volunteers/employees are recruited to plan and deliver programs.

In the New Brunswick program, after four years there was a significant increase in **protective factors** and a reduction in risk factors. The youths who were referred to the program had not been considered likely to complete Grade 9. At the end of the four years, more than half of the active participants had graduated on time, and an additional group (about 20 per cent) were set to graduate the following year.

With the use of the Juvenile Crime Prevention (JCP) Risk Assessment, the youth were assessed at the beginning of each year of the program to determine their level of risk as well as their strengths (the latter with the use of a Resilience Survey) (Ungar 2004). Significant correlations for each year of the program showed that as youths' level of risk decreased, their individual strengths increased (Reid 2014).

Critical Thinking Questions

What potential risk and protective factors are addressed in this program? How does this prevention program assist in reducing the likelihood of youth becoming entrenched in the youth criminal justice system?

encouragement of negotiation and choice in decisions that affected them, and that provided for their equal participation whenever it was reasonably available all supported young people becoming resilient (see Box 5.3).

Positive relationships with adults are essential as a protective factor for youth who may be enmeshed in the youth justice system. Throughout the province of Ontario, for example, they have become part of the "relationship custody" framework that guides the work with young persons in custody. The relationship custody approach requires staff not only to work from a strengths-based approach that reinforces the skills and talents of the young person but also to engage with young people and develop a rapport

Box 5.3   Youth Justice in Action

Teen Courts as a Restorative Justice Alternative

One example that has a strong component of youth engagement that has become popular in the United States is the "teen court"—also referred to as "student court" and "youth peer panel." The "Global Youth Justice Movement," as it is referred to, has recorded more than 1550 courts in operation in the United States and two other continents (Global Youth Justice 2014). These courts operate as a diversionary program for first-time minor offenders, apart from the formal youth justice system. In the majority of programs, the young person must admit guilt in order to participate. The main function of the teen court is to determine a restorative sentence for the youth that is fair and proportionate. In some teen courts, youth are required to "give back" after completing their disposition by sitting as a youth jury member.

The teen court is moderated by a justice official (usually a judge or lawyer) and is attended by a group of peer jurors who have been trained in the process of teen courts, the offender, and his or her parents or guardians. The initial meeting includes a meeting in a mock court setting to discuss the offence and have the young person comment on his or her willingness to participate in a disposition that might include assigned learning activities, letters of apology, counselling sessions, reflective essays, and restitution to the victim. Once the offender completes the assigned disposition, he or she returns to teen court for a review of the case and approval for case dismissal. Many of these programs have elements of restorative justice in that, within the process, the youth is given an opportunity to "repair relationships through voluntary face-to-face interactions between victims and offenders" (Laundra, Rodgers, and Zapp 2013, p. 23).

Smith and Chonody (2010) report that the young persons experienced significant improvements in positive identity, pro-social cognitions, and modelling positive behaviour. One youth reported:

> In a way I am kind of glad that this happened. It wasn't under the best of circumstances, but if it wasn't for this, then I would still be the little girl I was before the class . . . the little girl who didn't care where she ended up. The girl that was always mad at the world. Now I look back at my old self and ask, "Is that really who I want to be, the girl mad at the world?" (Choate and Manton 2014, p. 362)

Laundra et al. (2013) measured whether 38 teen court participants had learned principles of restorative justice as a result of completing the program. At the end of the program, there was a significant positive improvement with respect to the dimension "I feel responsible for improving my community." However, for other dimensions, the researchers noted no growth, and in some cases, there was a decrease in understanding—for example, in appreciating such restorative justice principles as decision-making and self-esteem. Other research has pointed out the benefits of learning about the process of the court system and of simply being a part of the process (Choate and Manton 2014).

Critical Thinking Question

What possible difficulties can you identify in having peers adjudicate other youth and hand out dispositions?

that helps them make more positive choices. It requires a balance between the dynamic security approaches (professional, positive relationships between youth and staff) and the static security approaches (physical barriers and surveillance) (Ontario, Provincial Advocate for Children and Youth 2013). Implementation of the framework has not been smooth. In 2009, a 192-bed secure-custody facility, called the Roy McMurtry Centre, was opened in Brampton, Ontario. But soon, complaints made to the Office of the Child and Youth Advocate resulted in an investigation that uncovered numerous deficiencies. While the majority of young persons could identify at least one staff person who sufficiently embodied the philosophy behind the framework, 52 per cent told of staff who left them feeling disrespected. They gave examples of rules not being followed, of being changed, or of being disregarded depending on who was on shift (Ontario, Provincial Advocate for Children and Youth 2013).

Schubert et al. (2012) report that youth who do not feel they can turn to staff for help are more likely to have difficulty in post-release outcomes. Marsh and Evans (2009) found, as well, that when youth in a closed-custody setting were asked to identify the qualities of the staff members they respected, high levels of trust, positive effects on youth, high levels of engagement, and effective problem-solving skills were cited. Those youth who spoke of staff who had these qualities were also more likely to believe they would achieve significant success after their release (see Box 5.4).

Box 5.4   Youth Justice in Action

Adult Ally Training with Correctional Staff in Closed-Custody Facility

In 2013, all of the staff involved with young offenders at the New Brunswick Youth Centre participated in a half-day training seminar led by young people on how to be an adult ally to the youth in the facility (Reid 2013b). Wong et al. (2010, p. 100) point out that a great deal of the child and adolescent research has been constructed using an "adult lens" where the perspectives and real life experiences of young people are frequently overlooked, and the delivery of a training session by young people shifted the focus so that the staff gained a better appreciation of what the young people might be experiencing. In one of the activities, staff were asked to write down one experience they had with a youth at the facility where they were proud to be an adult ally. The responses were then randomly handed out to the participants and read aloud to debrief the exercise (Reid 2013b). Here are some examples of the staff's experiences:

- "I had a conversation with an 'at risk/young offender' about him going to (program). He told me I was the first person to suggest it, and that he might even consider it."

- "Helped a female youth with low self-esteem learn to be more assertive with her peers."
- "Helped a young person feel better about themselves after they had an upsetting phone call from a family member who told them they were nothing."
- "Once I went through the process of showing a youth sympathy towards another youth. Encourage a youth to see that maybe that youth does not have the same opportunities as him."
- "I gave a youth an idea for a project and then saw him excel in creating a great product."
- "I've encouraged youth to join high school basketball team because of their potential."
- "I have taught different youth how to play the guitar. Taught a youth how to play a new song and made his day better!"

Critical Thinking Question

What kinds of activities can you think of that might fall under the category of adult ally?

To actively engage young people (**youth engagement**), adults need to work as partners with them in a supportive manner. Rather than young people working in isolation, away from the individuals and communities whose perceptions and actions they seek to transform, they can be engaged with "adult allies" who support them and act as their advocate every day (Fletcher and Vavrus 2006).

Strong youth–adult partnerships serve a variety of different purposes: they protect youth rights for participation, particularly in terms of decision-making; they facilitate positive youth development; and they work to steer youth toward improving their communities and civil society (Zeldin, Camino, and Mook 2005; Stolle and Hooghe 2004).

Developing Youth Policy with Youth Voice

Bessant (2005, p. 5) argues that the problem with discussions about youth policy is that adult policy-makers try to "imagine what young people want or what they believe they ought to want or need." This, she argues, has produced a history of youth policy-making where "policy makers create knowledge about young people" and act as spokespersons for them and as a "substitute for young people" (ibid., p. 5).

Brank and Lane (2008) suggest that even though young people have a unique perspective, they are rarely asked for their opinion. The UNCRC outlines, in Articles 12, 13, and 14, the right of children under 18 years of age to fully participate in decisions that affect them, to express their ideas and concerns in any way that is appropriate for them, and to have access to full information about situations that affect them.

Franke (2010) outlines an analytical framework for youth-related policy development and research in Canada, suggesting that it is essential to decompartmentalize how researchers and policy-makers view youth and adopt a holistic approach that builds on the strengths and contributions that youth make to society as opposed to the deficit-based approach that was common in earlier approaches.

In an effort to understand what young people had to say about improving the youth justice system, a focus group with 15 young persons was held at the New Brunswick Youth Centre (see Box 5.5). They described lives filled with risk factors and very few protective factors, and they shared very disturbing details of their home life and the pains of imprisonment (Reid 2009).

In terms of the reasons the youth at the NBYC gave for their crime, many of them felt that drugs had a large role to play in the commission of the offence. One young person commented, "We're all unique," and this was underscored by a later comment about how they had to wear uniforms and they had no individuality left. Family factors were important to young people, and one youth pointed out that not enough attention was paid to those young persons who were also parents. One youth felt that being a father was a protective factor, helping him to stay away from drugs and crime. Another young person also discussed the importance of family and how his incarceration was having an impact on his younger brother; he felt he had lost touch with him but also regretted the inappropriate role model that he had become since his incarceration. One youth stated, "If I had a family it would have saved me from this; foster care that's what messed me up."

youth engagement
"The meaningful participation and sustained involvement of a young person in an activity, which has a focus outside of him or herself" (Centres of Excellence for Children's Well-Being, www.tgmag.ca/centresnew/files/Whatis_WEB_e.pdf). Full engagement consists of a behavioural component, an affective component, and a cognitive component.

Box 5.5   Youth Justice in Action

Youth Matters: Conferences and Leadership Groups in Closed Custody

Youth Matters is a youth-led leadership group that brings together—in conferences, youth forums, and discussion groups—traditional and non-traditional leaders from high school and university to discuss issues of importance to young people. Since its inception, Youth Matters has had the mandate of engaging non-traditional leaders, as they are often young people with great abilities and a sense of agency who have just not yet had the chance to exercise them. One provincial conference was held in the same city as the NBYC, and two young offenders attended, supported by correctional staff who blended in with Youth Matters facilitators. The youth were so inspired that they asked whether they could develop a similar event for their peers inside the youth jail. The university students worked with these young persons in a series of meetings, and a two-day youth conference was hosted for all young offenders at the institution. The youth explored issues of substance abuse and bullying inside youth custody, and at the end of the event, they requested that a chapter of Youth Matters be established within the youth jail (see Reid 2013b). At the outset, the youth set out the following principles that would govern the work at NBYC:

Principles Governing Youth Matters (NBYC Chapter)

1. Non-judgmental
   - Good work ethic
   - Confidentiality
   - Look out for one another, make sure what is talked about within the conference/meeting does not go back to the units
2. Inclusive
   - Introduce it to new youth
   - Make it clear everyone is equal regardless of background
   - Work together, strengths and weaknesses male/female/compatibility with each other to create positive environment
3. Safe and meaningful
   - Show them (YP) the right way with help from leaders
   - Meaningful topics
   - Good representation from all units
4. Every voice heard
   - Everyone has the right to be a leader in Youth Matters

- Respect
- Every voice has a chance to speak

The value of this group to the young people at the centre is perhaps best summarized by the following comment made by one of the leaders who worked on the development of the first conference: "Youth Matters has changed my life. It has made me feel accepted, and helped me have a better sense of belonging. I'm grateful for having Youth Matters find me, it has/will be an amazing experience."

Since 2012, Youth Matters (Miramichi chapter) has created a video inside one of the units on institutional bullying so that it can be shown to new young persons when they arrive at NBYC. Funding was received from Status of Women Canada and the Meighen Family Foundation to continue the work at the centre. As part of a national grant, a weekly program on gender-based violence was offered to explore the issue of violence in young women's lives. While the anchoring topic always relates back to violence against women, this group has explored topics such as gendered bullying, sport culture and violence, the root causes of violence, and ways to engage young people on the topic. Hosting a group of young people in custody has unique challenges, as the population is constantly changing and facilitators must operate within the boundaries of the policies and procedures of the facility. Participation in the meetings is open to all residents of the centre, and youth attend on a voluntary basis.

The weekly meetings have yielded positive outcomes on many levels. First, many of these youth have never before had the opportunity to engage in decision-making processes, often because of their involvement in the youth criminal justice system. A number of the participants started attending meetings out of curiosity but soon developed a sense of ownership and a desire to create change. In their feedback about the weekly meetings, youth have said that the meetings have made them feel "more comfortable to speak in crowds" and be "more open to talking in groups." Others have commented that the meetings have "helped [them] take responsibility" and "show interest in other people's views."

Critical Thinking Question

What are some of the benefits that you see to having young people manage a group such as Youth Matters inside a carceral setting?

His sense of abandonment was further evidenced not only through the number of place-ments he had experienced but also through his opinion about his foster parents: "I'll take in this troublesome kid so I can get a couple hundred dollars for keeping him." Youth also commented about reintegration, and it was clear that some of these young people were afraid of breaching their multiple conditions of release: "While we are in here we work on levels, and if you achieve points you get more privileges. When you are released you start back at nothing with a 6 o'clock curfew, requirements to attend programs, attend school, attend counselling and no opportunity to improve, all the while not being able to talk to your friends because of a non-association order." Another youth said, "We're not robots, we can't go from being in here for six months or a year talking to our friends, to having no friends to talk to. We can't change overnight." There was acknowledgement from the youth that the probation officers had a job to do in terms of reporting to the court, but their complaints stemmed from the inability of officials to have the time to "see the posi-tive things" and be able to "cut some slack."

While these comments only scratch the surface of the myriad issues related to youth in custody, it is essential that there are provisions for "alternatives" for those young people who are completing their term of custody and reintegrating back into their communities. Without choice, services, and resources, there is a strong likelihood that these young people will breach their many conditions and return to custody.

Summary

There is no one ideal way to approach youth at risk. Youth justice legislation and youth-at-risk programming cannot be developed as a one-size-fits-all model because if this were done, the needs of so many youth would not be met. This chapter presented many of the unique challenges of developing effective policies for youth.

The binary function of the youth justice system, as it is designed today, does not permit the best interests of youth to be addressed. This chapter made the point that, increasingly, youth have been pushed into the adult system through a variety of loopholes prior to reaching the age of majority. This phenomenon is known as *adulteration*. With the 2012 amendments to the YCJA, concerns have emerged about a further entrenchment of youth into a life of crime owing to the provisions that allow the imposition of an adult sentence in the case of a serious offence. As has been pointed out throughout this chapter, a key challenge is to protect public safety while ensuring that the principles of effective correctional intervention are applied to maximize the likelihood that young people will make a healthy developmental transition to a non-criminal adulthood.

Throughout the evolution of youth criminal justice, the fundamental belief was that all avenues should be exhausted to prevent youth from embarking on a life of crime. As the research demonstrates, this is best achieved by reserving custodial sentences for the most severe of cases and, instead, imposing meaningful consequences that will promote rehabilitation and reintegration. Extrajudicial measures, diversion, and non-custodial sentences limit the occurrences of stigmatization and labelling and are more in line with serving the best interests of the child. This need to focus on non-custodial sentences is most apparent with youth with highly complex needs. High numbers of incarcerated youth have been shown to have mental illness or conduct disorders, and their needs cannot be met in a correctional facility. Mental health diversion programs were discussed as one avenue to help these youth. The case of Ashley Smith was held up as a key example of how the system has failed youth with mental health challenges.

Individualized programs must be developed for youth to help them overcome their dynamic risk factors. Evidence-based principles must be used to capitalize on each youth's strengths in order to promote resiliency. One such program is the Quantum Opportunities Program, which helps youth work within their strengths and pushes them to develop new ones to facilitate positive outcomes.

Finally, so that we might truly understand the needs of youth, youth themselves must be consulted. The UN Declaration on the Rights of the Child demands this, and as a signatory to this human rights treaty, Canada must respond. Allowing youth to have a voice in their own experience empowers them and encourages them to take ownership of their own path. This was exemplified through the youth-led group Youth Matters, which operates in a closed-custody facility. The value of strong adult–youth partnerships to enhance the voice of young people in closed custody was shown through examples of successful youth-led projects on institutional bullying and gender-based violence.

Key Terms

adulteration	rehabilitation
best interests of the child	reintegration
criminogenic	resiliency
custodial sanctions	risk factors
evidence-based principles	secure custody
labelling	youth engagement
protective factors	youth justice

Review Questions

1. What is meant by the "best interests of the child"? How does this concept relate to the current legal regulations of young persons?

2. What is meant by "adulteration"?

3. Describe the type of youth justice model that best describes the JDA and YOA. How do these models differ from the youth justice model that characterizes the YCJA?

4. What is the significance of the Nunn Commission and its recommendations?

5. Describe three to four of the key characteristics for effective youth-at-risk programs. How do they compare to the effective treatment principles for young offenders?

Critical Thinking Questions

1. How important do you think it is to maintain a separate system for young offenders in Canada?

2. To what extent do you feel the UN Convention on the Rights of the Child is, or is not, important for empowering and protecting young persons?

3. What are the critical factors that differentiate programs that work v. those that don't work? Briefly discuss the implications of these (if any) differences.

4. How might we best address the challenges that youth at risk face today?

5. What are ways to foster positive adult–youth partnerships with youth at risk?

References

Andrews, D., and Bonta, J. (2010). *The psychology of criminal conduct* (5th ed.). Toronto/Newark: LexisNexis.

Bessant, J. (2005). Principles for developing youth policy. *Policy Studies, 26*(1): 103–16.

Brank, E., and Lane, J. (2008). An experimental juvenile probation program: Effects on parent and peer relationships. *Crime Delinquency, 54*(2): 193–224.

Canada. (1965). *Juvenile delinquency in Canada. The report of the Department of Justice Committee on Juvenile Delinquency*. Committee on Juvenile Delinquency. Ottawa: Queen's Printer.

Canada. (1996). *A review of the Young Offenders Act and the youth justice system in Canada: Report of the Federal Provincial Territorial Task Force on Youth Justice*. Ottawa: Department of Justice Canada.

Canada. (1998). *A strategy for the renewal of youth justice*. Department of Justice. Ottawa: Queen's Printer.

Child and Youth Advocate: Ombudsman. (2008a). *Connecting the dots: A report on the condition of youth-at-risk and youth with very complex needs in New Brunswick*. Fredericton: New Brunswick Ombudsman and Child and Youth Advocate.

Child and Youth Advocate: Ombudsman. (2008b). *The Ashley Smith report*. Fredericton: New Brunswick Ombudsman and Child and Youth Advocate.

Choate, L.H., and Manton, J. (2014). Teen court counseling groups: Facilitating positive change for adolescents who are first-time juvenile offenders. *Journal for Specialists in Group Work, 39*(4): 345–65.

CMHA (Canadian Mental Health Association). (2014). Fast facts about mental illness. Retrieved from http://www.cmha.ca/media/fast-facts-about-mental-illness/#.VJHpUzHF9ws.

Cullen, F.T., Blevins, K.R., Trager, J.S., and Gendreau, P. (2005). The rise and fall of boot camps: A case study in common sense corrections. *Journal of Offender Rehabilitation, 4*(3–4): 53–70.

Department of Justice. (1908). *Juvenile Delinquents Act*. Ottawa: Government of Canada.

Department of Justice. (1985). *Young Offenders Act*. Ottawa: Government of Canada.

Department of Justice. (2002). *Youth Criminal Justice Act*. Ottawa: Government of Canada.

Espinosa, E.M., Sorensen, J.R., and Lopez, M.A. (2013). Youth pathways to placement: The influence of gender, mental health need and trauma on confinement in the juvenile justice system. *Journal of Youth and Adolescence, 42*(12): 1824–36.

Evans-Cuellar, A., McReynolds, L.S., and Wasserman, G.A. (2006). A cure for crime: Can mental health treatment diversion reduce crime among youth? *Journal of Policy Analysis and Management, 25*(1): 197–214.

Farrall, S. (2002). *Rethinking what works with offenders: Probation, social context and distance from crime*. London: Willan.

Farrington, D. .(1996). *Understanding and preventing youth crime*. New York: Joseph Rowntree Foundation.

Fletcher, A., and Vavrus, J. (2006). *The guide to social change led by and with young people*. Olympia, WA: CommonAction.

Franke, S. (2010). *Current realities and emerging issues facing youth in Canada: An analytical framework for public policy research*. Ottawa: Government of Canada, Policy Research Institute.

Gilbert, J., Grimm, R., and Parnham, J. (2001) Applying therapeutic principles to a family- focused juvenile justice model. *Alabama Law Review*, 52(1153): 1196–7.

Global Youth Justice. (2014). Teen, peer, youth student court. Retrieved 15 December 2014 from http://www.globalyouthjustice.org

Guerra, N.G., and Williams, K.R. (2012). Implementing evidence-based practices for juvenile justice in communities. In E.L. Grigorenko (Ed.), *Handbook of juvenile forensic psychology and psychiatry* (pp. 297–307). New Haven, CT: Springer.

Hoeve, M., McReynolds, L.S., and Wasserman, G.A. (2013). Service referral for juvenile justice youths: Associations with psychiatric disorder and recidivism. *Administration and Policy in Mental Health and Mental Health Services Research*, 1–11 (online).

Hoge, R.D., Guerra, N.G., and Boxer, P. (2008). *Treating the juvenile offender*. New York: Guilford.

Kapp, S.A., Petr, C.G., Robbins, M.L., and Choi, J.J. (2013). Collaboration between community mental health and juvenile justice systems: Barriers and facilitators. *Child and Adolescent Social Work Journal*, 30: 505–17.

Koehler, J.A., Lösel, F., Akoensi, T.D., and Humphreys, D.K. (2013). A systematic review and meta-analysis on the effects of young offender treatment programs in Europe. *Journal of Experimental Criminology*, 9(1): 19–43.

Latessa, E.J., Cullen, F.T., and Gendreau, P. (2002). Beyond correctional quackery: Professionalism and the possibility of effective treatment. *Federal Probation*, 66(2): 43–9.

Laundra, K., Rodgers, K., and Zapp, H. (2013). Transforming teens: Measuring the effects of restorative justice principles in a teen court setting. *Juvenile and Family Court Journal*, 64(4): 21–34.

Layton-MacKenzie, D. (2013). First do no harm: A look at correctional policies and programs today. *Journal of Experimental Criminology*, 9(1): 1–17.

Liebenberg, L., and Ungar, M. (2014). A comparison of service use among youth involved with juvenile justice and mental health. *Children and Youth Services Review*, 39: 117–22.

Lipsey, M.W., and Cullen, F.T. (2007). The effectiveness of correctional rehabilitation: A review of systematic reviews. *Annual Review of Law and Social Science*, 3: 297–320.

Loeber, R., and Farrington, D. (1998). *Serious and violent juvenile offenders: Risk factors and successful interventions*. Thousand Oaks, CA: Sage.

Lösel, F. (2011). Towards a third phase of "what works" in offender rehabilitation. In R. Loeber and B.C. Welsh (Eds), *The future of criminology*. Oxford: Oxford University Press.

MacKenzie, D.L. (2006). *What works in corrections? Reducing the criminal activities of offenders and delinquents*. Cambridge: Cambridge University Press.

MacKenzie, D.L. (2013). First do no harm: A look at correctional policies and programs today. *Journal of Experimental Criminology*, 9(1): 1–17.

Madell, D., Thom, K., and McKenna, B. (2013). A systematic review of literature relating to problem-solving youth courts. *Psychiatry, Psychology and Law*, 20(3): 412–22.

Marsh, S.C., and Evans, W.P. (2009). Youth perspectives on their relationships with staff in juvenile correction settings and perceived likelihood of success on release. *Youth Violence and Juvenile Justice*, 7: 46–67.

Meade B., and Steiner, B. (2010). The total effects of boot camps that house juveniles: A systematic review of the evidence. *Journal of Criminal Justice*, 38(5): 841–53.

Mihalic, D., and Aultman-Bettridge, S. (2004). A guide to effective school-based prevention programs. In W.L. Turk (Ed.), *School crime and policing*. Englewood Cliffs, NJ: Prentice Hall.

National Crime Prevention Centre. (2008). *Promising and model crime prevention programs*. Ottawa: Public Safety Canada.

Nunn, D.M. (2005). *Spiraling out of control: Lessons learned from a boy in trouble*. Halifax: Government of Nova Scotia.

Olver, M.E., Stockdale, K.C., and Wormith, J.S. (2011). A meta-analysis of predictors of offender treatment attrition and its relationship to recidivism. *Journal of Consulting and Clinical Psychology, 79*(1): 6–21

Ontario, Provincial Advocate for Children and Youth. (2013). *"It depends who's working": The youth reality at the Roy McMurtry Centre*. Toronto: Office of Provincial Advocate for Children and Youth.

Petrosino, A., Turpin-Petrosino, C., and Buehler, J. (2003). Scared Straight and other juvenile awareness programs for preventing delinquency: A systematic review of randomized experimental evidence. *The Annals of the American Academy of Political and Social Science, 589*(1): 41–62.

Petrosino, A., Turpin-Petrosino, C., and Guckenburg, S. (2010). *Formal system processing of juveniles: Effects on delinquency*. Campbell Systematic Reviews.

Reid, S.A. (2009). 125 warnings: A review of extrajudicial measures and sanctions in the province of New Brunswick. Unpublished report for New Brunswick Department of Public Safety.

Reid, S.A. (2013a). Ashley smith Case study. In K. O'Regan and S. Reid (Eds), *Thinking about Criminal Justice*. Toronto: Emond Montgomery.

Reid, S.A. (2013b, August). *Creating youth–adult partnerships with youth in Custody*. Paper presented to the New Brunswick Department of Public Safety.

Reid, S.A. (2014, June). Quantum opportunities at John Howard New Brunswick. Presentation to the Atlantic Crime Prevention Conference, Moncton.

Schirm, A., Rodriguez-Planas, N., Maxfield, M., and Tuttle, C. (2003). *The Quantum Opportunity Program demonstration: Short term impact*. Washington, DC: US Department of Labor, Employment and Training. Mathematic Policy Research Inc.

Schubert C.A., Mulvey, E.P., Loughran, T.A., and Losoya, S.H. (2012). Perceptions of institutional experience and community outcomes for serious adolescent offenders. *Criminal Justice and Behaviour, 39*(1): 71–93.

Skeem, J.L., Manchak, S., and Peterson, J.K. (2011). Correctional policy for offenders with mental illness: Creating a new paradigm for recidivism reduction. *Law & Human Behavior, 35*: 110–26.

Skeem, J.L., Scott, E., and Mulvey, E.P. (2014). Justice Policy Reform for High-Risk Juveniles: Using Science to Achieve Large-Scale Crime Reduction. *Annual Review of Clinical Psychology, 10*: 709–39.

Skowyra, K.R., and Cocozza, J.J. (2007). *Blueprint for change: A comprehensive model for the identification and treatment of youth with mental health needs in contact with the juvenile justice system*. Delmar, NY: National Center for Mental Health and Juvenile Justice.

Skowyra, K. and Powell, S.D. (2006). *Juvenile diversion: Programs for justice-involved youth with mental health disorders*. Washington, DC: National Centre for Mental Health and Juvenile Justice.

Smith, S., and Chonody, J.M. (2010). The Teen Court Peer Influence Scale (TCPIS): Determining an effective way to measure and model positive peer influence. *Youth Violence and Juvenile Justice, 8*(2), 148–59.

Steinberg, L., Blatt-Eisengart, I., and Cauffman, E. (2006). Patterns of competence and adjustment among adolescents from authoritative, authoritarian, indulgent and neglectful homes: Replication in a sample of serious juvenile offenders. *Journal of Research on Adolescence, 16*: 47–58.

Stolle, D., and Hooghe, M. (2004). The roots of social capital: Attitudinal and network mechanisms in the relation between youth and adult indicators of social capital. *Acta Politica, 39*: 422–41.

Sullivan, C.J., Veysey, B.M., Hamilton, Z.K., and Grillo, M. (2007). Reducing out-of-community placement and recidivism: Diversion of delinquent youth with mental health and substance use problems from the justice system. *International Journal of Offender Therapy and Comparative Criminology, 51*: 555–77.

Taggart, R. (1995). *Quantum Opportunity Program*. Philadelphia: Opportunities Industrialization Centres of America.

Tustin, L.A., and Lutes, R. (2008). *A guide to the Youth Criminal Justice Act*. Toronto: LexisNexis.

Ungar, M. (2004). Resilience among children in child-welfare, corrections, mental health and educational settings: Recommendations for service. *Child and Youth Care Forum, 34*(6): 445–64.

Ungar, M. (2013). The impact of youth–adult relationships on resilience. *International Journal of Child, Youth and Family Studies*, 4(3): 328–36.

UN General Assembly. (1989). *Convention on the rights of the child.* United Nations, Treaty Series, vol. 1577.

US Surgeon General. (2001). *Youth violence: A report of the Surgeon General.* Rockville, MD: Office of the US Surgeon General.

Wexler, D.B. (2000). Just some juvenile thinking about delinquent behavior: A therapeutic jurisprudence approach to relapse prevention planning and youth advisory juries. *University of Missouri at Kansas City Law Review*, 69: 93–114.

Whitted, K.S., Delavega, E., and Lennon-Dearing, R. (2013). The youngest victims of violence: Examining the mental health needs of young children who are involved in the child-welfare and juvenile justice systems. *Child and Adolescent Social Work Journal*, 30: 181–95.

Whyte, B. (2005). Effectiveness, research and youth justice. *Youth Justice*, 4(1): 1–21.

Wiener, R.L., Winick, B.J., Skovran-Georges, L., and Castro, A. (2010). A testable theory of problem solving courts: Avoiding past empirical and legal failures. *International Journal of Law and Psychiatry*, 33: 417–27.

Wilson, H.A., and Hoge, R.D. (2013). The effect of youth diversion programs on recidivism: A meta-analytic review. *Criminal Justice and Behavior*, 40(5): 497–518.

Winick, B. (2003). Therapeutic jurisprudence and problem solving courts. *Fordham Urban Law Journal*, 30: 1055–76.

Winterdyk, J. (2015, 8 March). Age of criminal responsibility: An illusive dilemma. *LawNow*, 39(4). Retrieved from http://www.lawnow.org/age-of-criminal-responsibility/

Wong, N.T., Zimmerman, M.A., and Parker, E.A. (2010). A typology of youth participation and empowerment for child and adolescent health promotion. *American Journal of Community Psychology*, 46: 100–14.

Zeldin, S., Camino, L., and Mook, C. (2005). The adoption of innovation in youth organizations: Creating the conditions for youth–adult partnerships. *Journal of Community Psychology*, 33(1): 121–35.

Youth Deviance and the Media: Mapping Knowledge and the Limits to Certainty

Chris McCormick

Overview

The media—including traditional print and electronic media, such as newspapers and television, and more recently social media on the Internet—are one of society's key sources of knowledge about crime. Despite the media's popularity and influence, however, over the years media scholars have been skeptical of the accuracy and usefulness of media representations of crime and justice, and have instead given more weight to officially produced data (like crime statistics) and data acquired through other data-collection techniques (like self-report and victimization studies). This chapter provides a somewhat different discussion of the media, acknowledging that although the media are often guilty of distorting and sensationalizing crime news stories, they nonetheless create a public arena in which youth crime and criminal justice are debated and understood.

Key Objectives

After reading this chapter, you should be able to:

- Understand different methods for measuring youth crime.
- Describe criticisms of those methods.
- Explain how new methods of counting youth crime arose from criticisms of official statistics.
- Apply your knowledge of the media to analyzing news stories about youth crime.

Introduction

Narrowly missing being designated a "young offender," an 18-year-old man has been charged with attempted murder and various weapons offences. Markel Downey's story, however, started before charges were laid against him in December 2014. He was a promising boxer who won gold at the Canada Winter Games in 2011. On track for the Olympics, he nonetheless lost contact with his coach and the sport he might have used as a ticket out of North Preston, a poor community outside Dartmouth, Nova Scotia. Charged along with two 17-year-old young offenders whose identity is protected under the law, the charges he faces have as much to do with his background as the decisions he made. To the public, however, he is simply the kid who had a great start but for whom things had inexplicably gone wrong (Global News 2014).

This chapter is a reflection on what we know about youth crime and juvenile deviance. Before we can do anything about a social problem, we must lay out the methods for acquiring knowledge about the problem and the limitations of those methods. In this chapter, the premise is that what we know about youth crime and juvenile deviance is based on the particular methods we use to map that knowledge. Although there are other methods, this chapter focuses specifically on an analysis of the role of media in the production of knowledge about youth crime and justice, contrasting it with other data-collection techniques, including official statistics, self-report, and victimization studies.

Three different sources of knowledge are official statistics, unofficial data, and the media. These three sources are complementary, although they differ both in kind and degree. Official statistics record in detail what is known and reported to the police, while self-report and victimization studies are used to fill out those incidents not reported to the police. The media, however, are the main sources of crime news information for the public (Surette 1998), but they highlight emotional and violent extremes of crime (Fishman 1981). Furthermore, the media create a feedback loop where discussions of youth crime influence public perception and to some extent public policy with calls for more punitive measures (Garofalo 1981).

Numerous studies by criminologists and media scientists have empirically supported the argument that the media play a significant role in shaping public attitudes toward youth crime (Best 1999; Cohen 1972; Faith and Jiwani 2002; Muncie 2004;

Schissel 1997, 2006). One of the earliest and most famous of these is Stanley Cohen's influential book *Folk Devils and Moral Panics: The Creation of the Mods and Rockers* (1972). Cohen's study, which involves field-research interviews and analysis of media reports, shows how rather haphazardly organized groups of youths (or "youth gangs") known as Mods and Rockers came to be famous in England in the 1960s through the sensationalist stories that were written about them in the newspapers of the day. Cohen coined the term **moral panic** to describe the exaggerated fears about youth deviance that were generated by the media, while he used the term **folk devils** to capture the idea that—much like witches in seventeenth-century New England—English youth of the 1960s came to be viewed by adults as a group that posed a potentially serious threat to the traditional values and institutions of English society (Smandych 2001, p. 66).

While the findings of researchers like Cohen (1972) have been influential in evoking skepticism about the accuracy and usefulness of information on youth crime and justice derived from the media, this does not mean that criminologists should entirely discount the value of examining the ways in which the media may contribute a very different knowledge to the public. Overall, in this chapter, we will come to see that the study of youth crime and deviance is more than just counting statistics, since the conditions for creating and knowing meaning are more complex. Knowledge of crime and deviance is both actuarial and interpretive, and it is known by police at the same time as it is socially constructed in the media. The topic of youth crime will be used here as a way to reflect upon our methods for knowing about crime and understanding its occurrence. By grounding the analysis of youth crime within the context of other ways of knowing, we may create a more adequate method of analyzing how our knowledge of youth crime and justice is generated in today's contemporary society.

moral panic
Exaggerated fears about social problems, including youth deviance, partly generated by the media.

folk devils
Any group that is perceived to pose a threat to the traditional values and institutions of society.

The Official Version: Statistics on Youth Crime

First, we will look at the official statistics on (youth) crime and consider what they do/do not tell us. Overall, these statistics attempt to portray crime as a pattern through uniform descriptions. However, in their doing so, artificial categories are often created that mask important details about events and processes connected with crime. Consequently, the attempt to know about youth crime from official crime statistics is like trying to dine out by reading restaurant reviews—entertaining but ultimately unfulfilling.

The Creation of an Official Statistic

The Canadian Centre for Justice Statistics (CCJS) has collected information on crime every year since 1962 in what is called the Uniform Crime Report (UCR) survey. It provides an aggregate count because it lumps crime into categories based on reports from over 1000 separate police detachments from over 200 different police forces across Canada. The UCR is the official source that represents crimes substantiated through police investigation.

UCR data are an invaluable resource for studying crime in society, and a revised version has even more detailed information on accused and victim characteristics (e.g., age, gender, alcohol and drug consumption, and victim–offender relationship) and incident characteristics (e.g., location, time, secondary violations, and weapons). The revised version, the UCR2, gives the police and the public a more specific sense of what offences occur.

Each month, police agencies report to the CCJS the number of crimes known to them, taken from all complaints of crime received from victims, from members of the public, or from officers who discovered the infractions. The initial reports of crime are investigated, and if they are unfounded, they are eliminated from the total. However, this crime total represents only what the police know about crime, because some crimes are never detected and many are not reported to the police at all. Called the "dark figure" of crime, such crimes are discovered in a different way, usually through victimization surveys or self-reports (see a more detailed discussion of this in Chapter 2).

The UCR thus does not reflect the total amount of crime in society, although it might be understood that way. It was originally created as a way to measure police work, although it is now used to compare crime across jurisdictions and to justify the use of police resources. And, of course, in order for the UCR to provide meaningful statistics, police have to count crime the same way, consistently and systematically, across jurisdictions.

The UCR uses several terms to express crime data. For homicide, the "actual number" is expressed as a raw figure. Second, the change in the amount of crime between years is computed. For example, homicide decreased from 543 homicides in 2012 (Statistics Canada 2014a). The change is important because it is read as an indicator of whether society is becoming more dangerous or safer. The rate of homicide in 2013 marks a downward trend and is the lowest rate since 1966. The change can also be read as a commentary on the effectiveness of the police, courts, and corrections, and the direction of public policy. If the crime rate increases, questions can be raised as to whether the police are doing a good job or whether politicians need to get tough on crime. Similarly, if the crime rate decreases, criticisms can be raised about whether we need to put resources into policing or whether political discourse on "getting tough on crime" is justified. The third way of expressing crime data is the crime "rate" per 100,000 people. The crime rate involves dividing the total crimes by the population (33 million), which creates a relative rate of changes in crime. For example, the homicide rate was 1.44 in 2013, which means that fewer than 2 people in every 100,000 were killed between 1 January and 31 December of that year. Thus, the likelihood of being murdered is very low in Canada (for further details, see Boyce, Cotter, and Perreault 2014), especially when compared to the United States (5), Russia (9), South Africa (31), or Jamaica (39) (World Bank 2014).

Overall, crime rates have continued to decline. This can be taken to mean that at the aggregate level Canadians have been enjoying an unprecedented level of safety, especially when seen with the new Crime Severity Index. This measure showed a decrease in crime overall of 8.9 per cent since 2006, and a decrease in violent crime of 9.97 per cent in 2013. Other crime patterns include low rates of violent crime compared with property crime, strong gender divisions in crimes committed, high rates of crime and victimization in Aboriginal communities, and geographic differences across the country.

In addition to incidence and crime rate, police agencies report the total number of "crimes cleared," which means the arrest and charging of at least one person, unless something prevents the physical arrest, such as when a suspect dies or leaves the country.

A case can also be "cleared otherwise" even if no charge is laid, as in the case of the diversion of a young offender to an extrajudicial measures program.

In general, the clearance rate for violent offences is around 70 per cent but for property crimes only about 20 per cent. The highest clearance rate is usually for homicide, while the lowest is often motor vehicle theft. Conversely, if 70 per cent of violent offences and 20 per cent of property violations were cleared, 30 per cent of violent crimes and 80 per cent of property violations are apparently unsolved. Violent crimes are more likely to be solved than property crimes because police devote more resources to these more serious acts (Cloninger and Sartorius 1979). Also, witnesses and the victims are available to identify offenders, since usually the victim and offender are previously acquainted.

The Youth Crime Statistic

In its annual publication on crime, Statistics Canada reports that about 104,000 youth (ages 12 to 17 years) were accused of a criminal offence in 2013. The youth crime rate had decreased by 16 per cent over the previous year and was down 40 per cent from when the Youth Criminal Justice Act was implemented a decade earlier. To put it in a larger time frame, the youth crime rate peaked in 1991, decreased substantially over the next decade, and then remained relatively stable until the recent downward trend. However, in contrast to the declining pattern of the youth crime rate, overall, the rate of *violent* youth crime has been steadily increasing since the mid-1980s. By 2007, this rate was double what it had been 20 years earlier and was largely made up of increases in common assault, which accounted for about 6 in 10 violent incidents committed by youth. This increase is accounted for in part by an actual increase in crime, but it also might be due to increased reporting and charging practices. By 2013, however, the rate was 16 per cent lower than the previous year and 39 per cent lower than a decade before.

The number of youth accused of homicide rose from 35 in 2012 to 40 in 2013, although the rate was lower than the 10-year average (Statistics Canada 2014b; see also Chapter 3). Youth homicide rates can vary considerably from one year to the next because of the relatively small number of offences. This can lead to a misinterpretation, especially if such a change is reported in the media without the underlying absolute change. And, as was seen in the opening news story about Markel Downey, the aspiring young boxer from Preston, youth homicide can be portrayed as "out of character."

In addition, in 2013, almost 18,000 youth were accused of a drug violation under the Controlled Drugs and Substances Act (CDSA), the majority (81 per cent) of which involved possession of cannabis. While the rates of youth accused of drug offences decreased for most drugs, rates for certain drug violations remained higher than a decade ago. For instance, while possession of cannabis decreased slightly between 2012 and 2013 (–1 per cent), the rate remained 30 per cent higher than in 2003 (600 youth accused per 100,000 youth population versus 462 youth accused per 100,000 youth population) (Statistics Canada 2014b). Part of this increase is artificial in that the CDSA, which was introduced in 1997 and which replaced the Narcotic Control Act, strengthened law enforcement. The CDSA also broadened the range of illegal substances to include amphetamines, LSD, and anabolic steroids (CanLII 1996).

Before we move on to discuss the limits of statistics, what also deserves mention in terms of the official statistics on youth crime is that many youth who could have been charged with an offence are handled outside the formal justice system. In 2013, 55 per cent of youth accused were dealt with by other means, while the remaining 45 per cent were formally charged by police. The decline in charges against youth accused of a crime followed the introduction of the Youth Criminal Justice Act (YCJA) in 2003. Since the YCJA was introduced, the proportion of accused youth who were cleared by means other than a charge increased for most offences. As discussed in Chapter 3, a primary objective of the YCJA was to divert youth involved in minor, non-violent crimes from the formal justice system, creating procedures for the police use of discretion. Obviously, charges are still the norm for serious offences, such as homicide, but less serious offences, such as minor theft, are more likely to be diverted from the criminal justice system (Barnhorst 2004).

For reasons associated with these legal changes, the youth crime rate can increase while the charge rate itself drops. Obviously, this means that accused youth are dealt with through means other than the formal system. Since about 2000, the proportion of youth apprehended but not charged has been on the rise, but this trend increased sharply after the introduction of the YCJA (as discussed in Chapter 3).

When it comes to some cases, however, such changes can lead to the charge that the system is now too lenient when it comes to young offenders. For example, in October 2004, 16-year-old Archie Billard ran a red light and crashed into Theresa McEvoy, a teacher's aide and mother of three, killing her instantly. He was speeding, was driving a stolen car, and was being chased by police. He was so high he had no memory of the incident, but he pled guilty to negligence causing death in 2006. The public was outraged because he had a string of convictions and was awaiting trial on other offences (CTV 2006). The circumstances surrounding the case led to a provincial inquiry (the Nunn Inquiry) that recommended changes to the federal Youth Criminal Justice Act. After pleading guilty to criminal negligence in McEvoy's death, Billard was sentenced to four years in prison, was released in 2009, and was then readmitted twice for statutory violations in that and the following year. Typical comments at the time were that he was unremorseful, that he was irresponsible, and that he was playing the system.

Limits of the Official Version of Youth Crime

Official crime statistics are produced through work—through people reporting crime to police, who then investigate, record, and lay charges that are then prosecuted in court. The machinery of (law and) order, so to speak, creates the product of crime, for until a crime is accepted, defined, and convicted, it is not a tangible thing. Crime is, as noted at the outset of this chapter, a social construct, an actuarial product. However, the quality of the raw material going into the crime machine is affected by five factors because (1) crime is report-sensitive, which means that the willingness of the victim to report the crime determines whether the police know about it; (2) crime is policing-sensitive, which means that the level of police enforcement determines whether the crime gets counted; (3) crime is definition-sensitive, which means that a change in the law affects whether something is called a crime; (4) crime is media-sensitive, which means that if crimes are publicized, a "feedback loop" can change the public's perceptions and their willingness to report; and (5) real trends in the number of crimes in society change over time (McCormick 2008). Let's deal with three of these issues briefly, as they are relevant to the topic of youth deviance: law enforcement, legal definitions, and media practices.

Law Enforcement Practices

The ways in which police departments enforce and record criminal activity also affect the UCR statistics. These practices can range from low clearance rates to police discretion (Black 1970). Ironically, increasing police efficiency can also increase crime rates, as departments adopt more sophisticated computer technology, hire better-trained employees, and improve record-keeping ability. In addition, discretion affects the way in which police enforce the laws on prostitution, drug crimes, traffic offences, and Internet crimes. For example, cannabis possession went from 2300 cases in 1968 to 44,000 cases in 2006 owing to increased use but also to increased police enforcement. Drug enforcement is higher in jurisdictions where forfeiture laws allow police to retain seized assets, raising drug arrest rates by about 18 per cent (Mast, Benson, and Rasmussen 2000). This enforcement disproportionately affects the young, and in many jurisdictions the law allows for discretion in traffic stops, which can then lead to so-called out-of-sight offences, such as police finding marijuana in the car.

Legal Definitions

Changes to the law affect the crime rate. For example, broadening the Criminal Code's definition of arson 20 years ago to include mischief or suspicious fires resulted in an increase of 17 per cent in the arson rate (McCormick 2008). An even more dramatic example was sexual assault in 1983, 1988, and 1991, when changes were made to remove barriers affecting a victim's willingness to report, thus increasing the rate. Another legislative change worth study is the YCJA, which diverts youths who have committed non-violent crimes from the formal criminal justice system. Early on, the charge rate dropped from 56 per cent to 42 per cent, resulting in an apparent decrease in youth crime, while in fact the number of youth who came into contact with police actually increased.

Media Practices

The media too have played a role in the distortion of crime knowledge as measured by what is known by the police. For example, news of crimes committed in public by strangers against innocent victims encourages the perception that crime is random, sensitizing the public to fear crime, perhaps causing changes in police enforcement or legislative changes (Kappeler 1996). News about crime and deviance can also desensitize the public in the opposite direction. For example, in the 1990s when sex-trade workers started disappearing on the Lower Mainland in Vancouver, media accounts ran stories about "hookers" who police said had simply moved away. This became a predominant version to account for the disappearances even though others insisted that a serial killer was to blame. Years before the name *Robert Pickton* became common knowledge, the message the public got was one that encouraged apathy and disinterest in missing and murdered women (McCormick 2010).

When we extrapolate this theme to youth crime, if there is a disproportionate number of articles on the topic or a disproportionate stress on violent crimes, for example, this is the version the public has knowledge of. Whether it is an accurate version is irrelevant because it becomes the template for reporting and policing youth crime. In the media analysis discussed later in this chapter, the national news almost consistently reports only on homicides committed by youth; thus the reader gets the predominant impression of violent youth, again as in the example of Downey at the beginning of the chapter. This impression has little to do with the conditions that produced the "young offender" in the first place. In that example, what is left unsaid is that North Preston is the oldest black community in Canada, settled by Loyalists who were not allowed to settle in white communities. The experience of segregation and racism is the background that is left out of the story.

Interestingly, the CCJS *Juristat* series is an important source of data for the media, as it presents complex information in a way that makes it appealing for the media to report the facts. The creation of UCR statistics originally was as much about providing journalists with information about crime as it was about measuring police workload. Today, the media influence the timing and wording of press releases, the types of statistics used, and the types of information presented. Furthermore, "information officers" provide the media with crime stories, as it is often beyond the scope of a reporter's ability to gather such information otherwise.

In conclusion, the official version of crime is the normative version, being the authoritarian representation of crime. Its character as mathematically produced and textually presented contributes to its authenticity. However, its limit is that it represents what the state knows and decides is worthy to count as crime. The official version is a pallid facsimile and aggregated conglomerate of youth crime and gives little voice to the practices that produced youth crime or to the violence that is often at its core. Understanding the limits of official statistics, however, does not mean that they are easily rectified, although other attempts to discover the more accurate reality of crime have been tried.

The Unofficial Version: Alternative Methods of Measuring Youth Crime

The various limits of official statistics have led criminologists to seek alternative sources of information to measure behaviour not reported to police and also to measure victimless crimes such as substance abuse. The assumption is that techniques can be devised to catch the dark figure of crime missed in official statistics and thus to supplement and expand official data. As discussed in Chapter 2, unreported crime is measured through victimization surveys, and deviant behaviour can be measured through self-report surveys. Moreover, it is relevant to comment further on these data-collection methods in connection with a discussion of the comparable role of the media in generating knowledge about youth crime.

Self-Report and Victimization Surveys

Self-report surveys ask participants to reveal information about deviance that may have been committed by or against them. Through interviews, telephone surveys, or anonymous questionnaires, self-reports are viewed as a way to get at delinquency in particular, which is often missed by official statistics.

Using self-report studies to collect information on young offenders in school is convenient and practical because many young people can be questioned at the same time. And because school attendance is mandatory up to the age of 16, a school-based self-report survey provides a fairly reliable snapshot of a cross-section of the population. Self-reports have also been used to examine the offence histories of prison inmates, drug users, and other groups (e.g., see Cantor and Lynch 2000). While self-reports are not used very often, perhaps because of the reliance on official statistics, they provide a broader picture of the distribution of deviance than do official data. They also provide a check on that data. For example, racial bias may be present if surveys indicate that white and non-white people report unequal levels of police attention, while official data indicate similar rates of whites and non-whites being arrested or stopped by police. It is in the self-reports that disclosure about police treatment of minorities is made available. Such surveys are also a way to see the distribution of criminal behaviour across racial, class, age, and gender lines (e.g., see Smart and Adlaf 1991).

A 1999 self-report study surveyed 2001 students ages 12 to 18 in 67 Alberta junior and senior high schools on perceptions of violence and personal safety, their own victimization and delinquent behaviour, and weapons possession. The survey revealed more information than would generally be known through other means (Gomes, Bertrand, Paetsch, and Hornick 2003). A similar study surveyed 3400 high school students and 400 street youth in Toronto about victimization, youth crime, and participation in gangs. What was revealing about this study was how criminality was often chosen as a means of survival (Tanner and Wortley 2002).

In 2010, the Canadian Alcohol and Drug Use Monitoring Survey of 3989 Canadians ages 15 years and older found that the prevalence of cannabis use had decreased significantly since 2004, from 37 to 25 per cent; the average age of initiation for cannabis use was approximately 15 years; and 7 per cent reported using at least one of five illicit drugs (cocaine, crack, speed, ecstasy, hallucinogens), down 11.3 per cent since 2004. Alcohol use declined from 83 per cent in 2004 to 72 per cent in 2010. Youth are more likely to report harm from substance abuse, and the International Youth Survey found that delinquent behaviour was significantly more prevalent among youth who consumed alcohol (35 per cent), took drugs (60 per cent), had delinquent friends (27 per cent), or had little parental supervision (56 per cent) (Health Canada 2010).

In line with that study, the Centre for Addiction and Mental Health conducted a national random survey of alcohol and drug use (the Canadian Campus Survey 2004) of over 6000 undergraduate students from Canadian universities. It showed heavy drinking (16 per cent), cannabis use (32 per cent), and other illicit drug use (9 per cent). There is no victim in the traditional sense in such deviance, and so self-report studies are almost the only way to collect such information. Various other drug use surveys include those done by the Addiction Research Foundation and the Canadian Centre on Substance Abuse, the Canadian Community Health Survey, and the Canadian Addiction Survey.

Victimization data have also been collected alongside self-report data in international youth surveys. Mentioned above, the International Youth Survey is conducted in over 30 countries. One cycle of the survey of more than 3200 youth in middle school revealed that 37 per cent of Toronto students had committed acts of violence, property crime, or drug dealing (Savoie 2007). Over 40 per cent of the students said they had been victimized at least once in the previous year but many did not report the incidents to the authorities. The findings of this survey would be surprising to anyone whose knowledge of youth crime was confined to official statistics. For example, in the previous year, 20 per cent of youth also reported committing at least one delinquent act, and they were often responsible for a high number of repeated acts of deviance. Overall, about 13 per cent of Toronto youth reported violent behaviour, and about the same number of students reported property-related crime. Carrying a weapon and participating in fights accounted for 88 per cent of violent acts, and vandalism and shoplifting were common property offences. Delinquency was highest in public places where there was less supervision, an obvious risk factor.

Other research has shown that the early onset of delinquency is a significant factor in repeat offences, with youth who began their "court career" at age 12 having an average of about 8 incidents. In comparison, those whose first incident was at age 21 had an average of about 1 incident. Most of the time these youth were with other people when they committed delinquent acts, such as arson (92 per cent), vandalism (81 per cent), breaking and entering (80 per cent), threatening someone (70 per cent), and assault (60 per cent). In 58 per cent of the cases, the delinquency was undiscovered, but when it was, it was punished (67 per cent). Youth reported being victimized by theft (28 per cent) or bullying (21 per cent), but reported the incidents in only 14 per cent of the cases. The reasons given for not reporting to the police were "not important enough" (36 per cent) or that it was dealt with another way (20 per cent). Delinquency itself appeared to contribute significantly to victimization, with 56 per cent of delinquent youth reporting being victimized compared to 36 per cent of those who did not (Carrington, Matarazzo, and deSouza 2005).

The risk factors for delinquency have also been studied using data from self-report and victimization surveys (Savoie 2007). Risk factors included being in step- or single-parent families (35 per cent and 25 per cent, respectively), rather than in double-parent families. Not surprisingly, over one-third of youth who reported that they did not get along with their parents had engaged in delinquency, compared to 20 per cent of youth who reported that they did get along well with at least one of their parents. Even less surprisingly, delinquency was relatively rare among youth who said their parents always knew who they were with when they went out (12 per cent), compared to youth (56 per cent) who said their parents never knew. Delinquency was highest among those who used drugs (60 per cent) and alcohol (35 per cent), compared to those who didn't use drugs (16 per cent) or those who didn't drink (9 per cent). Overall, what is significant is the much higher rate of both offending and victimization than the rate reported in official crime statistics. Specifically, the official rate of 7 per cent is far lower than that admitted in the self-report survey population of 37 per cent in both offending and victimization. Also, what we see is that youth commit both violent and property offences relatively equally, quite often undetected, in the company of others with predictable underlying risk factors. And, finally, we also see that most offences are committed by a disproportionally smaller portion of the population.

Overall, official statistics and unofficial data are complementary sources of information. Official statistics reflect those crimes that come to the attention of the police, while self-report and victimization studies reflect a wide range of incidents that might not. In addition, some forms of unofficial data get at a broader range of behaviour, since the deviance under study is quite often soft, such as drug use or truancy, for example. Moreover, these types of studies show the importance of asking people directly about crime, deviance, and victimization.

Youth Crime in the Media

We have looked at youth crime in two ways, discussing both official statistics (represented by police data) and unofficial data (collected through surveys). Official statistics show a steady decline in youth crime, except for a gradual increase in violent crime. Much youth crime has been property related and gender biased, and reflects an interest in diversion since the introduction of the YCJA. On the other hand, unofficial data show that youth commit property and violent crime almost equally and show a much higher rate of offending than is disclosed in official statistics. The data are complementary in that they fill out the details of crime not reported to the police and also begin to reveal some of the context in which youth crime occurs. However, the difficulty with both sources of information is that they are not how most people know about youth crime. For most people, media coverage is the main way of knowing about youth crime. For example, a recent government report on the primary source of information used by Canadians to learn about the youth justice system shows that the vast majority derive their information from newspapers, TV or radio news, and other media (see Figure 6.1). Consequently, it is important to see if youth crime in the media is portrayed in a way that is similar to or different from the other two ways of knowing discussed here.

Social scientists have frequently looked at media coverage of crime and deviance (see, generally, Chiricos, Eschholz, and Gertz 1997; Fishman 1981). They have looked at the media more as a source of misinformation than as a source of information, because it often exaggerates the impact of street crime (Fishman 1978) or misconstructs the nature of corporate crime. This helps explain how there is a discrepancy between dropping rates of youth crime and the perception that youth crime is out of control. It is caused by the fact that media coverage is distorted (Schissel 1997). Whether in the reporting of freeway crashes, shark attacks, serial killers, or youth super-predators, the media can be blamed for getting it wrong and misinforming the public (Best 1999).

The misrepresentation of crime in the media, for example, can cause fear and anxiety by distorting the frequency or severity of youth crime, thereby creating the impression that youth crime is more of a problem than it really is. However, to rest with the academic criticism that the media simply gets it wrong is inadequate, as it assumes that the media should do as good a job in portraying crime as we do in knowing it as criminologists. What is more important is to understand the consequences of the (distorted) portrayals the public receives.

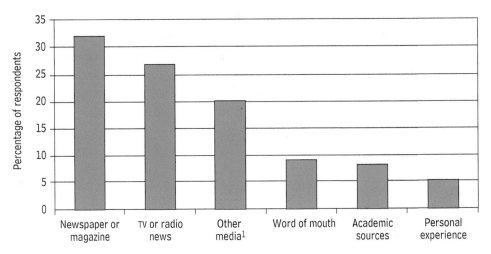

FIGURE 6.1 Primary Source of Information about the Canadian Youth Criminal Justice System

1. Includes movies, TV shows, and the Internet

Note: Respondents were also asked to identify their primary source of information about the youth criminal justice system in Canada. More than half (59 per cent) relied primarily on newspapers, magazines, or news stories from television or radio. Very few (8 per cent) relied on more academic sources, such as university courses, government reports, or books, and even fewer relied on first-hand experience (5 per cent).

Source: *The 2008 National Justice Survey: The Youth Justice System in Canada and the Youth Criminal Justice Act*. Figure 1: Primary Source of Information about the Youth Criminal Justice System, page 4, http://www.justice.gc.ca/eng/rp-pr/cj-jp/yj-jj/rr08_yj1-rr08_jj1/rr08_yj1.pdf. Department of Justice Canada, 2008. Reproduced with the permission of the Department of Justice Canada, 2015.

The Construction of the Research

There is not much research on media coverage of youth crime. Most crime and media research focuses on more hot-button, social-panic issues, such as child abuse and abduction, diseases, and homicide (Best 1993; Jenkins 1994)—crimes where it is easy to see that the media distort the danger of strangers, the risks to children, and the frequency of serial homicide in society. However, Jane Sprott (1996) gives a good example of how we can begin an analysis using a **context analysis**. Based on the premise that the reality constructed by the news media might not reflect other images of reality, she compared newspaper articles on youth crime in three Toronto papers over a two-month period to the so-called Bala and Lilles Young Offenders Reporting Service over a two-year period.

Sprott found that the youth court cases were broken down as follows: charges involving violence (22 per cent), property crime (50 per cent), other Criminal Code offences (18 per cent), YOA offences (7 per cent), and other federal offences (3 per cent). In comparison, the media (*Globe and Mail*, *Toronto Star*, and *Toronto Sun*) focused almost exclusively on violent crime (94 per cent). Homicide, for example, constituted 0.02 per cent of youth court cases, was summarized in the Bala and Lilles Report slightly more often (7.8 per cent), and composed a weighty 70.4 per cent of Toronto newspaper coverage. On the other hand, property crime was reported in the news far less often than it appeared in court (5.3 per cent compared to 50 per cent) or than was summarized in the reports (19.7 per cent). We might surmise, then, that property crime is not as interesting to cover, but the consequence of the "if it bleeds, it leads" approach is the over-sensitization of the public to issues of violent youth crime.

context analysis
Analyzing media content for themes such as sensationalism or distortion.

This type of research methodology is quite simple. Take a sample of media coverage and compare the incidence of its stories to another source of information. In this case, youth court statistics were used, but the source could have been police reports or even self-report survey results. The objective will always be to see if media coverage is distorted in comparison to the more objective information, and if it is, one could conclude that the media exaggerate crimes of violence. The objective will never be to show that court statistics are not entertaining or interesting to read.

As well as a context difference, Sprott also noticed a content difference between the newspaper articles and the sentencing reports: the articles focused more on the impact of the crime, while the sentencing reports focused more on the reasons for judicial disposition. Privileging the latter, she criticized the media for not giving enough information for the public to understand the reasons for sentencing. If the media did that, then the public would have a better understanding of how the courts work, the reasons for sentencing, and thus the need (sometimes) to be "soft" on youth crime. However, the newspapers focused on the affective dimension by foregrounding the victim, while the sentencing report did not. Which was doing the better job?

In this vein, because the news media distort the proportion of youth violent crime, it is useful to measure the public perception of youth crime as it probably affects policy changes. Sprott found that those who thought sentences were too lenient were usually thinking specifically of repeat offenders and were slightly more likely to want harsher sentences. Those who believed that sentences were too lenient were also more likely to overestimate the amount of violent youth crime and to think that it has increased. Again, as we will see in the media analysis, this is an easy conclusion to come to when the majority of youth crime stories are about violence. Consequently, the public cannot be blamed for having little knowledge of how youth court works or for thinking violent youth crime is out of control, because the media do such a poor job in reporting cases.

This research dovetails nicely with a survey conducted by Baron and Hartnagel (1996), who found that respondents were quite punitive toward juvenile justice issues. This attitude was not based on experience of victimization but coincided with more conservative social values, which Baron and Hartnagel hypothesize were the result of how the media constructed youth crime. Fully 78 per cent of their respondents felt that youth courts were too lenient, but their own level of victimization was only 22 per cent. Baron and Hartnagel speculate that high-profile coverage surrounding the YOA combined with simplistic coverage of sensational cases brings to awareness "latent public fears," the first step in the spiral of events that can lead to a full public crusade. This is called the "amplification of deviance." While their study was not intended to be a systematic analysis of media coverage, it fits within the "distorted coverage produces public fear" equation proposed by social constructionists.

A more recent study of juvenile homicide in Chicago newspapers (see Boulahanis and Heltsey 2004) between 1992 and 2000 found that juvenile homicide rates declined but the number of cases receiving media coverage increased. There is no good reason for one to reflect the other, but it does mean that the media can overrepresent the amount of violent crime and thus distort public perception. Furthermore, this study found that news articles do a good job of covering youth crime but tend to focus on atypical cases. Most homicides are committed by males (90 per cent), but females make up 30 per cent of media coverage. Additionally, homicides committed against females were covered more than twice as often as cases involving male victims. In Chicago, black youth commit the most murders, but a case gets more coverage if it is committed by a white youth. Specifically, more than 59 per cent of cases involving Caucasian offenders received media coverage, compared to those involving African-Americans (21 per cent) and Latinos (17 per cent). The study also found that every one-year increase in offender age corresponded to a 28 per cent reduction in the odds of getting newspaper coverage, and homicides involving victims younger than 14 were 480 per cent more likely to receive coverage than homicides involving victims aged 20 to 29.

cultivation hypothesis
The hypothesis that the media inundate the public with ideas about crime.

After establishing these patterns and using a model called the **cultivation hypothesis** (Gerbner, Gross, Morgan, and Signorielli 1980; Hawkins and Pingree 1980), the researchers felt that distorted media coverage made people more fearful. It was not that atypical cases were getting covered and typical cases were not, rather that there was a mix of coverage with atypical cases getting disproportionately more coverage than the typical cases. The researchers conclude that this mixture makes it difficult to see patterns of victimization, just as Sprott (1996) concluded that media coverage makes it difficult for the public to understand sentencing patterns. Boulahanis and Heltsey (2004, p. 155) say that this "uncertainty produces a fear that anyone can be a victim and anyone can be a perpetrator," but go on to state that the resulting distortions include the perception that homicides committed by young persons represent a growing problem, which may or may not be the case.

As mentioned before, the rate of youth crime has been steadily dropping. In addition, since the introduction of the YCJA in 2003, the proportion of apprehended youth formally charged with crimes has dropped because the YCJA diverts youth from the court system. However, as this is perhaps not general knowledge, it does not reassure the public when they hear news reports of youth violence.

The Social Constructionist Analysis

social constructionism
An approach that sees social problems as constructed in the media; see *moral panic*.

A large literature on **social constructionism** has developed over the past 40 or so years (see, for example, Altheide 2006; Goode 2009). This approach is more complicated than the context analysis approach mentioned above in that we are not comparing indices, so to speak, or asking how well the media report some objectively constructed reality. Rather, we are looking more closely at the discursive constructions used in media texts. In the analysis of prostitution in the Vancouver news in the 1980s, for example, it is argued that the word *hooker* desensitizes viewers and actually destroys any empathy the public might have for the victims of a serial killer (McCormick 2010). This discursive construction contributed to what John Lowman (2000) calls the "discourse of disposal"—that is, how media descriptions of the attempt of politicians, police, and residents' groups to get rid of street prostitution from residential areas actually contributed to a sharp increase in murders of street prostitutes in British Columbia after 1980. A geographic and political marginalization of street prostitution was aided by the symbolic marginalization created in the media, which ultimately led to violence against street prostitutes.

Social constructionist analysis usually has several main themes. First, there is the suggestion that the media present violence as a growing social problem, much like an epidemic or plague (see Best and Horiuchi 1985). Second, there are usually innocent victims and guilty predators who prey on those victims (see D'Arcy 2007). Third, there is also usually a link or **convergence** between a new problem and an existing one—for example, stalking and domestic violence, or Internet luring and pedophilia (see Doyle 2000). And fourth, there are claims-makers, such as police, politicians, or advocates, who advance the idea that the described social problem is growing, is out of control, or needs attention (see Dowler 2003). These are all basic elements of a constructionist approach that are easily applied to an analysis of youth crime in the media.

In the first example of constructionist research considered here, Spencer (2005) looks at select high-profile coverage of youth violence in 1994. In contrast to accounts that focus simplistically on media distortions that create a sense of (un)certainty in the audience, Spencer adopts the view that the media trades on the ambiguous culpability of youth in that they are both victimizer and victimized. He chose 1994 because it was prior to the Columbine school shooting, youth violence had peaked, and several sensational cases (in the US and abroad) were the focus of media attention. He chose commentary sections of the news, in venues such as *The New York Times*, *Time* magazine, *Newsweek*, and *US News & World Report*.

Spencer found that youth violence was promoted as though it was at a crisis level, that numerical estimates of its magnitude portrayed it as growing, that it was spreading geographically and could strike anyone and anywhere, and that atrocity tales were used to highlight the sensationalism of the issue. The crisis of youth violence was also linked to existing social problems, such as unemployment, single-parent families (single-mom or missing-dad), crack cocaine, child abuse, and the increasing use of guns. These are standard elements of a constructionist analysis, and they show how the public can get a distorted perception of youth crime.

Moreover, contextualizing the issue in this way raised issues of how culpable these youth were and how the audience was to relate to them emotionally. This raised the issue of whether they were victims or victimizers, or both. These are two contradictory images: are they to be feared or sympathized with; are they responsible or lost? Spencer (2005) calls this an **ideological flexibility**, and he suggests that the ambiguity in portrayal might be extended to analysis of other topics, such as mothers who kill their children, female partners who kill their abusive partners, or people who (knowingly) transmit the AIDS virus. This is a stronger version of "uncertainty" in media portrayal than was suggested earlier, and it presents a more complicated reality for the public to digest, as displayed in the opening news story of this chapter. This ideological flexibility also creates confusion when we cannot easily distinguish the victims from the villains.

In general, constructionist analysis would say that violent youth crime is overrepresented in the media, while youth property crime is under-represented. The public gets the message that violent youth crime is a significant problem, and it connects these patterns through an inordinate focus on victims. This message distorts perception and in doing so affects the reported rates of youth crime and the public's willingness to press charges,

convergence
When a current issue is framed in terms of its relation to a previous one.

ideological flexibility
Where the portrayal of persons is ambiguous—for example, a young offender is portrayed as both villain and victim.

the eventual result being added pressure on politicians to change the law. Even when elements of youth's background might help portray them in a more sympathetic light, because of ideological flexibility they help portray youth's fall as all the more tragic.

The Implication of the Patterns in Media Coverage of Youth Crime

As we have seen, there are certain patterns in media coverage of youth crime. Violent youth crime is overrepresented in the media, while youth property crime is under-represented; atypical cases get disproportionately more coverage than typical cases, emotion gets more foreground than structural background, and the resulting product is a public misperception about youth crimes. However, simply comparing media coverage to police statistics or court cases and criticizing the former presumes that the media have an obligation to report faithfully what is known by those other entities; that is, critics often argue that if the media's coverage of crime is distorted and sensationalized in comparison to that of other sources, then the media are inaccurate and responsible for the public's more punitive attitudes and, inevitably, for politicians seeking to cash in on those fears.

This method of characterizing the relationship between media knowledge and crime knowledge makes the mistake of privileging the latter while ignoring the problems inherent in generating official and unofficial crime data. As we saw earlier, there are problems with both police information and self-report studies, but they are complementary in giving us different images of what is putatively the same universe of behaviours: youth deviance. But they are images only, each with its own benefits and limit. Media knowledge is similarly a window on the world (see McCormick 2010), but there seems to be no ready reason why the media should mirror what is known by the police any more than police statistics should mirror juvenile self-reports. I suggest that instead of being antagonistic bodies of knowledge, they are imbricated scales, ways of measuring behaviour that are slightly overlapping (as shown in Figure 6.2).

Thinking of media knowledge in this way gives it a legitimacy that is often lacking in shallow versions of social constructionism, such as context analysis. Instead of seeing how well the media conform to a different way of measuring youth crime, we can use an alternative model such as **frame analysis** to see how the media frame or portray youth crime and how the media allow us to develop deeper cultural understandings of youth, especially when we combine frame analysis with a **critical discourse analysis** (Fairclough 2003; Wodak and Meyer 2000) to see the link between those portrayals and the larger political structure of society.

Using such an approach also opens the door to analyzing in more detail the role of the media in the public sphere. And for there to be a role for the media in the public sphere, the media have to be construed as more than a simple conduit for political opinion or police knowledge. Rather, the media have to be seen as a forum for debate, right or wrong, just or unjust. Debates that are divided and difficult do not rely on the idea that hegemony does not somehow simply exist; instead they show us how it is accomplished through discourse. Making claims about putative conditions and about the persons who it is suggested are responsible for those conditions, especially if we are not quite clear about their responsibility, is a good case study in the building of consensus.

frame analysis
Analyzing media content to see how crime and criminals are depicted.

critical discourse analysis
An approach in sociolinguistics that links discourse with political structure.

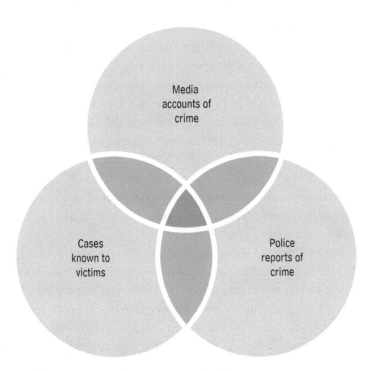

FIGURE 6.2 Different Ways of Knowing Youth Crime

A study that has looked at this issue of public debate in more detail is Hogeveen (2005). Through an analysis of House of Commons debates and some media reports, he explores the construction of the category of "the punishable young offender." According to his analysis, media reports of debates in the House of Commons in the late 1990s created a new discursive category that emphasized protecting the public from risks associated with youth crime. The public concern about young offenders in Parliament and in the media centred on replacing the YOA with a tougher law based on accountability—the YCJA. The shift in how juvenile offenders are characterized is all the more glaring when the YCJA is compared to the Juvenile Delinquents Act of 1908, where the dominant model was a family-centred, welfare, rehabilitative approach.

The selection of media articles that Hogeveen uses is not systematic, however, but is especially appropriate in showing how there is a valorization of victims in media coverage. For example, several years ago, former Alliance MP Jay Hill from British Columbia was able to name victims (who would have been in the news) as if everyone knew who they were, as in the following:

> In my home province of British Columbia, the names of Reena Virk, Dawn Shaw, and Trygve Magnusson represent just a few victims who died at the hands of violent youth. Their senseless deaths demand laws from the government that punish and deter those who commit violent acts and provide mandatory rehabilitation programs during incarceration. (*Hansard*, 21 October 1999, cited in Hogeveen 2005, p. 84)

These names would not make sense as anchors in a political argument if they were not well known to the public. As well, the late British Columbia MP Chuck Cadman, an important critic of the YOA, championed victims' rights after his son was a victim of an unprovoked attack in Surrey. In late October 1992, Cadman's 16-year-old son Jesse was stabbed to death in a so-called random street attack by a group of young people. In response to that event, Cadman and his wife Dona created the group Crime Responsibility and Youth, and he decided to enter politics to campaign for tougher juvenile justice legislation. In 1997 he introduced a private member's bill, saying, "It's a crapshoot, basically. If I'm successful with it, then we get a lot of good stuff done. If I'm not . . . at least we start to get some discussion." He called for changes to the Criminal Code allowing that there be formal recognition of victims in the justice system, that victims be kept informed of the progress of police investigations, and that restitution by the offender be given for psychological harm done to victims (*The Province* 1997).

Joe Wambach became another important claims-maker after his son was victimized in Toronto. These claims-makers are important for their role in the valorization of victims and for laying the groundwork for establishing that juveniles are "getting away with crime." They have used their experiences as media fodder in a way that other victims might not be able to, capitalizing and politicizing those experiences for a public unable to know how normative those experiences might be.

Hogeveen argues that the construction of the "punishable young offender" in political and media discourse is based on the perceived inadequacy of current law, on the centrality of victims, on a get-tough discourse, and, of course, on emotionality, as in former MP Mark Crawford's comments: "Where does it end? Local parents and other citizens are calling for vigilante justice. They do not trust our current system of justice that it lets off criminals with a slap upon the wrist while the victims are left in limbo for the rest of their lives" (*Hansard*, 2 May 1994, cited in Hogeveen 2005, p. 79). This comment from 1994 perhaps does not reflect current discourse, but it is uttered in the lead-up to changing juvenile justice legislation. This symbiotic relationship between violent offenders, valorized victims, and calls for tougher legislation is accomplished through debate (in the media). And I argue here that it is through the public arena of the media that this building of consensus happens. It is not as simple as privileging one form of knowledge over another—say official statistics over media stories. That is too easy a criticism. The media is a site for sensationalism and exaggeration, and at the same time it is a place of debate and correction. For example, in a letter to the editor written in June 1998, Anthony Doob, a leading University of Toronto criminologist, made the following point:

> It is not surprising to see a *Globe and Mail* editorial (March 16) suggesting, once again, that the Young Offenders Act be toughened up. . . . What is surprising, however, is that the *Globe and Mail* editorial board used patently false information . . . to support its editorial position. . . . The manner in which we as a society deal with young offenders is important. We have to decide, for example, whether we are interested in focusing more on ways to make Canada a safer place to live or on making symbolic gestures that make older people feel that they are being tough. These are legitimate choices that should be debated. The debate is not served, however, by dishonest (or incompetent) reporting of what the current law is.

A challenge, indeed.

In the next section, we introduce research findings from an ongoing critical discourse analysis media study of newspaper reporting on young offenders in Canada. This sample of findings from ongoing research supplements the data reported by Hogeveen (2005) and helps us to further appreciate the key role that the media play in producing knowledge about youth crime.

An Example of the Media Analysis of Newspaper Articles on Youth Crimes

The following media analysis research findings are derived from a study carried out by the author that involved searching the *National Post* newspaper from 1995 to 2003 for the term *young offender*. The study is based on Hogeveen's suggestion (2005) that media reports of debates in the House of Commons in the late 1990s created a new discursive category that emphasized protecting the public from risks associated with youth crime—the so-called "punishable young offender." The search yielded 121 relevant articles. The results were separated by year and by subject matter, and were analyzed for discursive trends using critical discourse analysis, a qualitative approach that looks for themes in media discourse related to structural issues. The intent was to see what themes, if any, could be found in this national newspaper that would support a tougher approach to juvenile offenders. Five themes were identified: editorializing, moral outrage, atrocity tales, problem defining events, and the valorization of victims, as shown in Box 6.1.

Although the *National Post*, being a national newspaper, was found not to have as many local stories about young offenders as local papers did, it did contain articles that reflected the national debate over youth crime and the lack of effectiveness of the youth justice system and the disproportionate attention given to youth violent crimes. In this sense, the national paper was both reflecting and reproducing a national "reader." Between 1995 and 1998, there were no stories in the *National Post* directly related to young offenders. However, from 1999 onward stories about young offenders began to appear more frequently, and they dealt typically with more national trends and issues and youth violent crimes.

Description of Findings

There were ten stories about young offenders in 2000; three in 2001; four in 2002; and six in 2003. Stories with little length were put into "briefs"; articles that were really about something else, such as the accidental shooting of an officer by another during pursuit of young offenders, were put into "tangents"; and articles making comments on some aspect of the system were put into "overviews." Some briefs, such as "Ontario: Teen Convicted of Animal Cruelty after Barbecuing Dog" (*National Post*, 29 November 2001, p. A7), are horrifying because of their briefness (see Box 6.1), but in general there was little to comment on. So-called tangential articles were about prison reform, young offender facilities, and politicians inadvertently releasing the names of young offenders, which is against the law.

It was in the category of "overviews" that general comments were often the most measured and the most interesting, such as comments on the law being too soft on young

Box 6.1   Youth Justice in Action

Media Sample

1. Editorializing

"A Young Killer Gets Kid-Glove Treatment: Special Hearing May Set Murderer Free after Just 29 Months"

"He may be the luckiest young killer in Canada, and if his luck continues to hold, he could end up serving only 29 months for the vicious murder of an elderly Holocaust survivor he stabbed nine times in the throat in broad daylight. . . ." (1106 words)

Byline: Christie Blatchford, *National Post*, Page: A1, Feb. 26, 1999.

2. Moral Outrage

"Dead Girl's Dad Says Youth's Sentence a 'Joke': Dangerous Driving: Teenager Gets One Year for Accident that Killed Two"

" . . . he was driving struck and killed two other teens. Court heard that the accused, who can not be named as he is a young offender, drank six beers in two hours before getting behind the wheel. He was originally charged with impaired driving causing . . ." (326 words)

Byline: Kelly Egan (*Ottawa Citizen*), *National Post*, Page: A10, May 11, 1999.

3. Atrocity Tales

"Teen Convicted of Animal Cruelty after Barbecuing Dog"

"A 17-year-old girl was convicted this week of animal cruelty after she beat and then barbecued her family's Pomeranian. The 12-year-old dog, named Peppy, had been a family pet for the past seven years. The young offender could face up to six months in jail, but the horrific case has renewed calls for stiffer penalties." (57 words)

Source: Brief, *National Post*, Page: A7, Nov. 29, 2001.

4. Problem Defining Event

"'Killer Kelly' Was Toughest Girl in the Gang, Friends Said: Results of Psychiatric Examinations Contradictory"

" . . . At the time of the fatal attack, Ellard was 15 and could have been tried as a young offender. In deciding whether to try her as an adult, the court turned to the evidence of a battery of experts, including . . ." (563 words)

Byline: Mark Hume, *National Post*, Page: A8, Apr. 1, 2000.

5. Valorization of Victims

"Bill to Give Victims of Crime More Rights: Offenders Would Pay into Fund to Help Injured Party"

" . . . Reform MP who has campaigned for increased victims' rights since his 16-year-old son, Jesse, was murdered by a young offender almost seven years ago, welcomed the new legislation. Mr. Cadman noted MPs from all parties supported victims . . . " (461 words)

Byline: Tim Naumetz (Southam News), *National Post*, Page: A7, Apr. 16, 1999.

We emphasize once again that this kind of media-based editorializing has been shown in many research studies to have measurable impacts on public perceptions and legislation affecting at-risk youth, young offenders, and the youth justice system.

offenders or Anthony Doob's dispute with Ontario's justice minister over the effectiveness of boot camps in reducing recidivism (Doob and Cesaroni 2004). The government had taken the recidivism statistics from a boot camp facility and had then compared them to those in regular jails and found a significant difference. However, the government had taken out those who had dropped out of the program before comparing the two groups statistically, artificially inflating its success. And in 2001, Vic Toews, the then new Canadian Alliance justice critic, voiced his wide-ranging objections to the youth justice reform bill that was to be tabled by Anne McLellan, the justice minister. On 5 February 2001, it was reported in the *National Post* that

[h]e opposes the new law's emphasis on cautions and out-of-court sanctions and its end to the practice of sending the worst offenders to adult court. "If we don't bring accountability into our youth justice system, we are breeding criminals in youth courts," he said. "Violent, repeat offenders need to be held accountable in adult court." He also wanted broader publication of names of young offenders. "I think it's wrong that people in a community can't be warned about a young offender living among them."

Similarly, David Young, the attorney general of Ontario, was quoted as saying on 15 June 2001 that "[n]one of these concerns [about the YCJA] were addressed in the bill. [The] Act is weak-kneed. It fails to protect the public." These "overview" articles, with their comments on the system at large, contextualize individual stories that might be published or aired about young offenders committing crimes. The year 2001 confirmed the suspicion that unusual cases are highlighted. There was a story about a Quebec teenager with racist tendencies and psychotic delusions who lured a Cuban-born girl to a gravel pit to kill her, and another about a girl who barbecued the family dog.

Between 2000 and 2003, the *National Post* contained 23 stories on young offenders. Because of this small sample it is difficult to generalize about the overall nature of media coverage. However, using an inductive method, we can see if there are any patterns. The year 2000 saw an article about the murder of a cross-dressing teenager; two articles on the extradition hearing of an Israeli soldier wanted for murder in a park; one on a carjacking in Forest Hill; one on a first-degree murder case in Newfoundland; two on the trial for the accused in the case of the Chatham, Ontario, boy found hanging from a hook in a school bathroom; two on the swarming death trial of Reena Virk's assailants; and one on the trial of the youth who killed a shop owner by stabbing him 50 times. These cases, mostly murder, are also fairly unusual and highly violent.

Given the number of youth crimes in Canada in 2000 and the number that went to court, the "national reader" is left reading a highly select group of articles. The *Juristat* publication on crimes in Canada that year reported that 22,635 youths were charged with violent crime, of which 16,404 were assaults. Of those charged with homicide, 8 per cent were youths, for a total of 41 cases.

One year, however, stands out in comparison to the rest in the 1995 to 2003 period. In 1999, there were a total of 50 articles, about half of which were primarily about crimes. This represents a remarkable spike in coverage in sheer numbers alone. One article was about a man who threatened police; the police arrived at his home to arrest him; a scuffle ensued; and people were shot. Another was about the shooting of an 11-year-old boy by a 13-year-old neighbour after a disagreement. Two articles were on a 16-year-old driving a van who struck and killed a police officer who was trying to lay down a nail belt to stop a high-speed chase outside Sudbury. Another concerned an 11-year-old who was set ablaze with kerosene and a lighter. There was an article about a 14-year-old boy who murdered a taxi driver with a baseball bat on a Hobbema reserve while his friends stole the alcohol he was delivering. There were two about the so-called Reena Virk case, two about a young woman who killed her parents on a ranch in Alberta, and one on a young man who severed the hand of another with a machete outside a bar in North York. Again, these articles were almost all about murders, unusual enough events in themselves, and all were told in a sensationalistic style.

In 1999, there were several more general pieces on victims, including one about greater compensation for crime victims; one on a new section of the YCJA that would punish parents if their children continued to commit crimes while at home (6 March), introduced in 1997 by Chuck Cadman; a comment by Priscilla de Villiers (9 March) on the need to get tough on the causes of crime; and several on recidivism in youth-care facilities. Chuck Cadman also spoke out on the need to lift publication bans in the cases of young offenders (12 March) and was criticized by then justice minister Anne McLellan for not understanding the youth crime legislation. There were also many other general articles on provisions of the YCJA and its implementation, and there were two on the rise in female offenders and overall trends in juvenile offenders.

What sense can we make of this? If we look at the sheer frequency of articles, 1999 is an important turning point. Examined critically, newspaper reporting shows a connection between individual crime stories and the larger political structure. Several features of the 1999 coverage bear this out. There are a lot of overview pieces—more than half of the coverage for 1999—with commentary by experts, by claims-makers who wished to advocate certain points of view about youth crime and its treatment, and by politicians. These articles create a discursive context within which to see youth crime. This is enhanced by primary news articles that also serve as platforms for the valorization of victims and the vilification of young offenders. In one article, "Dead Girl's Dad Says Youth's Sentence a 'Joke': Dangerous Driving: Teenager Gets One Year for Accident that Killed Two" (11 May), for example, a youth is given a sentence of open custody for dangerous driving causing death. The victim's father, who is by extension also a victim, uses the occasion of a specific crime to criticize the larger workings of the criminal law. Similarly, the use of headlines to accomplish a quick reading of the cases is easily demonstrated, as in "Daughter Charged in Brutal Slaying of Parents: First-Degree Murder: Two Teens Also Face Charges in Killing of Alberta Couple" (26 May); "15-Year Sentence Given in Home-Invasion Attack: Judge Calls Assault on Elderly Couple Horrific" (1 July); and "Beating Victim Still Comatose: 'Gang-Style Attack'" (10 July), which involved the beating of Jonathan Wamback. There was also the Forest Hill carjacking, "Teen in Forest Hill Carjacking Gets 3 Years: Lawyer and Wife Kidnapped, Beaten and Robbed" (3 September); and "Women Asked to Identify Their Underwear: Teen Charged after Bedroom Search Turns up Booty" (5 November).

The headlines draw in the national reader, who reads about salacious and horrific crimes in the context of a general commentary that is pro-victim and critical of the way youth are treated by the court and under the law. The year 1999 was a year for headlines above articles about highly violent and senseless crimes but also an opportunity for those who wished to make young offenders a social and political issue. In this way, specific crime discourse is tied to a larger political discourse, one that reflects and promotes a view of the world and of young offenders. The media then becomes a forum of debate, a punitive forum that is symbolic and communicative, regardless of youths' actual crimes or their ultimate dispensation. For most, the public forum of the media is the forum of the spectacle, and it is very real.

The key themes identified in this study, as well as examples of specific newspaper articles in which they appear, are highlighted in Box 6.1. These themes arguably frame the claim that the law on young offenders needed to be changed to make it less lenient on youth. The findings show that overall the *National Post* often served as a venue for giving voice to the claim that youth crime was out of control. Despite the lack of official corroboration by crime statistics, however, it is not simply that the media gets it wrong. The fact is that both sensationalism and correction, outlandish exaggeration and sober caution, are part of the public sphere that is the media. This debate, carried on in the public arena, creates a different way of knowing than is available through official crime statistics and/or self-report and victimization studies. It is important to see how the media constructs the reality that is youth crime, and at the same time it is important to realize that, for most people, that *is* their reality, whether it is grounded in objective information or not. In this case, as Hogeveen says, the media creates the category of "punishable young offender." It is a public criminology.

Summary

It is easy to privilege one way of knowing youth crime over another by using, for example, official statistics to criticize the way in which the media portray youth crime. Similarly, we could use self-report surveys to criticize police statistics, as if the former were better than the latter. Such approaches as context analysis are useful in using one measure to understand the limits of another. However, such approaches suggest that one way of "knowing" youth crime is inherently better than another.

Instead of privileging one way of knowing youth crime over the other, I suggest here that they are, at best, complementary forms of knowledge and, even better, different ways of knowing the world of youth crime. Yes, the media exaggerate and distort youth crime (from the perspective of official statistics), but perhaps the media is contributing to the public debate in a way that is unaccountable to official statistics and self-report surveys.

Some analysts (e.g., see McCormick 2010) have begun to get at some of the reasons this happens by suggesting that the media are part of a public debate at the beginning of the twenty-first century that is not accountable to official ways of knowing. And in the process we have moved to a harsher way of categorizing and conceptualizing youth crime, and the media constitute an important forum for that public debate.

Key Terms

context analysis

convergence

critical discourse analysis

cultivation hypothesis

folk devils

frame analysis

ideological flexibility

moral panic

social constructionism

Review Questions

1. This chapter describes three ways of knowing youth crime. What are these ways of knowing and how do they overlap?

2. What are the major problems with official statistics on youth crime as outlined in this chapter?

3. This chapter emphasizes the media as an important way for the public to know about youth crime. What do they learn from the media?

4. How do "atrocity tales" and other media patterns create a distorted reality of youth crime for the public?

Critical Thinking Questions

1. The valorization of victims in the media anchors the claim that politicians should get tougher on youth crime. Does this benefit the cause of victims in our society?

2. What would be a way to revise media coverage of youth crime to make it more accurate, less sensationalistic, and more educational for the public?

3. Imagine that you were a journalist who was asked to explain and defend why youth crime is reported in the media in the way that it is. How would you do this? What kinds of arguments would you put forth?

4. If you could work with high school students to design a public education project to highlight youth contributing to the community, what would you suggest? Specific elements would be a topic, such as the environment, venue, or media approach, and creative cultural materials. What would you do?

References

Altheide, D. (2006). Terrorism and the politics of fear. *Cultural Studies*, 6(4): 415–39.

Barnhorst, R. (2004). The Youth Criminal Justice Act: New directions and implementation issues, *Canadian Journal of Criminology and Criminal Justice*, 46(3): 231–50.

Baron, S., and Hartnagel, T. (1996). "Lock 'em up": Attitudes toward punishing juvenile offenders. *Canadian Journal of Criminology*, 28(2): 191–212.

Best, J. (1993). *Threatened children: Rhetoric and concern about child victims*. Chicago: University of Chicago Press.

Best, J. (1999). *Random violence: How we talk about new crimes and new victims*. Berkeley: University of California Press.

Best, J., and Horiuchi, G. (1985). The razor blade in the apple: The social construction of urban legends. *Social Problems*, 32(5): 488–99.

Black, D. (1970). Production of crime rates. *American Sociological Review*, 35(4): 733–48.

Blatchford, C. (1999, 26 February). A young killer gets kid-glove treatment: Special hearing may set murderer free after just 29 months. *National Post*, A1.

Boulahanis, J., and Heltsey, M. (2004). Perceived fears: The reporting patterns of juvenile homicide in Chicago newspapers. *Criminal Justice Policy Review*, 15(2): 132–60.

Boyce, J., Cotter, A., and Perreault, S. (2014, 4 December). Police-reported crime statistics in Canada, 2013. Retrieved from http://www.statcan.gc.ca/pub/85-002-x/2014001/article/14040-eng.htm

Canadian Campus Survey. (2004). Retrieved from http://www.camh.ca/en/research/research_areas/social-epiresearch/Documents/CCS_2004_report.pdf

Canadian Centre on Substance Abuse. (2011). Canadian Addiction Survey (CAS). Retrieved from http://www.ccsa.ca/eng/priorities/research/canadianaddiction/pages/default.aspx

CanLII. (1996). Controlled Drugs and Substances Act, 1996. Retrieved 23 December 2010 from http://www.canlii.org

Cantor, D., and Lynch, J. (2000). Self-report surveys as measures of crime and criminal victimization. *Criminal Justice, 4*.

Carrington, P.J., Matarazzo, A., and deSouza, P. (2005). Court careers of a Canadian birth cohort. Crime and Justice Research Paper Series. Statistics Canada Catalogue No. 85-561-MIE, no. 006. Ottawa.

CBC 2010. Archie Billard back in prison. Retrieved from http://www.cbc.ca/news/canada/nova-scotia/story/2010/10/25/ns-archie-billard-release-revoked.html

Chiricos, T., Eschholz, S. and Gertz, M. (1997). Crime, news and fear of crime: Toward an identification of audience effects. *Social Problems, 44*(3): 342–57.

Cloninger, D., and Sartorius, L. (1979). Crime rates, clearance rates and enforcement effort: The case of Houston, Texas. *American Journal of Economics and Sociology, 38*(4): 389–402.

Cohen, S. (1972). *Folk devils and moral panics: The creation of the mods and rockers*. London: MacGibbon and Rae.

CTV. (2006, 11 January). N.S. teen gets adult sentence for woman's death. Retrieved from https://www.treatingyourself.org/showthread.php?8935-N-S-teen-gets-adult-sentence/

D'Arcy, S. (2007). The "Jamaican criminal" in Toronto, 1994: A critical ontology. *Canadian Journal of Communication, 32*: 2.

Doob, A. (1998, 1 June). Young Offenders Act. *Globe and Mail*, Letter to the editor.

Doob, A., and Cesaroni, C. (2004). *Responding to youth crime in Canada*. Toronto: University of Toronto Press.

Dowler, K. (2003). Media consumption and public attitudes toward crime and justice: The relationship between fear of crime, punitive attitudes, and perceived police effectiveness. *Journal of Criminal Justice and Popular Culture, 10*(2): 109–26.

Doyle, V. (2000). Lead us not into temptation: The London, Ontario, "kiddie-porn ring" and the construction of a moral panic. *International Journal of Canadian Studies, 21*.

Egan, K. (1999, 11 May). Dead girl's dad says youth's sentence a "joke": Dangerous driving: Teenager gets one year for accident that killed two. *National Post (Ottawa Citizen)*, A10.

Fairclough, N. (2003). *Analyzing discourse: Textual analysis for social research*. London: Routledge.

Faith, K., and Jiwani, Y. (2002). The social construction of "dangerous" girls and women. In B. Schissel and C. Brooks (Eds), *Marginality and condemnation: An introduction to critical criminology* (pp. 83–107). Halifax: Fernwood.

Fishman, M. (1978). Crime waves as ideology. *Social Problems, 25*(5): 531–43.

Fishman, M. (1981). Police news: Constructing an image of crime. *Urban Life, 9*(4): 371–94.

Garofalo, J. (1981). Crime and the mass media: A selective review of research. *Journal of Research in Crime and Delinquency, 18*: 319–50.

Gerbner, G., Gross, L., Morgan, M., and Signorielli, N. (1980). The mainstreaming of America: Violence profile no. 11. *Journal of Communications, 30*: 10–29.

Global News. (2014, 2 December). Former Nova Scotia boxing prodigy charged in Cole Harbour triple shooting, by Rebecca Lau.

Gomes, J., Bertrand, L., Paetsch, J., and Hornick, J. (2003). Self-reported delinquency among Alberta's youth: Findings from a survey of 2,001 Junior and senior high school students. *Adolescence, 38*.

Goode, E. (2009). *Moral panics: The social construction of deviance*. Oxford, UK: Blackwell.

Hawkins, R., and Pingree, S. (1980). Some progress in the cultivation effect. *Communication Research, 7*: 193–226.

Health Canada. (2010). Canadian Alcohol and Drug Use Monitoring Survey. Retrieved from http://www.hc-sc.gc.ca/hc-ps/drugs-drogues/stat/_2010/summary-sommaire-eng.php

Hindelang, M.J. (1974). Public opinion regarding crime, criminal justice, and related topics. *Journal of Research in Crime and Delinquency, 11*: 101–16.

Hogeveen, B. (2005). "If we are tough on crime, if we punish crime, then people get the message": Constructing and governing the punishable young offender in Canada during the late 1990s. *Punishment and Society*, 7(1): 73–89.

Hume, M. (2000, 1 April). "Killer Kelly" was toughest girl in the gang, friends said: Results of psychiatric examinations contradictory. *National Post*, A8.

Jenkins, P. (1994). *Using murder: The social construction of serial homicide*. New York: Aldine de Gruyter.

Kappeler, V. (1996). *The mythology of crime and criminal justice*. Prospect Heights, US: Waveland Press.

Lowman, J. (2000). Violence and the outlaw status of (street) prostitution in Canada. *Violence against Women*, 6(9): 987–1011.

McCormick, C. (2008). *Criminology in Canada: Theories, patterns and typologies*. Toronto: Nelson.

McCormick, C. (2010). *Constructing danger: The mis/representation of crime in the news*. Halifax: Fernwood.

Mast, B., Benson, B., and Rasmussen, D. (2000). Entrepreneurial police and drug enforcement policy. *Public Choice*, 104(3–4): 285–308.

Muncie, J. (2004). *Youth and crime* (2nd ed.). London: Sage.

Naumetz, T. (1999, 16 April). Bill to give victims of crime more rights: Offenders would pay into fund to help injured party. *National Post* (Southam News), A7.

Province, The. (1997, 5 December). Cadman introduces victims' rights bill, by Keith Fraser.

Savoie, J. (2007). Youth self-reported delinquency, Toronto, 2006. Statistics Canada Catalogue No. 85-002-XPE, vol. 27, no. 6.

Schissel, B. (1997). *Blaming children: Youth crime, moral panic and the politics of hate*. Halifax: Fernwood.

Schissel, B. (2006). *Still blaming children: Youth conduct and the politics of child hating*. Halifax: Fernwood.

Smandych, R. (2001). *Youth justice: History, legislation, and reform*. Toronto: Harcourt.

Smart, R., and Adlaf, E. (1991). Substance use and problems among Toronto street youth. *British Journal of Addiction*, 86(8): 999–1010.

Spencer, J. (2005). It's not as simple as it seems: Ambiguous culpability and ambivalent affect in news representations of violent youth. *Symbolic Interaction*, 28(1): 47–65.

Sprott, J. (1996). Understanding public views of youth crime and the youth justice system. *Canadian Journal of Criminology*, 38(3): 271–90.

Statistics Canada. (2014a, 4 December). Homicide offences, number and rate, by province and territory. Retrieved from http://www.statcan.gc.ca/tables-tableaux/sum-som/l01/cst01/legal12a-eng.htm

Statistics Canada. (2014b). Police-reported crime statistics in Canada, 2013. Retrieved 4 December 2014 from http://www.statcan.gc.ca/pub/85-002-x/2015001/article/14211-eng.htm

Surette, R. (1998). *Media, crime, and criminal justice: Images and realities*. New York: Wadsworth Publishing.

Tanner, J., and Wortley, S. (2002). *The Toronto youth crime and victimization survey: Overview report*. Toronto: Centre of Criminology, University of Toronto.

Wodak, R., and Meyer, M. (2000). *Methods of critical discourse analysis*. Thousand Oaks, CA: Sage.

World Bank. (2014, 4 December). List of countries by intentional homicide rate. Retrieved from http://data.worldbank.org/indicator/VC.IHR.PSRC.P5

Canadian Girls and Crime in the Twenty-First Century

Lorinda Stoneman and Sibylle Artz

Overview

This chapter offers a broad overview of the ways in which girls who encounter the criminal justice system are dealt with in Canada. Readers are presented with material that will help them understand and critique the response of the Canadian youth justice system to female youth crime and also help them identify promising new directions for dealing with female youth offenders. Readers will also learn that in Canada, despite the shift in legislation initiated by the Youth Criminal Justice Act (YCJA) in 2003, far too many girls, notably Aboriginal girls, are being locked up and that Aboriginal girls are vastly overrepresented in Canada's youth justice system. This overrepresentation is a perpetual problem in Canada, a problem that the YCJA seems to have exacerbated at least in part because the funding necessary to administer extrajudicial measures has not been distributed in ways that make community-based intervention possible, especially in less affluent and remote communities. As a result, Canadian custody centres now mostly contain marginalized, under-resourced female and male youth who are often victims of childhood abuse and neglect, with the additional trauma of sexual abuse for many females (Smith, Cox, Poon, Stewart, and McCreary 2013). As Moretti, Odgers, and Reppucci (2011) found in their longitudinal study, "exposure to adversity, early in development and repeatedly over time, contributes to the development of problematic social cognitive and emotional processing and, in turn, to mental health problems, substance use, and physical health problems" (p. 143). Thus, young people confined to custody, as well as those youth diverted from formal processing into often under-resourced communities, bring with them tremendous and complex adversities. As a result youth justice professionals are tasked with finding ways to work with youth who have multiple needs and challenges (Mann, Senn, Girard, and Ackbar 2007). Recommendations are provided for instituting policies and practices to reverse systemic and personal discrimination based on gender and racial inequity and for keeping neo-liberal and neo-conservative crime-control policies in check.

Key Objectives

After reading this chapter, you should be able to:

- Identify and discuss Canadian female youth offending patterns.
- Understand and critique Canadian justice system responses to female youth crime.
- Outline traditional and contemporary explanations of female crime.
- Identify promising new directions in responding to female youth crime.

Introduction

In order to understand and respond to girls and crime, it is necessary to examine what we know about female young offenders as well as patterns of crime and trends in youth justice. We begin this chapter by discussing some characteristics of girls in conflict with the law and by examining girls' offending patterns using official statistics and self-report surveys. Next, we present a brief review of the theories that help to explain female crime and delinquency along with a critique of the ways in which female youth crime is conceptualized. The chapter ends with a discussion about the challenges of working effectively with delinquent girls in a system that, since 2006, has been under considerable political pressure from the Harper Conservative federal government with its "tough on crime" agenda, an agenda that has been heavily criticized by experts for being wasteful, counterproductive, and ultimately ineffective in dealing with youth crime (Cesaroni and Bala 2008).

Most delinquent girls commit minor crimes. Any apprehension or conviction, however, can have costly implications for girls, their families, their friends, and society. Looking at the various ways that female crime is understood and responded to in law and practice can help reveal how social order is established and held in place, sometimes despite the fact that solid research suggests that the opposite of what is being done should be done. Examining crime and punishment critically shows that crime is not a static phenomenon but one that changes as our ideologies and knowledge about crime and punishment change.

Patterns of Crime and Trends in Youth Justice

Girls, like boys, break the law but not often. While girls certainly engage in illegal behaviours, they rarely develop crime specialties (Chesney-Lind and Pasko 2004). Self-report data on delinquency in the US show that incidence rates have not substantially changed in more than a decade. Indeed, rather than showing increases in serious behaviours such as engaging in fights, girls are reporting lower, not higher, rates of the use of aggression and violence in recent years (Chesney-Lind 2010). In Canada, Barron and Lacombe

(2005) argue that public concern that girl violence is increasing is largely a social construction and a "product of a moral panic" (p. 52). They also note that data that support the notion of a rising violent crime rate among girls fail to take into account policy changes in the ways we count crime. Still, despite relatively low rates, the study of girls' offending remains an important social science task because, if not considered separately, girls easily become lost in comparison to boys (Kong and AuCoin 2008). Although girls join with other girls and with boys to commit crime, they may do so for reasons that are different from the reasons that boys have for engaging in these actions (Davidson 2013). However, as we discuss later in the chapter, we should exercise caution when framing girls as being different from boys because "gender differences are often pathologized" (Irwin and Chesney-Lind 2008, p. 842) through locating differences in girls as weaknesses in their biological and psychological chemistry.

The Female Young Offender

There is no typical female young offender, but there are some similar challenges that female young offenders face that help to draw a picture of this population; many of these challenges shape the pathways girls take into offending. We know that an overwhelming number of youth involved in the criminal justice system face a constellation of challenges, including those related to violence, abuse and trauma, mental and physical health, social and familial dysfunction, and sometimes cognitive difficulties (Chesney-Lind and Jones 2010; Chesney-Lind and Pasko 2013; Moretti et al. 2011). In the province of British Columbia, researchers from the McCreary Centre Society (MCS) periodically conduct one of the most extensive surveys done on incarcerated youth with a view to understanding some of the complex factors facing them. The 2012 MCS survey found that virtually all incarcerated girls had suffered physical abuse compared to slightly more than half of incarcerated boys (57 per cent) (Smith et al. 2013). Further, 57 per cent of girls (0 per cent of boys) reported physical abuse by an intimate partner and 75 per cent of incarcerated girls (32 per cent of boys) reported having been sexually abused. Incarcerated girls were also more likely to have reported having a mental health condition (e.g., depression) or an emotional condition and were more likely to suffer from multiple conditions than boys. Also, while 18 per cent of both girls and boys reported having engaged in self-harm, girls were four times more likely to report having harmed themselves six or more times. Additionally, the study showed that twice the proportion of girls (50 per cent) than boys (25 per cent) reported having been kicked out of their homes.

These self-reports show us that female young offenders, particularly those who become incarcerated, suffer from severe mental, emotional, physical, and social challenges and in many cases are victims as well as offenders. The dual victim and offender status experienced by female young offenders and the more numerous and severe needs and risks they must deal with present significant concerns for intervention and treatment. These will be discussed at the close of this chapter.

Canadian Justice System Responses to Female Youth Crime

Official Charges

An accurate summary of the amount of crime committed by youth of either sex is—like that for adults—illusive. Official police and court statistics, however, can provide key indicators of how the Canadian judicial system responds to some of the illegal behaviours of some girls (see Figure 7.1). To ensure a reliable estimate of Canadian girls' involvement in crime, it is necessary to use more than one indicator and more than one source and to interpret indicators in a comparative context—over time and as a ratio of the general population.

As Figure 7.1 suggests, only 3 per cent of all Canadians charged and brought to court in 2012 were girls (Statistics Canada 2014a, 2014e). It is not youth, but adults, especially adult men, who are likely to enter the court system for crimes against persons, property, or the public order. Additionally, although there are nearly equal numbers of girls and boys under the age of 18 in the Canadian population, the vast majority of charges laid by the police and Crown continue to be against boys. In the early 1980s, one in ten cases in youth courts were against girls. Twenty years later, the gender ratio narrowed to one in five, and in 2012, data showed that one-quarter of youth criminal court cases involved girls (Statistics Canada 2014e). While youth crime for both genders peaked in the mid-1990s, significant year-over-year decreases in crime rates—the rate of youth accused of Criminal Code offences (excluding traffic offences)—are evident (Statistics Canada 2014b). Over

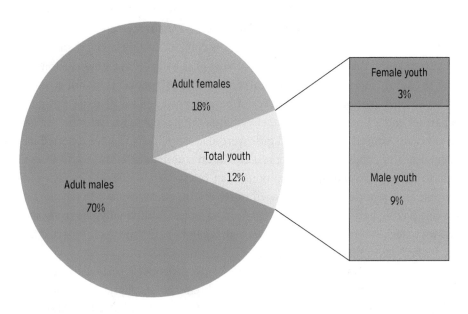

FIGURE 7.1 2012 Total Canadian Criminal Court Cases

Note: For 6 per cent of adults and 1 per cent of youth, sex was not reported.

Sources: Statistics Canada, 2014e, CANSIM Table 252-0064, Youth Courts, Number of Cases and Charges by Type of Decision; 2014a CANSIM Table 252-0053, Adult Criminal Courts, Number of Cases and Charges by Type of Decision.

this period of time, girls have seen a 43 per cent decrease in the rate of charges for property offences and a 25 per cent decrease in the rate of charges for violent offences. Boys have seen a similar decrease in violent offences and a slightly greater decrease in rate of charges for property offences. Further, although the causes of the increase in the late 1980s and into the mid-1990s remain unclear, it is widely agreed that statistics gathered during that time did not indicate an explosion of female crime and that at least some of the rise in crime during that period can be explained by legislative changes in the upper age limits for minors in the youth justice system, which changed from 16 to 18 years of age in 1985 (Doob and Sprott 1998; Estrada 2001). Current trends certainly indicate a clear decline in crime (see Chapter 2). These changes, like previous changes, cannot be explained by any single factor and, like previous trends, must be understood in terms of variations in criminal behaviour, legislative changes, and the demographic and policy changes that continue to contribute to fluctuations in youth accused rates and youth charge rates (Doob and Sprott 2004). The current decline therefore, should be understood at least in part as reflecting a decrease in rate of police charges because of the increased use of informal and pre-charge diversion under the YCJA (Dauvergne 2013).

In 2005, Steffensmeier, Schwartz, Zhong, and Ackerman found that the upward trend of girls' offending behaviour seen in the 1990s could not be replicated using unofficial longitudinal sources. They hypothesized that changes in enforcement, in youth justice policy, and in culture are better explanations of the changing charge rates. Because policy had changed in a more expressive and punitive direction (Steffensmeier et al. 2005), actions that previously would not have come to the attention of police were reclassified as criminal matters. These exacerbating and net-widening policies included zero tolerance policies in schools, a lower threshold for what constitutes criminality in domestic arguments, and the inclusion of parent–child and sibling altercations as chargeable domestic offences (Woolford 2009), along with the additional net-widening effect of using criminal charges for minor offences to prevent anticipated future criminal risk (Steffensmeier et al. 2005). Such policy changes might also help to explain why there appeared to be an upward trend in female major and minor assault charges from 1991 to 2001 that only began to level off and decrease in 2009.

Further, despite the data showing that girls are "catching up" to boys in their commission of criminal offences, Sprott and Doob (2009) affirm that this is not so. In fact, because fewer boys are becoming involved in the justice system as compared to the early 1990s, it is only the ratio of girls to boys that is narrowing. Sprott and Doob suggest that what is really a difference in offending patterns for boys tends to be interpreted as a reason to become alarmed about girls. Instead, they show quite convincingly that delinquent adjudication for girls has remained stable and even dipped slightly, while that for boys has noticeably declined. For these reasons, we need to be cautious when assessing female offending rates as if male offending rates were the accepted benchmark[1] (Sharpe and Gelsthorpe 2009). Another reason that caution is required as we examine girls' delinquency as represented by percentage-based quantitative statistics is that the base number of girls involved in crime is so small (Heidensohn and Silvestri 2012). For example, in 2005, only four girls were charged with homicide. The following year, six girls faced homicide charges (Statistics Canada 2006), accounting for a 50 per cent jump in these violent offences but representing the involvement of only two more girls. This example illustrates clearly that where small raw numbers are concerned, we need to refrain from making distorted extrapolations.

The rates of females charged started to decline late in the 1990s, and the comparable rate for boys has dropped even more. The number of females charged in 1996 was 2230 per 100,000 Canadian female youth, and the number charged in 2013 was 987 per 100,000 (Statistics Canada 2014b, 2014g). Overall, according to Statistics Canada, between 2004 and 2013, there was a 30 per cent decrease in charges for female youth and a 36 per cent drop in charges for boys.

Table 7.1 presents the types of crimes for which girls and boys made court appearances in 2011/12 by principal charge, listed in descending order of seriousness. Most frequently, charges resulting in court appearances for girls focus on **administrative offences**, followed closely by charges for theft and minor assault. Together, these offences amount to 64 per cent of charges for girls in court. For boys, the most frequent charges

administrative offences
Offences against the administration of justice—that is, violations of court-ordered behavioural requirements, such as complying with a curfew, attending mandated programs, and following through on all manner of bail conditions and probation orders.

Table 7.1	Specific Youth Court Cases, 2011/2012, by Gender		
Specific Youth Court Cases—Principal Charge for 2011/12		**Female %**	**Male %**
Murder and Attempt		0.03	0.10
Robbery		2.4	5.8
Against Person Major*		6.8	5.6
Against Person Minor**		**18.8**	**12.6**
Sexual Offences		0.4	3.3
Theft		**20.9**	**12.2**
Break and Enter		3.7	8.8
Fraud		1.8	0.9
Possess Stolen Goods		6.0	5.9
Drug Trafficking/Possession***		4.9	9.9
Mischief		5.5	7.6
Administrative/Against YCJA****		**24.3**	**20.4**
Other Property Crimes		0.4	1.0
Criminal Code Traffic		1.3	1.9
Other Criminal Code		2.6	5.8
Residual Federal Statutes		0.2	0.2
Total by Gender		**100%**	**100%**

* Major assault; assault with a weapon (s. 267), aggravated assault (s. 268), and other assaults (assaulting a police officer and unlawfully causing bodily harm). Excludes murder, attempted murder, and robbery.
** Common assault, harassment, and other crimes against the person.
*** Includes drug trafficking, production, importation, exporting, and possession.
**** Includes failure to comply with disposition, failure to comply with undertaking, assist/interfere/other, contempt against youth court, breach of recognizance, failure to appear, failure to comply with probation order, escape custody, unlawfully at large, and charges against the YCJA.

Source: Statistics Canada 2014e, CANSIM Table 2520064.

resulting in court appearances are also for administrative offences (a trend that has held for several years). Next in frequency for boys are charges for minor assaults followed closely by theft. Both girls and boys are infrequently charged with major serious violent crimes (9.2 per cent for girls and 11.5 per cent for boys).

For over 30 years, Canadian girls have been charged with fewer than 20 murders per year and usually far fewer than 10 (see also Reitsma-Street 1999)—a frequency that holds in the most recently available data (Statistics Canada 2014e). In 2011/12, female youth were responsible for 18 per cent of violent youth crime, 17 per cent of property crime involving youth, and 8 per cent of other Criminal Code offences involving youth (Statistics Canada 2014e). However, as we noted earlier, these percentages are difficult to interpret because of the decline in male charges and the stability in female charges. We cannot, therefore, use simple arithmetic to make sense of our computations.

For some time, there has been a lack of connection between the picture painted by official statistics and that portrayed in the media of youth crime and, more specifically, crime committed by female young offenders. Likely, neither record has captured a perfect picture of reality. An important issue with the data is that the category of "violent" crime suggests acts of terror and serious harm. But media reports on overall violent crime can be misleading, as they often include in the same category both the more frequent minor assault charges and the infrequent major aggravated assaults with deadly weapons and murder. Sensational media portrayals of female involvement in crime have fuelled the popular perspective of females acting more like males, a perspective that has been refuted by research over the past two decades (Chesney-Lind and Pasko 2004; Males 2010). Chesney-Lind and Irwin (2008) argue that the media disseminate a "misogynistic framing of girlhood" (p. 3) that perpetuates the oppression and subservience of girls and young women by attempting to make them fearful of the repercussions for non-normative female behaviour. In essence, the media perform a strong social control role. Further, when public perception is informed solely by media accounts of violence, the very important contexts for violence are usually missing, leading to the scapegoating of youth for family and societal problems that are beyond their control (Green and Healy 2003) and the development of moral panics that exaggerate girls' involvement in violent and serious crimes (Dean 2005; Males 2010).

Administrative Offences

What is perhaps most surprising is how often Canadian girls have been charged with administrative offences in the past three decades. In 1985–86, about 1 charge in 20 (5.1 per cent) against girls were for failure to comply with administrative orders. Since that time, there has been a sharp increase in the proportion and rate of administrative offence: in 2013, for example, 27 per cent of charges for girls were related to administrative offences (Statistics Canada 2014e). Though not as dramatic as the increases for girls, the proportion of administrative charges against boys has also risen rapidly, from 3.9 per cent in 1985 to 27 per cent of all charges in 2013 (Statistics Canada 2014e).

The striking increase in administrative charges that began in the 1990s and seems to be growing incrementally year-over-year illustrates how difficult it can be to obtain an accurate picture of girls and crime. We need to appreciate that changes in laws and regulations and problematic practices have implications for crime rates and our perceptions of reality. Sprott and Doob (2009) suggest that the increase in administrative charges that began in 1990s is continuing and that, in North America, these kinds of charges are still being used disproportionately with girls. Such charges can push girls further into the youth justice system, turning them into recidivists and leaving them with sizable criminal records (Sprott 2012).

The increase in the charges against girls (and boys) for technical administrative violations under the Young Offenders Act (YOA) was a trend much recognized and examined in research (Doob and Sprott 1998; Reitsma-Street 2005). A central question was: What is the reason for this trend—especially among girls? The answer to this question is that judges were adding more conditions to probation orders than before. These conditions included mandating girls' attendance in drug use prevention and intervention programs, attending school, keeping sometimes unreasonable curfews, and not associating with certain peers (Sprott 2012). Failure to comply with these probation conditions, then, became the new offences. In their research on bail orders in one Toronto court, Sprott and Doob (2010) found that while nearly all girls and boys were required to live at a particular location as a condition of bail, girls were much more likely to be given the condition of treatment (e.g., counselling; anger management) (51 per cent) than boys (34 per cent) prior to being convicted. As well, Sprott and Doob (2010) indicate that although girls usually commit non-violent offences and have shorter histories of criminal involvement than their male peers, girls are typically given more conditions upon their release from remand and custody. Those girls who commit non-violent offences are also just as likely as those who commit violent offences to receive counselling or treatment orders. This disproportionate use of treatment for girls may signal the persistence of a patriarchal response to girls in the justice system.

The Youth Criminal Justice Act

One of the reasons for the development of the YCJA in 2003 was to respond to the growing youth incarceration rate in Canada throughout the 1990s. Canada's incarceration rate for youth was one of the highest in the Western world, higher even than that of the United States. The Department of Justice approached the new youth justice legislation "with a more inclusive framework, focusing on public awareness, crime prevention, education, child welfare, health, family and the community" (Calverley 2007, p. 2). An important success of the YCJA has been a clearer delineation of serious and minor offences such that the most serious interventions (such as custody) are given to the most serious offenders, while minor offenders have the opportunity to be diverted from the formal system and take part in a community-based program or receive a warning (Sprott 2012). The result, a decrease in charges, guilty findings, and custodial sentences for both boys and girls, has been undeniable (Bala, Carrington, and Roberts 2009), and in British Columbia, was first seen in the closure of two girls' custody units and later in the complete closure of one youth custody centre (British Columbia 2014). While this reduction in custody spaces might be seen as a positive development, it is clear that resources have not been redirected into the community.

In a qualitative study of the BC context undertaken by Stoneman (forthcoming), less serious offenders were reportedly faced with trying to access non-existent or inappropriate programs in their communities, while more serious offenders were faced with incarceration further away from their families and home communities. The resulting phenomenon described by Stoneman as **net narrowing** occurs when youth who have been diverted struggle to access adequate resources. In her study, many of the participating youth-serving professionals reported that before they were able to gain access to resources such as clinical assessments, programming, financial assistance, and one-to-one support for their clients, they had to show that these clients were seriously entrenched in the system. This is perhaps the most pressing disadvantage of diversion, since resource allocation only follows after system involvement and is not available if clients are diverted. Paradoxically, then, under these conditions, serious criminal behaviour is almost desirable because it has become one of the keys to unlock desperately needed resources.

As noted above, an initial key feature of the YCJA was the intent to decrease custody for minor and administrative offences and with it net-widening (Bala et al. 2009). However, as the Act was moving through the legislative process on its way to becoming law, many expressed concern that the YCJA's post-custody supervision regulations might increase the number of administrative charges, as new charges might be laid and a return to custody made possible if supervision conditions were not complied with. These concerns have in part materialized: though the number of administrative charges for girls has decreased under the YCJA, it is decreasing at a much slower pace than other charges. Although the YCJA has made it tougher to sentence youth to custody—with guidelines in s. 39(1) stating that custody may only be used for youth in limited circumstances, including when they have been charged for a violent offence or have failed to comply with non-custodial sentences—incarcerating non-violent youth is still permitted. In fact, some custodial sentences resulting from failure to comply may be lengthier than 93 per cent of custodial sentences. Sprott and Doob (2009) speculate that such occurrences signal the existence of cases where, despite the YCJA's clarity that youth cannot be held in custody for welfare purposes, detention—especially for girls—is still being used for this reason instead of solely for the protection of the public.

Sharpe and Gelsthorpe (2009) discuss community-based alternatives to custody (diversion) but also highlight the concern that girls who fail community programs will then be "fast-tracked into custody" (p. 202). However, recent research in British Columbia (Artz and Amorim 2013) has found that police, probation officers, and judges share a sense of frustration about the lack of resources and programs to which they can divert or adjudicate young women and that they invoke administrative charges only as a last resort when "all else fails." Artz and Amorim underline a sense of duty of care rather than a need for control and suggest that higher incidence of referrals of girls to programs reflect their greater and more complex needs, while their higher rates of administrative charges reflect a dearth of services (see also Box 7.1).

Current Responses Have Led to an Overrepresentation of Aboriginal Girls

One glaring issue that has a long history in Canada is the overrepresentation of Aboriginal female youth in custody. In 2012, about 6 per cent of all female youth in this country were Aboriginal (Munch 2012). However, in 2011/12, Aboriginal female youth represented

net narrowing
A phenomenon that occurs when youth who have been diverted from the criminal justice system struggle to access adequate resources.

Box 7.1   Youth Justice in Action

Resource Deficits under the YCJA—"We've done everything we can"

In her study involving the use of diversion under the YCJA, Stoneman (forthcoming) spoke to professionals in the youth justice field, many of whom recounted numerous cases where they had simply run out of appropriate and meaningful resources with which to treat youth—in particular, young women. One youth worker described a situation where a young woman on her caseload had exhausted all means of treatment available in the community.

> I have a youth on my caseload right now. She's been on my caseload for four years. She's very highly addicted to all sorts of drugs, heroin being one of the most pressing ones. She's been in care all through her life, she's gone through, I believe, 25 foster homes. So really, I don't even know how these kids have a chance when they've already suffered through so much. We've sent her away to programs, given her all sorts of treatment and tried to help her in the community and we're finding that it's just not possible. We just don't have the resources to help her. She said her addictions are too strong. The last thing she said to us was "you guys want me to be normal, I'm just not normal, this is my normal." She is currently in jail and her probation actually expires in February and she's aged out. So, ya. It's bad. It tears on my heartstrings a little bit. . . . We've done everything we can. (N.p.)

Critical Thinking Question

What are the implications of these resource deficits for the treatment of girls under the YCJA?

---

40 per cent of girls admitted to total correctional services, 45 per cent of girls admitted to pre-trial detention, 63 per cent of girls admitted to remand, and 46 per cent of all female youth sentenced to custody (Statistics Canada 2014c). Conversely, Aboriginal girls make up 36 per cent of females admitted to community sentences. In all five categories, Aboriginal girls are overrepresented at a greater rate than Aboriginal boys. While the number of females admitted to remand has increased and the number of females admitted to sentenced custody has decreased overall, the decline has been much smaller for Aboriginal females. Taking the province of British Columbia as an example—a province that reported the lowest youth incarceration and community supervision rates of any province (Munch 2012)—58 per cent of girls in BC custody centres are Aboriginal while only 8 per cent of the BC youth population is Aboriginal (Sharpe and Gelsthorpe 2009). In fact, Aboriginal girls, many of whom are intergenerational survivors of the residential school system, are the fastest growing population in youth custody (NWAC 2012). Canada's current youth service and youth justice practices seem to be especially problematic for Aboriginal girls, who experience very high rates of administrative charges.

Court Decisions and Correctional Admissions for Convicted Girls

Not all girls who are charged are convicted and sentenced in youth court. Every year a substantial proportion of girls—49 per cent in 2011/12—have their cases withdrawn, dismissed, or stayed (this category includes referrals by the court to restorative justice programs and extrajudicial measures) (Statistics Canada 2014e). As with the rest of the justice system, where female youth are found in far fewer numbers than male youth, female youth are admitted to correctional services at a much lower rate than male youth. Research concludes that the trend of admissions to correctional services has been declining for nearly a decade and was hastened by the YCJA. About one in every five youths sentenced is a girl. In 2011/12, female youth made up 18 per cent of all youth admitted to probation, 14 per cent of those sentenced to custody, 46 per cent of those given conditional sentences, and nearly a quarter (23 per cent) of those sentenced to intensive support and supervision (Statistics Canada 2014f). While the incarceration rate for female youth in 2011/12 was 26 per 10,000, the rate for male youth was nearly 3.5 times higher, at 89 per 10,000. Although the total incarceration rates for both boys and girls have been declining since 2003/4, a closer look yields an increase in the rate of girls in pre-trial detention who are either awaiting trial or sentencing. This rate has increased by 33 per cent while at the same time, we have a decline in the number of youths who are sentenced to custody (–42 per cent for girls and –54 per cent for boys in 2011/12) (Statistics Canada 2014d).

The most common sentence or disposition for girls, like boys, continues to be probation. With the introduction of the YCJA, several new community corrections sanctions are available with the aim of correcting the upward trend in youth incarceration rates. In order to allow for reintegration following a custodial sentence, youth are sentenced to community supervision that commences once they are released from custody (akin to statutory release after serving a third of the sentence in the adult system). Along with the YCJA, in 2003, deferred custody and supervision orders (similar to adult conditional sentences) were introduced. In 2007, Taylor-Butts and Bressen investigated the hypothesis that conjoined sentencing—that is, linking custodial sentencing with community supervision—would decrease the use of probation under the YCJA, since the community portion of the custodial sentence is now automatic. These sanctions provide judges with another sentencing option to impose conditions where the penalty for non-compliance is custody (Kong 2009). And indeed, since the passage of the YCJA, there has been a marked decrease not only in charge rates for all youth but also in court rates (Taylor-Butts and Bressen 2007).

Theories of Female Crime and Delinquency

Before the 1970s, few mainstream sociological and criminological theorists concerned themselves with female crime and delinquency. Those that did grounded most of their thinking in male experience and in the notion that if females were delinquent, it was most likely because they were sexually deviant and pathological. When females *were* considered, the focus was generally on the **gender gap** (i.e., the proportionally lower crime participation of females in comparison to males), rather than on either the conditions or the motivations that move females toward crime and delinquency (Artz 1998; Tanner 1996).

Three categories of theory emerged from the early literature: (1) those theories that explain the gender gap in crime and delinquency as given in the biological differences between the sexes; (2) those that explain the gender gap as derived from differences in gender role socialization; and (3) those that focus on increased female deviance relative

gender gap
Acknowledges the difference in the rates at which males and females do things. In the field of criminology, there exists a persistent and well-documented difference in the arrest rates for males and females, with males consistently committing significantly more crime than females.

to males and explain this rise in terms of a "masculinization" of women brought on by women's liberation and the feminist movement (see Adler 1975; Simon 1975). All three categories of theory explain female crime and delinquency as a move away from the feminine toward the masculine and support the notion that delinquency and crime are in effect masculine pursuits (Cohen 1955). Claims that feminism has perpetrated a rise in delinquency in children as mothers leave their homes and the domestic realm to pursue careers have been carefully examined and shown to be erroneous (Chesney-Lind and Shelden 1998; Miller 1986). Still, it was not until the mid-1980s and afterward that theorists called for a shift away from theories of delinquency that are uncritically grounded in male behaviour (Campbell 1991; Chesney-Lind and Shelden 1998; Reitsma-Street 1998; Chesney-Lind and Pasko 2004; Zahn 2009; Chesney-Lind and Jones 2010). While the question of the gender gap still remains, the focus among researchers has shifted quite considerably toward understanding female delinquency as it pertains to females rather than merely as compared to males.

Biological Theories

Early theories of crime, whether focused on males or females, were largely informed by the notion that biology was destiny. Cesare Lombroso (1835–1909), for example, suggested that if females did become criminals, it was largely because they were degenerate, unwomanly aberrations without maternal instinct. Lombroso's explanations regarding biology and criminal behaviour have long fallen into disrepute, although even well into the twentieth century criminologists continued to explain girls' and women's lower involvement in delinquency and crime in terms of females' supposed biological inferiority— some even proposed premenstrual syndrome (PMS) as a cause for female criminality (see Binder, Geis, and Bruce 1988; Cowie, Cowie, and Slater 1968; Pollack 1950; Wilson and Herrnstein 1985).

Gisela Konopka (1966, 1983) was one of the first to turn directly to adolescent girls to examine with them their involvement in delinquency. While she emphasized the effects on female behaviour of the sexual double standard, psychosocial problems, and women's changing cultural position, she still assumed that girls and women were largely controlled by biology and sexuality.

Current work on biology and crime continues, but in a different vein. For example, in research on aggression and violence, Tremblay (2003) argues that "all humans are at risk for using physical aggression given the appropriate circumstances" (p. 195), and makes the case that aggression is innate rather than learned as was widely claimed in the 1980s and 1990s (see Reiss and Roth 1993). Tremblay states that aggression is "a natural behavior that one learns to control" (p. 183); that is, aggression and violence must be unlearned. He further suggests that variability in early aggression is due, in part at least, to some genetic effects (Dionne, Tremblay, Boivin, LaPlante, and Pérusse 2003) and cites the example of fetal exposure to testosterone as playing a role in how easily a child learns to control physical aggression (Rubinow and Schmidt 1996). Additionally, Tremblay suggests that there is good evidence that low levels of serotonin are implicated in impulsive and aggressive behaviour (see Moffit et al. 1998; Raine 2002). Interestingly, while

Tremblay emphasizes the need to understand the physiological underpinnings of behaviour that influence the ability to unlearn the use of aggression and violence—the behaviours of greatest concern when we consider youth crime—his theory ultimately turns on the use of socialization to shift what is biologically given. In further work, Tremblay et al. (2005) underline the importance of learning to regulate physical aggression in early childhood and emphasize the contribution of parental conflict and anti-social behaviour, low income, early child bearing, and maternal smoking to later problematic outcomes for children.

We have certainly learned to reconsider notions of biological determinism when it comes to understanding human behaviour and have learned to appreciate the importance of understanding the ways in which biologically based sensitivities and potentials intersect and interact with psychological and social factors in the lives of delinquent youth. So, for example, Kenneth Dodge and Gregory Pettit (2003) offer us a **biopsychosocial model** to explain chronic anti-social and delinquent behaviour in adolescents and show us that we need to pay attention to the reciprocal influences of biological and socio-cultural contexts on behaviour. These researchers show that for both girls and boys, biological dispositions influenced by prenatal factors—such as exposure to toxic substances—along with autonomic nervous system hyperactivity, intelligence potential, and temperament can be mediated positively or negatively in a child's life by socio-cultural context variables. Such variables may include family income, occupation and education, age of the mother, the absence or presence of parental conflict, divorce, and family violence; and, as the child matures, variables may include the mediating effects of positive or negative peer, school, and neighbourhood influences. As well, Dodge and Pettit note that these dispositions and socio-cultural interactions are not merely linear but reciprocal so that a child's sensitivities and temperament can influence parenting behaviour and the behaviour of other significant children and adults in the child's life. In this way, the child's early experiences serve to set in place a child's cognitive models and beliefs, that is, the child's social knowledge frameworks for how the world works. These internalized social knowledge frameworks influence how the child makes sense of what is expected and what is acceptable and exert a strong influence on behaviour and personal choice where delinquency is concerned, thus adding to the interactive nature of the development of delinquency.

Fishbein, Miller, Winn, and Dakof (2009), in their extensive examination of biopsychological factors, gender, and delinquency found that, for girls, the most salient biological disposition and vulnerability for delinquency appears to be early pubertal maturation. But as Fishbein et al. point out, early pubertal maturation is not simply a matter of fixed individual biological timing; it also involves heredity, body weight, and weight-to-height ratio, the hormonal and other biopsychological effects of stressful life events, and the quality of a girl's family relations, including the absence or presence of an adult male in the girl's household. Nor is early maturation by itself a causal factor for delinquency. Whether an early maturing girl becomes involved in delinquency depends on the quality of her home life, her school, and her neighbourhood; the effects of context and relationships and interpersonal trauma, such as sexual and other forms of abuse, deprivation on her mental health and wellness, and the presence and influence of older males who may seduce her and include her in their criminal activities. The interplay of multiple

> **biopsychosocial model**
> An approach used to study the involvement of girls in the criminal justice system that addresses biological, psychological, and social risk factors related to female criminality.

influences and their effect on mental health play an enormous role in how an early maturing girl, or for that matter any girl, becomes involved in delinquency and crime. As Fishbein and colleagues also note, the incidence of mental illness and of co-morbidity—that is, two or more psychiatric disorders—is extremely high in delinquent girls. These disorders are not merely intrinsic to some girls and not others; they have their origins in a complex interplay of personal, relational, social, and cultural factors and can by no means be explained by biological disposition alone.

Sociological and Gender Role Theories

Socialization theories of delinquency and crime emerged in the 1950s (Grosser 1951) and have grown in strength and number to the present day (Chesney-Lind and Shelden 1998; Chesney-Lind and Jones 2010; Hagan, Gillis, and Simpson 1985; Zahn 2009). **Gender role theories** explain the difference in male and female participation in delinquent behaviour as the outcome of differential gender socialization that imposes higher moral expectations and greater social controls on girls and women. Three mainstream sociological approaches to crime and delinquency that fit with a gender role analysis are (1) differential association or social learning theories, (2) social control theories, and (3) strain theories.

gender role theories
Those explanations of delinquent and criminal behaviour that focus on the role that gender plays in the lives and behaviours of both females and males.

Social Learning and Differential Association Theories

The primary source of social learning is, of course, the family—however variously constructed and defined families may be in the twenty-first century. In an extensive review of the research on family and youth delinquency and crime, Kruttschnitt and Giodarno (2009) found that girls and boys both suffer the negative consequences of family conflict, harsh and coercive parenting, and other problematic emotional family dynamics, including exposure to crime by family members, abuse within the family, divorce, and living in stressed lone-parent households. These researchers found few consistent gender differences with regard to the effects of these factors on the socialization of children except in the area of sexual abuse, where girls consistently suffer far higher rates of such abuse and, with that, the long-term negative effects of this kind of trauma, especially when combined with family criminality. Kruttschnitt and Giordano's analysis of the research on family and delinquency in girls calls into question the commonly held belief that girls have stronger connections with their families and are thus more positively socialized and less inclined to become involved in crime and delinquency. They point instead to a better, more nuanced understanding of the acquisition of gender roles and the consequent learned gender performance for dealing with emotional and interpersonal processes as a more promising area for further research. Whatever their social location, girls learn early that being "nice" and being "good" have enormous social value and they may therefore internalize greater constraints on delinquent behaviour.

Peer influence has for some time been known to be significant for delinquency. On the basis of observations that delinquents appear to gather in groups and gangs and have more interaction with those who engage in crime than with those who do not, Sutherland (1939) and others (Sutherland and Cressey 1978) argued that the techniques, motives, and values that facilitate criminal behaviour are transmitted through social and anti-social learning opportunities that arise from close association with others who engage in delinquency and crime. Although Sutherland and his associates studied only males, differential association (or learning theory) holds some promise with regard to explaining female delinquency and is supported by research that indicates that females who have frequent contact with other deviant youth appear to engage in deviant behaviour to a greater degree than those who do not (Giordano, Cernkovich, and Pugh 1986).

In her extensive examination of peer influences and crime, Giordano (2009) shows that some socialization practices seem to be involved in protecting girls from greater involvement with delinquent peers: girls generally spend more time in structured social activities than boys and less time simply "hanging out." As well, while the norms of the friendship group they most identify with help to shape the behaviour of both girls and boys, more girls than boys report affiliating with and knowing a greater range of peers and therefore girls experience a wider range of possible social norms and models than boys do. Giordano's assessment of the current literature on delinquency and peers suggests that the girls who are more vulnerable to negative peer influences are those who gravitate toward delinquent friends, especially mixed-gender groups of delinquent friends, and who become involved with delinquent romantic partners. Still, Giordano cautions us to refrain from overemphasizing the corrupting influence of males as an explanation for female delinquency.

So, is delinquency learned—that is, is it the outcome of exposure to delinquent models—or is the capacity for delinquency present in all humans, thereby placing the onus not on learning deviant behaviour but on learning self-restraint, deferred gratification, empathy, self-regulation, and positive social skills? As we saw earlier, Tremblay (2003) and Tremblay et al. (2005) point out the importance of self-regulation of the negative behaviour for which all humans have the capacity; in so doing, they align with social control theories.

Social Control Theories

Social control theories of crime and delinquency focus on the capacity of all human beings to engage in deviance and crimes. For social control theorists, personal control or inner containment of deviant urges grounded in a positive and socially conventional self-concept is central to the containment of delinquency and crime (Reckless 1961; Reiss 1951), as are effective family functioning and the existence of a positive social structure (Nye 1958; Toby 1957) and the presence of a social bond (Hirschi 1969). Positive bonds with family, friends, peers, school, and neighbourhood are of central importance to social control theorists, as they are to learning theorists.

Hirschi (1969) describes the social bond that keeps deviance in check as made up of four components: (1) attachment, (2) commitment, (3) involvement, and (4) belief. In applying Hirschi's notions to research with girls, Jensen and Eve (1976) and Cernkovich and Giordano (1987) found that attachment to conventional others and a belief in the legitimacy of rules have predictive power for both male and female delinquency. Cernkovich and Giordano also found that lower rates of female delinquency could be partly explained by higher levels of parental supervision and more intimate communication between parents and daughters.

Hagan, Gillis, and Simpson (1985), Hagan, Simpson, and Gillis (1987), and Hagan (1988, 1990), who developed **power-control theory**, a variant of social control theory, suggest that social control, power, and constraint vary across gender. Specifically, power-control theory suggests that patriarchal families are structured such that they support, and thus provide greater access for, males' risk-taking behaviour. In contrast, much tighter restrictions are placed on the behaviours of female children, thus lending some explanatory power to the impacts of familial gender socialization and lower rates of girls' involvement in crime. Conversely, in an egalitarian family, one that sets an equal threshold of risky behaviour for both boys and girls, one might expect more similar involvement in delinquency between the sexes. In the various articles by Hagan and his colleagues discussed above, they point out that females generally experience more social control and constraint and less power, especially in more traditional, patriarchal families. Sons, on the other hand, experience fewer controls, are expected to take risks, and are therefore more likely to be involved in risky, deviant, and delinquent behaviour and victimization than girls. Further, this theory suggests that as families move away from traditional models toward systems where adult women take up more equal power with males or find themselves in the position of being single heads of households, girls will become more like boys and, as a consequence, will also take more risks, including deviant risks, and may experience more victimization.

Such theorizing seems to suggest that women's labour force entry and female equality contribute to higher delinquency and higher victimization rates for girls. In fact, based on self-report and official statistics, female delinquency typically declines or remains stable in spite of the rise in the number of female-headed households (Chesney-Lind and Shelden 1998). Further, power-control theory also falls short in explaining victimization. Despite the consistent finding that boys are more likely than girls to be victims and offenders, patriarchal households do not necessarily protect girls from victimization (Blackwell, Sellers, and Schlaupitz 2002). Girls who are victimized are often victimized in their homes by those closest to them and may be more vulnerable than boys to abuse at home. Ethnographic work by Artz (1998) suggests that patriarchal households where fathers exert dominance through intimidation and fear may in fact contribute to delinquency and aggression in girls. Additionally, there appears to be a consistent and strong relationship between females' sexual and emotional victimization in the context of misogynist (i.e., one who hates all women) and stereotypical gender relations based on hierarchies of power dominated by males and female participation in delinquency and crime (Acoca and Dedel 1998; Chesney-Lind and Okamoto 2001; Means 2002).

In a study on girls' use of aggression, Artz, Nicholson, and Magnuson (2008) note that both males and females use aggression to hold in place males' expectations of female sexual behaviour in that females actively participate in the privileging of males' sexual expectations of their own sex and in containing their own resistance to male domination. Where dominance and aggression is concerned, both males and females carry what Holland, Ramazanoglu, Sharpe, and Thompson (1998) call "the male in the head" and enact the involuntary and asymmetric institutionalization and regulatory power of males and patriarchy in heterosexual relations (p. 171).

Strain Theory

Arising out of Durkheim's (1933) anomie concept, strain theory builds on the notion that delinquency can be explained as a response to being denied access to socially and conventionally approved opportunities for power and material success (Cloward and Ohlin 1960; Cohen 1955; Miller 1958) (see Chapter 8).

Strain theory has, however, been critiqued as not readily applicable to girls and women because females continue to suffer from unequal opportunities and more limited means for achieving success than males while at the same time committing significantly fewer crimes than males (see Agnew 1995; Artz 1998). But the theory has also been favourably reconsidered by those who argue for an expanded version, one that takes into account the different strains experienced by males and females and their different adaptations and responses to strain (Agnew 1992; Berger 1989; Naffine 1987; see also Chapter 8). Broidy and Agnew (1997) suggest that Agnew's (1992) general strain theory (GST) offers potential for explaining both higher rates of male crime and the causes of female crime because it extends the focus of classic strain theory on the failure to achieve positively valued material goals. GST incorporates not only blocked access to monetary success and middle-class status but also the loss of family, friends, and romantic partners and experiences with all forms of abuse and deprivation as part of strain.

In their own application of general strain theory, Broidy and Agnew (1997) argue along lines similar to those proposed by social control theorists regarding constraint: that the overall differences in female and male rates of crime can be explained by the differences in types of strain to which females and males are subjected. Because of gender-role stereotypes, males are more often subject to material- and status-related strains, and females are more subject to oppression in the forms of family violence, sexual abuse, and high levels of social controls and restrictions, including restrictions related to criminal opportunity.

Additionally, Broidy and Agnew (1997) suggest that the female and male differences in crime rates can be further explained by gender differences in the processing of the negative emotions associated with strain. Males "act out" with other-directed overt anger, aggression, and violence. Females, in contrast, "act in" with depression, guilt, and shame and inner or relationally directed, more covert aggression. Females also disperse their negative emotions by gaining support from others in their more developed social networks, and they have been socialized to espouse values and use coping styles that discourage the commission of crimes. Males, on the other hand, are typically rewarded for their displays of aggression and encouraged to use coping styles that support the commission of crime. It seems that, on occasion, the distinction between constraint and strain appears to blur, but strain focuses more on what is withheld than on how one is controlled.

No single factor is known to predict delinquent behaviour, and no single path to delinquency is known to exist either for girls or for boys, although the strains that contribute to both have by now been well documented. As well, no homogeneous set of strains or conditions applies to all girls or all boys, and within-group differences in strain also need to be considered (see, for example, Katz 2000, 2004). Lanctôt, Émond, and Le Blanc (2004) note that previous approaches in research and intervention that treat delinquent females as a homogeneous group have done little to further our knowledge about delinquent females.

Feminist criminology, like general strain theory, takes aim at the fear-based contention that greater self-determination and full equality somehow pose a criminogenic risk for girls and women. In fact, the opposite of this has been borne out: girls who perpetrate crime, especially those who engage in aggressive and violent crime, are embedded in gender stereotypical life-worlds and entrapped in seeking male approval and have only attenuated notions of feminism, where the best they can hope for is to be accepted by males (Artz 1998; DeKeseredy 2000; Chesney-Lind, Artz, and Nicholson 2002; Artz et al. 2008). As Miller and Mullins (2009) state, feminist criminology is informed by theories of gender and examines "the role that gender inequality plays in shaping girls' risks for delinquency, as well as how gender inequality affects the nature of girls' delinquent activities" (p. 31).

Promising Directions: Toward Gender-Specific Interventions and Social Justice

Although we may have made considerable advancements from the rehabilitative, treatment-focused paternalism of the early twentieth century as it concerns boys involved in the justice system, progress for girls has lagged somewhat (Sprott and Doob 2010). We propose that promising directions regarding girls' delinquency must focus both on personal and on social conditions that lead to anti-social behaviour and crime to arrive at interventions that address the strains faced by girls, their complex and varied pathways (for a recent discussion on the gendered pathways to crime, see Jones, Brown, Wanamaker, and Greiner, 2014) to social and delinquent behaviours, and the overarching and systemic structural issues that persist. Such a perspective demands attention not only to the individual youth and what can be done to minimize and remove their risks and marginalities (e.g., addictions, gang involvement, and family dysfunction), but also to wider social/structural inequalities and dysfunction (e.g., racism, poverty, and lack of education) (Barron 2011).

intersectionality
Refers to a movement away from thinking categorically and toward thinking about the connections and crossroads between social facets. Intersectional thinking and theorizing recognizes the multiple, changing, and often overlapping dimensions, demographics, roles, and identities of criminals, victims, other individuals, and collectives.

Intersectionality refers to a movement away from thinking categorically and toward thinking about the connections and crossroads between social facets (e.g., race, sexuality, and gender) (Daly 2008); it draws upon the theoretical concepts of feminist criminology as we have discussed earlier in this chapter (e.g., gender as a social construct and the individual lived experience of gender as opposed to the label of gender). As such, intersectional thinking and theorizing recognizes the multiple, changing, and often overlapping dimensions, demographics, roles, and identities of criminals, victims, other individuals, and collectives (Berger and Guidroz 2009). This approach moves beyond "essential," uniform identities and appreciates that the lives of girls who partake in delinquency are much more complex than the label "delinquent/bad girl" implies. For example, those engaged in crime may also suffer from social marginalization and/or victimization.

Intersectionality as a theoretical concept emerged in the 1980s and is now prevalent in feminist criminology (Daly 2010). This approach holds that gender, race, class, ethnicity, sexuality, age, and local and national political arrangements and their intersections are crucial to understanding one's position in society (Berger and Guidroz 2009) and, especially, the positions of criminalized girls (Chesney-Lind and Jones 2010). By rejecting the "universal" girl in favour of the "inessential" girl (an approach from Elizabeth Spelman's 1988 book *Inessential Woman*), we highlight the need to refrain from focusing only on discrete aspects of girls, such as their sex, and move toward a more nuanced understanding. This approach necessitates (1) theoretical and practical attention to demographic intersections experienced by girls, (2) an expansion of practices based on intersectionality, and (3) the mobilization of political change.

Attending to Demographic Intersections

There are several directions to pursue as part of attending to these intersections:

- Discontinue the use of stereotypes and overly simplistic theories.

- Eradicate the use of stereotypical punitive policies and inhumane practices.

- Stop ignoring girls' fundamental requirements for survival, safety, and well-being.

Attending to demographic intersections means not placing Aboriginal girls in centres thousands of miles from their home and culture. It means radically changing correctional practices to reflect Aboriginal respect for spirit and land (Monture-Angus 2000). It means not charging one in three Canadian girls for administrative offences. It means rescinding the ineligibility of youth for welfare or time limits on assistance. Research demonstrates that harsh punishment is ineffective and inefficient (e.g., Green and Healy 2003, p. 139). Moreover, punitive approaches are inhumane and violent and merit no place in a civil society.

Girls, like boys, are not responsible for the family, race, class, or neighbourhood into which they are born. Whether they commit major or minor crimes or none at all, girls are entitled to the requirements for well-being: economic survival, clean air and water, good education, adequate health services and housing, and protection from violence inside and outside homes. These requirements are necessary so that girls do not trade the dangers and hurt of insecure or violent families for dangerous streets and networks (Joe-Laidler and Hunt 1997; Jones 2010). Research indicates that quality education, apprenticeship, income assistance, and housing programs that meet the essential requirements of convicted girls are more effective in reducing recidivism and increasing girls' well-being than the general, short-term counselling for primarily emotional, cognitive, or family problems (e.g., Baines and Alder 1996; Chesney-Lind and Pasko 2004).

One simple intervention that avoids reducing persons into a select few behaviours that they may exhibit is to stop using shorthand phrases such as "violent girl," as the words reinforce inaccurate, hurtful, static stereotypes. The alternative phrase, "a girl who acted violently when . . . ," suggests there is an interaction between context and behaviour and that change and growth are possible. Every girl is a complex person, struggling against restrictive stereotypes, including pervasive messages that boys are more important than girls. Every girl lives her life at the nexus of several intersecting factors, including biology, psychology, and social dynamics. She cannot be placed in stereotypical, generalized categories according to a single factor or in accordance with crime typologies but instead must be recognized as an individual. Gaarder and Belknap (2002) speak about the value of "blurred boundaries," as girls are often both victims and offenders. They find that girls convicted of serious violent offences may never have been allowed to be young and yet are expected to act like responsible, rational adults. Abolishing the simplistic stereotypes and "one-size-fits-all" intervention frees up energy to develop individualized, flexible approaches.

Expanding Practices Based on Intersectionality

gender-sensitive responses
Responses that recognize that the pathways to criminal involvement and the needs of female offenders are different from those of male offenders. Such approaches include risk assessments, treatments, and supervision.

Gender-sensitive responses work under the well-established assumption that the pathways to and from crime and the needs of girls are unique (Chesney-Lind and Pasko 2004; Davidson 2013; Taylor and Blanchette 2009). Feminist criminology demands not only that the varying pathways of female offenders be recognized, but also that risk assessment, treatment, supervision, and other responses taken by the criminal justice system likewise take gender into account (Chesney-Lind and Pasko 2013). Davidson (2013) reminds us that these gendered pathways also have specific implications for those girls who are sentenced to custody and for how they deal with their time. For these reasons, a gender-sensitive approach to practice must be undertaken.

Gender-sensitive responses to female offenders should match the needs and learning styles of individual offenders and must be flexible (Blanchette and Brown 2006). There are some specific examples of gender-sensitive treatment. For girls convicted of an offence who live with serious mental illness, trauma from abuse, and heavy substance use, dialectical behavioural therapy (DBT)—a collaborative, therapeutically based intervention that helps clients to achieve cognitive and emotional self-knowledge and self-regulation and strengthens their ability to deal with stress and trauma—seems to be especially effective. DBT was first developed by Linehan (1993a, 1993b) and further developed and applied by Linehan, Head, and Armstrong (1993); Linehan et al. (1999); Linehan et al. (2002); and others (see Trupin et al. 1999; Verheul et al. 2003; McDonagh, Taylor, and Blanchette 2009). DBT has been extensively researched and well established as a positive intervention, especially because it is based on a strong alliance between client and therapist and on the principle that clients are capable of understanding their own processes and participating in the creation of their own well-being.

In addition to treatment, a key concern of gender specificity is risk assessment. In assessing the complex situations of offenders and making predictions about future criminal and anti-social behaviour, risk assessments can be important tools. Considerable research on the benefits of risk/need assessment tools that have now been widely implemented as part of correctional practices across offender populations in Canada, including young female offenders, exists (Worrall and Gelsthrope 2009). Despite the support and extensive use of the tools, some experts regard them with concern, raising questions ranging from their (non)applicability to female and non-white populations (Moretti et al. 2011; Hannah-Moffat and Maurutto 2003) to their tendency to focus too heavily on individual risk factors rather than on systemic structural inequalities (Barron 2011). Because, as Barron (2011) argues, risk analysis has as its focus the present and the future and, specifically, what can be done now to affect the future, the risk system necessarily zeroes in on individuals and on whether they are willing to change their identified personal risk factors while paying little or no attention to the systemic inequalities that may have laid the groundwork for the emergence of these personal risk factors.

In her research in the province of Saskatchewan, Barron (2011) found that the theory underlying risk assessments was heavily contradicted in correctional practice. For example, incarcerated girls in one institution were scored negatively for a lack of pro-social extracurricular activities (they frequently spent leisure time committing crimes or socializing with delinquent peer groups/gangs). In this instance, the risk assessment tool and the interpretation of it by correctional staff failed to acknowledge the resources required for participation in pro-social activities. So, while the tool was employed in an attempt to measure pro-social connections, it instead illuminated an absence of resources, a clear offshoot of poverty. Worse, within the custody environment, extracurricular activities such as exercise were held as privileges instead of as factors that contribute to individual health. As such, correctional staff held back these privileges as a consequence for non-compliance. Risk assessments used in this way may feed into a correctional culture of control rather than promote a view of the correctional institution as a place where youth's basic needs are met so that they can learn how to care for themselves and leave custody better equipped with the knowledge and skills that will assist them to remain free of crime. As long as risk assessment tools confuse worrisome behavioural symptoms—for example, the use and misuse of substances—with causes of crime rather than recognize that the same underlying factors are involved in both substance misuse *and* criminal behaviour, these tools may well be contributing to poor risk assessment and treatment choices. Thus, treating an addiction that began as a result of a need to cope with negative circumstances will not address criminal behaviour unless the underlying causes of the addiction and the criminal behaviours are addressed. If we are to see the continued employment of risk/need assessment tools, the copious and overlapping needs faced by at-risk girls as discussed throughout this chapter demand that these risk assessments be gender sensitive and focused on actual risk, not just on symptoms that demonstrate the presence of risk (Moretti et al. 2011).

It is now well established that gender must be a factor not only in understanding the pathways of females into criminal behaviour but also in understanding the current situations of female young offenders—situations that may include family reunification, birth control, and care for children—that have relevance for their successful reintegration (Davidson 2013). This means that in addition to gender-sensitive risk assessments, correctional supervision, reintegration planning, and community supervision must also be gender sensitive. Thus, as Davidson (2013) states, "The system needs to recognize the disproportionate histories of abuse faced by female offenders while not overly controlling them for factors that are or were beyond their control" (p. 180).

Gender-sensitive approaches designed for females in conflict with the law must also take seriously the strains that racism, chronic violence or illness, and inadequate schooling inflict on girls who are poor, disabled, and of marginalized groups. Compensatory practice acknowledges the damage and aims to repair it. These interventions can be family based (e.g., Moretti, Holland, Moore, and McKay 2004), school based (e.g., Artz and Nicholson 2010), group-home based (e.g., Brown 2010), and neighbourhood based (e.g., Jones 2010; Morash, Park, and Kim 2010). Expanding these types of interventions means fostering community practices and social policies that focus directly on one or more aspects of the well-being requirements for all children and youth in a family, school, neighbourhood, or province.

Mobilizing Political Change around Equity and Human Rights and Social Justice

Throughout this chapter, the importance of addressing the behaviours and marginalities of female young offenders as well as social/structural inequalities has been highlighted. The intersectional approach to girls and crime offers the potential to make important changes to policy (Daly 2008), including the following:

- Institute policies and practices to reverse systemic and personal discrimination.

- Demand gender and racial parity in resources.

- Keep neo-liberal and neo-conservative crime-control policies in check.

Girls who are charged or convicted of crimes have hopes similar to those not charged. They want to stop violence and the destruction of their bodies, health, spirit, and community; they want to get a good education and job; they want to love and care for people; and they want fun and adventure (Nicholson and Artz 2003; Reitsma-Street and Offord 1991). If we take seriously what girls (and boys) say, we then need to ask how particular interests are served by ignoring what girls, their families, and communities tell us. What was the benefit of forcing Aboriginal girls to attend residential schools against the wishes of children and parents (see Chapter 11)? Why are services to girls so inadequate and minimalist? What privilege makes possible the systematic abuse of girls such as those documented in the inquiry of the Ontario Grandview Training School for Girls (Kershaw and Lasovich 1991)? Unmasking the injustice and the unequal access to decision-making helps to account for what is of benefit or not, and to whom, and clarifies the political contested nature of policies and practices.

Mobilizing political change around equity and human rights goes beyond unmasking differences in power. It moves toward dismantling inequitable policies—for example, toward ceasing to scrutinize and judge the sexual histories of girls but not boys. It means above all an insistence that funding and legislative resources for girls in the justice system are proportionate to their numbers and adequate for their well-being (Bloom, Owen, Deschenes, and Rosenbaum 2002; Green and Healy 2003). Politicizing equity would mean that at least one-fifth of Canadian youth justice funds and resources are explicitly tied to girls and their well-being, and proportionately more to Aboriginal and Métis girls. But these funds should not be used to pay for longer custody sentences or more courts and police officers. Rather, resources must be aimed at community interventions and other gender-specific supports.

Summary

Girls are involved in all manner of anti-social, deviant, and criminal behaviours. But their criminal behaviour is infrequent despite fears that youth crime and violence by girls are increasing. Girls commit few serious crimes of violence—a trend that has been remarkably steady for decades. We argue that we need to study crime and our responses to girls and crime as a political project that reveals how social order and gender inequity are established and how they can be changed.

Girls' minimal involvement in crime has led to theories about female crime and delinquency that, until the 1970s, largely overlooked girls' experiences. Alternatively, some theorists attempted to explain girls' criminal behaviour as an aberration of "normal" femininity, or they proposed gender-neutral explanations that decontextualized the complex reality of girls living in a gendered, racist, and unequal world. With the rise of feminism in academia and a concomitant groundswell in gender studies, more attention is being paid to the need for differential explanations of deviance, delinquency, and crime.

Theorists like Artz (1998), Chesney-Lind and Pasko (2004), Reitsma-Street (2004), Zahn (2009), and Chesney-Lind and Jones (2010) remind us that crime is not just a function of interactions within an established order (see Daly 1997; Katz 2000; Schissel 2010). We need to understand illegal and other behaviours as part of active struggles within a changing social order in which power and privilege are unequally distributed and frequently contested. In order to develop a fully delineated theory of girls' crime, we must resist applying the pervasive male standard to female behaviour. Rather, we need to examine our expectations of girls and our fears and values in relation to them. This means that we must question approaches to constructing knowledge about girls while paying close attention to the impact of different laws and regulations on girls and society. Most of all, we must be willing to attend to what girls themselves say if we are to learn more about girls' crime and to respond positively.

In this chapter, we have considered intersectionality and what it means for gender-sensitive responses as a promising theoretical and practical approach that will help us address the complex intersections in the gendered, racist world in which girls live, and will aid policy-makers in building the just, humane, and effective possibilities that girls hope for.

Key Terms

administrative offences

biopsychosocial model

gender gap

gender role theories

gender-sensitive responses

intersectionality

net narrowing

power-control theory

Review Questions

1. Do official crime statistics support the claim that female crime is increasing? Can you ever know the "truth" about crime rates?

2. What are administrative offences and why have they increased?

3. What are the prevailing themes about girls in the theories of female crime and delinquency? What do the theories not explain?

4. What is the intersectional approach to intervention and inquiry? What aspects of the intervention apply to boys? What are its strengths and limitations?

Critical Thinking Questions

1. How would you describe and explain the context in which girls commit minor crimes? Serious crimes? How is the context for girls different than for boys?

2. Imagine yourself to be a member of the opposite sex. The police have caught you breaking into a neighbour's house. How would you explain yourself to your family? To your friends? How do you think the police would respond to you? What do you believe should happen to you?

3. What research questions about girls, policies, and crime need to be studied?

4. Should girls who fail to comply with previous non-custodial dispositions under the YCJA be sentenced to custody?

Endnote

1. We could also ask why females' lower crime rates are not the benchmark against which males' rates are measured and why the overall objective in crime prevention is not to aim to reduce male rates to those much lower rates consistently recorded for females. In other words, why distract ourselves with moral panics about girls instead of asking what continues to work for girls that we can also use with boys?

References

Acoca, L., and Dedel, K. (1998). *No place to hide: Understanding and meeting the needs of girls in the California juvenile justice system*. San Francisco: National Council on Crime and Delinquency.

Adler, F. (1975). *Sisters in crime*. New York: McGraw-Hill.

Agnew, R. (1992). Foundation for a general strain theory of crime and delinquency. *Criminology*, 30: 47–87.

Agnew, R. (1995, 15–18 November). *Gender and crime: A general strain theory perspective*. Paper presented at the 1995 annual meeting of the American Society of Criminology, Boston.

Artz, S. (1998). *Sex, power and the violent school girl*. Toronto: Trifolium.

Artz, S., and Amorim, T. (2013). *Girls in custody, a final report prepared for the Law Foundation of BC Legal Research Fund*. Submitted to the Law Foundation of British Columbia, 31 January 2013.

Artz, S., and Nicholson, D. (2010). Reducing aggressive behavior in girls by attending to school climate. In M. Chesney-Lind and N. Jones (Eds), *Fighting for girls: Critical perspectives on gender and violence* (pp. 149–74). New York: State University Press of New York.

Artz, S., Nicholson, D., and Magnuson, D. (2008). Examining sex differences in the use of direct and indirect aggression. *Gender Issues*, 25(4): 267–88.

Baines, M., and Alder, C. (1996). Are girls more difficult to work with? Youth workers' perspectives in juvenile justice and related areas. *Crime and Delinquency*, 42(3): 467–85.

Bala, N., Carrington, P.J., and Roberts, J.V. (2009). Evaluating the Youth Criminal Justice Act after five years: A qualified success. *Canadian Journal of Criminology and Criminal Justice*, 51(2): 131–67.

Barron, C. (2011). *Governing girls: Rehabilitation in the age of risk*. Winnipeg: Fernwood.

Barron, C., and Lacombe, D. (2005). Moral panic and the nasty girl. *Canadian Review of Sociology and Anthropology*, 42(1): 51–69.

Berger, M.T., and Guidroz, K. (2009). Introduction. In M.T. Berger and K. Guidroz (Eds), *The intersectional approach: Transforming the academy through race, class and gender* (pp. 1–22). Chapel Hill: North Carolina Press.

Berger, R. (1989). Female delinquency in the emancipation era: A review of the literature. *Sex Roles*, 21(5/6): 375–99.

Binder, A., Geis, G., and Bruce, D. (1988). *Juvenile delinquency: Historical, cultural, legal perspectives*. New York: Macmillan.

Blackwell, B., Sellers, C., and Schlaupitz, S. (2002). A power-control theory of vulnerability to crime and adolescent role exits—revisited. *Canadian Review of Sociology and Anthropology*, 39(2): 199–218.

Blanchette, K., and Brown, S.L. (2006). *The assessment and treatment of women offenders: An integrative perspective*. New York: Wiley.

Bloom, B., Owen, B., Deschenes, E.P., and Rosenbaum, J. (2002). Improving juvenile justice for females: A statewide assessment in California. *Crime and Delinquency*, 48(4): 526–52.

British Columbia. (2014). Information bulletin. Retrieved August 2014 from http://www2.news .gov.bc.ca/news_releases_2013-2017/2014CFD0018-000771.htm

Broidy, L., and Agnew, R. (1997). Gender and crime: A general strain theory perspective. *Journal of Research in Crime and Delinquency*, 34(3): 275–306.

Brown, M. (2010). Negotiations of the living space: Life in the group home. In M. Chesney-Lind and N. Jones (Eds), *Fighting for girls: New perspectives on gender and violence* (pp. 175–99). New York: SUNY Press.

Calverley, D. (2007). Youth custody and community services in Canada, 2004/2005. *Juristat*, 27(2). Statistics Canada Catalogue no. 85-002.

Campbell, A. (1991). *The girls in the gang* (2nd ed.). New York: Basil Blackwell.

Cernkovich, S., and Giordano, P. (1987). Family relationships and delinquency. *Criminology*, 25: 295–321.

Cesaroni, C., and Bala, N. (2008). Deterrence as principle of youth sentencing: No effect on youth, but significant effect on judges. *Queen's Law Journal*, 34: 447.

Chesney-Lind, M. (2010). Jailing "bad" girls: Girls' violence and trends in female incarceration. In M. Chesney-Lind and N. Jones (Eds), *Fighting for girls: New perspectives on gender and violence* (pp. 57–79). New York: SUNY Press.

Chesney-Lind, M., Artz, S., and Nicholson, D. (2002). Violence patterns in girls' delinquency and gender responsive programming in the United States and Canada. In L. Rapp-Paglicci, A. Roberts, and J. Wodarski (Eds), *Handbook of violence* (pp. 278–320). New York: Wiley & Sons.

Chesney-Lind, M., and Irwin, K. (2008). *Beyond bad girls: Gender, violence and hype*. New York: Routledge.

Chesney-Lind, M., and Jones, N. (2010). *Fighting for girls: New perspectives on gender and violence*. New York: SUNY Press.

Chesney-Lind, M., and Okamoto, S. (2001). Gender matters: Patterns in girl's delinquency and gender responsive programming. *Journal of Forensic Psychology Practice*, 1(3): 1–28.

Chesney-Lind, M., and Pasko, L. (Eds). (2004). *Girls, women and crime: Selected readings*. Thousand Oaks, CA: Sage.

Chesney-Lind, M., and Pasko, L. (2013). *The female offender: Girls, women and crime*. Thousand Oaks, CA: Sage.

Chesney-Lind, M., and Shelden, R. (1998). *Girls, delinquency and juvenile justice* (2nd ed.). Belmont, CA: West/Wadsworth.

Cloward, R., and Ohlin, L. (1960). *Delinquency and opportunity.* New York: Free Press.

Cohen, A. (1955). *Delinquent boys: The culture of the gang.* New York: Free Press.

Cowie, J., Cowie, V., and Slater, E. (1968). *Delinquency in girls.* London: Heinemann.

Daly, K. (1997). Different ways of conceptualizing sex/gender in feminist theory and their implications for criminology. *Theoretical Criminology, 1*(1): 25–51.

Daly, K. (2008). Seeking justice in the 21st century. In H. Ventura Miller (Ed.), *Restorative justice: From theory to practice.* Bingley, UK: Emerald Group.

Daly, K. (2010). Feminist perspectives in criminology: A review with Gen Y in mind. In E. McLaughlin and T. Newburn (Eds), *The Sage handbook of criminological theory* (pp. 225–46). Thousand Oakes, CA: Sage.

Dauvergne, M. (2013). Youth court statistics, 2010/2011. *Juristat, 33*(1). Statistics Canada Catalogue no. 85-002.

Davidson, J.T. (2013). Female offenders, community supervision, and evidence-based practices. In M. Chesney-Lind and L. Pasko (Eds), *The female offender: Girls, women and crime* (pp. 153–87). Thousand Oaks, CA: Sage.

Dean, A.R. (2005). Locking them up to keep them "safe": Criminalized girls in British Columbia: A systemic advocacy project conducted for Justice for Girls. Vancouver: Justice for Girls. Retrieved 15 August 2010 from http://www.justiceforgirls.org/publications/pdfs/jfg_complete_report .pdf

DeKeseredy, W. (2000). *Women, crime and the Canadian criminal justice system.* Cincinnati OH: Anderson Publishing Company.

Dionne, G., Tremblay, R., Boivin, M., Laplante, D., and Pérusse, D. (2003). Physical aggression and expressive vocabulary in 19-month-old twins. *Developmental Psychology, 39*(2): 261–73.

Dodge, K.A., and Pettit, G.S. (2003). A biopsychosocial model of the development of chronic conduct problems in adolescence. *Developmental Psychology, 29*(2): 349–71.

Doob, A., and Sprott, J. (1998). Is the "quality" of youth violence becoming more serious? *Canadian Journal of Criminology, 40*(2): 165–84.

Doob, A., and Sprott, J. (2004). Youth justice in Canada. In M. Tonry and A. Doob (Eds), *Crime and justice: A review of the research*, Vol. 31 (pp. 185–242). Chicago: University of Chicago Press.

Durkheim, E. (1933). *The division of labor in society.* (G. Simpson, trans.) New York: Free Press.

Estrada, F. (2001). Juvenile violence as a social problem: Trends, media attention and societal response. *British Journal of Criminology, 41*: 639–55.

Fishbein, D., Miller, S., Winn, D.M., and Dakof, G. (2009). Biopsychological factors, gender and delinquency. In M. Zahn (Ed.), *The delinquent girl* (pp. 84–106). Philadelphia: Temple University Press.

Gaarder, E., and Belknap, J. (2002). Tenuous borders: Girls transferred to adult court. *Criminology, 40*(3): 481–517.

Giordano, P. (2009). Peer influences on girls' delinquency. In M. Zahn (Ed.), *The delinquent girl* (pp. 127–45). Philadelphia: Temple University Press.

Giordano, P., Cernkovich, S., and Pugh, M. (1986). Friendships and delinquency. *American Journal of Sociology, 91*: 1170–202.

Green, R. and Healy, K. (2003). *Tough on kids: Rethinking approaches to youth justice.* Saskatoon: Purich.

Grosser, G. (1951). *Juvenile delinquency and contemporary American sex roles.* Unpublished doctoral dissertation, Harvard University.

Hagan, J. (1988). *Structural criminology.* Saint John, NB: Polity Press.

Hagan, J. (1990). The structure of gender and deviance: A power-control theory of vulnerability to crime and the search for deviant role exits. *Canadian Review of Sociology and Anthropology, 27*(2): 137–56.

Hagan, J., Gillis, A., and Simpson, J. (1985). The class structure of delinquency: Toward a power-control theory of common delinquent behaviour. *American Journal of Sociology, 90*: 1151–78.

Hagan, J., Simpson, J., and Gillis, A. (1987). Class in the household: A power-control theory of gender and delinquency. *American Journal of Sociology, 92*: 788–816.

Hannah-Moffat, K., and Maurutto, P. (2003). *Youth risk/need assessment: An overview of issues and practices*. Ottawa: Department of Justice Canada. Retrieved August 2014 from http://www .justice.gc.ca/eng/rp-pr/cj-jp/yj-jj/rr03_yj4-rr03_jj4/rr03_yj4.pdf

Heidensohn, F., and Silvestri, M. (2012). Gender and crime. In R. Morgan and R. Reiner (Eds), *The Oxford Handbook of Criminology* (5th ed., pp. 336–69). Oxford: Oxford University Press.

Hirschi, T. (1969). *Causes of delinquency*. Berkeley: University of California Press.

Holland, J., Ramazanoglu, C., Sharpe, S., and Thomson, R. (1998). *The male in the head: Young people, heterosexuality and power*. London: Tufnell Press.

Irwin, K., and Chesney-Lind, M. (2008). Girls' violence: Beyond dangerous masculinity. *Sociology Compass*, 2(3): 837–55.

Jensen, G., and Eve, R. (1976). Sex differences in delinquency. *Criminology*, 13: 427–48.

Joe-Laidler, K., and Hunt, G. (1997). Violence and social organization in female gangs. *Social Justice*, 24: 148–69.

Jones, N. (2010). "It's about being a survivor . . .": African American girls, gender, and the context of inner-city violence. In M. Chesney-Lind and N. Jones (Eds), *Fighting for girls: New perspectives on gender and violence* (pp. 203–18). New York: SUNY.

Jones, N.J., Brown, S.L., Wanamaker, K.A., and Greiner, L. (2014). A quantitative exploration of gendered pathways to crime in a sample of male and female juvenile offenders. *Feminist Criminology*, 9(2): 113–36.

Katz, R. (2000). Explaining girl's and women's crime and desistance in the context of their victimization experiences. *Violence against Women*, 6(6): 633–60. Reprinted with permission in M. Chesney-Lind and L. Pasko (Eds), (2004), *Girls, women and crime* (pp. 24–41). Thousand Oaks, CA: Sage.

Katz, R.S. (2004). Explaining girls' and women's crime and desistence in the context of the victimization experiences: A developmental test of revised strain theory and the life course perspective. In M. Chesney-Lind and L. Pasko (Eds), *Girls, women and crime: Selected readings* (pp. 24–41). Thousand Oaks, CA: Sage.

Kershaw, A., and Lasovich, M. (1991). *Rock-a-bye baby: A death behind bars*. Toronto: McClelland & Stewart.

Kong, R. (2009). Youth custody and community services in Canada, 2007/2008. *Juristat*, 29(2). Statistics Canada Catalogue no. 85-002-X.

Kong, R., and AuCoin, K. (2008). Female offenders in Canada. *Juristat*, 28(1). Statistics Canada Catalogue no. 85-002-XIE.

Konopka, G. (1966). *The adolescent girl in conflict*. Englewood Cliffs, NJ: Prentice-Hall.

Konopka, G. (1983). *Young girls: A portrait of adolescence*. New York: Hayworth Press.

Kruttschnitt, C., and Giordano, P. (2009). Family influences on girls' delinquency. In M. Zahn (Ed.), *The delinquent girl* (pp. 146–63). Philadelphia: Temple University Press.

Lanctôt, N., Émond, C., and Le Blanc, M. (2004). Adjudicated females' participation in violence from adolescence to adulthood: Results from a longitudinal study. In M. Moretti, C. Odgers, and M. Jackson (Eds), *Girls and aggression: Contributing factors and intervention principles*. Boston: Kluwer.

Linehan, M.M. (1993a). *Cognitive behavioural treatment of borderline personality disorder*. New York and London: Guilford Press.

Linehan, M.M. (1993b). *Skills training manual for treating borderline personality disorder*. New York and London: Guilford Press.

Linehan, M.M., Heard, H.L., and Armstrong, H.E. (1993). Naturalistic follow-up of a behavioral treatment for chronically parasuicidal borderline patients. *Archives of General Psychiatry*, 50: 971–4.

Linehan, M.M., Schmidt, H., Dimeff, L.A., Craft, J.C., Kanter, J., and Comtois, K.A. (1999). Dialectical behavior therapy for patients with borderline personality disorder and drug-dependence. *American Journal on Addiction*, 8(4): 279–92.

Linehan, M.M., Dimeff, L.A., Reynolds, S.K., Comtois, K.A., Welch, S.S., Haggerty, P., and Kivlahan, D.R. (2002). Dialectical behavior therapy versus comprehensive validation plus 12-step for the treatment of opioid dependent women meeting criteria for borderline personality disorder. *Drug and Alcohol Dependence*, 67(1): 13–26.

McDonagh, D., Taylor, K., and Blanchette, K. (2009). Correctional adaptation of dialectical behaviour therapy (DBT) for federally sentenced women. Correctional Services of Canada Forum on Corrections Research. Retrieved from http://www.csc-scc.gc.ca/text/pblct/forum/e142/e142i-eng.shtml

Males, M. (2010). Have "girls gone wild"? In M. Chesney-Lind and N. Jones (Eds), *Fighting for girls: New perspectives on gender and violence* (pp. 13–32). New York: SUNY Press.

Mann, R.M., Senn, C.Y., Girard, A., and Ackbar, S. (2007). Community-based interventions for at-risk youth in Ontario under Canada's Youth Criminal Justice Act: A case study of a "runaway" girl. *Canadian Journal of Criminology and Criminal Justice, 49*(1): 37–74.

Means, R. (2002). Decreasing the raise [sic] in female delinquency through gender specific program [sic] and proactive police involvement. Unpublished report, Department of Interdisciplinary Technology as part of School of Police Staff and Command Program Eastern, Michigan University.

Miller, E. (1986). *Street women: The illegal work of underclass women.* Philadelphia: Temple University Press.

Miller, J., and Mullins C.W. (2009). Feminist theories of girls' delinquency. In M. Zahn (Ed.), *The delinquent girl* (pp. 30–49). Philadelphia: Temple University Press.

Miller, W. (1958). Lower class culture as a generating milieu of gang delinquency. *Journal of Social Issues, 14*: 5–19.

Moffitt, T., Brammer, G., Caspi, A., Fawcett, J., Raleigh, M., Yuwiler, A., and Silva, P. (1998). Whole blood serotonin relates to violence in an epidemiological study. *Biological Psychiatry, 43*(6): 446–57.

Monture-Angus, P. (2000). Aboriginal women and correctional practice. In K. Hannah-Moffat and M. Shaw (Eds), *An ideal prison?: Critical essays on women's imprisonment in Canada* (pp. 52–60). Halifax: Fernwood.

Morash, M., Park, S., and Kim, J. (2010). The importance of context in the production of older girls' violence: Implications for the focus of interventions. In M. Chesney-Lind and N. Jones (Eds), *Fighting for girls: New perspectives on gender and violence* (pp. 219–40). New York: SUNY Press.

Moretti, M., Holland, R., Moore, K., and McKay, S. (2004). An attachment-based parenting program for caregivers of severely conduct-disordered adolescents. *Journal of Child and Youth Care Work, 19*: 170–9.

Moretti, M.M., Odgers, C., and Reppucci, N.D. (2011). Serious conduct problems among girls at risk: Translating research into intervention. *International Journal of Child, Youth and Family Studies, 1* and 2: 142–61.

Munch, C. (2012) Youth correctional statistics in Canada, 2010/2011. *Juristat, 32*(1). Statistics Canada Catalogue no. 85-002-X.

Naffine, N. (1987). Female crime: *The construction of women in criminology.* Sydney: Allen and Unwin.

Nicholson, D., and Artz, S. (2003). Preventing youthful offending: Where do we go from here? *Relational Child and Youth Care Practice, 16*(4): 32–46.

NWAC (Native Women's Association of Canada and Justice for Girls). (2012). *Gender matters: Building strength in reconciliation.* Retrieved July 2014 from http://www.nwac.ca/gender-matters/

Nye, F. (1958). *Family relationships and delinquent behaviour.* New York: Wiley.

Pollack, O. (1950). *The criminality of women.* New York: Barnes.

Raine, A. (2002). Annotation: The role of prefrontal deficits, low autonomic arousal, and early health factors in the development of antisocial and aggressive behavior in children. *Journal of Child Psychology and Psychiatry, 43*: 417–34.

Reckless, W. (1961). *The crime problem* (3rd ed.). New York: Barnes.

Reiss, A. (1951). Delinquency as the failure of personal social controls. *American Sociological Review, 16*: 196–207.

Reiss, A., and Roth, J. (Eds). (1993). *Understanding and preventing violence.* Washington: National Academy Press.

Reitsma-Street, M. (1998). Still girls learn to care; girls policed to care. In C. Baines, P. Evans, and S. Neysmith (Eds), *Women's caring: Social policy in Canada* (rev. ed., pp. 87–113). Toronto: Oxford University Press.

Reitsma-Street, M. (1999). Justice for Canadian girls: A 1990s update. *Canadian Journal of Criminology, 41*(4): 335–63.

Reitsma-Street, M. (2004). Connecting policies, girls, and violence. In M. Moretti, C. Odgers, and M. Jackson (Eds), *Girls and aggression: Contributing factors and intervention principles* (pp. 115–30). Boston: Kluwer.

Reitsma-Street, M. (2005). Radical pragmatism: Prevention and intervention with girls. In M.L. Hoskins and S. Artz (Eds), *Working relationally with girls: Complex lives/complex identities* (pp. 119–38). New York: Haworth Press.

Reitsma-Street, M., and Offord, D.R. (1991). Girl delinquents and their sisters: A challenge for practice. *Canadian Social Work Review, 8*(1): 11–27.

Rubinow, D., and Schmidt, P. (1996). Androgens, brain, and behavior. *American Journal of Psychiatry, 153*(8): 974–84.

Schissel, B. (2010). Ill heath and discrimination: The double jeopardy for youth in punitive justice systems. *International Journal of Child, Youth and Family Studies, 1*(2): 157–78.

Sharpe, G., and Gelsthorpe, L. (2009). Engendering the agenda: Girls, young women and youth justice. *Youth Justice, 9*(3): 195–208.

Simon, R. (1975). *Women and crime*. Lexington, MA: Lexington Books.

Smith, A., Cox, K., Poon, C., Stewart, D., and McCreary Centre Society (2013). Time out III: A profile of BC youth in custody. Vancouver: McCreary Centre Society. Retrieved July 2014 from http://www.mcs.bc.ca/pdf/Time_Out_III.pdf

Spelman, E. (1988). *Inessential woman: Problems of exclusion in feminist thought*. Boston: Beacon Press.

Sprott, J. (2012). The persistence of status offences in the youth justice system. *Canadian Journal of Criminology and Criminal Justice, 54*(3): 309–32.

Sprott, J.B., and Doob, A.N. (2009). *Justice for girls? Stability and change in the youth justice systems of the United States and Canada.* Chicago: University of Chicago Press.

Sprott, J.B., and Doob, A.N. (2010). Gendered treatment: Girls and treatment orders in bail court. *Canadian Journal of Criminology and Criminal Justice, 52*(4): 427–41.

Statistics Canada. (2006). Youth court survey, number of cases, by sex of accused, annually. CANSIM Table 2520048.

Statistics Canada. (2014a). Adult criminal courts, number of cases and charges by type of decision. CANSIM Table 2520053.

Statistics Canada (2014b). Estimate of population, by age group and sex for July 1, Canada, provinces and territories. CANSIM Table 0510001.

Statistics Canada. (2014c). Youth custody and community services (YCCS), admissions to correctional services, by sex and Aboriginal identity, 1997/1998 to 2011/2012. CANSIM Table 2510012.

Statistics Canada. (2014d). Youth custody and community services (YCCS), admissions to correctional services, by sex and age at time of admission, 1997/1998 to 2011/2012. CANSIM Table 2510011.

Statistics Canada. (2014e). Youth courts, number of cases and charges by type of decision 1997/1998 to 2011/2012. CANSIM Table 2520064.

Statistics Canada. (2014f). Youth courts, guilty cases by type of sentence 1997/1998 to 2011/2012. CANSIM Table 2520067.

Statistics Canada. (2014g). Incident-based crime statistics, by detailed violations. CANSIM Table 252-0051.

Steffensmeier, D., Schwartz, J., Zhong, H., and Ackerman, J. (2005). An assessment of recent trends in girls' violence using diverse longitudinal sources: Is the gender gap closing? *Criminology, 43*(2): 355–406.

Stoneman, L. (forthcoming). *Community-based responses to youth offending: Politics, policy and practice under the YCJA*. Doctoral dissertation, University of Victoria, Victoria, BC.

Sutherland, E. (1939). *Principles of criminology*. Philadelphia: Lippincott.

Sutherland, E., and Cressey, D. (1978). *Criminology* (10th ed.). Philadelphia: Lippincott.

Tanner, J. (1996). *Teenage troubles: Youth and deviance in Canada*. Toronto: Nelson Canada.

Taylor-Butts, A., and Bressen, A. (2007). Youth crime in Canada, 2006. *Juristat, 28*(3). Statistics Canada Catalogue no. 85-002-XIE.

Taylor, K.N., and Blanchette, K. (2009). The women are not wrong: It is the approach that is debatable. *Criminology and Public Policy, 8*(1): 221–9.

Toby, J. (1957). Social disorganization and stake in conformity: Complementary factors in predatory behaviour in hoodlums. *Journal of Criminal Law, Criminology and Police Service, 48*: 12–17.

Tremblay, R. (2003). Why socialization fails: The case of chronic physical aggression. In B. Lahey, T. Moffitt, and C. Avshalom (Eds), *Causes of conduct disorder and juvenile delinquency* (pp. 182–224). New York: Guilford.

Tremblay, R.E., Nagin, D.S, Séguin, J.R., Zoccolillo, M., Zelazo, P.D., Boivin, M., Pérusse, D., and Japel, C. (2005, February). Physical aggression during early childhood: Trajectories and predictors. *Journal of the Canadian Academy of Child and Adolescent Psychiatry, 14*(1): 3–9. Retrieved from http://www.ncbi.nlm.nih.gov/pmc/articles/PMC2538721/

Trupin, E., Stewart, D., Boesky, L., McClurg, B., Beach, B., Hormann, S., and Baltrusis, R. (1999, February). Evaluation of a dialectical behavior therapy with incarcerate female juvenile offenders. Paper presented at the 11th annual research conference, "A system of care for children's mental health: Expanding the research base," Tampa, FL.

Verheul, R., van den Bosch, L.M.C., Koeter, M.W.J., de Ridder, M.A.J., Stijnen, T., and Van den Brink, W. (2003). Dialectical behaviour therapy for women with borderline personality disorder: 12-month, randomised clinical trial in the Netherlands. *British Journal of Psychiatry, 182*: 135–40.

Wilson, J., and Herrnstein, R. (1985). *Crime and human nature.* New York: Simon and Schuster.

Woolford, A. (2009). *The politics of restorative justice: A critical introduction.* Halifax: Fernwood.

Worrall, A., and Gelsthrope, L. (2009). "What works" with women offenders: The past 30 years. *Probation Journal, 56*(4): 329.

Zahn, M.A. (Ed.). (2009). *The delinquent girl.* Philadelphia: Temple University Press.

New Theoretical Perspectives on Youth Crime

Stephen W. Baron

8

Overview

This chapter will review six of the new theoretical perspectives that have emerged in the past two decades to explain youth crime. The chapter will examine each of these perspectives in the order in which they were developed, beginning with the general theory of crime, then turning to general strain theory, the age-graded theory of social control, control balance theory, differential coercion theory, and situational action theory. The chapter will begin with an examination of each perspective, outlining the main theoretical premises offered by the theorists; that is, it will scrutinize the way that each of the different theorists attempts to explain how youth become involved in crime. This will include an examination of how certain factors might lead to other factors, which in turn can lead to crime. The chapter also discusses the way that certain causal factors may work together with other factors or may require that other factors be present before they will increase the risk that youth will become involved in illegal activities. In addition to a review of each theoretical perspective, attention is given to examining the empirical status of each theory, with particular attention given to the research that has been undertaken on the theory to date. This overview will determine whether each theory works as an explanation of youth crime, where future research is needed to clarify the causal mechanisms outlined in the particular perspective, and whether theoretical revisions are required for the theory to better explain youth involvement in criminal activities.

Key Objectives

After reading this chapter, you should be able to:

- Identify and distinguish the new theoretical perspectives developed to explain youth crime.
- Better understand the way different theoretical concepts can be integrated to improve our understanding of youth crime.
- Appreciate the complexity required to understand youth crime.
- Recognize some of the empirical weaknesses of theoretical approaches offered to explain youth crime.

Introduction

In this chapter, we examine a number of the more recent theoretical perspectives that have been offered to help explain and better our understanding of youth crime. Until quite recently, explanations of youth crime were dominated by theoretical perspectives developed prior to the 1970s (e.g., social control and strain theories, discussed in Chapter 7). Researchers who explored these perspectives, however, discovered that these explanations of crime provided only a limited account of the behaviour. This lack of empirical support suggested that additional thinking was required to help us understand how youth became involved in crime. In response, the past two decades have seen a growth in the number of, and complexity in, explanations for youth crime. Here we will review six of the newly offered theoretical viewpoints in the historical order in which they emerged. Contained in our assessment will be the general theory of crime, general strain theory, the age-graded theory of social control, control balance theory, differential coercion theory, and situational action theory. Some of these perspectives build on past perspectives, while others attempt to put together, or integrate, a number of the previously developed perspectives with innovative, new causal concepts to create novel explanations of criminal behaviour. Our goal is to explore the main causal factors that each perspective outlines as leading to criminal behaviour. We will also be interested in the more indirect and less obvious ways that these factors may lead to crime. We will be following the causal trail of each perspective, investigating how certain factors lead to other factors, which in turn lead to crime. Further, we will be paying attention to the role that combinations of factors play together in helping us to understand crime. Here we want to be aware of how the central causal factor may work better when other factors are also present. As our agenda suggests, these recent theoretical developments can be both simple and sophisticated, reflecting the evolution of the understanding of crime.

The General Theory of Crime: Self-Control

The general theory of crime, as outlined by Michael Gottfredson and Travis Hirschi (1990), focuses on the key concept of self-control. Self-control refers to the ability to restrain oneself from momentary temptations. People who develop self-control are said to be less likely to engage in criminal activities. In contrast, the failure to develop this characteristic leaves one more at risk of engaging in crime and also increases the likelihood of involvement in other negative activities. While viewed as an overarching concept, **low self-control** is argued to be made up of six different characteristics. While these six elements are distinct, Gottfredson and Hirschi argue that they tend to come together in the same people, operate in tandem, and persist over the lifespan to produce a stable, coherent construct (see Figure 8.1).

low self-control
A trait made up of impulsivity, short-sightedness, risk-taking, physicality, insensitivity, and low frustration tolerance, which leaves individuals less able to refrain from activities that provide short-term pleasure or gain.

Characteristics of Low Self-Control

Impulsivity

The first characteristic of those who lack self-control is the tendency to be impulsive. Impulsivity can be summarized as the inability to defer gratification or to control impulses as well as the inclination to focus on events that are taking place in the here and now. For those who are impulsive, criminal activities can serve to satisfy various personal desires easily and immediately. For example, crime can lead to the quick acquisition of property without putting in the effort to secure resources to purchase the desired goods, it allows quick revenge against others without waiting for resolution through the courts or intervention of others, and potentially it provides a simple and quick method to satiate sexual or other desires.

Lack of Diligence

The second characteristic indicative of a deficiency in self-control focuses on the lack of diligence. Those who have developed self-control show a tendency to be persistent, industrious, and tenacious in a course of action. The theory suggests that people naturally wish to accomplish their goals through the simplest, easiest means possible. People who lack diligence will choose the quickest path to satisfy their desires even if the long-term consequences are negative. Crimes allow people to satisfy desires more easily, with minimal effort, and to bypass some of the more complicated methods of reaching goals through more conventional avenues.

Risk-Taking

The third element of low self-control is the tendency to be a risk-taker. People with low self-control enjoy engaging in activities that provide adventure, thrills, and excitement. Criminal

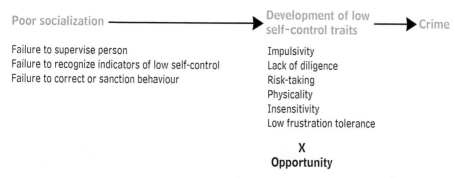

FIGURE 8.1 The General Theory of Crime

acts involve elements of excitement and risk. Breaking into a house, stealing a car, and/or getting into a fight all provide exciting adventures that are appealing to those with low self-control. Those who have high self-control are more likely to be risk averse and more cautious and careful in their behaviour, all of which discourage involvement in criminal activities.

Physicality

The fourth characteristic of low self-control is the tendency to be physical as opposed to valuing or possessing cognitive or academic skills. Gottfredson and Hirschi note that most crimes do not require much skill, training, or elaborate planning. Instead, the cognitive requirements for crime are argued to be slight. Most criminal acts simply entail physically hurting others or taking their property and are undertaken impulsively based on in-the-moment decisions. Thus, crime becomes an attractive pursuit for those who do not wish to be challenged cognitively.

Insensitivity

The fifth element of self-control focuses on the degree of a person's self-centredness or insensitivity. Those who lack self-control are egotistical and unconcerned about the needs of others. Criminal acts often leave victims in pain if physically harmed, or feeling violated if their property has been stolen. Individuals who consider the feelings of others prior to their actions adjust their behaviour to minimize hurting others.

Low Frustration Tolerance

Finally, Gottfredson and Hirschi argue that those with self-control are able to control their frustrations when faced with difficult circumstances. In contrast, those with low self-control have low frustration tolerance and respond negatively to events that they interpret as irritating. Thus, slights from people can lead to assaults, frustrating tasks can lead to property damage, and difficult interpersonal interactions can lead to violence rather than verbal resolution. In contrast, those people with self-control have the ability to cope with frustrating situations and respond to interpersonal conflicts with non-physical responses.

Convenience and Opportunity

Although low self-control leaves one more likely to commit crime, a person also requires the convenience and opportunity to commit crime. Gottfredson and Hirshi argue that criminal events contain features that appeal to persons with low self-control. In effect, they argue that low self-control constitutes a disposition to act in a certain way, triggered by circumstance.

While Gottfredson and Hirschi propose that the lack of self-control is the main cause of crime, they also suggest that it is linked to a range of other analogous behaviours that require little planning, provide immediate gratification, and offer a great deal of excitement. Low self-control, therefore, will leave one more likely to smoke, drink, speed, be involved in more traffic accidents, gamble, have illicit sex, and have children out of wedlock. Further, Gottfredson and Hirschi argue that low self-control has "social consequences" that shape people's ability to succeed in social institutions and to form **social bonds**. Thus, those

social bonds
The degree to which individuals, through socialization, have connections to people and institutions in a society and believe in the rules of the society. These connections serve as restraints against criminal opportunities and behaviour.

lacking self-control will be more likely to become divorced, to be unemployed, and to drop out of school. Gottfredson and Hirschi argue that since low self-control is the cause of various social failures, these failures themselves actually have no causal impact on crime. Thus, the negative impact that low self-control has on people's lives is extremely broad.

Causes of Variation in Self-Control

How does someone end up with low self-control? Gottfredson and Hirschi argue that low self-control is the result of an absence of training or ineffective or incomplete socialization. While Gottfredson and Hirschi admit that there will be variations in the degree to which children demonstrate the traits associated with low self-control, they note that effective socialization to develop self-control is always achievable. So how do we ensure effective socialization? Teaching self-control requires that caregivers (1) monitor a child's behaviour; (2) recognize the characteristics of low self-control, demonstrated in the forms of impulsiveness, lack of diligence, risk-taking, physicality, insensitivity, and low frustration tolerance, when exhibited; and (3) sanction and correct those behaviours indicative of low self-control. This child-rearing strategy will increase the child's capabilities in delaying gratification, develop his or her sensitivity to the feelings and wishes of others, create more tolerance for frustration, promote diligence and focus on cognitive development, and build an aversion toward risky, dangerous activities.

Gottfredson and Hirschi note, however, that this child-rearing process can be undermined in a number of ways, including situations where there is a lack of emotional attachment between the parents and the child and/or where the parents lack the time or resources to supervise the child's activities and conduct. Parents also may not recognize the characteristics of self-control or make a connection between these traits and later problematic behaviour, and they therefore may not view the behaviours negatively. Gottfredson and Hirschi stress that without proper socialization, low self-control becomes difficult to alter, and that between the ages of 8 and 10, it becomes relatively stable and will influence behaviour across the life course.

Current Empirical Research into the General Theory of Crime

The general theory of crime has generated a considerable amount of empirical research. Empirical research has generally been supportive of the perspective, finding that those with low self-control tend to engage in crime and analogous behaviours (Pratt and Cullen 2000). Work also suggests that low self-control is predictive of negative social consequences, such as unemployment, homelessness, accidents, criminal associates, and criminal victimization (Baron 2003; Miller, Schreck, and Tewksbury 2006; Pratt, Turanovic, Fox, and Wright 2014). However, the theory has not necessarily been shown to be a general theory of crime, nor has it been shown to be the only possible explanation of crime. For example, the theory has shown little success in explaining white-collar offending (Miller et al. 2006). There has also been considerable debate regarding the stability of low self-control. Of late, research suggests that self-control is malleable (Piquero, Jennings, and Farrington 2010) and may be influenced by levels of social control (Na and Paternoster 2012; Ray, Jones, Loughran, and Jennings 2013). Recent work also suggests that the level of self-control of one's peers can influence an individual's level of self-control (Meldrum, Young, and Weerman 2012; Ray, Jones, Loughran, and Jennings 2013). Certain work also indicates that experiences with victimization can lower a person's self-control (Agnew et al. 2011).

The unidimensionality of low self-control has also been questioned. Some research suggests that the six characteristics of low self-control do not come together as one measure of self-control; rather, they remain separate, distinct indicators of impulsivity, lack of diligence, risk-taking, physicality, insensitivity, and low frustration tolerance. This is important because some work suggests that some of the individual components are better predictors of certain behaviours. For example, low frustration tolerance appears to have a strong link with violent offending, while risk-taking has been linked to property offending (Baron, Forde, and Kay 2007). In sum, while there is general support for the link between low self-control and crime, the theory has generated a great deal of debate and provides a fruitful ground for further research.

General Strain Theory (GST)

Robert Agnew (1992, 2001) provides a theory that focuses on how a broad number of negative situations can lead to criminal behaviour. He focuses on emotional reactions to negative situations or **strains** and details how other factors can influence people in their choice to cope with strain through either criminal or non-criminal means. The GST focuses squarely on people's negative relationships with others. These are situations where people do not like the way that they are being treated, and it is this experience that pressures people into committing crime as a means of coping with the strain. In his perspective, Agnew outlines three broad areas of strain that are thought to lead to crime (see Figure 8.2).

Types of Strains

Failure to Achieve Goals

The first broad area of strain outlined in the GST is the failure to achieve positively valued goals. Within this broad area are three sub-areas that, as Agnew summarizes, can possibly

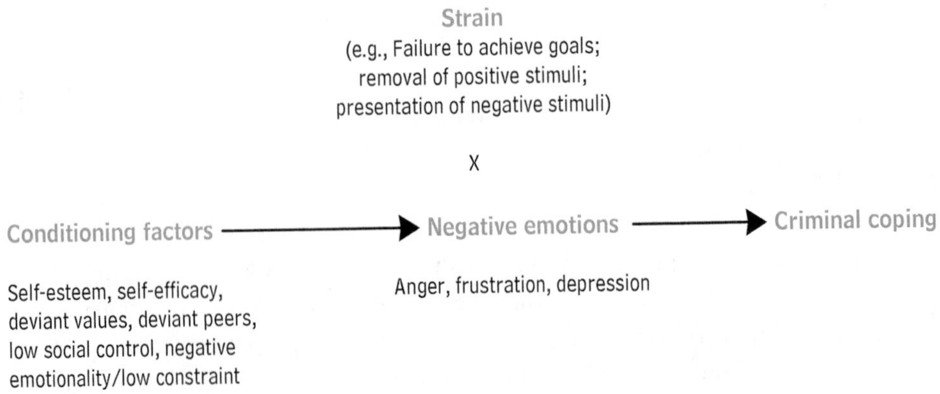

> **strains**
> Experiences or situations that individuals perceive as being negative, creating a negative emotional reaction that provides the possible incentive for using crime as a coping mechanism.

Strain
(e.g., Failure to achieve goals;
removal of positive stimuli;
presentation of negative stimuli)

X

Conditioning factors ⟶ Negative emotions ⟶ Criminal coping

Self-esteem, self-efficacy,
deviant values, deviant peers,
low social control, negative
emotionality/low constraint

Anger, frustration, depression

FIGURE 8.2 General Strain Theory

lead to criminal behaviour. The first form of strain encompasses the disjunction between aspirations and expected achievements and is similar to the version of strain that Merton (1938) outlines in his classic perspective. Here the gap between what people desire and what people expect to achieve leads to unpleasant feelings, pressuring them to utilize criminal means to achieve those aspirations. Thus, if someone aspires to extreme wealth but expects more modest success, then he or she can be led to adopt crime as a potential avenue to success.

The second type of strain under the rubric of the failure to achieve positively valued goals is the disjunction between expected achievements and actual achievements. This form of strain moves away from focusing on aspirations (e.g., acquiring a fortune), which are sometimes unrealistic. Instead, it centres on people's expectations of achievement, which are formed from their past achievement experiences and/or their observations of the achievements of others like them. Thus, expected achievements can be viewed as more realistic in terms of accomplishment than are aspirations. If there is a gap between these more realistic expectations for achievement and what is actually achieved, this failure motivates individuals to turn to crime as a method of addressing this gap.

The third form of strain under this category is the disjunction between just or fair outcomes and actual outcomes. In contrast to the two previous forms of strain, some individuals may not necessarily have specific expectations regarding outcomes when they enter into a situation. Instead, they may enter into circumstances believing that rewards will be allocated fairly. When the actual outcome in a situation is different from what people believe to be a fair or just outcome, then crime may be one response to attempt to adjust their outcomes. Crime can be viewed as a method where people can gain more rewards for themselves while the rewards for others are decreased, meaning the allocation of outcomes can be shifted to where the individual perceives them to be more equitable. Thus, an individual who gets a poorer grade than a classmate who puts in less effort may steal from, or assault, the classmate or the teacher who distributed the outcomes in an attempt to alter outcomes.

Removal of Positive Stimuli

The second broad source of strain that Agnew outlines is the removal of positively valued stimuli. This removal can be actual or it can be anticipated. There are a range of positively valued stimuli that can cause individuals to turn to crime if they are removed, including property and relationships. Agnew outlines a number of potential responses to these types of losses. In some cases, people may try to prevent the loss of the valued item, such as by defending themselves and their property if being robbed. Second, the person who loses a positively valued item might seek revenge against those who stole their property by assaulting the guilty party. Third, those who lose positively valued stimuli may attempt to recover or reclaim the lost stimuli, or perhaps search out a replacement for the stimuli, in both cases through theft. Finally, Agnew notes that losing positively valued stimuli can generate negative emotions, and these emotions may be addressed through the use of alcohol or drugs.

Presentation of Negative Stimuli

The third broad source of strain outlined in the GST is the presentation of negative stimuli. Again, either the anticipation of a negative experience or the actual experience with some sort of negative stimuli can lead individuals to cope with a criminal response. Examples of negative stimuli might include criminal victimization, child abuse, and a negative school environment. Similar to the removal of positively valued stimuli, there are a number of potential avenues for coping with this form of strain. First, individuals who experience negative stimuli may attempt to avoid or escape from the source of the stimuli. For example, a person who dislikes school or is being abused at home may become truant or run away from home. Second, that person may seek revenge against the source of the negative stimuli or against a displaced target that represents the source of the negative stimuli. For example, such individuals may assault the teacher if they dislike school or the parent who is abusing them. Third, individuals experiencing negative stimuli may attempt to bring an end to the source of the negative stimuli. Finally, the experience of negative stimuli will give rise to negative emotions, which can be dealt with by using drugs and/or alcohol.

Overlapping Strains

While these types of strains outlined in the GST are theoretically distinct from one another, they may often be viewed as overlapping. School failure can lead to a gap between expectations and achievements, perceptions of unjust outcomes, and the presentation of negative stimuli. Agnew also notes that it is important to distinguish between "objective strains" and "subjective strains." Objective strains are conditions, situations, or episodes that a majority of a given group will dislike, while subjective strains allude to the conditions, situations, or episodes that are not liked by the individuals who are experiencing them or have experienced them in the past. Examples of objective conditions or events that most people dislike might include school failure, a lack of shelter and/or food, and violent victimization. However, people differ in their subjective evaluation of the same objective strains. Thus, one person may find living in poverty, failing school, or being the victim of crime as more of a strain than another person. The subjective evaluation can be influenced by a number of factors, including values, social resources, and life circumstances. Therefore, we must consider both the objective situations that individuals encounter and their perceptions and interpretations of those situations.

Agnew also suggests that the impact of strain may vary depending upon the severity/magnitude, duration, recency, and centrality of the strain. Strains that are severe or high in magnitude influence actors' abilities to cope in a non-criminal manner by decreasing the perceived costs of criminal coping and increasing the disposition to engage in criminal coping. Strains that are of a long duration and/or high frequency are expected to have a greater negative impact on the individual. As well, more recent strains are expected to have a greater impact on judgments of magnitude than older strains, although certain types of strains, including severe childhood strains, may have long-term effects and potentially contribute to later criminal behaviour. In terms of the "centrality" of the strain, negative experiences, particularly extreme or severe traumatic events that jeopardize central values, goals, needs, identities, and activities, are argued to be more criminogenic because they undermine the ability to cope in a non-criminal fashion.

Agnew also notes that strains associated with or caused by low social control can increase the probabilities of a criminal coping strategy because the costs of crime are reduced. Further, individuals who lack conventional commitments, attachments, and supervision are less likely to have access to the resources that promote non-criminal coping. Agnew also argues that strains that are viewed as unjust increase the probability of criminal coping because they are particularly conducive to creating anger. Agnew adds that certain forms of strain also produce some inducement, stimulus, or motivation to utilize crime as a method of coping. For example, certain strains (e.g., criminal victimization and physical abuse) provide access to values or beliefs that support criminal coping strategies and models that reinforce criminal coping strategies. Further, in some environments, the best, or perhaps lone, strategy to cope with strain is through criminal means.

Negative Emotions

The various forms of strain are thought to elevate the probability that the person will react with a possible array of negative emotions. Some of the possible emotions that strain might call forth include fear and depression. However, the critical emotion outlined in this perspective is anger. People are more likely to respond to strain with anger when they blame the experiences on other people because anger amplifies their feeling of injury. It is an emotional response that generates a need for revenge or retaliation or some sort of corrective action. Anger can also invigorate a person to actually take some sort of action. At the same time, anger lowers inhibitions and reduces any fear of punishment for engaging in crime, in part because strained, angry individuals suppose that others will consider their response to strain as justified. Those who respond to strain with greater levels of anger will be more likely to engage in crime. Crime can be interpreted as a means of easing the negative emotions generated by strain as well as a method of altering the strain itself.

Conditioning Factors

According to Agnew, a number of different factors may increase or buffer the effect of strain, influencing whether a person will adopt a criminal or non-criminal coping strategy in response to strain. First, Agnew notes the importance of levels of *self-efficacy*. In particular, he suggests that those high in self-efficacy will be more likely to feel they can cope with strain in a non-delinquent manner. Those lacking self-efficacy will be more sensitive to events and believe that they will be unable to alter those events through the use of non-criminal means. Second, *self-esteem* will influence individuals' sensitivity to strain and their ability to engage in various coping strategies. High self-esteem will buffer individuals from strain, leaving them less likely to use criminal coping strategies. Third, those who associate with deviant criminal peers and hold values supportive of deviant behaviour are more likely to react to strain with illegal behaviour. Deviant peers may strengthen the link between strain and delinquency by interpreting as strain certain experiences they share in common with their associates. In doing so, deviant peers can supply further support for criminal behaviour, for example, by modelling criminal behaviour, defining certain deviant activities as appropriate responses to strain, and serving as instigators of criminal behaviour. Moral values against crime may dampen the effect of strain on crime, while deviant attitudes that support criminal coping may increase the effect of strain on crime. Fourth, Agnew argues that people are more likely to engage in crime when they blame their adversity on others. Fifth, the availability and quality of social support that people have at their disposal will also influence whether they deal with strain in a criminal or a conventional fashion. Social support may come in the form of financial assistance, guidance, and emotional support that steer strained individuals clear of crime. Those without conventional, instrumental, and social support are more likely to adopt criminal coping strategies. Criminal coping is also more likely when the benefits of utilizing crime are great and the costs of utilizing criminal coping are low.

Finally, Agnew argues that the personality traits of negative emotionality and low constraint will influence whether an individual deals with strain through criminal or non-criminal means. Individuals with negative emotionality are easily upset and angered and tend to have aggressive interaction styles. Those with low constraint tend to be impulsive risk-takers, with little empathy for others. These characteristics are likely to increase the relationship between strain and crime because individuals with low constraint and negative emotionality are more likely to be sensitive to strain, to interpret situations as strain, and to view situations as unjust. Individuals with these characteristics care little about the reactions of others and give little thought to the consequences of their own actions, leaving them more likely to adopt criminal coping strategies. The aggressive interaction style and proneness for risk that characterize individuals with these traits also increase the likelihood of an illegal response in reaction to strain. In sum, those individuals who experience a strain when they have low self-efficacy, low conventional social support, greater access to deviant peers and deviant values, and greater negative emotionality/low constraint, and who see the costs of criminal coping to be minimal and who blame the strain on others will be more likely to engage in crime. Box 8.1 provides an example of research that applies the GST in explaining crime.

Current Empirical Research into General Strain Theory

General strain theory has generated a great deal of research. There is much support for linkages between various negative experiences and criminal coping (Agnew 2006) including the following:

- The failure to achieve core goals that can easily be achieved through crime (including quick money, masculine status, and autonomy)

- Parental rejection

- Emotional and physical abuse in various settings (including the family, school, and criminal justice system)

- Negative school experiences

- Poor employment conditions (that involve unpleasant, physically demanding, and repetitive work; minimal autonomy; low wages; absent benefits; and limited prospects for advancement)

- Abusive peer relationships

- Criminal victimization

- Youth homelessness

Box 8.1   Youth Justice in Action

Agnew's General Strain Theory

Moon and Jang set out to examine whether Agnew's GST could help explain the bullying that goes on in schools. The researchers were interested in discovering if different types of strains and different forms of negative emotions were associated with different forms of bullying. The researchers asked about 300 school youths to report on their experiences with strain, such as family conflict, emotional punishment from teachers, racial discrimination, and criminal victimization. They also gathered information on the respondents' negative emotions, asking about experiencing episodes of anger and/or depression in the previous year. To explore whether the impact of these strains and emotions on bullying behaviour might be swayed by other factors, Moon and Jang also asked the students questions that would tap into their levels of self-control (e.g., risk-taking and impulsivity), associations with peers who engaged in illegal activities, levels of parental support, affection, and interest, and the degree to which their behaviour was monitored by parents. The researchers also asked the youths to recall how often they engaged in psychological (e.g., making fun of other students) and physical (e.g. pushing or physically attacking other students) bullying.

Moon and Jang found that the strains examined were related to certain forms of bullying, and their associations were mediated by anger and depression. This meant that the strains were related to the negative emotions, and the negative emotions were in turn more likely to lead to bullying. Further, the results indicated that the effects of strain, anger, and depression were less likely to lead to certain types of bullying when the youths had high levels of parental control. In contrast, strain and anger were more likely to lead youths to participate in certain forms of bullying when they associated with peers who were involved in offending.

Critical Thinking Question

What other factors may influence whether strain and/or negative emotions lead to school bullying?

Source: Byongook Moon and Sung Joon Jang. (2014). "A General Strain Approach to Psychological and Physical Bullying: A Study of Interpersonal Aggression at School." *Journal of Interpersonal Violence*, 29(2): 2147–71.

There is also evidence for the link between these negative experiences and negative emotions, such as anger. In turn, there is some evidence that anger is related to criminal coping, particularly for more aggressive forms of offending. Some debate has emerged here regarding the type of anger that has been explored, which has often been more of a measure of trait anger (a stable personality trait) than of state anger (an emotion generated by the situation) (Agnew 2006). The minimal research conducted so far suggests that there may be differences. There is also some debate regarding whether the effects of strain leading to crime should flow primarily through anger or whether they have some independent impact (ibid.). Finally, there are now calls for work to explore other types of emotions— depression, for example—and to determine which types of strains might generate these alternative emotions and the types of coping that these reactions might generate (ibid.).

Recent work has also established that strain can lead to a reduction of self-control and a seeking of illegitimate social support that are related to crime. This research suggests that strain can have an indirect impact on crime through its relationship with other important factors (Baron 2014). The work that is exploring the role of the conditioning factors has generated uneven results. Overall, there is limited support for the moderating roles of self-efficacy, self-esteem, social control, deviant values, deviant beliefs, negative emotionality/low constraint, external attribution, and low risk of apprehension. However, the results often vary across studies, populations examined, the type of strain examined, and the form of crime to be explained (Agnew 2006, 2013; Baron 2004). Agnew (2013) has recently suggested that it is the combination of the various characteristics detailed in the description of the conditioning factors that creates the strong propensity for offending rather than each factor in isolation. Overall, this sporadic support beyond the basic relationships between various forms of strain and crime, together with fresh theoretical guidance, suggests that more work is required to help us more accurately understand how the conditioning factors and emotions will work with which form of strain and within which type of population.

Age-Graded Theory of Social Control

informal social control
The control over people's behaviour that develops as a result of relationships and attachments to significant others and investments in conventional activities that could be damaged by engagement in illegal activities.

Sampson and Laub (1993; Laub and Sampson 2003) offer an age-graded theory of **informal social control**. The theory emerges from the broader life-course perspective in sociology that stresses the importance of examining individuals over time. The life course is identified as a path through the lifespan and comprises a series of culturally expressed age-graded transitions and positions to be performed throughout an individual's life (Elder 1985). The life-course perspective allows one to understand continuity as well as change in people's behaviour across time by connecting prior experiences, episodes, and events to current situations. At the framework's core is the degree of behavioural continuity as one moves from childhood through to adulthood while at the same time focusing on experiences and events that alter or disrupt the behavioural patterns. The theory is an example of developmental criminology. It can be distinguished from the other perspectives being reviewed in that it is more temporal in its approach and focuses on within-individual changes as opposed to the other perspectives, which focus more on explaining differences between individuals and their participation in crime (Sampson and Laub 1997).

In light of this context (Sampson and Laub 1993; Laub and Sampson 2003), the theory seeks to explain how people become involved in offending in the first place (the onset of offending), why people keep offending (continuity in offending), and later changes that lead individuals to move from offending to non-offending (desistance) or from non-offending to offending. The theory focuses on the manner in which informal social controls at different stages of a person's life influence continuity and change in offending behaviour as a person moves from childhood to adolescence to young adulthood and beyond (see Figure 8.3).

Mechanisms of Adolescent Informal Social Control

The theory begins by identifying three mechanisms of informal social control within the context of the family: attachment to the family, monitoring, and consistent discipline. The degree to which the child is connected to the family inhibits or allows for delinquency. These three methods of informal control can buffer youth against participating in delinquency through the presence of strong emotional bonds or by means of the more direct control of supervision and punishment. School provides an additional significant

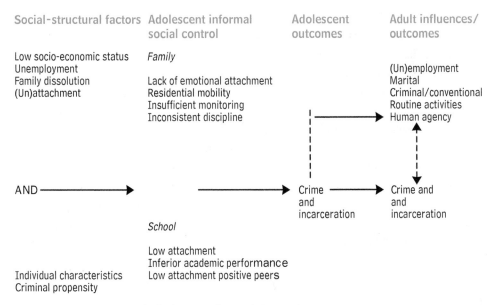

FIGURE 8.3 Age-Graded Theory of Social Control

socializing institution where the degree of attachment, as well as academic performance, reduces or allows for participation in delinquency.

Social-Structural Factors

The age-graded theory suggests that social-structural factors influence the quality and levels of these social bonds; that is, socio-economic status, unemployment, family dissolution, and residential mobility can undermine social bonds. In fact, Sampson and Laub suggest that these types of factors affect the probability of delinquency through social bonds rather than through there being any direct link to crime. For example, socio-economic disadvantage may have a negative impact on parents, increasing the likelihood of parental difficulties in coping and impeding parenting behaviour that facilitates social control. The stress associated with living in poverty and dense households may undermine the attachment between the child and the parent, reducing emotional social control, while the attraction of the less crowded streets can interrupt monitoring.

Disrupted social control can destroy attachments to school and, along with the lack of monitoring and supervision where homework is checked and attendance confirmed, can lead to educational deficits. In turn, it is the lack of connection to the school and the lack of social bonds in the family that have a direct effect on crime in youth, mediating the impact of poverty and social disadvantage.

Social bonds can also be undermined by individual differences in criminal propensity. These individual differences can be characterized by early conduct disorder, difficult temperaments, and persistent tantrums. Positive parenting styles are disrupted by the child's anti-social behaviour. Displays of anti-social behaviour can provoke angry and hostile reactions from parents and inhibit or destroy social bonds, creating additional negative behaviour from the child. Similarly, poor school attachment can be a consequence of misbehaviour as well as a cause. Teachers may react negatively to difficult

disrupted social control
Events or life circumstances that weaken or destroy the relationships, attachments, and activities that provide barriers to engaging in criminal activities.

and disruptive children, which leads to damaged student/teacher relationships. These damaged relationships can lead to a decreased attachment to the school and potentially undermine the child's academic performance, thereby increasing the potential for criminal activities. A child's display of anti-social characteristics can also lead to rejection by more conventional peers. Peer rejection means that another potential source of positive socialization is destroyed, as those with negative traits move into groups containing others who display similar anti-social characteristics.

Sampson and Laub suggest that adult crime can be understood in terms of **cumulative continuity**, where behaviour is sustained by the process of its consequences. According to Sampson and Laub, weak social bonds account for continuity in criminal activities beyond childhood and into adolescence and adulthood. Early negative behaviours, such as crime and the anti-social characteristics outlined in the previous section, are associated with negative adult behaviours, including participating in crime and using drugs. Further, criminal behaviour persists into adulthood because such behaviour affects prospective life chances and undermines adult social control. Negative life experiences associated with earlier criminal participation, arrest, conviction, and incarceration may lead to school failure and unemployment, thereby decreasing future opportunities. Moreover, previous criminal involvement can also jeopardize informal social bonds with family, friends, and school and make vulnerable the creation and progress of adult social bonds. Thus, childhood criminal behaviour leads indirectly to adult criminal behaviour by undermining adult social bonds.

Adult Influences/Outcomes

While Sampson and Laub argue that there is continuity in criminal behaviour as a result of the link between crime and social control, they also stress that socialization experiences and significant life events in adulthood can offset or neutralize the sway of earlier life events and experiences. The theory outlines **life-course turning points**, such as employment and marriage that can modify and shift life **trajectories**. In particular, the theory outlines that these transitions potentially contain social ties, monitoring, and social support that can supply social control that alters a person's trajectory from offender to non-offender. Alternatively, transitions that destroy these sources of social control may lead a person to move from non-offender to offender. In either case, individual pathways to both crime and conformity, independent of prior criminal propensity, can be modified by key social control institutions.

In 2003, Laub and Sampson revised their perspective, identifying a number of additional causal factors, including structured routine activities and human agency, to better the understanding of desistance from crime in adulthood as well as continuity. The type of routine activities that individuals engage in influence their involvement in crime. Different routines influence the behavioural choices available to individuals. For example, spending time out on the street at night with other offenders increases the likelihood that someone will become involved in crime. In contrast, spending time with extended family or spending significant amounts of time at work, where an individual is monitored, might be expected to decrease behavioural choices that involve crime. Thus, having a family, or not, and having employment, or not, can influence routine activities that can either

cumulative continuity
A developmental model that outlines how crime in adolescence has negative consequences for future life chances in areas such as education, relationships, and employment, and increases the likelihood that criminal behaviour will continue into adulthood. These in turn undermine further life chances, escalating the probability of continued, persistent criminal behaviour.

life-course turning points
Events such as marriage/divorce or employment/unemployment that serve to direct an individual's developmental criminal career path toward either desistance or onset.

trajectories
Paths or avenues of development throughout the lifespan. These are long-term patterns of behaviour that often consist of marriage, parenthood, employment, and involvement in criminal activities.

promote desistance from crime, even if the individual in question has a history of prior offending, or encourage persistence for those already involved in offending. Further, individuals whose social controls become damaged or undermined in adulthood are likely to have changes in their routine activities, which increases their likelihood of practising anti-social behaviour.

Human agency is the last factor offered to shape offending trajectories across the life course. This concept suggests that individuals are actively involved in actions to transform their situations. Here Sampson and Laub introduce the idea of **situated choice**. People make choices to get involved in certain relationships, be they work or personal, but these choices are situated under certain structural and historical conditions. At the same time, the choices that people make under these conditions will influence their behaviour. Thus, people make decisions regarding offending or desistance, and in turn those decisions influence outcomes. These outcomes, however, according to the theory, are not necessarily predictable. Nevertheless, Sampson and Laub offer a perspective showing how, independent of prior criminal propensity (e.g., low self-control), behaviour can negatively influence people's future outcomes but can still be modified across the life course by the availability of social control and alternative routine activities associated with social control and choice.

situated choice
The choices individuals make to become involved in certain relationships, be they work or personal, that are situated under certain structural and historical conditions and that can influence future behaviour.

Current Empirical Research into the Age-Graded Theory of Social Control

The age-graded theory of social control has been subject to theoretical verification through a range of research. The empirical work on deviance in childhood and adolescence provides a great deal of support for the association between family and school bonds and youth crime (Laub, Sampson, and Sweeten 2006; Sampson and Laub 1993). Furthermore, there is work that outlines the negative impact that social-structural factors have on these social bonds, as well as the largely indirect relationship to crime that these larger structural factors have through their destruction of social bonds (see Laub et al. 2006). There is also considerable support for the argument that criminal behaviour continues from adolescence into young adulthood and beyond. Part of this is explained by the continuing effect of a previous anti-social propensity, such as low self-control. But research has also detailed the indirect effects this propensity and other anti-social behaviours have on undermining adult social bonds. Moreover, there is evidence that offending in adolescence undermines adult opportunities. Thus, in support of the perspective, the empirical evidence shows that to some degree anti-social behaviour in childhood and adolescence is associated with a number of negative adult outcomes and is relatively stable across stages of the life course (Laub et al. 2006; Sampson and Laub 1993).

There is also support for the arguments about changes in behaviour. In regard to youth involved in serious offending, work suggests that a person's creating a social bond through education while incarcerated can lead to a continued participation in education upon release, leading to a reduction in criminal behaviour (Blomberg, Bales, Mann, Piquero, and Berk 2011). Other work has shown that while gang participation leads to transitions in attitudes, associations, and routine activities that increase crime and have a long-term impact on people's life chances (Melde and Esbensen 2014; Pyrooz 2014), a reduction in association with gangs is a process that decreases criminal participation (Pyrooz, Decker, and Webb 2014; Sweeten, Pyrooz, and Piquero 2013). Adult tests of the age-graded theory show that important life events that create social bonds in adulthood can lead to desistance from criminal activities. In particular, getting married (where an attachment bond is formed with a conventional partner) or having a stable job (that establishes a social bond) leads to changes from criminal to non-criminal behaviour, even if the person has a criminal history and criminal propensity (Laub et al. 2006; Sampson and Laub 1993). The combination of both types of bonds has a very strong impact on a person's behaviour (Berg and Huebner 2011). The relevant literature shows that those who are involved in conventional activities will be less likely to become involved in anti-social behaviour. In addition, social control relationships offer routine activities that reduce opportunities for criminal offending. Finally, work on the agency component of the perspective suggests that people make decisions to desist or persist in offending and that these decisions are often influenced by outside factors of which the individual is unaware (Laub and Sampson 2003; Laub et al. 2006). At the same time, work suggests that changes often begin to take place prior to some of the turning points (e.g., employment), indicating that people prepare and make an effort to seek change and that the change in social bonds serves to reinforce and facilitate the change (Skardhamar and Savolainen 2014).

Control Balance Theory

control balance
The degree of control that individuals perceive they have over their environment relative to the degree of control they perceive their environment has over them.

Charles Tittle (1995, 2004) offers a theory—the **control balance** theory—whose central concept is "control." The idea of *being controlled* focuses on how an individual's behavioural choices are restricted to some degree by some other person or group of people who have the power or resources to impede or assist that individual in achieving his or her goals or in satisfying his or her motivations. Being controlled can also include the degree to which physical or social-structural arrangements make attaining one's goals more problematic. *Exercising control*, in contrast, focuses on how people, alone or with others, escape the limitations of the behavioural restrictions imposed by others. Exercising control also refers to a person's capacity to overcome structural or physical obstacles in order to realize his or her personal goals. It can also include the ability to help or impede others in one's quest to reach one's goals.

Tittle's Original Theory

According to Tittle's original theory proposed in 1995, the amount of control that a person experiences relative to the amount of control a person can exercise is referred to as a *control ratio*. This ratio influences whether a person will engage in deviance and what form of deviance they might engage in. People are said to have a number of specific control ratios associated with their various roles, statuses, and environments, in addition to a general control ratio reflecting their overall ability to control and be controlled. Thus, people can have a control ratio for their friendships, jobs, school, and family, as well as a general control ratio that encompasses all of these various situations.

When the amount of control that individuals exercise is equal to the amount of control they experience, their control ratio is balanced, a condition that is unlikely to lead to deviance. In contrast, control ratio imbalances, which can take two forms, leave individuals more likely to consider deviance as a method of altering that imbalance. Individuals will have a *control surplus* when the amount of control they exercise is greater than the amount of control they experience. Therefore, if you perceive that you have more control over your friendships than they have over you, then you would have a control surplus in that domain. *Control deficits* arise where the amount of control that a person experiences exceeds the amount of control the person exercises. For example, if you felt that school had greater control over you than you had over it, you would have a control deficit for that domain. The two types of control imbalance predispose a person to undertake deviance to improve control ratios. However, this predisposition will only transform into a motivation for deviance under circumstances where people experience a provocation that reminds them, or makes them aware, of their control imbalance.

Motivation created by control ratio imbalances and provocation, however, will only lead to criminal activity if there is opportunity to carry out criminal activity. The person cannot, for example, break into a car or assault someone when there are no vehicles or human targets present. Given motivation and opportunity, individuals will review a range of deviant acts, including those that they perceive will lead to the greatest change in their control ratio. The act that the individual actually chooses will be influenced by *constraint*.

Constraint is a complex variable that represents the seriousness of the act being considered and the situational risk. Seriousness is related to the amount of counter-control that the act might elicit. Those acts that are thought to lead to greater punishment will be viewed as more serious. Situational risk is the concern about being caught engaging in the act and actually experiencing the counter-controlling reactions. Thus, individuals will be sensitive to constraint when reviewing possible avenues to address imbalances and are more likely to choose those acts where the probabilities of detection are lower and the penalties less severe.

Tittle also took into account differences in individual levels of self-control in the causal process of deviant behaviour. In particular, he proposed that low self-control makes people vulnerable to provocation, leaving them more apt to become motivated for crime, more likely to react instantly, less likely to consider the counter-control associated with their acts, and less likely to consider gains. In contrast, those high in self-control can restrain themselves from taking instantaneous action, which leaves them more likely to consider different types of acts than those with low self-control. These acts may have more impact on altering control balance ratios.

Contingencies

Tittle's (1995) theory also recognized that the causal process of deviant behaviour may be influenced by various contingencies, including moral beliefs, self-efficacy, prior deviant experience, and subcultural involvement. For example, thinking certain activities are wrong will mean that there is less likelihood that a control imbalance will be addressed through illegal means. In contrast, when a person faces control imbalance, higher self-efficacy may leave her or him more likely to confront controls and/or take advantage of deviant opportunities that others would find risky. Prior experience with deviance can also act as a contingency because people can recall previous successes in altering control imbalances through crime and recognize the low potential for counter-control. Similarly, subcultural involvement may produce motivations for deviance beyond those stemming from imbalanced control ratios, as people are exposed to various forms, excuses, rationalizations, and expectations of deviance.

Types of Deviance

The manner in which control balance theory deals with different forms of deviance has evolved over its development. The original version of the theory sketched discrete forms of deviant activities linked to different control ratio imbalances. People who experienced control balance deficits were argued to be at risk for "repressive" deviant practices. Individuals who experienced small deficits were thought more likely to engage in predation. Acts of predation involved direct personal involvement in such offences as violence and theft. Those who experienced moderate control balance deficits were thought more likely to display acts of defiance (e.g., vandalism and drug use). Defiant behaviours communicated contempt for the values and norms of the broader conventional society. Finally, large deficits were argued to be linked to submission or behaviours characterized by extreme passive obedience to others.

Individuals with control balance surpluses were argued to seek out "autonomous" forms of deviance. Individuals who experienced small surpluses were argued to undertake acts of exploitation where they benefited by using others to engage in illegal activities. These others coerced, manipulated, or stole for the benefit of the exploiter. Moderate surpluses were linked to acts of "plunder" (e.g., environmental destruction for profit)—activities that displayed minimal care for others. Finally, the theory outlined that people with large control balance surpluses were more likely to engage in impulsive, irrational, and unpredictable acts of decadence (e.g., sex with children).

Tittle's Revised Theory

Research showed little empirical support linking control balance ratio differences (small, moderate, and large deficits or surpluses) and specific acts of repressive or autonomous forms of deviance. In response, Tittle (2004) revised the perspective, discontinuing the distinctions in forms of deviance. The theory now focuses on conformity, deviance, and submission. Further, control imbalances are argued to explain all forms of deviance. Different deviant acts are now distinguished by their *control balance desirability*. Control balance desirability has two components. The first surrounds the potential long-term change in the control ratio that may result from the act. The second focuses on the degree to which the offender needs to be personally or directly involved with the victim. Acts with little direct contact with victims and that allow for long-term changes in control balance ratios have the greatest control balance desirability. Acts that involve direct contact and have shorter-term impact on control balance ratios are seen to have less control balance desirability. Tittle suggests that acts can be sorted on a continuum based on these characteristics. He argues, however, that the theory does not permit the precise estimate of particular behaviours; rather, it can help explain the choosing of a certain act from behaviours with similar control balance desirability scores.

Actors who have substantial control surpluses, who are high in self-control, and who are presented with opportunities and few constraints will be most likely to undertake behaviours high in control balance desirability (e.g., commit a sophisticated white-collar crime or lead an organized crime syndicate). In contrast, acts low in control balance desirability are more likely to be accessed by people who have small-to-medium control deficits, who are low in self-control, and who face constraints in committing acts high in control balance desirability but have opportunities for low-desirability acts (e.g., assaulting a boss or robbing a convenience store). Acts around the middle of the desirability continuum may point toward various levels and amalgamations of the causal variables. Those with extreme deficits, however, are most likely to resort to *submission*, which will include passive rather than active responses, and therefore, they are not included on the continuum (see Figure 8.4).

Current Empirical Research into Control Balance Theory

Most of the empirical work on the control balance perspective has found that both control balance deficits and control balance surpluses are related to a range of deviant behaviours, including assault, theft, drug and alcohol use, deviant sexual practices, eating disorders, stalking, the use of others' school work, cheating, and criminal victimization (Baron and Forde 2007; Nobles and Fox 2013). To date, there has been little focus on the relationships between control ratio imbalances and different behaviours that might have different control balance desirability (Baron 2010; Hughes, Antonaccio, and Botchkovar 2014; Nobles and Fox 2013). Limited research has also examined the moderating effects of the contingency variables. This research shows mixed support for the impact of self-control. The findings on the moderating impact of constraint or risk on the control balance ratio have also been mixed. Limited research has indicated that the impact of control imbalances on deviance is greater at higher levels of deviant peer association. Generally, support for the contingency variables depends on the sample used and the offence being examined (Baron and Forde 2007). Thus, a review of the research suggests that while the basic, direct causal process appears to be related to deviance as a new emerging perspective with a number of potential avenues for research, support for the more nuanced causal process is yet to be determined.

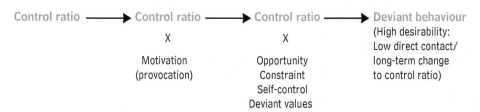

FIGURE 8.4 Control Balance Theory

Differential Coercion Theory

Mark Colvin (2000) has offered a theory that integrates several of the perspectives outlined in his book and in this chapter, including social control theory, social learning theory, general strain theory, the general theory of crime, and control balance theory, as well as Marxist perspectives explaining youth offending. Central to the perspective are two dimensions of control. The first surrounds **coercion**, which can range from extremely coercive to completely non-coercive. Coercion is viewed as punitive because of the emotional and/or physical pain it can cause and because it can take away vital sources of instrumental and social support. The second dimension of control is the consistency with which it is delivered. Consistency can range from highly erratic to extremely consistent (see Figure 8.5).

coercion
A personal or an impersonal force that compels or frightens individuals to behave in a certain way.

Direct and Indirect Coercion

When examining these dimensions, it is important to recognize that coercion can be either direct or indirect. For example, control developing from a tangible interpersonal relationship (e.g., the family) would be direct coercion. Control emerging from forces beyond an individual's control can be viewed as indirect coercion (e.g., economic conditions).

Both direct and indirect coercion can be consistent or erratic. For example, a parent who punishes a child for every single infraction can be seen to be engaging in consistent direct control. The parent who sanctions irregularly is engaging in inconsistent direct control. Broad labour market conditions that move an individual in and out of employment are erratic and indirect. Those that provide long-term or permanent exclusion from the labour market can be seen as more consistent and indirect.

There can be ties between interpersonal and impersonal forms of coercion. The ability to escape coercive *interpersonal* relationships may depend on the nature of *impersonal* coercive relationships. For example, people's ability to leave their family or their undesirable employment might be disrupted by poor labour markets and the lack of employment. Therefore, impersonal economic forces can emerge as coercive in and of themselves when they have an impact on the interpersonal coercive forces.

Colvin observes that coercion has numerous sources—including the family, peers, and criminal justice and social service agencies, as well as the broader economy. In these

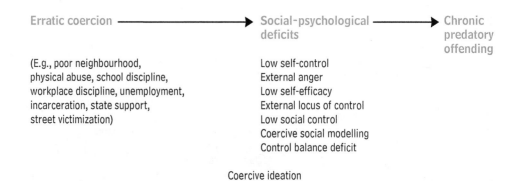

FIGURE 8.5 Erratic Coercion and Chronic Predatory Offending

settings, individuals are said to differ in the degree to which they experience coercion. In families where force, intimidation, and threats are used with some frequency to gain compliance, children are understood to experience coercion. Individuals who participate in peer groups where they continually encounter violent victimization and verbal degradation and disparagement at the hands of others are also viewed as suffering coercion. Impoverished individuals under the formal supervision of state agencies that can remove or threaten to remove financial support and threaten or impose sanctions are exposed to coercion. Being incarcerated, since it entails being held in a confined space by force against one's wishes, is viewed as coercive. Finally, poverty and economic necessity and the stress and desperation that surface from economic pressure are thought to be extremely coercive. Colvin notes that often individuals experiencing coercion in one setting move to other settings where they again experience coercion.

Types of Control Structures

Colvin argues that four types of control structures can be identified based on the degree of coercion (coercive/non-coercive) and the consistency (consistent/erratic) with which the coercion is delivered. The different types of control structures influence the development of a number of social-psychological mechanisms. The extent of coercion and the degree of consistency in its delivery will have an impact on levels of social bonds, self-efficacy, locus of control, self-control, social learning of behaviour, and control balance deficits. In turn, the type of control experienced and the type of psychological mechanism developed will influence whether an individual will become involved in crime and in what type of crime that person will likely become involved.

A Consistent, Non-coercive Environment

The first type of control structure outlined by Colvin is one where the individual experiences a consistent, non-coercive environment. Here, any sort of control is applied in a manner that is firm and fair and accompanied by explanations that outline the reasoning for the application of control. Further, the use of instrumental means, like offers of money or gifts, to gain compliance is avoided. This type of environment offers no opportunities to observe aggressive models, and because of the fairness in applying control, it is unlikely to generate anger or provide provocation to remind people that they have a control imbalance. However, because of the bonds that are developed by using this form of control, this type of environment does lead to higher levels of social control, self-control, self-efficacy, and an internalized locus of control. As a result, people who experience this type of control structure will show an inclination toward pro-social behaviours, leaving them less likely to become involved in criminal activities.

An Erratic, Non-coercive Environment

The second type of control structure is referred to as erratic and non-coercive. This form of control can best be described as lenient, negligent, or weak. The controller tends to exhibit an indifference or detached involvement with the individual who is being controlled. When the controller does intervene, the control is weak as well as inconsistent or erratic. The lack of interest on the part of the controller results in intermittent emotional social support at best. There may be some instrumental support as controllers attempt to influence the subject's actions through the use of money and other incentives, but this support still will take place erratically. Again, because this type of control does not involve coercion, it will not generate anger; nor will it provide provocation that will remind people of imbalanced control ratios. In this particular situation, individuals may have a control balance surplus, since the person who is controlling rarely exerts control. Furthermore, these individuals are likely to develop high levels of self-efficacy and an internal sense of control. The failure of consistent emotional support to develop and the erratic recognition and correction of anti-social behaviour mean, however, that people under this control regime will have low social control and low self-control. The lack of social control and self-control along with the sense of self-efficacy will, Colvin argues, lead to a greater likelihood that individuals will experiment with pleasurable deviant activities, such as drinking, drug use, and illicit sex. Further, because of their history of exchanging compliance for instrumental rewards, they will have the tendency to lie to and manipulate authority figures. Finally, because their control history does not involve anger-generating coercion, such individuals are more likely to engage in minor forms of street crime than in more serious predatory street offending. Colvin argues that this type of control structure and the types of offending it produces account for the majority of offenders.

A Consistent, Coercive Environment

The third type of control structure is referred to as consistent coercive control. This pattern of control is regularly and repeatedly delivered and highly coercive, creating a highly punitive relationship between the controller and the object of control. These types of relationships usually lack instrumental and emotional support and guidance. To the extent that emotional and instrumental social supports are available, they are continuously in danger of being eliminated or taken away as an additional method of coercion. This type of consistent, coercive-control relationship incites a control ratio deficit—often to such an extent that the subject of control will become resigned to his or her negative situation. Additional fallout from these experiences includes a low sense of self-efficacy and an external locus of control. Furthermore, the coercion involved incites anger, but because the coercion is consistent and any external reaction to coercion is punished, the anger is self-directed. The coercion also provides a model for the social learning of coercive behaviour. Finally, since the social supports are weak and constantly under threat of removal, the social bonds that develop are moderate and calculative, and the consistent supervision and discipline lead to high self-control.

Consistent, coercive control limits the probability of criminal behaviour, but its nature also leads to a low probability of pro-social behaviour. The highly restrictive environment does not allow for deviance, and fear of the consequences resulting from the failure to comply leads to highly self-monitored behaviour. Highly self-monitored behaviour inhibits the initiative, creativity, or development that is necessary for success in education and other pursuits. Instead, consistent, coercive control leads to an increased likelihood of mental health problems, including chronic depression. Moreover, Colvin suggests that it is possible that in situations where the consistent constraints are loosened or removed from these individuals, the self-directed anger may be rerouted externally, leading to violent behaviour.

An Erratic, Coercive Environment

The final type of control structure is the erratic, coercive type. In this type, control takes the form of irregular punitive responses to transgressions. On occasion, serious misbehaviour is overlooked, while minor misconduct is severely punished. There may be other circumstances where punishment is meted out when no violation has occurred. The experience of erratic and what appear to be arbitrary punishment practices leads youth to develop feelings of injustice and externally directed anger. Furthermore, the erratic nature of the coercion leads to low self-efficacy and an external locus of control. This inconsistency leaves these youths feeling that events are beyond their control, unrelated to their behaviour, and that they have little chance of changing the circumstances. Erratic coercion allows the victims intermittent periods of reprieve that leave them feeling humiliated and debased. The experience leads such individuals to recognize that they have control balance deficits—that they have less control than they are subject to—which fuels deviant motivation. The inconsistent nature of the punishment also means that self-control fails to develop, allowing negative traits such as risk-taking, temper, and impulsiveness to be exhibited unfettered. The coercive experience also provides extreme avenues for learning coercive behaviour. Here, youths learn how to use coercion themselves as a method for controlling and gaining the compliance of others. Finally, since in these situations emotional and instrumental social supports tend to be minimal or completely absent, there is little opportunity for social bonds to develop. In fact, any bonds that do develop are negative.

Taken together, the experiences of coercion along with the social-psychological deficits—that is, negative social bonds, low self-control, low self-efficacy, external locus of control, coercive behaviour modelling, and control balance deficits—lead to the generation of *coercive ideation* (see Figure 8.5 above). Coercive ideation occurs when the individual comes to interpret the world as an environment enveloped in coercion and to believe that the only way to combat the coercion he or she experiences is through the use of coercion.

Colvin argues that the psychological ramifications that emerge from erratic coercion increase the likelihood of chronic involvement in predatory street crime, intimidation and coercion of others, and hostility and defiant behaviour directed toward those in authority. Colvin argues that offenders drawn from the erratic/coercive-control structure begin their offending at an early age and are more likely to become involved in violent offending because of their exposure to coercive modelling and to their coercive ideation. Colvin notes that individuals who have experienced erratic and extreme coercion are often drawn to the street and the culture it offers, which tends to match the social-psychological deficits produced by inconsistent coercion.

Current Empirical Research into Differential Coercion Theory

As a new perspective, differential coercion theory has been subjected to limited empirical research to date—all of which has focused on the crime-causing impact of erratic coercive control. This research is extremely supportive of the perspective. It shows that different forms of coercion, including parental coercion, a coercive school environment, coercive neighbourhoods, incarceration, state support, and street victimization, are related to crime generally and to violent offending specifically (Baron 2009; Unnever, Colvin, and Cullen 2004). However, this research also shows that coercion that is delivered more to the consistent end of the erratic continuum is related to these behaviours, which suggests that further theoretical refinement is required. The social-psychological deficits of social control, low self-control, trait anger, control imbalances, coercive social models, and coercive ideation have also been shown to be related to crime (ibid.). Limited work also reveals that erratic coercion toward the more consistent end of the continuum is related to the development of low self-control, anger, coercive modelling, and coercive ideation. In contrast, erratic coercion does not appear to be related to the development of control imbalances (Baron 2009).

While generally supportive, there is still room for research on the other types of control structures and their relationships with social-psychological deficits and together how these are related to other forms of behaviour. Theoretical work is already being extended to include the idea of social supports and the degree to which they are offered in a consistent or an erratic fashion (Antonaccio, Tittle, Brauer, and Islam 2014; Baron 2014). Early research in this area is uneven, but some shows how levels of conventional social support can influence social control, self-control, anger, and whether or not one enters into illegitimate social support networks. These factors in turn influence criminal participation (Baron 2014). Future empirical work will need to more fully explore the role of social support in tandem with the degree and erratic or consistent nature of coercion. Such research will also have to investigate the relationships of these various combinations with different forms of behaviour, including crime (Colvin, Cullen, and Vander Ven 2002).

Situational Action Theory

Situational action theory (SAT), as developed by Wikström (2006, 2012), strives to understand the various personal and environmental factors that influence people to engage in crime. SAT outlines that crimes can best be understood as **moral actions**, or as behaviours that are shepherded by moral rules. These moral rules outline what is acceptable and unacceptable to do in specific situations. Crimes, then, are viewed as violations of moral rules that are outlined by laws.

moral actions
Actions steered by moral rules that outline what behaviours are allowed or disallowed in particular circumstances.

Action Alternatives

SAT suggests that people's actions are the result of how they perceive their "action alternatives," which set the boundaries for behavioural choices. Individuals are thought to differ in the manner in which they perceive action alternatives. This explains why people will respond differently in the same environmental setting. The perception-choice process may take on a form of habitual action or it may involve more deliberation. Habitual action describes situations where the individual perceives there to be only one applicable action alternative and so automatically selects this act. Habitual reactions are developed

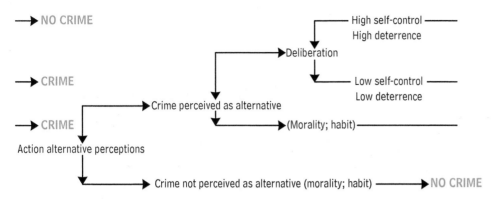

FIGURE 8.6 Situational Action Theory

through repeated experiences in specific situations, leading actions to become automated in these and other comparable situations. In contrast, cases that involve deliberation have no perceived prominent action alternative. The choice of actions in these situations, therefore, is the result of calculating the positives and negatives of the range of perceived alternatives.

The central characteristic guiding perceptions of action alternatives is an individual's morality. This is made up of a person's moral rules and the emotions attached to these rules. A person's moral rules and moral emotions may foster or dissuade the breaking of particular rules defined as wrong by the law. Some individuals will hold moral beliefs against breaking the law and will display shame or guilt if they violate a moral rule or express satisfaction if they abide by a moral rule. Others may hold moral beliefs that allow the breaking of the law and display no negative emotional responses for violating the rules. Morality can create moral habits where individuals act in accordance with moral rules, automatically without deliberation, because of the familiarity of the circumstances and a previously established perception of a favoured action alternative.

Wikström contends, however, that when an individual's morality has not developed into a habit, it permits the consideration of action alternatives when presented with a motivation for crime. This motivation may emerge as a result of either a provocation that leads to anger or annoyance or a temptation that presents itself to satisfy some desire. Here, individuals with weaker levels of law-relevant morality may or may not engage in crime, depending on other factors.

Self-Control

The first of these factors is self-control. Self-control influences whether those whose morality allows them some deliberation of action alternatives will engage in crime. Those with lower self-control will be the ones most likely to engage in crime, while those with higher self-control will be less likely to engage in crime. Self-control is not likely to influence the choices between action alternatives for those who have developed certain moral habits, since they are less likely to consider action alternatives. Box 8.2 provides an example of research on the specific relationship between morality and low self-control.

Box 8.2   Youth Justice in Action

Wikström's Situational Action Theory

Wikström and Svensson explored one of the central processes outlined in situational action theory. They investigated the roles morality and self-control play in the restriction and generation of youth crime. They were interested in determining if a youth's morality was the most important element in understanding why people break the law and uncovering if and when self-control is important in this development. Wikström and Svensson hypothesized that those youths with strong moral reservations would be unlikely to engage in illegal activities no matter what level of self-control they had. They also expected, however, that when morality was lower, levels of self-control would be very important in determining if youths would engage in crime.

To investigate this, they surveyed over 1500 British youths ages 14–15, asking them questions about moral rules surrounding certain behaviours, including how wrong they thought it was for someone their age to hit someone with the idea of hurting them or steal items worth various amounts of money. The youths were also asked about how ashamed they would be if their parents, teachers, or friends found out about their participation in a number of these specific crimes. The researchers then created a measure of morality combining the responses based on the questions on moral rules and shaming. The researchers also asked the youths about various aspects of their self-control, including questions that tapped into anger, impulsivity, and risk-taking. Finally, they queried the youths on how many times in the prior year they had engaged in a number of property and violent offences.

From the answers the youths provided to these questions, the researchers were able to determine that both weak morality and low self-control were strong predictors of crime, with weak morality being a stronger factor. The results also showed that for those who had high morality, self-control had no influence on offending, since crime was not viewed as something to engage in. As levels of morality dropped, however, levels of self-control became important. Those with high self-control were still less likely to engage in crime because of their ability to restrain themselves even without moral reservations about breaking the law, while those with low self-control were much more likely to engage in crime when the moral restraints were reduced.

Critical Thinking Question

What other factors might be important in interacting with morality to help us understand crime?

Source: P.H. Wikström and R. Svensson. (2010). "When Does Self-Control Matter? The Interaction between Morality and Self-Control in Crime Causation." *European Journal of Criminology, 7*(5): 395–410.

Fear of Sanctions

The second factor is deterrence. Wikström argues that, similar to self-control, the fear of sanctions can influence whether individuals engage in crime under conditions where they may deliberate over action alternatives. Where individuals act out of habit and do not see deviant behaviour as an action alternative, the potential sanctions for deviance are irrelevant. When individuals engage in deviance out of moral habit, there is little consideration of action alternatives, again leaving the evaluation of consequences immaterial. However, the action alternatives considered by those with lower morality may be influenced by potential sanctions, while those with higher morality will be less likely to be influenced by these, since they view criminal action alternatives as wrong.

Wikström and Treiber (2006) also suggest that individuals with lower levels of self-control must be exposed to stronger deterrent cues for the probabilities of deviance to decrease. Therefore, for those who perceive illegal action alternatives, the criminogenic impact of low self-control can be undermined by the restrictive influence of potential sanctions.

Environments and Moral Habits

According to situational action theory, as well, environments vary in the features that influence whether or not a crime can take place. Settings vary in their moral norms, which may either promote or deter the breaking of rules defined as illegal. Further, settings vary in the degree to which they monitor for moral rule violations and sanction these violations. These are the "deterrent qualities" of the setting. Those settings perceived to be more highly monitored for rule violations and where sanctions for moral violations are sensed to be severe influence deliberation of action alternatives.

When individuals enter into settings, they recognize a range of action alternatives. The recognition of action alternatives is influenced by their own "moral perception" of each environment. This moral perception will be swayed by the individual's own morality and the morality of the setting. When moral habits and personal morality are strong and in line with the moral rules of the setting, then the action alternatives that emerge for the individual will be consistent with moral rules of the setting. Thus, in situations where moral habits and the moral rules of the setting discourage law breaking, illegal action is unlikely. Similarly, in circumstances where morality, moral habits, and the moral rules of the setting encourage law breaking, criminal acts are likely. However, in situations where individuals hold or have developed moral habits that are weak or in conflict with the moral rules of the setting, perceptions of possible illegal action alternatives will emerge.

In situations where there is a conflict between personal morality and the moral rules of the setting, the factors of self-control and deterrence become important. In situations where a person's morality discourages deviance but the moral rules of the setting encourage this action alternative, self-control will influence the choice. Those with greater self-control will be less likely to choose the illegal action alternative, while those with lower self-control will be more likely to select the illegal option. In those circumstances where the individual's morality is in support of illegal action but the moral rules of the setting discourage illegal action, the perceived risk of apprehension and the severity of the sanctions will influence decisions. Here, when the sanctions are seen as potentially certain and severe, the likelihood of an illegal action being selected is reduced. Where perceptions of sanctions are more uncertain or the costs viewed as insubstantial, then illegal action alternatives will be more likely to be selected.

Current Empirical Research into Situational Action Theory

Much of the research on SAT has been supportive of the perspective. The work examining the morality component of the theory shows that those with greater morality are less likely to engage in crime, while those with weaker morality are more likely to commit offences (Antonaccio and Tittle 2008; Wikström and Svensson 2008, 2010). Research has also established that self-control tends to have a direct impact on the undertaking of criminal action alternatives. Further, it also suggests that self-control does not influence the behaviour of those with strong morality. In contrast, whether those with weaker morality break the law or not appears to be influenced by the ability or inability of the individual to execute self-control (Wikström and Svensson 2010). Results on the role of deterrence suggest that the threats of detection and the degree of monitoring have a direct effect on behaviour (Gallupe and Baron 2014; Haar and Wikström 2010). Further, it is those who have low self-control or a higher propensity for crime who are most influenced by deterrence (Wikström, Tseloni, and Karlis 2011). Initial evidence also suggests that environments are important, so those with morality-based criminal propensities who frequent locations where crime is likely to take place are more likely to engage in crime (Wikström and Svensson 2008). While this is suggestive, more work is required on this perspective, work that will explore all the possible connections between morality, self-control, deterrence, environment, and habit, and how these influence people's decision-making.

Summary

Our review of emerging theoretical perspectives on youth crime has provided us with a breadth of possible explanations. The general theory of crime outlines how low self-control leaves individuals unable to refrain from temptation, increasing their risk for crime when opportunities present themselves. The general strain perspective focuses on how not being treated the way individuals would like to be treated leads to negative emotions that encourage people to engage in crime to address these emotions. Such experiences are more likely to lead to crime when their subject has any of various characteristics, including deviant values, deviant peers, negative emotionality/low constraint, low self-esteem, and low self-efficacy. The age-graded theory of social control focuses on the manner in which informal social controls at different stages of a person's life influence continuity and change in the offending behaviour. This theory outlines the impact, leading to crime, that structural conditions and early anti-social propensities have upon social control factors in the family and school. This theory also explains how criminal participation in one's youth undermines social control mechanisms in adulthood, leading to continuity in crime. The age-graded theory of social control also delineates how, through concerted efforts and employment and marriage, individuals can re-establish social control and alter their criminogenic routine activities to achieve a desistance from illegal activities. The control balance perspective cues us to the importance of having a sense of control over various domains in our lives. When we have too much or too little control, we are more likely to engage in crime when we are reminded of our situation and encounter the proper opportunity. The type of crime we pick and its impact on our sense of control will be influenced by the way deviant values, deviant peers, low self-control, self-efficacy, and perceptions of risk of apprehension shape our perceptions of control. The differential coercion perspective outlines how personal and impersonal forces of coercion that are delivered in different ways can produce a variety of social-psychological mechanisms that lead to crime. More erratic coercion will lead to the development of low self-control, low social control, anger, values supporting coercion, an external locus of control, and low self-efficacy, which in turn increase the likelihood of offending. Finally, situational action theory outlines how morality guides behaviour and influences people's perceptions of how they should act. For those whose morality allows them to consider crime, their behaviour will be influenced by their level of self-control and the potential for detection and sanction. Individuals with lower reservations against committing crime will be more likely to choose this option under conditions where they also have low self-control and perceive the chances of getting caught to be minimal.

Our review of some of the more recent theoretical developments in youth crime shows the variety of ways that scholars have approached the topic. Some, such as the general theory of crime, have focused on a monocausal approach. Others have outlined perspectives that incorporate a broader range of factors that attempt to more clearly specify how the central factor will lead to crime and under what conditions. Further, some of these approaches have adopted a strategy for theoretical development whereby they attempt to bring in useful pieces of other theoretical perspectives. Rather than viewing different theoretical perspectives as competitors, we would do well to recognize that, to successfully understand youth crime, we must recognize and include ideas not normally viewed as complementary. These ideas need to be gathered up and incorporated in the causal process, allowing for a more complex and nuanced understanding of how youth crime emerges and evolves. This strategy enables researchers to establish various possible entry points for youth to explore crime; it also establishes that there may be more than one possible causal path to crime. As we think about youth crime, we must provide a number of possible answers to the many questions we might pose. Then, theories provide a number of insights into how we might answer such questions.

Key Terms

coercion	low self-control
control balance	moral actions
cumulative continuity	situated choice
disrupted social control	social bonds
informal social control	strains
life-course turning points	trajectories

Review Questions

1. Gottfredson and Hirschi's argument suggests that low self-control leads not only to crime but also to analogous acts. Why would this be the case?

2. Using general strain theory, outline the type of young person who would most likely turn to criminal activities in an attempt to cope with his or her strain.

3. Tittle argues that a number of conditions must converge for an imbalanced control ratio to lead to crime. Review these conditions and outline why the individual's control ratio will be central to these conditions.

4. Outline the main causal process that could lead a youth to desist from crime, according to the age-graded theory of social control.

5. Summarize Colvin's four types of controls and discuss which of the four types is most likely to lead to serious offending and for what reasons.

6. Outline the conditions under which a person with few moral reservations will and will not engage in crime.

Critical Thinking Questions

1. In Colvin's theory of crime and coercion, a number of social-psychological deficits are identified. How do these deficits relate to some of the other perspectives that we have read about or discussed in class? Do we benefit from including various perspectives together?

2. Gottfredson and Hirschi's general theory of crime sees self-control as a trait that is relatively stable and unchangeable, leading to a life of participation in crime and other negative activities. Compare this with how Sampson and Laub might view this issue.

3. Explore the ways in which different types of contingency variables (e.g., peers, values, self-efficacy) may be more important in moderating the impacts of certain forms of strain on crime than others.

4. Tittle argues that different criminal acts will have different levels of control balance desirability. Explore which types of acts you think will fall along the continuum of control balance desirability and which types of individuals will be more likely to commit these types of acts.

References

Agnew, R. (1992). Foundation for a general strain theory of crime and delinquency. *Criminology*, 30(1): 47–87.

Agnew, R. (2001). Building on the foundation of general strain theory: Specifying the types of strain that most likely lead to crime and delinquency. *Journal of Research in Crime and Delinquency*, 38(4): 319–61.

Agnew, R. (2006). *Pressured into crime: An overview of general strain theory*. Los Angeles: Roxbury.

Agnew, R. (2013). When criminal coping is likely: An extension of general strain theory. *Deviant Behavior*, 24: 653–70.

Agnew, R., Scheuerman, H., Grosholz, J., Isom. D., Watson, L., and Thaxton, S. (2011). Does victimization reduce self-control? A longitudinal analysis. *Journal of Criminal Justice*, 39: 169–74.

Antonaccio, O., and Tittle, C.R. (2008). Morality, self-control, and crime. *Criminology*, 46(2): 479–510.

Antonaccio, O., Tittle, C.R., Brauer, J.R., and Islam, M.Z. (2014). Supported or coerced? A cross-site investigation of the effects of social support and coercion on criminal probability. *Journal of Quantitative Criminology*. doi:10.1007/s10940-014-9224-7

Baron, S.W. (2003). Self-control, social consequences, and criminal behavior: Street youth and the general theory of crime. *Journal of Research in Crime and Delinquency*, 40(4): 403–25.

Baron, S.W. (2004). General strain, street youth and crime: A test of Agnew's revised theory. *Criminology*, 42(2): 457–83.

Baron, S.W. (2009). Differential coercion, street youth, and violent crime. *Criminology*, 47(1): 239–68.

Baron, S.W. (2010). Street youths' control imbalance and soft and hard coming drug use. *Journal of Criminal Justice*, 38: 903–12.

Baron, S.W. (2014). Differential social support, differential coercion, and organized criminal activities. *Justice Quarterly*, 1–29. doi:10.1080/07418825.2014.887760

Baron, S.W., and Forde, D.R. (2007). Street youth crime: A test of control balance theory. *Justice Quarterly*, 24(2): 335–55.

Baron, S.W., Forde, D.R., and Kay, F.M. (2007). Self-control, risky lifestyles, and situation: The role of opportunity and context in the general theory. *Journal of Criminal Justice*, 35(2): 119–36.

Berg, M.T., and Huebner, B.M. (2011). Reentry and the ties that bind: An examination of social ties, employment, and recidivism. *Justice Quarterly*, 28(2): 382–410.

Blomberg, T.G., Bales, W.D., Mann, K., Piquero, A.R., and Berk, R.A. (2011). Incarceration, education, and transition from delinquency. *Journal of Criminal Justice, 39*: 355–65.

Colvin, M. (2000). *Crime and coercion: An integrated theory of chronic criminality.* New York: St Martin's Press.

Colvin, M., Cullen, F.T., and Vander Ven, T. (2002). Coercion, social support, and crime: An emerging theoretical consensus. *Criminology, 40*(1): 9–42.

Elder, G.H., Jr. (1985). Perspectives on the life course. In G.H. Elder Jr. (Ed.). *Life course dynamics* (pp. 23–49). Ithaca, NY: Cornell University Press.

Gallupe, O., and Baron, S.W. (2014). SAT and street youths' drug use. *Crime and Delinquency, 60*(2): 284–305.

Gottfredson, M.R., and Hirschi, T. (2000). *A general theory of crime.* Stanford: Stanford University Press.

Haar, D.H., and Wikström, P.H. (2010). Crime propensity, criminogenic exposure and violent scenario responses: Testing situational action theory in regression and Rasch models. *European Journal of Applied Mathematics, 21*(4–5): 307–23.

Hughes, L.A., Antonaccio, O., and Botchkovar, E.V. (2014). How general is control balance theory? Evidence from Ukraine. *Justice Quarterly.* Retrieved from http://dx.doi.org/10.1080.07418825 .2013.864696.

Laub, J.H., and Sampson, R.J. (2003). *Shared beginnings, divergent lives: Delinquent boys to age 70.* Cambridge: Harvard University Press.

Laub, J.H., Sampson, R.J., and Sweeten, G.A. (2006). Assessing Sampson and Laub's life-course theory. In F.T. Cullen, J.P. Wright, and K.R. Blevins (Eds), *Taking stock: The status of criminological theory: Advances in criminological theory*, Vol. 15 (pp. 313–33). New Brunswick, NJ: Transaction Publishers.

Melde, C., and Esbensen, F.A. (2014). The relative impact of gang status transitions: Identifying the mechanisms of change in delinquency. *Journal of Research in Crime and Delinquency, 51*(3): 349–76.

Meldrum, R.C., Young, J.T.N., and Weerman, F.M. (2012). Changes in self-control during adolescence: Investigating the influence of the adolescent peer network. *Journal of Criminal Justice, 40*: 452–62.

Merton, R.K. (1938). Social structure and anomie. *American Sociological Review, 3*(5): 672–82.

Miller, J.M., Schrek, C.J., and Tewksbury, R. (2006). *Criminological theory.* Toronto: Pearson.

Na, C., and Paternoster, R. (2012). Can self-control change substantially over time? Rethinking the relationship between self- and social control. *Criminology, 50*(2): 427–62.

Nobles, M.R., and Fox, K.A. (2013). Assessing stalking behaviors in a control balance theory framework. *Criminal Justice and Behavior, 40*(7): 737–62.

Piquero, A.R., Jennings, W.G., and Farrington, D.P. (2010). On the malleability of self-control: Theoretical and policy implications regarding a general theory of crime. *Justice Quarterly 27*(6): 803–4.

Pratt, T.C., and Cullen, F.T. (2000). The empirical status of Gottfredson and Hirschi's general theory of crime: A meta-analysis. *Criminology, 38*(3): 931–64.

Pratt, T.C., Turanovic, J.J., Fox, K.A., and Wright, K.A. (2014). Self-control and victimization: A meta-analysis. *Criminology, 52*(1): 87–116.

Pyrooz, D.C. (2014). From colors and guns to caps and gowns? The effects of gang membership on educational achievement. *Journal of Research in Crime and Delinquency, 51*(1): 56–87.

Pyrooz, D.C., Decker, S.H., and Webb, V.J. (2014). The ties that bind: Desistance from gangs. *Crime & Delinquency, 60*(4): 491–516.

Ray, J.V., Jones, S., Loughran, T.A., and Jennings W.G. (2013). Testing the stability of self-control. *Criminal Justice and Behavior, 40*(6): 588–607.

Sampson, R.J., and Laub, J.H. (1993). *Crime in the making: Pathways and turning points through life.* Cambridge: Harvard University Press.

Sampson, R.J., and Laub, J.H. (1997). A life-course theory of cumulative disadvantage and stability of delinquency. In T. Thornberry (Ed.), *Developmental theories of crime and delinquency: Advances in criminological theory*, Vol. 7 (pp. 1–29). New Brunswick, NJ: Transaction Publishers.

Skardhamar, T., and Savolainen, J. (2014), Changes in criminal offending around the time of job entry: A study of employment and desistance. *Criminology, 52*(2): 263–91.

Sweeten, G., Pyrooz, D.C., and Piquero, A.R. (2013). Disengaging from gangs and desistance. *Justice Quarterly, 30*(3): 469–500.

Tittle, C.R. (1995). *Control balance: Toward a general theory of deviance.* Boulder, CO: Westview.

Tittle, C.R. (2004). Refining control balance theory. *Theoretical Criminology, 8*(4): 395–428.

Unnever, J.D., Colvin, M., and Cullen, F.T. (2004). Crime and coercion: A test of core theoretical propositions. *Journal of Research in Crime and Delinquency, 41*(3): 244–68.

Wikström, P.H. (2006). Individuals, settings, and acts of crime: Situational mechanisms and the explanation of crime. In P.H. Wikström and R.J. Sampson (Eds), *The explanation of crime: Context, mechanism, and development* (pp. 61–107). New York: Cambridge University.

Wikström P.H. (2012). Does everything matter? In C.J. Sullivan, J.M. McGloin, and L.W. Kennedy (Eds), *When crime appears: The role of emergence* (pp. 53–72). New York: Routledge.

Wikström P.H., and Svensson, R. (2008). Why are English youths more violent than Swedish youths? A comparative study of the role of crime propensity, lifestyles and their interactions in two cities. *European Journal of Criminology, 5*(3): 309–30.

Wikström P.H., and Svensson, R. (2010). When does self-control matter? The interaction between morality and self-control in crime causation. *European Journal of Criminology, 7*(5): 395–410.

Wikström P.H., and Treiber, K. (2007). The role of self-control in crime causation. *European Journal of Criminology, 4*(2): 237–64.

Wikström P.H., Tseloni, A., and Karlis, D. (2011). Do people comply with the law because they fear getting caught? *European Journal of Criminology, 8*(5): 401–20.

Critical Criminology and Youth Justice in the Risk Society: Issues of Power and Justice

Bryan Hogeveen and Joanne Minaker

9

Overview

This chapter highlights the importance of critical criminology for the study of youth justice and attends to important questions concerning social (in)justice, choice, and power. We encourage readers to think critically about youth justice issues and engage in what Minaker and Hogeveen (2009, p. 5) call "social justice praxis." Critical scholarship attends to the systemic inequality, marginalization, and social exclusion that underpins and is often at the centre of young people's encounters with the law. To explore what might constitute justice for young people and meaningful societal changes, the chapter draws heavily on the theoretical work of scholars like Jacques Derrida and Michel Foucault. At the same time, it encourages students to ask themselves some questions: *What is to be done? What is my responsibility to this end?* Critical criminology offers a unique location from which to consider what a humane, hospitable, and just Canadian society might entail.

Key Objectives

After reading this chapter, you should be able to:

- Explain what it means to be critical.
- Explore how young people, especially Indigenous peoples, are marginalized in Canada.
- Highlight the political dimensions of space.
- Describe Jacques Derrida's understanding of deconstruction and hospitality as it relates to critical criminology.
- Highlight Foucault's unique understanding of power.
- Describe the "risk society" and the place of young people therein.
- Illustrate cultural criminology and its contribution to critical scholarship.

Introduction

> We are not content to teach our students about the social world—to pass on knowledge claims about what is—without also encouraging a process of critical reflection and social engagement about what *could* be.
>
> — Minaker and Hogeveen 2009, p. 5

Youth, crime, and justice are contentious; we seem to lack definitive answers to these pressing concerns. Nevertheless, newspaper headlines and nightly news stories caution about "troubling kids" and advocate punishment as the solution. Obscured from this picture are the inequalities, discrimination, abuse, and neglect that characterize the life histories of many of the young people who make their way into the youth justice system.

critical criminology
Scholarship on crime and justice that seeks to examine and alter inequalities, marginalization, and social exclusion.

While mainstream criminology does its part to examine the causes, consequences, and control of youth crime, **critical criminology** begins from a very different perspective. One strand of critical scholarship takes contemporary criminal justice processes to task for their part in contributing to structural inequalities that marginalize young people. Others presume that Canadian society is organized in hierarchies of age, gender, race, ethnicity, class, sexuality, and ability. Recognizing the impact of difference and disadvantage under law has been the passion of feminist writers like Carol Smart (1989). Since the 1960s, feminist scholars have clearly articulated the disadvantaged social position of women and girls in the justice system and in society. In more recent decades, their analyses have extended beyond the singular emphasis on gender. They have examined how criminology as a "decidedly male-centred enterprise" considers girls and women involved in crime as "monsters, misfits and manipulators" (Balfour and Comack 2006, p. 22).

Like feminist scholarship, critical criminology begins from the perspective that the lives of the most marginalized in contemporary society are lived out in circumstances not of their own choosing. They are thrown into a world that is discriminatory, racist, and sexist. These conditions structure the life chances of the marginalized other—Aboriginal youth, the poor, and racial minorities—and translate into overrepresentation in the contemporary youth justice system. This chapter will explore the unique insights of such scholars as Henri Lefebvre, Jacques Derrida, and Michel Foucault, and of cultural criminologists. We encourage you to think critically about the issues presented. Minaker and Hogeveen (2009, p. 5) suggest that this kind of inquiry is a first step toward "social justice praxis," which is aimed at "addressing the systemic conditions of **marginalization**, exclusion and social inequality that lead to the involvement of youth in crime in the first place." Critical criminology is dedicated to making meaningful changes to improve the life chances of young people. It asks, *What is to be done?* and *What is my responsibility to this end?* As you will see, critical criminology offers unique opportunities to envision a more just, humane, hospitable, and inclusive society.

marginalization
The exclusion of certain groups from mainstream society who routinely suffer as the result of gross inequalities.

What Does It Mean to Be Critical? Why Is It Important?

To say all this is deconstructable does not amount to disqualifying, negating, disavowing, or surpassing it, of doing the critique of critique (the way people wrote critiques of the Kantian critique as soon as it appeared), but of thinking its possibility from another border, from the genealogy of judgment, will, consciousness or activity, the binary structure, and so forth.

— Derrida 1995, p. 357

What does it mean to be critical? Criticism routinely appears as negative judgment. From this broad perspective, in one way or another, all of us are critical. Not long ago, the federal gun registry was the subject of scorn among some Canadians. Others have condemned the massive destruction of land and water by excavation in the Alberta oil sands. We need look no further than our own daily lives for "critiques": "This traffic light takes far too long to change colour"; "The dress she is wearing is far too short"; "This professor gives far too much homework." Critique and criticism, it seems, is all around us. One group never far from criticism is young people, particularly criminalized youth.

If critique is something we all do, what sets critical scholars apart? Put another way, how are critical criminologists distinct in their critiques? Some strands of criminology and criminal justice studies are concerned with criticizing government policy and suggesting alternative approaches that might better respond to youth crime, to offenders, and to victims. In recent years, for example, restorative justice advocates have successfully argued that traditional youth justice processing fails victims of crime and alienates communities from the process (Minaker and Hogeveen 2009; also see Chapter 16 in this book). Restorative justice scholarship calls traditional and existing governmental process into question and proposes (perhaps) a more effective alternative (e.g., circle sentencing). At a more practical level is the Edmonton-based Youth Restorative Justice Project (YRAP). A diverse group of young people (ages 14 to 24) grew concerned that young people were silent in youth justice matters and were otherwise alienated from the process. In response, YRAP administers the world's first restorative justice committee for and by youth and challenges the Western status quo whereby adults alone are responsible for delivering and administering justice (Hogeveen 2006).

YRAP and other restorative justice groups who oppose traditional criminal justice orthodoxy are certainly critical in the conventional sense of casting judgment upon existing programs and suggesting that the object of criticism falls somewhat short of an established ideal. Nevertheless, youth justice officials can comfortably incorporate this flavour of critique (critique as modification) within existing processes without much concern that the established infrastructure will crumble to the ground. Indeed, without fear of significantly altering contemporary mandates and with the goal of streamlining existing practices, many youth justice systems encourage this form of intervention.

In our contemporary ethos, judgment is most closely associated with critique. Such judgmental criticism derives its meaning and its efficacy from an established mean or aesthetic. Consider, for example, current television programming, such as *American Idol*, *America's Got Talent*, and, but not limited to, *So You Think You Can Dance*. All are premised upon experts (supposedly) offering sage banter in the wake of a competitor's performance. Much to the delight of the viewing audience, the expert stands before this group conferring witty and (often) acrimonious critique upon the performer. The program would be rather dull without the expert's judgments, which make the show a success. How many regular viewers of *American Idol* can remember the winner of each season? By contrast, how many people, whether viewers or not, would recognize Jennifer Lopez as one of the show's judges? We speculate that many more would answer the latter correctly. What does it say about our society when the judges who often heap lamentable criticism on unwitting contestants are the "real" stars?

Criterion provides the impetus for judgment and suggests that we make an assessment of something (i.e., a performance, beauty, or youth justice programming) against a normative standard that has been put forth as the ultimate by which those things should be measured. For example, the *Mona Lisa*, Sidney Crosby, and Luciano Pavarotti are routinely considered the criterion upon which all else in their particular field is measured. Youth justice officials, too, employ normative standards to judge programming and the behaviour of criminalized youth. Recidivism rates are seemingly objective measures of a program's success. Whether a subject who has been adjudicated by YRAP, for example, has reoffended is an ostensibly even-handed means through which to determine this Youth Justice Committee's (YJC) effectiveness. Two problems become immediately evident, however. On the one hand, other favourable outcomes may not be readily observable in re-arrest rates. Indeed, a young person may acquire a skill set in the adjudication process that will keep him or her off the streets. On the other hand, police administrative policies and severity of the offence of record for entry into the program tend to affect recidivism rates. As a result, the recidivism rates for this program are artificially higher than for more traditional YJCs. Employing standardized criterion often leads to overlooking programmatic nuances that may qualitatively and positively affect the young person. Consider, for instance, a street-entrenched youth who finds secure housing and a stable job through the assistance of YRAP but misses a court appearance because her employer insists she work a shift. The young person may be charged with "failure to appear." In this instance, the case would be logged as a failure because it resulted in a new charge. Such an approach to determining the success of a program misses how the young person was unquestionably affected by her or his involvement with YRAP.

Critical criminology stands in stark contrast to those forms of critique that seek to improve the functioning and efficacy of the existing youth justice system. Instead of chasing down programming that will work effectively within contemporary justice processes, critical criminology seeks "to take the system to task rather than tinker with its parts" (Ratner 1971). Since Ratner's keen insight, which differentiated a critical brand of Canadian criminology some 40-odd years ago, much debate has emerged concerning what counts as pushing the system hard enough or long enough or what kind of critique qualifies as doing more than merely criticizing the system for reinforcing race, class, gender, age, and other hierarchies. A critical approach examines systemic issues of power and justice vis-à-vis youth crime and society. Critical scholars reject traditional assumptions of mainstream criminological theory (i.e., emphasis on crime control and law and order) and direct their gaze at structural inequalities within and outside of the criminal justice system (CJS). As we hope you will come to see, critical scholars are concerned with more than exposing systemic conditions of marginalization. They are dedicated to opening up more ethical ways of being with others and are not content with the social world as it is. Instead, they encourage critical and serious reflection about how things could be otherwise. Critical criminology engages "with the challenges and contradictions involved in making ameliorative changes in our social world that offer hope instead of despair, compassion instead of intolerance, and justice instead of marginalization, exclusion, and suffering" (Minaker and Hogeveen 2009, p. xiii).

Critical criminology attempts to avoid the trap of collusion with criminal justice processes that serve only to further marginalize the least powerful in society. Hogeveen and Woolford (2006) encourage scholars to become intensely creative in their approaches and to conjure up alternatives that will push beyond established limits of youth justice orthodoxy. It is this reticence to avoid the trap of complicity with contemporary systems of governance, no matter how auspicious, that sets critical criminology apart. Drawing on the scholarship of Derrida, Foucault, Lefebvre, among others, and cultural criminology, critical criminology emphasizes the desirability of interventions that push beyond established hegemony. Instead of well-worn strategies, these scholars and their interlocutors promise an art of critique that unsettles, disrupts, or otherwise challenges contemporary relations (both inside and outside the CJS) in the name of justice and amelioration to come. They suggest more-just ways of being with others in a world bent on racism and exclusion of the marginalized other.

Marginalization and Aboriginal Youth Crime

Lost among sensational headlines concerning the recalcitrance of young people today and efforts by the federal government to "get tough" on youth crime by overhauling contemporary legislation is the number of young people who suffer crime's ill effects. Media images colour our understanding of crime and criminals. Television shows, such as *Law and Order* and the evening news, would have us believe that the average young offender is a gun-toting gangbanger who preys on the unwitting. Many in Western society would be surprised to hear that the majority of reported crime is property related and non-violent in nature. But this misperception is not surprising given that for the vast majority of Canadians the media are their primary sources of crime information (see Chapter 6). When the conception of youth crime and young offenders is stockpiled with violent images, intrusive and carceral solutions are most often proposed as the only viable alternatives to the violent young offender (see, e.g., Harper 2008; see also Box 9.1).

According to a recent Statistics Canada report, young people were the most likely group to divulge violent victimization during the previous 12 months. Indeed, individuals between the ages of 15 and 24 were almost "15 times more likely than those aged 65 and older to report being a victim of violent" crime (Perreault and Brennan 2010). More disconcerting is how Aboriginal peoples, especially Aboriginal women, are disproportionately represented as victims of crime. Consider, for example, that Aboriginal peoples were three times more likely to be victims than non-Aboriginals and five times more likely than other Canadians to have been the victim of sexual offending (Chartrand and McKay 2006). Indeed, Chartrand and McKay (2006) report that "while victimization of Aboriginal people is much higher than non-Aboriginal people, statistics demonstrate that it is Aboriginal women and children who are largely bearing the burden of victimization" (see also Scrim 2013). McGillivray and Comaskey (1996) maintain that the violence experienced by Aboriginal women is appalling. A staggering 1017 Aboriginal women were murdered between 1980 and 2012 (Royal Canadian Mounted Police 2014).

Why is it that violence disproportionately affects Aboriginal peoples? While a full accounting of the conditions that have given rise to this lamentable situation is beyond the scope of this chapter, we can consider the impact of colonialism on contemporary Indigenous life. Systemic racism is conspicuous in the gross overrepresentation of Indigenous young people in Canadian carceral institutions. Donna Calverley (2007) reports that in 2004 and 2005 Aboriginal young people made up approximately 5 per cent of the entire Canadian population yet constituted 25 per cent of young people admitted to custody. This situation becomes more egregious when we turn our gaze to young Aboriginal girls, who constitute 49 per cent of all admissions to female facilities (Statistics Canada 2014; also see Chapter 11 in this book). This reprehensible condition shows no signs of abating.

Canada has a long history of confining Aboriginal peoples. They have been held captive on reserves through a shameful pass system and in residential schools where the tutelage they received inculcated Euro-Canadian norms and mores. Residential school officials, most often with religious ties, forcibly removed Aboriginal children from their parents and cultural milieu for years at a time while they attempted to indoctrinate them with Euro-Canadian ideals (Miller 1996). The effects were devastating and predictable. Torn from their parents and elders and forced to live at some distance from their traditional lands, they experienced a manner of being in the world that was almost completely shaped by residential school officials, who were notoriously physically violent and sexually abusive. Aboriginal authors such as Fournier and Crey (1997) maintain that the intergenerational impact of residential schools, particularly as it relates to sexual and physical abuse, has collectively contributed to high rates of alcohol and drug abuse among Aboriginal peoples and is manifested in countless social, health, and psychological problems (Royal Commission on Aboriginal Peoples 1996; Aboriginal Healing Foundation 2003). The Aboriginal Healing Foundation argues in its report on domestic violence that

> [t]he legacy of the residential school experience has been well documented and is clearly linked to symptoms of post traumatic-stress disorder, as well as to a wide range of social problems, including addiction and physical and sexual abuse. . . . In general, this body of research, theories and models all point to the same general conclusion—family violence and abuse in Aboriginal communities has its roots, at least in part, in historical trauma and in the social realities created by those historical processes. (2003, p. 22)

It is into this ethos of violence conditioned by a dismal colonial heritage that many Aboriginal people are born. A review by the Aboriginal Healing Foundation (2003) found that colonialism, specifically the residential school system, bears much of the burden for the economic, cultural, and political inequalities faced by Aboriginal people today.

Buttressing this tragic condition are the dire levels of poverty experienced by this group. Despite increasing and growing demand, social welfare rates and services have not kept pace. Aboriginal groups are increasingly in need of social service support only to find what they need harder to access. While poverty and homeless rates among Indigenous peoples are snowballing, the social welfare net that has traditionally been in place to cushion the blow of unemployment and homelessness has been repeatedly stripped away (Scott 2003). Cuts to social welfare are a recurrent theme in the contemporary ethos. Indeed, a burgeoning group of homeless Aboriginal people are being forcibly moved to the back of social assistance lines, while industries that the government deems as having more pressing needs (i.e., horse racing) get their cut (Hogeveen 2007).

The Aboriginal population today is much younger than the Canadian average. Statistics Canada reports that in 2011 the median age for Aboriginal groups was 28 years, which is 13 years younger than that for non-Aboriginals. Moreover, children 14 and under made up 33 per cent of the Aboriginal population compared to just 19 per cent for non-Indigenous peoples (Anderson 2003). Appallingly, this group is most likely to live in poverty.

While it is horrendous that 1 in 10 Canadian children live below the poverty line in this land of plenty, more intolerable still is that 1 in 4 Aboriginal children experience poverty's ill effects. Further, it is reported that 49 per cent of Aboriginal children who are under age 6 and living off-reserve live in poverty, compared to just 18 per cent of non-Aboriginal children (Campaign 2000 2009).

Not only is the Aboriginal population becoming younger, it is becoming increasingly urban. According to Andersen (2009), between 2001 and 2006 population growth among Aboriginal people in Edmonton far outpaced that of all other groups (25 per cent compared to 9 per cent). Most (60 per cent) live in the inner city where the space is run down and the community is overwhelmed by crime and disorder (Andersen 2009). Urban landscapes are marked not only geographically, but racially.

Outcast Spaces

In Canada, an Aboriginal person is more likely than a member of any other group to be detained in state institutions of control and, at the same time, to be impoverished, homeless, and anchored in undesirable and outcast space (Mallea 2010). Although Karl Marx was relatively silent on the question of space, Marx-inspired authors like Edward Soja, Henri Lefebvre, and David Harvey have drawn critical attention to its importance in class relations. Marx's relative silence on this issue may have been because cities were just beginning to take on their current configuration during his lifetime (Elden 2007). Lefebvre (1996) famously took up this gap in Marx's work and argues that space is political. He maintains that city spaces become divided up in very definite ways that betray their ethos. That is, space is socially constructed rather than being naturally constituted. This condition has a dramatic impact on the actors living out their lives in particular areas. Social space, Lefebvre suggests, is allocated along class lines such that city planning reproduces and buoys the existing class structure. It follows that the quality of space allotted provides obvious clues as to its owners (Elden 2007). The inner-city spaces and core areas of town, such as Winnipeg's North End, are older, crowded, and often abandoned, yet are also over-policed. By contrast, sprawling suburbs complete with white picket fences and open "green" spaces are reserved for the more affluent. Whereas children growing up in suburbia enjoy new schools and growing recreational centres, the "playground" for poor children and their families looks more like a grey concrete mass and is shared with the mentally ill, the criminal, and the drug user. Harvey (1989, p. 237) maintains that the history of capitalism is the history of a struggle for the command of space: "[T]he whole history of territorial organization, colonialism and imperialism, of uneven development, of urban and rural contradictions, as well as of geopolitical conflict testifies to the importance of such struggles within the history of capitalism."

All people are contained in their space so as to better facilitate rule and control of the recalcitrant and marginalized other. Consider how space is allocated and lived in Edmonton, Alberta. Rather than providing open spaces where strangers may intersect and interact, Edmonton's city planners have seemed to sweep away and confine the poor within spaces of disorder. As "blots" on the otherwise serene and tranquil city, the impoverished roam the streets and are routinely shooed and shunted into the least coveted and most dangerous places. Most people never see where the truly marginal live, as they are tucked away in spaces long forgotten and out of the way of the business classes, who scurry back to the suburbs hopeful that the disorder will not touch their lives.

Even when the capitalist state seeks to ameliorate the marginalized other's suffering, its programs are carried out not in the centres of affluence but in the most downtrodden and overburdened areas of the city. Following the lead of Calgary and Seattle, Edmonton is in the midst of a "Housing First" initiative. Under this plan, the chronically homeless are allotted housing for a one-year period, during which they are provided with a residence and a limited amount of support to help manage and deal with their addictions and other social problems (see Edmonton Committee to End Homelessness 2009). What will happen to these residents after the time limit runs out has yet to be determined. However, units to house the marginalized—including but not limited to street-involved youth who have left home to escape abuse, former inmates who have left prison and who have no family or work to go to, and drug-addicted clients who are no longer welcome in detoxification centres—are not evenly spread throughout the city. Indeed, there are no group homes for the homeless and drug addicted in affluent neighbourhoods. Instead, the city has dumped these units in the city's most economically depressed spaces. What's more, even before the Housing First initiatives, these outcast spaces were already saturated with social services, as well as crime, disorder, drug addiction, and homelessness (Kleiss 2010). It seems the city is willing to help only so far as doing so does not upset the tranquility of suburban space.

Jacques Derrida (1930–2004) and Justice

So far, we have spent much time discussing and contemplating (in)justices facing young people today, especially as they pertain to Aboriginal peoples. Clearly, marginalized populations are excluded from full and meaningful participation in contemporary Canadian society. Quite simply, racial divisions are reflected spatially and assist in underwriting patterns of exclusion (Herbert and Brown 2006). What is to be done about the heinous social injustices marginalized youth face? Can we envision alternative practices that challenge the existing social conditions that exclude, punish, and "other" young people? Instead of shunting the marginalized other into cities' least desirable spaces, what if the approach was one of welcome? Consider how this shift in perspective could affect how these young people view themselves and their sense of feeling cared for and cared about? Toward this end, we suggest the deconstructive work of Derrida (2005, 2002, 1999; Derrida and Dufourmantelle 2000). Derrida's understanding of **hospitality** and **justice** has much conceptual and practical applicability.

Although Derrida has become widely known as the philosopher of **deconstruction**, he was rather reticent when it came to spelling out its nuances. In fact, the word *deconstruction* rarely appears in his many works. Deconstruction is not synonymous with destruction. Derrida was concerned with opening up taken-for-granted words and works and subjecting them to intense scrutiny. He argued that "deconstruction, if such a thing exists, should open up" (Derrida 1987, p. 261). Thus, if there is such a thing as deconstruction it is intended to "re-construct, re-constitute or re-affirm" a given word structure (Bradley 2008). Deconstruction works to unbolt language and reveal its silent, hidden, or repressed elements that provide them with their meaning. On the rare occasion where Derrida (1985) did articulate a meaning for deconstruction he maintained that it represented the undoing of language to disclose "how an 'ensemble' was constituted." We extend this notion of an "ensemble" to include ways of speaking and thinking about, and being with, young people.

Language dramatically affects what happens at the level of society. How things are named holds significance for how they are understood and acted upon. Derrida maintains that to understand what is going on at the heart of language, we must comprehend the **trace**, which refers to the silent components of our language that assign meaning. However, this quiet element is tremendously slippery and difficult to grab ahold of. Trace is present in all flows of conversation and in all language, but is constantly deferred and silent. Each sign (word) must always already contain *traces* of other signs through which

hospitality
An unrestrained welcome to a stranger. It calls for open spaces that welcome the other as he or she arrives.

justice (Derrida)
For Derrida, justice is a messianic promise of a more just future "to come."

deconstruction
Involves opening up words to their hidden or closed-off possibilities in an attempt to reveal what is going on behind language.

trace
The silent elements that provide words with their essential meaning (Spivak 1976) and that underlie all language.

the original sign derives meaning. For example, marginalization has traces in words like social order, power, and freedom.

For Derrida, everything that is present before us contains traces of other elements that are ostensibly absent or not readily apparent (Bradley 2008). Contemporary discussions of the overrepresentation of Indigenous youth in the YCJS and/or in the child welfare system may not overtly recognize colonization (the historical and ongoing processes that began with the arrival of Europeans to Canada and various attempts to dominate and assimilate Indigenous peoples). The trace remains hidden, but it still there. Derrida claims that all things oscillate between being present and absent without ever being wholly at hand or wholly silent.

Deconstructing "Hospitality"

Let us consider deconstruction at work or what happens when we examine our everyday language more closely. Consider, for example, the term *hospitality*. It might conjure images of welcome mats, dinner parties, or a weekend guest who is visiting from out of town. In the Western world, it is customary to invite people into our places of residence with the greeting "Make yourself at home." We do not, for the most part, mean this in the literal sense. Not immediately evident in this seemingly gracious term is an inalienable tension—between a welcome to a stranger and an uncertain hostility concealed within that welcome. Quite simply, the welcome itself already assumes a stranger in its very utterance. Fashioning the other as "other" in the instance of the welcome sets in motion and entrenches relations of dominion over space. Anyone who has hosted particularly odious houseguests can begin to understand the duality endemic to hospitality. A guest who has overstayed his or her welcome becomes a source of stress for the host (e.g., their children, pets, household schedule). Welcoming a guest into one's home is conditional upon the guest's accepting and attending to established rules of decorum. When I say "Welcome, please make yourself at home," I am actually commanding my guest to be comfortable in a space that belongs to me and over which I am sovereign. Hospitality, as we know and practise it in the West, contains a trace of restraint and hostility that "preserves the distance between one's own and the stranger, between owning one's own property and inviting the other into one's home. So, there is always a little hostility in all hosting and hospitality" (Derrida and Caputo 1997, p. 110). Opening language to its silent but essential elements is at deconstruction's core.

Over the summer months of 2010, the Edmonton Police Service (EPS) increased its **surveillance** and presence in Churchill Square, which is situated firmly within the city's downtown core and is also the site of countless festivals that attempt to attract the affluent and their dollars. Marginalized young people, as you might imagine, were not similarly welcomed into this site. Instead, police officers stationed around the square were instructed to stop, question, and search any "suspicious-looking" young people (read: Aboriginal). With their rather unkempt appearance and lack of surplus income, these youths were unwelcome in Churchill Square and were constituted as "other" to the affluent suburbanites that city officials were attempting to attract (Hogeveen and Freistadt 2012). State responses to these marginalized young people were hostile (see Box 9.1).

surveillance
The direct or indirect observation of conduct, which is intended to produce a desired outcome (i.e., conformity).

| Box 9.1 | **Youth Justice in Action** |

Library Loiterers Given Lesson in Crime and Punishment: Frequent Police Patrols among Efforts to Make Patrons Feel Safer

Edmonton Journal, Saturday, 15 May 2010
By Andrea Sands

Police officers patrolling the area around Sir Winston Churchill Square on Friday stopped often to talk with groups of teens loitering near the Stanley A. Milner Library.

The beefed up police presence is one of several tactics civic leaders will use to make library patrons feel safer after several recent assaults were reported in the area.

"There's lots (more police). We always get talked to, every single day," said Tyson Kakakaway, 16, after a pair of officers on bikes spoke to him and his friend, Randall Alexander. "It's all right. It's kind of weird, because I don't like talking to cops."

The teens, students at the Centre High campus a few blocks away, were standing at the south end of Churchill Square across from the library entrance when the officers approached them.

"They just stop by and ask what's going on, and check you out," said Alexander, 18.

"I think it will help with all the drama that's going on around here."

A recent rash of assaults and violence in the city's core has sparked worries about public safety around the library doors. Two stabbings involving teenage victims happened within five hours last week outside the City Centre Mall and the library.

Mayor Stephen Mandel met Friday morning at City Hall with police Chief Mike Boyd and Edmonton Public Library CEO Linda Cook to figure out how to make patrons of the Stanley A. Milner Library feel more secure.

The leaders agreed in the private meeting that increasing police patrols, getting rid of newspaper boxes, and removing or reducing the size of the bus shelter in front of the downtown library will happen immediately to make the area safer.

"We need to ensure that our citizens feel safe and secure when they're walking in that area—and they don't right now—and we have to change it and we will," Mandel said after the meeting in the city manager's office. "We all agreed there's a problem and we have to fix it and so we'll work together to fix it."

The mayor had previously suggested moving the library entrance, which faces Churchill Square, to the south side of the building to ease congestion in front of the library along 102nd Avenue.

That won't go ahead for now, although Mandel said he still likes the idea.

Police presented a report at the meeting asking to remove obstacles around the library entrance and keep pedestrian traffic moving to reduce crime.

Plans that will proceed immediately include removing about seven newspaper boxes and either removing or narrowing the bus shelter in front of the library, Cook said.

"The whole idea is to make it a wider sidewalk."

Cook said officials want to get at the root of the problem to solve it, not just move it.

"My opinion is that, I think there are a lot of 16- to 22-year-olds that have fallen through the cracks, so far as social services is concerned. We have lots of youth in there who simply don't have homes, they don't have a place to sleep, they don't have enough food, and they come to the library because they feel welcome there. Their behaviour sometimes can get out of hand, but they do understand that if their behaviour isn't acceptable, if they are causing problems for the comfort of our other customers, they will be asked to leave and they may be banned for the day or they may be banned for the year, depending on what they've done."

Extra police will patrol the square and interact more with the public, plainclothes officers will visit the area regularly and police will work with other security officials to make sure troublemakers are removed, said Boyd.

"One of the other things that we talked about was trying to do some programming on the square to invite and welcome more people in the area to the square at lunchtime and in the morning and afternoon hours, because we think that will be helpful as well," he said.

City bureaucrats are working on ways to draw more activity to Churchill Square, and have advertised asking for ideas. City councillors expect to receive a report at the end of June, Mandel said.

"I think that will make a difference too—with more people there, you have less problems."

What would a politics of hospitality look like in this instance? Hospitality without the trace of hostility and exclusion would stretch established limits and work toward welcoming all without any imposed limitations. It would, at the same time, encourage "others" to be as they are and as they arrive (Derrida 2005, p. 66). Hospitality demands acts of *extreme generosity* and opening of space to an unknown and unknowable other: "It is a politics that does not accept limits imposed upon itself, but always asks 'what's next?' and in response relentlessly pushes against established exclusionary boundaries of being" (Carroll 2006, p. 825). Such a way of being in the world is founded in a reverence for the other who appears at a person's threshold whether or not he or she may even be perceived as unpredictable or dangerous. In the case of Churchill Square and in the spirit of hospitality, the city might open the square to the marginalized other and establish venues that encourage the other's unique interests. Instead of closing down this space and employing the state's policing arm to repress the other's manner of expression, a genuine unrestricted welcome would invite young people to share the space on their own terms.

For two days in the summer of 2010 the city did, in fact, open the square to young people and encouraged them to express their unique identities. Youth organizers of Edmonton's Urban Games fashioned an open space of welcome for youth "at-risk" to showcase their talents. The games featured hip-hop battles, skateboarding, dance competitions, and graffiti walls that were spread throughout the square. Instead of being excluded and pushed out of prime consumer space, for one weekend marginalized youth were welcomed and encouraged to make themselves at home. Nevertheless, the city's hospitality was short-lived. Following the allotted time, graffiti walls, much like the at-risk youth who participated in the games, were quickly removed and the square was returned to its previous exclusionary state. While the games gestured in the direction of an open hospitality, they did not go nearly far enough. Enduring sites of inclusion that welcome the other ought to be fashioned.

Searching for "Justice"

Opening up new ways of being and understanding to what lies beyond them encourages adherents of deconstruction to think outside of contemporary mentalities that imprison and exclude others in favour of more-just practices and social relations. If that is what we are after, should we now deconstruct or open up "justice"? It might be extremely rewarding and intellectually expedient if this were indeed possible. Unfortunately, Derrida insists that justice is *impossible*. It does not exist because it must forever remain in the future (Derrida 2002). If justice does not and cannot exist, why does Canada have a youth justice system, justices of the peace, and the Youth Criminal Justice Act (YCJA)? Surely, these are all instances of justice. Derrida and others maintain that these are merely instruments of vengeance that imprison and confine and do little to ameliorate suffering (see Hogeveen and Woolford 2009). That is, the youth justice system is authorized under the YCJA to deliver pain to juvenile offenders as payment for this or that harm caused. Jails and penitentiaries are run based on this misdirected understanding of justice. Justice that finds its end in retribution is not just—it is a form of revenge and is fully at odds with the logic and spirit of justice that Derrida encourages. Further, it is the marginalized other who is typically on the receiving end of this brand of vengeance, masquerading as justice. What we have, then, is a so-called justice system predicated on punishing the poor and marginalized.

Derrida has something much different in mind. He understands justice to be a "promise" that is "beyond law, and is itself incalculable, infinite and undeconstructable" (Pavlich 2007, p. 989). Understood from Derrida's perspective, justice becomes an ideal that exists beyond current ontological limits and must be doggedly pursued. Maintaining that our system of punishment is just would be to claim that all of our hard work is done. Suggesting that the youth criminal justice system is just because it administers the laws of Canada would be to deny the suffering of the indigenous other who is overrepresented at all stages of the "justice" system.

Justice does not exist and does not lend itself to the infinite play of signifiers in the fashion of hospitality, community, or violence. Caputo (Derrida and Caputo 1997, p. 139) argues that it "would be the height of injustice to think that justice exists [or] existed." Justice is not and cannot be a "thing." The potency of this manner of thinking lies in how it stimulates us to fight for the other. "Justice haunts us, disturbs our sleep, stalks us like the specter of old Marx whom we can't quite bury, keeps us up pacing the floors well into the night, has us seeing ghosts" (ibid., p. 139). Derrida was involved in a variety of justice struggles that seemed to trouble his slumber. As one of the world's most well-known philosophers, he levied his celebrity to rally against racism, apartheid, and practices of discrimination that plagued French immigration policy. Thus, to say that justice is impossible or messianic is not to inspire nihilism. Rather, the spectre of justice aims at provoking restlessness. If we return to our previous example of the Urban Games, justice would call upon us to push contemporary limits and refuse to allow Churchill Square to return to its previous configurations. Despite a weekend of welcoming the marginalized youthful other, the square continues to be a site where young people are routinely excluded. Justice calls us to be infinitely responsible, without calculation or vengeance, to all others.

Michel Foucault (1926–1984) and Power

Like Derrida, Michel Foucault was a highly influential French philosopher. His many books include *The History of Sexuality* (three volumes), *Power/Knowledge*, and the *Archaeology of Knowledge*. Given his disdain for the discipline, it may seem odd to include a section on Foucault in a book on youth crime and criminology. Foucault thought criminology to be replete with "garrulous discourse" and "endless repetition" and was convinced that the discipline's primary and perhaps only function was to relieve criminal justice officials of their guilt for delivering pain and suffering upon the other (Foucault 1980, p. 47). That is, he was certain that criminology only served to make judges, for example, feel better about sending young people away from their families and communities because doing so was for "their own good" and a protection for society. Nevertheless and despite Foucault's distaste for criminology, scholars interested in the subject have successfully drawn on his voluminous work to render contemporary systems of governance intelligible. Foucault's book *Discipline and Punish* and his series of articles on governmentality have been particularly influential.

Foucault's work has been prominent in several studies that attend to how young people are governed and disciplined. As we have seen already, youth, and particularly recalcitrant and marginalized young people, are increasingly the targets of surveillance. Ericson and Haggerty (1999) have examined this phenomenon through a governmentality lens. They argue that "governance is organized in terms of risk management technologies that identify dangers" and maintain that police collaborate with other agencies to provide knowledge about youth (i.e., using street-stop recording systems and missing persons registries) (ibid., p. 163). The authors maintain that police function as "the fulcrum of risk communication systems for governing the young" (ibid., p. 164). Predictably, it is marginalized youth and those identified as having the highest levels of **risk** that are subjected to the most intensive surveillance.

Foucault's Understanding of Power

Scholars have been particularly drawn to Foucault's unique understanding of **power**. Prior to Foucault's interdiction, many writers were convinced that power was concentrated in the hands of a few. By contrast, Foucault maintains that power extends beyond a particular class or state and is evidenced only when it is exercised. From this view, power is not something that can be held, accumulated, or stored up for later use. It is only ever evident when it is being put to use. Think about this for a minute. Can you show me power? Can you hold it in your hands and bring it to me? Money as power is a common theme in contemporary music.

Consider, for example, the song "Money, Power and Respect" by Lox (featuring Lil' Kim and DMX) (www.youtube.com/watch?v=YAOgWDLo--w). In the song, the artist makes it clear to the listener that becoming powerful is dependent on first acquiring money. For this group, "it's the key to life." Foucault disagrees with Lox's assessment. For Foucault, money becomes power only when it is spent; it has no power in and of itself.

Foucault (1991, 1980, 1977) was deeply interested in how power shaped the conduct and lives of those subjected to its disciplinary effects. In his classic work on the rise of the prison and punishment, Foucault (1977) traces the emergence of a new economy of discipline that continues to dominate our thinking about how best to govern and train human beings. He was convinced that discipline was characterized by micro-powers that shaped human subjects in preferred ways. These micro-powers, Foucault argues, operate at the minutiae of our existence but are nevertheless momentous in their effects. Every bit of our being is shaped through the exercise of this kind of micro-power. All things, from holding a pencil, to martial arts, to riding a bike, are taught to us through an exacting discipline. Instead of punishing the body via capital punishment or the stock and pillory for that matter, discipline takes hold of the soul and shapes it in ways that are functional and desirable. Thus, rather than seeing power as being repressive or negative, Foucault suggests that power is creative and positive: not in terms of being good or exceptional but in terms of producing some desirable behaviour or outcome. He argues that "we must cease once and for all to describe the effects of power in negative terms. . . . In fact, power produces; it produces reality; it produces domains of object and rituals of truth" (Foucault 1979, p. 194). In this way, Foucault urges scholars to avoid the trap of examining how power dismantles social relations and instead consider what is created through power's exercise.

risk
The calculated probability of an event or a circumstance. Risks are calculated and managed through class, gender, age, and race categories.

power (Foucault)
Rather than as a quantity held or possessed by the state, Foucault understood power to be relational, positive, and exercised.

Foucault was convinced that these micro-powers are not confined to the prison but have been diffused into the larger social world. Following Foucault (as well as David Garland 1985), Chunn (1992) has demonstrated how disciplinary powers were disseminated throughout early twentieth-century Canadian society to create a dense and interlocking web of surveillance intended to discipline the working classes. We encourage you to think about your everyday lives. What forms of discipline are acting upon you? What forms of surveillance are encouraging you to act appropriately? Are there closed-circuit television cameras at your college or university? Will you pass a photo radar vehicle on your way home? How does your behaviour change as a result?

Foucault's work has been routinely challenged for conceptualizing human subjects as "docile" bodies who are the subject of discipline without at the same time resisting incursion into their lives. Foucault addresses this criticism in a 1982 essay entitled "The Subject and Power," where he argues that power operates on individuals so long as they are free. For Foucault (1982), power operates on the actions and behaviour of others, which implies that power can only ever work on a subject who is capable of action and who is (relatively) free. Power seeks to structure subjects' choices in ways that bring their behaviour in line with the needs and desires of governors. For example, during their trip to Disney World, Clifford Shearing and Phillip Stenning (1984) noticed that, despite the hordes of people and without overt signs of discipline and control, the amusement park seemed to function like clockwork. They found that "designed-in" features, like carefully marked roadways and smiling employees, control and shape behaviour in ways conducive to good order at the park. One does not have to travel to Florida to witness similar effects. One of the authors of this chapter recently visited IKEA to purchase an item for his home. When he arrived, he knew exactly what he wanted and where he could find it (in the warehouse). Despite this knowledge, the configuration of the store shaped his actions such that he was "encouraged" by the partition separating the entrance (on one side) from the warehouse (on the opposite side) to venture through the entire store. Those familiar with the massive size of IKEA can imagine his frustration.

Today micro-powers abound and assist in ordering contemporary life. Policing has been bolstered by the promulgation and circulation of micro-power. Consider how you adjust your driving after noticing a police car in your vicinity. Whether or not the officers are directly observing your behaviour is secondary to how their presence alters your conduct. Returning to our example of Churchill Square further reveals the contemporary distribution of micro-powers. In 2010, the City of Edmonton released its blueprint for the future of the square and the larger downtown area (Edmonton 2010). Edmonton city planners call this a "bold vision for Edmonton's downtown" that enhances the "overall aesthetic quality of Sir Winston Churchill Square" (Edmonton 2010, p. 162). Mention of spaces for marginalized young people is conspicuously absent. Instead, the report spotlights several strategies to address crime and disorder. Among the plans is a call for all major downtown streets to be open, to be designed with continuous store-front retail, and to have wide sidewalks. You might be wondering how this relates to crime control. Such tactics expand "natural surveillance" through having more "eyes on the street" and creating unobstructed lines of site throughout the space (ibid., pp. 82, 102). City planners are convinced that this will have the intended effect of improving "safety and security in the Downtown" (ibid., p. 26).

As you can now see, Foucault's work helps crime scholars understand modern configurations of power by alerting them to how the behaviour of active subjects is shaped and contoured in ways often hidden from view, but that have very real effects.

Risk and the Risk Society

Risk is seemingly ubiquitous today. Consider, for example, how the University of Alberta boasts a department of Risk Management Services (RMS). Campus security, emergency management, and insurance and risk management all fall under the RMS rubric. The very existence of this unit suggests that there are numerous risks at the university and that they require some form of regulation. According to the RMS's website, its "vision is to make risk management an integral part of all decision making, at all levels, across the University." It seems that managing risk is such a fundamental part of the contemporary ethos at the university that all decisions require an assessment of risk levels.

It is not only at universities that discourses concerning risk have become omnipresent. It seems that almost everything we do can be understood in risk terms. A quick search of the Internet returns countless websites dedicated to providing information on all manner of diseases. Not only does such a site provide knowledge about the problem, it is also an instrument for you to ascertain your individual level of risk for such calamities as heart disease, sexually transmitted diseases, stroke, breast cancer, and, but certainly not limited to, diabetes. There is nothing inherently risky about having sexual intercourse or eating a diet rich in fat. Rather, it is only when these problems are translated into statistics via actuarial techniques for determining probability that they become risky. That is, only when we are able to accumulate sufficient data on a problem and then assemble that data into a form amenable to calculation do seemingly random events become constituted into the language of risk. Patterns of probability emerge when incidents are tabulated across time and space. Without this ability to translate events and actions into probabilities, events would only be as they are or as we encounter them.

Awareness of predictable crime patterns often shapes our decision-making processes. How many readers, or parents of readers, of this chapter have purchased a burglar alarm for their homes? What prompted this decision? Or how many have altered their diet because of the latest research tying cancer to this or that food category? Ewald (1991, p. 199) maintains that there is nothing in our world that is in and of itself a risk; rather, "it all depends on how one analyses the danger, considers the event." Thus, the invention of instruments that calculate risk orders our social world through technologies that render risk knowable and thus governable. In other words, if we know that having a burglar alarm, trimming the hedges around our homes, purchasing quality locks, and turning on lights at night reduce our risk of victimization, we can take steps to lower the probability that our home will be targeted.

Risk is the probability of an event or an action occurring (Ewald 1991). Insurance agents ask a number of probing questions that are intended to determine a person's level of risk and that are used to provide a quotation for their services: *How old are you? What gender? Have you ever had an "at fault" accident? How many traffic tickets?* By comparing your answers to data aggregated across time (i.e., accident reports and police statistics), insurance companies determine your level of risk and the probability that they will be called upon to pay a claim on your behalf. Young, unemployed, and undereducated males with several traffic tickets are likely to pay much more for their coverage than married women with no blemishes on their driving record. Calculating risk in this way orders seemingly random occurrence in a form that can be used to definite ends (Dean 1999).

Risk and Youth Justice

Contemporary calculations of risk are not the exclusive domain of the insurance industry. They are central to the administration of Canadian youth justice. The perceived ability of these technologies to efficiently and accurately match disciplinary practice to offender characteristics has meant that risk governance strategies have become ubiquitous (O'Malley 1996). Youth, it seems, are at risk for a greater number of predicaments and misadventures than any other segment of the Canadian population (Health Canada 1998). Studies of young people have revealed a series of risk factors that may increase their probability of being victimized or of developing behavioural problems that may then lead to crime and other anti-social behaviour (Howell 2005; Hawkins and Pollard 1999; Shader 2003; Wyrick and Howell 2004). Canada's National Crime Prevention Centre (2007) has identified a variety of risk factors that may lead to gang involvement. Based on accumulated knowledge and data, the centre argues that the following are predictive of gang involvement: overreliance on anti-social peers, poor parental supervision, prior delinquency, aggression, and, but not limited to, early or precocious sexual activity. Risk factors such as these do not stand alone but are often combined toward a variety of ends. For example, Hoge and Andrews (2010) have aggregated risk factors into the latest incarnation of the Youth Level of Service/Case Management Inventory (YLS/CMI), which, they maintain, now takes into account gender and cultural factors. Hoge and Andrews (2010, para. 1) argue that the "YLS/CMI helps probation officers, youth workers, psychologists, and social workers identify the youth's major needs, strengths, barriers, and incentives; select the most appropriate goals for him or her; and produce an effective case management plan."

Risk has come to order our social world to such an extent that social theorist Ulrich Beck (1992) has deemed our contemporary ethos the **risk society**. Whether through advertising, television programming, or word of mouth, citizens in the West are increasingly made aware of their risks for all manner of calamity and are taking steps to remedy these seemingly inevitable ends. For Beck (1992) and others (Ferrell and Hayward 2011), this practice is very much characteristic of a reflexive modern society that is consistently reflecting back upon itself with a wary eye toward the future. Whereas previous societies were constantly looking backward and were reactive, the risk society is preoccupied with allaying future harms. Because contemporary citizens are very much aware of looming risks, they trim their hedges, install burglar alarms, remove all of the valuables from their vehicles, avoid the wrong part of town, and eat a diet free of harmful pesticides and hormones. However, Beck (1992) does not argue that contemporary society is any more at risk than society at any other point in history. Rather, insurential technologies have organized our lives according to risks that are seemingly ubiquitous.

Because risk has become increasingly pervasive in contemporary society, it has also become a subject of study for critical scholars, including youth justice researchers

risk society
This refers to a break with modernity into an emerging societal form characterized by the production of risks and of tools for their management. In contrast to the view that social problems are to be solved, issues in the risk society (i.e., crime) are risks to be managed.

(Hannah-Moffat 2001). While risk orders our contemporary manner of being in the world, critical criminologists recognize that there are inherent problems with applying risk management thinking in the youth justice system. In particular, when risk structures our thinking about social problems (i.e., poverty, drug use, violence, youth crime, and punishment), these unfortunate conditions cease to be obstacles to a more just ordering of the social world. Instead, such issues become constituted as risks that require management (Hogeveen and Woolford 2009). For example, a 10-year-old Aboriginal boy living in poverty is determined to be at risk for joining a gang because of his family history of crime, his low birth weight, and, since he lives in poverty, his poor performance in school. When risk is calculated without consideration for structural conditions that buoy marginality, poverty (for example) is constituted as a risk factor rather than as an intolerable condition that demands redress and amelioration (Minaker and Hogeveen 2009).

Cultural Criminology

Beck's (1992) and Ferrell and Hayward's (2011) works, among others, alert us to the growing importance and seeming omnipotence of risk in contemporary societies. However, this scholarship does little to help criminologists understand and conceptualize how young people on the ground experience and understand this phenomenon. Evidence suggests that young people today are engaging in and enjoying more risky behaviours simply because they are constituted to do so (Hunt, Evans, Moloney, and Bailey 2009; Sanders 2005). Sean Morrissey (2008), in his examination of voluntary risk-taking behaviour among a Scottish dance education company, suggests that young people find risk-taking to be particularly alluring. He argues that transgressive conduct is particularly tempting in societies of caution, where young people are heavily surveilled and policed (Morrissey 2008). Indeed, risk-taking behaviour among young people is evident in a number of divergent and diverse domains of youth culture, from BASE jumping (using a parachute to jump from buildings, antennas, spans, and earth) to ecstasy use in the rave scene.

Contemporary criminological theories have difficulty accounting for these seemingly absurd and baseless choices. Rational choice theory, for example, is among the most prominent perspectives in criminology for understanding youthful offending. It posits that young people are rational actors who make informed and rational decisions about rule-breaking. While criminologists have widely applied this theory in the context of crime, other scholars have attended to how almost all behaviour (e.g., purchasing a television) can be understood in relation to how we understand perceived costs and benefits. Nevertheless, such a perspective does little to account for the emotional and visceral elements of crime and deviance. Cultural criminology, by contrast, is attentive to what renders "transgression and the consumption of transgression so seductive" (Hayward 2002).

Transgressive Elements of Youth Deviance

Cultural criminologists are less concerned with state definitions of crime and the pragmatism of crime control than with the adrenaline surge and emotion that accompany the commission of crime. Fenwick and Hayward (2000) suggest that this insight challenges one of the most widely held and central assumptions of criminology: that crime is "routinized" and rather "banal." They maintain that this "is undoubtedly the case if one adopts the perspective of the police . . . however, it is not necessarily true for those participating in criminal activity, for whom the most innocuous transgression may well represent an exhilarating form of experience" (ibid., p. 36). Thus, while home invasion may not make rational sense to the average crime scholar, cultural criminologists may argue that this crime is more often the result of the adrenaline rush emerging from the commission of the crime than of reasoned forethought.

Cultural criminology enjoys considerable intellectual momentum at present (Ferrell and Young 2004; Ferrell and Hayward 2011). This group of scholars, all of whom are critical of the methods and orthodox criminology and its inability to conceptualize the adrenaline and emotions intrinsic to offending, interweave a number of intellectual threads. These include cultural studies, postmodern theory, critical theory, textual/media analysis, and ethnographic methodologies (Ferrell 1999). Considered more broadly, the very notion of cultural criminology indexes the increasing attention crime scholars lend to popular culture constructions of crime and its control (McCormick 2010; Ferrell 1999). Through innovative theoretical and methodological precepts, cultural criminologists aim to expand and enliven the discipline (Ferrell and Sanders 1995, p. 17).

Innovative methodologies provide cultural criminologists with unique insight into the visceral nature of crime and deviance. According to Kane (2004, p. 303), "participant observation remains the methodological touchstone for the culture-worker." Ethnographic research is particularly appropriate for the subject of cultural criminology. This method attends to the "nuances of meaning within particular cultural milieux" (Ferrell 1999, p. 399). Deep immersion in criminal or deviant fields encourages researchers to formulate pithy and textured descriptions of these worlds, which are often hidden from view. However, cultural criminologists do not only employ participant observation to their academic ends. Maggie O'Neill (2004), for example, uses a method she calls "ethno-mimesis" to capture the complexity of lived reality. For example, she had sex workers use art and prose to detail not only their life experiences but their ideas for social change (O'Neil 2004).

Cultural criminology possesses much potential for transgression. Like the other critical projects discussed in this chapter, cultural criminology unflaggingly challenges taken-for-granted assumptions about crime and its study so as to expose how these are "culturally constructed and delimited by a particular world view" (Hogeveen and Woolford 2009, p. 354; Morrison 2004). Jock Young (2004, p. 1) maintains that because we are "confronted at this moment with an orthodox criminology which is denatured and desiccated," the need for a cultural criminology that captures the phenomenology of crime—"its adrenaline, its pleasure and panic, its excitement, and its anger, rage and humiliation"—has never been more pressing.

Summary

Critical criminologists direct attention to the structural inequalities within and outside of the criminal justice system. They advocate social engagement in ways that would transform marginalization and bring about justice for the other. Critical criminologists recognize that young people are marginalized through power relations along age, class, gender, and racial lines. In Canada, while marginalization is widespread, the situation facing Aboriginal youth is particularly egregious; this is evident in incarceration rates and homelessness, and in the tragic history and impact of colonialism that continues unabated in contemporary society.

Deconstruction, as understood by Derrida, opens language to its hidden and its silent elements. While almost all language can be deconstructed, justice resists our attempts, as it is forever "to come." Considered in this way, justice encourages tireless ameliorative efforts on behalf of marginalized others.

Foucault's impact on critical scholarship is particularly significant. He attuned scholars to new ways of thinking about and understanding power. Instead of seeing power as solely repressive, he thought it was creative and productive. Foucault argued that rather than being housed in some place or entity (i.e., the state), power is evident only in its exercise. Through discipline, surveillance, and governmentality, Foucault maintained that power shapes individuals in ways that render them more amenable to governance.

Critical criminologists have also made use of the concepts of risk, actuarialism, and the risk society to critically examine contemporary society's preoccupation with insurance-like predictions of potential harm. Because of their age, level of maturity, and propensity for precarious behaviour, young people are particularly likely subjects of such forms of calculation. Critical scholarship attends to the social contexts that produce the risk society and encourages academics to draw attention to how marginalization is camouflaged in risk management approaches to juvenile justice. Similarly, cultural criminology is critical of contemporary scholars who reject crime as a visceral phenomenon. Scholars working in this tradition direct academic attention to crime as a lived experience that can best be understood through **ethnography**. Critical scholarship on youth justice is aimed at both critical reflection and social engagement toward a more just and caring social order (Minaker and Hogeveen, 2009).

ethnography
A form of participatory research that involves immersion in the field of study. Because it allows for rich and descriptive findings on areas that are often hidden from view, ethnographic research is fundamental to cultural criminology.

Key Terms

critical criminology	power (Foucault)
deconstruction	risk
ethnography	risk society
hospitality	surveillance
justice (Derrida)	trace
marginalization	

Review Questions

1. Explain how critical criminologists understand and operationalize critique.
2. Highlight and provide examples of how colonialism has contributed to social suffering and to the marginalization of Aboriginal people.

3. Describe and provide examples of how cultural criminology is critical.
4. Explain and provide an example of deconstruction (pay particular attention to the trace).
5. Explore why Derrida claims justice is not deconstructable.

Critical Thinking Questions

1. Explain what being critical means to you. Discuss the differences and similarities between your understanding of being critical and that of critical criminology.
2. Marginalization of the other is found in every Canadian city. Discuss what responsibility, if any, you might have to ameliorate the suffering experienced and lived by the other.
3. How might the insights of the various scholars outlined in this chapter be implemented in the real world?
4. Recall Foucault's understanding of power. How does this conception differ from more widely held beliefs about power in Western society? Explore how your everyday behaviour is disciplined, is the subject of surveillance, and is governed. To what ends is this governance exercised?

References

Aboriginal Healing Foundation. (2003). *Aboriginal domestic violence in Canada*. Ottawa: Anishinabe Press.

Andersen, C. (2009). *Aboriginal Edmonton: A statistical story—2009*. Edmonton: City of Edmonton Aboriginal Relations Office.

Anderson, J. (2003). *Aboriginal children in poverty in urban communities*. Ottawa: Canadian Council on Social Development.

Balfour, G., and Comack, E. (2006). *Criminalizing women: Gender and (in)justice in neoliberal times*. Halifax: Fernwood.

Beck, U. (1992). *Risk society: Towards a new modernity*. London: Sage.

Bradley, A. (2008). *Derrida's of grammatology*. Bloomington: Indiana University Press.

Calverley, D. (2007). Youth custody and community services in Canada, 2004/2005. *Juristat, 27*(2).

Campaign 2000. (2009). *2009 report card on child and family poverty in Canada, 1989–2009*. Toronto: Campaign 2000.

Carroll, D. (2006). "Remains" of Algeria: Justice, hospitality, politics. *Modern Language Notes, 121*(4): 808–27.

Chartrand, L., and McKay, C. (2006). *A review of research on criminal victimization and First Nations, Métis and Inuit People, 1990 to 2001*. Ottawa: Department of Justice.

Chunn, D. (1992). *From punishment to doing good: Family courts and socialized justice in Ontario, 1880–1940*. Toronto: University of Toronto Press.

Dean, M. (1999). *Governmentality: Power and rule in modern society*. London: Sage.

Derrida, J. (1985). Letter to a Japanese friend. In D. Wood, and R. Bernasconi (Eds), *Derrida and différance* (pp. 1–6). Warwick: Parousia.

Derrida, J. (1987). Some questions and responses. In N. Fabb, D. Attridge, and C. MacCabe (Eds), *The linguistics of writing: Arguments between language and literature* (pp. 252–64). Manchester: Manchester University Press.

Derrida, J. (1995). *Points—interviews, 1974–1994*. E. Weber (Ed.). (P. Kamuf, Trans.). Stanford: Stanford University Press.

Derrida, J. (1999). Hospitality, justice and responsibility: A dialogue with Jacques Derrida. In R. Kearney and M. Dooley (Eds), *Questioning ethics: Contemporary debates in philosophy* (pp. 65–83). New York: Routledge.

Derrida, J. (2002). Force of law: The "mystical foundation of authority." In G. Anidjar (Ed.), *Jacques Derrida: Acts of religion* (pp. 229–98). London: Routledge.

Derrida, J. (2005). *The principle of hospitality. Paper machine* (R. Bowbly, Trans.) (pp. 66–9). Stanford: Stanford University Press.

Derrida, J., and Caputo, J.D. (1997). *Deconstruction in a nutshell: A conversation with Jacques Derrida.* New York: Fordham University Press.

Derrida, J., and Dufourmantelle, A. (2000). *Of hospitality.* Stanford, CA: Stanford University Press.

Edmonton. (2010). *Capital City Downtown Plan.* Retrieved from http://www.edmonton.ca/residential_neighbourhoods/Capital_City_Downtown_Plan_May_27_2010.pdf

Edmonton Committee to End Homelessness. (2009, 29 January). *Edmonton Committee to End Homelessness releases 10-year plan.* Edmonton Committee to End Homelessness news release. Retrieved from http://www.endedmontonhomelessness.com/docs/mediapackagewithgoals.pdf

Elden, S. (2007). There is a politics of space because space is political: Henri Lefebvre and the production of space. *Radical Philosophy Review, 10*(2): 101–16.

Ericson, R., and Haggerty, K. (1999). Governing the young. In R. Smandych (Ed.), *Governable places: Readings on governmentality and crime control* (pp. 163–90). Aldershot, UK: Ashgate.

Ewald, F. (1991). Insurance and risk. In G. Burchell, C. Gordon, and P. Miller (Eds), *The Foucault effect: Studies in governmentality* (pp. 197–210). Chicago: University of Chicago Press.

Fenwick, M., and Hayward, K. (2000). Youth crime, excitement and consumer culture: The reconstruction of aetiology in contemporary theoretical criminology. In J. Pickford (Ed.), *Youth justice: Theory and practice* (pp. 31–50). London: Glasshouse.

Ferrell, J. (1999). Cultural criminology. *Annual Review of Sociology, 25*(1): 395–418.

Ferrell, J., and Hayward, K. (2011). *Cultural criminology.* Surrey, UK: Ashgate.

Ferrell, J., and Sanders, C. (1995). *Cultural criminology.* Boston: Northeastern University Press.

Ferrell, J., and Young, J. (2004). Cultural criminology: Some notes on the script. *Theoretical Criminology, 8*(3): 259–73.

Foucault, M. (1977). *Discipline and punish.* New York: Vintage.

Foucault, M. (1979). *The history of sexuality.* New York: Vintage.

Foucault, M. (1980). *Power/knowledge: Selected interviews and other writings.* New York: Pantheon.

Foucault, M. (1982). The subject and power. In H. Dreyfus and P. Rabinow (Eds), *Michel Foucault: Beyond structuralism and hermeneutics* (pp. 208–26). Chicago: University of Chicago Press.

Foucault, M. (1991). Governmentality. In G. Burchell, C. Gordon, and P. Miller (Eds), *The Foucault effect: Studies in governmentality* (pp. 87–104). Chicago: University of Chicago Press.

Fournier, S., and Crey, E. (1997). *Stolen from our embrace: The abduction of First Nations children and the restoration of Aboriginal communities.* Vancouver: Douglas and McIntyre.

Garland, D. (1985). *Punishment and welfare: A history of penal strategies.* London: Gower.

Hannah-Moffat, K. (2001). *Punishment in disguise: Penal governance and federal imprisonment.* Toronto: University of Toronto Press.

Harper, S. (2008). Prime Minister Stephen Harper delivers remarks at the 6th Annual Gala and Fundraiser for the Canadian Crime Victims Foundation. Retrieved from http://pm.gc.ca/eng/media.asp?id=2145

Harvey, D. (1989). *The condition of postmodernity: An inquiry into the origins of cultural change.* London: Blackwell.

Hawkins, D., and Pollard, J. (1999). Risk and protective factors: Are both necessary to understand diverse behavioural outcomes in adolescence? *Social Work Research, 23*(3): 145–58.

Hayward, K. (2002). The vilification and pleasures of youthful transgression. In J. Muncie, G. Hughes, and E. McLaughlin (Eds), *Youth justice: Critical readings* (pp. 80–93). London: Sage.

Health Canada. (1998). *Meeting the needs of youth-at-risk in Canada: A summary of the learnings.* Ottawa: Health Canada.

Herbert, S., and Brown, E. (2006). Conceptions of space and crime in the punitive neoliberal city. *Antipode, 38*(4): 755–77.

Hoge, R.D., and Andrews, D.A. (2010). YLS/CMI: Youth level of service/case management inventory 2.0. Retrieved from http://www.mhs.com/product.aspx?gr=safandprod=yls-cmiandid=overview

Hogeveen, B. (2006). Unsettling youth justice and cultural norms: The Youth Restorative Action Project. *Journal of Youth Studies*, 9(1): 47–66.

Hogeveen, B. (2007). Is there justice for youth? In G. Pavlich and M. Hird (Eds), *Questioning sociology: Canadian perspectives* (pp. 210–25). Don Mills, ON: Oxford University Press.

Hogeveen, B., and Freistadt, J. (2012). Youth justice and hospitality: Overcoming "scarecrow policing." In R. Jochelson and K. Gorkoff (Eds), *Thinking about justice: A book of readings*. Halifax: Fernwood.

Hogeveen, B., and Woolford, A. (2006). Critical criminology and possibility in the neoliberal ethos. *Canadian Journal of Criminology and Criminal Justice*, 48(5): 681–702.

Hogeveen, B., and Woolford, A. (2009). Contemporary critical criminology. In R. Linden (Ed.), *Criminology: A Canadian perspective* (6th ed.) (pp. 339–70). Toronto: Pearson Education.

Howell, J. (2005). Moving risk factors into developmental theories of gang membership. *Youth Violence and Juvenile Justice*, 3(5): 334–54.

Hunt, G., Evans, K., Moloney, M., and Bailey, N. (2009). Combining different substances in the dance scene: Enhancing pleasure, managing risk and timing effects. *Journal of Drug Issues*, 39(3): 495–522.

Kane, S. (2004). The unconventional methods of cultural criminology. *Theoretical Criminology*, 8(3): 303–21.

Kleiss, K. (2010, 11 October). Housing dollars fuel social chaos: Residents. *Edmonton Journal*. Retrieved from http://www.edmontonjournal.com/business/Housing%20+dollars+fuel+social+chaos+residents/3653120/story.html

Lefebvre, H. (1996). *Writing on cities*. London: Blackwell.

McCormick, C. (2010). *Constructing danger: Mis/Representation of crime in the news*. Halifax: Fernwood.

McGillivray, A., and Comaskey, B. (1996). *Black eyes all the time: Intimate violence, Aboriginal women and the justice system*. Toronto: University of Toronto Press.

Mallea, P. (2010). *The fear factor: Stephen Harper's "tough on crime" agenda*. Ottawa: Canadian Centre for Policy Alternatives.

Miller, J.R. (1996). *Shingwauk's vision: A history of Native residential schools*. Toronto: University of Toronto Press.

Minaker, J., and Hogeveen, B. (2009). *Youth, crime, and society: Issues of power and justice*. Toronto: Pearson Prentice Hall.

Morrison, W. (2004). "Reflections with memories": Everyday photography capturing genocide. *Theoretical Criminology*, 8(3): 341–58.

Morrissey, S.A. (2008). Performing risks: Catharsis, carnival and capital in the risk society. *Journal of Youth Studies*, 11(4): 413–27.

National Crime Prevention Centre. (2007). *Youth gang involvement: What are the risk factors?* Ottawa: National Crime Prevention Centre of Public Safety Canada.

O'Malley, P. (1996). Risk and responsibility. In A. Barry, T. Osborne, and N. Rose (Eds), *Foucault and political reason: Liberalism, neoliberalism and rationalities of government* (pp. 189–208). Chicago: University of Chicago Press.

O'Neill, M. (2004). Crime, culture, and visual methodologies: Ethno-mimesis as performative praxis. In J. Ferrell, K. Hayward, W. Morrison, and M. Presdee (Eds), *Cultural criminology unleashed* (pp. 219–29). London: Glasshouse.

Pavlich, G. (2007). Deconstruction. In G. Ritzer (Ed.), *Blackwell encyclopedia of sociology* (pp. 986–89). Malden: Blackwell.

Perreault, S., and Brennan, S. (2010). Criminal victimization in Canada, 2009. *Juristat*, 3(2).

Ratner, R. (1971). Criminology in Canada: Conflicting objectives. Unpublished manuscript.

Royal Canadian Mounted Police. 2014. *Missing and murdered Aboriginal women: A national operational overview*. Retrieved from http://www.rcmp-grc.gc.ca/pubs/mmaw-faapd-eng.pdf

Royal Commission on Aboriginal Peoples. (1996). *Report of the Royal Commission on Aboriginal Peoples*. Ottawa: Indian and Northern Affairs Canada.

Sanders, B. (2005). In the club: Ecstasy use and supply in a London nightclub. *Sociology*, 39(2): 241–58.

Scott, K. (2003). *Funding matters: The impact of Canada's new funding regime on nonprofit and voluntary organizations*. Ottawa: Canadian Council on Social Development.

Scrim, K. (2013). *Aboriginal victimization in Canada: A summary of the literature*. Ottawa: Department of Justice.

Shader, M. (2003). *Risk factors for delinquency: An overview*. Washington, DC: Office of Juvenile Justice and Delinquency.

Shearing, C., and Stenning, P. (1984). From the panopticon to Disney World: The development of discipline. In A. Doob and E. Greenspan (Eds), *Perspectives in criminal law* (pp. 335–49). Toronto: Aurora.

Smart, C. (1989). *Feminism and the power of law*. London: Routledge.

Spivak, G. (1976). Translator's preface. In J. Derrida, *Of grammatology* (G. Spivak, Trans.) (pp. ix–lxxxvii). Baltimore: Johns Hopkins University Press.

Statistics Canada. (2011). *Statistics Canada: Aboriginal Peoples in Canada: First Nations People, Métis and Inuit*. Retrieved from http://www12.statcan.gc.ca/nhs-enm/2011/as-sa/99-011-x/99-011-x2011001-eng.cfm#a6

Statistics Canada. (2014). *Admissions to Youth Correctional Services in Canada, 2011/2012*. Retrieved from http://www.statcan.gc.ca/pub/85-002-x/2014001/article/11917-eng.htm

Wyrick, P., and Howell, J. (2004). Strategic risk based response to youth gangs. *Juvenile Justice Journal, 9*(1): 20–9.

Young, J. (2004). Voodoo criminology and the numbers game. In J. Ferrell, K. Hayward, W. Morrison, and M. Presdee (Eds), *Cultural criminology unleashed* (pp. 13–27). London: Glasshouse.

Part III

At-Risk and Criminalized Youth in Canada: Selected Types and Problems

When the subject of delinquency, criminalized youth, or youth at risk is discussed, most conversations inevitably shift toward specific subject areas (e.g., Aboriginal youth, substance abuse, gangs, violence, bullying). This swing is seen as a natural progression owing to the imprecise meaning of the concept of young offenders, youth at risk, or delinquency. Furthermore, any discussion about the different expressions of youth at risk, or criminalized youth, can be examined from a variety of different perspectives—generally reflecting the complexity of delinquency and the interdisciplinary and/or multidisciplinary nature of the study of youth crime. Practical constraints do not allow us to cover all the key topics that we might aspire to address in a book of this nature. Therefore, in this section we focus on four different types of delinquent behaviour and/or phenomena. Collectively, the chapters serve to illustrate not only that young persons' behaviour is complex but that any efforts to prevent, control, treat, or otherwise respond to it are both challenging and fraught with varying degrees of controversy. The topics covered in this section also serve to illustrate that we cannot rely on blanket solutions, programs, or treatment techniques to (re)solve youth crime.

The themes and topics included in Part III tend to reflect themes and topics that have dominated the youth crime and youth justice literature for several generations now. In fact, entire books have been written on each of the topics presented. Therefore, while we do not profess to provide a comparable level of depth of analysis, each of the chapters offers a concise and yet enriched and enlivened overview of the subject matter being addressed.

The first chapter (Chapter 10), by Jordon Diplock, Darryl Plecas, and Ronda Trumper, provides an engaging and diverse discussion on the topic of substance abuse and related crime in adolescence. In addition to spending the first part of their chapter providing some factual details around the extent and nature of adolescent substance use among Canadian youth, the authors also provide a contextual framework as to why young people experiment with and/or use drugs, and they discuss a range of the risks (e.g., physical health, psychological health). Diplock, Plecas, and Trumper then succinctly describe how substance use and abuse are related to various youth crimes as a result of such risk factors as impaired judgment, social pressure, the lure of "fast money," and so on. In recognizing the varied harms of substance use and abuse, Diplock, Plecas, and Trumper then examine a range of formal and informal intervention and prevention strategies (most of which are school-based) that have been successfully used to prevent youth from ever experimenting and to "just say no." The authors conclude by reiterating that while in recent years there appears to have been a general decrease in substance use and abuse among young people across Canada, the topic remains complex and one that requires us to "build upon existing knowledge" to better inform prevention strategies.

The next chapter (Chapter 11) in Part III was written by Hirsch Greenberg, Jana Grekul, and Rhonda Nelson. The focus of the chapter is on Aboriginal youth, who, like other minority groups around the world, are overrepresented in the Canadian youth justice system. After providing some disheartening statistics of the nature and type of this overrepresentation, the authors move on to provide a sound historical context by which to understand how and why Aboriginal youth have become so closely aligned with youth crime. Through an assortment of clear examples they show how "specific historical policies and processes have contributed to intergenerational experiences of trauma" and overrepresentation in the youth criminal justice system. Then, by drawing on the Aboriginal perspective, the authors show how using Aboriginal-based approaches to justice may better fit the needs and values of Aboriginal youth. The overarching approach that is expressed through this chapter may be referred to as a social justice–based approach. For readers not familiar with the contextual framework of Aboriginal youth, the authors present a critically compelling argument for major reforms in how we have traditionally dealt with young Aboriginal offenders.

In Chapter 12, Mark Totten tackles the topic of gang-involved youth in Canada. While a topical and controversial subject matter, "youth gangs" are generally not well understood owing to their nature and complexity. Couched within the context that there are very limited reliable data on the actual nature and number of gangs in Canada, Totten begins by describing the three major types of gangs that exist in Canada: street gangs, mid-level gangs, and organized crime groups. By referring to specific type of gangs, he provides, among other elements, a clear examination of their structure, history, prevalence across Canada, and criminal activity. Based on available information and a number of case studies, Totten offers a descriptive overview of such topics as recruiting, exiting, and criminal activity. He then goes on to point out that while the legislation (i.e., Bill C-24, which came into effect on 1 February 2002) has attempted to define gang-related activity, it "has not been successfully applied in many cases." Totten then explores a range of theories that have been used to explain gang engagement and provides an overview of certain key risk factors, such as family, school peer group, and community, which can all contribute to predisposing a young person to joining a gang. The final section of the chapter summarizes some of the key intervention and prevention programs that have been introduced across Canada to combat youth gangs or deter young people from joining gangs. Yet in spite of the image many might have of gangs or gang members, Totten reminds the reader that for many it is not a lifestyle choice and that they are often "troubled youth" in need of support.

Bruce MacLaurin and Catherine Worthington co-authored Chapter 13, which focuses on street-involved youth in Canada. Although the topic is regularly overlooked or given only passing attention in most books on young offenders, the authors offer clear insight into the important relationship between street-involved youth and youth crime. Through their careful review of the different typologies of street involvement, they identify the various risk factors (i.e., pathways) that may result in street youth turning to delinquent behaviour for myriad reasons. In addition to discussing the impact of street involvement on the education system and child welfare, MacLaurin and Worthington include an examination of the impact of street involvement on the criminal justice system. And, as with all the chapters in this section, they discuss intervention and prevention strategies but point out that such services are underutilized.

However, drawing on their related work, they offer some examples that have proven promising. The chapter concludes by reiterating that not only are street youth a marginalized group, they are also a diverse and complex group of young people who, despite their resilience, have their own unique challenges that deserve careful attention.

The final chapter in this section (Chapter 14) was prepared by Susan McIntyre and Anne Miller. The authors address a long-standing concern but from a unique perspective. While there exists a rich body of literature on female adolescent prostitution, McIntyre instead directs her attention to the sexual exploitation of young men. As reflected in the title of their chapter, it is a topic that has remained largely "under the radar." Yet over the years the authors, in particular McIntyre, have accumulated the most comprehensive data set of its kind in Canada. The authors use the data set to provide a detailed and expansive overview of sexually exploited young men. Most of the data used are based on first-person accounts of sexually exploited males rather than on service-provided insight/feedback. Their discussion shows that the nature, extent, and characteristics of sexually exploited young men are different from those of their female counterparts. McIntyre and Miller's discussion also shows that the risk factors for young males also differ from those of their female counterparts and hence require different intervention and prevention strategies. For example, males are more likely to be victims of gay bashing and violence. The chapter concludes by pointing out that, as with most types of youth crime and problems, young males do not enter the sex trade by choice but, once involved, "it is not easy to leave the trade." In fact, the authors note that "comparatively nothing has been done for young males."

Issues of Substance Abuse and Related Crime in Adolescence

Jordan Diplock, Darryl Plecas, and Ronda Trumper

10

Overview

This chapter provides an overview of some of the major issues surrounding substance use and abuse among youth in Canada and the link to involvement in criminal behaviour. To provide background for these issues, the first half of the chapter presents information on the nature and extent of adolescent substance use, the reasons young people use drugs and alcohol, and the potential harms of substance use for adolescents. The chapter then discusses how adolescent substance use and abuse relates to crime in this age group. The sections focus specifically on the theories and evidence suggesting a link between substance use and crime and the nature and extent of adolescent participation in drug-specific crimes. Finally, the chapter discusses the most promising practices for substance abuse prevention and treatment for adolescents. Case studies based on interviews with addiction counsellors working within the youth justice system are presented to illustrate some of the key concepts discussed in the chapter. This chapter allows students to critically assess the current situation surrounding substance use among youth in Canada to inform their opinions about the future steps that policy-makers, researchers, and law-enforcement officials should take to deal with these many issues.

Key Objectives

After reading this chapter, you should be able to:

- Identify which substances are most commonly used by adolescents in Canada and discuss trends in substance use.
- Recognize some of the reasons youth become involved with drugs and have an understanding of the issues surrounding this topic.
- Identify the potential harms to adolescents from substance use.
- Discuss the link between adolescent drug use and criminal behaviour.
- Discuss best and promising practices for substance abuse prevention and treatment with youth in general and youth involved in the justice system specifically.

Introduction

As is the case in most parts of the world, the use and abuse of licit and illicit substances has become a part of the social landscape in Canada. For example, although there has been considerable and ongoing success in reducing rates of smoking across Canada (a decrease of 9 per cent from 1999 to 2012), one-sixth (16 per cent) of Canadians over the age of 15 were current smokers in 2012 (Health Canada 2012b). Alcohol consumption represents a major component of leisure-time culture, with Canadians ranking among the world's top 50 in per capita alcohol consumption (World Health Organization 2014). In addition to legal substance use, illegal drugs have become a serious concern in Canada. In recent years, the United Nations (UNODC 2010) has named Canada as a source country for the exportation of both marijuana and designer drugs such as methamphetamine and ecstasy. The country is also home to more than 100,000 intravenous drug users, many living in urban areas such as Vancouver's infamous Downtown Eastside (Urban Health Research Initiative 2009). These issues have occurred concurrently with a general increase in the number of Canadians who believe that marijuana possession should no longer be illegal (Milnor et al. 2009). This current reality inevitably exposes young Canadians to these substances and contributes to the ongoing concern that Canadian youth may face serious life problems related to **substance abuse**.

The most recent National Anti-Drug Strategy from the Government of Canada (Canada 2014) was unveiled in 2007 and has a strong focus on the prevention and treatment of youth substance abuse. One initiative is a national awareness campaign, "drugsnot4me," which includes television commercials and websites with information targeting young people and their parents with the focus of discouraging drug use and experimentation (Health Canada 2009). Accompanying the awareness campaign is increased funding for drug treatment as well as enforcement and intervention for youth struggling with substance abuse (Canada 2014). Such a national strategy and the millions of dollars in funding (ibid., 2010) in addition to private and government websites, programs, and other information resources indicate that substance abuse among youth is a Canadian priority.

substance abuse
Excessive, unhealthy use of a substance such as alcohol, tobacco, or illicit drugs.

Are the hundreds of millions of dollars spent annually across the country on prevention initiatives, research, policing, courts, corrections, and treatment programs in the hope of discouraging youth from starting or continuing drug and alcohol use warranted? Or, conversely, is more emphasis needed on youth substance abuse issues, with increased enforcement powers, more and better treatment options, and more pervasive educational programs? This chapter will provide the reader with some of the information needed to begin to answer these and other related questions.

Substance Abuse among Canadian Youth

There is significant concern among the general public about the level of substance abuse among adolescents in Canada (Teed 2009), but is this concern warranted? Contrary to popular belief, the majority of Canadian adolescents do not report using illicit drugs, and use of alcohol and tobacco are on the decline (Health Canada 2012). However, a significant percentage of adolescents are still using substances and that is alarming, as youth are more likely than adults to engage in risky alcohol and drug use behaviour and experience greater harms associated with that use (Adlaf, Begin, and Sawka 2005). In addition, research has shown that early initiation of substance use is predictive of later substance abuse behaviours, with as much as four times greater risk for those who drank to intoxication before the age of 15 over those who started drinking after age 20 (de Girolamo, Dagani, Purcell, Cocchi, and McGorry 2012). Further, for every year an adolescent delays drug use, the risk of developing a serious problem with substance abuse is reduced by 5 per cent (Behrendt, Wittchen, Holfer, Lieb, and Beesdo 2009).

Drug Use Trends

Surveys of youth in Grades 7–12 are conducted regularly in 9 of our 10 provinces as well as in the nationally administered Youth Smoking Survey (YSS), a school survey of youth smoking and other drug use. For the first time the *Cross-Canada Report of Student Alcohol and Drug Use* (CCSA 2011) has collected these data in a single report, allowing the comparison of information for this age group across the country. In addition, the Canadian Alcohol and Drug Use Monitoring Survey (CADUMS) has been collecting information on the substance use behaviours of people 15 years of age or older since 2008, separating out the results for people aged 15–21, which allows us to follow societal substance use trends over that time period (Health Canada 2011).

The CCSA (2011) reported consistent patterns of alcohol and drug use across the provinces as well as at the national level when comparing youth of the same gender and grade. The results from these surveys are reported in a range to demonstrate the variance in reported use across the provinces. Some of the consistencies found in the report were that "more males appear to engage in daily or almost daily cannabis use and males appear to more often report driving after drinking" (CCSA 2011, p. 3), and the not unexpected increase in substance use from early to late high school. "For example, in Grade 7, depending on the province, 3–8% report past use or almost daily use versus 30–53% of their Grade 12 counterparts" (ibid., p.3).

Alcohol Use

Alcohol is the most common substance used by youth. While alcohol is a legal substance, there are age restrictions and other regulations to control its use in Canada. The legal minimum age to purchase and consume alcohol is 19 in all provinces other than Alberta, Manitoba, and Quebec, where the legal minimum age is 18. In a survey of students in Grades 7–12, 52.6 per cent reported using alcohol at least once and between 19 and 30 per cent reported consuming 5 or more drinks on a single occasion in the past year (CCSA 2011).

Tobacco Use

Although much less common than drinking alcohol, tobacco smoking is also one of the most commonly used substances by youth. As with alcohol, each province has a minimum age of 18 or 19 to purchase tobacco products. Tobacco use has greatly declined over recent years, with the majority of youth (76 per cent) in Grades 6–12 reporting having never tried smoking and only 2 per cent of all youth in Grades 6–12 reporting being daily smokers (Health Canada 2014). Although tobacco use among youth appears to be declining (ibid.), the addictive quality of nicotine, the stimulant drug within tobacco, and the numerous negative health consequences associated with long-term cigarette smoking make its use among youth a continued major concern in Canada.

Marijuana Use

Marijuana is the most commonly used illicit drug among adolescents in Canada. Across Canada, between 20.9 and 36.8 per cent of students in Grades 7–12 have reported using marijuana in their lifetime (CCSA 2011). Past-year usage is lowest among students in the younger grades and increases with the age of the students. Approximately, 1 in 20 Grade 7 students reported past-year marijuana use, while the rate of past-year use for Grade 12 students was between 1 in 2 and 1 in 3. Between 2.2 and 5.3 per cent of youth in Grades 7–12 report daily use of marijuana. Importantly, the most recent Canadian Alcohol and Drug Use Monitoring Survey reports a decrease in past-year marijuana use by 15–24-year-olds from 37 per cent in 2004 to 20.3 per cent in 2012 a drop of 16.7 per cent (ibid.).

Other Drug Use

With the exception of marijuana use, illicit drug use is not common within the general youth population in Canada, although some youth do report worrisome substance abuse behaviours. The Youth Smoking Survey (Health Canada 2014) is the most comprehensive source of information on substance use from youth across the country. According to this study, ecstasy is the second most commonly used drug by adolescents, with 3 per cent of youth reporting use in the past year. Simultaneous polysubstance use—the use of a combination of two or more substances at the same time—is also common among some adolescent drug-using populations, with alcohol, marijuana, and tobacco the most commonly mixed substances (Barrett, Darredeau, and Pihl 2006). A very positive trend across Canada and among youth in particular is a decrease in the use of these substances and of combinations of substances, and a resulting reduction in the harm caused to youth by their involvement with these substances (Health Canada 2012a) (see Table 10.1).

Table 10.1	Changes in Past-Year Substance Use among Canadian Youth* from 2004 to 2012		
Substance	**% Past-Year Use (2004)**	**% Past-Year Use (2012)**	**% Change**	
Alcohol	82.9	70.0	−12.9	↓
Cannabis	37.0	20.3	−16.7	↓
Tobacco				
15–19 years	18.0			
20–24 years	28.0			
Any 5 drugs (cocaine/crack, speed, ecstasy, hallucinogens incl. salvia, heroin)	15.4	6.5	−8.9	↓
Any drug harm to self—of total population*	9.5	1.6	−7.9	↓

* At least one of eight harms physical health; friendship and social life; financial position; home life or marriage; work, studies, or employment opportunities; legal problems; difficulty learning; housing problems.

Source: Health Canada 2012a.

Inherent Challenges of Measuring Adolescent Drug Use in Street-Involved Youth

Drug and alcohol surveys are inherently unable to procure information from the entire youth population. The information obtained through these types of surveys typically comes from the youth who attend public schools or from youth who can be contacted through telephone surveys and who agree to participate in the surveys. In addition to an array of potential methodological problems with these types of self-report surveys—such as **social desirability effects**, errors in memory, exaggeration, and deception (Palys and Atchinson 2014)—the selection biases necessarily exclude the drug use of those youth who do not attend school or rarely attend school, and those youth who are homeless or otherwise marginalized. In Canada, estimates of the number of **street-involved youth** have been cited at 150,000 (Public Health Agency of Canada 2006, also see Chapter 13). While these adolescents do not compose a substantial portion of the age group, researchers who have studied these populations have found that they are at greater risk than mainstream youth to use both non-injection and injection drugs and to engage in unsafe sexual behaviour, and that they suffer from various health problems and mental illnesses (Werb et al. 2008).

Without information obtained from these marginalized youth, the official rates of national drug use likely underestimate to some degree the true extent of adolescent usage. Perhaps, as some commentators (see Saewyc 2007) have suggested, focusing on measuring and discouraging substance abuse in mainstream youth is misguided, as most of the problems related to substance abuse will manifest within the most at-risk populations— populations that are currently difficult to study and that are targeted by law-enforcement

social desirability effects
Biases in research caused by respondents' desire to provide what they feel is the socially acceptable response or "what the researcher wants to hear."

street-involved youth
A heterogeneous population of youth between ages 12 and 24 who lack adequate shelter and are considered to live outside the mainstream youth population.

anti-drug measures while being largely ignored by anti-drug awareness campaigns. This issue will be further explored in the prevention and treatment section at the end of this chapter.

Reasons Youth Use Alcohol and Other Drugs

Most adolescents experiment with different attitudes and behaviours as part of the process of developing a sense of self separate from their family and other authority figures (Newcomb and Bentlar 1989). Neuroscience researchers suggest that the differing maturation patterns of the areas of the brain responsible for emotions and reasoning may significantly contribute to risk-taking and novelty-seeking behaviour by youth (Steinberg 2004). Although this willingness to take risks and try new things is normative and functionally adaptive, it can lead to substance use that can be problematic with the developing brain (Winters and Arria 2011). Although many youth indicate that their original use of substances was provoked by curiosity and the majority will not continue to use these substances, a significant percentage will. The question becomes: "What motivates adolescents to continue to use substances?"

For Pleasure

One key rationale that adolescents offer for substance use in self-report surveys is "enjoyment" (Terry-McElrath, O'Malley, and Johnston 2009). Such enjoyment is generally equated with increasing positive experiences while at parties or other social events. While there may be other underlying reasons, such as a lack of enjoyable pro-social alternatives, many young people are drawn to the promise of leisure offered by drugs. They may also have an overly positive expectation of the effects of drugs, as researchers have found that users may downplay the negative aspects of their drug use experiences (Hayaki et al. 2010). Since adolescents may perceive substance use as a normative method of enjoyment, the role of pleasure should not be overlooked by the assumption that all substance abuse necessarily stems from an underlying pathology (Hunt, Moloney, and Evans 2009).

As a Result of Peer Pressure

Researchers generally accept that young people are influenced by their peers as they seek to establish their identity and that much socialization occurs within these groups (Harris 1995). Feeling pressure from peers is often emphasized as a reason for adolescent substance use. This is exacerbated by the tendency for youth to regularly overestimate the prevalence and regularity of alcohol and drug use among their peer group (Martens, Page, Mowry, Damann, Taylor, and Cimini 2006). Peer pressure, or the perception thereof, may play a role in substance use despite existing prohibitions. If drug and alcohol use is perceived as normative, young people may view the social consequences of not partaking as more detrimental than the consequences prescribed by the law or others in authority.

Social factors may, however, be less important to continuation than the perceived psychological and physical effects of the drug (Cooper, May, Soderstrom, and Jarjoura 2009), as those youth who do not enjoy their first experience are likely to make the choice to discontinue. While it is common that youth with friends who use alcohol and drugs also tend to be involved with these substances, it is also true that youth who abstain tend to associate with peers who also abstain (Bauman and Ennett 1996). Therefore, while peer pressure may influence a young person's decision to try alcohol and other drugs, the interplay between social factors and personal choices becomes more complex as youth decide whether or not to continue.

As a Means of Coping

Adolescence is a time of transition and experimentation, often causing a number of struggles for youth as they navigate the changes (Wolfe, Jaffe, and Crooks 2006), and some adolescents turn to drug use as a coping mechanism for other difficulties and challenges in their lives (Terry-McElrath et al. 2009). While perhaps not as common as experimenting with drugs and alcohol for excitement and social approval, difficulty coping with life stressors could be related to initiation into substance use. For example, some youth struggling with a difficult home life, poor school performance, or any number of other issues may perceive drugs and alcohol as an escape after witnessing other youth experiencing enjoyment and social rewards. Coping may also be a potential reason for continuation of substance use because even if a young person first tries drugs for excitement or as a result of peer pressure, he or she may eventually begin to equate the positive feelings associated with alcohol and drug use with a method of coping with life stressors.

Potential Negative Effects of Adolescent Substance Abuse

Consequences of Impairment

Substance use places youth at risk of serious negative consequences because of impairment and intoxication. Accidents and self-induced injuries were among the most common causes of alcohol- and illegal drug-related hospitalizations and death in Canada in 2002 (Rehm et al. 2006a). While injuries owing to alcohol alone or in combination with drugs represented only a small proportion (0.6 per cent) of overall visits to Canadian emergency rooms for young people between 2000 and 2003, the rates increased with age and increased annually for all age groups (Lea, Black, and Asbridge 2009).

In addition to injuries, young people often experience other potentially negative consequences of substance use. Substance use may result in unplanned, or unprotected sexual activity; a drive in a car driven by an intoxicated driver; an inability to remember events; an argument with family; and criminal acts (Centre for Addictions Research in BC 2009). Even if the intention of consuming drugs and alcohol is to have fun, youth run the risk of engaging in behaviours that can have immediate and long-term negative repercussions.

General Health Risks

Both the type of substance used and the **method of administration** can have serious adverse effects on the health of users young and old. The most serious potential harm of drugs and alcohol use is death, which occurred in 4258 cases related to alcohol, in 1695 cases related to illegal drugs, and in 37,209 cases related to tobacco use in Canada in 2002 (Rehm et al. 2007). Health-related alcohol-related deaths were most commonly linked to cirrhosis of the liver (1246), esophageal cancer (501), and cardiac arrhythmias (449). Tobacco-related deaths were typically caused by lung cancer (13,401), ischemic heart disease (5343), and respiratory diseases such as chronic obstructive pulmonary disease (7533). More than half of all deaths related to illegal drug use were as a result of overdose (958), while hepatitis C (165) or HIV (87) was also a major cause of death (ibid.).

Other negative health conditions linked to substance abuse can range from debilitation to inconvenience. For example, the nicotine in tobacco can cause the narrowing of arteries, reducing the blood supply to the heart and making it work harder (Benowitz 2009). Cocaine and other stimulants produce a similar effect on the cardiovascular system and can lead to increased respiration, rapid and irregular heartbeat, increased blood pressure, and hyperthermia (NIDA 2011). These symptoms increase the risk of heart attack and stroke (Treadwell and Robinson 2007). Heroin and other opioids (e.g., codeine, morphine, and oxycodone) can slow respiration to dangerous levels (NIDA 2011). And heavy alcohol use, or **binge drinking**, has also been linked to liver and kidney diseases, various cancers, heart disease, and malnutrition (Rehm et al. 2006b).

The method of administration of the drug can also be a factor in the negative health consequences of consumption. For substances administered through smoking combusted plant matter, such as tobacco or marijuana, the majority of the harm stems from the introduction of chemicals into the lungs (see Diplock and Plecas 2009). Intravenous injection of drugs such as heroin, cocaine, and methamphetamine not only can be damaging to the veins, but can also put the user at a greatly increased risk of contracting illnesses such as hepatitis B and C, HIV, and other infections (Thorpe et al. 2002). Intranasal administration, or snorting, can cause irritation to the nasal lining, chronic running or bleeding nose, loss of ability to smell, and difficulty swallowing (NIDA 2011). Therefore, while it is important to stress the negative health consequences of the drugs themselves to discourage use among adolescents, it is equally important to disseminate information about the harms associated with particular methods of consuming those drugs and to offer alternatives that will reduce the potential for harm caused by the method of administration (see Table 10.2).

method of administration
The path by which a drug or other substance is brought into contact with the body. Common methods include smoking, ingestion, injection, and intranasal inhalation.

binge drinking
Heavy alcohol consumption over a short period of time for the purpose of becoming intoxicated. Generally, the concept is operationalized as the consumption of five or more drinks on one occasion (four or more for females).

Effects on the Developing Brain

Consuming alcohol and other drugs may result in serious negative effects on the adolescent, as the developing brain may be more vulnerable to the effects of these substances (Vaccarino 2007). Recent research has suggested that substance use in adolescents can lead to abnormalities in brain functioning (Squeglia, Jacobus, and Tapert 2009). However, because few adolescent drug users do not also use alcohol, challenges arise in separating the effects of various substances on adolescent brain development (ibid.). Thoma et al. (2010) found that heavy alcohol and marijuana use in adolescents leads to reduced

Table 10.2	Commonly Abused Drugs and Their Effects

Category and Street Names	Acute Effects and Health Risks
Alcohol (ethyl alcohol)	Low doses: euphoria, mild stimulation, relaxation, lower inhibitions.
	High doses: drowsiness, slurred speech, nausea, emotional volatility, loss of coordination, visual distortions, impaired memory, sexual dysfunction, loss of consciousness, increased risk of injuries, violence, fetal damage (in pregnant women), depression, neurologic deficits, hypertension, liver disease, addiction and fatal overdose.
Marijuana Blunt, dope, ganja, grass, herb, joint, bud, Mary Jane, pot, reefer, green, trees, smoke, sinsemilla, skunk, weed, boom, gangsta, hash, hash oil, hemp.	Euphoria, relaxation, slowed reaction times, distorted sensory perception, impaired balance and coordination, increased heart rate and appetite, impaired learning and memory, anxiety, panic attacks, psychosis, cough, frequent respiratory infections, possible mental health decline, addiction.
Tobacco Found in cigarettes, cigars, and smokeless tobacco (snuff, spit tobacco, and chew).	Increased blood pressure and heart rate, chronic lung disease, cardiovascular disease, stroke, cancers of the mouth, pharynx, larynx, esophagus, stomach, pancreas, cervix, kidney, bladder, and acute myeloid leukemia, adverse pregnancy outcomes, addiction.
Cocaine Cocaine hydrochloride, blow, bump, C, candy, Charlie, coke, crack, flake, rock, snow, toot.	Increased heart rate, blood pressure, body temperature, metabolism, feelings of exhilaration, increased energy, mental alertness, tremors, reduced appetite, irritability, anxiety, panic, paranoia, violent behaviour, psychosis, weight loss, insomnia, cardiac or cardiovascular complications, strokes, seizures, addiction, nasal damage from snorting.
Methamphetamine Desoxyn, meth, ice, crank, chalk, crystal, fire, glass, go fast, speed.	Increased heart rate, blood pressure, body temperature, metabolism, feelings of exhilaration, increased energy, mental alertness, tremors, reduced appetite, irritability, anxiety, panic, paranoia, violent behaviour, psychosis, weight loss, insomnia, cardiac or cardiovascular complications, strokes, seizures, addiction, severe dental problems.
Amphetamine Biphetamine, Dexedrine, berries, black beauties, crosses, hearts, LA turnaround, speed, truck drivers, uppers.	Increased heart rate, blood pressure, body temperature, metabolism, feelings of exhilaration, increased energy, mental alertness, tremors, reduced appetite, irritability, anxiety, panic, paranoia, violent behaviour, psychosis, weight loss, insomnia, cardiac or cardiovascular complications, strokes, seizures, addiction.

Table 10.2 *(Continued)*	
MDMA Methylenedioxymethamphetamine, Ecstasy.	Mild hallucinogenic effects, increased tactile sensitivity, empathic feelings, lowered inhibitions, anxiety, chills, sweating, teeth clenching, muscle cramping/sleep disturbances, depression, impaired memory, hyperthermia, addiction.
Anabolic Steroids Anadrol, Oxandrin, Durabolin, Depo-Testosterone, Equipoise, roids, juice, gym candy, pumpers.	No intoxication effects, hypertension, blood clotting and cholesterol changes, liver cysts, hostility and aggression, acne, in adolescents—stoppage of growth, in males—prostate cancer, reduced sperm production, shrunken testicles, breast enlargement, in females—menstrual irregularities, development of beard and other masculine characteristics.
Inhalants Solvents (paint thinners, gasoline, glue), gases (butane, protane, aerosol, propellants, nitrous oxide), nitrates (isoamyl, isobutyl, cyclohexyl), laughing gas, poppers, snappers, whippets.	(Varies by chemical)—stimulation, loss of inhibition, headache, nausea or vomiting, slurred speech, loss of motor coordination, wheezing/cramps, muscle weakness, depression, memory impairment, damage to cardiovascular and nervous systems, unconsciousness, sudden death.

Source: Excerpted from the NIDA (National Institute on Drug Abuse) 2011.

attention and executive functions and to memory detriments, respectively. While further research is necessary, these changes to the structure and processes in young developing brains may put early-onset substance users at greater risk of acquiring long-term cognitive impairment, mental illness, and addiction.

Psychological Risks

Substance use can lead to serious negative consequences for a person's mental health. In 2002, substance abuse led to 2058 alcohol-related and 1517 illegal drug–related psychiatric hospitalizations in Canada (Rehm et al. 2006a). There is some evidence that the use of stimulants—such as cocaine, amphetamines, and methamphetamine—can cause **psychosis** (Dore and Sweeting 2006). Furthermore, marijuana use might also trigger the onset of psychosis in those people with an existing predisposition (Degenhardt and Hall 2006). In other cases, prolonged or heavy substance use can result in drug-induced psychosis, a condition where the user exhibits psychotic symptoms, such as hallucinations, delusions, memory loss, and confusion, for a temporary period (CAMH n.d.). Drug use, particularly exposure at an earlier age, may put users at a greater risk of developing psychosis resulting from or triggered by substance abuse (Smith, Thirthalli, Ben Abdallah, Murray, and Cottler 2009).

As is the case with psychosis, studies have found high levels of **co-morbidity** of substance abuse and mental health problems among adolescents similar to levels among

psychosis
A symptom of mental illness involving a substantial alteration to an individual's personality and a loss of contact with objective reality.

co-morbidity
Two or more independent and coexisting medical conditions.

adults (Chan, Dennis, and Funk, 2008). Other mental health problems co-occurring with substance abuse include depression and anxiety (O'Leary-Barret 2014). However, trying to determine whether substance abuse is a causal factor in mental illness presents researchers with a considerable challenge. Studies are often limited because it is difficult to determine if substance abuse caused a change to brain functioning that in turn led to mental illness, or if the onset of mental illness was a factor in the initiation of drug use (Degenhardt, Hall, and Lynskey 2002). While the sequence of events that explain the link between substance abuse and mental illness requires continued study, the evidence suggests that some substances may trigger mental illness in those already predisposed and may exacerbate symptoms in those already experiencing mental illness (O'Leary-Barret 2014).

Addiction

Some researchers believe that substance abuse during the adolescent stage of brain development may put the user at a greater risk of changes to brain structure and functioning that could lead to addiction (Squeglia et al. 2009). Addiction, also called **dependence**, generally refers to either psychological or physical dependence on a substance. According to the Centre for Addiction and Mental Health (CAMH 2009), psychological dependence exists when a substance abuser feels that she or he needs the drug in order to function or feel normal. Physical dependence occurs when a substance abuser's body has developed a tolerance, meaning that a higher dose of the drug is necessary to get the same effect. Furthermore, when substance abuse stops, the user may feel symptoms of withdrawal (ibid.). Dependency symptoms can range from tolerance, to withdrawal, to taking the drug for longer periods of time or in larger doses than intended, to an increase in the time spent obtaining the drug and recovering from its effects, to ignoring other important activities, or to continuing use despite undesirable consequences (Looby and Earleywine 2007).

According to Statistics Canada, in 2012 approximately 21.6 per cent of Canadians met the criteria for a substance abuse disorder in their lifetime (Pearson, Janz, and Ali 2012). This included not only people who met the criteria for dependency but also those who met the criteria for **abuse**. Youth aged 15–24 years had the highest rate of substance abuse among all the age groups, at 11.9 per cent (ibid.).

Despite the low rates of dependence in Canada, addiction is a serious concern. The compulsive drug seeking that accompanies addiction compels the addicted substance abuser to take greater risks to obtain the substance, to use more, and to continue to use despite negative experiences (Friedman 2009). Continued drug use puts the user at greater risk of developing the health and mental health afflictions discussed earlier. These consequences are exacerbated by the social **stigma** surrounding drug abuse—a stigma fuelled by the self-destructive, burdensome, and victimizing behaviour that can result from addiction (Room 2005). Therefore, while addiction may be uncommon, the consequences are dire because it is a condition where the drug user may require a great deal of support and yet be separated or marginalized from the mainstream sources of that support (Mooney 2005).

dependence
When an individual feels that use of a substance is necessary for normal daily functioning or when substance use leads to tolerance. Abruptly stopping use may lead to symptoms of withdrawal.

abuse
Characterized by a pattern of recurrent use of a substance where at least one of the following occurs: failure to fulfill roles in major life areas, use in physically dangerous situations, recurrent alcohol- or drug-related problems and continued use despite this use contributing to social or interpersonal problems.

stigma
A behaviour or an attribute that causes an individual to be discredited, rejected socially, or negatively stereotyped.

Adolescent Substance Abuse and the Link to Criminal Behaviour

The link between substance use and crime has been well studied. Data on federal and provincial inmates, as well as on arrestees, indicate that more than half of offenders from each of these groups were intoxicated by illicit drugs, alcohol, or both during the commission of their most serious crimes (Pernanen, Cousinea, Brochu, and Sun 2002). While this study does not specify the proportion for youth offenders, the connection between substance abuse and delinquent activity in adolescents has been well documented (Dowden 2003). Adolescents involved in the justice system tend to initiate substance abuse at earlier ages (Murray and Belenko 2005), use a greater variety of substances, and use more frequently and at higher doses than their peers the same age (Erickson and Butters 2005). In general, research has found a strong relationship between adolescent substance abuse and crime, although other underlying factors likely contribute to both (Harrison, Erickson, Adlaf, and Freeman 2001).

The link between substance abuse and crime is often explained through the tripartite drug-crime model first discussed by Goldstein (1985), suggesting that drug use causes crime through three distinct modes: (1) psychopharmacological, (2) economic compulsive, and (3) systemic. The first, psychopharmacological, refers to the idea that the intoxicating effects of the substances change a person's behaviour, causing that person to act out and break the rules. A person may also use the drug to inhibit feelings of nervousness or fear in order to partake in crime (Brunelle, Brochu, and Cousineau 2000). The second mode, economic compulsive, posits that some drug users commit crime to obtain the money to support expensive drug use. The third mode, systemic, suggests that the nature of the drug market requires those involved to commit crime, generally violent crime, to protect territory, maintain supply, and retrieve debts. The first two modes have been found to be most relevant to crime committed by adolescent substance users (ibid. 2000).

Adolescent Crime Caused by Impairment

Crimes such as property damage, public disorder, violent offences, shoplifting and other thefts, and driving offences are some of the most common offences committed by adolescents and adults under age 25 (Diplock and Plecas 2010). These offences are also commonly linked to alcohol and drug use (Felson, Savolainen, Aaltonen, and Moustgaard 2008). In his research on adolescent male offenders in Toronto and Montreal, Brochu (2013) found that intoxication was the main factor that led to their violence and offending, although often the youths indicated that they used intoxication to make it possible for them to commit crimes that they would find difficult to do sober. The argument that impairment causes crime is generally more applicable to substances, such as alcohol, that have a disinhibiting effect. For example, research has found that rates of alcohol use were statistically significantly related to rates of violent offending, but the same was not true for rates of cocaine use (Martin, Maxwell, White, and Zhang 2004). However, the same study found that neither cocaine use nor alcohol use was statistically significantly associated with property crime. Therefore, while the psychopharmacological argument may make sense, there are likely confounding variables that explain both the criminal behaviour and the substance abuse of these youths independently.

There are also offences that involve drug impairment as a major component of the offence. The most obvious example is impaired driving, which necessitates the consumption of alcohol or drugs. While there is no legally prescribed limit for drug consumption prior to driving, the law includes impairment by drugs. Police have the power to perform a **drug recognition expert (DRE) evaluation** to test potentially impaired drivers for signs of drug intoxication. In a recent roadside survey of BC drivers, results indicated that 8.3 per cent and 10.1 per cent had been drinking or using drugs, respectively, although the rate of drivers with a blood-alcohol level above 50mg/dl was less than 6 per cent (Beasley and Beirness 2012). The study found that no participants under 18 years of age had been drinking, and less than 5 per cent of those under 18 years of age had been using drugs. Among those cases where drug use was found, marijuana was the most frequently used, followed by cocaine and then opiates (ibid.).

Drug and alcohol impairment may also lead to crime in another way: youth may become easier targets of violence, thefts, and sexual assaults when they are impaired by substance use. According to research by McClelland and Teplin (2001), alcohol intoxication contributes substantially to violent offending, particularly increasing the risk to those who would otherwise be unlikely victims. Another study (Shepherd, Sutherland, and Newcombe 2006) found that alcohol use, independent of other factors, increased the vulnerability of adolescents to victimization. Alcohol intoxication is also a major contributing factor in rapes of young college women (Testa and Livingston 2009). While drug use is also related to victimization, other factors such as heavy drinking are also often present. Research indicates that heavy drinking puts young males at a greater risk of victimization than young females, but that young female illicit drug users are at a greater risk of victimization as a result of their substance abuse than are their male counterparts (Wells and Thompson 2009).

Adolescent Crime Resulting from the Search for Drugs

Economic compulsion posits that substance abusers commit crimes to obtain money to get drugs. These crimes may include thefts of money, thefts of items to sell to obtain drugs, thefts of items to save legitimate money for drugs, or other illegal money-making activities such as prostitution or selling drugs (Bennet and Holloway 2009). Brunelle et al. (2000) suggest that the economic powerlessness of adolescents is a factor that might push them toward crime so that they could consume even less expensive drugs. Youth have fewer opportunities to make money through work, employment insurance, social welfare, or selling possessions and, therefore, may be more likely to resort to crime to acquire money. However, Brochu (2013) found that the youth in his samples were least likely to explain their offending as having been caused by the need to obtain drugs because of their dependency. This explanation may be more likely for those youth already comfortable

---

drug recognition expert (DRE) evaluation
A standardized procedure performed by a trained drug recognition expert—involving visual cues, vital signs, questioning, and the provision of bodily fluids by the potentially impaired driver—that is used for determining impairment by drugs or by a drug in combination with alcohol.

with delinquent behaviour or for those who are addicted or in withdrawal (Bennet and Holloway 2009).

Youth Involvement in Drug Crimes

Many of the activities involved in the use of drugs are illegal, as outlined in Canada's Controlled Drugs and Substances Act (CDSA 1996). The possession, production, distribution, importation, and exportation of specifically scheduled substances are prohibited, each of them having its own criminal sanctions that vary by the type (or schedule) of the substance. For some offences, such as trafficking, importation or exportation, and production (again depending on the schedule of the substance), the maximum penalty is imprisonment for life (CDSA 1996).

Approximately 98,000 incidents of drug crimes occurred in Canada in 2009 (Dauvergne and Turner 2010). The vast majority of drug offences are related to marijuana, mainly resulting from possession (Dauvergne 2009). Many drug offences go undetected, with most reported offences resulting from **proactive police work**. Therefore, the statistics are largely a product of the direction of police focus on drug crimes (Warner and Wilson-Coomer 2003).

proactive police work
Enforcement activities that are police initiated rather than in response to a call for service.

In 2007, of the over 90,000 people accused of drug offences, approximately 19 per cent were youths (ages 12 to 17) (Dauvergne 2009). Young people have much higher rates of involvement in drug offences than other age groups, particularly for marijuana-related crimes (Dauvergne 2009). However, only 38 per cent of the files with accused adolescents went forward with charges, demonstrating an effect of Canada's Youth Criminal Justice Act, which encourages police to divert youth involved in drug offences away from charges toward extrajudicial measures (Dauvergne 2009).

Possessing Drugs and Alcohol

Possession offences are the most common drug offences (Dauvergne 2009), and official rates of possession offences represent only a fraction of the actual offences committed. Based on the rates of self-reported youth drinking, smoking, and drug use, adolescents clearly are regularly in possession of prohibited substances or are at least collaborating together to have these substances available. Therefore, substance use itself necessarily implicates the youth in criminal or delinquent behaviour. While possession alone may seem like a minor offence, it can be accompanied by other related rule-breaking deviant behaviour such as using fake identification, stealing from family or friends, hiring bootleggers, or buying from people involved in the criminal lifestyle. Also, since possession is likely to lead to use and intoxication, possession offences can be seen to be linked to the crimes that may result.

Selling Drugs

The fact that adolescents have a higher likelihood of using illicit drugs than adults do (Health Canada 2012a) provides an opportunity for some youths to get involved in the distribution of these drugs to other youth. While most youth access illicit drugs through social sources and very few exclusively buy their own drugs, a majority of youths who use drugs have bought drugs from people they know, often their friends (Harrison, Fulkerson, and Park 2000). This creates opportunities for youths to sell drugs to their peers.

Shook, Vaughn, and Salas-Wright (2013) found three main categories of youth involved in drug trafficking: dabblers, who had elevated rates of alcohol, tobacco, and marijuana use but low levels of actual drug selling, violence, other offending, and "harder" drug use; delinquents, who had higher rates of violence and offending, but moderate levels of drug selling, moderate use of alcohol, tobacco, and marijuana, and very low rates of other substance use; and externalizers, who had higher levels of drug selling, as well as high rates of violence and offending, substance use, and the use of "harder" drugs. For mainstream youth, selling drugs appears to be dependent on close peer connections and is largely limited to marijuana (Harrison et al. 2000).

Dealing in "harder" drugs or dealing outside of the close peer group is more common among youths who are more entrenched in drug cultures and already involved in criminal activity. In street-level dealing as well as in selling to mainstream youth, those young people who sell drugs are generally also drug users (Floyd et al. 2010) and involved in other risky activities (Shook et al. 2013). Research has indicated that selling drugs is common among chronic youth offenders (MacRae et al. 2008) and street-involved youth (Werb, Kerr, Li, Montaner, and Wood 2008). Although some research suggests that improving access to legitimate job opportunities would effectively reduce levels of drug dealing among youth (Ihlanfeldt 2007), since many drug dealers are also drug users, addressing issues of addiction and other substance abuse problems among adolescent drug dealers may also be necessary (Floyd et al. 2010; see also Box 10.1).

Box 10.1   Youth Justice in Action

The Story of Kirk

Kirk grew up on the family farm, living with his mother and stepfather. He had a difficult home life and was expected to attend school as well as work long hours on the farm. There was poor emotional connection between Kirk and his parents and little supervision of his time away from work. Kirk began using marijuana and alcohol when he was 13. The local police were aware of Kirk, as they often found him inebriated in their small rural town and would return him home. Initially, Kirk was able to pay for his substance abuse habit with

his farm wages, but as his substance use progressed to OxyContin and cocaine, he began to sell drugs to other youth in his community to support his habit. At 16 years of age Kirk was picked up for trafficking and incarcerated at the Young Offenders Centre.

Critical Thinking Question
What factors may have contributed to Kirk's decision to sell drugs to his peers?

Producing and Trafficking Drugs

Because drug markets are typically controlled by adult offenders, adolescent participation in drug distribution markets is largely dependent on whether young people are needed (Bouchard, Alain, and Nguyen 2009). Youth fill a niche in markets that are either inaccessible to adults, such as schools, or where the market exceeds the capacity of adult drug offenders, sometimes as a result of law-enforcement efforts (ibid.). The large number of growing operations have provided opportunities for high school–age youth to enter into a potentially lucrative illegal industry as labourers for adult growers or as operators of their own operations. The opportunity to enter into the drug production industry, moreover, extends beyond those youths who are already involved in other criminal activity, and it can lead to future criminal offending for youths who are successful and develop a criminal network (Nguyen and Bouchard 2010).

Organized criminals are often major players within the illegal drug production and trafficking industry (Royal Canadian Mounted Police 2010). These organized criminal groups can use youths to sell drugs to their peers, to work as **sitters**, or labourers in drug production operations, and to smuggle drugs, alcohol, and contraband tobacco across provincial or international borders (Richter-White 2002). For these youth, this involvement may seem like an opportunity to make money, while for adult organized criminals it is an opportunity to increase profits and reduce personal risk through low-cost and convenient labour (Bouchard et al. 2009).

The majority of youth involved in the drug industry have been found also to be drug users (Bouchard et al. 2009). They may become involved because doing so helps to support their drug use or because they do not perceive the drugs or the illegal activity to be particularly harmful, given the messages of decreasing support for the criminalization of marijuana possession (Milnor et al. 2009), the misinformation arising from the prohibition–legalization debate (Diplock, Cohen, and Plecas 2009), or the general confusion about the legal status of marijuana in the country (MacCoun, Pacula, Chriqui, Harris, and Reuter 2009). These youth may also lack enough of what they perceive to be good, legitimate opportunities for work at their age, which makes illegal drug crime an appealing option (Ihlanfeld 2007). There may be a need to improve employment opportunities and to have more consistent messaging about not just the negative effects of drug use but also the societal impact of the entire drug industry.

sitters
Individuals who are paid to tend to and protect the plants in a marijuana growing operation. Sitters may also appear to legitimately occupy a residence to avoid drawing suspicion.

Adolescent Substance Abuse Prevention

The significant harm to individuals and to society as a whole warrants considerable effort on preventing adolescent substance abuse. Research on effective prevention programs has shown a cost saving of $15–$18 on every dollar spent on substance abuse prevention (CCSA 2013). To get the most benefit possible from prevention efforts, it is imperative that these efforts be focused on strategies that incorporate evidence informed practices.

What Works?

Considerable time and effort have been spent in researching key factors in effective prevention programs. According to the CCSA's Compendium of Best Practices (Roberts et al. 2001), keys to effective substance abuse prevention programs include building a strong framework, striving for accountability, understanding and involving young people, and creating an effective process. These components emphasize the need for the message to be credible and based on accurate information that recognizes adolescent development and perceptions. Also, since many programs rely on teachers, student leaders, law-enforcement officers, and other professionals to take part as facilitators, those who lead or facilitate the programs must be competent, credible, empathetic, and able to interact well with youth (Roberts et al. 2001).

The Canadian Standards Task Force, in partnership with the CCSA, has developed the Canadian Standards for Youth Substance Abuse Prevention. The key principles expressed in these standards are as follows:

1. Prevention is most successful when schools, families, and organizations throughout the community are involved.

2. School-based prevention is most successful when it's integrated into the school's core mission and links to community initiatives.

3. Family skills training should be included in prevention initiatives (CCSA 2014).

The United Nations Office on Drugs and Crime (UNODC 2014) reviewed prevention programs for all age groups and identified programs and policies that were found to have positive prevention outcomes. Its review concluded that substance abuse prevention should ideally be delivered continuously over a lifetime with programs matched for the developmental and situational needs of the individual and group (ibid.). These effective prevention programs included a variety of approaches—universal, selective, and indicated programs. *Universal* prevention programs include initiatives that are appropriate for the population at large. *Selective* prevention programs include strategies appropriate for groups that are particularly at risk. *Indicated* prevention programs include strategies appropriate for individuals at risk.

School-Based Initiatives

Since most eventual drug users and those with substance abuse problems started their substance abuse before adulthood and because early initiation is a risk factor for later problems (Lubman, Hides, Yucel, and Toumbourou 2007), adolescence is an appropriate time to implement substance abuse prevention. Schools present an ideal setting for the delivery of all types of prevention programming—universal, selective, and indicated. Some types of universal prevention that were broadly delivered, such as Drug Abuse Resistance Education (DARE), have had disappointing results (Pan and Bai 2009), although the newly released curriculum appears to show more promise than in the past (see DARE 2014). Other programs, such as Life Skills Training and Project ALERT, have been found to be effective at reducing the levels of substance use, although not necessarily at preventing initiation (National Crime Prevention Centre 2009). The most effective type of universal school-based substance abuse prevention programs are skill-based, where youth are taught resistance skills and learn about the social influences of substance use while receiving other life skills training (UNODC 2014).

A combination of universal and selective prevention in schools results in school policies and culture that support prevention goals. Reviews of the effects of school policies and culture on adolescent substance abuse have found that ideal policies are created in consultation with all key stakeholders (e.g., students, parents, and staff). These policies include the mandate that substances will not be used on school property or at school events by anyone and include selective components such as cessation support and referral to promote healthy behavioural change rather than a focus on punishment (UNODC 2014). There are also prevention benefits to addressing the school environment; these entail increased commitment to school, student participation, and positive relationships, all of which show a positive effect in reducing substance abuse and other risk behaviours (ibid.).

Indicated prevention can include programs to support individual adolescents who have specific psychological vulnerabilities to substance abuse. Certain internalizing problems, such as mood and anxiety disorders, and externalizing disorders, such as ADHD and conduct disorders, can greatly increase the likelihood of a person's developing substance abuse disorders (Abu-Shakra and Cox 2014). These prevention programs are based on identifying youths at greater risk for substance abuse and training them to cope positively with difficult emotions. There is mounting evidence that these personality-centred interventions are effective in delaying the onset of alcohol and drug use (Conrod, Castellanos-Ryan, and Mackie 2011).

Although one of the benefits of school-based interventions is that these programs will reach the majority of adolescents, some of the high-risk adolescents who could most benefit from prevention programming may not be attending school and therefore do not have access to the programs (Saewyc 2007). These youths are often in greater need of prevention services (e.g., Bodnarchuk et al. 2006). Therefore, to reach this population, it is important that other prevention initiatives are in place, such as multi-faceted community-based interventions and family-based interventions.

Community-Based Multi-component Initiatives

Opportunities to prevent substance abuse and increase positive developmental outcomes for adolescents occur in many different settings and contexts. Positive prevention outcomes are most likely when prevention initiatives take a comprehensive approach that links school and families with other settings and organizations in the community (CCSA 2014). These community-based initiatives can be universal or selective in their targeting for the prevention initiative. Key components of successful community initiatives include supporting the enforcement of tobacco and alcohol policies; working in a range of community settings (families and schools, workplace, entertainment venues, etc.); and involving universities in the implementation of evidenced-based programs and their monitoring and evaluation (UNODC 2014). One example, the Communities That Care Program (CTC), in which community coalitions are developed and members receive training and support to address specific community-based issues, has shown success (Hawkins et al. 2012).

Family-Based Initiatives

Brotnow and Sinha (2014) pointed out, "[S]table and supportive family structures buffer the impact of stress and promote resilience in the child. Without that stability and support, the impact of other risk factors can be intensified." Family-based initiatives can be universal or selective prevention. Characteristics of an effective family-based initiative include enhancing family bonding; supporting parents in taking a more active role in their children's lives; supporting parents on how to provide positive and developmentally appropriate discipline; supporting parents in how to be role models for their children; and, making it easier for parents to participate (out of office hours, meals, child care, etc.). The Strengthening Families Program (SFP) is an example of a well-established family intervention program that focuses on family communication and parenting skills to reduce a variety of negative outcomes, including substance abuse. This program has been found to reduce children's problematic internalizing and externalizing behaviours, reduce parent and child substance abuse, and improve family communication and interaction styles (Trudeau, Spoth, Randall, Mason, and Shin 2012).

Anti-drug Media Campaigns

The message of substance abuse prevention is often spread through mass media campaigns, as they are highly visible and can carry a universal or selective prevention message. The "drugsnot4me" campaign (Canada 2014) involves television commercials and websites targeted at both youth and their parents. These media campaigns are intended to reach a wide audience and present messages that will resonate with youth as well as with adults. Media campaigns have traditionally involved television and print ads but have expanded by incorporating other media and technology such as websites, social networking websites, and cellphones. While there may be potential for media campaigns to effectively change the beliefs and behaviours of youth, improperly guided campaigns could simply be wasting resources (Palmgreen and Donohew 2003). Based on an understanding of the characteristics of youth who are most likely to use illicit drugs, anti-drug media campaigns may be more effective if they appeal to sensation-seeking youth by having novelty or "shock value" (ibid.). Effective media campaigns are those that precisely identify target groups; are grounded in a solid theoretical basis; have messages designed on the basis of strong formative research; strongly connect to existing drug prevention programs in the home, school, and community; achieve adequate exposure to the target group; are systematically evaluated throughout the campaign and adjusted for maximal effect; target parents as well as children; aim to change cultural norms about substance abuse; and/or educate about the consequences of substance abuse and suggest strategies to reduce substance abuse (UNODC 2014).

Alternatives to Fear-Based Communication

fear-based communication Messages used to frighten youth away from experimentation with substances by emphasizing the potential negative effects of use.

Researchers generally agree that **fear-based communication** is an ineffective approach to dissuading youth from using substances such as alcohol, tobacco, and marijuana (National Crime Prevention Centre 2009). The fear-based approach, although not untruthful in presenting information, overemphasizes the potential harms, highlighting worst-case scenarios and intentionally increasing the perceptions of the likelihood of harm. These messages contradict what the majority of youth will later or already know about the effects of substance abuse, potentially causing the messenger to lose credibility (Tupper 2008).

Perhaps, rather than emphasizing what youth should not do, messages should instead focus on promoting healthy living in general. The challenge is in finding ways to dissuade problematic substance use among adolescents without resorting to strategies that rely on fear and on the condemnation of the substances and substance users.

There is still value in credible and well-designed substance abuse prevention messages, directed at youth through school-based and mass media programs, that emphasize the potentially serious consequences of substance use, but these messages should be accompanied by a full complement of additional messages and alternative approaches. Tupper (2008) suggests that drug education should adopt the discourse of drugs as "tools," which, when used properly and for the right reasons, may be very beneficial, but when misused, can be socially harmful. Ideally, messaging would change the perception that unhealthy behaviours are "just part of growing up," perhaps by emphasizing that substance use is actually less normative than many youth perceive (Martens et al. 2006). Other prevention approaches might include increased taxation of unhealthy substances, regulation to ensure appropriate use and deter unsafe use, and **harm-reduction strategies** to address factors that contribute to the negative consequences associated with substance abuse (Toumbourou et al. 2009). These efforts could promote healthy lifestyles while providing the support necessary for those who are struggling with substance abuse issues. Consistency in the social messages across the lifespan is also important to consider, since the portrayal of substance use as normative for adults through advertising, entertainment, and actual consumption will influence adolescents (American Academy of Pediatrics 2010).

harm-reduction strategies
Any policies or programs that are designed to reduce the level of harm associated with substance use and abuse without requiring the cessation of use.

Substance Abuse Treatment for Young Offenders

Research has demonstrated the need for substance abuse treatment for young people involved in the justice system. Substance use among young offenders has been linked to high-risk sexual behaviour, violence, accidents, and harm to fetal development among pregnant women (Chassin 2008) and contributes to their criminal activity as well as negatively affecting their academics, peer-group involvement, and family relationships (Dowden 2003). Yet, both male and female young offenders show positive outcomes from participating in treatment programs (ibid. 2003). Unfortunately, even though many justice programs for adolescents contain in-house substance abuse treatment programs or link to community-based treatment programs, there has been very little focus on the effectiveness of the strategies used in the programs (Chassin 2008). As there are limited resources, it is important to ensure that the programs that are implemented are based on evidenced-based best practices.

Adolescent Substance Abuse Treatment Best Practices

No single treatment produces the best outcomes, but many approaches can be effective, including multi-systemic therapy, cognitive-behavioural therapy, contingency management, family therapy, motivational enhancement, and residential therapeutic communities

(Chassin 2008). Programs that were originally designed for adults are often delivered to youth, which may not be appropriate, so it is important to identify best practices for adolescent treatment. Health Canada (2008) has suggested best practices for substance abuse treatment for adolescents based on a review of relevant research, interviews with key experts, and focus groups with youth.

The following were identified as strategies for strengthening service delivery orientations:

- Use a readiness-to-change model. A widely accepted model for understanding and assessing treatment readiness was developed by Prochaska and Diclimente (1986) and outlines the stages that people go through when making major life changes. The stages include pre-contemplation, contemplation, preparation, action, maintenance, and relapse. Understanding the stage that a youth is in allows the program to match the youth appropriately to a treatment strategy most likely to increase his or her chance of succeeding in the behaviour change. This model is often paired with brief interventions that incorporate cognitive-behavioural approaches, motivational interviewing, and a focus on the youth's strengths (Levy, Vaughn, and Knight 2002).

- Strength-based programs that are designed to promote positive change by recognizing and engaging the strengths of youths, their families, and their communities.

- Youth perspectives should be pursued and youth leadership encouraged when organizing and delivering community-based, youth-focused services and programs. This includes the perspectives of non-users as well as those at risk of substance abuse issues.

- Youth-specific services should be offered rather than adult-oriented services that youths can also attend. These services should be developmentally appropriate, easily accessible, and available, with quick response times when youths express a desire to change their behaviour.

- Inclusive v. exclusive policies should be formulated that foster relationship development with positive adults and peers to encourage a sense of belonging and attachment to school and community.

Treatment Best Practices with Young Offenders

Many of the principles that apply to substance abuse treatment for the general youth population can be applied to youths who are involved in the justice system, but some unique needs and experiences should be taken into consideration when implementing treatment programs for young offenders. Dowden (2003) identified the importance of considering client characteristics, in-treatment factors, and post-treatment factors.

Key Client Characteristics

Key client characteristics to take into consideration when implementing a substance abuse treatment program for young offenders include age, gender, race/ethnicity, psychopathology, and risk (Dowden 2003). Programs for young offenders that have substance abuse treatment as one of their goals show greater success in reducing reoffending when they engage younger participants (ibid.). This supports the argument for the early identification and treatment of substance abuse problems in the adolescent population. In regard to gender differences in treatment outcomes, a meta-analytic database review found that for adult and youth offenders both males and females have positive outcomes from participation in substance abuse treatment programs. Research on the impact of race/ethnicity and treatment outcomes for young offenders is lacking, but the existing research suggests that treatment that is culturally appropriate has improved outcomes (ibid.).

As noted earlier in this chapter, psychopathology plays a role in the development of substance abuse problems and research supports the need to address co-occurring disorders within treatment programming. Level of risk is another important client characteristic to take into consideration when planning substance abuse treatment strategies. Treatment effectiveness is enhanced by matching the youths' needs with the appropriate treatment approach, and in the case of young offenders, this includes matching the young offender's level of involvement in substance abuse and criminal offending with intensity of treatment programming (Chassin 2008; see Box 10.2).

Box 10.2   Youth Justice in Action

The Story of Joanna

Joanna grew up in a large urban centre with her mother and sister. Joanna's father has not been involved with the family since she was 3 years old. Her mom has a history of substance abuse and has been diagnosed with bipolar disorder. Joanna and her sister were removed from their mother's care for two years and placed in foster care. Joanna's mother tries to be a good parent, but her own substance abuse and mental health issues limit her success. When she was only 9 years old, Joanna started using alcohol and marijuana. By the age of 16, she was also using crystal methamphetamine, cocaine, and OxyContin. She had traded sex for drugs before but did not consider that prostitution. Joanna was picked up by the police under the Protection of Sexually Exploited Children Act (PSECA) in Alberta. PSECA legislation allows for youths who are considered at immediate risk of engaging in prostitution to be apprehended by police or a delegated Enhancement Act caseworker and taken to a protective safe house. Joanna's mother did not support the PSECA order, and Joanna was released. Joanna later became involved with the criminal justice system when she was caught selling marijuana and crystal methamphetamine. Joanna met with an addictions counsellor while in custody, and when released she returned home and started an intensive drug and alcohol day-treatment program. Joanna attended the program six days before she left her mother's home, and she began living on the streets and using substances again. She was picked up again for selling drugs and admitted she had also been prostituting. She was returned to the Young Offenders Centre. She began seeing an addictions counsellor in custody. This time the focus was on ensuring that Joanna was matched with the appropriate level of support, and emphasis was on including a relapse prevention plan and a transition plan to help Joanna successfully reintegrate into the community. On her second release, she attended a residential program for young women who had been involved with prostitution, one that included substance abuse counselling. Joanna is now 18 years old, has returned home, and has not had any probation breaches or new criminal charges up to the time of the writing of this chapter.

Critical Thinking Question
What contributed to making Joanna's second attempt at substance abuse treatment more successful?

In-Treatment Factors

In-treatment factors to be considered in planning effective substance abuse treatment programs for adolescents include program content, delivery, and the organizational environment in which the program was delivered. Dowden (2003) found that, to increase program effectiveness, content should target multiple areas for young offenders, including family, academic, and peer problems, and incorporate elements of relapse prevention and cognitive-behavioural therapy. For program delivery, key factors for improving program effectiveness include program staff training, monitoring, and minimizing turnover (Chassin 2008). Organizational environment includes the setting and context of program delivery. Research into the ideal setting for substance abuse treatment for young offenders has found little difference in outcomes for in-patient versus out-patient substance abuse treatment (Annis 1990). This lends credence to the value of treatment matching—where the needs of the individual client are matched with the appropriate treatment program. It is important to have a number of treatment options available to assist in the matching of each individual adolescent with the appropriate program. Some adolescents would find treatment in a residential wilderness setting helpful as an opportunity to be removed from drug-using peers and/or family members and be exposed to experiential learning opportunities, while other youths, unfamiliar and uncomfortable with being in a wilderness setting, may see the location as a barrier to treatment. Similarly, attending a treatment group on-site in a justice setting may be a positive connection point for some adolescents, giving them the opportunity to deal with some difficult issues in a controlled setting, while other adolescents would feel unsafe sharing information about trauma and abuse with their peers in custody.

Post-treatment Factors

Two post-treatment factors that correlated with reductions in offending are aftercare services and initiatives that enhance protective factors (Dowden 2003). Aftercare services include activities and supports designed to help adolescents maintain their behaviour change following treatment. The substantial relapse rates associated with substance abuse have prompted some researchers to suggest that substance abuse should be managed as a chronic disorder characterized by relapse and remission (Chassin 2008). Therefore, researchers have argued that enhancing protective factors, or inherent strengths of youths, their families, and communities, should be an important goal of post-treatment interventions (Dowden 2003).

Summary

Despite the perception that drug use among youth is rising "out of control" (Saewyc 2009), there have recently been general decreases in rates of adolescent substance use across Canada (CCSA 2011; Health Canada 2012a). When considering the trend toward these lower rates, we must not allow them to overshadow the fact that alcohol, marijuana, and, to a lesser but still notable degree, tobacco use is common among adolescents and that usage rates are substantially higher than those of adults (Health Canada 2012a). In fact, when considering adolescent populations outside the mainstream population, even the use of so-called hard drugs is common (Public Health Agency of Canada 2006). While experimenting, coping with the struggles of adolescence, and generally fitting in all act together to produce "past-year" adolescent substance use rates above those of adults, the lifetime use of many substances is similar among adolescents and adults. Indeed, those substances with relatively higher past-year usage rates among young people are generally the same substances that exhibit higher rates among adults (Health Canada 2012a). This suggests that not only will the majority of adolescents who experiment with substances abstain in the future but also that the substance use of adolescents is largely reflective of adult substance use.

Adolescent substance abuse, its consequences on the future of Canada's young people, and its potential to create problems associated with crime and criminality are ongoing concerns in this country. Hundreds of millions of dollars are spent on law-enforcement efforts, education, research, and media campaigns to get youth to say that drugs and alcohol are "not for me." Students in the field of crime control, policing, and criminology must critically assess the direction of drug policies, other prevention strategies, and treatment programs, and work toward improving these programs where needed and forging new directions when existing ones prove inadequate, inappropriate, or counterproductive.

Key Terms

abuse	proactive police work
binge drinking	psychosis
co-morbidity	sitters
dependence	social desirability effects
drug recognition expert (DRE) evaluation	stigma
fear-based communication	street-involved youth
harm-reduction strategies	substance abuse
method of administration	

Review Questions

1. Although it is recognized that marijuana is not a "gateway drug" leading directly to the use of other drugs, are there ways that marijuana use might contribute to other drug use?

2. What are the potential physical and psychological harms that adolescents may experience with substance abuse?

3. Consider Goldstein's tripartite drug-crime model. Which, if any, of the three modes do you feel best fits the relationship between adolescent substance use and criminal behaviour?

4. As was discussed in this chapter, some Canadian youth become involved in drug crime beyond "simple" possession (drug dealing, working in marijuana growing operations, joining gangs who traffic in drugs, etc.). What factors might lead young Canadians to engage in this type of criminal behaviour?

5. What are the differences between universal, selective, and indicated prevention?

6. What are the key components of a substance abuse treatment program for adolescents?

Critical Thinking Questions

1. In your opinion, what are the reasons that adolescents use drugs and what causes experimentation to lead to substance abuse?

2. Many schools and law-enforcement agencies in Canada work in concert to provide drug prevention information to children and adolescents, with police officers taking on the role of drug prevention educators. What might be some advantages and disadvantages of police officers' taking on this role in substance use prevention?

3. If you were responsible for designing a program in your community to dissuade youth from impaired driving, what would you focus on?

4. In your opinion, how well do your province's alcohol and tobacco regulations (minimum-age limits, rules surrounding advertising, licensing of drinking establishments, anti-smoking regulations, etc.) reduce adolescent substance use or make it less harmful? In what ways do you feel these regulations inadvertently contribute to adolescent substance use or make it more harmful?

5. As a result of the association between substance use/abuse and crime, substance use issues become of concern to health-care and criminal justice systems, among others. What do you think would be the ideal balance between the health-care and criminal justice systems to reduce and prevent the harms associated with substance use?

References

Abu-Shakra, M., and Cox, S. (2014). The externalizing developmental pathway to substance use disorders. In M. Leyton and S. Stewart (Eds). (2014). *Substance abuse in Canada: Childhood and adolescent pathways to substance use disorders* (pp. 27–47). Ottawa: Canadian Centre on Substance Abuse.

Adlaf, E.M., Begin, P., and Sawka, E. (Eds). (2005). *Canadian Addictions Survey (cas): A national survey of Canadians' use of alcohol and other drugs: Prevalence of use and related harms: Detailed Report*. Ottawa: Canadian Centre on Substance Abuse.

American Academy of Pediatrics. (2010). Policy statement—Children, adolescents, substance abuse, and the media. *Pediatrics, 126*(4): 791–9.

Annis, H.M. (1990). Effective treatment for drug and alcohol problems: What do we know? *Forum on Corrections Research, 2*(4): 18–23.

Barrett, S.P., Darredeau, C., and Pihl, R.O. (2006). Patterns of simultaneous polysubstance use in drug using university students. *Human Psychopharmacology: Clinical and Experimental, 21*: 255–63.

Bauman, K.E., and Ennett, S.T. (1996). On the importance of peer influence for adolescent drug use: Commonly neglected considerations. *Addiction, 91*(2): 185–98.

Beasley, E.E., and Beirness, D.J. (2012). *Alcohol and drug use among drivers following the introduction of immediate roadside prohibitions in British Columbia: Findings from the 2012 roadside survey*. Ottawa: Beirness & Associates.

Behrendt, S., Wittchen, H.U., Holfer, M., Lieb, R., and Beesdo, K. (2009). Transitions from first substance use to substance use disorders in adolescence: Is early onset associated with a rapid escalation? *Drug and Alcohol Dependence, 99*(1–3): 68–78.

Bennet, T., and Holloway, K. (2009). Causal connection between drug misuse and crime. *British Journal of Criminology, 49*(4): 513–31.

Benowitz, N.L. (2009). Pharmacology of nicotine: Addiction, smoking-induced disease, and therapeutics. *Annual Review of Pharmacology and Toxicology, 49*: 57–71.

Bodnarchuk, J., Patton, D., and Rieck, T. (2006). *Adolescence without shelter: A comprehensive description of issues faced by street youth in Winnipeg.* Winnipeg: Addiction Foundation of Manitoba.

Bouchard, M., Alain, M., and Nguyen, H. (2009). Convenient labour: The prevalence and nature of youth involvement in the cannabis cultivation industry. *International Journal of Drug Policy, 20*(6): 467–74.

Brochu, S. (2013). When youth combine drugs and violence: An explosive cocktail. *Istanbul Universitesi Huku Fakultesi Mecmuasi, 71*(1): 177–93.

Brotnow, L., and Sinha, R. (2014). *A developmental approach to prevention and intervention.* Ottawa: Canadian Centre on Substance Abuse.

Brunelle, N., Brochu, S., and Cousineau, M. (2000). Drug-crime relations among drug-consuming juvenile delinquents: A tripartite model and more. *Contemporary Drug Problems, 27*: 835–66.

CAMH (Centre for Addiction and Mental Health). (2009). *Do you know . . . tobacco.* Retrieved from http://www.camh.net/About_Addiction_Mental_Health/Drug_and_Addiction_Information/tobacco_dyk.html

CAMH. (n.d.). *Psychosis.* Retrieved from http://www.camh.ca/en/hospital/health_information/a_z_mental_health_and_addiction_information/psychosis/Pages/Psychosis.aspx

Canada. Department of Justice. (2014). *National anti-drug strategy: Backgrounder.* Retrieved from http://news.gc.ca/web/article-en.do?nid=811359

CCSA (Canadian Centre on Substance Abuse). (2011). *Cross-Canada report on student alcohol and drug use: Technical report.* Ottawa: Author.

CCSA. (2013). *A case for investing in youth substance abuse prevention.* Retrieved from http://www.ccsa.ca/Resource%20Library/2012-ccsa-Investing-in-youth-substance-abuse-prevention-en.pdf

CCSA. (2014). *Drug prevention standards.* Retrieved 13 September 2014 from http://www.ccsa.ca/Eng/topics/Children-and-Youth/Drug-Prevention-Standards/Pages/default.aspx

CDSA (Controlled Drugs and Substances Act, S.C., c.19). (1996). Retrieved from http://laws-lois.justice.gc.ca/eng/acts/C-38.8/FullText.html

Centre for Addictions Research BC. (2009). *Adolescent substance use and related harms in British Columbia.* Victoria, BC: Author.

Chan, Y., Dennis, M.L., and Funk, R.R. (2008). Prevalence and co-morbidity of major internalizing and externalizing problems among adolescents and adults presenting to substance abuse treatment. *Journal of Substance Abuse Treatment, 34*(1): 14–24.

Chassin, L. (2008). Juvenile justice and substance use. *Future of Children, 18*(2): 165–83.

Conrod, P.J., Castellanos-Ryan, N., and Mackie C. (2011). Long-term effects of personality-targeted intervention to reduce alcohol use in adolescents. *Journal of Consulting and Clinical Psychology, 79*(3): 296–306.

Cooper, K., May, D., Soderstrom, I., and Jarjoura, G.R. (2009). Examining theoretical predictors of substance use among a sample of incarcerated youth. *Journal of Offender Rehabilitation, 48*(8): 669–95.

DARE (Drug Abuse Resistance Education). (2014). Retrieved from http://drugawareness.bc.rcmp-grc.gc.ca/ViewPage.action?siteNodeId=651&languageId=1&contentId=-1

Dauvergne, M. (2009). Trends in police-reported drug offences in Canada. *Juristat, 29*(2). Retrieved 28 September 2010 from http://www.statcan.gc.ca/pub/85-002-x/2009002/article/10847-eng.pdf

Dauvergne, M., and Turner, J. (2010). Police-reported crime statistics in Canada, 2009. *Juristat, 30*(2). Retrieved from http://www.statcan.gc.ca/pub/85-002-x/2010002/article/11292-eng.pdf

Degenhardt, L., and Hall, W. (2006). Is cannabis use a contributory cause of psychosis? *Canadian Journal of Psychiatry, 51*: 556–65.

Degenhardt, L., Hall, W., and Lynskey, M. (2002). Testing hypotheses about the relationship between cannabis and psychosis. *Drug and Alcohol Dependence, 71*: 37–48.

Diplock, J., Cohen, I., and Plecas, D. (2009). A review of the research on the risks and harms associated to the use of marijuana. *Journal of Global Drug Policy and Practice, 3*(2). Retrieved from http://www.globaldrugpolicy.org/3/2/3.php

Diplock, J., and Plecas, D. (2009). *Clearing the smoke on cannabis: Respiratory effects of cannabis smoking.* Ottawa: Canadian Centre on Substance Abuse.

Diplock, J., and Plecas, D. (2010). Revisiting age and crime. *Journal of Criminal Justice Research, 1*(2).

Dore, G., and Sweeting, M. (2006). Drug-induced psychosis associated with crystalline methamphetamine. *Australasian Psychiatry, 14*(1): 86–9.

Dowden, C. (2003). *The effectiveness of substance abuse treatment with young offenders.* Ottawa: Department of Justice Canada.

Erickson, P.G., and Butters, J.E. (2005). How does the Canadian juvenile justice system respond to detained youth with substance associated problems? *Substance Use and Misuse, 40*(7): 953–73.

Felson, R., Savolainen, J., Aaltonen, M., and Moustgaard, H. (2008). Is the association between alcohol use and delinquency causal or spurious? *Criminology, 46*(3): 785–808.

Floyd, L.J., Alexandre, P.K., Hedden, S.L., Lawson, A., Latimer, W.W., and Giles, N. (2010). Adolescent drug dealing and race/ethnicity: A population-based study of the differential impact of substance use on involvement in drug trade. *American Journal of Drug and Alcohol Abuse, 36*(10): 87–91.

Friedman, D.P. (2009). Drug addiction: A chronically relapsing brain disease. *North Carolina Medical Journal, 70*(1): 35–7.

Goldstein, P.J. (1985). The drugs-violence nexus: A tripartite conceptual framework. *Journal of Drug Issues, 15*: 493–506.

Harris, J.R. (1995). Where is the child's environment? A group socialization theory of development. *Psychological Review, 102*(3): 458–89.

Harrison, L.D., Erickson, P.G., Adlaf, E., and Freeman, C. (2001). The drugs-violence nexus among American and Canadian youth. *Substance Use and Misuse, 36*(14): 2065–86.

Harrison, P.A., Fulkerson, J.A., and Park, E. (2000). The relative importance of social versus commercial sources in youth access to tobacco, alcohol, and other drugs. *Preventive Medicine, 31*: 39–48.

Hawkins, J.D., Oesterle, S., Brown, E.C., Monahan, K.C., Abbott, R.D., Arthur, M.W., et al. (2012). Sustained decreases in risk exposure and youth problem behaviors after installation of the Communities That Care prevention system in a randomized trial. *Archives of Pediatrics and Adolescent Medicine, 166*(2): 141–8.

Hayaki, J., Hagerty, C.E., Herman, D.S., de Dois, M.A., Anderson, B.J., and Stein, M.D. (2010). Expectancies and marijuana use frequency and severity among young females. *Addictive Behaviours, 35*: 995–1000.

Health Canada. (2008). *Best practices: Early intervention, outreach and community linkages of youth with substance abuse problems.* Retrieved from http://www.hc-sc.gc.ca/hc-ps/alt_formats/pacrb-dgapcr/pdf/pubs/adp-apd/bp-mp-intervention/Youth_Outreach.pdf

Health Canada. (2009). *Not4Me: Youth drug prevention.* Retrieved from http://www.hc-sc.gc.ca/hc-ps/drugs-drogues/youth-jeunes/index-eng.php

Health Canada. (2012a). *Canadian alcohol and drug use monitoring survey.* Retrieved from http://www.hc-sc.gc.ca/hc-ps/drugs-drogues/stat/_2012/tables-tableaux-eng.php#t4

Health Canada. (2012b). Canadian tobacco use monitoring survey (CTUMS) 2012. Retrieved from http://www.hc-sc.gc.ca/hc-ps/tobac-tabac/research-recherche/stat/ctums-esutc_2012-eng.php

Health Canada. (2014). Summary of the results of the Youth Smoking Survey 2012–2013. Retrieved from http://www.hc-sc.gc.ca/hc-ps/tobac-tabac/research-recherche/stat/_survey-sondage_2012-2013/result-eng.php

Hunt, G., Moloney, M., and Evans, K. (2009). Epidemiology meets cultural studies: Studying and understanding youth cultures, clubs and drugs. *Addiction Research and Theory, 17*(6): 601–21.

Ihlanfeldt, K.R. (2007). Neighborhood drug crime and young males' job accessibility. *Review of Economics and Statistics, 89*(1): 151–64.

Lea, S., Black, K., and Asbridge, M. (2009). An overview of injuries to adolescents and young adults related to substance abuse: Data from Canadian emergency departments. *Canadian Journal of Emergency Medicine, 11*(4): 330–6.

Levy, S., Vaughn, B.L., and Knight, J.R. (2002). Office-based interventions for adolescent substance abuse. *Pediatric Clinics of North America, 49*: 329–43.

Looby, A., and Earleywine, M. (2007). Negative consequences associated with dependence in daily cannabis users. *Substance Abuse: Treatment, Prevention, and Policy, 2*: 3.

Lubman, D.I., Hides, L., Yucel, M., and Toumbourou, J.W. (2007). Intervening early to reduce developmentally harmful substance use among youth populations. *Medical Journal of Australia*, 187: S22–S25.

McClelland, G.M., and Teplin, L.A. (2001). Alcohol intoxication and violent crime: Implications for public health policy. *American Journal on Addictions*, 10: s70–s85. doi: 10.1080/10550490150504155

MacCoun, R., Pacula, R.L., Chriqui, J., Harris, K., and Reuter, P. (2009). Do citizens know whether their state has decriminalized marijuana? Assessing the perceptual component of deterrence theory. *Review of Law and Economics*, 5(1): 347–71.

MacRae, L.D., Bertrand, L.D, Paetsch, J.J., and Hornick, P. (2008). *A profile of youth offenders in Calgary: An interim report*. Prepared for the City of Calgary and the Alberta Law Foundation. Calgary: Canadian Research Institute for Law and the Family.

Martens, M.P., Page, J.C., Mowry, E.S., Damann, K.M., Taylor, K.K., and Cimini, M.D. (2006). Differences between actual and perceived student norms: An examination of alcohol use, drug use, and sexual behaviour. *Journal of American College Health*, 54(5): 295–300.

Martin, S.E., Maxwell, C.D., White, H.R., and Zhang, Y. (2004). Trends in alcohol use, cocaine use, and crime: 1989–1998. *Journal of Drug Issues*, 4(2): 333–60.

Milnor, M., Monaghan, M., Montero, D., Reyes, M., Roman, T., Tollasken, R., et al. (2009). North Americans' attitudes toward illegal drugs. *Journal of Human Behaviour in the Social Environment*, 19(2): 125–41.

Mooney, G.H. (2005). Addictions and social compassion. *Drug and Alcohol Review*, 24: 137–41.

Murray, L.F., and Belenko, S. (2005). CASASTART: A community-based school-centered intervention for high-risk youth. *Substance Use and Misuse*, 40(7): 913–33.

National Crime Prevention Centre. (2009). *School-based drug abuse prevention: Promising and successful programs*. Ottawa: Author.

Newcomb, M.D., and Bentlar, P.M. (1989). Substance use and abuse among children and teenagers. *American Psychologist*, 44(2): 242–8.

Nguyen, H., and Bouchard, M. (2011). Need, connections, or competence? Criminal achievement among adolescent offenders. *Justice Quarterly*, 30(1): 44–83.

NIDA (National Institute on Drug Abuse). (2011). Commonly abused drugs. Retrieved from http://www.drugabuse.gov/drugs-abuse/commonly-abused-drugs/commonly-abused-drugs-chart

O'Leary-Barrett, M. (2014). The internalizing developmental pathway to substance use disorders. In M. Leyton and S. Stewart (Eds), *Substance abuse in Canada: Childhood and adolescent pathways to substance use disorders*. Ottawa: Canadian Centre on Substance Abuse.

Palmgreen, P., and Donohew, L. (2003). Effective mass media strategies for drug abuse prevention campaigns. In Z. Sloboda and W.J. Bukoski (Eds), *Handbook of drug abuse prevention: Theory, science, and practice*. New York: Kluwer Academic/Plenum Publishers.

Palys, T.S., and Atchinson, C. (2014). *Research decisions: Quantitative and qualitative perspectives* (5th ed.). Toronto: Harcourt Brace & Company.

Pan, W., and Bai, H. (2009). A multivariate approach to a meta-analytic review of the effectiveness of the DARE program. *International Journal of Environmental Research and Public Health*, 6: 267–77.

Pearson, C., Janz, T., and Ali, J. (2011). *Statistics Canada: The 10 leading causes of death 2011*. Retrieved from http://www.statcan.gc.ca/pub/82-625-x/2014001/article/11896-eng.htm

Pernanen, K., Cousinea, M., Brochu, S., and Sun, F. (2002). *Proportions of crimes associated with alcohol and other drugs in Canada*. Ottawa: Canadian Centre on Substance Abuse.

Prochaska, J., and DiClimente, C. (1986). Towards a comprehensive model of change. In W.R. Millet and N. Heather (Eds), *Treating addictive behaviours: Process of change* (pp. 3–27). New York: Plenum.

Public Health Agency of Canada. (2006). *Street youth in Canada: Findings from enhanced surveillance of Canadian street youth, 1999–2003*. Ottawa: Author.

Rehm, J., Baliunas, D., Brochu, S., Fischer, B., Gnam, W., Patra, J., et al. (2006a). *The costs of substance abuse in Canada 2002*. Ottawa: Canadian Centre on Substance Abuse.

Rehm, J., Geisbrecht, N., Popova, S., Patra, J., Adlaf, E., and Mann, R. (2006b). *Overview of positive and negative effects of alcohol consumption-implications for preventive policies in Canada*. Toronto: Centre for Addiction and Mental Health.

Rehm, J., Gnam, W., Popova, S., Baliunas, D., Brochu, B., Fischer, B., et al. (2007). The costs of alcohol, illegal drugs, and tobacco in Canada, 2002. *Journal of Studies on Alcohol and Drugs* 68: 886–95.

Richter-White, H. (2002). The direct and indirect impacts of organized crime on youth, as offenders and victims. *Trends in Organized Crime*, 7(4): 79–111.

Roberts, G., McCall, D., Stevens-Leavigne, A., Anderson, J., Paglia, A., Bollenbach, S., et al. (2001). *Preventing substance use problems among young people: A compendium of best practices*. Ottawa: Canadian Centre on Substance Abuse.

Room, R. (2005). Stigma, social inequality and alcohol and drug use. *Drug and Alcohol Review, 24:* 143–55.

Royal Canadian Mounted Police. (2010). *Report on the illicit drug situation in Canada—2009*. Ottawa: Author.

Saewyc, E.M. (2007). Substance use among non-mainstream youth. In *Substance abuse in Canada: Youth in focus*. Ottawa: Canadian Centre on Substance Abuse.

Saewyc, E.M. (2009). Alcohol and other drug use among BC students: Myths and realities. *Visions Journal*, 5(2): 8–9.

Shepherd, J.P., Sutherland, I., and Newcombe, R.G. (2006). Relations between alcohol, violence and victimization in adolescence. *Journal of Adolescence*, 29: 539–53.

Shook, J.J., Vaughn, M.G., and Salas-Wright, C.P. (2013). Exploring the variation in drug selling among adolescents in the United States. *Journal of Criminal Justice*, 41: 365–74.

Smith, M.J., Thirthalli, J., Abdallah, A.B., Murray, R.M., and Cottler, L.B. (2009). Prevalence of psychotic symptoms in substance users: A comparison across substances. *Comprehensive Psychiatry, 50*(3): 245–50.

Squeglia, L.M., Jacobus, J., and Tapert, S.F. (2009). The influence of substance use on adolescent brain development. *Journal of Clinical eeg and Neuroscience*, 40(1): 31–8.

Steinberg, L. (2004). Risk taking in adolescence: What changes and why? In R.E. Dahl and L.P. Spear (Eds), *Adolescent brain development and opportunities*, Vol. 1021 (pp. 51–8). New York: Annals of New York Academy of Sciences.

Teed, R. (2009, 26 February). Adolescent use of drugs, liquor nears epidemic. *Star-Phoenix*. Retrieved 17 September 2010 from Canadian Newsstand.

Terry-McElrath, Y.M., O'Malley, P.M., and Johnston, L.D. (2009). Reasons for drug use among American youth by consumption level, gender, and race/ethnicity: 1976–2005. *Journal of Drug Issues, 39*(3): 677–714.

Testa, M., and Livingston, J.A. (2009). Alcohol consumption and women's vulnerability to sexual victimization: Can reducing women's drinking prevent rape? *Substance Use and Misuse, 44:* 1349–76.

Thoma, R.J., Monnig, M.A., Lysne, P.A., Ruhl, D.A., Pommy, J.A., Bogenschutz, M., et al. (2010). Adolescent substance abuse: The effects of alcohol and marijuana on neuropsychological performance. *Alcoholism: Clinical and Experimental Research*. doi: 10.1111/j.1530-0277.2010.01320.x

Thorpe, L.E., Ouellet, L.J., Hershow, R., Bailey, S.L., Williams, I.T., Williamson, J., et al. (2002). Risk of hepatitis C virus infection among young adult injection drug users who share injection equipment. *American Journal of Epidemiology, 155*(7): 645–53.

Toumbourou, J.W., Stockwell, T., Neighbors, C., Marlatt, G.A., Sturge, J., and Rehm, J. (2009). Interventions to reduce harm associated with adolescent substance use. *Lancet, 369:* 1391–401.

Treadwell, S.D., and Robinson, T.G. (2007). Cocaine use and stroke. *Postgraduate Medical Journal*, 83: 389–94.

Trudeau, L., Spoth, R., Randall, G.K., Mason, A., and Shin, C. (2012). Internalizing symptoms: Effects of a prevention intervention on developmental pathways from early adolescence to young adulthood. *Journal of Clinical Child and Adolescent Psychology*, 42(3): 287–301.

Tupper, K.W. (2008). Drugs, discourses and education: A critical discourse analysis of a high school drug education text. *Discourse: Studies in the Cultural Politics of Education, 29*(2): 223–38.

UNODC (United Nations Office on Drugs and Crime). (2010). World Drug Report 2010. Retrieved from http://www.unodc.org/unodc/en/data-and-analysis/WDR-2010.html

UNODC. (2014). International Standard on Drug Prevention. Retrieved from https://www.unodc.org/unodc/en/prevention/prevention-standards.html

Urban Health Research Initiative. (2009). *Drug situation in Vancouver*. Vancouver: British Columbia Centre for Excellence in HIV/AIDS.

Vaccarino, F. (2007). Drug abuse, addiction and youth: A neuroscience perspective. In *Substance abuse in Canada: Youth in focus*. Ottawa: Canadian Centre on Substance Abuse.

Warner, B.D., and Wilson-Coomer, B. (2003). Neighborhood drug arrest rates: Are they a meaningful indicator of drug activity? A research note. *Journal of Research in Crime and Delinquency, 40*(2): 123–38.

Wells, S.L., and Thompson, J.M. (2009). Alcohol-related victimization among young adult Canadian drinkers: The explanatory roles of hazardous drinking and illicit drug use. *Canadian Journal of Public Health, 100*(1): 55–9.

Werb, D., Kerr, T., Li, K., Montaner, J., and Wood, E. (2008). Risks surrounding drug trade involvement among street-involved youth. *American Journal of Drug and Alcohol Abuse, 34*: 810–20.

Winters, K.C., and Arria, A. (2011). Adolescent brain development and drugs. *Prevention Researcher, 18*(2): 21–4.

Wolfe, D.A., Jaffe, P.G., and Crooks, C.V. (2006). *Adolescent risk behaviours: Why teens experiment and strategies to keep them safe*. New Haven, CT: Yale University Press.

World Health Organization. (2014). *Global status report on alcohol and health 2014*. Geneva: Author.

Aboriginal Youth Crime in Canada

Hirsch Greenberg, Jana Grekul, and Rhonda Nelson

Overview

This chapter explores historical policies that influenced Aboriginal youth crime and youth justice in Canada, outlining both the historical relationship between Aboriginal and non-Aboriginal peoples and the intergenerational effects of this relationship on Aboriginal youth. It is founded on an understanding of Aboriginal youth crime, outlining specific historical policies and processes that have contributed to the intergenerational trauma of lived experiences expressed as a loss of identity, family dysfunction, substance abuse, violence, lack of education, unemployment, poverty, experiences of racism and discrimination, gang involvement, and overrepresentation in the criminal justice system. Furthermore, the chapter draws on Aboriginal authors and representations to explore the possibility and value of using Aboriginal-based approaches to justice that more appropriately fit with, and address, the traumas that lead to criminal behaviours in the first place.

Key Objectives

After reading this chapter, you should be able to:

* Understand the complexities of youth and crime in an Aboriginal context.
* Contextualize Aboriginal youth crime with respect to individual risk factors, protective factors, and social environmental factors.
* Understand complex Aboriginal youth crime behaviours from individual, community, and historical perspectives.
* Review Canadian judicial responses to Aboriginal youth crime.
* Compare mainstream responses with alternative justice approaches.
* Identify future avenues for intervention that are culturally sensitive and socially responsible, that hold individuals accountable, and that can positively affect Aboriginal youth.

Introduction

Crime, committed by a youth or an adult, is often reported by mainstream media as ubiquitous. Criminals are painted as faceless strangers invading our communities. Media reports neglect to mention that criminals are members of our communities and are a creation of our communities (see Box 11.1). Is crime everywhere? Maybe it just appears that way.

This outlook drives a wedge between "law-abiding citizens" and those who "choose" to commit unlawful acts. A "get tough" approach is considered by some to be the definitive answer to crime.

Yet, while we recognize and acknowledge the suffering of victims, the suffering and victimization of many offenders passes unnoticed. For example, many offenders feel that they do not or cannot meet the social and economic expectations of society, and as a consequence, these individuals can be identified by their disengagement and detachment from acceptable social participation. Punishment in the form of incarceration confirms their world view that social acceptance is biased and unjust, that they are outsiders and unworthy of belonging. While "getting tough" on offenders is a popular approach in some circles to dealing with crime, Dietrich Bonhoeffer (1906–1945), a Lutheran minister and anti-Nazi dissident whose experiences emerged from the concentration camps of World War II, suggests a different response: "We must learn to respond to people less in the light of what they do or omit to do, and more in the light of what they suffer" (in Braswell et al. 2005, p. 447).

If we are to recognize the suffering caused by crime and compassionately respond to victims and offenders, we must acknowledge all those who suffer.

Box 11.1   Youth Justice in Action

Crime Is Everywhere

By Daphne Branham
Vancouver Sun, **29 December 2010**

I'm done with my life of crime. All those murderers, drug dealers, rapists, serial killers. Sure, in the end justice is usually done, but I'm finished with that as well.

Crime crept so stealthily into my life that I scarcely noticed it.

But I've had it.

No more *Mentalist*. No more csı, regardless of the location. No more *Blue Bloods, Hawaii Five-O,*

Lie to Me or any of those others. I don't have to give up *Dexter* because even at my worst, I could never bear even the idea that a psychopathic serial killer could be a "hero."

Television is so stuffed with blood, guts, murder, torture, gang fights, rapes and all manner of evil. Crime has become a prime source of all entertainment, even though most is nearly devoid of the mystery that makes whodunits so appealing. . . .

Source: Retrieved 3 February 2011 from http://www.canada.com/vancouversun/news/westcoastnews/story.html?id=07267aa8-7f9f-4282-8de0-e82c3d8f124a

It would appear that one can, with empirical support, talk about broad changes in the US population in support of punitive policies. However,

> that the increase in support for punitive policies occurred at the same time as the public turned away from [social] solutions to poverty is no coincidence. . . . The ups and downs of punitive sentiment are driven by important political factors such as the construction of crime by political leaders. The framing of crime as a problem of a permissive system and increasing perceptions of racial integration increased public demand for punitive policies. (Ramirez 2013, p. 357)

Aboriginal
Includes individuals who identify as First Nations, Métis, or Inuit.

The approach taken in this chapter is to understand **Aboriginal** youth crime as an outcome of historical policies, practices, and processes that have resulted in severe and entrenched trauma among generations of Aboriginal peoples in Canada. The underlying contributing factors in Aboriginal youth crime are varied and reflect a complex web of historical and existing conditions that in some ways sets these actions apart from other criminal events. Car theft by a 13-year-old Aboriginal youth whose home and other socio-economic environments are unhealthy is not equivalent to the same criminal offence committed by a 56-year-old, white, middle-class male income earner.

As we explore the issues, we will observe that for some Canadians crime is not about an act committed against the queen or about a law broken (see Chapter 2); rather, it is about harm and harmed relationships. Often these harms or criminal offences are heavily influenced by relationships between individuals, families, and communities and intersect with broader societal processes. These behaviours and harmed relationships, while often defined as criminal by Western judgment, are an expression of the traumatizing and victimizing experiences of Aboriginal peoples and Aboriginal youth in particular. They are manifestations of anomie, strain, or normlessness—in other words, of feelings of being lost. **Values** from Aboriginal knowledge and experience inform us that expressions of anomie are essentially about broken relationships, a consistent theme throughout Aboriginal justice perspectives. If we take this approach to understanding youth misbehaviour, it becomes more difficult to "get tough" and becomes more relevant to explore responsive alternatives to crime. Understanding the offender and the context within which he or she has "chosen" to commit an offence leads us to consider the value of a healing perspective that focuses on the reparation of the harms done instead of exacerbating already damaged relationships.

Who is an offender? Is it someone who shows little regard for the law or who disregards right relationships, demonstrating little respect for others? Navajos say of such a person, "He acts as if he has no relatives." So, what do you do when someone acts as if they have no relatives? You bring in the relatives (Chief Justice Robert Yazzie, Navajo First Nation, in McCaslin 2005, p. 85).

How we define crime—by a law or by a relationship harmed—decides the path we take toward understanding, explaining, intervening, and resourcing solutions. We are reminded of an Aboriginal youth who shared his story with the second author when he was apprehended with a weapon while attending school: "Why do you have a weapon?" I asked. "For protection!" the youth responded. "Protection from what?" I responded quizzically. "Someone wants to beat me up," stated the youth. "Why?" I asked. "Because my brother beat him up!" Pursuing his logic, I explored the story further: "Why did your brother beat him up?" "Because," said the youth, "he stole my brother's bike!" Pausing, I thought about the youth's responses. "So, why is the boy going after you, and not your brother?" (I thought there was a hole in his story.) "Because my brother is bigger than he is!" he argued. Ah . . . retribution, I thought. I asked, "Who do you think is winning this fight, you, the boy who is after you, or your brother?" "My brother! Because he beat up the boy who stole his bike." "Yes, I can see that," I said, "but your brother doesn't have a bike!" The youth was silent.

In this anecdote, the three Aboriginal youths did not turn to any legal or school authority, or even to an adult with their problem of a relationship harmed. They simply took matters into their own hands. We can speculate as to how many times this story plays out among Aboriginal youth. Cousins's reflects that before the "Great Law" was introduced, the Haudenosaunee lived pretty much as these three youths: engaged in blood feuds and revenge and repeating the cycle of vengeance. In response to this internal violence and strife, the Creator sent the Peacemaker to convince the Haudenosaunee to accept the Great Law of Peace and to establish one of the most powerful political alliances on the North America continent (as cited in McCaslin 2005, p. 145).

Injustices in the lives of young Aboriginals beckon redress, but with nowhere to turn, retribution, either against each other or against those with more social privilege, seems the only answer. This is an outcome of processes set in motion centuries ago and is reflective of the destruction of social, cultural, and economic well-being since contact with Europeans. What happened to this once flourishing and rich social fabric comprising "a variety of languages, cultures and social traditions" (Royal Commission on Aboriginal Peoples 1996, p. 6), existing in social cohesion and characterized by group conformity, reverence for nature and community, and awareness of the Creator (Dumont 1996)?

values
A collective conception of what is considered proper, desirable, and good—or improper, undesirable, and bad—in a culture.

Understanding the Complexities of Aboriginal Youth Crime

> This report is for Lawrence Wegner, Rodney Naistus, Pamela George, Leo La Chance, and the many unnamed Aboriginal men and women who have paid the ultimate price for ignorance and neglect. . . . While these men, and women, who were sons, daughters, fathers and mothers, are gone . . . they are not forgotten.
>
> —Commission on First Nations and Métis Peoples and Justice Reform, 2003–04. Final Report, vol. 2 (2003), (s. 1, p. 1)

The complexities of Aboriginal youth crime interlace two main features. First is the shared experience of Aboriginal peoples—historically, culturally, socially, and economically—as defined by their relations with the settlers—relations marked by racism, broken treaties, assimilation attempts, and domination. A second feature is intergenerational trauma and the repercussions felt in daily lived experiences of Aboriginal youth. Effects include poverty, underemployment, dropping out of school, family violence, high rates of substance abuse, poor health, overrepresentation in the criminal justice system, and experiences of racism and discrimination.

The *common experience* and the resulting individualized traumatic experiences are so tightly woven together in the life stories of Aboriginal communities and individuals that they should be observed as one. This has been a failing of intervention strategies, which are, in the main, "programming fixes" for the problem of crime, all the while ignoring root causes for such behaviours. Margaret Wheatley writes: "When we start a conversation by asking, 'What's wrong and how can we fix it?' we spark criticism, and not necessarily of the healthy sort. . . . When we ask questions like, 'Who cares and what is possible?' we immediately open ourselves to one another" (as cited in Borne 2008, p. 49). Shared community and individual healing must occur concurrently (as we will discuss later in the chapter). First, however, we briefly discuss the historical context critical to understanding the **criminalization** of Aboriginal youth.

criminalization
The process whereby individuals are assigned the label of "criminal."

Historical Context

Broken Relations and Promises

The historical context illustrates the link between Aboriginal youth's common experience—traumatization and victimization—and criminalization. Relationships between Aboriginal and non-Aboriginal (settlers) peoples have been marred by broken relations and promises. After some 500 years of a relationship that has swung from partnership to domination, from mutual respect and co-operation to paternalism and attempted assimilation, Canada must now work out fair and lasting terms of coexistence with its Indigenous people (Royal Commission on Aboriginal Peoples 1996, p. 4) (see Figure 11.1).

There is little doubt that there is a relationship problem between Canadians of European ancestry and the first peoples of North America. Figure 11.1 provides a brief

Provincial/Regional	Title
1989	The Royal Commission on the Donald Marshall Inquiry
1990	The Osanburgh/Windigo Tribal Council Justice Review (Northern Ontario)
1991	Report of the Aboriginal Justice Inquiry of Manitoba
1991	The Task Force on the Criminal Justice System and Its Impact on the Indian and Métis People of Alberta
1991	Policing in Relation to the Blood Tribe (Southern Alberta)
1992	Indian Justice Review Committee and Métis Justice Review Committee (Saskatchewan)
1993	The Caribou Chicoltin Justice Report (Interior British Columbia)
1995	Report and Recommendations of the Advisory Committee in the Administration of Justice in Aboriginal Communities (Quebec)
2001	Aboriginal Justice Implementation Commision, Manitoba
Federal	
1969	Statement of the Government of Canada on Indian Policy (The White Paper)
1990	Indian and Northern Affairs Canada: Indian Policing Policy Review
1991	Correctional Services Canada: Task Force on Federally Sentenced Women
1991	Law Reform Commission of Canada: Aboriginal Peoples and Criminal Justice
1996	Royal Commission on Aboriginal Peoples: Bridging the Cultural Divide
2009	Truth and Reconciliation Commission of Canada
2015	A National Inquiry into Missing and Murdered Aboriginal Women (Phase 1)

FIGURE 11.1 Justice Inquiries and Commissions

Source: Adapted from A Review of Research on Criminal Victimization and First Nations, Métis and Inuit Peoples 1990 to 2001 (2006). Appendix A: List of Justice Inquiries and Commissions, 106. Retrieved from: http://www.justice.gc.ca/eng/rp-pr/aj-ja/rr06_vic1/rr06_vic1.pdf. Department of Justice Canada, January 2006. Reproduced with the permission of the Department of Justice Canada, 2015.

chronology of attempts to redress this relationship. These broken relations and promises included policies of domination and assimilation. The establishment of reserves isolated and impoverished Aboriginal peoples. "[The Indian Act] has . . . deprived of us of our independence, our dignity, our self-respect and our responsibility," stated Katherine June Delisle of Kanien'kehaka First Nation, Kahnawake, Quebec, to the Royal Commission on Aboriginal Peoples (1996, p. 10). Ceremonies such as the potlatch—giveaways or gifting—were outlawed; a pass system for reserves was instituted, forbidding outsiders from doing business with Aboriginal peoples without permission of the Indian agent; and in 1849 residential schools were created to deal with Aboriginal independence and "savagery" (Royal Commission on Aboriginal Peoples 1996, p. 11). Along with imposed poverty and economic, social, cultural, and linguistic marginalization, non-compliant behaviours were defined as illegitimate. For example, Aboriginal students in residential schools were forbidden to speak their own language or allowed to grow their hair long (an important element of self-identity for Aboriginal males).

Indeed, from a historical analysis of Aboriginal peoples and the criminal justice system, the Canadian Criminal Justice Association (CCJA 2000, p. 3) summarizes its findings:

> [T]he historical problems of many Aboriginal peoples stem directly from assimilation, which fundamentally changed the economic, political, and social life—indeed the very culture—of First Nations people. Assimilation policies were based partly on the European belief that Aboriginal people were uncivilized and incapable of governing themselves. As a result of the devaluation of their language, traditions, and customs after this experience, Aboriginal people began to suffer cultural uncertainties. This cultural crisis can be linked to specific internal problems that currently plague Aboriginal communities, including disproportionate levels of Aboriginal incarceration, poverty, unemployment, alcohol abuse, domestic violence, and an absence of economic self-sufficiency and business infrastructure.

colonization
Refers to historical and ongoing processes that began with the arrival of Europeans to the country and that include attempts to dominate and assimilate Indigenous peoples.

For Aboriginal youth, the intergenerational effects of **colonization** are felt to this day. Robert Yazzie, a chief justice emeritus of the Navajo Supreme Court, writes, "In time of legend, Navajos slew monsters. Today, Navajos [youth] face new monsters . . . domestic violence, child abuse, and neglect . . . alcoholism. . . . These problems are today's monsters . . . which get in the way of success (Yazzie, in Boyes-Watson 2008, p. 23).

Historical policies aimed at "civilizing" and "assimilating" Aboriginal peoples have created a legacy wherein Aboriginal youth are confronted with "violence, fear, abandonment, neglect, economic hardship, discrimination and displacement" (Boyes-Watson 2008, p. 23). As Youngblood (2008) notes, these disadvantages create self-identity issues and frustration for Aboriginal youth: "In the perplexing context of settler states [Canada] and their concept of legal systems, the implementation of human rights and fundamental freedoms will not come easy" (p. 95).

Traumatization

Lack of freedom to gain independence, powerlessness to engage in healthy choices because of a lack of decent housing, safety, clothing, and diet, as well as the absence of a sense of belonging (intergenerational violence and substance abuse, lack of family cohesion) create an overwhelming sense of oppression. Herman explains:

> Traumatic events call in question basic human relationships. They shatter the construction of the self that is formed and sustained in relation to others [crime behaviour, for example]. They undermine the belief systems that give meaning to human experience. They violate the victim's faith in natural or divine order and cast the victim into a state of existential crisis. (Herman 1997, p. 51)

Five and a half centuries after the Europeans arrived in the Americas "Indigenous populations [today] are characterized by poverty, subsistence holdings [reserves]" (Youngblood 2008, p. 28). Such conditions have undermined Indigenous culture, languages, self-governance, and relations (e.g., residential schools), the end result being a profound sense of loss about how the Indigenous world should work. Positive self-identity has been diminished by colonialism, and racism has made acceptance within the larger social and cultural space challenging. This has had an impact "not only on individual psychological structures of the self (e.g., Aboriginal youth who commit crime) but also on the systems of attachment and meaning that link individual and community" (Herman 1997, p. 51). Policies, programs, and activities that the government implemented over the history of colonization have undermined Aboriginal traditions, identity, and social cohesion.

Lane, Bopp, Bopp, and Norris (2002) state:

> It becomes clear when considering these various sources of trauma, that the eventual impact of trauma originating from outside Aboriginal communities was to generate a wide range of dysfunctional and hurtful behaviours (such as physical and sexual abuse) which then began to be recycled generation after generation inside communities.

There is a long history of deliberate disenfranchisement of a great proportion of Aboriginal people in Canada, resulting in not only barriers to prosperity but post-colonial stress expressed through addiction, depression, health problems, suicide, and violence. As Episkenew (2009, p. 25) observes, "Because those steeped in imperial ideology believed without question in their superiority over the Indigenous people, neither the regime nor colonial society in general was willing to welcome the Indigenous peoples into its midst. To do so would have required tolerance of difference, and the colonizers interpreted difference as evidence of inferiority."

Educational and Socio-economic Implications of Crime

For youth and young adults who are of First Nations heritage, historical and current societal power structures have predisposed them to pervasive disadvantage and to a suppression and repression of personal value that are apparent across many contexts, one of which is the experience of "schooling."

Individuals' experience of school varies greatly. Personal characteristics, including gender, social class, religious creed, and ethnicity, not only affect students' objective chances of academic success but also have an impact on the subjective experience of school, including attitudes toward the institution. In addition, education systems differ according to the context and culture in which they are located (Raveaud 2005, p. 460). Essentially, educational institutions based on academic or vocational streams that reflect Judeo-Christian values demonstrate a vacuum of perspectives, processes, and supports that can address the personal characteristics and subjective experiences of Aboriginal children and youth (e.g., the impoverishment and racism that can affect learning).

Aboriginals are also disadvantaged socio-economically. The Aboriginal population is younger on average than other groups in Canada, and Aboriginals have higher unemployment rates than other ethnic groups in Canada. They are more likely to live in crowded conditions and have higher residential mobility, and their children are more likely to be members of a lone-parent family. In addition, they have lower levels of education (Statistics Canada 2006; Deane, Bracken, and Morrissette 2007; Kelly and Caputo 2007). For policy-makers, focusing on crime (managing the symptom) may be more practical than addressing the social problems, including the **marginalization** of people on economic and racial grounds (the

marginalization
The partial exclusion of certain groups from mainstream society who routinely suffer as the result of gross inequalities.

causes), from which crime emerges. Band-Aid solutions (i.e., "getting tough on crime") are quick fixes that divert attention from the broader issues that require more sustained attention, more critical analysis, more resources, and more comprehensive social change.

Contemporary Context

Victimization: A Statistical Profile

trauma
Experience that is psychologically painful, distressful, or shocking (such as suffering sexual abuse or witnessing serious violence) and that often results in long-term mental or physical problems (such as depression, anxiety, or insomnia). Also, the community-level and individual-level damage, pain, and suffering of Indigenous peoples—physically, spiritually, emotionally, and psychically—as a result of the historical and current processes of colonization.

victimization
The experience of being a victim, which can be linked to future criminalization.

Trauma and **victimization** characterize Aboriginal populations, yet observers point to a noticeable lack of information on Aboriginal victimization. Research shows that the link between victimization and future criminalization is a significant one (Minaker and Hogeveen 2009). Although a person can be a victim one day and an offender the next, most reports focus on the role of Aboriginal youth as offenders rather than as victims (Chartrand and MacKay 2006, p. 20) (see Figure 11.2).

Chartrand and McKay (2006, pp. 25–32), for example, report the lack of comprehensive data on Aboriginal youth victimization. Further, Kingsley and Mark (2000, p. 42) and Elliot (1997) caution "that historical, cultural and economic factors experienced by Aboriginal children and youth are different and unique and that 'these factors limit application of the non-Aboriginal research, programs and policy to Aboriginal youth-at-risk'" (in Chartrand and McKay 2006, p. 31). As Chartrand and McKay (2006, p. 32) explain, "while Aboriginal youth often become engaged in criminality [gangs, sex-trade, etc. . . .], their involvement is often a component of their continued victimization."

Figure 11.2 illustrates the relative victimization of Aboriginal peoples compared to non-Aboriginal peoples. While there are no specific studies we are aware of that focus on comparative Aboriginal youth victimization, it is clear from Figure 11.2 that Aboriginal youth victimization is likely similar to that of their families. According to one report, in 2009 young people between the ages of 15 and 24 accounted for almost half (47 per cent)

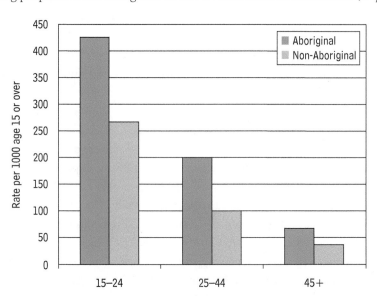

FIGURE 11.2 Aboriginal People More Likely to Be Victims of Violent Crime, 2009[1]

1. Includes robbery and excludes all incidents of spousal sexual and physical assault. Includes incidents that occurred during the 12 months preceding the survey.

Source: Statistics Canada, General Social Survey, 2009.

of violent incidents reported by Aboriginal peoples, yet this age group represents only 22 per cent of the Aboriginal population that is over the age of 15 (Perreault 2011). This would seem to suggest that Aboriginal youth are overrepresented in violent victimizations within the Aboriginal population.

Victimization, Criminalization, and Justice System Involvement

Victimization in the form of family violence and abuse, bullying, and other types of assault is far too common in the lives of far too many Aboriginal youth. And the link between victimization and criminalization means that many of these victimized youth are at risk of adopting criminal behaviours.

While youth 12 to 17 years old who self-identified as Aboriginal represent about 7 per cent of youth in Canada, in 2011/12 they made up about 39 per cent of youth admitted to custody (Perreault 2014). Female Aboriginal youth are overrepresented in the system compared to non-Aboriginal female youth, and they experience greater overrepresentation than their male counterparts (ibid.). Figure 11.3 illustrates the relative proportion of Aboriginal female and male youth in the correctional system, compared to non-Aboriginal youth.

There are also geographical patterns indicating the overrepresentation of Aboriginal youth in the correctional system. As Figure 11.4 shows, in all of the provinces for which data were collected, Aboriginal youth are overrepresented in correctional system admissions, with the exception of Newfoundland and Labrador. This overrepresentation becomes more pronounced as one moves from east to west and north in the country.

The disturbing number of Aboriginal youth coming into conflict with the law occurs even though certain "rights" are constitutionally guaranteed: "Section 15: (1) every individual is equal before and under the law . . . without discrimination and, in particular, *without discrimination based on race* [author's emphasis], national or ethnic origin, colour, religion, gender, age, or mental or physical disability" (Roberts and Doob 1997, p. 471). The disproportionate representation of Aboriginal youth in the youth justice system is likely to be a consequence of some combination of higher rates of offending by the Aboriginal population, higher use of the criminal justice system in some Aboriginal communities to

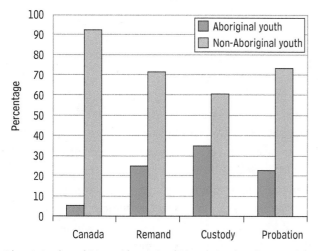

FIGURE 11.3 Aboriginal and Non-Aboriginal Youth in the Correctional System

Source: Calverley, Cotter, and Halla, 2010.

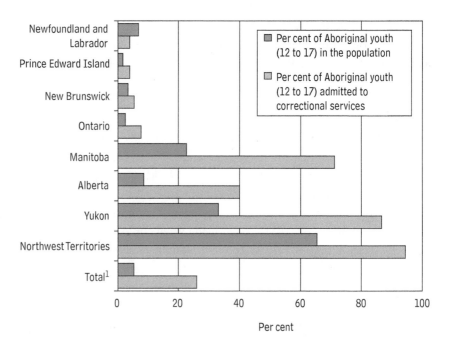

FIGURE 11.4 Provincial and Territorial Aboriginal Youth Admissions to Correctional Services, 2010/2011

Source: Statistics Canada, Canadian Centre for Justice Statistics, Youth Custody and Community Services Survey.

deal with certain types of crime, direct and indirect discrimination by the criminal justice system, and the *socially disadvantaged role occupied by Aboriginals* in Canadian society (ibid., p. 482). Indeed, the problem is systemic. Aboriginal people, both adults and youth, are disproportionately represented as offenders and as victims of crime in our country (Brzozowski, Taylor-Butts, and Johnson 2006).

Aboriginal youth crime must, then, be explained within and under historical, social, cultural, and economic conditions—indeed, these realities must be the prima facie conditions under which we examine, and understand, the victimization and criminalization of Aboriginal youth.

Understanding the Causes/Influences of Crime

There is resistance to considering offenders as victims, yet the link between victimization and criminalization is well established (Minaker and Hogeveen 2009). This link can be understood more clearly if we consider the following question: How much suffering does one individual have to undergo before he or she retaliates against another human being (Gilligan 1996, p. 50)? Gilligan, an experienced psychiatrist, reports that he has not encountered an individual who has harmed another who was not first him- or herself a victim of harm: "Children who fail to receive sufficient love from others fail to build those reserves of self-love and mostly feel numb, empty, and dead" (ibid., p. 50). Feelings of low self-worth often lead to a sense of shame: "The shame that oppressed Indigenous minorities . . . is central to understanding the persistence of their domination" (Ahmed,

Harris, Braithwaite, and Braithwaite 2001, p. 4). This shame, according to Brown (2007), is a sense of not fitting in. Aboriginal youth, lacking a cohesive socio-cultural history, retreat to finding "worth" where it is available. Then, since marginalization and disenfranchisement mean there are limited options for finding self-worth, Aboriginal youth turn to criminal behaviours and gang involvement to provide such an option.

Identity, Self-Esteem, and Risk-Protective Factors

Part of the attraction of gangs is the sense of belonging and identity they promise to provide their members. Identity is a life story or a set of stories that adults have internalized in order to make sense of their life to themselves and others. Youth are expected to develop a core identity that is reasonably stable and sustainable while living within a society that is characterized by change. This is an enormous task. Aboriginal youth today inherit the legacy of the residential school experiences of previous generations, as well as the intergenerational trauma that is the legacy of colonization (see, for example, Wesley-Esquimaux and Smolewski 2004).

Identity issues have implications for self-esteem. Recent reports find strong connections between low self-esteem and problems such as aggression and anti-social behaviour (see Donnellan, Trzesniewski, Robins, Moffitt, and Caspi 2005). The term *at risk* has come to be a general descriptor of young people who are considered to be "on a trajectory toward a myriad of problems that threaten their present and future adjustment" (Schonert-Reichl 2000, p. 3). Previously, it was the word *disadvantaged* that was used to describe factors that were thought to play a critical role in placing young people in jeopardy: poverty, ethnic minority status, community or family characteristics (i.e., single-parent family), parents' education, inadequate housing, child abuse, home–school breakdown, inadequate knowledge of the country's official language(s), and the type and geographic location of schools (Wotherspoon and Schissel 2001).

Even though the very conception of the term *at risk* rests on the premise of deficit, various interpretations of what composes that deficit do exist. Yessine and Bonta (2009), for example, found that chronic high-offending Aboriginal offenders shared common background characteristics, including an impoverished background, an unstable family environment, substance use, and negative peer associations. Considering the historical and contemporary life circumstances of many Aboriginal youth, the validity and applicability of the "at risk" label is worth exploring. But "risk protective" factors are not solely about risk. Protective factors refer to those elements in a young person's life that offer insulation against negative influences: a healthy family situation, a positive role model, pro-social friends, involvement in positive activities, and positive educational experiences (Totten 2012). For many Aboriginal youths, the situation is such that risk factors tend to outweigh the protective factors. One particularly salient risk factor that Aboriginal youth face is the trauma referred to throughout this chapter.

Much has been acknowledged about the trauma of Aboriginal youth as a result of their common experience. Joe Solanto, a faculty member of the Justice Institute of British Columbia, lectures widely on intergenerational trauma and healing. In his presentation to the Public Business and Law Institute Aboriginal Justice Forum (Solanto 2008), he outlined how the trauma of residential schools is experienced not only by those who attended them, but also by family and community who never attended, as the experience is passed on from parents to children and grandchildren. Substance abuse becomes an attempt to nullify the pain of the residential school experience and is a learned behaviour to cope with poverty, violence, and family breakdown (also see Chapter 7).

This intergenerational experience has a role in producing symptoms that contribute to higher rates of risk among Aboriginal youth. A speaker from the Saskatchewan First Nations Women's Council, in a presentation to the Commission on First Nations and Métis Peoples and Justice Reform, describes the intergenerational experience: "When some parents feel their lives are spiraling out of control, that parent is more likely to direct a form of violence, verbal, emotionally, physical, sexual, neglect or abandonment towards their child. This form of adult bullying can transfer down to sibling abuse and parental attack" (Commission on First Nations and Métis Peoples and Justice Reform, Vol. I, 2004, s. 3, p. 2).

Kelly and Totten (2002) present a summary of youth violence risk factors, including individual factors, family factors, school factors, peer-related factors, and community and neighbourhood factors (see Chapter 12), that makes it clear there are numerous dimensions and layers to issues of crime and criminalization. Up to this point, we have emphasized the role of history and social processes in the marginalization of Aboriginal youth and have attempted to show how the line between victimization and criminalization is a porous one. We have discussed the importance of the discriminatory policies and practices that have created a context within which criminal behaviour becomes a viable option for some youth, as well as how the criminal justice system is more apt to label Aboriginal youth as offenders and to treat them more harshly than their non-Aboriginal counterparts:

> Through an exploration of a portion of the ample literature base, it is clear that, as human beings, we are far more complicated than simply our biology, our environment or our psychology. It is the complex interaction of factors within us and outside of us mixed with the intangible of human agency that makes accurate predictions of human behaviour difficult. (Nelson 2011, p. 5)

A number of different perspectives take into account other influences on behaviour. We will touch on some of these next.

Biological/Genetic Influences

A wide assortment of behavioural problems and personality and mood disorders have been determined to be influenced by genes, many of which are related to criminal behaviour. Intellectual functioning, personality characteristics (e.g., negativity), and temperamental factors (e.g., impulsivity) all have genetic roots. Behavioural precursors to delinquency and crime (e.g., attention deficit hyperactivity disorder [ADHD]) have also been traced in the behavioural genetics research (Wright, Tibbetts, and Daigle 2008). While substantial importance is attached to what is inherited, genes do not operate in isolation. The environment into which a child is born holds considerable sway.

Psychological Influences

From a psychological perspective, it is critical how people perceive themselves, how they understand what they experience and the meaning they place on that experience within the context of their life, and how valued they feel as a person (Harms and Pierce 2011). We seek to understand why some people do terrible things to other people and what makes violent people different from "us." Classifications have been created to distinguish one type of offender from another and to make sense of the statistics that show that crime is more often located in one group than in another. These classifications may be based on characteristics that lead to stereotypical depictions of who is, and who is not, a criminal (Hollin 2007).

Socio-cultural Influences

Explanations for criminal behaviour that rest on social control look outside the individual to the social systems that surround her or him. From this perspective, delinquent behaviour results from the failure of personal and social controls to produce behaviour that conforms to the norms of the social system. Delinquency occurs when those norms have not been internalized (e.g., due to marginalization, anomie). The common thread among the socio-cultural explanations for criminal behaviour is the critical importance of the interaction between an individual and others in her or his immediate and extended social world. Children with peer relationship difficulties are at an increased risk for aggression, academic problems, anxiety, depression, and loneliness, all of which can contribute to delinquent or criminal behaviour (Ooi, Ang, Fung, Wong, and Cai 2006) and can lead to membership in gangs owing to a desire for social belonging and social identity (White 2008; also see Chapter 9 in this volume).

Demographic Influences

The influence of the interrelationship between demographic variables, such as poverty, race, and neighbourhood, has been explored (Spano, Rivera, Vazsonyi, and Bolland 2008). The sense of physical and social disorder that can be characteristic of neighbourhoods that house large numbers of poor, marginalized people has been shown to exert damaging influences on an individual's social, physical, and psychological health (Weyers et al. 2008; Farrington 2007). With poverty restricting people's access to supports, their present is compromised and their future is uncertain. Such absence of resources has been implicated in the likelihood of criminalization (Reiman 2013).

The Influence of Fetal Alcohol Spectrum Disorder (FASD)

One group of individuals that is at a higher risk of criminalization includes individuals diagnosed as having **fetal alcohol spectrum disorder (FASD),** the result of maternal alcohol consumption during pregnancy. The degree to which prenatal exposure to alcohol affects the fetus is dependent on a number of factors, including genetics, maternal characteristics, nutrition, duration and exposure to alcohol, as well as a number of other factors. FASD can affect an individual's physical, cognitive, behavioural, and social functioning. This disorder provides a poignant example of the ways in which biological, psychological, and social influences coalesce in such a manner as to heighten the risk of both victimization and criminalization. For Aboriginal youth, histories marred by neglect, abuse, and violence exemplify the victimization–criminalization connection. FASD serves to complicate the situation and increase the risk of both.

fetal alcohol spectrum disorder (FASD) Refers to a medical diagnosis of fetal alcohol syndrome (FAS), partial fetal alcohol syndrome (pFAS), alcohol neurodevelopmental disorder (ARND), and alcohol-related birth defects (ARBD), all of which refer to some degree of permanent central nervous system damage to a fetus as a result of maternal alcohol consumption during pregnancy.

The diagnosis of FASD is challenging. This is partly because it is a relatively new disorder, having only been identified in the early 1970s, and also because not all physicians are trained in the area. Assessments ideally involve a team of specialists, including a geneticist or pediatrician experienced with FASD, a clinical psychologist, a speech-language pathologist, and a school or social worker (Chudley et al. 2005). The specialized nature of the diagnosis process means that the availability of obtaining such a diagnosis is lacking. To complicate matters, provincial health-care plans do not cover the cost of the assessment, which ranges from about $3000 to $4500 (Popova et al. 2013). Given the prevalence of family violence in Aboriginal communities, diagnosis in these communities is further complicated by the overlap of FASD symptoms with post-traumatic stress disorder symptoms (see Table 11.1).

As estimating the incidence and prevalence of FASD is difficult, largely because of difficulties in diagnosis, it is likely that the disorder is highly under-diagnosed. There is, however, some indication that rates of FASD are higher in Aboriginal populations. According to one estimate, the incidence of FASD within the Canadian Aboriginal population ranges from 25 to 200 per 1000 births compared to the estimated incidence rate of 1 to 10 per 1000 births in the general Canadian population (Adler, Mueller, Laufer, and Grekul 2009). What appears to be clearer is the link between FASD and criminalization. Recent studies in Saskatchewan and Manitoba report that at least 50 per cent of young offenders were born

Table 11.1	Examples of How the Cognitive and Behavioural Characteristics of FASD Apply to Offenders, Victims, and Witnesses in Court[1]	
Category	**Characteristic**	**Difficulty in Court**
Intellect	Do not learn from previous experiences	Difficulty understanding legal terms
	Difficulty generalizing from one event to another	Confused by sarcasm or abstract examples used by lawyers
Attention	Restless	Distracted by others entering and leaving courtroom
		Unable to focus on questions being asked
		Easily frustrated or overwhelmed in court setting
Memory	Impaired short- and long-term memory	Forgetful of time of day
		Difficulty recollecting events
		Unsure of time frames or duration of events
		Unknowingly adding false statements when trying to remember events
Language	Speech difficulties	Unable to articulate thoughts effectively
Social communication	Social cues	Going along with whatever argument the Crown, police, or lawyer is saying in order to please them
	Shy	Easily agreeing to leading questions

1. The information in this table was adapted from "Victims and Fetal Alcohol Spectrum Disorder (FASD): A Review of the Issues," by Charlotte Fraser, *Victims of Crime Research Digest*. Retrieved from http://www.justice.gc.ca/eng/pi/rs/rep-rap/rd-rr/rr07_vic4/p4.html

with FASD. Another in British Columbia found that of 415 individuals with FASD, 60 per cent ages 12 and over had been in trouble with the law (Adler et al. 2009).

FASD, however, also appears to increase the risk of victimization. Because of the nature of the disorder and the problems associated with it, individuals with FASD are particularly vulnerable to being taken advantage of, especially by family members and friends. Complicating matters is the fact that some victims with FASD may not realize that certain behaviours are wrong (i.e., sexual advances and inappropriate touching), may not fully understand what it means to be a victim of crime, and may have difficulty navigating through the court process as a victim or witness (see Table 11.1). Researchers, professionals, and communities alike emphasize the need for more research on FASD and its impact on individuals, as well as more support for prevention programming and diagnostic assessment. An emerging concern is that gangs have begun to target youth with FASD because these young people are vulnerable, eager to please, and easily influenced.

Investigating the Aboriginal Youth Gang Phenomenon

Many gang members started selling illegal drugs when they were quite young. Jerry said to us: "I grew up on this corner here [near the Merchants Hotel] selling drugs." He was about twelve years old when he started. He got some drugs from his older brother, and "We sold that shit in ten minutes." Soon Jerry was selling while in school: "An hour of selling drugs at lunchtime, you know, put a hundred dollars in your pocket."

— Comack, Deane, Morrissette, and Silver 2013, p. 103

In *"Indians Wear Red": Colonialism, Resistance, and Aboriginal Street Gangs* (2013), Elizabeth Comack and her co-authors provide an in-depth look at the links between colonization, racism, poverty, trauma, and masculinity and their complex connections to the emergence and perpetuation of Aboriginal street gangs. The authors show how many of the risk-protective factors discussed thus far manifest themselves in criminal behaviours, but they can also lead to the formation of gangs. Gangs in turn contribute to further criminal behaviours. Risk of victimization within these groups at the hands of rival gang members and members of one's own gang is extremely high. Recent years have witnessed a growing concern with Aboriginal youth gangs, in part because of the perceived growth in these groups and the increasingly violent nature of their activities. Aboriginal over-incarceration has also led to a strong connection between street and prison gangs for this population. This is not to suggest that all Aboriginal youth are involved in gangs, nor that all Aboriginal youth crime is gang related. Investigating the gang phenomenon, however, provides an opportunity to explore the complex ways in which risk and protective factors combine with social, cultural, and historical processes to influence the formation of this type of response to community-level and individual-level issues and problems (Totten 2014).

Part of the attraction to gangs felt by young people from all ethnic groups is based on the media sensationalization of these groups. Movies, music, and Internet representations present a glamorous "gangsta" identity and lifestyle that appear to provide an endless supply of money, drugs, women, sex, and status to its members. Arguably this search for identity is one of the main underlying causes of gang association for Aboriginal youth who have, as we saw earlier, lost an important part of their identity—their culture—as a result of historical and current discriminatory processes. This element of gang membership may be particularly influential for a group that is defined by cultural identity. In other words, for Aboriginal groups whose culture is integral to "who they are," experiencing cultural loss has forced some members to seek an alternative source of cultural identity. Gangs may serve that function.

As noted in Chapter 12, a number of risk factors can lead to gang involvement among youth. The gang promises to serve as a substitute family for its members. It promises to provide money and excitement, and it serves as a source of identity, prestige, and status for members. For young Aboriginals, many of whom experience violence inside and outside the home, gangs promise protection and loyalty. Protection as a reason for joining a gang becomes more significant for incarcerated youth. Some research suggests that many Aboriginal youth first join a gang inside prison as a means of protection (Grekul and LaBoucane-Benson 2008). Over-incarceration of Aboriginal youth, then, becomes additionally problematic in that it ostensibly contributes to growth in gangs.

Also related to the unique configuration of social-structural and individually based factors that contribute to gang involvement among Aboriginal youth is recruitment by family members (Grekul and LaBoucane-Benson 2008). Aboriginal gangs were first identified as a growing concern in the early 1990s in Manitoba. Now, 25 years later and as a result of official government and correctional policies that led to the flourishing of these groups across the Prairie provinces, Aboriginal communities are witnessing intergenerational gang involvement.

In some cases, youth are even expected to follow in the footsteps of gang-involved parents, uncles, or family members and become members. In one case, for example, a gang-member father involved his two teenage sons in a conspiracy to commit murder. The sons ended up going to jail (as young offenders) for the offence (but the father did not). Out of jail now, the two boys have Facebook pages proudly stating their gang affiliation. In other cases, reports exist of babies being welcomed into their father's gang. Nimmo (2001), in her study on the role of females in Winnipeg's Aboriginal gangs, found that "blessing-in ceremonies" were an important ritual in some groups. Along similar lines, "a Native Syndicate member has a picture of his child with a Native Syndicate 'dew rag' done up in the knot—the Native Syndicate-style knot—on Facebook as his profile picture" (interview with gang unit detective). Totten (2012) reports that some of his participants had "multiple family members in different, rival gangs—cousins, uncles, stepbrothers" (p. 145). While most of these participants reported having 10 or more gang-involved family members, a minority claimed that over 20 of their family members were involved with gangs (ibid.). At the same time, an Alberta report on gangs in that province that was based on interviews with 207 (ex)gang members, the majority of whom were Aboriginal, found that 93 per cent of participants would not want their child to become involved with a gang (Cazal, Garnett, Chalas, Wiredu, and Grekul 2013).

The intergenerational element is perhaps a sign of the entrenchment of gangs in some Aboriginal communities and in the lives of some Aboriginal families. As one of the men in Comack et al.'s study (2013, p. 93) explains:

> When I was younger, all I looked up to was gang members, right, 'cause of my family and my older cousins and uncles. And I just wanted to be something, you know. But I didn't only want to be part of it. I wanted to be someone . . . so I thought that if I went there [the penitentiary] that it would help me, help out my record of, you know, gangsters, you know what I mean?

The suggestion is that this entrenchment is occurring as a result of the "almost-institutionalization" of the issues faced by Aboriginal communities. Social-structural problems of the type discussed earlier have led to social-structural responses that have become long-term and enduring. A gang unit detective (whose father and brother are also police officers) who works closely with these groups explains:

> You have a guy like [name] of the Redd Alert sitting there with his kid in a red bandana showing the gang sign in pictures . . . I have pictures of me and my brother wearing police hats when we were 10 and 8, or 5 and 3 and it's the same thing. We've allowed this thing to get to the level of where you have generational gang membership.

The gang unit detective goes on to explain the significance of this, not only as a commentary or reflection on the entrenched nature of social-structural factors but in terms of ways of addressing the gang issue: "Intervention strategies on generational gang membership aren't going to work . . . you're not going to get to those youth before anyone else gets to them because they're being taught from a young age: police are bad, gangs are good, this is what you're in." The implication is that Band-Aid solutions—programs or policies that target individual-level issues and risk factors—cannot operate successfully without efforts to address the structural level or broader factors that contribute to the general social-structural disadvantage faced by Aboriginal communities and that manifest themselves in gang involvement.

Many, if not all, of these social-structural issues arise out of colonization. It follows that an effective response to dealing with the issues should be rooted in decolonization (Comack et al. 2013)—undoing the impact of forced assimilation and all that has come with it. Comack and her co-authors show how gangs are a manifestation of colonization and in fact are a form of collective resistance, albeit a negative one, on the part of some Aboriginal peoples. In speaking with elders from Aboriginal communities, the authors show how programming alone is not sufficient to prevent and intervene in gang involvement. Rather, a broader approach to dealing with gangs effectively involves, for example, challenging stereotypes about Aboriginal peoples and gangs, drawing on Aboriginal ways of knowing, teaching young Aboriginal men about a kind of "masculinity" that is not rooted in the gang version of what it means to be a man, teaching Aboriginal peoples about who they are and where they have come from, and reconnecting them with their culture (Comack et al. 2013). Importantly,

Aboriginal people need to be at the centre of a process of building communities in which they can safely live and work as Aboriginal people, aware of and proud of their identity, while making a living in ways consistent with their traditional values. (ibid., p. 146)

Members of Aboriginal communities and researchers are increasingly turning to an understanding of intergenerational trauma as a framework for contextualizing the social-structural and individual-level risk factors we have been discussing. The suggestion is that a root contributing factor to youth crime and gangs in Aboriginal communities can be found in the generational "piling up" of trauma and grief that originated centuries ago with the arrival of the colonizers. Yet this kind of thinking is somewhat at odds with the approach to justice currently informing our criminal justice system.

Attribution of Responsibility: The Youth Justice System

We live in a society whose members must take personal responsibility for criminal action according to the law: "You do the crime, you do the time." However, this personal responsibility is not only for the criminal action itself but also for the conditions and the response to the conditions that gave rise to the criminal behaviour in the first place: "Criminal law rests on the notion of attributing personal responsibility for the crime . . . consequently the social, political and cultural context in which the problem occurred disappears into the background" (Law Commission of Canada 2003, p. 13).

A multitude of factors and influences can place an Aboriginal youth at risk and promote negative outcomes, one of which is incarceration. The desire to understand why youth become disengaged and involved in delinquent and criminal activity has propelled inquiry into the situation. As indicated earlier, research into criminal behaviour has provided a variety of interpretations. These causal interpretations stem from a belief that factors either internal or external to the individual play a significant role in determining outcomes. Biological/genetic, psychological, socio-cultural, and demographic conditions exist that have been correlated with an increased likelihood that a child growing up and experiencing a combination of these conditions, each weighing in differentially, will be vulnerable to engaging in criminal behaviour (Walsh and Beaver 2009).

Researchers may find it highly desirable to "find" the critical element(s) that promote criminal activity, their aim being to significantly reduce the occurrence of criminal activity by changing those elements. However, to focus only on the influence that certain experiences, conditions, or substances have on promoting criminal behaviour ignores the added complexity brought by a person's own perceptions, motivations, and beliefs in the outcomes of his or her life. The potentially critical influences that adolescents and young adults will have been, or currently are, exposed to, together with the experiences that those influences will have brought with them, are mediated by how young people perceive and interpret them in relation to themselves. It is this incredibly intricate and individualized interrelationship that provides a basis for attaching considerable significance to a process that affirms their life journey.

Healing: A More Appropriate Alternative to Aboriginal Youth Crime?

There has been a focus in the literature on causality of crime, on the characteristics of those who get involved in criminality, on the success or failure of interventions, and on the identification of the educational needs of youth involved in criminal activity. Some studies look at the problems of youths coming out of custody from the perspective of those youths (Mazzotta 2004) or consider the societal perceptions of race, class, and gender that engender inadvertent bias toward youth who are at risk (Crenshaw 2005). Rarer are studies that seek to understand through the voices of youth and young adults how they perceive themselves as learners within the socially constructed experience of "schooling" (Duke 1977) and how a change or shift in one's self-perception as "learner" may be facilitated (Butler 2002). What appears to be under-explored is how a sense of "self as learner" could potentially be enhanced through recognition of past experiences and the learning that has resulted. It is within that gap that we now turn our attention to some Aboriginal perspectives and explanations.

Aboriginal Perspectives

The destruction of Aboriginal peoples' way of life changed their relationships with one another and with the larger society. We have presented how the lives of Aboriginal youth are affected by both historical conditions and contemporary insights. From Aboriginal perspectives—especially those of Aboriginal youth—in order to take a vibrant and meaningful step toward healing, the dominant culture must break down the barriers it has created.

The most unfruitful response, from a healing perspective, would be for non-Native readers to dismiss, or refuse to deal with, what Aboriginal youth have expressed. It has been this particular sense of white privilege that has contributed to such a gap in awareness in the first place. The fact that Natives often "speak the truth" in these ways and that non-Natives often are unfamiliar with this level of truth-telling suggests where the healing process might start—namely, with listening to voices and views that are often not heard (Breton, in McCaslin 2005, p. 19). In this sense, the Royal Commission on Aboriginal Peoples (1996) strikes a chord for the future: "The starting point is recognition that Aboriginal people are not as some Canadians think, an inconsequential minority group with problems that need fixing and outmoded attitudes that need modernizing. They are unique political entities, whose place in Canada is unlike that of any other people" (p. 67).

The number of Aboriginal perspectives, values, and beliefs is far too great and rich to discuss in this chapter. However, some shared beliefs and values include the following:

- Having a connection to nature and to each other

- Knowing the importance of circles and ceremonies

- Resisting justice as force

- Healing broken relations with mainstream society

- Peacemaking and respecting community

James Dumont (1990) contrasts Aboriginal values with non-Aboriginal values (see Table 11.2) and emphasizes the importance of understanding and respect.

Rupert Ross (1995), Canadian Crown prosecutor and author of *Returning to the Teachings: Explorations in Aboriginal Justice*, learned that he was routinely misinterpreting the behaviour of Aboriginal victims, witnesses, and offenders, both in and out of court. He discovered that he regularly drew incorrect conclusions when he encountered witnesses who would not make eye contact, victims who would not testify in the presence of the accused, and parents who showed great reluctance to interfere in their children's offending behaviour. With the assistance of Aboriginal teachers, he began to see that behind such behaviour lay a complex web of coherent cultural commandments that he had never suspected, much less understood (Ross 2006, p. 5).

What Ross (1992) learned—discussed in this chapter—was that trauma is a fundamental experience of Aboriginal peoples and, importantly, of Aboriginal youth. For example, Ross found "that Aboriginal witnesses often describe traumatic events in flat emotionless fashion" (1992). The resulting perception is that Aboriginal youth are unresponsive, do not care, and are cavalier about the criminal justice process. Former deputy minister of justice and attorney general of Saskatchewan Robert Mitchell mentioned, after attending the Royal Commission on Aboriginal Issues in the early 1990s, that Aboriginal peoples are less concerned with who committed the crime (guilt) and more concerned with how to repair the harm. The concern is not really with punishment (personal communication). Table 11.3 offers a comparison of the manner in which Western society and traditional Aboriginal cultures understand and approach "justice."

Table 11.2 Contrasting Values	
Aboriginal Values	**Non-Aboriginal Values**
Gets along with group (conformity)	Gets ahead; or on top of the group
Gets ahead for the group	Gets ahead for oneself
Focuses on the present	Focuses on the future
Does not show fear when faced with difficult situations	Does not always face difficult situations with an impassive face
Uses nature and maintains reverence for it (has respect for and relationship with the land)	Uses nature for personal use
Awareness of the Creator	Spirituality is often in the background of one's life
Acts of religion are spontaneous and can occur at any time	Religion is compartmentalized (e.g., religious acts are restricted to certain days of the week)

Source: Dumont in Canadian Criminal Justice Association (2000)

	Western Justice	Traditional Aboriginal Justice
Table 11.3 Western Justice v. Traditional Aboriginal Justice		
Justice system	Adversarial	Non-confrontational
Guilt	Europe concept of guilty/not guilty	No concept of guilty/not guilty
Pleading guilty	The accused has the right against self-incrimination. Thus it is not seen as dishonest to plead not guilty when one has actually committed the offence.	It is dishonest to plead not guilty if one has committed the crime.
Testifying	As part of the process witnesses testify in front of the accused.	Reluctance to testify. It is confrontational to testify against the accused while in his/her presence.
Truth	Expectation to tell the "whole truth"	It is impossible to know the "whole truth" in any situation.
Witnesses	Only certain people are called to testify in relation to specific subjects	Everyone is free to have their say (witnesses do not want to appear adversarial and often make every attempt to give answers that please counsel, thus often change their testimony).
Eye contact	Maintaining eye contact conveys that one is being truthful	In some Aboriginal cultures, maintaining eye contact with a person of authority is a sign of disrespect.
Verdict	Accused is expected to show, during proceedings and upon a verdict of guilty, remorse and a desire for rehabilitation	Accused must accept what comes to him/her without a show of emotion
Incarceration/probation	Means of punishing/rehabilitating offender	Completely absolves Aboriginal offender of responsibility of restitution to victim
Function of justice	Ensure conformity, punish deviant, and protect society	Heal the offender; restore peace and harmony to the community; reconcile the offender with victim/family that has been wronged; punishment is not the objective

Source: CCJA 2000, pp. 5–6.

The barriers Aboriginals encounter—poverty, substance abuse, family violence, limited education and recreational opportunities—almost guarantee hopelessness, despair, and boredom and certainly contribute to criminal offences (CCJA 2000, p. 6). In the second author's contact with the closed- and open-custody facilities in Regina, Saskatchewan, many staff reported that Aboriginal youth will commit crimes just to escape the harsh realities of their world on the outside or will commit a breach within the institutions, such as running away during an outing just prior to their release date, to extend their stay. At least then the Aboriginal youth will have a warm and safe place, a school, food, and a sense of positive relationships—with staff.

Summary

When it comes to moving health-care practices forward efficiently, Canada is a country of perpetual pilot projects. We seldom move proven projects into stable, funded programs, and we rarely transfer the outcomes of pilot projects across jurisdictions. This approach is not serving our health-care system well.
—Bégin, Eggertson, and Macdonald 2009, p. 1185

Esteemed Norwegian criminologist Nils Christie writes, "My suspicion is that criminology to some extent has amplified a process where conflicts [criminal offences] have been taken away from the parties directly involved and thereby have either disappeared or become other people's property [professionals, researchers]. In both cases a deplorable outcome" (1977, p. 1). The sentiment of both these scholars, Bégin and Christie, informs us of two problems with "programs": (1) programs come and go as ideas wax and wane in popularity; and (2) programs are not owned by the participants but, rather, are owned by the professionals. In the case of the latter, an Aboriginal youth stated to the Commission on First Nations and Métis Peoples and Justice Reform (2004), "In many instances I think we would have experiences of bureaucracies who want to maintain control and power over programs that are under various departments" (p. 2–1). Another youth addressing the commission speaks to the former point:

And we did a bit of play with words here and thought that maybe we could use, instead of saying crime prevention all the time, we could maybe start talking about community promotion and create a sense of that among our youth, and from an early age—whether we're talking about the far North, in a small community, or a large city, or your part of the city, that we could be promoting our part of the communities to our children, our youth, so that sense of pride and self esteem is attached to that. (s. 2, p. 1)

Many programs start with good intentions but end up with unintended consequences for Aboriginal youth. Sections 4 and 5 of the Youth Criminal Justice Act provide for alternative interventions. For the first author (a board member of an alternative measures program in Regina, Saskatchewan), it is of constant concern that the number of youth being referred is dropping and that fewer Aboriginal youth are being referred. From a national perspective, referrals to alternative measures have not been widely used in cases involving Aboriginal young offenders (CCJA 2000, p. 6).

Many programs can be identified across the country. If we draw on Hester and Miller's (1995, p. 1) idea that there is no "one true light" explanation or effective response for substance abuse and we extrapolate this observation to the broader set of issues, the implication is that successful interventions into the human condition require considerate and "multivariate" explanations and responses. Dr. Rod McCormick, an Aboriginal psychologist and mental health consultant, speaks to this understanding: "Not all strategies will work for everyone as each community is different. That is why it is necessary to explore different strategies and adapt and modify them so that it fits the needs of your [our] youth" (McCormick, in White and Jodoin 2007, p. ii).

One approach that is particularly impressive and that confirms the belief that change is about ownership, resilience, self-esteem, community, and then individuals, is found in the *First Nations Community Justice Guidebook*, developed and published by the Restorative Justice Unit (2010) of the File Hills Qu'Appelle Tribal Council (a member of Treaty 4). The book states that a "program" is a "facilitated learning process [that] allows for the full and active involvement of all participants and so enriches learning, promotes community development and enables change" (p. 9) and is "[t]he art of leading people through processes towards agreed-upon objectives in a manner that encourages participants, ownership and creativity by all those involved" (p. 10). The guidebook is an important document, as many of the Treaty 4 (Southern Saskatchewan and Western Manitoba) languages are incorporated, as is important First Nation artwork by Lawrence (Henry) Shepherd. In the guidebook, 12 elements are presented in a circle and are equally represented at each hour of the clock (p. iii):

- The Youth Criminal Justice Act (12:00)

- Policing and Peacekeeping (1:00)

- Community Justice Committees (2:00)

- First Nations Law (3:00)

- Nurturing Leadership (4:00)

- Wellness and Balance (5:00)

- Inherent Authority and Treaty Relationships (6:00)

- Lands and Resources (7:00)

- Ancestral Laws (8:00)

- Restoring Balance (9:00)

- Justice and Healing (10:00)

- The Legal System and Legislation (11:00)

Surrounding the clock are the nations of their community, written in English, and the language representing each nation. What the guidebook has successfully accomplished is the integration of history, mainstream thinking, expertise, and practices with a strong sense of community, harmony, the land, and their own knowledge, experience, and expertise. Punishment is not a response: "In the Commission on First Nations and Métis Peoples and Justice Reform report, Willie Littlechild spoke of people who are 'Champions of Change' in our communities who are true leaders" (2010, p. 3). It is not about a single successful program or one that failed; it is instead about developing the culture for change, working collaboratively across "broken promises and relationships" to reduce effectively the social-structural and individual-level challenges faced by Aboriginal youth that contribute to their victimization and criminalization in this country.

We have briefly discussed and made a case for the importance of understanding the complexities of Aboriginal youth crime. The historical context illuminates the policies of domination and assimilation, phrases we equate with broken relationships and promises. We suggest that to address Aboriginal youth crime, any intervention must incorporate elements that address poverty, racism, and self-determination. Further, interventions must include family and community as part of the process.

We have also discussed a number of approaches to understanding the factors that contribute to criminal behaviour and criminalization, including those based in biology, sociology, and psychology. We suggest that the criminalization of "deviant" Aboriginal youth behaviours is largely a result of victimization at the individual and social-structural levels. Finally, our conclusion is that any effort to deal effectively with the issues facing Aboriginal youth and Aboriginal offenders must be based on an understanding of Aboriginal culture, values, and justice. Ultimately, any approach to reducing the criminalization of Aboriginal youth must be situated against a backdrop against which social-structural issues are also addressed.

Key Terms

Aboriginal
colonization
criminalization
fetal alcohol spectrum disorder (FASD)

marginalization
trauma
values
victimization

Review Questions

1. What happened to once flourishing First Nations societies that contributed to Aboriginal youth crime?
2. Aboriginal youth experience victimization in greater numbers than their non-Aboriginal counterparts. Explain.

3. Aboriginal youth experience criminalization in greater numbers than their non-Aboriginal counterparts. Discuss.

4. What are the arrays of influences or explanations that contribute to Aboriginal youth crime?

5. How do Aboriginal perspectives on justice differ from non-Aboriginal perspectives?

Critical Thinking Questions

1. If Aboriginal youth are to succeed in Canada, partake as full citizens in the economy and educational system, and reduce their undesirable position in the criminal justice system, what critical changes would you make to policies? To legislation? To public education?

2. There have been numerous federal and provincial inquiries and reports on the historical relationships between First Nation and Métis peoples and European settlers. Yet Aboriginal children and youth today remain disadvantaged in many ways. Can the damaged relationships between First Nation and Métis peoples and European settlers ever be healed? Is the criminal justice system the vehicle for such change?

3. Carol LaPrairie is one of Canada's most prolific authors on Aboriginal justice. She was a committed advocate for Aboriginal justice reform. She applied sound empirical evidence and research practices to evoke change (Murphy and Stenning 2014). Here is a question LaPrairie might challenge us to think about: "What are the community-based reforms that would address the policies and practices needed for Aboriginal youth who are involved in the criminal justice system?"

References

Adler, F., Mueller, G.O.W., Laufer, W.S., and Grekul, J. (2009). *Criminology* (Canadian ed.). Toronto: McGraw-Hill Ryerson.

Ahmed, E., Harris, N., Braithwaite, J., and Braithwaite, V. (2001). *Shame management through reintegration.* Cambridge, UK: Cambridge University Press.

Bégin, M., Eggertson, L., and Macdonald, N. (2009, June). A country of perpetual pilot projects. *Canadian Medical Association Journal, 180*(12).

Borne, P. (2008). *Community conversations.* Toronto: BPS Books.

Boyes-Watson, C. (2008). *Peacemaking circles and urban youth: Bringing justice home.* St Paul, MN: Living Justice Press.

Braswell, M.C. (2005). Criminal justice: An ethic for the future. In M.C. Braswell, B.R. McCarthy, and B.J. McCarthy, *Justice, crime, and ethics.* Conklin, NY: Matthew Bender & Company.

Brown, B. (2007). *Shame resilience theory.* In S.P. Robbins, P. Chatterjee, and E.R. Canda (Eds), *Contemporary human behavior theory: A critical perspective for social work* (rev. ed.). Boston: Allyn and Bacon.

Brzozowski, J.A., Taylor-Butts, A., and Johnson, S. (2006). Victimization and offending among the Aboriginal population in Canada. *Juristat, 26*(3). Statistics Canada, Catalogue no. 85-002-XIE.

Butler, D. (2002). Individualizing instruction in self-regulated learning. *Theory into Practice, 41*(2): 81–92.

Calverley, D., Cotter, A., and Halla, E. (2010). *Youth Custody and Community Services in Canada, 2008–2009. Juristat* (April): 1–29. http://www.statcan.gc.ca/pub/85-002-x/2010001/article/11147-eng.pdf

Cazal, T., Garnett, T., Chalas, D., Wiredu, E., and Grekul, J. (2013). *Alberta gang study*. Edmonton: Alberta Solicitor General.

CCJA (Canadian Criminal Justice Association). (2000). Aboriginal people and the justice system. *Aboriginal Peoples and the Criminal Justice System*. Retrieved from http://www.ccja-acjp.ca/en/aborit.html

CCJA. (2008, Spring/Summer). *Youth Justice, 23*(2–3). Ottawa.

Chartrand, L., and McKay, C. (2006). *A review of research on criminal victimization and First Nations, Métis and Inuit peoples 1990–2001*. Ottawa: Policy Centre for Victim Services, Department of Justice Canada.

Christie, N. (1977). Conflict as property. *British Journal of Criminology, 17*(1): 1–15.

Chudley, A.E., Conry, J., Cook, J.L., Loock, C., Rosales, T., and LeBlanc, N. (2005). Fetal alcohol spectrum disorder: Canadian guidelines for diagnosis. *Canadian Medical Association Journal, 172*(supplement 5): s1–s21.

Comack, E., Deane, L., Morrissette, L., and Silver, J. (2013). *"Indians wear red": Colonialism, resistance, and Aboriginal street gangs*. Winnipeg: Fernwood.

Commission on First Nations and Métis Peoples and Justice Reform. (2004). *Legacy of hope: An agenda for change*. Final Report, Vol. I. Saskatchewan.

Commission on First Nations and Métis Peoples and Justice Reform. (2003–04). *Submissions to the commission*, Vol. II. Saskatchewan.

Crenshaw, S.J.N. (2005). *The role of systemic public education in the retention and attrition of students placed at risk: Closing or creating the achievement gap*. In *Dissertation Abstracts International*, 66/04, 1220.

Deane, L., Bracken, D.C., and Morrissette, L. (2007). Desistance within an urban Aboriginal gang. *Probation Journal, 54*(2): 125–41.

Donnellan, M.B., Trzesniewski, K.H., Robins, R.W., Moffitt, T.E., and Caspi, A. (2005). Low self-esteem is related to aggression, anti-social behaviour and delinquency. *Psychological Science, 16*(4): 328–35.

Duke, D.L. (1977). What can students tell educators about classroom dynamics? *Theory into Practice, 16*(4): 262–71. Retrieved from http://www.jstor.org

Dumont, J. (1990). "Justice and Aboriginal Peoples." In *Aboriginal Peoples and the Justice System*, edited by the Royal Commission on Aboriginal Peoples. Ottawa: Ministry of Supply and Services.

Dumont, J. (1996). Justice and Aboriginal People. In Royal Commission on Aboriginal Peoples, *Bridging the cultural divide. A report on Aboriginal peoples and the criminal justice system in Canada* (p. 69). Ottawa: Queen's Printer.

Elliot, D. (1997). Social and health-care pilot project for sex trade workers: Interim report. In L. Chartrand and C. McKay, *A review of research on criminal victimization and First Nations, Métis and Inuit peoples 1990–2001*. Ottawa: Policy Centre for Victim Services, Department of Justice Canada.

Episkenew, J. (2009). *Taking back our spirits: Indigenous literature, public policy and healing*. Winnipeg: University of Manitoba Press.

Farrington, D.P. (2007). Advancing knowledge about desistance. *Journal of Contemporary Criminal Justice, 23*(1): 125–34.

Gilligan, J. (1996). *Violence: Our deadly epidemic and its causes*. New York: Putman Books.

Grekul, J., and LaBoucane-Benson, P. (2008). Aboriginal gangs and their (dis)placement: Contextualizing recruitment, membership and status. *Canadian Journal of Criminology and Criminal Justice, 50*: 31–57.

Harms, L., and Pierce, J. (2011). *Working with people: Communication skills for reflective practice*. Don Mills, ON: Oxford University Press.

Herman, J. (1997). *Trauma and recovery*. New York: Basic Books.

Hester, R.K., and Miller, W.R. (1995). *Handbook of alcoholism treatment approaches: Effective alternatives* (2nd ed.). Needham Heights, MA: Allyn and Bacon.

Hollin, C.R. (2007). Criminological psychology. In M. Maguire, R. Morgan, and R. Reiner (Eds), *The Oxford handbook of criminology* (4th ed., pp. 43–77). New York: Oxford University Press.

Kelly, K., and Caputo, T. (2007). Health and street/homeless youth. *Journal of Health Psychology*, *12*: 726–36.

Kelly, K.D., and Totten, M. (2002). *When children kill: A social psychological study of youth homicide*. Peterborough, ON: Broadview Press.

Kingsley, C., and Mark, M. (2000). "Sacred lives: Canadian Aboriginal children & youth speak out about sexual exploitation," in S. McKay, D. Fuchs, and I. Brown (2009), *Passion for action in child and family services: Voices from the Prairies*. Regina, SK: Canadian Plains Research Centre.

Lane Jr., P., M. Bopp, J. Bopp, & J. Norris. (2002). *Mapping the healing journey: The final report of a First Nation research project on healing in Canadian Aboriginal communities*. Ottawa, ON: Solicitor General of Canada and the Aboriginal Healing Foundation.

Law Commission of Canada. (2003). *What is a crime? Challenges and alternatives*. Retrieved from http://www.lcc.gc.ca

McCaslin, W. (2005). *Justice as healing: Indigenous ways*. St Paul, MN: Living Justice Press.

Mazzotta, M.A. (2004). Perceptions about schooling and substance abuse treatment success from court mandated adolescent males. In *Dissertation Abstracts International*, *65*(02): 412. Retrieved from http://www.proquest.umi.com

Minaker, J.C., and Hogeveen, B. (2009). *Youth, crime, and society: Issues of power and justice*. Toronto: Pearson Prentice Hall.

Murphy, C., and Stenning, P. (2014). Introduction. In *Essays to Honour the Life and Work of Dr. Carol LaPrairie*. Toronto: University of Toronto Press. Special issue of *Canadian Journal of Criminology and Criminal Justice*, *56*(4).

Nelson, R. (2011). *Reconstruction of a learner self: A phenomenological study with youth and young adults post-incarceration*. Doctoral dissertation in the Faculty of Education and the Faculty of Graduate Studies and Research, University of Regina.

Nimmo, M. (2001, June). *The "invisible" gang members: A report on female gang association in Winnipeg*. Canadian Centre for Police Alternatives.

Ooi, Y.P., Ang, R.P., Fung, D.S.S., Wong, G., and Cai, Y. (2006). The impact of parent-child attachment on aggression, social stress and self-esteem. *School Psychology International*, *27*: 552–66.

Perreault, S. (2011). Violent victimization of Aboriginal people in the Canadian provinces, 2009. *Juristat*. Statistics Canada Catalogue no. 85-002-X.

Perreault, S. (2014). Admissions to youth correctional services in Canada, 2011/2012. *Juristat*. Statistics Canada Catalogue no. 85-002-x. Retrieved from http://www.statcan.gc.ca/pub/85-002-x/2014001/article/11917-eng.htm

Popova, S., Lange, S., Burd, L., Chudley, A.E., Clarren, S.K., and Rehm, J. (2013). Cost of fetal alcohol spectrum disorder diagnosis in Canada. PLOS ONE8 (4): e60434. doi: 10.1371/journal.pone.0060434

Ramirez, Mark D. (2013). Punitive sentiment. *Criminology*, *51*(2): 329–64. In *Criminological Highlights*, Vol. 14, No.1, January 2014, Centre for Criminology and Sociolegal Studies, University of Toronto.

Raveaud, M. (2005). Hares, tortoises and the social construction of the pupil: Differentiated learning in French and English primary schools. *British Educational Research Journal*, *31*(4): 459–79.

Reiman, J. (2013). *The rich get richer and the poor go to prison* (10th ed.). New York: Pearson.

Restorative Justice Unit, File Hills Qu'Appelle Tribal Council. (2010). *First Nations community justice handbook*. Saskatchewan: File Hills Qu'Appelle Tribal Council.

Roberts, J., and Doob, A.N. (1997). Race, ethnicity, and criminal justice in Canada. In M. Tonry (Ed.), *Ethnicity, crime and immigration: Comparative and cross-national perspectives*, Vol. 21 (pp. 469–522). Chicago: University of Chicago Press.

Ross, R. (2006). *Dancing with a ghost*. Toronto: Penguin Group.

Royal Commission on Aboriginal Peoples. (1996). Highlights from the report *People to people, nation to nation*. Ottawa: Indian and Northern Affairs Canada.

Schonert-Reichl, K. (2000, April). *Children and youth at risk: Some conceptual considerations*. Paper presented at the Pan-Canadian Educational Research Agenda Symposium "Children and Youth at Risk," Ottawa. Retrieved from http://www.educ.ubc.ca/research/ksr/docs/schonert-reichl_childrenatrisk2000.pdf

Solanto, J. (2008). Aboriginal Justice Forum presentation: *Intergenerational trauma and healing. Found on the National Day of Healing and Reconciliation, January 28, 2010.* Forum organized by Pacific Business and Law Institute with support from the Aboriginal Directorate, Justice Canada. Retrieved from: http://ndhr.ca/wordpress/?s=solanto

Spano, R., Rivera, C., Vazsonyi, A.T., and Bolland, J.M. (2008). The impact of exposure to violence on a trajectory of (declining) parental monitoring: A partial test of the ecological-transactional model of community violence. *Criminal Justice and Behavior, 35*(11): 1411–28.

Statistics Canada. (2006). Aboriginal people as victims and offenders. *The Daily,* 6 June 2006. Government of Canada. Retrieved from http://www76.statcan.gc.ca/stcsr/query.html?style=ecl-f&qt=Aboriginal+people+as+victims+and+offenders&charset=utf-8&ct=300800001&qm=1&qp=topic%3A113113165%2C+topic%3A300800000%2C&oq =&rq=1

Totten, M. (2012). *Nasty, brutish, and short: The lives of gang members in Canada.* Toronto: James Lorimer.

Totten, M. (2014). *Gang life: 10 of the toughest tell their stories.* Toronto: James Lorimer.

Walsh, A., and Beaver, K.M. (2009). *Biosocial criminology: New directions in theory and research.* New York: Routledge.

Wesley-Esquimaux, C.C., and Smolewski, M. (2004). *Historic trauma and Aboriginal healing.* Ottawa: Report prepared for the Aboriginal Healing Foundation.

Weyers, S., Dragano, N., Mobus, S., Beck, E., Stang, A., Möhlenkamp, S., et al. (2008). Low socio-economic position in association with poor social networks and social support: Results from the Heinz Nixdorf Recall Study. *International Journal for Equity in Health, 7*(13): 1–13.

White, J., and Jodoin, N. (2007). *Aboriginal youth: A manual of promising suicide prevention strategies.* Centre for Suicide Prevention, Canadian Mental Health Association, Alberta Division.

White, R. (2008). Disputed definitions and fluid identities: The limitations of social profiling in relation to ethnic youth gangs. *Youth Justice, 8:* 149–61.

Wotherspoon, T., and Schissel, B. (2001). The business of placing Canadian children and youth at-risk. *Canadian Journal of Education, 26*(3): 321–39.

Wright, J.P., Tibbetts, S.G., and Daigle, L.E. (2008). *Criminals in the making: Criminality across the life course.* Thousand Oaks, CA: Sage.

Yessine, A.K., and Bonta, J. (2009). The offending trajectories of youthful Aboriginal offenders. *Canadian Journal of Criminology and Criminal Justice, 51*(4): 435–72.

Youngblood, H.J. (Sa'ke'j). (2008). *Indigenous diplomacy and the rights of peoples: Achieving un recognition.* Saskatoon: Purich Publishing.

An Overview of Gang-Involved Youth in Canada*

Mark Totten

Overview

This chapter will provide an overview of youth gangs in Canada, focusing on three major types of gangs: (1) street gangs, (2) mid-level gangs, and (3) organized crime groups. The primary differences between these gangs include hierarchical structure, level of sophistication, degree of organization, seriousness of criminal activity, breadth of influence, and longevity. We will also discuss the different roles in gangs, along with gender issues. Many young women involved in gangs experience sexual exploitation and other forms of violence. In general, most young women play tertiary roles in gangs. In addition, this chapter will present a biopsychosocial model for understanding gang involvement. This model explores key risk and protective factors in the following areas: biological and genetic, psychological, family, peer group, and community. Finally, we will investigate high-quality prevention, intervention, and suppression strategies.

---

* Given the subject area, some of the language may appear tactless, but in order that it be authentic and without sensationalism, some terms from gang life are included.

Key Objectives

After reading this chapter, you should be able to:

- Present an overview of the study of youth gangs.
- Examine internalized and externalized patterns of violence for gang-involved youth.
- Review Canadian judicial responses to gang crimes.
- Outline biopsychosocial explanations of gang involvement.
- Identify high-quality prevention, intervention, and suppression models.

Introduction

Last year I got shot, rolled up in a plastic sheet and thrown in a bathtub and left to die. I was all caught up. I paid out what I had to pay out [money made from crack dealing] and I took my share. I loaded up my rig and took it [crack, intravenously] and was chillin' and I looked up and he [a member of the same gang] had a gun pointed at my head. The next thing I knew it felt like I had been punched really hard. I felt my gut and I was bleeding and I fell down. I was stoned so I didn't feel any pain and I got up and they wrapped me in plastic and threw me in the tub—to die I guess.

—Totten 2012a, p. 205

To understand and address youth involvement in gangs, we must examine pathways into and out of gang life. Qualitative research provides an excellent opportunity to hear the voices of young gang members and to shed light on the *how* and *why* of gang life. We begin this chapter by providing an overview of gang research in Canada. Next, we explore the differences between street gangs, mid-level gangs, and organized crime groups. We investigate why marginalized Aboriginal and minority young people are overrepresented in Canadian gangs and look at female involvement in gangs. Next, we examine a biopsychosocial model for understanding gang involvement. Finally, we explore high-quality prevention, intervention, and suppression approaches. Unfortunately, Canada's "get tough" policies preferred and introduced by the previous Conservative government do not work. As will be demonstrated, we cannot incarcerate our way out of the gang problem.

Gang-involved youth are not born "bad." Instead, they are trained by violent and unhealthy adults to engage in violent offending. When we take the time to sit down with gang members and hear their life stories, a clear picture emerges. We see that instead of just being "gang members," these young people have endured tremendous suffering and, despite this, many have hidden talents and skills. Some are talented singers and rappers; others are poets and writers. Many have acute business savvy—skills that can be applied to the business world outside of gang life. Many are parents, struggling to raise children in impoverished and marginalized circumstances. Finally, most have very serious health problems, such as brain damage, developmental delays, learning disabilities, and terminal illnesses. When we see the human face of gang-involved young people, it is much easier to develop good strategies to prevent gang involvement, support exit from gangs, and implement effective criminal-justice-system responses (see Totten 2014).

Overview of Gang Research in Canada

How Many Are There?

Even though youth gangs have existed since Canada was first settled (see Carrigan 1998), it is difficult to find accurate data on the actual number of gangs in Canada. Police-based estimates are likely inflated for two main reasons: (1) there is no commonly accepted definition of a gang; and (2) levels of funding are in part dependent on how large the gang problem is. In addition, there is a lack of academic research that focuses on the prevalence of gangs across the country. Most studies have directed their attention to specific regions of Canada.[1] In addition, it is difficult to come up with a list of gang names and members because low-level street gangs are in a state of constant flux. Names and membership frequently change.

In 2006, the Criminal Intelligence Service of Canada identified 344 street gangs with 11,900 members. Three per cent of the identified gangs were organized crime groups. Most street gang members were between 21 and 30 years of age, and almost all the gangs had youth and adult members. Roughly 6 per cent were youths only—18 years and younger. These gangs were active in 166 urban, rural, and Aboriginal reserve areas. At that time, gangs were active in all parts of the country with the exception of Prince Edward Island, Yukon, and Nunavut (CISC 2007). In 2010, the Criminal Intelligence Service of Canada (CISC) reported that there could be as many as 900 gangs in Canada (CISC 2010). Although this may seem like a large increase in the number of gangs since 2006, we should interpret these figures with caution. It could be that new gangs are forming, but it could also be that police are counting gangs differently (for example, organized crime groups could be identified as street gangs, and cells from larger gangs could be identified as new gangs). As well, street gangs could break apart, forming smaller groups, and gangs could be changing names. The CISC no longer publishes annual reports on organized crime owing to these challenges.

Western Canada has consistently had higher violent crime rates and gang activity compared to central and eastern Canada (Perreault 2013). This is likely due to pockets of high crime in cities such as Vancouver (the Downtown Eastside), Winnipeg (West End, West Broadway, Centennial, and North End neighbourhoods), Regina (the North Central neighbourhood), and Saskatoon (including Pleasant Hill and Riversdale communities). These areas are populated by transient young men who are high school dropouts, by single-parent families with high rates of violence and abuse, and by addicts. They are characterized by high poverty, poor housing, and drug dealing.[2]

Where Are They Located?

Gangs can be found throughout Canada, and their level of activity and membership varies by region.[3] Most street gangs are based in ethnically marginalized neighbourhoods and on reserves, and they do not expand their territory outside of their immediate turf. However, a few gangs have higher levels of sophistication and have expanded to other parts of Canada or to the United States. Gangs with inter-provincial connections include, among others, Indian Posse, Native Syndicate, Independent Soldiers, Manitoba Warriors, and North Preston's Finest. Transnational gangs identified in Canada include the MS-13 and the 18th Street Gang.

Given that gang membership is very fluid and actual gangs come and go quickly, the following data should be interpreted with caution. One of the reasons behind the rapidly changing composition of gangs is that the gangs of today are more likely to co-operate with each other. Although there are gang wars in Canada (e.g., the Galloway Boys and the Malvern Crew in Toronto), gang members understand that wars are bad for business—they attract the police and also eat into profits. Another complicating factor lies in the definitional problem of what exactly constitutes street gangs, mid-level gangs, and organized crime groups.

The Maritimes

Outlaw motorcycle gangs present the biggest problem in the Maritimes, and youth are unlikely to be affiliated with these gangs. Although gang activity is very limited in Newfoundland and Labrador, the Bacchus motorcycle gang has recently been active. In Nova Scotia, street gangs are a concern, though nowhere near the extent they are in central and Western Canada. Gaston Road Gang, G-Lock, Murda Squad, North End Dartmouth, Money Over Bitches, Wolf Pack, and the Woodside Gang have had a presence historically. In addition, a small number of gangs have connections to other parts of Canada (such as North Preston's Finest), primarily through the sex trade. In New Brunswick, outlaw motorcycle gangs have been active, along with various factions of the Crips and the Bloods. Some of these also have links to gangs in other parts of Canada, including Ontario and Quebec. Prostitution and the trafficking of young women are the main criminal activities of these gangs.

Quebec

There are approximately 50 known gangs in Quebec, most being Haitian, Jamaican, or Hispanic based. Most gangs are ethnically homogeneous and tend to be aligned with Red or Blue factions. Gangs that have a high degree of criminal sophistication and that are linked to outlaw motorcycle gangs or the Italian Mafia include Bo-Gars, Crack Down Posse, Syndicates, and the Wolf Pack. Most gangs in Quebec are in the Montreal area, with the remainder based in Gatineau, Laval, Longueil, and Quebec City.

Ontario

Although estimates vary considerably, conservative approximations suggest that there are roughly 180 gangs in Ontario, with the largest concentration in the Greater Toronto Area but also on northern reserves. Of these gangs, a handful are criminally sophisticated, highly organized, and linked to groups in other parts of Canada. They include the Quebec-based Crack Down Posse (Niagara Falls) and Bo-Gars (Niagara Falls); Jamestown Crips, Valvettithurai (V.V.T., a Tamil gang), Asian Assassins, Galloway Boys, Sick Thugz, and Dixon City Bloods (Toronto); and the Ledbury-Banff Crips (Ottawa). Meanwhile, in northern Ontario, the Native Syndicate street gang is a concern. Outlaw motorcycle gangs are also major concerns in Ontario.

Manitoba

There are more or less 25 known street gangs in Manitoba. A majority of these are Aboriginal, along with smaller numbers of African- and Asian-based groups. These latter gangs are primarily active in the Winnipeg area (including the Mad Cowz, African Mafia, and Asian Bomb Squad), whereas Aboriginal gangs are also based in Winnipeg (such as Native Syndicate and Indian Posse) and in rural areas and on reserves (including Manitoba Warriors, Indian Posse, and Native Syndicate).

Saskatchewan

There are approximately 20 street gangs in this province, and almost all are Aboriginal. Indian Posse (IP) and Native Syndicate (NS) are the most sophisticated, with cells in Manitoba and Northern Ontario. The Hells Angels and their puppet club (the Freewheelers) have been in conflict with the NS over the lucrative drug trade. Saskatoon, Regina, and Prince Albert have the highest number of active gangs, including Brown Premise, Crazy Cree, Crazy Dragons, Indian Mafia, Crips, Tribal Brotherz, Terror Squad, and Scorpion Brothers, among several others. Fort Qu'Appelle, Yorkton, and many reserves also have gang activity.

Alberta

There are around 30 known street gangs in Alberta. The Crazy Dragons is likely among the most sophisticated given its many cells across Alberta, in other provinces, and in the Northwest Territories. Most other gangs are Asian based (such as the former Fresh Off the Boat and Fresh Off the Boat Killers) and Aboriginal (including Indian Posse, Redd Alert, and Alberta Warriors). The Maskwakis (formerly known as Hobbema) community in central Alberta, which includes Samson, Ermineskin, Montana, and Louis Bull Cree Nations, has had a very high rate of gang activity historically, with a handful of gangs competing for control of the drug trade. The Edmonton-based White Boy Posse is a white supremacist gang, well known for its co-operation with the Hells Angels in the trafficking of drugs.

British Columbia

There are approximately 30 active gangs in this province, with most based in the Lower Mainland (including the 18th Street gang, Bloods, Crazy Dragons, Crips, MS-13). Some of these gangs have migrated to smaller cities such as Prince George and Cranbrook. Aboriginal gangs are active on some reserves and in the Downtown Eastside of Vancouver. The most sophisticated gangs include the United Nations Gang, Independent Soldiers, and Game Tight Soldiers. Many low-level gangs buy drugs from organized crime groups, such as Asian groups and the Hells Angels.

Northwest Territories, Yukon, and Nunavut

There is very little gang activity north of the 69th parallel, although cells of the Crazy Dragons, Indian Posse, Alberta Warriors, White Boy Posse, and Redd Alert have been active in Yellowknife and Whitehorse. These gangs are primarily based in Alberta and British Columbia and have migrated north due to the lucrative drug trade.

Gang Typology in Canada

The multi-dimensional frameworks developed by Totten (2009a, 2009b) and Mellor, MacRae, Pauls, and Hornick (2005) highlight the different types of Canadian gangs involving young adults.[4] Street gangs are visible, hard-core groups that come together for profit-driven criminal activity and often severe violence. Gang-related communication rituals and public displays of gang-like attributes are common, such as tattoos (Totten 2012b; Gordon 2000). Gang involvement exists on a continuum, and types of gangs can be conceptualized using a pyramid diagram (see Figure 12.1). The degree of organization in the gang is defined by the following:

- The gang's structure and hierarchical nature

- The gang's connection to larger, more serious organized crime groups

- The gang's sophistication and permanence

- The existence of a specific code of conduct or set of formal rules

- The gang's initiation practices

- The level of integration, cohesion, and solidarity among the gang's members (Totten 2008)

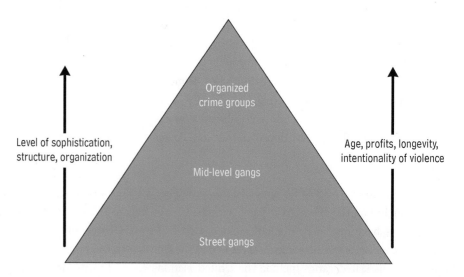

FIGURE 12.1 Gang and Organized Crime Group Typology

Source: Based on the work of Shinder Kirk, B.C. Integrated Gang Task Force

This integrated model allows for a general typology that can be applied and adapted to identify specific types of gangs. The common structure is very similar to that identified in the United States (Block and Block 2001), Europe (Klein 2002), and other countries (see Covington 2010; Grennan, Britz, Rush, and Barker 2000). The continuum includes street gangs, mid-level gangs, and organized crime groups.

Street Gangs

Almost all youth gang members in Canada belong to street gangs. The following are some characteristics common to most street gangs:

- Street gangs are involved in serious crime and violence—this differentiates gangs from non-criminal youth groups.

- Street gangs have some stability over time, yet membership is fluid.

- Typically, they claim an area/turf, which they protect from rival gangs. This may be a housing project or an area they claim to be their own for drug distribution (Hemmati 2006; NCPC 2007).

- Members identify themselves through a common name, symbols, colours, signs, graffiti, clothing styles, bandanas, and hats.

- They rely on violent entry and exit rituals to protect the gang from outsiders.

- Marginalized ethnic and racial minorities, including Aboriginal youth, dominate membership. While some gangs have members mainly from a single ethnic group, an increasing number have a multi-ethnic membership. One key factor that differentiates those who become gang involved from those who do not is the experience of severe poverty.

- Drug and alcohol abuse is common.

The case of Jafar is illustrative of the chaotic, fluid nature of many street gangs in Canada. Jafar is a 29-year-old man from sub-Saharan Africa whose family escaped a civil war by coming to Canada. He is facing deportation because of his gang crimes. He was the leader of a rival gang that had just splintered off from the main gang. He described the unpredictable, volatile nature of his gang:

> It was crazy . . . at first. We had dysfunctional alliances on the street, with no connection, and there was a major power struggle. It grew so fast and no one seen it. . . . It took everybody by surprise. There was no established leadership in the beginning, just a few individuals, and no one had overall responsibility. We had four or five guys in charge, whose rank was higher, and then just a really large number of other guys under them. (Totten 2014, p. 177)

Mid-level Gangs

Mid-level gangs have characteristics of both street gangs and organized crime groups:

- These gangs can be multi-ethnic, although some groups in the Prairie provinces are exclusively Aboriginal.

- Members may come from different socio-economic backgrounds, but Aboriginal and African gang members have lived in extreme poverty.

- These gangs are frequently rooted in school, justice, and child welfare settings—family blood lines and neighbourhoods are important.

- Compared to organized crime groups, mid-level gangs are made up of unstructured smaller groups or cells.

- Like street gangs, their relationships with other groups are fluid and opportunistic—often organized around lucrative criminal opportunities.

- These gangs are involved in serious crimes: extortion, kidnapping, drug dealing, smuggling, homicide, extreme violence, and trafficking.

- Violence is often initiated in response to perceived threats from other groups, whether real or not.

- Members rely on violent entry and exit rituals to protect the gang from outsiders.

- Mid-level gangs are frequently sophisticated and disciplined (Totten 2012a).

Organized Crime Groups

According to the Canadian Security Intelligence Service and Public Safety Canada,[5] organized crime groups have a number of common characteristics. It is relatively rare for teens to be involved in these sophisticated organizations. Typical features include the following:

- Organized crime groups are highly structured and hierarchical—they are often modelled after successful companies.

- They have flourished over time and are recognized, feared, and respected.

- Membership is exclusive and is based on family, race, and ethnicity.

- They are complex enterprises with rules, bylaws, and constitutions.

Street Gang Membership, Roles, and Characteristics

Who Is Involved in Street Gangs?

Youth gang membership can be conceptualized using a concentric circle diagram: wannabees/posers and "floaters" (youth who are marginally involved but have friendships with confirmed gang members—the term was first used by Spergel [1990]) are on the

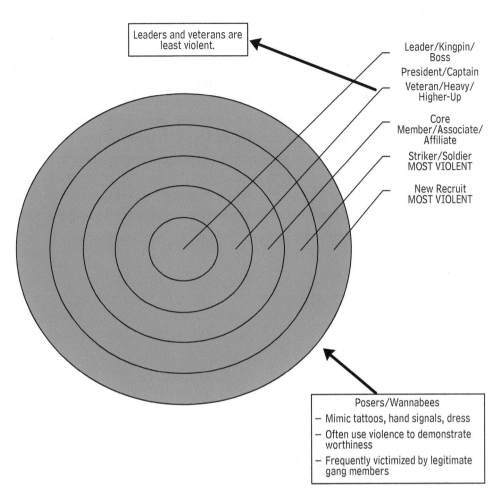

FIGURE 12.2 Roles in Street Gangs and Levels of Violence

Source: Totten 2012b.

outside; new recruits are in the outermost ring; and leaders are in the innermost ring (see Figure 12.2). The leadership structure is made up of the original founder and core members who started the gang. Membership commitment can be measured in a hierarchical ranking system within the gang (Totten and Dunn 2012a, 2012b). Often, there is not one person who directs other members, although older members have more influence compared to young members. Leaders (also called "kingpins," bosses, presidents, or captains) actively promote and participate in serious criminal activity. These males are generally in their mid-twenties or early thirties. Veterans (also called heavies or higher-ups) decide which criminal activities the gang will participate in and are considered to be faithful in their loyalty to the gang. Along with leaders, they are responsible for settling internal conflicts within the gang. These conflicts typically arise from members having friendships with rival gang members, from those who engage in sexual relations with girlfriends of fellow gang members without their expressed consent, or from those who steal money from criminal profits or illicit drugs. Consequences range from severe beatings to death. Core members (also called associates or affiliates) usually have been with the gang since it started and are experienced, proven members. Wannabees are at a particularly high risk of being victimized by violence at the hands of legitimate gang members. These youth are looking for a sense of belonging and family, and go to great lengths to mimic gang membership through tattoos, dress, display of colours, and hand signals.

There are some common indicators of membership. The more indicators there are, the greater the likelihood that a young person is gang involved. They include such indicators as stylized dress and haircuts; jewellery; tattoos; gang slang; graffiti and drawings; monikers or nicknames; hand signs; claiming or "repping" (representing a gang using their dress, hand signals, graffiti, etc.); association with known gang members; burns and scars, particularly those that are stylized (e.g., cigarette burns in the form of a triangle); branding (including burning a gang tattoo off); and gang photos on social media sites. Another indicator of membership is the correct use of slang. The following are some examples of gang slang:

- Cap: bullet

- Piece/heat/biscuit: gun

- Heat source: attracting police attention

- Crib: home

- 187: murder

- 81: Hells Angels

- 1%: outlaw bikers

- Eight ball: 8 oz. bag of drugs

- Busta cap: shoot a gun

- Slanging: dealing drugs

- Hound: sex offender

- Holla back: call me

- Feigning: craving drugs

- Slamming: injecting drugs

Many of these terms are used in hip-hop as well.

What Are the Primary Activities of Street Gangs?

Hanging Out

Contrary to popular belief, gang members spend the majority of their time hanging out, meeting basic needs such as food and shelter, partying, and being incarcerated (Sheldon, Tracy, and Brown 2004). A primary activity is heavy drug and alcohol use and generally a withdrawal from mainstream social interaction. Such drug use results in property crimes and crimes of violence, often on an impulsive and senseless basis (White 2007).

Making Profits from Serious Crime

Making money through serious crime may be episodic for disorganized street gangs, but it usually involves complex relationships and an organized division of labour for mid-level gangs and organized crime groups. As street-level robberies and rival gang violence increase, victims are made aware of the "turf war" as gangs establish their territory. Street gangs generally prey upon communities in which they reside through threats, violence, and intimidation to garner respect and fear. It is common for rival gangs to take control of separate high-rise apartment buildings in social housing communities and use them as a base for dealing chemicals, pimping young women, selling and storing firearms, and shooting at rival gang members from upper floor apartments. These gangs sometimes extort money from residents in return for protection from enemy gangs (Totten 2012a). As members become entrenched in violence and crime, the complexity of their behaviour increases and they assume a permanent place in specific geographic spaces. They come to acquire a steady supply of chemicals to sell (e.g., crack cocaine, crystal methamphetamine) and a sophisticated arsenal of guns to protect themselves and kill off rivals. The frequency and seriousness of violence and crime escalate over time, and by intimidating witnesses to their criminal activities, gang members enhance their status and increase their control over community residents and rivals, which is what we will discuss next.

Engaging in Severe Violence

Violence within and between gangs is associated with gaining social status and reputation. There is an emphasis on honour, personal integrity, and territoriality. Issues of self-esteem, gender identity, and self-protection help explain the onset and escalation of gang violence. Violence often occurs over seemingly insignificant incidents that are perceived as disrespectful by rival gang members; such incidents include crossing out a rival's graffiti or painting it upside down, showing a rival's hand signs upside down, or crossing out a rival's hand signs with another finger (Totten 2012a). There are numerous examples in Canada of street gangs splintering into different groups as a result of internal conflict. These groups then engage in severe violence, including murder, against each other (e.g., Native Syndicate and Native Syndicate Killers; Fresh Off the Boat and Fresh Off the Boat Killers).

Jeremy's case is indicative of the extreme violence engaged in by many gang members.[6] He was 32 years old when I first interviewed him. An enforcer for both an Asian organized crime group and a prison gang, he looked white but told me that he was part Aboriginal. He used his appearance to his benefit: when working for a white supremacist prison gang, he claimed he was Caucasian; when hanging with Aboriginal gangs, he claimed he was Sioux. He told me about a particularly violent attack he delivered, at the direction of a prison gang: "I was nineteen and stabbed someone who ratted [a gang member] out. He was a snitch and I stabbed him with a hanger. Everyone stood around and were kicking him and just letting him bleed. I kept on stabbing him, poking holes in him" (Totten 2014, p. 157).

What Are the Distinguishing Characteristics of Gangs?

Hand Signals and Dress

The Bloods and Crips are two good examples of how different gangs use hand signals and dress to represent their gang. Both gangs have adopted specific cultural forms and public presentations of their attributes. Bloods' identifiers and symbols include the colour red, red bandanas ("rags"), crossed-out *C* in words as disrespect for Crips, and other disrespectful anti-Crips graffiti. Crips identifiers and symbols include the colour blue, blue bandanas, using the letter *C* in place of *B* in writing in disrespect for Bloods, and calling themselves "Blood Killas" (BK).

Most Bloods gangs use one hand to form a variation of the lower-case letter *b* to represent or lay claim to their territory or faction. This form of "repping" is used in many situations where other gang identifiers may not be possible or appropriate (such as graffiti), and it can also show that a gang member is in the area to conduct gang business as opposed to just passing through. These hand signs can serve to relay more specific information, such as what faction gang members represent within a larger gang or in which activities they are currently taking part. Individual letters can be used to tell stories when flashed in rapid succession, each representing a word beginning with that letter. Some gang-related hand signals are similar to other common hand signs, which can result in confusion between gang members as well as for individuals who are not affiliated with gangs. Sometimes the result is violent victimization (Totten 2012a; Watkins and Ashby 2007).

Tattoos

Street gang members use tattoos for several reasons. Most gang members have numerous tattoos, particularly if they have spent time in young offender facilities, jails, or prison (Totten 2012b). Tattoos portray one or more symbols that the gang has adopted as something unique to represent the gang. Tattoos are also worn and used for intimidation. Members of violent gangs usually have the gang name tattooed in large, bold letters so that other persons or gang members will know what gang the person represents. Wearing an unauthorized tattoo typically results in the wearer being severely beaten or killed.

Crosses between the knuckles on both hands are meant to signify the number of years served in federal facilities (one cross is equivalent to one year served). Three dots or cigarette burn marks forming a triangle (usually near the thumb or wrist or next to one eye) signify *mi vida loca* or "my crazy life" (Knox 2000). Gang members in Canada report that the teardrop tattoo signifies to fellow gang members and rival gangs that the gang member killed a rival, had a member of his or her gang or family killed, or has served time. A primary function that young gang members attribute to this tattoo is to communicate the message that they are dangerous and must be respected (Totten 2012b).

Gang Recruitment and Exit

There are a handful of different routes into gang involvement for young people. Some members are "born in," others are "jumped in," some are actively recruited, some get "sexed in" or raped in, and yet others form their own gang (Original Gangster). Some of these routes are characterized by a high degree of motivation and choice; others involve no choice and are forced onto youth. For marginalized, abused, and vulnerable youth, there are many positive aspects of gang life. Many gang members talk about having a sense of family and belonging in their gangs, a safe place to hang out with friends, an identity, and a good source of income. For many youths who grow up in communities characterized by high unemployment, entrenched poverty, and violence, gang involvement is a rational choice (Totten 2009a). Gangs can also provide a shelter for young people who have suffered from racism, war atrocities, and the adverse effects of colonization (e.g., having dysfunctional parents who suffered abuse in residential schools), helping them to fight back against social injustice.

Recruitment refers to the process whereby youths are brought into a gang or the method by which they gain access to gangs. The recruitment process is different depending on gang type. For example, in family-based gangs, there is no recruitment outside of the immediate family. Joining the gang is seen as a normal thing to do, as prospective members are sometimes exposed to the gang by family members.

In other instances, street gangs and criminal organizations require recruits to perform specific tasks. Youths are required to prove themselves worthy of being taken into the gang by committing acts of severe sexual and physical violence and/or serious crimes. Leaders are responsible for this. Tasks include armed robbery, aggravated assault, murder (which is often referred to as being "murdered-in" and involves killing a rival when ordered to do so by a higher-up), chemical dealing, and pimping (CISS 2005). There is a standard process for being recruited in each gang. Recruitment is common in young offender or adult facilities.[7]

Most youth gangs require prospective recruits to meet certain criteria and perform criminal acts before they are allowed into the gang. This is called "crime-in." Younger gang members are most likely to be involved in the most serious crimes of violence as they are in the process of being recruited into the street gang. These youths want to prove themselves and rise through the ranks; they often earn serious money for gangs. To gain entry, a recruit generally requires sponsorship. These members often have their loyalty tested by gang members and are "put in work" by undertaking criminal activities when directed by leaders (Sanders, Lankenau, and Jackson-Bloom 2010; Valdez 2000). Before recruits are allowed entry into the gang, they are often required to pass three initial tests:

1. Perform a series of criminal acts called *strikes* at the direction of superiors in the gang to prove their loyalty.

2. Produce *paperwork* (a copy of their criminal record) for members of the gang.

3. Endure a beating from the other gang members to prove their strength and loyalty (this is called *beating-in*, *jumping-in*, or *boot-fucking*).

Gender plays a crucial role in determining routes into gang involvement. Many female gang members get "sexed-in" or raped into male-dominated gangs, where they are forced to endure sexual assaults by multiple gang members. The following example illustrates the unique ways in which young women become gang involved. Julie, 21 years old, was the only female in an all-male street gang from the age of 15 to the age of 19. She had to show the male gang members that she was deserving of their respect and was tough. She also needed a strategy to avoid being forced to work in the sex trade and to bring money into the gang. She resorted to pimping out a stable of anywhere from six to ten 15- to 17-year-old girls over a three-year period. She was widely feared on the streets because of her propensity to engage in severe violence. She continued this lucrative operation until she was charged and incarcerated for four years in both youth and adult facilities. She explained how treatment by her caregivers set the stage for gang membership:

> Coke and morphine. That's what I remember when I was young. Always lots of people coming and going, lots of girls and needles and alcohol. . . . My Dad was a dealer and a pimp—that's why there were always lots of girls and drugs around. That's how they took me (child protection). I brought a friend home when I was like five or six and my Dad and all those people were doing needles and then my friend went home and told her Mom and child welfare came to get me later that day. The cops picked my Dad up . . . (and) I got put in foster care. I've been everywhere—I've stayed in different places—until I went to jail—pretty much all my life. . . . They took me from the ghetto and put me into a rich neighbourhood. I was the only Indian in an all-white school. . . . Then I started to act out and went to (secure custody facility) lots. (Totten 2012a, p. 37)[8]

For many, the gang exit process can be just as difficult as, if not more difficult than, joining the gang. Methods of leaving can involve the following:

- *Blood out*: "Doing minutes" (suffering a beating) at the hands of a couple of gang members.

- *Gang rape*: Being sexually assaulted by multiple gang members.

- *Getting pregnant, having kids, or getting married*: Many gangs purport to have honourable and romantic ideals, including permitting members to leave in order to start their families.

- *Honouring-out*: loyal members, particularly those in leadership positions, are invited to a party to pay tribute to their membership in the gang.

- *Gang exit program*: Joining a comprehensive program that supports leaving the gang. This can be dangerous because higher-ups do not want you to leave.

- *Death*: Unfortunately, being killed or committing suicide is a common way to end gang membership.

Legislation and Official Response to Gangs

Bill C-24 is the only section of the Criminal Code related to crimes committed by gangs and organized crime groups. The Criminal Code does not, however, make reference to "gangs." The legal treatment of gangs is covered by provisions for "criminal organizations." This section of the Criminal Code has not been successfully applied in many cases. However, an increasing number of young offenders are being charged with involvement in organized crime. This is a matter of concern because most youth gangs are not criminal organizations. Rather, they are loosely organized, non-hierarchical, and fluid groups that come together and dissolve rapidly after profitable crimes have been committed.

Female Involvement in Gangs

Canada has few all-female gangs. Gang-involved young women have unique and special risks, including a history of victimization (mainly physical and sexual abuse); academic failure, truancy, or dropout; repeated running away and prostitution; unstable family life (lack of connectedness, isolation, other family members involved in the justice system); a history of unhealthy, dependent relationships, primarily with older males; mental health issues; and a history of substance abuse. Compared to males, young women report having experienced significantly higher rates of physical and sexual violence and victimization in their childhood (Totten 2012a).

There are three categories of young women who are involved in gangs: (1) female members of all-women street gangs; (2) women who are affiliated with male-dominated gangs; and (3) street women in the sex trade (Moore 2007; Totten 2012a). Young women who are members of all-female gangs are not in the same social situation as those who are affiliated with male gang members. The latter group is more vulnerable. These are the girlfriends and partners of the male gang members. Their affiliation and status are defined by their "man." They are likely to experience extreme physical and sexual violence from their male partners and are dominated by them. If these women are rejected by their partners, they become the property of other male gang members. Often, these females monitor the behaviours of other affiliated women, ensuring that they are not intimate or flirting with their "man." They do not experience the same sense of belonging and family as members of all-female gangs. Gang-affiliated women are in a position of dependency and are very isolated. Because of the "code of silence," they must demonstrate loyalty and cannot talk about their violent victimization.

Young women in male-dominated gangs play tertiary roles, such as being the lookout for the police, dealing drugs, or working in the sex trade (Totten 2014). They are typically required to carry weapons and drugs because they have a lower chance of being searched by male police officers (Abbotsford Youth Commission 2010; Dorais and Corriveau 2009), especially given the female anatomy (i.e., carrying drugs in their vagina). Women also are likely to act as escorts, drivers, and intelligence gatherers. They are involved in debit- and credit-card scams. Some manipulate rival male gang members into thinking they want a romantic relationship, when in fact these women are gathering intelligence on the rival gang. Young women who do not have prior criminal records are particularly attractive for gangs because they are off the police radar (Totten 2014).

On the other hand, young women who are members of all-female gangs report that they are relatively safe and free from violence and belong to mutually supportive peer groups. Anne Campbell (1987, pp. 463–4) writes, "Gang girls see themselves as different from their peers. Their association with the gang is a public proclamation of their rejection of the lifestyle which the community expects from them." Girls in all-female gangs are likely to resist and negotiate their gender roles outside of traditional femininity; the gang provides a social space to do gender differently.

There are at least two types of all-female gangs: those that are auxiliaries to male-dominated gangs and those that are independent of other gangs. Canada has had very few members of either type. Both types of female gangs are likely to have their own hierarchy and status (Nimmo 2001). Examples include the Winnipeg-based Sisters in Action gang and Native Sistahs (reported to be related to NS). The Indian Posse Girls are reported to be the auxiliary to the Indian Posse Gang and have exerted control over the Edmonton and Hobbema sex trade in the past. The Sisterhood Gang has been identified as affiliated with IP.

Unaffiliated street women/girls are by far the most vulnerable group of females. They are not respected or valued by the male gang members. These women hang out with gangs but do not have relationships with male gang members. Instead, they find themselves attracted to the gang and are treated as sex objects. Many are addicts and sex-trade workers, often referred to as "party girls." Some are wannabees or posers. See, for example, the case of Janie in Totten 2014 (pp. 108–9).

So far, we have provided an overview of the nature and characteristics of the different forms of youth gangs in Canada. Next, we will explore some of the explanations for and descriptions of their actions.

A Biopsychosocial Theory of Youth Gangs

A biopsychosocial perspective addresses the multiple risk factors related to gang involvement. Pathways into gang life are best understood through an integration of biological, psychological, and social factors, including biophysiological and psychological characteristics, as well as family, school, peer, and social variables. Within each category, social inequalities such as poverty, gender, and race are significant risk factors that can lead to unhealthy child and adolescent development. Protective factors such as access to high-quality health, recreation, education, and other social services and supports can improve the outcomes for children and youth who are vulnerable.

Children have different social, psychological, and familial experiences. They face different risks, and resiliency varies tremendously. Although all children have a right to an environment that is hospitable and nurturing, a significant minority grow up in one that is hostile and threatening. The playing field is far from level. Resilience is the ability to live in adverse conditions to achieve positive outcomes (Ungar 2007; Luthar, Cicchetti, and Becker 2000). It is through resilience that the combination of societal-level, institutional, and individual factors (Barankin and Khanlou 2011; Gutman and Midgley 2000; Smokowski, Reynolds, and Brezruczko 1999) to which young people are exposed results in positive and negative outcomes. It is important to recognize that diverse outcomes can be expected for young people living in similar negative life situations. The key is the ability of individuals, families, schools, and communities to mitigate the risk factors.

Biological and Genetic Factors

Biological and genetic factors can be key determinants of gang involvement. Children are born with different sets of abilities and potential as a result of these attributes in combination with other psychosocial factors. Factors such as resiliency, intelligence, cognitive functioning, physical ability, physical attributes, and body type are important protective factors in determining healthy child and adolescent development (see, generally, Santrock 2007).

The presence of one or more of these attributes can go a long way in protecting a young person from involvement in gang life. Developmental problems, learning disabilities, intellectual limitations, fetal alcohol spectrum disorder (FASD), brain injuries, predisposition to mental health problems, and certain personality traits are important risk factors that can lead to poor child and adolescent health in the absence of key buffers against these risks (Resnick, Ireland, and Borowsky 2004; World Health Organization 2002).

Personality traits that influence child behaviour are complex and the product of the co-occurrence of several genes (Plomin and Crabbe 2000). Temperament (whether children are fussy or calm, upset or happy) and other characteristics such as irritability, low self-control, and irresponsibility are moderately genetic (Moffitt et al. 2001). Children's capacity to learn the social use of language, to interact with others, and to regulate their emotions is influenced by genetic inheritance as well. These factors are directly influenced by a mother's behaviour when pregnant. For example, malnutrition, smoking, alcohol/drug consumption, and victimization by violence during pregnancy all contribute to negative health outcomes for the fetus. FASD, which results in infant brain damage to areas responsible for planning and self-control (Buxton 2004; Kyskan and Moore 2005), is a particular concern in Aboriginal communities. Risky behaviours during pregnancy are more common in low-income mothers. This is primarily due to a lack of education and other behavioural risk factors (Totten 2009c; Stark 2004).

It has been estimated that roughly 40 per cent of a child's anti-social behaviours may be related to genetic factors (Rhee and Waldman 2002; Moffitt 2005). However, genes interact with important environmental dynamics. For example, so-called bad genes inherited by a child (e.g., cognitive impairment and low intelligence) most likely will not negatively affect psychosocial functioning in the context of positive parenting, high-quality schooling, and a pro-social peer group.

In the preschool years, children with difficult temperaments, hyperactivity, impulsivity, oppositional and defiant behaviour, early-onset aggression, and social difficulties are at high risk of serious and violent offending trajectories. Without comprehensive early intervention to address risk and protective factors, these children will likely grow into the 5 per cent of all adolescents who are responsible for committing over half of all serious youth crime (Shaw 2001; Sprott, Doob, and Jenkins 2001).

Psychological Factors

Certain psychological factors are key determinants of mental health. Intellectual and interpersonal abilities, positive self-esteem, personal responsibility, and pro-social behaviours are key protective factors that can shelter young people from the risks of gang involvement. However, risk factors such as poor mental health status, low self-esteem and body image, learning disabilities, internalizing disorders (e.g., withdrawal, anxiety, eating disorders, and suicidal behaviour), and externalizing disorders (e.g., hyperactivity, concentration problems, and aggression) can compromise children's healthy development, particularly if they live in poverty and do not have protection from some of these risks. Children and youth with emotional and behavioural disorders are significantly more likely to be involved in gangs (see Totten 2012a).

Family Factors

In the vast majority of cases, the seeds of violence and gang involvement are planted at home. Simply put, children with strong bonds with their parents have better mental and physical health (Fabricius and Luecken 2007; McCreary Centre Society 1999) and are highly unlikely to become involved in gangs.

In Canada, child maltreatment is a major public health epidemic (MacMillan 2000) that affects many more children than cancer or AIDS. Many maltreated kids have impaired physical, emotional, cognitive, and social functioning. Suffering serious and prolonged child maltreatment is strongly related to experiencing youth violence and mental health problems (MacMillan 2000). All aspects of children's lives are affected when they grow up in violent homes. Domestic violence can make children less likely to succeed in school, more likely to suffer and commit violence, and more likely to face a host of health problems that can last throughout their lives (ibid.). Depression, low self-esteem, self-destructive and criminal behaviour, delayed cognitive development and poor school performance, and aggression are common (Gold, Wolan Sullivan, and Lewis 2011; Wolak and Finkelhor 1998). Severity, frequency, and duration of child abuse are crucial factors in the extent to which these youths experience emotional and behavioural difficulties in their lives (Lazenbatt 2012; Hecht and Hansen 2001). Children who witness and hear chronic and severely abusive behaviour between care-givers can show the same effects as children who directly experience such abuse (Sudermann and Jaffe 1999). In general, female victims internalize distress (substance abuse, eating disorders, self-mutilation, suicide attempts, and depression), and most male victims externalize distress. Boys have higher levels of conduct symptoms (e.g., destroying things, bullying, and cruelty) and externalized violence (e.g., homicide, physical and sexual assaults, homophobia, and racism).

Twenty-three-year-old Michael, a long-standing street gang member, was victimized by chronic and severe physical, sexual, and emotional abuse growing up. His poem is representative of the mental health problems experienced by many gang members, resulting from untreated childhood **trauma**. He wrote this poem while serving time for a serious crime of violence he had committed.

trauma
Experience that is psychologically painful, distressful, or shocking (such as suffering sexual abuse or witnessing serious violence) and that often results in long-term mental or physical effects (such as depression, anxiety, or insomnia) (Corcoran 2010).

Suicide

Thoughts of suicide once came into play
Sobbing with pain holding the string
Managed to tie,
But just couldn't end my life,
Reminiscence of family and friends,
And how it could be the end,
Contaplating [sic] on taken [sic] the next step,
Towards an ending life feeling like thiers [sic] nothing left,
A childhood which wasent [sic] the greatest,
A ruined life I just couldn't take it,

With the noose around my neck,
And the tears dripping like sweat,
Really hoping somebody would help me,
To stop my pain and to stop all the misery,
Was dealt a cruel hand and lived my 22 years sad,
Reasons to live for, I wish I had.

Most maltreated children are not violent, however, and some violent youth have not experienced maltreatment as children. A key moderating variable in this link is the resiliency of abused children: their individual, familial, and community protective factors that offset the impact of child maltreatment. Key protective factors at the family level include strong attachment to parent(s) and caregivers, bonding with other adults, effective family management practices (positive reinforcement, consistent structure and discipline, good supervision), residential stability (adequate housing, few moves), and good health of parent(s) and caregivers (Ungar 2007).

School Factors

School success and bonding, participation in extracurricular activities, and low delinquency rate of students at school are key protective factors for young people. These youth are highly unlikely to become gang involved. Risk factors include academic failure, low literacy, frequent school transitions, truancy and dropping out of school, and a high delinquency rate of students at school. These risks are linked to negative health outcomes in the absence of protective factors in other areas of a young person's life (Bridgeland, DiIulio, and Morison 2006).

Staying in school provides structured daytime activities and supports a healthy socialization process. However, many gang members spend long periods of time outside of school; they are frequently suspended or expelled, have high rates of absenteeism, and frequently drop out.

Peer-Group Factors

Key protective factors at the peer-group level that lead to positive health outcomes include pro-social siblings and peers and positive peer-group membership. Evidence suggests that most healthy peer networks are organized around hobbies, interests, and other activities shared by friends (Totten 2000). Positive social support is related to lower rates of emotional and behavioural disorders, crime, and violence. Risk factors at the peer-group level include delinquent siblings and peers and membership in anti-social peer groups. Researchers who have studied violence and youth crime in the social context of peer-group processes argue that peers play a significant role in enabling and sustaining these anti-social behaviours (Brechwald and Prinstein 2011; Warr 2002). Associations with people who are violent role models can result in violent behaviour. These problems can interact and feed off genetic, biological, family, and school risk factors.

Community and Neighbourhood Factors

The risk factors at this level related to gang involvement include community disorganization (e.g., gangs, poor housing, high unemployment), poverty, exposure to violence, and racial discrimination. Social infrastructures to promote inclusion and participation in high-quality health, social, and recreation services are minimal compared to those in more affluent neighbourhoods (Jackson et al. 2001). There are usually few social networks and ties, with a disproportionate number of single-parent families and individuals experiencing mental or physical health problems. These neighbourhoods tend to have low social capital. Immigrants, ethnic and visible minorities, and Aboriginal people make up a disproportionate share of many social housing communities. Protective factors include living in a community with mixed socio-economic backgrounds of families, organized and accessible community and social infrastructure (e.g., recreation facilities and activities, adequate housing, high employment), bonding to institutions outside of family and school, and strong cultural identity and racial harmony (Totten 2008).

Today, roughly one in ten young people in Canada lives in poverty. A large body of research on human development shows that health and well-being are linked to financial resources. Children and youth from low-income families are more vulnerable: they generally experience more physical, behavioural, and mental health problems; they suffer more neglect and physical violence; and they do less well at school, are more likely to drop out, and experience less labour market success than people from more affluent family backgrounds.[9] The vast majority of gang members grow up experiencing severe poverty. The negative effects of poverty can be overcome by a positive family environment (e.g., good parenting skills and stable family unit), by positive community supports (e.g., regular involvement in structured, skill-building recreational activities that develop self-esteem; an adult mentor who provides unconditional support and models healthy behaviour) (Williams Shanks and Danziger 2010; Currie 2006; Offord, Lipman, and Duku 1998), by access to high-quality health and social services and positive school experiences (e.g., high engagement, good grades, supportive teachers, development of future academic and vocational interests), or by particular individual attributes.

Prevention, Intervention, and Suppression Approaches

What Doesn't Work?

prevention
Approaches that prevent young people from joining gangs.

intervention
Approaches that address the needs of youth once they are involved in gangs.

Historically, in Canada, gang suppression and community safety strategies have won out over evidence-based treatment and **prevention**. Unfortunately, scarce resources have been spent on "get tough" approaches, where young gang members are incarcerated at huge financial cost. Ironically, the best gang **intervention** programs cost a fraction of the "lock 'em up" approach yet have not been implemented in a systematic fashion across the country. Approaches described below have proven to be ineffective and should be stopped. They typically are not part of a broad continuum of integrated services and include the following:

- *Curriculum-based prevention programs* targeting youth at risk for gang involvement, such as the American Gang Resistance Education and Training program (G.R.E.A.T.) and Drug Abuse Resistance Education (DARE), effect modest, short-term change. However, follow-up studies have found program participants to be as likely as non-participants to become gang members in the long term.

- *Traditional detached-worker programs*, which use social workers, youth and recreation workers, or Aboriginal leaders to outreach into gangs, are ineffective and can do more harm than good by increasing gang cohesion (Vigil 2010; Howell 2000). More modern detached-worker programs (such as the Broader Urban Involvement and Leadership Development) have included curriculum components that address consequences of gang involvement, peer pressure, and substance abuse. These programs remain ineffective in preventing youth from joining gangs.

- *Gang suppression program* evaluations have had mixed results (e.g., Howell 2010; Klein and Maxson 2006). These programs are based on the prosecution and conviction of gang members, especially targeting gang leaders. Although effective in decreasing gang-related crime in the short term, gang **suppression** programs fail to address important psychosocial issues, such as child maltreatment, mental health, substance abuse, education, and employment. Suppression initiatives should only be utilized if other prevention and intervention programs have not been successful. Even then, suppression should be used to complement a range of interventions.

suppression
Policing approach to dealing with gangs.

- *Incarcerating gang members* does not reduce future criminal behaviour (Aos, Miller, and Drake 2006). Studies in the United States demonstrate that locking up gang members can actually increase the chances of their reoffending and staying in the gang (FBI 2012; DeLisi 2003; Olson, Dooley, and Kane 2004). Likewise, grouping early-onset, high-risk youth together can increase the negative bonding among members and lead to even more entrenched anti-social and criminal behaviour. In Canada, a comparison study of 1955 gang members and inmates who were not gang involved found that the incarcerated gang members were more likely to re-offend (gang-related violent offences), to have employability problems, to associate with criminal peers, and to be involved in assaults on prison staff and inmates and alcohol seizure (Nafekh 2002; Nafekh and Stys 2004).

What Does Work?

In Canada, a small minority of all children and families with the most complex mental health needs take up a large portion of all available human services resources in traditional services (e.g., Offord, Boyle, and Racine 1990). The long-term outcomes for these traditional, high-cost services (primarily residential and out-of-community) are poor in most cases (e.g., Fechter-Leggett and O'Brien 2010; Duchnowski, Hall, Kutash, and

Friedman 1998). These young people usually have early-onset aggression prior to age six years. If left untreated, most turn into serious and violent offenders and gang members. It is less costly and more effective to prevent youth from joining gangs than it is to provide the resources to help members exit a gang. The programs that have the best outcomes are those that combine primary, secondary, and tertiary prevention in a multidisciplinary and multi-systemic community approach. Some research indicates that positive outcomes depend more on the individual young person (e.g., motivation and resiliency) than on his or her engagement in gang activities (see Aos et al. 2006).

Primary prevention focuses on the entire child and youth population at risk and the biological, personal, social, and environmental risk factors linked to criminal behaviour. Gang prevention focuses on awareness and education. It is assumed that if resiliency is enhanced and youth develop a capacity to recognize risky situations, then they may be better equipped to resist engaging in gang-related activity. Secondary prevention services target individuals and groups identified as being at greater risk of becoming gang members. Community assessments frame these strategies. The focus is on reducing risk factors rather than on variables that are not changeable (Offord and Bennett 2002). Both social problems and individual risk factors are targeted. Tertiary prevention targets gang members and recruits directly to rehabilitate or incapacitate youth, address the needs of victims, and provide exit strategies and support to help youth leave and stay out of gangs.

The initiatives described next are proven to be effective in preventing youth from joining gangs and intervening with gang-involved youth. The National Crime Prevention Centre (NCPC of Public Safety Canada) has provided five-year funding for a variety of evidence-based gang prevention and intervention projects across Canada. The projects it funds fit within Irving Spergel's (1924–2010) Comprehensive Gang Model. The funding is typically between $4 million and $5 million per project, including for a comprehensive evaluation. Ironically, the majority of these projects have not secured other sources of funding since NCPC began giving its support.

Spergel's model is a community-wide response to gangs and has been adopted by the Office of Juvenile Justice and Delinquency Prevention (OJJDP) across the United States. This model consists of five core strategies that flow from an integrated and team-oriented problem-solving approach using secondary and tertiary prevention. The model is based on the belief that a lack of social opportunities and the degree of social disorganization in a community explain the youth gang problem. Contributing factors such as poverty, institutional racism, poor social policies, and a lack of or misdirected social controls are important. The following are five core strategies: community mobilization; social intervention; provision of academic, economic, and social opportunities; gang suppression; and facilitation of organizational change and development.

Other programs that have demonstrated success include the following:

- *Multi-systemic therapy* (MST) is highly effective with serious, violent, and chronic juvenile offenders (Henggeler, Schoenwald, Borduin, Rowland and Cunningham 2009; Henggeler 1997). It is a cost-effective program that provides gang members with intensive therapy, supervision, and monitoring. MST focuses on the multiple determinants of criminal and anti-social behaviour and provides services in the youths' own neighbourhood. Offending is viewed as having many causes; therefore, interventions focus on the multitude of factors influencing anti-social behaviour. There is an average of 60 hours of contact with families over a four-month period.

- *Wraparound* is a complex, multi-faceted intervention strategy designed to keep youthful offenders at home and out of institutions whenever possible. Rather than young people being forced to fit into categorical, inflexible therapeutic programs, a comprehensive continuum of individualized services and support networks is "wrapped around" them (Portland State University Research and Training Center 2003). Individual case management is a cornerstone (Burchard, Bruns, and Burchard 2002). Wraparounds conducted in Canada and the US have been effective in reducing the frequency of residential or institutional placement of children and youth, and in reducing recidivism and arrests of seriously violent youth (e.g., see the Wraparound Surrey Project; Totten and Dunn 2012b; Milwaukee County Behavioral Health Division 2003; Walker et al. 2004).

- The *California Repeat Offender Prevention Program* (ROPP, also referred to as the "8% Solution") is a multi-site early-intervention program targeting young offenders at high risk of becoming serious repeat offenders and gang members. Originally developed by the Orange County, California, probation department in the early 1990s, the program integrates intensive supervision with Wraparound services. Evaluations showed that control-group youth significantly improved their academic performance and were twice as likely to complete probation orders compared to comparison-group youth (State of California Board of Corrections 2002). Replication of the ROPP has had mixed results, largely because of a failure to implement the program fully (Zhang and Zhang 2005; Schumacher and Kurz 2000; State of California Board of Corrections 2002).

- The *Philadelphia Youth Violence Reduction Partnership* (YVRP) targets offenders who are at high risk of being killed or of killing others. Youth-serving organizations and criminal justice agencies collaborate to balance intensive supervision with comprehensive therapeutic support. YVRP provides youth with increased supervision and supports their access to relevant resources (employment, mentoring, school bonding, counselling, health care, and drug treatment). Street workers and police help probation officers supervise participants, the result being almost daily contacts with seriously violent youth and smaller caseload sizes. Street workers mentor youths and brokers in other services. A key goal is to stabilize the families of participants through such efforts as finding jobs for parents and locating housing. Analysis of youth homicide rates in Philadelphia suggests that the YVRP is effective (Fight Crime: Invest in Kids 2004; McClanahan 2004; McClanahan, Kauh, Manning, Campos, and Farley 2012).

- *Warrior Spirit Walking Project* (WSW), Prince Albert Outreach Program Inc. (PAOPI), is a Canadian leader in evidence-based prevention and intervention for gang-involved Aboriginal youth. NCPC provided rich funding for this project between 2007 and 2012. WSW also serves youth at high risk of gang involvement. It is nested within the broader PAOPI agency and serves youth aged 10 to 24 years in daily intensive services. Key programs include the Youth Activity Centre, the Won Ska Cultural School, intensive counselling, street outreach to youth in the sex trade, and court outreach. Evaluation data demonstrated statistically significant reductions in overall levels of risk for treatment-group participants over time. In addition, statistically significant positive changes were found in levels of gang involvement, substance abuse, violent and non-violent offending, and employment. The treatment sample of 147 youths was matched to a control group of 48 youths. Most participants were followed over a three-year period (Totten and Dunn 2012a).

- *Regina Anti-Gang Services Project* (RAGS), North Central Community Association (NCCA), is a unique initiative targeting gang-involved Aboriginal youth and young adults aged 16 to 30 years in Regina's North Central neighbourhood. It is the only comprehensive gang exit project in Canada. NCPC provided rich funding for this project between 2007 and 2012. The program engages clients in intensive daily services aimed at reducing their involvement in gang life and facilitating their exit from gangs. The four core programs are life skills programming for young men; circle keeper program for young women; intensive gang exit counselling; and outreach to schools and institutions. As with the Warrior Spirit Walking Project, RAGS evaluation data demonstrated statistically significant reductions in overall levels of risk for participants. In addition, statistically significant positive changes were found in levels of gang involvement, substance abuse, and offending. The treatment sample of 74 young adults (18 of whom had been convicted of murder, attempted murder, or manslaughter) was matched with a control group of 29 high-risk gang members. Most participants were followed over a three-year period (Totten and Dunn 2012b).

- Oshkiiwaadizag Mino Niigaaniiwad—Youth Leading in a Good Way—is another successful project. It targets approximately 100 Aboriginal youths per year in the care of the West Region Child and Family Services (WRCFS), a large Aboriginal child welfare agency in Manitoba. Both males and females, ages 13 to 21, living on and off reserve, who are at high risk of gang involvement and/or are known to be gang involved have been recruited. The youths, all of whom are in foster care or treatment homes, come from local First Nations communities (Pine Creek, Skownan, O-Chi-Chak-Ko-Sipi, Tootinaowaaziibeeng, Ebb and Flow, Keeseekoowenin, Rolling River, Waywayseecappo, and Gambler First Nations), and some live in the cities of Winnipeg, Brandon, and Dauphin in Manitoba. It is the only youth gang project in Canada that uses a randomized controlled trial design with a longitudinal follow-up. The Wraparound model is being used (Totten, Bennell, and Ferns 2013) (see Box 12.1).

Box 12.1 Youth Justice in Action

Examples of Promising Approaches

homeboyindustries.org

Homeboy Industries is a not-for-profit organization that started up in 1988 in Los Angeles (see Boyles 2010). It serves high-risk, formerly gang-involved men and women with a continuum of free social services and programs, and operates several social enterprises that serve as job-training sites.

saferschoolstogether.com

Vancouver-based Safer Schools Together trains schools throughout North America in bullying and violence prevention and intervention strategies.

Their goal is to promote safe, caring schools through the development of effective practice, policy, protocols, and programs.

reachedmonton.ca

The WrapEd youth gang prevention project was created by REACH Edmonton and works in collaboration with the Africa Centre, Edmonton John Howard Society, Edmonton Police Services, Native Counselling Services of Alberta, and YOUCAN. The goal of this five-year project, funded by NCPC, is to prevent at-risk youth from falling into a life of drugs, violence and gangs.

Summary

The primary purpose of this chapter is to provide an overview of youth gangs in Canada. Since the previous edition of this book, the gang landscape in Canada has changed and evidence-based practices in the areas of prevention, intervention, and criminal justice have evolved. We identify differences between street gangs, mid-level gangs, and organized crime groups. The primary differences between these three types of gangs include hierarchical structure, level of sophistication, degree of organization, seriousness of criminal activity, breadth of influence (i.e., local, regional, provincial, national, international), and longevity. The chapter also provides a summary of gang activity across different provinces and the territories. A handful of gangs are identified as having high levels of sophistication and influence across different regions of Canada (e.g., including Indian Posse, Native Syndicate, Crazy Dragons, North Preston's Finest, Independent Soldiers, and various factions of the Crips and Bloods).

We discuss different roles in organized gangs, including new recruits, strikers and soldiers, associates and affiliates, captains and higher-ups, and leaders. Gender is identified as a key factor that influences young people's experiences in gangs. The sexual assault and objectification of young women is common in gangs. For the most part, female youth play tertiary roles in male-dominated gangs, and it is rare for women to occupy leadership positions. The chapter also investigates Canadian judicial responses to gang crimes and addresses the problematic nature of the official definitions of street gangs and organized crime groups.

In addition, the chapter presents a biopsychosocial model for understanding gang involvement. Finally, the chapter identifies high-quality prevention, intervention, and suppression strategies. The best models include all three strategies and address problems at various levels of the biopsychosocial framework.

Gang-involved youth have suffered greatly throughout their young lives. Although many have committed serious crimes and must be held accountable, we must not forget the human face of these troubled youth. They are much more than merely gang members; many have unique talents and skills that are often buried underneath their violent and anti-social behaviour.

Key Terms

intervention	suppression
prevention	trauma

Review Questions

1. What are the main differences between street gangs, mid-level gangs, and organized crime groups?
2. What are some of the key risk and protective factors related to gang involvement?
3. What are some examples of high-quality prevention programs for youth?
4. What are some examples of high-quality intervention programs for youth?

Critical Thinking Questions

1. How does gender affect pathways into and out of gangs?
2. How does gender influence roles played in gangs?
3. Why are Aboriginal youth overrepresented in gangs?
4. Why are young people who come from war-torn countries susceptible to gang involvement?
5. Do suppression and correctional approaches work?
6. What aspects of these programs make them more promising than their predecessors?
7. What do you think the implications are of official gang and organized crime definitions for the treatment of youth under the Youth Criminal Justice Act (YCJA)?

Endnotes

1. For example, Gordon 2000; Nimmo 2001; Totten 2009a, 2008, 2000.
2. For example, see Totten and Dunn 2012a, 2012c; Totten 2012a.
3. These data on gang activity come from a number of sources, including interviews conducted by Totten with gang members across Canada; CISC and RCMP reports; and confidential interviews with municipal, provincial, and federal law-enforcement organizations.

4. Young adults are defined as those between 12 and 30 years of age.
5. For example, see CISC 2007; Public Safety Canada 2012.
6. Pseudonyms are used to protect the identity of participants.
7. Although youth under the age of 18 years who are charged with a criminal offence are typically dealt with under the Youth Criminal Justice Act, a small number are transferred up to the adult system if they have committed very serious offences. If convicted, these latter youth usually serve their sentence in adult jails or prisons.
8. Permission granted by all participants to reproduce their narratives in publications by Totten.
9. For example, see Offord and Bennett 2002.

References

Abbotsford Youth Commission. (2010). *Gangs, girls and sexual exploitation in British Columbia: Community consultation paper.* Abbotsford, BC: Victim Services and Crime Prevention, Ministry of Public Safety, and Solicitor General/National Crime Prevention Centre, Public Safety Canada.

Aos, S., Miller, M., and Drake, E. (2006). *Evidence-based public policy options to reduce future prison construction, criminal justice costs, and crime rates.* Olympia: Washington State Institute for Public Policy.

Barankin, T., and Khanlou, N. (2011). *Growing up resilient: Ways to build resilience in children and youth.* Toronto: CAMH.

Block, C., and Block, R. (2001). Street gang crime in Chicago. In J. Miller, C.L. Maxson, and M.W. Klein (Eds), *The modern gang reader.* Los Angeles: Roxbury.

Boyle, G. (2010). *Tattoos on the heart: The power of boundless compassion.* New York: Free Press.

Brechwald, W., and Prinstein, M. (2011). Beyond homophily: A decade of advances in understanding peer influence processes. *Journal of Research on Adolescence,* 21: 166–79.

Bridgeland, J., DiIulio, J., and Morison, K. (2006). *The silent epidemic: Perspectives of high school dropouts.* A report by Civic Enterprises in association with Peter D. Hart Research Associates for the Bill & Melinda Gates Foundation.

Burchard, J., Bruns, E., and Burchard, S. (2002). *The wraparound process: Community-based treatment for youth.* Oxford: Oxford University Press.

Buxton, B. (2004). *Damaged angels.* Toronto: Knopf Canada.

Campbell, A. (1987). Self-definition by rejection: The case of gang girls. *Social Problems,* 34: 451–66.

Carrigan, D. (1998). *Juvenile delinquency in Canada: A history.* Toronto: Irwin Publishing.

CISC. (2007). *Project spectrum: 2006 situational overview of street gangs in Canada.* Ottawa: Author.

CISC. (2010). *2010 annual report on organized crime.* Ottawa: Author.

CISS (Criminal Intelligence Services Saskatchewan). (2005). *2005 intelligence trends: Aboriginal-based gangs in Saskatchewan.* Regina, SK: Author.

Corcoran, J. (2010). *Mental health treatment for children and adolescents.* New York: Oxford University Press.

Covington, H. (2010). *Street gangs throughout the world* (2nd ed.). Springfield, IL: Charles C. Thomas.

Currie, J. (2006). *The invisible safety net: Protecting the nation's poor children and families.* Princeton, NJ: Princeton University Press.

DeLisi, M. (2003). Criminal careers behind bars. *Behavioral Sciences and the Law,* 21: 653–69.

Dorais, M., and Corriveau, P. (2009). *Gangs and girls: Understanding juvenile prostitution.* Montreal and Kingston: McGill-Queen's University Press.

Duchnowski, A., Hall, K., Kutash, K., and Friedman, R. (1998). The alternatives to residential treatment studies. In M. Epstein, K. Kutash, and A. Duchnowski (Eds), *Outcomes for children and youth with behavioral and emotional disorders and their families* (pp. 55–80). Austin, TX: Pro-Ed.

Fabricius, W., and Luecken, L. (2007). Postdivorce living arrangements, parent conflict, and long-term physical health correlates for children of divorce. *Journal of Family Psychology,* 21(2): 195–205.

FBI. (2012). *2011 National gang threat assessment: Emerging trends.* Washington, DC: National Gang Intelligence Centre.

Fechter-Leggett, M., and O'Brien, K. (2010). The effects of kinship care on adult mental health outcomes of alumni foster care. *Children and Youth Services Review, 32*(2): 206–13.

Fight Crime: Invest in Kids. (2004). *Caught in the crossfire: Arresting gang violence by investing in kids.* Washington, DC: Author.

Gold, J., Wolan Sullivan, M., and Lewis, M. (2011). The relation between abuse and violent delinquency: The conversion of shame to blame in juvenile offenders. *Child Abuse & Neglect, 35*(7): 459–67.

Gordon, R. (2000). Criminal business organizations, street gangs and "wanna-be" groups: A Vancouver perspective. *Canadian Journal of Criminology,* January: 39–60.

Grennan, S., Britz, M., Rush, J., and Barker, T. (2000). *Gangs: An international approach.* Upper Saddle River, NJ: Prentice Hall.

Gutman, L.M., and Midgley, C. (2000). The role of protective factors in supporting the academic achievement of poor African American students during the middle school transition. *Journal of Youth and Adolescence, 29*(2): 223–48.

Hecht, D., and Hansen, D. (2001). The environment of child maltreatment: Contextual factors and the development of psychopathology. *Aggression and Violent Behavior,* 6: 433–57.

Hemmati, T. (2006). *The nature of Canadian urban gangs and their use of firearms: A review of the literature and police survey.* Ottawa: Department of Justice Canada, Research and Statistics Division.

Henggeler, S. (1997). The development of effective drug abuse services for youth. In J. Egertson, D. Fox, and A. Leshner (Eds), *Treating drug abusers effectively* (pp. 253–79). New York: Blackwell Publishers.

Henggeler, S., Schoenwald, S., Borduin, C., Rowland, M., and Cunningham, P. (2009). *Multisystemic therapy for antisocial behaviour in children and adolescents.* New York: Guilford Press.

Howell, J. (2000). *Youth gang programs and strategies.* Washington, DC: US Department of Justice, Office of Justice Programs, Office of Juvenile and Delinquency Prevention.

Howell, J. (2010, December). Gang prevention: An overview of research and programs. *OJJDP Juvenile Justice Bulletin,* NCJ 231116.

Jackson, A., Hanvey, L., Tsoukalas, S., Buckland, L., Roberts, E., and Perkins, N. (2001). *Recreation and children and youth living in poverty: Barriers, benefits and success stories.* Ottawa: CCSD.

Klein, M. (2002). Street gangs: A cross-national perspective. In C. Huff (Ed.), *Gangs in America III.* Thousand Oaks, CA: Sage.

Klein, M., and Maxson, C. (2006). *Street Gang Patterns and Policies.* New York: Oxford University Press.

Knox, G. (2000). *An introduction to gangs* (5th ed.). Chicago: New Chicago School Press.

Kyskan, C., and Moore, T. (2005). Global perspectives on foetal alcohol syndrome (FAS): Assessing practices, policies, and campaigns in four English-speaking countries. *Canadian Psychology,* 46: 153–65.

Lazenbatt, A. (2012) Impact of abuse and neglect on the health and wellbeing of children and young people. In G. Wilmer et al., *Understanding and treating the life-long consequences of childhood sexual abuse.* Leeds, UK: The Lantern Project, Kilburn Prints.

Luthar, S., Cicchetti, D., and Becker, B. (2000). The construct of resilience: A critical evaluation and guidelines for future work. *Child Development, 72*(3): 543–62.

McClanahan, W. (2004). *Alive at 25: Reducing youth violence through monitoring and support.* Philadelphia: Public/Private Ventures.

McClanahan, W., Kauh, T., Manning, A., Campos, P., and Farley, C. (2012). *Illuminating solutions: The YVRP.* Philadelphia: PPV.

McCreary Centre Society. (1999). *Healthy connections: Listening to BC youth. Highlights from the Adolescent Health Survey II.* Burnaby, BC: McCreary Centre Society.

MacMillan, H. (2000). Child maltreatment: What we know in the year 2000. *Canadian Journal of Psychiatry,* 45: 702–9.

Mellor, B., MacRae, L., Pauls, M., and Hornick, J. (2005). *Youth gangs in Canada: A preliminary review of programs and services.* Prepared for Public Safety and Emergency Preparedness Canada. Calgary: Canadian Research Institute for Law and the Family.

Milwaukee County Behavioral Health Division. (2003). *Wraparound Milwaukee: 2002 annual report.* Milwaukee, WI: Milwaukee County Behavioral Health Division, Department of Health and Human Services.

Moffitt, T. (2005). The new look of behaviour genetics in developmental pathology: Gene-environment interplay in antisocial behaviour. *Psychological Bulletin, 131*: 533–54.

Moffitt, T., et al. (2001). *Sex differences in antisocial behaviour.* Cambridge, UK: Cambridge University Press.

Moore, J. (2007). Female gangs. In J. Hagedorn (Ed.), *Gangs in the global city: Alternatives to traditional criminology.* Chicago: University of Illinois Press.

Nafekh, M. (2002). *An examination of youth and gang association within the federally sentenced Aboriginal population.* Ottawa: Correctional Services Canada.

Nafekh, M., and Stys, Y. (2004). *A profile and examination of gang affiliation within federally sentenced inmates.* Ottawa: Correctional Services Canada.

NCPC (National Crime Prevention Centre). (2007). *Building the evidence: Youth gangs.* Ottawa: Public Safety Canada.

Nimmo M. (2001). *The invisible gang members: A report on female gang association in Winnipeg.* Winnipeg: Canadian Centre for Policy Alternatives.

Offord, D., and Bennett, K. (2002). Prevention. In M. Rutter and E. Taylor (Eds), *Child and adolescent psychiatry* (4th ed., pp. 881–99). Oxford: Blackwell Science.

Offord, D., Boyle, M., and Racine, Y. (1990). *Ontario child health study.* Toronto: Queen's Printer.

Olson, D., Dooley, B., and Kane, C. (2004). The relationship between gang membership and inmate recidivism. *Research Bulletin, 2*(12). Chicago: Illinois Criminal Justice Research Authority.

Offord, D., Lipman, E., and Duku, E. (1998). *Which children don't participate in sports, the arts, and community programs?* Ottawa: Human Resources Development Canada.

Perreault, S. (2013, 25 July). Police-reported crime statistics in Canada, 2012. *Juristat, 30*(2). Statistics Canada, Catalogue no. 85-002-X.

Plomin, R., and Crabbe, J. (2000). DNA. *Psychological Bulletin, 126*: 806–28.

Portland State University Research and Training Center. (2003). Quality and fidelity in wraparound. *Focal Point.*

Public Safety Canada. (2012). *Organized crime research brief 28: Data mining for possible organized crime.* Ottawa: Public Safety Canada.

RCMP (Royal Canadian Mounted Police). (2006). *RCMP environmental scan: Youth gangs and guns.* Ottawa: Strategic Policy and Planning Directorate, RCMP.

Resnick, M., Ireland, M., and Borowsky, I. (2004). Youth violence perpetration: What protects? What predicts? Findings from the National Longitudinal Study of Adolescent Health. *Journal of Adolescent Health, 35*: 424.e1–e10.

Rhee, S., and Waldman, I. (2002). Genetic and environmental influences on antisocial behavior: A meta-analysis of twin and adoption studies. *Psychological Bulletin, 128*(3): 490–529.

Sanders, B., Lankenau, S., and Jackson-Bloom, J. (2010). Putting in work: Qualitative research on substance use and other risk behaviours among gang youth in Los Angeles. *Substance Use and Misuse, 45*(5): 736–53.

Santrock, J. (2007). *A topical approach to human life-span development* (3rd ed.). St Louis, MO: McGraw-Hill.

Schumacher, M., and Kurz, G. (2000). *The 8% solution—Preventing serious repeat juvenile crime.* Thousand Oaks, CA: Sage.

Shaw, M. (2001). *Investing in youth 12–18: International approaches to preventing crime and victimization.* Montreal: ICPC.

Sheldon, R., Tracy, S., and Brown, W. (2004). *Youth gangs in American society.* Belmont, CA: Wadsworth.

Smokowski P., Reynolds, A., and Brezruczko, N. (1999). Resilience and protective factors in adolescence: An autobiographical perspective from disadvantaged youth. *Journal of School Psychology, 37*(4): 425–48.

Spergel, I. (1990). *Youth gangs: Problems and responses.* Arlington, VA: US Department of Justice, Office of Juvenile Justice and Delinquency Prevention, National Youth Gang Information Centre.

Sprott, J., Doob, A., and Jenkins, J. (2001). Problem behaviour and delinquency in children and youth. *Juristat, 21*(4).

Stark, J. (2004). Breaking the cycle: A community approach to prevention of low-birth weight babies. *Leadership in Health Services, 17*(4): 1–8.

State of California Board of Corrections. (2002). *Repeat offender prevention program.* Sacramento, CA: State of California Board of Corrections.

Sudermann, M., and Jaffe, P. (1999). *A handbook for health and social service providers and educators on children exposed to woman abuse/family violence.* Ottawa: Minister of Public Works and Government Services Canada.

Totten, M. (2000). *Guys, gangs and girlfriend abuse.* Peterborough, ON: Broadview Press.

Totten, M. (2008). *Promising practices for addressing youth involvement in gangs.* Vancouver: British Columbia Ministry of Public Safety and Solicitor General.

Totten, M. (2009a). Aboriginal youth and violent gang involvement in Canada: Quality prevention strategies. *Institute for the Prevention of Crime Review,* 3: 135–56.

Totten, M. (2009b). Preventing Aboriginal youth gang involvement in Canada: A gendered approach. In J. White and J. Bruhn (Eds), *Aboriginal policy research: Exploring the urban landscape,* Vol. 8. Toronto: Thompson Educational Publishing.

Totten, M. (2009c). *Investigating the linkages between FASD, gangs, sexual exploitation and women abuse in the Canadian Aboriginal population: A preliminary study.* Ottawa: Native Women's Association of Canada.

Totten, M. (2012a). *Nasty, brutish and short: The lives of gang members in Canada.* Toronto: James Lorimer.

Totten, M. (2012b). Use of the tear drop tattoo by young street gang members. *Journal of Gang Research,* 19(1): 37–52.

Totten, M. (2014). *Gang lives: Ten of the toughest tell their stories.* Toronto: James Lorimer.

Totten, M., Bennell, C., and Ferns, A. (2013). *Evaluation plan for the Oshkiiwaadizag Mino Niigaaniiwad—Youth Leading in a Good Way Project.* Toronto: Mark Totten & Associates.

Totten, M., and Dunn, S. (2012a). *Final evaluation report for the Prince Albert Outreach Program Inc. Warrior Spirit Walking Gang Project* (Year 5). Gatineau, QC: Mark Totten & Associates.

Totten, M., and Dunn, S. (2012b). *Final evaluation report for the North Central Community Association Regina Anti-Gang Services Project* (Year 5). Gatineau, QC: Mark Totten & Associates.

Ungar, M. (2007). *Playing at being bad: The hidden resilience of troubled teens.* Toronto: McClelland & Stewart.

Valdez, A. (2000). *A guide to understanding gangs.* San Clemente, CA: LawTech Publishing.

Vigil, J. (2010). *Gang redux: A balanced anti-gang strategy.* Long Grove, IL: Waveland Press.

Walker, J., Bruns, E., Rast, J., VanDenBerg, J., Osher, T., Koroloff, N., et al. (2004). *Phases and activities of the wraparound process.* Portland, OR: National Wraparound Initiative, Regional Research Institute, Portland State University.

Warr, M. (2002). *Companions in crime: The social aspects of criminal conduct.* Cambridge, UK: Cambridge University Press.

Watkins, D., and Ashby, R. (2007). *Gang investigations: A street cop's guide.* Sudbury, MA: Jones and Bartlett Publishers.

White, R. (2007). *Youth gangs, violence and anti-social behaviour.* West Perth, WA: Australian Research Alliance for Children and Youth.

Williams Shanks, T., and Danziger, S. (2010). Antipoverty policies and programs for families and children. In J. Jenson and M. Fraser (Eds), *Social policy for children & families: A risk and resilience perspective* (2nd ed., pp. 25–56). Thousand Oaks, CA: Sage.

Wolak, J., and Finkelhor, D. (1998). Children exposed to partner violence. In J.L. Jasinski and L.M. Williams (Eds), *Partner violence: A comprehensive review of 20 years of research* (pp. 73–112). Thousand Oaks, CA: Sage.

World Health Organization. (2002). *World report on violence and health.* Geneva: WHO.

Zhang, S., and Zhang, L. (2005). An experimental study of the Los Angeles repeat offender prevention program: Its implementation and evaluation. *Criminology and Public Policy,* 4: 205–36.

Street-Involved Youth in Canada

Bruce MacLaurin and Catherine Worthington

13

Overview

This chapter provides an overview of street-involved youth in Canada. It focuses specifically on definitions and typologies of street involvement; pathways to the street from home or alternative care; key risk and protective factors associated with street involvement; institutional experiences with the education, child welfare, and juvenile justice systems; and street services and strategies for effective intervention.

Key Objectives

After reading this chapter, you should be able to:

- Discuss why there is such a significant number of street-involved youth in Canadian cities.
- Identify key risks and concerns for youths living on the streets.
- Describe why youth may become involved in street life.
- Outline types of services required by street youth.

Introduction

Street-involved youth are visible living on the streets of most major Canadian urban centres. This is not a recent phenomenon; nineteenth-century literature popularized Huckleberry Finn and Oliver Twist in stories of street children existing and surviving on their own. Street-involved youth may be more visible today, however, as newspapers during the past decade have consistently highlighted the lives of young street teens, describing them as runaways, throwaways, panhandlers, squeegee kids, or teen parents (Abate 2001; Anonymous 2010a, 2010b; Cuthbertson 2012; Derworiz 2010; Goar 2009; McCarter 2010). Despite this increase in recognition and awareness, the plight of street-involved youth arguably continues to deteriorate in Canada.

underhoused
Youth who are underhoused live in housing that is temporary in nature, inadequate for space, does not meet safety or health thresholds, or has high risk for eviction.

Street-involved youth are generally defined as individuals who are 25 years of age or younger, who are either runaways, homeless, or **underhoused** (i.e., living in temporary or unreliable housing). A variety of typologies, or classifications, of street-involved youth has been developed to describe this population. This chapter will describe some of the typologies documented in current North American research to provide a comprehensive overview of street-involved youth. These typologies are based on the intent, or purpose, of the street involvement, the time spent on the street, the factors associated with street involvement, and whether there is a choice of returning home. In spite of some limitations, such as being too simple or vague, typologies can assist us in understanding this population and the specific risks that street-involved youth face on the street.

Street-involved youth experience a decrease in rights, opportunities, and social supports (Grover 2007; Worthington et al. 2008), and this may exacerbate the risks associated with living on the streets. Street-involved youth are also at higher risk of developing mental health problems, some of which can lead to suicide (Boivin, Roy, Hayel, and Galbaud du Fort 2005); becoming involved in survival or obligatory sex (Haley, Roy, Leclerc, et al. 2004b); developing physical health concerns, including contracting sexually transmitted diseases (Public Health Agency of Canada 2006a); getting involved in criminal and delinquent activity (Baron and Hartnagel 2006); using and abusing drugs (Roy 2002b); and simply not meeting their basic physical needs for food, clothing, and shelter (Dachner and Tarasuk 2002). A review of the literature will illustrate how these risk factors have a significant impact on youth when on the streets.

Insufficient attention has been given to the service needs of street-involved youth. Services are needed that will support these youth while they are on the streets and when they try to leave the street life. As well, we need to focus more on prevention if we are to understand the factors that provide the earliest indications of risk of street involvement. While much literature has described street youth populations over the past decades, more attention is required to develop rigorous intervention research to determine what services are best for what groups. This chapter describes effective forms of intervention available to street-involved youth in Canada as well as barriers to service utilization.

Defining Street-Involved Youth v. Homeless Adults

As mentioned, the literature generally defines **street-involved youth** as being young people 25 years of age or younger who do not have a safe home or are underhoused; have been forced to leave their family of origin (**throwaway**); who have run away from their home without the consent of their parents or guardian; or who left foster- or group-care placements (runaway) (Hammer, Finkelhor, and Sedlak 2002). These youth may be described as the most street entrenched; however, recent evidence indicates that additional youth are becoming involved in street life who are less recognized or understood, who have significant and specific risks, and who would benefit from prevention and support services. Recent definitions of street-involved youth have expanded on the runaway and homeless definition to include youth who are not living on the street but who experiment and engage in street-involved activities and identify with street culture and street peer groupings (Worthington et al. 2008). In this chapter, the term *street-involved youth* will be used to describe this entire population.

Youth living on the streets present as a unique service population distinct from the adult homeless population. Homelessness for adults is described first and foremost as a housing and poverty issue, which establishes the context in which individual risk factors can trigger a homeless episode (Burt 2001, as cited by Tutty et al. 2010). Four specific structural issues contribute to adult homelessness: (1) an increasing number of people are being priced out of the affordable housing market; (2) employment opportunities for those individuals with secondary education are dwindling; (3) institutional supports have been reduced for those people with severe mental health and addiction concerns; and (4) people are excluded from affordable housing owing to racial, ethnic, and/or class discrimination (Burt 2001). Street-involved youth have experienced many of the same individual risk factors associated with the adult homeless population, including high rates of childhood maltreatment, child welfare involvement, mental health concerns, incomplete education, and drug use; however, the factors that trigger their street involvement are different (Tutty et al. 2010).

street-involved youth
Youths 25 years of age or younger who do not have a safe home or are underhoused; who have been forced to leave their family of origin; who have run away from their home without the consent of their parents or guardian or who left foster- or group-care placements; or who are not living on the street but who experiment and engage in street-involved activities and identify with street culture and street peer groupings.

throwaways
Youths who are asked, or encouraged, to leave home by their parents/guardians, with the purpose of ending parental responsibility for the well-being of the youths.

Typologies of Street-Involved Youth

A number of typologies have been developed in Canada and the United States over the past 30 years to help researchers and practitioners better understand the unique characteristics of youth who are involved in the street and to develop services designed to meet their current needs (Adlaf and Zdanowicz 1999; Kufeldt and Nimmo 1987b). Typologies generally include, but are not limited to, youth who experiment with street life by occasionally running away or practising truancy, children who run away from home to escape maltreatment and harm, and those young people who have spent years living on the streets and are firmly entrenched in the street lifestyle.

A recent ethnographic study based in San Francisco developed a **life-cycle model** that has proven to be useful in understanding the duration and range of street involvement that youth experience (Auerswald and Eyre 2002). This model proposes a series of stages that youth encounter on the street and includes an initial engagement in street life, a stage where youth become more comfortable with street life, and, finally, periods of crisis during which some youths may transition off the street. A cyclical pattern is noted, however, in that many youths who exit the street may become re-involved. The model describes key influences at each stage, including street mentors who provide youth with basic street survival skills and assist them in understanding the culture of street life.

The Auerswald and Eyre (2002) life-cycle model, and other typologies, assist practitioners and researchers in understanding the Canadian street youth population and the specific risks that are associated with the street lifestyle. These classification systems consider pathways to the street, the frequency and duration of street involvement, the level of individual choice for being on the street, and options for leaving the street. While these classifications provide an understanding of the range of street-involved youth, further work is required to test and validate these typologies (see Figure 13.1).

life-cycle model
This model proposes a series of stages that youth encounter on the street and includes an initial engagement in street life, a stage where youth become more comfortable with street life, and, finally, periods of crisis during which some youths may transition off the street. A cyclical pattern is noted, however, in that many youths who exit the street may become re-involved.

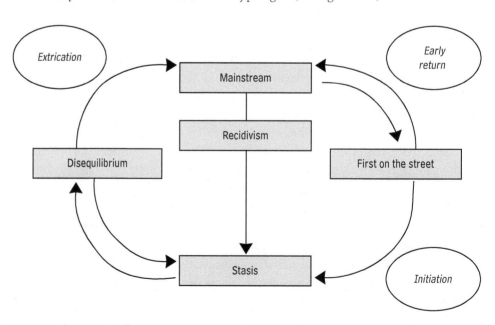

FIGURE 13.1 The Life-Cycle Model of Youth Homelessness

Source: Auerswald and Eyre 2002, p. 1501.

Numbers of Street-Involved Youth

To date, there are no accurate estimates of the Canadian street-involved youth population. It is difficult to estimate these numbers because of the challenges in defining street-involved youth, the unique differences within this population, and differential service use by sub-groups of street-involved youth. Recent estimates based on the national incidence studies of missing youth in the United States suggest that more than 1.6 million youths in the US can be described as street involved (i.e., those who left home or were asked by a parent or guardian to leave the home) (Hammer et al. 2002). The number of street-involved youth in Canada, those who are homeless or living in shelters on any given day, is frequently suggested to be approximately 150,000 (Public Health Agency of Canada 2006). The 150,000 estimate is attributed to DeMatteo et al. (1999), but these numbers were generated in 1988 for an earlier study (Radford, King, and Warren 1989) and based upon an appropriate percentage of US street youth. It is clear that the numbers of street-involved youth as well as the factors that lead to youth homelessness have changed dramatically over the past 25 years, and there is no accurate estimate for the total number of street-involved youth in Canada.

Gaetz, O'Grady, and Vaillancourt (1999) report that the Toronto Hostel Division estimated an average of 325 to 340 youths between the ages of 16 and 24 were living in shelters on any given night in Toronto in 1999; however, Toronto street surveys indicate that this figure was less than one-quarter of the total street-involved youth population in that city (Gaetz et al. 1999). This is supported by a recent US study that found that approximately 7 per cent of the street youth population used shelters (Carlson, Sugano, Millstein, and Auerswald 2006).

Other cities in Canada face similar challenges when estimating the number of youth who are street involved. For example, in Calgary, **homeless youth** currently represent approximately 20 per cent of the entire homeless population (City of Calgary 2008). On 10 May 2006, there were 355 youths under the age of 18 and an additional 327 youths between the ages of 18 and 24 staying on Calgary's streets, in emergency or transitional facilities, or at other non-shelter service agencies such as hospital emergency departments—a significant increase over the past 12 years (City of Calgary 1996, 2008). However, this figure does not represent all street-involved youth in Calgary, including those who sleep in public areas, those who rely on friends for short-term accommodation (couch surfing), or those who engage in the street lifestyle only during the day.

In Halifax, the numbers of homeless adults and youths have increased dramatically over the past decade (Community Action on Homelessness 2009; Nova Scotia Housing and Homelessness Network 2012). Youth ages 16 to 19 made up 9.8 per cent of the 1973 homeless individuals using shelters in 2011, while those under age 16 composed roughly 4.5 per cent (Nova Scotia Housing and Homelessness Network 2012). These numbers describe only a part of the youth homeless population, as a higher percentage of children and youth do not access shelter services. A study by the Halifax Regional Municipality (2005) reported that in 2004 youth under age 18 made up 12 per cent of homeless respondents and those aged 19 to 24 composed 22 per cent. Seven per cent of youth under age 18 and 12 per cent of youth aged 19 to 24 lived in shelters, while 20 per cent of youth under 18 and 43 per cent of youth aged 19 to 24 lived on the streets.

Cross-sectional counts of those on the streets, in shelters, or in other service agencies do not capture the fluidity or diversity of the street-involved youth population, and

homeless youth
Youth who either have left or have been urged to leave home with the full knowledge or approval of legal guardians. They have no alternative home in which to live.

the majority of street-involved youth report moving to large Canadian cities and spending time in different cities (Gaetz et al. 1999). Counts of the actual street-involved youth population in Canada will continue to be conservative estimates of this at-risk population. The range in the estimates of street-involved youth in Canada and the United States raises several questions about the accuracy of estimates. These variations can definitely be attributed to the methodological challenges of developing an accurate count and estimate (Peressini, McDonald, and Hulchanski 1995). The following are several critical issues to consider when planning an estimate or count of the number of street-involved youth:

- What criteria determine street involvement? Definitions of who should be counted need to be established. For example, if runaway youth are included in the street-involved youth counts, should those who have run away but are staying with friends and not on the streets be included?

- How should street-involved youth be contacted? Some estimates of street-involved youth have used street counts at random periods over the course of a year, while other estimates have been based upon counts submitted by service providers. Different methods of contact will run the risk of missing different types of street-involved youth.

- Should shelter numbers be used as a basis for predictions of the uncounted street-involved population who do not use shelters or services? Estimates may be generated to include youths who do not use traditional street resources; however, the accuracy of these estimates remains unknown. This group would typically include youths involved in the formal sex trade, youths who access adult services, or highly transient youths who do not use any services.

Perspectives on Street-Involved Youth

The lens, or perspective, with which we view street-involved youth in Canada has a great impact on the way we respond to the needs of this population. The lens has shifted constantly over the past half century. Prior to the 1960s, youth on the street were seen as delinquents who were there as a result of their own individual pathology and deviant nature (Appathurai 1987). This position shifted during the 1960s as the counter-culture movement saw an increased number of middle-class teens living on city streets. Factors related to the family and school were primary areas of concern in the literature on street-involved youth in the 1970s, while maltreatment of children became a paramount concern for research and service delivery during the 1980s and early 1990s (McCormack, Janus, and Burgess 1986). With the end of the twentieth century and the beginning of the twenty-first, structural factors now play an increasing role in our understanding of street-involved youth. The increase in HIV/AIDS (human immunodeficiency virus/acquired immunodeficiency syndrome), chronic poverty, inadequate housing, unemployment or underemployment, deinstitutionalization, and the challenged and overworked systems of child welfare all have a critical impact on street-involved youth in Canada (van der Ploeg and Scholte 1997; Worthington et al. 2008).

An ecological perspective has frequently been used as a theoretical framework for understanding the runaway and homeless phenomenon. The model described in this chapter was developed by Kufeldt and Burrows (1994), based on initial work by Bronfenbrenner (1974) and later expanded on by Garbarino (1982). Bronfenbrenner's influence was acknowledged in the authors' description of the ecological approach: "A child's development is influenced by a complex network of family, friends, school, community resources, and ultimately, by forces outside the child's immediate experience, such as government decisions and cultural or societal expectations" (Kufeldt and Burrows 1994, p. 13). This approach is useful for focusing the reader's attention on the interaction of the individual with different systems (e.g., school, peers, and child welfare) and within the predominant values, attitudes, and philosophies of society (see Figure 13.2).

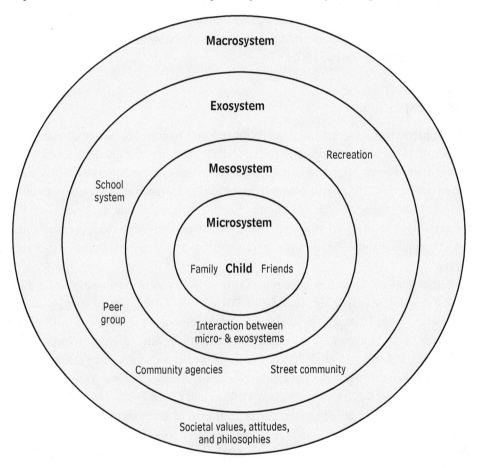

Microsystem	This is the immediate setting in which a person resides. For the street population, it can include family, school, child welfare placement, and the street culture itself.
Mesosystem	This represents the connections between the child's microsystems and exosystems. Risk and opportunity relate to the quality of connections and relationships and the congruencies of values within the microsystems.
Exosystem	Larger systems (school system, community agency) are exosystems in which policies and operations can enhance or detract from opportunities for homeless youth.
Macrosystem	This includes the culture and ideology of the society in which a person lives. The dilemma in leaving the street is the need to conform to predominant and straight culture without the means to incorporate and practise its values.

FIGURE 13.2 Ecological Framework

Source: Kufeldt and Burrows 1994, p. 14. Adapted from Bronfenbrenner 1979.

Pathways to the Street—The Vulnerable Population

Young people become involved with street life in a variety of ways. A significant proportion of street-involved youth say that they initially left home as a result of family conflict, disruption, and maltreatment (Chen 2004; Hyde 2005; McLean 2005). In addition, many youths leave home because they were thrown out or forced to leave, or because they sought further independence (McLean 2005; Public Health Agency of Canada 2006b). Other youths become street involved following an early exit from or aging out of the child welfare system (Lenz-Rashid 2006).

Family Experiences

A large percentage of street-involved youth report a history of child maltreatment at the hands of their caregivers. The Enhanced Surveillance of Canadian Street Youth (E-SYS) is an ongoing project to monitor behaviours, risk determinants, sexually transmitted infections (STIs), and related infections in the Canadian street youth population (Public Health Agency of Canada 2006b). The E-SYS reported that between 19 and 28 per cent of street-involved youth left home because of physical abuse, sexual abuse, and/or emotional abuse. In addition, 30 per cent reported experiencing neglect in their homes.

Other North American studies report that rates of maltreatment range from 12 to 50 per cent for sexual abuse, and 30 to 90 per cent for physical abuse (Adlaf and Zhanowicz 1999; Hyde 2005; MacLaurin, Worthington, Dittmann, and Kitt 2009b; Rotheram-Borus, Mahler, Koopman, and Langabeer 1996; Thrane, Hoyt, Whitbeck, and Yoder 2006; Worthington et al. 2008). The maltreatment experienced by street-involved youth is consistently reported to be chronic, extreme, and initiated at a young age (Cauce, Tyler, and Whitback 2004; Janus et al. 1995; Tyler and Cauce 2002).

MacLaurin et al. (2009b) found that 71 per cent of street-involved youth surveyed in Calgary reported at least one type of maltreatment while living at home, including physical abuse (43 per cent), sexual abuse (20 per cent), neglect (29 per cent), and emotional maltreatment (52 per cent). And abuse among street-involved youth is rarely a one-time occurrence. Of this group, 61 per cent reported that the maltreatment had consisted of multiple events during a period of more than six months, while an additional 31 per cent reported multiple events occurring within six months or less. Only 8 per cent reported that the maltreatment had been a single event. In addition, 54 per cent of surveyed street-involved youth reported having witnessed domestic violence between their parents (MacLaurin et al. 2009b).

Children who experience maltreatment within their family may resort to running away from home as an alternative to the abuse or neglect. More than 11 per cent of children and teens who experienced substantiated maltreatment in Alberta in 2003 had a history of running away from home at the time of the child welfare investigation, and the percentage of teens (ages 12 to 15) was significantly higher (MacLaurin et al. 2006) (see Box 13.1).

Box 13.1 Youth Justice in Action

Growing Up on Streets Trumps Dysfunctional Home Life; Family Dynamics—Not Drugs or Alcohol—Is the Main Reason Why Thousands of Teens Choose to Run Away from Home

By Bronwyn McCarter

Christopher Brown, a 19-year-old homeless man, stood barefoot in a damp black hoodie, shivering, one bleak afternoon on Granville Street. His hard-luck story began, he said, when he was kicked out of his home at a young age. He spent days sitting on the steps of the Vancouver Art Gallery until the police found him and put him in foster care, he recalled in an interview. As he grew older, Brown said he was tired of being shuffled from foster home to foster home, feeling that no one truly cared for him. At the age of 18, he turned to the streets. "It's a hard life out here," he said. Unfortunately, Brown isn't unique in feeling like the streets are the only place left to go. He is one of 65,000 homeless teenagers in Canada who struggle to find a safe, dry place to sleep each night. "You don't know if you're gonna wake up in a car with a bag over your head, or with a knife to your throat," said Brown, who mostly sleeps with a group of friends in various locations on Vancouver's sidewalks. On the streets, Brown said, teens make their own families. It is often difficult to find someone to trust, but when that connection is made on the streets, he said, the relationships are strong and more meaningful than those he made at school.

Brown has been trying to get a job for more than three years. He began his search while in foster care, but now that he is homeless he said it is impossible to find employment. "No one wants to hire someone like me," Brown said. Employers don't want to hire a person who looks dirty, or doesn't have an address. They worry such an employee would turn away customers, and potentially hurt their businesses. That traps teens in a vicious cycle: they have nowhere to go except the streets, but they can't get jobs because they don't have stable families to live with, or easy access to showers and clean clothes. Money is by far the hardest thing to come by for homeless teens. While food, used clothing, showers, and laundry facilities can be found in downtown Vancouver, young people often start trying to collect money through panhandling—until desperation forces them to consider more drastic measures, such as prostitution and drug dealing.

For many people, dropping a couple of quarters into someone's hat is a difficult decision. They are unsure where the money will be spent: will it go toward a new pair of shoes, an umbrella, or someone's next high? Directions Youth Services offers a job program that is Brown's personal favourite. The program is called Street Youth Job Action (SYJA), and allows young people to clean up the streets, do needle sweeps, and leave at the end of the day with some cash in their pockets. Brown and other teens who sleep on Vancouver's streets applaud the SYJA program because they get a chance to give back to the community. Many people believe it is drugs or alcohol that bring young people to the streets. While that may be true for some, experts say it is often family dynamics that drive teens to the wet streets of Vancouver. Some are runaways from home; others are kicked out. Drugs often become the problem after they reach the streets.

Many homeless young people also have mental health problems and turn to drugs as a way of self-medicating, said Michelle Clausius, associate director of development and communications at Covenant House, a facility for youth on Drake Street. Jennifer Hanrahan, a manager at Directions Youth Services Centre, said crystal meth is one of the leading drugs causing addiction among young people. It is the cheapest drug on the market, and easily available. However, not all teens on the street are involved with drugs. A group of homeless teenagers on Granville recently told the *Vancouver Sun* they would never smoke anything more harmful than marijuana because becoming addicted to a stronger drug often means "the drugs start doing you, you don't do the drugs." Some of Brown's friends said their biggest dream is one day to get off the streets, and they believe that doing hard drugs could make it harder to get a roof over their heads.

Brown's two biggest goals, he said, are to find a home and go to college to study culinary arts. When asked what he thought would get him off the streets, he said that if he was given $125 more a month on his welfare cheque, he would be able to

(Continued)

find a place to live. Then, he said, he could shower every day, feel safe sleeping, and try to pull himself together to get a job. Brown now gets the standard welfare rental rate of $375 a month for housing, but in Vancouver it is getting increasingly hard to find a place in which to live for that price. According to a recent report by the Carnegie Community Action Project, single-room occupancy hotel rooms in the Downtown Eastside rented at welfare-friendly rates have gone down from 29 per cent of available rooms in 2009, to 12 per cent this year.

Helping homeless teens may seem like a hopeless task. How does society know where to start? Is it housing, food, and employment? Or just someone to believe in them and to encourage them along the way? People who work with homeless teens say the solutions vary. Hanrahan believes young people need the help of people who are non-judgmental and who will convey they are worth caring for, because sometimes they feel they have little self-worth. Every teen has potential, if given the chance. If a community can help one teen follow his or her dream, advocates say, it can become a win-win situation for society and, most importantly, for the young person on the street.

Bronwyn McCarter is a Grade 11 student at West Vancouver Secondary School.

Source: Bronwyn McCarter, *Vancouver Sun*, 18 November 2010, p. A17.

Child Welfare Experiences

Children and youth who have experienced maltreatment and family conflict frequently become involved with child welfare and are referred to child welfare care (MacLaurin and Bala 2004). Children in the care of child welfare (e.g., foster care, group homes, or treatment centres) are overrepresented in most street youth populations (Barker et al. 2014; Biehal and Wade 2000; Duval and Vincent 2009; Fitzgerald 1995; Kulik, Gaetz, Crowe, and Ford-James 2011; Park 2005; Worthington et al. 2008). Worthington et al. (2008) reported that 62 per cent of street-involved youth surveyed in Calgary reported that their family had a history of child welfare involvement, and of this number 52 per cent had been placed in either foster or group care as a result of the involvement.

This overrepresentation may be a reflection of the number of youths who ran away from current child welfare care or of those youths who became homeless following emancipation from care (Lenz-Rashid 2006). Although less than 1 per cent of children in England were in foster care or group homes, more than 30 per cent of **runaways** reported as missing to the police were from care (Biehal and Wade 2000). This trend is also seen in Canada, with a high percentage of children reported missing to the police from institutional and foster care, and institutional care having the highest rate of repeat runners (Fisher 1989).

runaways
Youths who run away from their family or child welfare placement, at least overnight, without parental or caretaker permission. They often leave as a result of family conflict or maltreatment.

Child welfare agencies have the mandate to serve the transitional needs of youth effectively as they prepare for independence following their in-care placements. Research focusing on the health and housing outcomes of youth aging out of the child welfare system has identified that these young people are not consistently well served (Lenz-Rashid 2006). The percentage of youth emancipated from the care of child welfare who were described as homeless at the point of emancipation in the United States ranges from 25 to 66 per cent (Barth 1990; Courtney et al. 2001; California Department of Social Services 2002).

There are significant differences noted for youths who enter street life from foster or group care compared to those youths who enter the streets from home (Biehal and Wade 2000; Rees 1993). Rees (1993) found that street-involved youth who had left child welfare placements were more likely to run repeatedly, more likely to run for longer periods of time, and more likely to be apprehended by police.

Life on the Streets

Once youths make the transition from home to the street, they enter a new world with its own culture, norms, and rules. As Auerswald and Eyre (2002) point out, this initial experience of the street is characterized by feelings of loneliness, disorientation, and the need to survive. Their study suggests that youths find street mentors and become acculturated to the street, including the street's resources, economy, language, and drugs. Victimization on the street is extremely common among street-involved youth and can take the form of theft or robbery, sexual assault, physical assault, and assault with a weapon (Gaetz 2004). For minority groups like lesbian, gay, bisexual, trans, or questioning (LGBTQ) youth, the level of victimization can nearly double (Whitbeck, Chen, Hoyt, Tyler, and Johnson 2004). LGBTQ youth are clearly overrepresented in the street-involved population in Canada (Abramovich 2012). Furthermore, the mortality rate for street-involved youth is about 11 times the expected rate for the general youth population (Boivin 2005). Gaetz (2004) notes that a significant proportion of street-involved youth do not turn to anyone when they have experienced victimization on the street.

Social Support and Resilience

Street-involved youth develop social networks that can be a source of support (Bender et al. 2013; Johnson, Whitbeck, and Hoyt 2005). Nearly 80 per cent of youth have relationships that were formed prior to their time on the streets, and 66 per cent have friends from home, indicating that these youths still value the ties from their past (Johnson et al. 2005). Furthermore, nearly one-third (31 per cent) of street-involved youth report family members as part of their social network, including siblings (ibid.). Weaker family ties are associated with youths who have externalizing behaviour problems; with gay, lesbian, and bisexual youths; and with those who experience caregiver abuse prior to leaving home (ibid.; Milburn et al. 2005). In a qualitative study by Kidd (2003), one-quarter of street-involved youth mentioned significant support from friends on the street who taught them the rules of street culture. Street acquaintances provide an element of family support for street-involved youth and are described as being there for personal, financial, and emotional support (Worthington, MacLaurin, Dittmann, and Kitt 2009c).

Street-involved youth are resilient in a number of ways. Kidd (2003) found that a large number of Canadian youth had a strong sense of confidence in their own abilities, of security in their own beliefs, and of self-worth. Other research supports these findings and indicates that youth have both resource-related strengths (i.e., knowledge of the street environment and streetwise skills) and self-improvement skills (e.g., making healthier choices and gaining emotional maturity) (see Rew and Horner 2003). Beneficial coping mechanisms include having hope and goals for the future, having a sense of spirituality, having friends, having time alone to think, having positive thinking and humour, and having hobbies (Worthington et al. 2009c). A major theme in Kidd's (2003) interviews with street-involved youth was their desire for more opportunities to increase their self-worth. These youths, despite their history and circumstances, continue to have a sense of hope for their future.

Risks Associated with Street Involvement

Substance Use and HIV Risk

Substance use is primarily used as a coping mechanism for life on the streets, stress, and early family abuse, but it can also be used for social or recreational purposes (see Chapter 10). Substance use is common among street-involved youth and includes the use of tobacco, alcohol, marijuana, hashish, crack cocaine, powder cocaine, heroin, lysergic acid diethylamide (LSD), mushrooms, crystal meth, speed, crank, ecstasy, and glue (Clatts, Goldsamt, Yi, and Gwadz 2005; Robert, Pauze, and Fournier 2005). The rate of substance use among street-involved youth varies by specific substance, with between 70 and 94 per cent of youth overall reporting the use of any substance (MacLaurin, Worthington, Dittmann, and Kitt 2009c). Specific levels of reported substance use include alcohol (67 to 100 per cent), tobacco (96 per cent), and marijuana (43 to 93 per cent), although several other substances are also used by the majority of street-involved youth (Kulik et al. 2011; Thompson, Zittel-Palamara, and Maccio 2004; Tyler and Johnson 2006). Brands, Leslie, Catz-Biro, and Li (2005) found that substance use among street-involved youth is not only common but also tends to be extreme.

Most studies report rates of injection drug use among street-involved youth from 20 to 54 per cent (Clatts, Rees-Davis, Sotheran, and Atillasoy 1998; Leach, Wolitski, Goldbaum, Fishbein, and the AIDS Community Demonstration Projects 1997; Roy, Haley, Leclerc, Cedras, and Boivin 2002b. Furthermore, between one-quarter and three-quarters of youth who use injection drugs have shared drug-injection equipment (Gleghorn, Marx, Vittinghoff, and Katz 1998; Worthington et al. 2008).

Although some Canadian studies on street-involved youth have shown low risk of HIV infection through injection drug use, levels of injecting risk behaviours among street-involved youth require ongoing assessment. The majority of research shows that youth (defined as those under 30 years of age) who use injection drugs are at greater risk of HIV transmission than older users (Health Canada 2002b). This risk results from sharing contaminated needles, syringes, and other drug-use equipment and the tendency to engage in unsafe sex, often under the influence of drugs (Diaz, Conover, Edwards, Monterroso, and Susser 1998; Kral, Lorvick, and Edlin 1999; Marshall, Kerr, Qi, Montaner, and Wood 2010). Findings also indicate that youth who use injection drugs have a significantly higher rate of hepatitis C virus (HCV) (Boivin et al. 2005).

Physical and Mental Health Problems

Canadian research has consistently demonstrated that street-involved youth are a population at risk for physical and mental health problems. It has been suggested that street-involved youth face barriers to exercising their rights and the opportunities of their citizenship (e.g., access to health care, to shelter, to mental health support) while having the same basic needs as all Canadians, and that they are one of the most disenfranchised groups in our society (Bassuk, Rubin, and Lauriat 1984; Miller et al. 1980). A study of homeless Toronto **squeegee kids**, for example, suggests that the lives of this group of street-involved youth are characterized by a constant struggle to find safe, secure shelter, to generate income, and to find sufficient food (Dachner and Tarasuk 2002).

squeegee kids
A group of street-involved youth who are resourceful in attempting to develop and maintain a livelihood and means of survival by offering to clean windshields at major intersections.

Study findings indicate a higher prevalence of mental health problems for street-involved youth than for non-street-involved youth (Wong, Clark, and Marlotte 2014; Perlman, Willard, Herbers, Cutuli, and Eyrich-Garg 2014). Common mental health problems in this population include conduct and oppositional disorder, anxiety disorders, dissociative symptoms, and depression (Booth and Zhang 1997; Thompson et al. 2004; Tyler, Cauce, and Whitbeck 2004). However, Ayerst (1999) found that most street-involved youth felt less depressed and stressed on the street than when they were living at home. Street-involved youth are at a higher risk for attempted and completed suicide, and suicidal ideation often follows completed suicides of street friends (Perlman et al. 2014; Clatts et al. 2005; Wong et al. 2014; Yoder, Hoyt, and Whitbeck 1998). Documented rates of attempted suicide range from 25 to 46 per cent, with even higher rates noted for gay, lesbian, and bisexual youth (Clatts et al. 2005; Kidd 2006; Whitbeck et al. 2004; Worthington, MacLaurin, Dittmann, and Kitt 2009a). Mental health is a critical concern for all street-involved youth and specifically for select marginalized groups.

Given the lifestyle of street-involved youth, it is understandable that youth may not receive adequate health care and are frequently unable to obtain this care because of a lack of current health-care coverage (e.g., some may not have access to a health-care card) (Farrow, Deisher, Brown, Kulig, and Kipke 1992; Gaetz et al. 1999). Health concerns reported by street-involved youth include upper-respiratory-tract infections, skin disorders (including scabies and lice), gastrointestinal disorders, genitourinary disorders, and foot problems (e.g., fungus and blisters) (Dachner and Tarasuk 2002; Wright 1991). A higher percentage of street-involved youth with a current or previous history of living on the street reported physical health conditions than youth who had never lived on the street (Worthington et al. 2009b). And chronic health concerns for street-involved youth may be twice as high as those for youth who are not street involved (Wright 1991). Additional health concerns are identified for street-involved youth who have children while they are living on the street (Pennbridge, MacKenzie, and Swofford 1991; Ray 1993). The literature highlights a relationship between the duration of street involvement and health outcomes for youth—the longer the duration, the greater the risk of tuberculosis, dental problems, viral and sexually transmitted diseases (STDs), HIV/AIDS, hepatitis B virus (HBV), and hepatitis C virus (HCV) (Kraus, Eberle, and Serge 2001).

Sexual Health—STIs and HIV Risk

According to findings from the Canadian E-SYS study (Enhanced Surveillance of Canadian Street Youth, initiated in 1998), street-involved youth are at high risk of contracting sexually transmitted infections (STIs) (Public Health Agency of Canada 2006a). Compared to the general youth population, street-involved youth included in the E-SYS study are 10 times more likely to have chlamydia, and 20 to 30 times more likely to have gonorrhea. Among youth included in the E-SYS study, between the years 1999 and 2003, approximately 2.3 per cent of street-involved youth had HBV, 3.6 to 4.5 per cent had HCV, and 14.2 to 18.8 per cent had herpes simplex virus-2 (HSV-2), associated with genital herpes.

Canadian and American incidence and prevalence data, in conjunction with surveillance data, reveal that street-involved youth are at very high risk of HIV infection (Boivin 2005; DeMatteo et al. 1999; Hahn, Shafer, and Moss 1998; Kipke, Montgomery, Simon, and Iverson 1996; Larke 2001; Roy et al. 2002b; Roy et al. 2001; Sullivan 1996). The number of new HIV cases in youth between the ages of 15 and 19 years has remained relatively constant since 1999; however, the proportion of females among this group is growing (Health Canada 2002a, 2002b). Sexual activity is likely to present a major risk for HIV transmission among street-involved youth. St Lawrence, Crosby, and O'Brannon (1999) found that the average age at first intercourse for street-involved youth is 12 years old, while the average number of times street-involved youth have sexual intercourse each week ranges from two to three times for casual sex, up to 13 times for paying sex (Public Health Agency of Canada 2006a). Studies report high percentages of youth with multiple sexual partners, and young men who have sex with men represent the most at-risk subgroup among street-involved youth, with an average of 45 lifetime partners (Booth and Zhang 1997; Public Health Agency of Canada 2006a; St Lawrence et al. 1999).

Although young people are generally aware of HIV risks, research on sexual risk behaviours shows that youth are among the least likely to employ safer sex precautions. A large percentage of street-involved youth do not use condoms to protect themselves from HIV or other sexually transmitted diseases, with a low of 10 per cent of female street-involved youth who consistently use condoms (Clatts et al. 1998; De Rosa, Montgomery, Hyde, Iverson, and Kipke 2001; Haley, Roy, Leclerc, Boudreau, and Boivin 2004b; Weber, Boivin, Blais, Haley, and Roy 2002).

Pregnancy is also common among street-involved youth. Studies report that 42 to 50 per cent of all female youth living on the street have been pregnant (Haley 2004a; Weber 2002; Worthington, MacLaurin, Dittmann, and Kitt 2009d). Greene and Ringwalt (1998) examined the relationship between pregnancy in street-involved youth and street-involved youth's level of street involvement, and found that youth currently living on the street were most likely to become pregnant and to experience multiple pregnancies. There are significant risks for youth who experience a pregnancy while living on the street, including drug use, access to prenatal and medical services, financial resources, and infant health (Thompson, Bender, Lewis, and Watkins 2008); however, there is evidence that pregnancies among street-involved youth may provide motivation for some youth to establish more stable housing (Hathazi, Lankenau, Sanders, and Bloom 2009).

Involvement in Survival or Obligatory Sex

Survival or obligatory sex involves the bartering of sex for money or other necessities, such as food and shelter. Studies reveal that up to 25 per cent of street-involved youth have traded sex at some point in their lives and that females may be at higher risk for involvement (Clatts et al. 1998; Haley 2004b; Public Health Agency of Canada 2006a; Weber et al. 2002; Worthington et al. 2009d). Survival or obligatory sex may offer a way for street-involved youth to gain autonomy and independence while on the street. Many youth have left family or child welfare situations in a manner that does not allow their return, and survival or obligatory sex and eventual involvement in the sex trade is a way of establishing some immediate financial independence and autonomy from their former living situations (McIntyre 1999; also see Chapter 14 in this volume). Street-involved youth may participate in unprotected sexual activity in order to receive a greater amount of money than that offered for protected sex or for a secure place to stay for the night (de Oliviera 1992; Slonim-Nevo, Ozawa, and Auslander 1991; Swart-Kruger and Richer 1997). Among Canadian street-involved youth involved in survival or obligatory sex,44 per cent report not using a condom during their most recent obligatory sexual encounter (Public Health Agency of Canada 2006a; Swart-Kruger and Richer 1997).

Institutional Experiences of Street-Involved Youth

Education

Education for street-involved youth is a serious concern, as many of these youth may drop out of school or be expelled before finishing, or even reaching, high school. Without education, young people have difficulty finding and maintaining a steady job, making it even more difficult for them to transition off the street. This population also experiences a higher rate of learning difficulties (Barwick and Siegal 1996; Thompson et al. 2004). One study reported that more than half of all street-involved youth display evidence of a reading disability, nearly 30 per cent display evidence of arithmetic/written work disability, and 20 per cent are classified as "normally achieving" (Barwick and Siegal 1996). School attendance declines as youth get older. Approximately 65 per cent of early-adolescent street-involved youth reported attending school within the past month compared to27 per cent of older-adolescent street-involved youth (Unger et al. 1998). Reasons for not attending school are complex, but Thompson, Zittel-Palamara, and Maccio (2004) determined that more than half of street-involved youth were either suspended or expelled from school. A survey of Calgary street-involved youth found that 69 per cent of respondents reported an incomplete high school education and 46 per cent reported having been kicked out of school (MacLaurin, Worthington, Dittmann, and Kitt 2009a).

Child Welfare

A high percentage of street-involved youth have had previous child welfare experiences and foster-care placements (Clarke and Cooper 2000; Gaetz et al. 1999; Leslie and Hare 2000; Min Park, Metraux, and Culhane 2005). In 2003, 42 per cent of Canadian street-involved youth in the E-SYS study reported having been in foster care, and 47 per cent

Box 13.2   Youth Justice in Action

Canada Failing Homeless Youth, Report Charges—Stress on Emergency Assistance, Not Prevention, Solves Little in the Long Run, Professor Says

By Leslie Ferenc, *Toronto Star*, GTA, Monday, 3 March 2014

Canada falls short of meeting the needs of homeless youth by treating them as adults and expecting shelter care to solve the problem, according to a new report. Many youth find themselves "languishing in a shelter for four or five years when they should be in school learning to be an adult with the supports they need . . . instead of rushing them to be adults, living in poverty and becoming chronically homeless adults," says report author Stephen Gaetz, a professor in York University's education faculty and director of the Homeless Hub (Canadian Homelessness Research Network). "By continuing to emphasize emergency supports, as important as they are, rather than prevention or rapid rehousing, our strategy is simply to manage the problem," he said. Gaetz is author of *Coming of Age: Reimagining the Response to Youth Homelessness in Canada*, which was released Monday.

The report looks at remedies used in Canada and countries such as the United Kingdom and Australia which address youth homelessness differently. "Youth homelessness is distinct from adult because of conditions . . . it's not just an age difference," he said, adding that they are thrust into adult roles before their time and the transition is often traumatic. For one, they don't have the resources and support they need to be independent. "They leave a home where they were dependent on the care of adults." Family conflict can also be a factor with youth fleeing difficulties at home, including abuse. They land in shelters and "suddenly, they find themselves having to behave as adults." said Gaetz.

While he acknowledged there will always be a need for emergency services, they are not the solution. "We need to refocus our efforts on preventing it from happening in the first place," he wrote in the report. "For those who can no longer stay at home we must develop a crisis response that allows them to rapidly move into housing in a safe and planned way, with the supports they need to help them transition to a healthy and fulfilling adulthood." The report recommends an integrated system of care that reconnects youth to their families if possible, offers outreach mental health and harm reduction programs as well as legal support for youth in conflict with the law. To meet the needs of youth means looking at what others are doing "so we can put together a framework for responding to youth homelessness differently," said Gaetz, adding it will also mean a shift in thinking.

Australia's Reconnect program targets youth 12–18 and their families. School social workers and teachers help identify at-risk or homeless youth. A series of programs and services such as assessment, counselling, and practical support are available to help young people work through their problems. A shelter diversion program in the UK offers youth a bed and support from a family in their neighbourhood, a place to chill while they resolve their problems. An integrated system of care includes housing and, if possible, family reunification. The report also cites the Infinity Project, run by the Boys and Girls Clubs of Calgary, which offers young people 16–24 permanent housing, leading to greater self-sufficiency. In Niagara Region, Youth Reconnect is a community-based shelter diversion program to help homeless and at-risk youth stay in their communities and in school. In Toronto, outreach and harm reduction programs at front-line agencies such as Eva's Satellite help meet service needs of diverse groups.

For Gaetz, it's a start, but he wants every community in Canada to make ending youth homelessness a priority. "Moreover, outside of the Province of Alberta which is readying its strategic response to youth homelessness, most higher levels of government across the country are largely silent on the issue," he said. "This means in most communities the response is fragmented and ad hoc, and the focus is on managing the problem rather than ending it through a coordinated response that shifts the focus to prevention and rehousing."

The next step for Gaetz is to engage citizens, agencies, community groups, and all levels of government across the country to come to the table. "We are looking at developing a coalition model to support communities to end homelessness," he said. "It's not a cookie cutter response. Toronto's will be different from York Region's or Kenora's. I'm positive this can happen because there is a lot of momentum in Canada."

reported having been in group homes (Public Health Agency of Canada 2006b). In addition, between 12 and 38 per cent of youth transitioning out of foster care spend some time without a home shortly after discharge, either sleeping on the streets or in a homeless shelter (Cook 1994; Courtney 2001; Courtney and Dworsky 2006; Freundlich and Avery 2006). A number of studies have reported that youth with child welfare histories were two times more likely than other youth to be unable to pay their rent or utility bills and four times more likely to be evicted, and that, overall, youth transitioning out of care reported feeling poorly prepared for independent living (Courtney 2001; Leslie and Hare 2000; Reilly 2003).

Criminal Justice System

Extensive work by Baron has shown how crime is related to several factors in the lives of street-involved youth (Baron 2003, 2004; Baron and Hartnagel 1998, 2006). These factors include monetary dissatisfaction; unemployment; deviant/criminal peers; being a victim of robbery, violence, or theft; perception of blocked opportunities; drug/alcohol use; low self-control; and low self-esteem. All of these factors interact to increase the risk of crime involvement in street-involved youth. As can be seen, criminal involvement among street-involved youth is a complex interaction of numerous factors and cannot simply be explained as deviant behaviour (Gaetz, O'Grady, and Buccieri 2010).

Street-involved youth consistently report that selling drugs is a means of earning money while on the streets (Baron and Hartnagel 2006; Hagan and McCarthy 1997). A significant proportion of street-involved youth are involved in some form of gang activity while on the street (Yoder, Whitbeck, and Hoyt 2003), while violent crime such as assault is also commonly noted in Canadian and US studies (Baron and Hartnagel 2006; Gaetz 2004). Other criminal involvement includes shoplifting, theft, and property offences (Baron and Hartnagel 2006). A survey of Calgary street-involved youth found that 69 per cent of respondents reported that they had been charged with a crime at some point in their life, and of this group, 79 per cent were charged under the juvenile justice system, 48 per cent were charged under the adult system, and 75 per cent had spent time in jail or detention as a result of these charges (Dittmann, MacLaurin, Worthington, and Kitt 2009).

It has been suggested that street-involved youth do not necessarily prefer to be delinquent or elect to become involved in criminal activities; rather, they become involved in response to the situational demands and challenges of living on the streets (Hagan and McCarthy 1997). O'Grady and Green (2003) point out that the more disadvantaged a homeless person becomes, the more likely that person may opt to be involved in criminal activity. This is especially critical when appropriate avenues for earning are limited or criminalized. During the late 1990s, there was a noted increase in the number of people involved in squeegee cleaning on the streets of many large Canadian cities. Squeegee cleaning, like panhandling, was an income-generating activity that was seen as the domain of street-involved youth and resulted in the term "squeegee kids" (O'Grady and Bright 2002). In 2000, the Safe Streets Act was enacted in Ontario, and it resulted in the criminalization of squeegee cleaning as a means of income generation (Schneiderman 2002). O'Grady and Greene (2003) question the rationale of this move, as research found that squeegee-cleaning street youth were less involved in criminal activity and reported lower levels of hard-drug use and lower levels of psychological distress than that reported by street youth who did not participate in squeegee cleaning (O'Grady, Bright, and Cohen 1998).

Street Services and Intervention Strategies

Street-involved youth do not take advantage of available services in all circumstances. McLean (2005) found that, in a sample of youth in Calgary without child welfare status, just over half reported knowing about or using community outreach services for homeless youth, and that they primarily heard about these services from their friends. Of those surveyed in this study who used shelters, 29 per cent said they experienced difficulty accessing the service, while 32 per cent said they had been turned away because they did not meet certain shelter criteria (ibid.).

A San Francisco study that examined differential service use for street-involved youth at different stages of street involvement found that youth who were more entrenched in the street culture were less likely to access drug-related services while those attempting to leave the street were more likely to access medical services (Carlson et al. 2006). Regardless of the level of street involvement, virtually all street-involved youth in the study reported using at least one related service, 50 per cent used medical services, 45 per cent used outreach services, 21 per cent used drug-related services, and 7 per cent used shelters. This study demonstrated a high rate of service use overall but highlighted that the effectiveness of individual services truly differ for subpopulations (Carlson et al. 2006).

Worthington et al. (2008) report similar findings in Canada as use of specific services differed by type of street involvement. The three levels of street involvement included street-involved youth who were currently living on the street (Currently on Street); the second category included street-involved youth who were not currently living on the street but had a past history of living on the street (Not on Street—History); the third category included street-involved youth who were not currently living on the street and had no history of living on the street (Not on Street—No History). Youth currently living on the street reported higher use of shelters, drop-in centres, and outreach services, while street-involved youth who had not lived on the street reported higher use of alternative educational services (Worthington et al. 2008) (see Table 13.1).

The majority of street-involved youth speak very positively about the services available to them—specifically those services that are flexible, have employees with positive attitudes, offer a comfortable atmosphere, and provide a sense of safety and security (Worthington et al. 2008). A continued focus on high-quality assurance is needed, however, as street-involved youth continue to experience barriers to accessing timely and effective services. Karabanow (2004) provides an example of two Toronto-based shelters that have teamed with child welfare organizations. While these programs were originally designed to provide emergency housing and services to street-involved youth, they

Table 13.1	Use of Street Services by Current Level of Street Involvement							

Services Used in the Past Three Months (*N* = 333)	Current Level of Street Involvement							
	Not on Street— No History		Not on Street— History		Currently on Street		Total	
	%	#	%	#	%	#	%	#
Food banks	22	14	38	43	33	50	32	107
Shelters*	19	12	32	36	72	111	48	159
Drop-in centres*	12	8	30	34	68	105	44	147
Medical clinics	35	23	45	51	40	61	41	135
Outreach services*	9	6	32	36	53	81	37	123
Financial aid	6	4	15	17	8	13	10	34
Employment services	23	15	21	24	29	44	25	83
Educational services	20	13	16	18	10	16	14	47
Counselling services*	15	10	26	30	10	16	17	56
No services used*	22	14	17	19	2	3	11	36
Total	Column totals not provided because participants could choose multiple responses							

Calgary Youth, Health and the Street—Final Report

Note: Based on a sample of 333 responses with information about use of street services and current street involvement.

* Significance level $p \leq 0.05$.

Source: Worthington et al. 2008, p. 116.

are now providing long-term care facilities for young people experiencing difficulty with child welfare services. Other barriers to services identified in the literature include inadequate program funding, unavailable programs and services, low salaries, insufficient and inexperienced staff, and government policy (Brooks, Milburn, Rotheram-Borus, and Witkin 2004; Worthington et al. 2008). According to Brooks et al. (2004), most of the issues identified by agencies as problem areas for street involved youth are not well addressed by these agencies. Street-involved youth tend to respond best to service providers who are respectful, flexible, empathetic, supportive, encouraging, and empowering (Thompson et al. 2006).

Effective service development is not a simple prescription for meeting the needs of street-involved youth. Given the diversity of street youth—as noted in the discussions of the life-cycle model of street involvement and the level of street involvement (Worthington et al. 2008), as well as the inherent risks associated with street involvement—there is a critical need to establish a continuum of services to meet the diverse needs of street-involved youth. Services are required to assist young people at different points in their life: before youth become regularly involved in the streets; during street involvement; during a transition from the street locale; and as a follow-up to street involvement (Kufeldt and Burrows 1994). Services at each of these points need to address the physical needs (e.g., food, clothing, and shelter) of young people involved in street life as well as needs related to their physical and mental health, education, and employment (see Table 13.2). Studies advocate a **youth-centric programming model** that allows youth to play a significant role in developing and evaluating programs and in which the agencies continue to be flexible in adapting to the changing needs of street-involved youth (Baer, Peterson, and Wells 2004; Whitmore and McKee 2001).

Emerging research and advocacy are calling for a new response to street-involved youth and youth homelessness in Canada (Gaetz 2014; Raising the Roof 2009). Services at this point continue to focus on responding to crises and emergencies; however, a renewed emphasis on prevention services is required to reduce the growing numbers of street-involved youth. As well, a focus on supportive transitions and accommodations is required to support successful transitions to housing stability.

With these new and emerging practices for youth homelessness, there is a continuing call for a systematic and rigorous examination to determine what interventions work best for what children and youth, and for what time frame. Recent work by the Canadian Homelessness and Research Network proposes the development of a hierarchy of evidence for promising practice research that will highlight the benefits of emerging work evidence for populations at risk (Canadian Homelessness Research Network 2013). One critical element of promising practice research will continue to be work focused on intervention research (McCay and Aiello 2013).

youth-centric programming model
Youth play a significant role in developing and evaluating programs, and agencies continue to be flexible in adapting to the changing needs of street-involved youth.

Summary

Street-involved youth are a diverse, marginalized population that face multiple challenges and insufficient and fragmented support from institutions and services. Understanding the experience of street-involved youth and the risks associated with street involvement is critical to developing services to meet their needs at all stages of their involvement—from early contact with the street, during their extended time spent on the street, and following their decision to leave the street. Communities need to promote and support positive life choices among street-involved youth while respecting their independence. An increased focus on evidence-based intervention is required to better identify what can work best for what groups of this diverse population. Research has shown that while street-involved youth are at higher risk for a variety of issues related to survival, safety, and health, these youth possess resilience and a strong desire to develop a future for themselves. A male street-involved youth eloquently described this hope for the future during a study interview in Calgary: "It's not a dark road. I mean it's whatever I want to make of it. Wherever I want to go, I know I can get there. It's gonna take work, it's gonna take discipline, it'll take a lot of things, but it's not unreachable. So, I'm not hopeless" (Worthington et al. 2008, p. iii).

Table 13.2	Continuum of Services for Homeless Youth: Stage of Homelessness and Type of Service Required			
	Before the Street	**On the Street**	**Transitional Services**	**Off the Street**
Accommodation	– Affordable housing	– Emergency housing – Place to go during the day		– Affordable housing
Protection	– Community outreach – Child welfare services	– Secure treatment – Safe, protected accommodation – Emergency child welfare placements		
Food	– Adequate family income	– Daily meals		– Adequate income
Clothing	– Adequate family income	– Clothing – Storage and laundry facilities		– Adequate income
Health and hygiene	– Accessible, affordable health care	– Walk-in or mobile medical services – Showers	– Accessible, affordable health care	– Accessible, affordable health care
Mental health	– Crisis intervention counselling and/or mental-health services	– Crisis intervention	– Supportive counselling	– Informal social supports
Substance abuse	– Information counselling and/or treatment	– Detoxification services	– Substance abuse treatment and follow-up	– Informal social supports
Education	– Drop-out prevention – Specialized programs	– Walk-in schooling	– Transitional school programs	– Regular schools – Adult upgrading
Income	– Adequate family income		– Social assistance	– Job
Employment	– Job or school		– Life skills training – Employment training – Job-finding help	– Job

Source: Kufeldt and Burrows 1994, p. 14. Used with permission of the University of Calgary.

Box 13.3 Youth Justice in Action

Rising Youth Homelessness a Crisis We Mustn't Ignore

A New Survey Confirms That Youth Homelessness Is on the Rise. It's a Complex Problem That Requires a Concerted Solution
By Sean Kidd, *Toronto Star*, Monday, 12 May 2014

If you wanted to find me in the summer of 2000, I was most likely at a service for street youth—like the now-shuttered Street Outreach Services (SOS) and Youthlink Innercity in Toronto, or Covenant House in Vancouver. I was doing research on street youth suicide for my PhD. During that summer, I met a young woman who was only 18, but had already been working in the sex trade for years. She was tack sharp.

(Continued)

Through the skilful persistence of the staff at sos, and her own tough-mindedness, she had left the sex trade, crack addiction, and had a job and boyfriend who wasn't involved in the streets. She was able to imagine a different life for herself. She was tough, funny, and made light of a past that was nothing but violence and disappointment—at the hands of parents, through holes in the various so-called safety nets, until she hit the streets and entered a new landscape of violence and exploitation. I had interviewed her as a research participant, learned a lot about her life and hung with her and others in the sos waiting area cracking jokes and talking nonsense for hours.

Then came a moment I will never forget. I was sitting in the staff area chatting with the employment counsellor when one of the outreach staff came in and told us that this girl who had dug herself out of hell had died of a drug overdose in the bathtub of a crack house. It is something that has never left me—it cut through all of the rhetoric about homeless youth and somehow made it very personal and impossible to accept.

Meanwhile, well over a decade later, we continue to collect statistics. Eva's Initiatives, an organization dedicated to confronting youth homelessness, just released the findings of a national survey of over 1000 Canadian homeless youth. These young people are among the 30,000 to 60,000 youth on Canadian streets on any given day. The survey builds upon the rafts of data documenting the adversity that leads to homelessness, violence on the streets, and the tremendous difficulty leaving that life. Young people have to swim against the current to move from poverty and marginalization to housing and a good quality of life.

Very much in line with research showing that suicide and overdose are the leading causes of death for homeless youth in Canada, this latest survey found that 56 per cent of the youth who responded had major mental health issues. When coupled with addictions, this represents a major challenge when it comes to finding housing for homeless youth—a challenge not adequately addressed in our current system of services.

The complexity of youth homelessness makes it difficult to find solutions. Mental illness is an important piece in the puzzle, but it's not the whole story. Abusive and neglectful parents are sometimes a cause, but not always. Family poverty is often involved, but this is not true for all. Failed school, child protection, and criminal justice systems are often part of the problem, but again not always.

There is one clear and incontrovertible truth, however—the number of young Canadians on the streets is growing. And the longer they are on the streets, the more likely they are to die, be victimized, become mentally ill and addicted, and the more difficult they are to engage in services.

The solution involves better attention to mental health in schools, child protection services, and the criminal justice system—the places through which at-risk youth flow. We need greatly enhanced support for the many community organizations providing youth services on the thinnest of financial margins, and we need system-wide solutions that better address health, housing, and employment.

Governments need to do more: youth services are left with patching together motley collections of grants and donations, with staff often unsure from one year to the next if they will have a job. We need a strategy—one that will involve a modest investment relative to the high costs of prisons and hospitals, not to mention the social costs of failing to invest—and the human-rights implications.

Youth homelessness has always been a barometer of social and civic health. From the height of 1800s industrialization, to the Great Depression, to our current statistics, which rival those of earlier times, this is an issue that warns of high levels of poverty, social inequity, and inadequate social response. Let's stop losing our kids to the streets.

Dr Sean Kidd is head of the Psychology Service of CAMH Schizophrenia Services and assistant professor with the University of Toronto, Department of Psychiatry.

Key Terms

homeless youth
life-cycle model
runaways
squeegee kids

street-involved youth
throwaways
underhoused
youth-centric programming model

Review Questions

1. Identify structural factors that may contribute to the involvement of youth in street life in Canada.
2. Identify and describe key factors that contribute to young people becoming involved on the street.
3. Why might typologies be useful in providing a framework for working with street-involved youth in Canada?
4. What kinds of risks are street-involved youth exposed to? Why?

Critical Thinking Questions

1. How would you propose getting an accurate count of the number of street-involved youth currently living in a major Canadian city?
2. What factors, if any, do you think would be important in developing a public awareness program for street-involved youth?
3. How would you counter the view that shelters and outreach services make it too easy for children to remain living on the street and that there is no incentive for them to get off the street?
4. Identify a group of street-involved youth (e.g., youth involved in survival or obligatory sex, or injection drug use). If you were designing a new program, what program components would be a priority for meeting their immediate and long-term needs? How would you know if the program was successful?

References

Abate, G. (2001, 20 February). Squeegee ban violates charter, lawyer argues. *Globe and Mail*, p. A23.

Abramovich, I. (2012). No safe place to go: LGBTQ youth homelessness in Canada—Reviewing the literature. *Canadian Journal of Family and Youth*, 4(1): 29–51.

Adlaf, E.M., and Zdanowicz, Y.M. (1999). A cluster analytic study of substance abuse problems and mental health among street youths. *American Journal of Drug and Alcohol Abuse*, 25(4): 639–59.

Anonymous. (2010a, 20 October). Guest comment: Why youth homelessness is an important social issue. *Victoria News*, p. 1.

Anonymous. (2010b, 29 October). Scope of youth homelessness largely unknown. *Prince George Citizen*, p. 27.

Appathurai, C. (1987). *Runaway behaviour: A background paper.* Toronto: Ministry of Community and Social Services.

Auerswald, C.L., and Eyre, S.L. (2002). Youth homelessness in San Francisco: A life cycle approach. *Social Science and Medicine, 54*: 1497–512.

Ayerst, S.I. (1999). Depression and stress in street youth. *Adolescence, 34*(135): 567–85.

Baer, J.S., Peterson, P.L., and Wells, E.A. (2004). Rationale and design of a brief substance use intervention for homeless adolescents. *Addiction Research and Theory, 12*(4): 317–34.

Barker, B., et al. (2014). High prevalence of exposure to the child welfare system among street-involved youth in a Canadian setting: Implications for policy and practice. *Public Health, 14*(197): 1–7

Baron, S.W. (2003). Self-control, social consequences, and criminal behavior: Street youth and the general theory of crime. *Journal of Research in Crime and Delinquency, 40*(4): 403–25.

Baron, S.W. (2004). General strain, street youth and crime: A test of Agnew's revised theory. *Criminology, 42*(2): 457–83.

Baron, S.W., and Hartnagel, T.F. (1998). Street youth and criminal violence. *Journal of Research in Crime and Delinquency, 35*(2): 166–89.

Baron, S.W., and Hartnagel, T.F. (2006). Street youth, strain theory, and crime. *Journal of Criminal Justice, 34*(2): 209–23.

Barth, R.P. (1990). On their own: The experiences of youth after foster care. *Child and Adolescent Social Work, 7*: 419–40.

Barwick, M.A., and Siegal, L.S. (1996). Learning difficulties in adolescent clients of a shelter for runaway and homeless street youths. *Journal of Research on Adolescence, 6*(4): 649–70.

Bassuk, E.L., Rubin, L., and Lauriat, A. (1984). Is homelessness a mental health problem? *American Journal of Psychiatry, 141*(12): 1546–50.

Bender, K., Thompson, S., McManus, H., Lantry, J., and Flynn, P. (2007). Capacity for survival: Exploring strengths of homeless street youth. *Child Youth Care Forum, 36*: 25–42.

Biehal, N., and Wade, J. (2000). Going missing from residential and foster care: Linking biographies and contexts. *British Journal of Social Work, 30*: 211–25.

Boivin, J.F., Roy, E., Haley, N., and Galbaud du Fort, G. (2005). The health of street youth: A Canadian perspective. *Canadian Journal of Public Health, 96*(6): 432–7.

Booth, R.E., and Zhang, Y. (1997). Conduct disorder and HIV risk behaviors among runaway and homeless adolescents. *Drug and Alcohol Dependence, 48*: 69–76.

Brands, B., Leslie, K., Catz-Biro, L., and Li, S. (2005). Heroin use and barriers to treatment in street-involved youth. *Addiction Research and Theory, 13*(5): 477–87.

Bronfenbrenner, U. (1974). Towards an experimental ecology of human development. *American Psychologist, 52*: 513–31.

Brooks, R.A., Milburn, N.G., Rotheram-Borus, M.J., and Witkin, A. (2004). The system-of-care for homeless youth: Perceptions of service providers. *Evaluation and Program Planning, 27*(4): 443–51.

Burt, M. (2001). *What will it take to end homelessness?* Washington: Urban Institute.

California Department of Social Services (CDSS). (2002). *Report on the survey of the housing needs of emancipated foster/probation youth.* Independent Living Program Policy Unit, Child and Youth Permanency Branch. Sacramento, CA: Author.

Canadian Homelessness Research Network. (2013). *What works and for whom? A hierarchy of evidence for promising practice research.* Toronto: Canadian Homelessness Research Network Press.

Carlson, J.L., Sugano, E., Millstein, S.G., and Auerswald, C.L. (2006). Service utilization and the life cycle of youth homelessness. *Journal of Adolescent Health, 38*: 624–7.

Cauce, A.M., Tyler, K.A., and Whitback, L.B. (2004). Maltreatment and victimization in homeless adolescents: Out of the frying pan and into the fire. *Prevention Researcher, 11*: 12–14.

Chen, X., Tyler, K.A., Whitbeck, L.B., and Hoyt, D.R. (2004). Early sexual abuse, street adversity, and drug use among female homeless and runaway adolescents in the Midwest. *Journal of Drug Issues, 34*(1): 1–21.

City of Calgary. (1996). *The 1996 count of homeless persons*. Calgary: City of Calgary, Community Strategies.

City of Calgary. (2008). *The 2008 Biennial Count of Homeless Persons in Calgary*. Calgary: City of Calgary, Policy and Planning Division, Community and Neighbourhood Services.

Clarke, M., and Cooper, M. (2000). *Homeless youth: Falling between the cracks*. Calgary: Youth Alternative Housing Committee.

Clatts, M., Goldsamt, L., Yi, H., and Gwadz, V. (2005). Homelessness and drug abuse among young men who have sex with men in New York City: A preliminary epidemiological trajectory. *Journal of Adolescence*, 28: 201–14.

Clatts, M., Rees-Davis, W., Sotheran, J.L., and Atillasoy, A. (1998). Correlates and distribution of HIV risk behaviours among homeless youth in New York City: Implications for prevention and policy. *Child Welfare*, 77(2): 195–207.

Community Action on Homelessness. (2009). *Halifax report card on homelessness 2009*. Halifax: Community Action on Homelessness.

Cook, R.J. (1994). Are we helping foster care youth prepare for their future? *Children and Youth Services Review*, 16(3/4): 213–29.

Courtney, M.E. (2001). Foster youth transitions to adulthood: A longitudinal view of youth leaving care. *Child Welfare*, 80(6): 685–717.

Courtney, M.E., and Dworsky, A. (2006). Early outcomes for young adults transitioning from out-of-home care in the USA. *Child and Family Social Work*, 11: 209–19.

Cuthbertson, R. (2012, 5 December). For homeless youth, "We're here to help you. Whoever you are." *Calgary Herald*.

Dachner, N., and Tarasuk, V. (2002). Homeless "squeegee kids": Food insecurity and daily survival. *Social Science and Medicine*, 54: 1039–49.

DeMatteo, D., Major, C., Block, B., Coates, R., Fearon, M., Goldberg, E., et al. (1999). Toronto street youth and HIV/AIDS: Prevalence, demographics and risks. *Journal of Adolescent Health*, 25: 356–66.

de Oliviera, W. (1992, July). *Street children and safe sex: Opportunities and barriers for changing behaviors*. Paper presented at the International Conference on AIDS VIII. Amsterdam, The Netherlands.

De Rosa, C.J., Montgomery, S.B., Hyde, J., Iverson, E., and Kipke, M. (2001). HIV risk behavior and HIV testing: A comparison of rates and associated factors among homeless and runaway adolescents in two cities. *AIDS Education and Prevention*, 13(2): 131–48.

Derworiz, C. (2010, 5 April). "Plan within a plan" to end homelessness. *Calgary Herald*, p. A1.

Diaz, T., Conover, S., Edwards, V., Monterroso, E., and Susser, E. (1998, July). *Drug using behaviors of young and recent initiate injection drug users in New York City: A unique opportunity for prevention of HIV*. Paper presented at the International Conference on AIDS XII, Geneva, Switzerland.

Dittmann, D., MacLaurin, B., Worthington, C., and Kitt, O. (2009). *Criminal activities among Calgary's street-involved youth: Calgary youth, health and the street* (Fact Sheet #11). Calgary: University of Calgary.

Duval, D.M., and Vincent, N. (2009). Affect regulation of homeless youth once in the child welfare system. *Child and Adolescent Social Work Journal*, 26: 155–73.

Farrow, J.A., Deisher, R.W., Brown, R., Kulig, J.W., and Kipke, M.D. (1992). Health and health needs of homeless and runaway youth. *Journal of Adolescent Health*, 13: 717–26.

Fisher, J. (1989). *Missing children research project*. Vol. 1: *Findings of the study—A focus on runaways* (No. 1989-07). Ottawa: Solicitor General of Canada.

Fitzgerald, M.D. (1995). Homeless youths and the child welfare system: Implications for policy and service. *Child Welfare*, 74(3): 717–31.

Freundlich, M., and Avery, R.J. (2006). Transitioning from congregate care: Preparation and outcomes. *Journal of Child and Family Studies*, 15: 507–18.

Gaetz, S. (2004). Safe streets for whom? Homeless youth, social exclusion, and criminal victimization. *Canadian Journal of Criminology and Criminal Justice*, 46(4): 423–55.

Gaetz, S. (2014). *Coming of age: Reimagining the response to youth homelessness in Canada*. Toronto: Canadian Homelessness Research Network Press.

Gaetz, S., O'Grady, B., and Buccieri, K. (2010). *Surviving crime and violence: Street youth and victimization in Toronto*. Toronto: JFCY and Homeless Hub.

Gaetz, S., O'Grady, B., and Vaillancourt, B. (1999). *Making money: The Shout Clinic report on homeless youth and employment.* Toronto: Central Toronto Community Health Centres.

Garbarino, J. (1982). *Children and families in the social environment.* New York: Aldine DeGruyter.

Gleghorn, A.A., Marx, R., Vittinghoff, E., and Katz, M.H. (1998). Association between drug use patterns and HIV risks among homeless, runaway, and street youth in northern California. *Drug and Alcohol Dependence, 51*(3): 219–27.

Goar, C. (2009, 23 November). Street kids' toughness only skin deep. *Toronto Star*, p. A13.

Greene, J.M., and Ringwalt, C.L. (1998). Pregnancy among three national samples of runaway and homeless youth. *Journal of Adolescent Health, 23*(6): 370–7.

Grover, S. (2007). Homeless children and street involved children in Canada. In R.B. Howe and K. Covel (Eds), *Children's rights in Canada: A question of commitment* (pp. 343–72). Waterloo, ON: Wilfrid Laurier Press.

Hagan, J., and McCarthy, B. (1997). *Mean streets: Youth crime and homelessness.* Cambridge: Cambridge University Press.

Hahn, J., Shafer, K., and Moss, A.R. (1998, July). *High rate of HIV infection in homeless young injectors: Sex poses greatest risk.* Paper presented at the International Conference on AIDS XII, Geneva, Switzerland.

Haley, N., Roy, E., Leclerc, P., Boudreau, J-F., and Boivin, J-F. (2004a). Characteristics of adolescent street youth with a history of pregnancy. *Journal of Pediatric and Adolescent Gynecology, 17*(5): 313–20.

Haley, N., Roy, E., Leclerc, P., Boudreau, J-F., and Boivin, J-F. (2004b). HIV risk profile of male street youth involved in survival sex. *Sexually Transmitted Infections, 80*(6): 526–30.

Halifax Regional Municipality. (2005). *Homelessness in HRM: Portrait of streets and shelters*, Vol. 2. Halifax: Halifax Regional Municipality, Planning and Development Services.

Hammer, H., Finkelhor, D., and Sedlak, A.J. (2002). *Runaway/thrownaway children: National estimates and characteristics.* Washington, DC: Office of Juvenile Justice and Delinquency Prevention.

Hathazi, D., Lankenau, S., Sanders, B., and Bloom, J. (2009). Pregnancy and sexual health among homeless young injection drug users. *Journal of Adolescence, 32*(2): 339–55.

Health Canada. (2002a). *HIV/AIDS Epi update: Prevalent HIV infections in Canada: Up to one-third may not be diagnosed.* Ottawa: Centre for Infectious Disease Prevention and Control.

Health Canada. (2002b). *HIV/AIDS Epi update: HIV and AIDS among youth in Canada.* Ottawa: Centre for Infectious Disease Prevention and Control.

Hyde, J. (2005). From home to street: Understanding young people's transitions into homelessness. *Journal of Adolescence, 28*: 171–83.

Janus, M.D., Archambault, F.X., Brown, S.W., and Welsh, L.A. (1995). Physical abuse in Canadian runaway adolescents. *Child Abuse and Neglect, 19*(4): 433–47.

Johnson, K.D., Whitbeck, L.B., and Hoyt, D.R. (2005). Predictors of social network composition among homeless and runaway adolescents. *Journal of Adolescence, 28*: 231–48.

Karabanow, J. (2004). Changing faces: The story of two Canadian street youth shelters. *International Journal of Social Welfare, 13*(4): 304–14.

Kidd, S.A. (2003). Street youth: Coping and interventions. *Child and Adolescent Social Work Journal, 20*(4): 235–61.

Kidd, S.A. (2006). Factors precipitating suicidality among homeless youth: A quantitative follow-up. *Youth and Society, 37*(4): 393–422.

Kipke, M., Montgomery, S., Simon, T., and Iverson, E. (1996, July). *Homeless youth: Variations in HIV risk according to peer group affiliation.* Paper presented at the International Journal on AIDS XI, Vancouver.

Kral, A.H., Lorvick, J., and Edlin, B.R. (1999, August). *Differences between young and old injection drug users in San Francisco* (Abstract 533). Paper presented at the National HIV Prevention Conference, Atlanta, GA.

Kraus, D., Eberle, M., and Serge, L. (2001). *Environmental scan on youth homelessness.* Ottawa: Canada Mortgage and Housing Corporation.

Kufeldt, K., and Burrows, B.A. (1994). *Issues affecting public policies and services for homeless youth.* Calgary: University of Calgary.

Kufeldt, K., and Nimmo, M. (1987a). Kids on the street, they have something to say: Survey of runaway and homeless youth. *Journal of Child Care, 3*(2): 53–61.

Kufeldt, K., and Nimmo, M. (1987b). Youth on the street: Abuse and neglect in the Eighties. *Child Abuse and Neglect, 11*: 531–43.

Kulik, D., Gaetz, S., Crowe, C., and Ford-James, E. (2011). Homeless youth's overwhelming health burden: A review of the literature. *Paediatrics & Child Health, 16*(6): 43–7.

Larke, B. (2001). *HIV/AIDS surveillance*. Edmonton: Alberta Health, Disease Control and Prevention.

Leach, M.P., Wolitski, R.J., Goldbaum, G.M., Fishbein, M., and the AIDS Community Demonstration Projects. (1997). HIV risk and sources of information among urban street youth. *Psychology, Health and Medicine, 2*(2): 119–34.

Lenz-Rashid, S. (2006). Employment experiences of homeless young adults: Are they different for youth with a history of foster care? *Children and Youth Services Review, 28*: 236–59.

Leslie, B., and Hare, F. (2000). *Improving the outcomes for youth in transition from care*. Toronto: Working Group of the Children's Aid Society of Toronto, Covenant House, and Ryerson University Research Project.

McCarter, B. (2010, 18 November). Growing up on streets trumps dysfunctional home life; Family dynamics—not drugs or alcohol—is the main reason why thousands of teens choose to run away from home. *Vancouver Sun*, p. A17.

McCay, E., and Aiello, A. (2013). The need for early mental health intervention to strengthen resilience in street-involved youth. In S. Gaetz, B. O'Grady, K. Buccieri, J. Karabanow, and A. Marsolais (Eds), *Youth homelessness in Canada: Implications for policy and practice* (pp. 229–42). Toronto: Canadian Homelessness Research Network Press.

McCormack, A., Janus, M.D., and Burgess, A.W. (1986). Runaway youths and sexual victimization: Gender differences in an adolescent runaway population. *Child Abuse and Neglect, 10*: 387–95.

McIntyre, S. (1999). The youngest profession—the oldest profession: A study of sex work. In C. Bagley and K. Mallick (Eds), *Child sexual abuse and adult offenders: New theory and research* (pp. 159–92). Aldershot, UK: Ashgate.

MacLaurin, B., and Bala, N. (2004). Children in care. In N. Bala, M.K. Zapf, R.J. Williams, R. Vogl, and J.P. Hornick (Eds), *Canadian child welfare law* (pp. 111–38). Toronto: Thompson Educational Publishing.

MacLaurin, B., Trocmé, N., Fallon, B., McCormack, M., Pitman, L., Forest, N., et al. (2006). *Alberta incidence study of reported child abuse and neglect—2003 (AIS-2003): Major findings report*. Calgary: University of Calgary, Faculty of Social Work.

MacLaurin, B., Worthington, C., Dittmann, D., and Kitt, O. (2009a). *Education among Calgary's street-involved youth: Calgary youth, health and the street* (Fact Sheet #14). Calgary: University of Calgary.

MacLaurin, B., Worthington, C., Dittmann, D., and Kitt, O. (2009b). *Maltreatment among Calgary's street-involved youth: Calgary youth, health and the street* (Fact Sheet #1). Calgary: University of Calgary.

MacLaurin, B., Worthington, C., Dittmann, D., and Kitt, O. (2009c). *Substance use among Calgary's street-involved youth: Calgary youth, health and the street* (Fact Sheet #2). Calgary: University of Calgary.

McLean, L. (2005). *Seeking sanctuary: An exploration of the realities of youth homelessness in Calgary—2005*. Calgary: Broadview Applied Research Group.

Marshall, B.D.L., Kerr, T., Qi, J., Montaner, J.S.G., and Wood, E. (2010). Public injecting and HIV risk behaviour among street-involved youth. *Drug and Alcohol Dependence, 110*: 254–8.

Milburn, N.G., Rotheram-Borus, M.J., Batterham, P., Brumback, B., Rosenthal, D., and Mallett, S. (2005). Predictors of close family relationships over one year among homeless young people. *Journal of Adolescence, 28*: 263–79.

Min Park, J., Metraux, S., and Culhane, D.P. (2005). Childhood out-of-home placement and dynamics of public shelter utilization among young homeless adults. *Children and Youth Services Review, 27*(5): 533–46.

Nova Scotia Housing and Homelessness Network. (2012). *Halifax report card on homelessness in 2012*. Halifax: Nova Scotia Housing and Homelessness Network.

O'Grady, B., and Bright, R. (2002). Squeezed to the point of exclusion: The case of Toronto squeegee cleaners. In J. Hermer and J. Mosher (Eds), *Disorderly people: Law and politics of exclusion in Ontario* (pp. 79–90). Halifax: Fernwood.

O'Grady, B., Bright, R., and Cohen, E. (1998). Sub-employment and street youths: An analysis of the impact of squeegee cleaning on homeless youths. *Security Journal, 11*: 315–23.

O'Grady, B., and Greene, C. (2003). A social and economic impact study of the Ontario Safe Streets Act on Toronto squeegee workers. *Online Journal of Justice Studies* 1(1). Retrieved 21 January 2011 from http://web.archive.org/web/20060113223626/ojjs.icaap.org/issues/1.1/ogrady-greene.html

Pennbridge, J., MacKenzie, R.G., and Swofford, A. (1991). Risk profile of homeless pregnant adolescents and youth. *Journal of Adolescent Health, 12*: 534–8.

Peressini, T., McDonald, L., and Hulchanski, D. (1995). *Estimating homelessness: Towards a methodology for counting the homeless in Canada—Background report.* Toronto: Centre for Applied Social Research.

Perlman, S., Willard, J., Herbers, J., Cutuli, J., and Eyrich-Garg, K. (2014). Youth homelessness: Prevalence and mental health correlates. *Journal of the Society for Social Work and Research, 5*(3): 361–77.

Public Health Agency of Canada. (2006a). *Sexually transmitted infections in Canadian street youth: Findings from enhanced surveillance of Canadian street youth, 1999–2003* (No. HP5-14/2006). Ottawa: Minister of Health.

Public Health Agency of Canada. (2006b). *Street youth in Canada: Findings from enhanced surveillance of Canadian street youth, 1999–2003* (No. HP5-15/2006). Ottawa: Minister of Health.

Radford, J.L., King, A.J.C., and Warren, W.K. (1989). *Street youth and AIDS.* Ottawa: Health and Welfare Canada.

Raising the Roof. (2009). *Youth homelessness in Canada: The Road to Solutions.* Toronto: Raising the Roof Organization.

Ray, J. (1993). Survival methods of young street mothers. *Child and Adolescent Social Work Journal, 10*(3): 189–205.

Rees, G. (1993). *Hidden truths: Young people's experiences of running away.* London: Children's Society.

Reilly, T. (2003). Transition from care: Status and outcomes of youth who age out of foster care. *Child Welfare, 82*(6): 727–46.

Rew, L., and Horner, S.D. (2003). Personal strengths of homeless adolescents living in a high-risk environment. *Advances in Nursing Science, 26*(2): 90–101.

Robert, M., Pauze, R., and Fournier, L. (2005). Factors associated with homelessness of adolescents under supervision of the youth protection system. *Journal of Adolescence, 28*: 215–30.

Rotheram-Borus, M.J., Mahler, K.A., Koopman, C., and Langabeer, K. (1996). Sexual abuse history and associated multiple risk behaviour in adolescent runaways. *American Journal of Orthopsychiatry, 66*(3): 390–400.

Roy, E., Haley, N., Leclerc, P., Cedras, L., Bedard, L., and Allard, R. (2002a). Seroprevalence and risk factors for hepatitis A among Montreal street youth. *Canadian Journal of Public Health, 93*(1): 52–3.

Roy, E., Haley, N., Leclerc, P., Cedras, L., and Boivin, J.F. (2002b). Drug injection among street youth: The first time. *Addiction, 97*(8): 1003–10.

Roy, E., Haley, N., Leclerc, P., Boivin, J.F., Cedras, L., and Vincelette, J. (2001). Risk factors for hepatitis C virus infection among street youths. *Canadian Medical Association Journal, 165*(5): 557–60.

Schneiderman, D. (2002). The constitutional disorder of the Safe Streets Act: A federalism analysis. In J. Hermer and J. Mosher (Eds), *Disorderly people: Law and politics of exclusion in Ontario* (pp. 79–90). Halifax: Fernwood.

Slonim-Nevo, V., Ozawa, M.N., and Auslander, W.F. (1991). Knowledge, attitudes and behaviors related to AIDS among youth in residential centers: Results from an exploratory study. *Journal of Adolescence, 14*(1): 17–33.

St Lawrence, J.S., Crosby, R.A., and O'Brannon III, R. (1999). Adolescent risk for HIV infection: Comparison of four high risk samples. *Journal of HIV/AIDS Prevention and Education for Adolescents and Children, 3*(3): 63–86.

Sullivan, T.R. (1996). The challenges of HIV prevention among high-risk adolescents. *Health and Social Work, 21*(1): 58–65.

Swart-Kruger, J., and Richer, L.M. (1997). AIDS-related knowledge, attitudes and behaviour among South African street youth: Reflections on power, sexuality and the autonomous self. *Social Science and Medicine, 45*(6): 957–67.

Thompson, S., Bender, K., Lewis, C., and Watkins, R. (2008). Runaway and pregnant: Risk factors associated with pregnancy in a national sample of runaway/homeless female adolescents. *Journal of Adolescent Health, 43*(2): 125–32.

Thompson, S.J., McManus, H., Lantry, J., Windsor, L., and Flynn, P. (2006). Insights from the street: Perceptions of services and providers by homeless young adults. *Evaluation and Program Planning, 29*: 34–43.

Thompson, S.J., Zittel-Palamara, K.M., and Maccio, E.M. (2004). Runaway youth utilizing crisis shelter services: Predictors of presenting problems. *Child and Youth Care Forum, 33*(6): 387–404.

Thrane, L.E., Hoyt, D.R., Whitbeck, L.B., and Yoder, K.A. (2006). Impact of family abuse on running away, deviance, and street victimization among homeless rural and urban youth. *Child Abuse and Neglect, 30*: 1117–28.

Tutty, L., Bradshaw, C., Waegemakers-Schiff, J., Worthington, C., MacLaurin, B., Hewson, J., et al. (2010). *Risks and assets for homelessness prevention: A literature review for the Calgary homeless foundation.* Calgary: University of Calgary.

Tyler, K.A., and Cauce, A.M. (2002). Perpetrators of early physical and sexual abuse among homeless and runaway adolescents. *Child Abuse and Neglect, 26*: 1261–74.

Tyler, K.A. Cauce, A.M., and Whitbeck, L.B. (2004). Family risk factors and prevalence of dissociative symptoms among homeless and runaway youth. *Child Abuse and Neglect, 28*: 355–66.

Tyler, K.A., and Johnson, K.A. (2006). Pathways in and out of substance use among homeless-emerging adults. *Journal of Adolescent Research, 21*(2): 133–57.

Unger, J.B., Simon, T.R., Newman, T.L., Montgomery, S.B., Kipke, M.D., and Albornoz, M. (1998). Early adolescent street youth: An overlooked population with unique problems and service needs. *Journal of Early Adolescence, 18*(4): 325–48.

van der Ploeg, J., and Scholte, E. (1997). *Homeless youth.* London: Sage.

Weber, A.E., Boivin, J.F., Blais, L., Haley, N., and Roy, E. (2002). HIV risk profile and prostitution among female street youths. *Journal of Urban Health, 79*(4): 525–35.

Whitbeck, L.B., Chen, X., Hoyt, D.R., Tyler, K.A., and Johnson, K.D. (2004). Mental disorder, subsistence strategies, and victimization among gay, lesbian, and bisexual homeless and runaway adolescents. *Journal of Sex Research, 41*(4): 329–42.

Whitmore, E., and McKee, C. (2001). Six street youth who could . . . In P. Reasor and H. Bradbury (Eds), *Handbook of action research: Participative inquiry and practice* (pp. 396–402). London: Sage.

Wong, C., Clark, L., and Marlotte, L. (2014). The impact of specific and complex trauma on the mental health of homeless youth, *Journal of Interpersonal Violence.* Online journal, November 2014.

Worthington, C., MacLaurin, B., Dittmann, D., and Kitt, O. (2009a). *Mental health among Calgary's street-involved youth: Calgary youth, health and the street* (Fact Sheet #5). Calgary: University of Calgary.

Worthington, C., MacLaurin, B., Dittmann, D., and Kitt, O. (2009b). *Physical health among Calgary's street-involved youth: Calgary youth, health and the street* (Fact Sheet #6). Calgary: University of Calgary.

Worthington, C., MacLaurin, B., Dittmann, D., and Kitt, O. (2009c). *Resilience among Calgary's street-involved youth: Calgary youth, health and the street* (Fact Sheet #15). Calgary: University of Calgary.

Worthington, C., MacLaurin, B., Dittmann, D., and Kitt, O. (2009d). *Sexual health among Calgary's street-involved youth: Calgary youth, health and the street* (Fact Sheet #4). Calgary: University of Calgary.

Worthington, C., MacLaurin, B., Huffey, N., Dittmann, D., Kitt, O., Patten, S., et al. (2008). *Calgary, youth, health and the street—Final report.* Calgary: University of Calgary.

Wright, J.D. (1991). Health and the homeless teenager: Evidence from the National Health Care for the Homeless Program. *Journal of Health and Social Policy, 2*(4): 15–35.

Yoder, K.A., Hoyt, D.R., and Whitbeck, L.B. (1998). Suicidal behaviour among homeless and runaway adolescents. *Journal of Youth and Adolescence, 27*(6): 753–71.

Yoder, K.A., Whitbeck, L.B., and Hoyt, D.R. (2003). Gang involvement and membership among homeless and runaway youth. *Youth and Society, 34*(4): 441–67.

Under the Radar: The Sexual Exploitation of Young Men in Western Canada

Susan McIntyre and Anne Miller

14

Overview

This chapter offers an overview of the research on the issue of sexually exploited young persons, with specific attention directed toward young men in Western Canada. It focuses on the background of these young men prior to their involvement in the sexual exploitation trade (SET). The demographics of the 157 young men interviewed were considered in the areas of Aboriginal heritage, age, running away, education, and background of sexual or physical abuse. The chapter explores how an individual enters the trade, at what age, and for how long, and also discusses family relations. The chapter will review dangers for young men working in the SET, such as gay bashing, violence, lack of safety, and drug use. In closing, the chapter explores how young men are able to work in the trade, the services they need, and their attempts at exiting.

Introduction

Sexual exploitation has recently gained prominence as an issue in Canada, with challenges and changes to Canada's sex-trade legislation (*Bedford v. Canada*) and a new awareness and punishment of human trafficking in Canada (e.g., the Human Trafficking Taskforce, established June 2012). News media coverage of the issues surrounding sexual exploitation has increased significantly in recent years, raising public consciousness around violence, safety, and sex trafficking.

While awareness of sexual exploitation in Canada may be increasing, it is largely focused on female sex-trade workers. This leaves the sexual exploitation of males and transgendered individuals as an "under the radar" issue in Canada. This is true both in the media coverage of sexual exploitation issues and in the body of academic literature. For example, Dennis's 2008 review of 166 academic articles related to sexual exploitation revealed that 84 per cent of the articles discussed only females involved in the sex trade, while 10 per cent discussed only males and 6 per cent discussed both.

This lack of literature and media coverage is even starker with respect to *young* men. While the passing of legislation such as the Protection of Sexually Exploited Children Act (PSECA) in Alberta has highlighted the need for more attention to be paid to the experiences of sexually exploited children and youth, media dialogue and academic literature are often still focused on the victimization of females. This is despite the fact that gender is not a factor in the vulnerability of children and youth to sexual exploitation. According to Saewyc et al.'s (2013) article on media discourses on the sexual exploitation of youth in Canada,

> 93% of articles mentioned girls as victims of exploitation, and fewer than 30% mentioned boys. Yet findings from several studies . . . challenge the discourse that sexually exploited youth are mostly female. Among younger street-involved youth in Canada, 1 in 3 youth reported exploitation, and males and females were equally likely to be exploited. (p. 100)

After reviewing sexual exploitation literature and gender focus, Dennis (2008) found a similar trend indicating that "the teenage boy sex-worker is thus subject to redoubled invisibility, his gender and his age causing him to virtually vanish from scholarly scrutiny" (p. 21). According to ECPAT USA (2013),

> While there has been some increased awareness about sexually exploited boys in the U.S. over the past several years, most law enforcement and service providers often miss them entirely or view them as too few to be counted or not in need of services. The little notice given to boys primarily identifies them as exploiters, pimps and buyers of sex, or as active and willing participants in sex work, not as victims or survivors of exploitation. Discussion of boys as victims or survivors of CSEC is frequently appended to a discussion about commercially sexually exploited girls. (p. 2)

This has led to a body of literature that presents a greater understanding of female sexual exploitation than of male sexual exploitation. Pathways into sexual exploitation for females include vulnerabilities resulting from childhood maltreatment (including sexual abuse), family dysfunction, substance abuse and addiction, the need to provide for dependants, and overall basic-needs insecurity (including housing, food, etc.) (Reid and Piquero 2014).

With the limited literature related to sexually exploited men primarily focusing on sexual orientation and safety risks such as HIV, the pathways to exploitation, the violence and trauma experienced by young men in the sex trade, and the possibilities for exit are largely ignored (Dennis 2008). This leaves sexually exploited young men virtually invisible in our society. Given the under-representation of young men in research on sexual exploitation, this chapter will focus on the topic of **sexual exploitation** of young males.

First, we will provide the background that led to the study "Under the Radar: The Sexual Exploitation of Young Men in Western Canada." Second, we will discuss key demographics and findings from this study. Third, we will discuss the actual work life of sexually exploited young men. Fourth, we will examine the process of their attempting to exit the SET. In closing, we will provide an overview of the recommendations that emerged from this study.

sexual exploitation
The abuse of children and youth through the exchange of sexual activity for money, drugs, and/or basic needs.

Factors Leading to "Under the Radar: The Sexual Exploitation of Young Men"

Young men are virtually invisible and ignored when it comes to the issue of sexual exploitation. In the 2006 ECPAT Global Monitoring Report on Canada, young men were essentially ignored. The report spoke about children, but it spoke predominantly, if not exclusively, about young women, as illustrated in this quote: "The increase in prostitution of children is causing growing concerns. Young girls are seduced by pimps and subsequently conned into prostitution or forced to work in strip clubs. They are recruited in public places, such as shopping malls, metro stations and bus stops, even on the street" (ECPAT 2006, p. 11).

In 1994, Susan McIntyre released "The Youngest Profession, the Oldest Oppression," a study of sexual exploitation conducted in Calgary, Alberta. A total of 50 young people participated in the study: 41 young women and 9 young men were interviewed. At the time, these young people were typically viewed as criminals, many of them charged with prostitution-related offences, most likely under section 213 of the Criminal Code (see Box 14.1), which spoke to the issue of communicating for the purpose of prostitution. The "Youngest Profession" (McIntyre 1994) revealed that this population began working in the prostitution trade at the age of 14 and that over 80 per cent had a background of sexual abuse prior to their involvement with the sex trade. On the basis of these findings, it was clear that the involvement of these individuals in the SET could not be regarded as adults choosing a lifestyle. These were children and young adolescents who, by and large, had been either forced or coerced into the sex trade by an adult. In most cases, these young people did not identify their involvement with the sex trade as a "choice" but viewed it as a means of survival. Following the release of the study, there was a shift in the perception of this population, from the view that they were prostitutes to the view that they were sexually exploited. This shift in understanding resulted in various legislative initiatives, such as the Alberta PSECA, aimed at addressing the issue of child sexual exploitation. In 2002, McIntyre returned to interview some of the original participants in the 1992 study. Her report *Strolling Away*, released in 2002, included interview findings from a total of 41 (82 per cent) of the original 50 participants. A reoccurring observation in the study was that, until this point, the issue of sexual exploitation had focused primarily on the female perspective. It was for this reason that the study "Under the Radar: The Sexual Exploitation of Young Men in Western Canada" was launched in the provinces of Alberta, British Columbia, Saskatchewan, and Manitoba. A total of 157 young men in the four Western provinces of Canada were interviewed. This study involved 48 non-profit organizations, 6 research coordinators, and 20 research assistants. Eight of the research assistants self-identified as **experiential**: they had been involved with, and had exited, the SET. They brought with them invaluable insights into the realities faced by sexually exploited children and youth.

experiential
Refers to an individual who has worked and lived the lifestyle of a sex-trade worker.

Box 14.1 | Youth Justice in Action

Canada v. Bedford 2013 SCC 72

On 20 December 2013, the Supreme Court ruled that the laws under Canada's Criminal Code that had formerly criminalized aspects of the adult sex trade were unconstitutional. The Court then gave the Government of Canada one year to design new legislation that would comply with Canada's Charter of Rights and Freedoms.

The challenge to the laws claimed that the sections of the Criminal Code associated with the sex trade violated the constitutional rights of sex-trade workers under section 7 of Canada's Charter of Rights and Freedoms. After much debate, sections of the Criminal Code were struck down as being unconstitutional, including living off the avails of prostitution, keeping a bawdy house, and communicating for the purposes of selling sex.

In the one-year period from the Supreme Court ruling until the government tabled its new legislation, there was considerable debate over the shape the new laws could take. Two prohibition models were considered:

1. *Conservative* prohibition, which makes the buying and selling of sex illegal, as well as any third-party profit from the sex trade. This is the type of

(Continued)

law that exists in the United States, for example (except certain parts of Nevada);

2. *Demand-side* prohibition, also known as the "Nordic Model," which criminalizes buying sex and third-party profit from prostitution without punishment for selling sex. This model takes the approach that the seller of sex is a victim of violence and coercion. This is the type of law that was first adopted in Sweden in 1999.

Possibilities around the legalization of prostitution in Canada were also put forward by different groups:

1. *Legalization* whereby the sex trade is regulated but not specifically prohibited through the Criminal Code (although there may be a combination with certain criminal prohibitions). For example, in Nevada, selling sex in brothels is permitted and regulated.

2. *Decriminalization* whereby all references to selling and buying sex would be removed from the Criminal Code, leaving the sex trade to be regulated with business and other civil laws. Since 2003, New Zealand has had a decriminalized system around the sex trade in their country (see Lowman and Louie 2012).

On 4 June 2014, Canada's then justice minister Peter MacKay introduced amending legislation, Bill C-36, the Protection of Communities and Exploited Persons Act, in response to the Supreme Court's directive to the government that it create new laws around the sex trade in Canada.

The new law is being touted by the government as a *demand-side prohibition* or "Nordic" approach to selling sex in Canada. It criminalizes the purchase of sex but not the selling of sex, although communication in an area in which minors could reasonably be expected to be will be illegal along with advertising sexual services (e.g., on the Internet). The law maintains a section similar to the "living off the avails" section of the previous law, but excludes those in "legitimate living arrangements." The bill was passed in the House of Commons and the Act received royal assent on 6 November 2014. While the language of the bill positions sex workers as victims of exploitation and aims only to punish those perpetrating the acts of exploitation, many have argued that the bill does not address the initial concerns of the Supreme Court and that criminalizing the demand side of the sex trade will increase safety risks for sex-trade workers (see Chu and Glass 2013).

Terri-Jean Bedford, who brought forward the initial case against the government, vocally opposed the bill, bringing her opinions before the Senate committee reviewing the bill (*Globe and Mail*, 10 September 2014). Others organized demonstrations and rallies to bring the voices of sex trade workers to the fore as they express their concerns over the new laws.

The new laws also create a paradigm that further decreases the visibility of sexually exploited young men. The language of the current debate focuses largely on the victimization of women, to the exclusion of sexually exploited men. Furthermore, the criminalization of buying sex is largely based on the view of the seller as a victim of male violence against women. This could create further invisibility for men who are victims of sexual exploitation.

In addition, even while the original Communicating Law was in place (making communication for the purposes of selling sex illegal), males were virtually never charged with this offence. In order to bring about such a charge, a male undercover officer would have to pose as a **customer** seeking out a male sex-trade worker. Even though this has rarely happened, young men were virtually ignored from the enforcement position of the Communicating Law. With new legislation under Bill C-36 around communication for the purposes of selling sex, little will have changed for young men in the SET. (See References for additional readings.)

customer
An individual who is a consumer and pursues the opportunity to purchase activity from a sex-trade worker.

Consultations with Youth in Care Networks

During the development of earlier studies (2002 and 2004), the principal investigator had consulted with young people (18 to 24 years of age) in and from child welfare care to ensure that the views and experiences of "youth at risk" influenced the design and style of the questionnaires, as well as the interview format. As this approach had proven to be effective, youth in and from care were again consulted in the development of the "Under the Radar" study questionnaire. Primarily, these consultations were with members of the Alberta Youth in Care and Custody Network.

Provincial and local Youth in Care Networks can be found across Canada. These organizations are the outcome of a national movement started in 1985 by a small group of young people between the ages of 14 and 24 who were in, and from, child welfare/government care. It was their vision to develop a network that would connect their peers from all provinces and territories, so they would know they were not alone. This movement has taken many of the principles of social networking theory and brought them into practice.

Child welfare is a term used to describe a set of government and private services designed to protect children and encourage family stability. The main aim of these services is to safeguard children from abuse and neglect. Child welfare agencies typically investigate allegations of abuse and neglect (these activities are called "child protection services"), supervise foster care, and arrange adoptions. They also offer services aimed to support families so that they can stay intact and raise children successfully.

The relevance of **youth in care** to the "Under the Radar" study is important, as the findings revealed that 55 per cent of respondents reported some degree of child welfare intervention during childhood or adolescence. While not all young men, or women, involved with the SET have a child welfare background, we have learned that at least 55 per cent of respondents had a history of physical and/or sexual abuse, or had witnessed familial aggression during their childhood or adolescence. This would indicate that these young men should have received child protection services. In either case, it is clear that at some point these young men were failed by the very people who were supposed to care for them.

child welfare
In Canada, this term is used to describe a set of government and private services intended to protect children and encourage family stability. The main purpose of these services is to safeguard children from abuse and neglect. Hence, one of the primary activities of the child welfare agencies is the investigation of allegations of abuse and neglect.

youth in care
Refers to children and youth involved with Canada's child welfare system.

Key Demographics from the Study

The following sections provide key demographic findings from the study "Under the Radar: The Sexual Exploitation of Young Men in Western Canada." In addition to offering a descriptive review, the data speak to a number of the key risk factors for young male sexual exploitation victims: "Risk factors can be defined as life events or experiences that are associated with an increase in problem behaviors, such as drug use or gang activities. For example, being the child of a single-parent who is often absent from the home and lacks adequate support, can be considered a risk factor. The negative influence of a friend or sibling can be another" (Howell 2005, pp. 334–6).

Aboriginal Heritage

According to the 2011 National Household Survey in Canada, approximately 4.3 per cent of the Canadian population have Aboriginal ancestry. However, 27 per cent of offenders in provincial and territorial prisons are Aboriginal and approximately 20 per cent now serving federal sentences are Aboriginal (Dauvergne 2012, p. 11). In Western Canada, up to 78 per cent of individuals in custody are Aboriginal (British Columbia data unavailable, Alberta 41 per cent, Saskatchewan 78 per cent, and Manitoba 69 per cent). Research has shown that Aboriginal young people are sent to jail at a younger age and for longer periods of time (www.oci-bec.gc.ca/cnt/rpt/oth-aut/oth-aut20121022info-eng.aspx; also see Chapter 11).

"Under the Radar" (McIntyre 2009, p. 15) found that 61 per cent of the 157 youths interviewed identified themselves as Aboriginal. Aboriginal young men are at an alarmingly high risk of entering the SET and the criminal justice system (see Box 14.2).

Of the respondents who participated in the "Under the Radar" project who self-identified, 56 per cent indicated that they felt they were connected to their traditional Aboriginal culture, while 44 per cent indicated they had no connection to their Aboriginal culture. The provinces varied in the percentage of respondents claiming to be Aboriginal: British Columbia revealed the lowest percentage (40 per cent); 85 per cent of Saskatchewan respondents identified themselves as Aboriginal; and 65 per cent of Manitoba respondents and 54 per cent of Alberta respondents indicated an Aboriginal heritage (McIntyre 2009).

Involvement with Child Protection Services

It is estimated that over 200,000 children and youth are involved with child protection authorities annually in Canada (Trocmé et al. 2005). Mulcahy and Trocmé (2010) found that on any day within Canada there are 65,000 children and youth residing in or out of home care, with 67,000 in out-of-home care in 2007 according to the most recent available statistics from provincial and territorial child welfare agencies.

In relation to the current study, just over half of those interviewed had experienced some degree of intervention through government-legislated child welfare authorities. The remaining 45 per cent who had not experienced child welfare interventions were "at risk,"

Box 14.2 Youth Justice in Action

Aboriginal People in Canada and Their Involvement in the Sexual Exploitation Trade

In the same way that Aboriginal individuals are overrepresented in Canada's correctional systems, they are also estimated to be overrepresented in the SET (Sethi 2007). While exact numbers are not possible to obtain, a 2005 study by Farley and Lynne found that 52 per cent of their 100 street-based Vancouver sex-worker participants were Aboriginal, while approximately 1.7 per cent of Vancouver's general population were Aboriginal. Similarly, Currie (2000) estimated that 70 per cent of Vancouver sex workers were Indigenous in 2000.

This overrepresentation may be due to a number of factors, including fewer opportunities for Aboriginal youth, lower socio-economic status, effects of colonization, experiences of poverty and isolation, legacy from Canada's residential school system, gang involvement, and substance abuse (Saewyc et al. 2013). According to Hunt (2013, p. 94),

Poor quality of life is prevalent in many Indigenous communities, which can contribute to the level of choice Indigenous people can exercise about whether or not to engage in sex work . . . people in northern and isolated communities who lack transportation may exchange sex for a ride into a nearby town. Some argue that these conditions have led Indigenous women—as well as men and transgender people—to enter sex work without *real choice*. (Fletcher 2013)

Involvement in the SET for Aboriginal youth often also involves being trafficked for sexual exploitation within Canada, following a rotation of Canadian cities (Sethi 2007).

While an awareness is slowly growing of the plight of sexually exploited and trafficked Aboriginal women in Canada, sexually exploited young Aboriginal men are still largely ignored.

given backgrounds of abuse and running away, but they were not directly connected to the child welfare system.

Boys are not encouraged to talk about the changes that are happening to their bodies. They receive less guidance about their reproductive role despite being provided with information and support in conjunction with the experiences of puberty (Powelson 2004, p. 5). While most authorities assume that young men have received the knowledge about sexual biology and socialization that they require, this is not always the case.

The majority of the young men in the study said that they had not received adequate information on sexual development or health while growing up. This lack of information and knowledge has placed these young men in a vulnerable situation, as they have gaps and misinformation with reference to their sexual development.

Education

In the study, it was important to ascertain the level of education this population had completed and at the same time gain an understanding of the educational disruptions they had experienced. Thirty-five per cent of all the respondents indicated that they had completed high school, while 10 per cent of that population had completed either college- or university-level programs. On the other hand, 15 per cent of the total number of respondents indicated they had only completed grade school, while 85 per cent indicated they had completed some level of high school, varying from Grades 9 to 12.

Three significant education factors contribute to the disadvantages and vulnerabilities of young men at risk of sexual exploitation. First, young men are more likely to drop out of high school than young women. In fact, they represent 9.7 per cent of school dropouts, while young women represent only 5.9 per cent (Employment and Social Development Canada 2014). Second, 22.6 per cent of dropouts are Aboriginal young men, with 61 per cent of Aboriginal young people (aged 20 to 24) not having completed high school compared to 13 per cent of non-Aboriginal young people in Canada (Chief's Assembly on Education 2012). A third challenge for this group of young men relates to the fact that 55 per cent of them grew up in government care. The Alberta Child and Youth Advocate reported the following in reference to youth growing up in care while being educated:

> Children and youth in care are more likely to perform below Grade level and to fall behind their peers as they get older. They are over-represented in special education and vocational classes and are more likely to be identified as having behavioral disorders, severe learning disabilities or mild intellectual disabilities. They are more likely to be suspended or expelled from school and are less likely to complete high school. While we were unable to find data specific to the school experience of Alberta children and youth in care, it is safe to suggest their experiences mirror those reported for children and youth in other jurisdictions. (Child and Youth Advocate 2008, p. 5)

Running Away

While most young people threaten to run away from home at some time during their formative years, actually doing so is, fortunately, a relatively rare occurrence (also see

Chapter 13). Therefore, when young people do run away, it generally reflects considerable distress or conflict in the family (MacLaurin and Worthington 2012). Once they are away from the support of their homes, there is value in ascertaining how a young person ends up surviving on the streets. Over 83 per cent of the youth interviewed for this study had the experience of being runaways, throwaways, or both. According to MacLaurin and Worthington (2012), a runaway is a youth who leaves his or her place of residence without permission and is absent for at least one night, while a throwaway is a youth who is asked to leave and has no alternative accommodations provided for him or her.

Eighty-three per cent of the study's total respondents indicated that at some point they had run away or were made to leave the family home during childhood or adolescence. Sixty-one per cent of the total respondents indicated that when they ran away, they were offered food and shelter, and 45 per cent of those who were offered food and shelter had conditions attached, most of which were sexual in nature. A similar finding occurred in the Public Health Agency of Canada's study on street youth (2006), where 25.7 per cent of young male street youth took part in obligatory sex for food, shelter, money, gifts, and/or drugs.

Many of those interviewed indicated that their first introduction to hustling/working in the SET occurred while they were "on the run" and trying to survive. One young man said that when he was approached, it was "sex for food and shelter." When offered accommodation, another young man said it was clear he was to "put out or get out."

As evidenced by these quotations, the risks associated with being a runaway and being lured into the SET for survival are high. Obligatory sex is clearly a form of survival for the runaway and homeless male populations (Public Health Agency of Canada 2006; McIntyre 2009).

Getting Thrown Out

McIntyre (1994, 2002, 2009) clearly identified the population interviewed for the study as being at risk of running away. At the same time, this population was also at risk of being thrown out of their place of residence.

Fifty-one per cent of respondents indicated that they had been thrown out of the family home (i.e., told to leave). One young man said he was thrown out of the house because of his sexuality and "because I wanted to dress like a girl." As a result, these respondents sought temporary accommodation or places to sleep outdoors. Respondents indicated various reasons for being thrown out of the family home. These included not fitting in socially, spiritually, sexually, or culturally.

Sexual and Physical Violation

The topic of sexual and physical violation of young people in Canada received virtually no attention until the mid-1980s. David Finkelhor (1979) credits the women's movement with raising public awareness of sexual abuse in North America. The consequence of this awareness was the Canadian landmark study by the Badgley Commission (1985), which looked at the issue of sexual abuse and prostitution in Canada. It was thanks to this report that discussion began on the actual definitions of *abuse*. The following are the definitions that were agreed upon in 2009 by the Department of Justice Canada:

> *Physical child abuse* may consist of just one incident or it may happen repeatedly. It involves deliberately using force against a child in such a way that the child is either injured or is at risk of being injured. Physical abuse includes beating, hitting, shaking, pushing, choking, biting, burning, kicking or assaulting a child with a weapon. It also includes holding a child under water, or any other dangerous or harmful use of force or restraint. Female genital mutilation is another form of physical abuse.
>
> *Child sexual abuse and exploitation* involves using a child for sexual purposes. Examples of child sexual abuse include fondling, inviting a child to touch or be touched sexually, intercourse, rape, incest, sodomy, exhibitionism, or involving a child in prostitution or pornography. (Family Violence Initiative 2009)

Within the "Under the Radar" project, 75 per cent of respondents in all four Western provinces identified themselves as having been sexually abused prior to their involvement with the sex trade. These youths described being sexually violated many times and at very early ages as children. Eighty-five per cent reported a history of physical violation or physical abuse. We must caution, however, that not all who experience this degree of violation turn to sexual exploitation. Nevertheless, coupled with a runaway or throwaway experience, sexual and physical violation can increase the risk of possible recruitment into sexual exploitation as a mode of survival.

Overall, this is a population with a substantial history of both sexual and physical violation prior to their involvement with the SET. Furthermore, this population experienced extensive victimization within their homes and communities and within the SET.

Witnessing Aggression While Growing

In 1999, Statistics Canada produced the findings of "Children Witnessing Family Violence." According to the survey, 37 per cent of children heard or saw one parent assaulting the other. This report, by Dauvergne and Johnson (2001), determined that witnessing family violence is also linked to negative behaviours in children. These children are more likely to exhibit aggression, have emotional disorders and hyperactivity, and act in a delinquent manner toward property. Blanchette, Robinson, Alksnis, and Serin (1998) found that of those who had grown up witnessing violence, 56 per cent replicated this violence in their adult lives.

Indeed, the population interviewed for "Under the Radar" reported that 86 per cent of them had personally witnessed violence. This percentage is at least twice as high as the national average reported by Dauvergne and Johnson (2001). This population of sexually exploited young men spoke about seeing their mothers being beaten and the explosive nature of family gatherings that involved alcohol.

Involvement with Police

In our study, 79 per cent of respondents reported having a background involvement with the police. This police involvement resulted either from some aspect of their family of origin, from their involvement in the general community, or, more recently, from their involvement on the street. The data suggest that such criminal activities were primarily summary convictions and occurred in the context of social and community disorder. Of the 157 individuals interviewed, none had been incarcerated for any significant period of time.

However, it is important to understand that these young men had all experienced being "labelled." This labelling is further ingrained and illustrated as they become a population of runaways and throwaways. People vary in their vulnerability or sensitivity to the reactions of others; if the original self-image is not strong enough, the labelled person may come to accept the image offered by others and change the self-image accordingly. And the more frequently a person is labelled, the more likely it is that this change will take place (Williams and McShane 2013).

In summary, this population is characterized by several risk factors, such as a background of abuse, criminal activity, community disorder, and running away and/or being thrown away. Evidently, young males who are sexually exploited are significantly at risk of being victimized: "The evidence is clear. Those in prostitution have experienced extremely high rates of childhood trauma, violent victimization while in prostitution, substance abuse, and psychiatric disorders" (Ross, Farley, and Schwartz 2003, p. 202).

We will now shift to examine how young men enter into the SET.

The Work Life/Hustling of Sexually Exploited Young Men

Entering the Sexual Exploitation Trade

Research has highlighted many possible reasons for an individual to enter the SET. What we know for certain is that this is not attributable to any one factor but is often the outcome of multiple contributing factors, including physical, mental, and emotional health; necessity and survival (e.g., food, clothing, and shelter); drug and alcohol dependency; and family history. In other words, young men become sexually exploited for a number of complex, myriad personal and interpersonal reasons:

> Rotherham-Borus, Mahler, Koopman, and Langabeer (1996) estimate that street youth are five times as likely as domiciled youth to report having been victims of sexual abuse as children. These young people are likely to experience low self-esteem, an impaired ability to form affective and trusting relationships with adults, higher rates of depression and suicide attempts, running away or being kicked out of home. (Gaetz 2009, p. 2)

None of the respondents identified having had as "a goal" entering into, or to remaining involved with, the SET. In fact, over 69 per cent of the total respondents saw this activity as a short-term method to make money in order to survive. These respondents also shared that the SET was a means of escape from something and/or someone. Other responses indicated that individuals had a desire to feel wanted and to belong to a culture or peer group. Those who reported that they were "on the run" at the time they were first introduced to the sex exploitation trade recalled feeling a sense of **anomie**, isolation from their families and communities.

Social control theory speaks of deviance as a way of attaching and belonging and as a means of establishing commitment and involvement (see Williams and McShane 2013). Many participants in the study spoke about how they felt compromised, strange, or immoral in what they were doing. Through their involvement with the "trade," however, they found a camaraderie and level of acceptance they had not previously known or that had been missing from their lives. On the street, they found a place, an identity, and a social group to attach to; yet this presented challenges, as street life is not a healthy environment for those involved in it.

As noted earlier, 81 per cent of those who had run away were offered food and/or shelter. Of this group, 45 per cent reported that conditions were attached to this type of offer. These conditions were sexual in nature, and as such, these respondents identified them as their introduction to the SET. As one respondent noted, "it was survival, food, shelter then drugs."

It is important to gain some background information on exactly how someone discovers and enters the SET. With 83 per cent of study participants having a runaway or throwaway background, 51 per cent then learned about the sex trade through a "friend." Most of the responses indicate that while on the street a friend introduced them to the SET as a means of survival.

Thirty-four per cent of all the respondents explained that they learned the "protocol" of sex work by observing others and mimicking their actions. Fifteen per cent reported that they had met a customer, or "trick," who had offered to teach them how the sex trade works. Young men from the study spoke about how they just fell into the surroundings of the SET. For example, some learned about the trade from friends or from those who had violated them but then provided them with cash.

Age at Beginning to Hustle/Work

Strolling Away (McIntyre 2002) highlighted that males enter the SET earlier and stay at least twice as long as their female counterparts. Young men stay longer, as they have fewer options. By contrast, young women often leave the SET to birth a child. *Under the Radar* (2009) revealed that 73 per cent of youth entered the SET under the age of 18 (see Table 14.1). The youngest person entered the SET at 8 years of age and the oldest was 25. This reflects a vast differential in ages and personal development.

Overall, the SET was about economic survival for the population both over and under the age of 18. For older youth, lack of employment skills and work experience often led to a need for paid sex as a means of survival. Of the study group, 27 per cent entered when they were adults (over 18 years of age). This finding shows that the male SET is not one that only targets children and adolescents, rather that those under the age of 18 are at greater risk:

> When they do find work, it is often in short-term, dead-end jobs or in
> unregulated work on the margins of the economy. As a result they engage in

anomie
The sense of normlessness and frustration that is a product of the way society is organized. Anomie can be a source of deviance. The organization or disorganization of society causes anomie, which leaves people confused about what norms should regulate their behaviour. (Cao 2004, p. 71)

Table 14.1	Under the Radar: The Sexual Exploitation of Young Men in Western Canada, 2009
Age Started	**Per Cent**
8–9 years	3
10–11 years	4
12–13 years	15
14–15 years	22
16–17 years	29
18–19 years	16
20–21 years	6
22–23 years	2
24 years plus	3

Source: Based on S. McIntyre. (2009). *Under the Radar: The Sexual Exploitation of Young Men in Western Canada.* Calgary: Hindsight Group.

risky money making strategies, some of them illegal or quasi-legal, including the sex trade, panhandling (begging), squeegeeing (cleaning car windshields), and criminal acts such as theft and drug dealing. (Gaetz 2009, pp. 5–6)

As reported earlier, the majority of this population had a background of sexual and/or physical abuse. A child's experience of physical or sexual violation/abuse (particularly when untreated) can affect him or her later in adulthood, and the current study indicates, it might also trigger, or prompt, an individual's introduction into the SET at an early age.

Time Spent Hustling/Working

Understanding the length of time respondents had been hustling/working is important, as it affects the needs of and intervention plan for a person considering exiting. The majority of respondents (83 per cent) had been in the sex trade longer than two years. Only 9 per cent of the total population of respondents had been in the sex trade for less than one year. The reality for most of these young men, however, is that they eventually became entrenched in a long-term cycle of victimization and trauma.

As described earlier in this chapter, these young men remained largely out of sight, which may result in longer-term involvement in the SET. According to Saewyc et al. (2013, p. 102),

The absence of this information [about the sexual exploitation of young men] in media coverage is problematic, because it adds to the invisibility of these victims. It makes it difficult for such exploited youth to recognize what is happening to them. . . . Further, it potentially influences the availability of health and social service programs for sexually exploited boys and young men, or for sexual minority girls and young women, and makes it challenging to create services that will reach out to them, meet their specific needs, or to even see the need for services for such groups of sexually exploited youth.

These youth are not quickly identified, as they "work" in a rather underground manner; neither are these young men quick to self-identify themselves as "sex trade workers" or as individuals who are being exploited. Consequently, preventive support services and other forms of outreach services that may support them in their health needs and in exiting sexual exploitation are not as readily available or as accessible. As respondents suggested, such circumstances often limit the ability of social support services to connect with these individuals before they are fully entrenched in the SET, thereby prolonging their time in the trade.

Overall, there appears to be a general lack of understanding in terms of what is required to ease the transition from working to exiting the SET for young men. As noted, many young women exit to birth children, which brings with it family and state support. This is not an option for young men.

Work Locations

The study identified a variety of work locations. Most worked in cars, hotels, and apartments, while some worked at truck stops and parks. Young men working are often undetectable, as they wear everyday clothing. Also, young men work in various locations where potential customers are found, such as chat lines, house parties, bars, lobbies, washrooms, and the street (see Box 14.3).

Box 14.3 Youth Justice in Action

Prostitution on the Internet

Increasingly, selling sex is moving online. From apps like "grindr" that may introduce young men into "sugar daddy" relationships after plausible hookups, to sites that facilitate the selling of sex, the sexual exploitation of young men may be becoming even more invisible as their services move online. While some argue that sex bought and sold online potentially opens the door for increased safety (screening of buyers, choice of location) and liberal markets (decreased market control by pimps), others voice concern that online prostitution results in even more difficulty for service providers in facilitating safe exits (see Economist, 9 August 2014, p. 9).

From the buyer side, the Internet is a popular venue for seeking sex, since it provides greater anonymity, reducing the perceived stigma of buying sex from a man. It also promotes the commodification of racialized desires and fetishes, as well as an expanding client base that includes more heterosexual men and women as clients. From the seller side, Minichiello, Scott, and Callandar (2013) suggest that the Internet is popular not only because of reduced stigma but also because of decreased probability of arrest and increased control over marketing and client selection.

By interviewing men selling sex online, Parsons, Koken, and Bimbi (2004) found that many men started selling sex on the streets and moved online after gaining enough resources for consistent access to a computer and the Internet. The same study suggests that the Internet offers an opportunity for the promotion of safer sex through online channels as well as better options for negotiating safer sex prior to client encounters. Overall, the literature on male sexual exploitation online is sparse, pointing to a need for more research into the new implications of an online sex market.

Shelter Stays

Because members of this population are often runaways and throwaways, they will, out of necessity, seek out shelter. This often results in temporary homeless accommodations. Sixty-four per cent of total respondents reported staying in shelters. For many, shelters were the only option available to them. Entrance into, and continuation within, the SET often results in a distinct lack of options.

Homelessness is a reality for many of these young men. According to Hein (2011, p. 274), for youth, "homelessness is dangerous. The standardized mortality rate for Canadian homeless youth is currently three times that of non-homeless youth." For many young men, the sex trade can present a means to avoid homelessness. Hein (ibid., p. 275) goes on to point out that "the research on homeless adolescents is equally clear that these adolescents do not engage in sex work for any reason other than inordinate desperation: survival."

A small number of respondents reported negative or unsafe experiences within homeless shelters, which had discouraged them from accessing this service. For instance, respondents reported that because of the high-barrier structure of certain shelter services, they had been refused access to shelter beds once they had disclosed their involvement with the SET (see Gaetz 2009).

In summary, respondents reported that the sex trade is a means of making a living in the world and a way to obtain basic needs—food, shelter, and other material goods.

Dissociation

According to the trauma model of dissociation . . . pathological dissociation is a core element of the response to chronic, severe childhood trauma which includes sexual, emotional, and verbal abuse, neglect, loss of primary caretakers through death, divorce, addiction, mental illness or imprisonment, family chaos and violence, violence outside the home, medical and surgical trauma, and severely disturbed family dynamics. (Ross, Farley, and Schwartz 2003, p. 200)

The majority of these young men reported that they did not enjoy working in the SET. They felt victimized or traumatized in this lifestyle. Their responses reinforced the perception that their involvement in the activity was based on their need to survive rather than on enjoyment or lifestyle choice. Unresolved abuse issues were a clear theme in the accounts of young men discussing their thoughts and feelings while working and after working.

This is not an activity that people engage in proudly or with a strong sense of safety or security. As such, dissociating from one's reality is common for both young men and young women in the SET. Young men consistently spoke about how they felt "awful, full of shame," as well as sick, dirty, drained, and burned out. For example, one of the young men articulated how he would dissociate by saying "I mentally would send myself somewhere else, I was there in body and they were doing that to me but I wasn't there in mind."

Further compounding the dissociation experienced by young men can be the role of sexual orientation in their sexual exploitation (discussed further, below). Depending on demand, young straight men may pretend to be gay to attract buyers ("gay for pay"), or young gay men may pretend to be straight men working as "gay for pay" men. As adolescents move toward the development of their own sexual identity, these different roles may compound their experience of dissociation while they are involved in the SET (discussed further with respect to sexual orientation).

Family Relations

As noted earlier, for these young men, family relations are often strained and challenged; this is evident by the high rates of abuse, aggression, and child welfare experiences. With reference to family knowledge of a person's involvement in the SET, the following was discovered: 69 per cent of the population interviewed said that at least one family member was aware of their involvement with the SET. Respondents reported that initially they were able to keep their involvement a secret but that eventually family members became aware of what was occurring. Thirty-two per cent of those interviewed believed that their family was unaware of their involvement in the trade.

Fifty-four per cent of this population have difficult or non-existent relationships with their families. Once a family became aware of the SET in the child's life, anger, fear, and confusion typically resulted, and understanding/acceptance was difficult. People found it difficult to understand or accept the child's lifestyle. This experience was common among all youth regardless of gender. However, according to the respondents, when family members discovered that the customers of sexually exploited young men are predominantly male, this put further strain on the family relationship. As one young man stated, "It is no good my grandfather hates me and I told them all I was bi-sexual and they look down upon me."

Advice to Other Youth

Those immersed in a life of sexual exploitation clearly warn and challenge people to rethink their decision prior to entering the trade. They speak about the harm and shame they experience, yet this population often ended up staying in the SET.

All respondents were in agreement that the SET is not something one should become involved with. They spoke about the downsides and negative results and the loss of respect that comes from this continuous victimization with no clear escape route. Respondents strongly recommended that people explore alternative options for survival and income.

We will now shift to looking at those who stay in the SET for a period of time.

Experiences of Youth Who Stay in the Sexual Exploitation Trade

As noted earlier, the majority of respondents in the study had remained in the SET for long periods of time. Eighty-three per cent, in fact, had been in the trade for more than two years. These youth are subject to a variety of experiences and traumas, such as assault, sexual assault, gay bashing, drug and alcohol abuse, and stigmatization.

Common Fears

During the interviews, we asked individuals what they feared most while they were hustling/working. Twenty-nine per cent of the respondents indicated that their greatest fear was a "bad date," meaning a customer who would harm them and potentially kill them. Eighty per cent had experienced a "bad date." The threat of being beaten, raped, or attacked with a weapon is the most prominent worst experience reported by respondents in all four Western provinces. Even seasoned workers, like River Redwood, who advocate for the sex trade recognize the dangers for male sex workers. Redwood (2013) states, "Due to issues of masculinity, a man who has been sexually assaulted is rarely seen as a victim. It is more often the case that he will believe, or will be made to feel, that the assault was his own fault because he wasn't masculine enough. This situation can be doubly compounded if you're a male sex-worker and are assaulted by another man" (p. 52). He goes on to indicate that "[i]f a male sex-worker is assaulted, there are very few services and supports he can access. . . . The sad reality is that it's often better to deal with the situation on your own or with a close friend than to risk the ignorance and abuse of a professional" (p. 53). Almost unanimously, the participants also spoke of not being allowed to leave, of enduring threats of death, of being given drugs, of being kidnapped and taken out of town, and of the fear of a drive-by shooting taking place.

A total of 85 per cent of those interviewed saw hustling/working in the SET as always dangerous. They witnessed and personally experienced the dangers of the SET in varying degrees. They also spoke of the violence that friends had experienced, including murder. One young man stated, "I have seen people overdose, suicide, murdered and be bashed. I fear being raped and dumped outside the City." Youth are in constant fear of what could occur; they are always at risk and need to be prepared:

> Street youth are vulnerable to exploitation whether by petty criminals, sexual predators, unscrupulous landlords or employers, or a whole range of other individuals who can wield power over them because potential perpetrators recognize that young people who are homeless have few resources to defend themselves and little recourse to challenge them. (Gaetz 2009, p. 13)

While participants in this study clearly articulated that a fear of physical harm and violence was part of their experience in the SET, most academic literature continues to focus on sexually transmitted infections as the most feared and dangerous aspect of sex work for men (Dennis 2008). While HIV is a serious concern for all sex workers, the focus on this one potential outcome for male sex trade workers again moves their experiences and issues from a place of victimization to a place of agency, doing a serious disservice to these young men in the discursive process.

Common Preoccupations

Respondents shared that while hustling/working, their thoughts often turned to concerns for their own safety, as well as to how and when they would/might exit the trade. One individual feared that he would never get out of the trade. He also wondered if he would ever be able to find himself again. None of the respondents reported having positive thoughts about the activity of hustling/working. However, they did acknowledge the income the SET provided, whether for daily survival, for substance use, or for maintaining a lifestyle free of the dangers of absolute homelessness.

McIntyre (2009) found that 58 per cent reported that while not working, their thoughts often centred on ways to change and improve their lives, as well as the lives of their families. Respondents also shared their hopes and dreams for a safer and more rewarding lifestyle, one that they could take pride in. A resounding theme identified by all four provinces involved in this study was the respondents' desire to exit the trade successfully.

Sexual Orientation

What became clear to the principal investigator over time was the distinct difference between how individuals defined their sexual identity while working/hustling and what they were like in their personal "non-work" time. "Confused" was how one person identified his sexual identity, particularly while hustling or working. For both young women and young men in the SET, there was a big difference between who they were when they worked and who they were on their own time. For young women, this was demonstrated by their having a "working name" they only used during working hours. While female sex workers experienced a range of sexual identities, in Dennis's (2008) review of 166 related articles, the author found that female sex workers were always assumed to be heterosexual and engaged in heterosexual activities. On the other hand, articles addressing males in the SET always addressed sexual orientation and identity in relation to sexual exploitation (Redwood 2013).

The following three descriptors are particularly important in understanding sexual orientation and survival in the SET:

- **Gay for pay** refers to a young man who is heterosexual in his non-hustling/working life. During the time in which he is hustling/working, he is "gay for pay," meaning he will become involved in sexual activities with male customers. Respondents who identified as "gay for pay" reported that customers found the potential opportunity to alter a young man's heterosexual orientation very attractive.

- **Straight for pay** refers to a gay male who will take on the persona of a heterosexual male while hustling/working. Respondents reported that some male customers found it attractive to engage with these young men as this presents the challenge and potential to alter their sexual identity.

- A person will work as a heterosexual male "straight" but have a private identity of **transgender**. Often this reflects a need for safety—that is, it is safer to appear as a male, whether straight or gay for pay.

gay for pay
A person who is heterosexual but who, in order to survive, will work in the sex trade as a homosexual.

straight for pay
A person who is homosexual but who, in order to survive, will work in the sexual exploitation trade as a heterosexual.

transgender
A person who crosses gender roles in one way or another, including as a transsexual, drag queen, or transvestite.

Respondents of the study self-identified their *working* sexual orientation as shown in Table 14.2. As we have learned, some respondents described their sexual identity as different from their actual sexual identity or orientation.

Table 14.2	Sexual Orientation of Respondents of "Under the Radar: The Sexual Exploitation of Young Men in Western Canada"	
Working Sexual Orientation		**Non-working Sexual Orientation**
Gay (38%)		Gay (42%)
Gay for pay (14%)		
Straight for pay (3%)		Straight (19%)
Tranny (19%)		Tranny (16%)
Bisexual (18%)		Bisexual (14%)
Confused (7%)		Confused (8%)
Don't know (1%)		Don't know (1%)

Gay Bashing

Violence is an issue that both genders are subject to while in the SET. Humiliation and violence from customers and the general community were cited as a daily occurrence. In previous studies, women had reported more violence from customers, while males were at a higher risk of homophobia and **gay bashing** (McIntyre 2009) (see Box 14.4).

gay bashing
The humiliation and violence that sex-trade workers are at risk of from customers and the community.

The fear of gay bashing is prevalent at all times for young men involved in the SET. Forty-four per cent of the respondents had experienced gay bashing and indicated that their safety had been at risk each time they had worked. This potential fear is always top of mind for sexual exploitation workers. This risk of violence related to gay bashing and homophobia for male sex trade workers is heightened through the bar scene within the inner city: "Queer bashing by drunken revelers turned out from the bars after closing is

Box 14.4   Youth Justice in Action

Port Moody Man Arrested in Vancouver Gay-Bashing Case

By Simone Blais

A Port Moody man has been charged in an alleged gay-bashing incident near Tinseltown in early October. Vancouver police announced Wednesday that Port Moody's Michael Anton Hostland, 22, has been arrested.

Shortly after 3 a.m. on Oct. 8, police were called to an assault in progress near International Village at Abbott and West Pender streets. Two men were initially taken into custody at the scene, but were released while the case was being investigated.

Const. Lindsey Houghton said in a release that an extensive investigation was conducted, which led to charges against Hostland and another suspect, 20-year-old Dustin James Sciog from Fort St John.

Sciog has been charged with three counts of assault, while Hostland will face one count of assault. Houghton said neither Hostland nor Sciog were previously known to police.

They are scheduled to appear in the downtown community court on Nov. 22.

Source: Simone Blais, *Coquitlam now*, 19 November 2010.

Note: Cases of gay bashing occur in the communities where male sex trade workers ply their trade to survive. Gay bashing is a direct homophobic reaction to male sex trade workers, which often occurs after the bars shut down as was evidenced by the case outlined in this box. The men charged in this case had no history of previous criminal behaviour yet reacted in a homophobic rage in an inner-city, gay-friendly neighbourhood.

another danger" (West and de Villiers 1993, p. 84). Gay bashing is often cited as resulting from a fear of homosexuality and being a product of homophobia: "Hatred of homosexuality may induce some heterosexual 'queer bashing' to select a rent boy for victimization" (West and de Villiers 1993, p. 103).

Working Safely

Young men rely on specific techniques to maintain their safety while hustling/working. While these techniques are far from foolproof, respondents reported that they provided them with a sense of control and safety.

Thirty per cent of respondents indicated that they do not hustle/work alone. Usually they will work with friends close by and will stay in areas that are "safe" and "well lit." The respondents also spoke of the need to rely heavily on their own personal instincts or "intuition" in order to maintain their personal safety.

One of the challenges these workers face in trying to maintain their personal safety is their inability to call the police because of fear of arrest or potential homophobic reactions on the part of the police. River Redwood (2013, p. 52), a professional sex worker and porn producer, addressed this problem: "To this day, I would never call the police to help me in connection with a [sex] work-related issue. I shudder at the thought of how they would react and deal with the situation. If anything, I view the police as being more dangerous than the most horrendous trick."

Young men in the trade often seek out a "sugar daddy" for security. Respondents described how this type of "relationship" protects them and has the potential to limit the amount of time they would spend and risk they would experience on the street. A sugar daddy can provide a regular source of income as well as other material goods. One young man saw having a sugar daddy as an "opportunity to have my expenses taken care of for a number of months." While respondents did not suggest in any way that a sugar daddy relationship is one a young man should seek out, they perceived such a relationship to be safer than the alternative methods of hustling/working on the street.

Respondents also revealed that a sugar daddy would often target a particular type of young man, seeking him out in public places or at events. Most often the sugar daddy is seeking a public relationship with the chosen young man. Such a relationship often involves exclusivity and a live-in role and may be based on "gay for pay."

Hustling/Working and Drugs

The initial introduction to hustling/working is often driven by the need to obtain the basic means of survival: food, shelter, and clothing. This is the first stage of Maslow's hierarchy of needs (Maslow 1943)—physiological needs. However, these needs often become replaced by, or adjoined to, a need to feed a drug addiction. There is a strong relationship between drug use and the SET. For some respondents, substance use/abuse was first introduced to them when they began working in the trade.

Virtually all respondents reported that drugs eventually became a "way of life" once they had become entrenched in the trade. Initially, drugs were viewed as a reward, providing an escape from the continual exploitation and humiliation experienced while hustling/working. Respondents suggested that the longer they remained in the trade, the more interdependent the relationship became.

While close to half of those interviewed avoid using drugs while they are hustling/working on the street, nearly all of them spoke of some drug use in their private time. We learned that for these individuals drug use in their private life often fuels their need to work and enables them to remain in the trade.

Helping Young Men Exit the Sexual Exploitation Trade

Why Do They Stay?

Many might wonder why someone would remain in the sexual exploitation life. The following quote speaks to the challenges inherent in preparing to leave: "Regaining self-respect and recreating an emotional life is far more difficult. It is as hard as reconstructing a hundred crown bill from ashes" (Hoigaard and Finstad 1992, p. 115). If we are to be effective in assisting individuals to successfully exit the SET, we must understand what motivates them to continue hustling/working. Almost an equal number of individuals indicated either that they have no choice or options (48 per cent) or that their addictions are what keep them hustling (47 per cent). Responses across the four provinces varied significantly; in Alberta, a much higher number of respondents indicated the need to stay hustling because of addictions (65 per cent).

It comes as perhaps no surprise to the reader that everyone we interviewed wanted to leave the SET. This is consistent with both young women and young men (McIntyre 2002, 2005). No one person identified positive benefits or a desire to remain. In fact, all respondents reported that they had at some point attempted to leave the trade or had taken a break from it. However, most eventually returned, citing factors such as necessity, survival, or addiction to drugs and/or alcohol as the main reasons for returning. Individuals also often have difficulty leaving the SET because of their fear or experience of violence when they attempt to leave (from their exploiters or former community members) (see Cimino 2012).

Despite the support he received for working in the sex trade, Redwood (2013, p. 47) admits that "because of the stigma and stereotypes about my [sex] work, it can be very difficult for me to get a non-sex-industry job. Although I have a range of skills and experiences, I'm often forced to drop things off my resume or just plain lie in job interviews." For men entering the SET at a young age, the cost of losing the opportunity to work within the mainstream economy can make it extremely difficult to enter the mainstream workforce when attempting to exit the SET. This again compounds the experience of scarcity and poverty, leading many youths back to selling sex as a means of supporting their basic needs (survival).

What is important to understand about these youth is that they are a diverse, complex population surviving in whatever way they can in their personal and work lives. It is clear that this population needs supports and protective program strategies and services.

Services That Would Help

Throughout the interviews, we were curious about the type of services these young men felt should exist. A theme frequently voice was that existing services were predominantly female-oriented. Compared to studies on females working in the SET, there is little known about the unique needs, challenges, and "working style" of males. Therefore, it is not surprising that the delivery of appropriate and accessible services was viewed as limited or non-existent (see, for example, Saewyc et al. 2013; Dennis 2008, ECPAT USA 2013; Reid and Piquero 2014).

Respondents said that by participating in this study, they hoped to provide the clarity required to ensure that relevant services and supports were established for young men who are sexually exploited. Sexually exploited young men have been ignored in many settings across the world (see Harper and Scott 2005, p. 6).

Sixty-one per cent of respondents in the study put forward one of the strongest recommendations—the need for residential support services. Many of these respondents indicated that residential support services would or could eliminate the need to trade sexual favours for basic survival, such as a place to sleep. They also claimed that this type of service would help them develop their independence and, ultimately, exit the SET.

Attempts at Exiting

The group that emphasized the need for residential support services were committed to pursuing traditional and conventional lives. They expressed a clear sense of Hirschi's (1969) social control theory:

> Commitment represents the investment one has already built up in conventional society. This investment may take such forms as the amount of education, a good reputation, or the establishment of a business. Those with these forms of commitment to conventional society have more to lose if they are caught engaging in deviant behavior. (Williams and McShane 2013, p. 152)

Respondents did not perceive the sex trade as a long-term lifestyle. However, we need to understand what they know about leaving this life if we are to design supports accordingly. As noted by Gaetz (2009), homeless youth and sexually exploited youth have been socially isolated from home, family, education, employment, health and community support, and understanding. We need to be patient with this population and understand that exiting the sex trade is similar to quitting smoking—it often takes a number of attempts.

It is difficult to imagine anyone (regardless of age) wanting to be a victim of such violation. Reflecting on the primary focus of this chapter, however, some 24 per cent of the respondents said that limited resources and a change in the life circumstances they had grown used to were the most challenging aspects of leaving the trade. In addition, 20 per cent indicated that missing their friends, roommates, and others they had bonded with would entail a significantly difficult adjustment.

Returning to the Sexual Exploitation Trade

Almost half (48 per cent) of the respondents reported that they had returned to hustling/working because they were stranded, unemployed, and/or feared becoming homeless. Within this group, respondents shared their belief that hustling/working was the only thing they knew how to do to avoid becoming homeless or going hungry. This push and pull that occurs in the SET can be explained by Reckless's containment theory:

> Emphasizing inner containment, Reckless said that a self concept exists in people and is formed when they are quite young. This self-concept provides either a "good" or "bad" image of the self and acts as a buffer to outside influences. He also stressed that there are a variety of "pushes" and "pulls" toward deviant behavior that all individuals experience. (Williams and McShane 2013)

We must remember that all of these young men have lived either as runaways, throwaways, or were homeless people and have experienced the shelter system. Although they may decide to stop working/hustling, the majority choose to continue associating with friends and living with roommates who work in the sex trade (McIntyre 2002, 2009). Unfortunately, living on the periphery of this lifestyle can present challenges to a successful and permanent exit. We have learned from respondents that maintaining close ties to the trade (e.g., through friends) can result in returning to it.

Reactions after Exiting

The data used in preparing this chapter show that 63 per cent of all respondents experienced symptoms of stress once they stopped hustling/working. In most cases, this stress was a direct result of worrying about how they would provide for themselves and, in some cases, their families. Most of the individuals had limited experience with other forms of employment. Their experiences in the trade did not prepare them for the demands of mainstream or "legitimate" employment:

> Many sex-workers have great professional skills, but they can't put them on their resume for fear of stigma or the simple fact that their work isn't recognized as legitimate. If they worked in a strip club, escort agency, bathhouse, or massage parlour, they are forced to come up with a different name or alternative for how they've been employed. In other words, they are made to lie. (Redwood 2013, p. 48)

During periods of time when young men exited the trade, over 56 per cent experienced difficulty sleeping because of the late hours they were used to working. However, it was not just the adjustment to the change in waking/sleeping hours. Often difficulty sleeping had to do with other changes, including drug withdrawal, sleep disturbances, and nightmares.

Moreover, 58 per cent of the respondents experienced flashbacks once they left the street. Often these youths recalled some of the difficult times they'd had while in the SET, or they experienced unresolved issues they had suppressed while in the trade. These reactions are common for persons who have experienced trauma in their lives. Both young women and young men from the SET have had such experiences while attempting to exit and successfully exiting the SET (McIntyre 2009).

Messages for Service Providers

"Under the Radar" had a clear purpose: to understand sexually exploited young men and their need for services. It was important to hear what these young men wanted to tell service providers. An overwhelming number wanted to let service providers know that it is not easy to leave the trade. As McIntyre (2002) reported, nearly everyone had left at least once but had then returned. Therefore, we must understand that the process of leaving is a challenge, as these youth often do not have the resources or the skills to exit successfully. Compounded by substance addiction, lack of employment, and limited resources, attempts to exit "successfully" often resulted in homelessness and/or shelter stays.

The young men in this study reported that they did not feel understood by service providers and they did not believe that appropriate services were available to them. Sadly, little if anything has changed in the past 20-plus years, as was discussed by Visano (1987) in interviews with 33 young men in Toronto: "[E]stablished reception and therapeutic facilities were perceived by all prostitutes as ineffective and coercive. Very few opportunities exist for prostitutes to engage in positive programs directed toward skill development" (ibid., p. 329). For example, Hustle: Men on the Move, a Vancouver peers program initiated in 2007, is essentially the only program designed specifically for young male sex trade workers in Canada.

Sixty-six per cent of the respondents in this study explained the difficulty in leaving the trade, indicating that service providers, health-care providers, and the legal system need to understand the differences between being a male hustler and a female hustler and to recognize the lack of support for young men. The issue of drug rehabilitation and addictions treatment programs was critical. Young men engage in sexual exploitation at a very young age and remain in the trade longer than women, and consequently, they have longer and more severe experiences of addiction.

Through this study, however, the young participants felt that their pleas for services to meet their needs were finally being heard. While condoms and coffee programs may assist, there is clearly a desire for more substantive services.

Summary

This chapter set out to shed some light and awareness on the under-the-radar topic of sexually exploited young men. Sexual exploitation occurs regardless of gender. All of our street-trade youth—both young women and young men—have comparable backgrounds of sexual and physical abuse prior to the SET. These youths, who run away or are thrown away, are placed in vulnerable circumstances that can put them at risk within our communities. Young women and young men have a comparable risk of entering the SET in order to survive, and this lifestyle is often heavily associated with drugs.

It is perhaps ironic that in an age where the rights of women and children who are being sexually exploited, trafficked, and/or smuggled across borders or across jurisdictions are being championed at all levels of government, comparatively nothing is being done for young males. Society has enabled young men to be involved in the SET, as there remains a level of discomfort and confusion regarding male sexual exploitation—a form of reverse discrimination. We have supported and facilitated young men in flying under the radar. As evidenced in this chapter, the longer a young male stays street involved, the more distant and estranged he becomes from his family and community. As a society, we have looked at the issue of sexual exploitation through a female lens. Young men have specific service needs, and we need to recognize this and protect them and assist them in exiting the SET.

Researching justice issues is also about research policy. In the end, data and information gathered about any issue should bring about some fundamental return on investment to the community. In addition to facilitating the recognition and acknowledgement of the plight of young male sexual workers, the most effective strategies to address the problem should focus on all three levels of prevention/intervention—primary, secondary, and tertiary—in the following areas:

- Addiction treatment

- Counselling and clinical support

- Crisis services

- Education

- Employment

- Housing

Key Terms

anomie	gay for pay
child welfare	straight for pay
customer	sexual exploitation
experiential	transgender
gay bashing	youth in care

Review Questions

1. What role does running away play for young men in the sexual exploitation trade?
2. What do you believe are the risk factors that lead young men into the sexual exploitation trade?
3. Which of the theoretical explanations do you think best describe how and why young men become involved in the SET?
4. How might the risk factors differ from those of young females in the sex trade?

Critical Thinking Questions

1. Why do you think the issue of sexual exploitation of young men has been ignored?
2. What impact do you think government legislation can have on the issue of sexual exploitation in Canada?
3. Why do you think that Aboriginal young men are overrepresented in the population of sexually exploited young men in Canada?
4. What role do you think the Internet will play or is playing in the sexual exploitation of young men in Canada?
5. What do you think are the primary dangers for young men in the sexual exploitation trade?
6. What are the possible challenges to actualizing the proposed prevention/intervention strategies?

References

Bagley, C. (1985). Child sexual abuse and juvenile prostitution: A commentary on the Badgley report on sexual offences against children and youth. *Canadian Journal of Public Health*, 76 (January/ February): 65–6.

Blanchette, K., Robinson, D., Alksnis, C., and Serin, R. (1998). *Assessing treatment change among family violent offenders: Reliability and validity of a family violence treatment assessment battery.* Ottawa: Research Branch, Correctional Service Canada.

Canada. Committee on Sexual Offences against Children and Youths. (1984). *Sexual offences against children* (2 vols.; Chairman: R. Badgley). Ottawa: Minister of Justice and the Attorney General of Canada and the Minister of National Health and Welfare.

Cao, L. (2004). *Major criminological theories: Concepts and measurement.* Belmont, CA: Wadsworth/ Thomson Learning.

Chief's Assembly on Education. (2012, 1–3 October). *A portrait of First Nations and education.* Retrieved 6 October 2014 from http://www.afn.ca/uploads/files/events/fact_sheet-ccoe-3.pdf

Child and Youth Advocate. (2008). *Annual report 2006–2007.* Edmonton: Government of Alberta. Retrieved 8 June 2011 from http://advocate.gov.ab.ca/home/documents/AR2006to2007.pdf

Chu, S., and Glass, R. (2013). Sex work law reform in Canada: Considering problems with the Nordic Model. *Alberta Law Review*, 51(1): 101–24.

Cimino, A. (2012). A predictive theory of intentions to exit street-level prostitution. *Violence against Women*, 18(10): 1235–52.

Currie, S. (2000). Assessing the violence against street involved women in the Downtown Eastside/ Strathcona community. *Report for the Ministry of Women's Equality, Province of British Columbia.* Vancouver: unpublished report.

Dauvergne, M. (2012). Adult correctional statistics in Canada, 2010/2011. Statistics Canada, *Juristat*, Catalogue no. 85-002-X. Retrieved 6 October 2014 from http://www.statcan.gc.ca/pub/85-002-x/2012001/article/11715-eng.htm#a7

Dauvergne, M., and Johnson, H. (2001). Children witnessing family violence. *Juristat*, 21(6). Canadian Centre for Justice Statistics, Statistics Canada.

Dennis, J. (2008). Women are victims, men make choices: The invisibility of men and boys in the global sex-trade. *Gender Issues*, 25: 11–25.

ECPAT. (2006). Global monitoring report on the status of action against commercial sexual exploitation of children: Canada. Bangkok: ECPAT International. Retrieved from http://www.ecpat.net/A4A_2005/PDF/Americas/Global_Monitoring_Report-CANADA.pdf

ECPAT. (2013). *And boys too.* New York: ECPAT USA. Retrieved from https://d1qkyo3pi1c9bx.cloudfront.net/00028B1B-B0DB-4FCD-A991-219527535DAB/1b1293ef-1524-4f2c-b148-91db11379d11.pdf

Employment and Social Development Canada. (2014). Learning—School drop outs. *Indicators of Well-Being in Canada*. Retrieved 6 October 2014 from http://www4.hrsdc.gc.ca/.3ndic.1t.4r@-eng.jsp?iid=32

Family Violence Initiative. (2009). Ottawa: Department of Justice. Retrieved 8 June 2011 from http://www.justice.gc.ca/eng/pi/fv-vf/about-aprop/

Farley, M. (Ed.). (2003). *Prostitution, trafficking and traumatic stress*. San Francisco: Haworth Press.

Farley, M., and Lynn, J. (2005). Prostitution of Indigenous women: Sex inequality and the colonization of Canada's First Nations women. *Fourth World Journal*, 6(1): 1–29.

Finkelhor, D. (1979). *Sexually victimized children*. New York: Free Press.

Fletcher, T. (2013). Trans sex-workers: Negotiating sex, gender, and non-normative desire. In E. van der Meulen, E. Durisin, and V. Love (Eds), *Selling sex: Experience, advocacy, and research on sex work in Canada*. Vancouver: UBC Press.

Gaetz, S. (2009). Whose safety counts? Street youth, social exclusion and criminal victimization. In J.D. Hulchanski, P. Campsie, S. Chau, S. Hwang, and E. Paradis (Eds), *Finding home: Policy options for addressing homelessness in Canada* (pp. 1–23). Toronto: Cities Centre, University of Toronto.

Harper, Z., and Scott, S. (2005). *Meeting the needs of sexually exploited young persons in London*. Barkingside, Essex, UK: Barnardo's.

Hein, L. (2011). Survival strategies of male homeless adolescents. *Journal of American Psychiatric Nurses Association*, 17(4): 274–82.

Hirschi, T. (1969). *Causes of delinquency*. Berkeley, CA: University of California Press.

Hoigaard, C., and Finstad, L. (1992). *Back streets: Prostitution, money and love*. Cambridge: Polity Press.

Howell, J.C. (2005). Moving risk factors into developmental theories of gang membership. *Youth Violence and Juvenile Justice*, 3(4): 334–54.

Hunt, S. (2013). Decolonizing sex work: Developing an intersectional Indigenous approach. In E. van der Meulen, E. Durisin, and V. Love (Eds), *Selling sex: Experience, advocacy, and research on sex work in Canada*. Vancouver: UBC Press.

Lowman, J., and Louie, C. (2012). Public opinion on prostitution law reform in Canada. *Canadian Journal of Criminology and Criminal Justice*, 54(2): 245–60.

McIntyre, S. (1994). *The youngest profession: The oldest oppression*. Unpublished doctoral dissertation. Sheffield, UK: University of Sheffield.

McIntyre, S. (1999). The youngest profession—The oldest oppression: A study of sex work. In C. Bagley and K. Mallick (Eds), *Child sexual abuse and adult offenders: New theory and research* (pp. 159–92). Brookfield, VT: Ashgate Publishing.

McIntyre, S. (2002). *Strolling away*. Ottawa: Department of Justice Canada Research and Statistics Division.

McIntyre, S. (2009). *Under the radar: The sexual exploitation of young men—Western Canada*. Calgary: Hindsight Group.

MacLaurin, B., and Worthington, C. (2012). An overview of gang-involved youth in Canada. In J. Winterdyk and R. Smandych (Eds), *Youth at Risk and Youth Justice: A Canadian Overview*. Don Mills, ON: Oxford University Press.

Maslow, A.H. (1943). A theory of human motivation. *Psychological Review*, 50(4): 370–96.

Minichiello, V., Scott, J., and Callandar, D. (2013). New pleasures and old dangers: Reinventing male sex work. *Journal of Sex Research*, 50(3–4): 263–75.

Mulcahy, M., and Trocmé, N. (2010). Children and youth in out-of-home care in Canada. CECW Information Sheet. #78E. Montreal: McGill University, Centre for Research on Children and Families.

Parsons, J.T., Koken, J.A., and Bimbi, D.S. (2004). The use of the Internet by gay and bisexual male escorts: Sex workers as sex educators. *AIDS CARE*, 16(8): 1021–35.

Powelson, K. (2004). *A moment for boyz*. Vancouver: McCreary Youth Foundation.

Public Health Agency of Canada. (2006, March). *Street youth in Canada: Findings from enhanced surveillance of Canadian street youth, 1999–2003*. Ottawa: Government of Canada.

Redwood, R. (2013). Myths and realities of male sex work: A personal perspective. In E. van der Meulen, E. Durisin, and V. Love (Eds), *Selling sex: Experience, advocacy, and research on sex work in Canada*. Vancouver: UBC Press.

Reid, J., and Piquero, A. (2014). Age-graded risks for commercial sexual exploitation of male and female youth. *Journal of Interpersonal Violence*, 29(9): 1747–77.

Ross, C.A., Farley, M., and Schwatrz, H.L. (2003). Dissociation among women in prostitution. In M. Farley (Ed.), *Prostitution, trafficking and traumatic stress* (pp. 199–212). Binghamton, NY: Haworth Maltreatment & Trauma Press.

Rotherham-Borus, M.J., Mahler, K.A., Koopman, C., and Langabeer, K. (1996). Sexual abuse history and associated multiple risk behaviour in adolescent runaways. *American Journal of Orthopsychiatry*, 66(3): 390–400.

Saewyc, E., et al. (2013). Competing discourses about youth sexual exploitation in Canadian news media. *Canadian Journal of Human Sexuality*, 22(2): 95–105.

Sethi, A. (2007). Domestic sex trafficking of Aboriginal girls in Canada: Issues and implications. *First Peoples Child and Family Review*, 3(3): 57–71.

Trocmé, N., Fallon, B., MacLaurin, B., Daciuk, J., Felstiner, C., Black, T., et al. (2005). *Canadian incidence study of reported child abuse and neglect—2003*. Ottawa: Minister of Public Works and Government Services Canada.

Visano, L. (1987). *This idle trade: The occupational patterns of male prostitution*. Concord, ON: VitaSana Books.

West, D.J., and de Villiers, B. (1993). *Male prostitution*. Binghamton: Haworth Press.

Williams, F.P., and McShane, D.M. (2013). *Criminological theory* (6th ed.). Englewood Cliffs, NJ: Prentice Hall.

Part IV

Keeping Kids out of the System: Exploring Progressive Approaches to Youth Crime and Justice

To this point in the book we have studied the history of youth justice in Canada and the impact and evolution of youth justice legislation, provided an examination of youth crime, and discussed a number of key types of youth crime and problems. In this concluding section, we include two chapters that explore some unique, if not promising, approaches to dealing with youth crime and youth problems.

In Chapter 15, Louis-Georges Cournoyer, Jacques Dionne, Michèle Goyette, and Pierre Hamel provide a comprehensive overview of Quebec's unique approach to keeping young offenders out of the justice system. While many textbooks have given passing attention to the Quebec experience, this chapter represents one of the first (if not the first) detailed accountings of how and why Quebec has adopted a social welfare, psycho-educational approach toward dealing with youth at risk. While still operating within the parameters of the Youth Criminal Justice Act (YCJA), Quebec has managed to forge a model of juvenile justice that shows promise and that is gaining wider acceptance—indeed, a model that should serve as an example of what might be possible for Canada as a whole. The reader, we hope, will be inspired to debate and explore the potential of the Quebec model. And, as the authors note in their concluding remarks, the Quebec approach is "more in keeping with what is found in western European countries." We also hope that this in turn will also motivate you to explore and examine youth justice systems outside of Canada because, in the end, there is always room for improvement.

The final chapter, Chapter 16, authored by Brenda Morrison and Colleen Pawlychka, focuses on juvenile justice and the development of restorative justice in Canada. Although the authors draw on Canadian and some international material to ground their discussion, they rely on the situation in British Columbia to ground their overview and development of restorative justice. Restorative justice (RJ) is widely seen to represent a strong and viable alternative to conventional youth justice practices, not only in Canada but internationally. And now that the Youth Criminal Justice Act has legal provisions for the application of RJ, it is appropriate that, after the almost 15 years since its enactment, its relative merits be examined. Morrison and Pawlychka begin by providing a broad overview of the youth justice system in Canada, arguing that in spite of legislative reforms, young offenders are still largely subject to "a system of social control." The authors then provide a clear description of how several different models of RJ can be applied, and have been applied, in different strategic justice contexts. These strategic initiatives are also examined with a critical lens that helps to identify theoretical and practical issues that should be addressed if RJ is to become more mainstream. For example, Morrison and Pawlychka examine whether RJ programs should be state operated or supported through community-based NGO groups. The chapter concludes with a thought-provoking observation: referring to the commentary of other noted RJ champions, the authors point out that while RJ has a rich history in Canada, we do not appear to have capitalized on its potential for youth justice. Indeed, in the aftermath of the passing of the controversial crime bill—Bill C-10, also referred to as the Omnibus Crime Bill given that its primary focus is on accountability—RJ is likely to continue to struggle for acceptance within the youth justice system.

Although the textbook has endeavoured to cover a broad range of themes and issues, the information presented is in no respect the definitive word. Rather, we sincerely hope that the material presented will further stimulate your thinking as well as your desire to become involved in the quest to better understand and address youth crime, youth justice, and/or their related problems through one or more of the intervention, prevention, or control strategies discussed.

Quebec's Experience in Keeping Youth out of Jail

Louis-Georges Cournoyer, Jacques Dionne, Michèle Goyette, and Pierre Hamel

Overview

This chapter presents an overview of some key moments in the history of the efforts to rehabilitate young offenders in Quebec—key moments that have served to lay the foundation for how young offenders are dealt with in Quebec today. The chapter describes the evolution of Quebec's legislative youth justice framework, as well as the evolution of the province's various intervention strategies, and focuses particularly on the views of rehabilitation in the province that led to the actual structure of services offered to youth offenders. Together, these elements are intended to help explain why a majority of the Quebec population is opposed to some of the fundamental principles of the Youth Criminal Justice Act (YCJA). The chapter also provides the reader with insight into how and why Quebec's focus has shifted away from the gravity of the offence to try instead to address the needs and capacity of young persons who are recognized as at-risk youth.

Key Objectives

After reading this chapter, you should be able to:

- Define the logic behind the assertion "the right measure at the right time."
- Identify the key moments in the history of the rehabilitation of youth offenders in Quebec that determined the way such rehabilitation is organized today.
- Identify the values that guide offenders' rehabilitation in Quebec.
- Understand the reasons why Quebec opposed the YCJA.

Introduction

The Province of Quebec has a unique socio-political context in Canada. It is the only province to have French as the only official language. Under the provincial political system, Quebec also has a unique organization of public services (e.g., finance, justice, health, education). In addition, Quebec has maintained the Napoleonic Civil Code that it inherited from France, although in terms of criminal justice, the Canadian Criminal Code applies. This distinction goes back to the founding of Canada as the union of Upper and Lower Canada and has in some ways influenced the conceptualization of law as applied to youth offenders, as will be discussed herein.

The Quebec Intervention Model for Young Offenders: The Right Measure at the Right Time

Before 1950, in Quebec, as in the rest of Canada and some occidental countries, young offenders found themselves in adult prisons (Parizeau 1976; Foucault 1984). It was several decades before the incarceration of minors ended in Quebec. This chapter describes the evolution of this process from various perspectives over the past 100+ years. The changes made to the judicial system then were accompanied by new concepts of intervention and more extensive criminological, psychological, and psycho-educational research. The dynamic relationship between research and intervention has also played a major role in defining a **differential intervention** approach that has become more explicit and is now recognized as the basis of the Quebec intervention model used. We will describe the past and current organization of services for youth offenders in Quebec and the difficulties associated with the implementation of the Youth Criminal Justice Act (YCJA) in the province.

Evolution of Quebec's Legislative Framework

In 1857, Canada adopted the Act for the More Speedy Trial and Punishment of Juvenile Offenders in an effort to avoid long imprisonments before trial proceedings. It was at that time that the government decided to play a role in the protection of minors who had

differential intervention Based on the identification of the type of delinquency associated with the behaviours of young offenders, interventions must then be tailored to meet young offenders' treatment needs and the level of risk they pose to society (risk of recidivism). Takes into account that people do not come in one-size-fits-all packages and therefore refrains from applying the same approach to each person involved in a class, program, or other form of group-based change process.

committed an offence (see Chapter 1 in this textbook for further discussion). Between 1868 and 1925, more than 80,000 poor children were sent from England to Canada without family, some of them with delinquency issues. They were initially placed in asylums before being integrated into Canadian families as farm labourers or domestic servants. To protect these abandoned children from delinquency, in 1869 Quebec adopted two laws that established institutions to take charge of these children: the Industrial Schools Act, which ensured housing and education for children under 14 years old who had been abandoned or were not being properly taken care of; and the Reform School Act, which aimed to rehabilitate offenders under 16 years of age. Prisons were, at that time, overflowing with minors. This system remained in place until 1892, when a change in law obliged municipalities to pay for half of the cost for youth offenders placed in industrial and reform schools. Unfortunately, municipalities avoided paying these new costs, and once again, youth offenders were sent to adult courts and prisons (Joyal 2000).

In 1908, the adoption of the Juvenile Delinquents Act (JDA) marked a societal shift toward juvenile offenders. As described in Chapter 1, this law was based on a paternalistic philosophy whereby minors were no longer seen as criminals but as poorly raised and, therefore, not to be held responsible for their actions (see Platt 1977). Similar to abused and neglected children, delinquent children were seen as victims of their environment and deemed to need care, encouragement, and supervision. Intervention centred on helping these young people instead of reprimanding them for their delinquent behaviour. Constituting major social progress, this 1908 law conferred a special legal status on youth who had committed offences. Distinct tribunals and legal procedures for young offenders allowed them to receive help and remain with their family instead of being systematically incarcerated and/or treated like adults. Judges were now expected to act with reasonable and due care when it came to judicial proceedings involving young offenders.

By the beginning of the twentieth century in Quebec, religious institutions cared for abandoned children free of charge. The intention was to morally and physically "save" these children. Children were placed in big halls and dormitories, their basic needs were provided for, and they received minimal instruction. In 1951, Quebec passed the School Act of Youth Protection, a law that abolished reform and industrial schools. This new Act instituted youth protection schools and the court of social welfare, and judges were expected to hear the youth's situation. The spirit of this law favoured the substitution of the state for parents when the child was in need of protection. The tribunal responsible for administering this law was the same one responsible for the federal JDA. With the Act, however, the rules of law were minimal, since the legislation did not acknowledge the notion of rights for young people. The procedures in the court of social welfare were very basic, and the judge was expected to act with reasonable and due care. The principles of the Act were aligned with those of the federal law in effect at the time—the 1908 JDA. The procedures applied by the judge could be seen as a concrete implementation of the state as the *parens patriae*.

In 1977, Quebec adopted the Youth Protection Act (YPA), which came into effect in January 1979. Adopting this Act was a major step that influenced the course of intervening with young offenders. In addition to dealing with children in need of protection, this law also dealt with young persons charged with an offence under the Criminal Code or under provincial or municipal laws. Provisions were included that defined voluntary measures that could be offered to young offenders as an alternative to judicial proceedings and were deemed to be in their best interest. These provisions allowed the youth protection director to propose a voluntary measure, refer the matter to court, or close the case. This process was invalidated with the Supreme Court of Canada declaring in 1981 that criminal law, including procedures, is a federal jurisdiction (*Procureur général du Quebec c. Lechasseur et autre* [1981] 2 R.C.S. 253). However, the effect of this incursion of provincial legislation on federal jurisdiction has been to introduce a recourse for young offenders outside of judicial procedures. This legislation affirms the notion of the "precedence of social intervention over court intervention," which constitutes an important milestone for differential intervention.

It was at this time that the Quebec National Assembly held the Charbonneau Special Parliamentary Commission addressing youth protection. Taking into account the Supreme Court's decision and the enactment of the Young Offenders Act (YOA) in 1982, the commission proposed the adoption of an alternative measures program that balanced social and judicial obligations. In this program, the first step consists of an examination of the evidence by the solicitor followed by the youth protection director deciding which regime is applicable, either by proposing alternative measures to the youth or by recommending to the solicitor that charges be pressed against the offending youth. The Charbonneau Commission also recommended that the youth protection director be made provincial director under the YOA, thereby giving the youth protection network responsibility over the rehabilitation services provided to young offenders. Hence, the notion of precedence of social intervention was reaffirmed with the adoption of the YOA. As soon as the Act came into effect in 1984, Quebec adopted its Alternative Measures Program (Charbonneau Commission, part II). As detailed in Chapter 3, the YOA considered that youth were able to assume responsibility for their actions but it also insisted on protecting society. At the same time, the YOA emphasized the principle of considering adolescents' special needs in treating delinquency (see s. 3(1)(c)).

The nature and gravity of the offence are not the only elements considered when imposing judicial decision: a juvenile's needs and circumstances must also be taken into account when explaining his or her behaviour. Inspired by Quebec's experience using extrajudicial measures, the YOA instituted the Alternative Measures Program (AMP), which allowed Quebec and other jurisdictions of Canada to elaborate on and implement these measures. Quebec rapidly adopted a decree to institutionalize this option. Under the AMP, the prosecutor was expected to evaluate the evidence and determine if an offence had been committed. If such was the case, for the majority of offences each jurisdiction was obliged to transfer the young offender to the director of Youth Protection Services (YPS) for assessment and to determine how best to apply the program options. For some offences or specific situations, the prosecutor had the discretion either to refer the offender to the director of YPS or to proceed directly with legal proceedings.

The methods of intervention used with young offenders and the place the non-judicial measures occupy are the result of the experience and thinking of the 1960s and 1970s (to be discussed subsequently). In 1984, Quebec became one of the first provinces to take advantage of these provisions by adopting the decree "the Alternative Measures Program" as a program outside of the court that was part of the YOA. Since 1984, the directors of YPS have been designated provincial directors according to the YOA and, consequently, have responsibility to oversee the Alternative Measures Program. And since 2003, the provincial directors have the same responsibilities under the new YCJA. In the same manner, the rehabilitation centres responsible for youth protection were designated detention centres for young offenders with custodial sentences.[1]

Since 1984, the number of juveniles who have benefited from alternative measures has continued to grow. In 2014, 5261 teens were given extrajudicial sanctions compared to 5907 juveniles who received sentences and who were under the responsibility of the provincial director. Indeed, since 2000, approximately 8000 young offenders a year have been supervised by **alternative justice agencies** in Alternative Measures Programs.

In **extrajudicial programs**, the assessment carried out by the provincial director must examine certain key factors: the offence committed as well as who is responsible for the offence; the character of the offender and of his/her family; and the social environment. This allows the director to identify not only the nature of the action but also its meaning and significance for the young person, as well as the risk to society. This program is still in effect and has been extended under the YCJA as the Extrajudicial Sanctions Program.

When implementing the YCJA, the provincial directors confirmed their support for a differential approach to the intervention option. A differential intervention is based on identifying the type of delinquency associated with the young offender's behaviours. The distinction here is between a "common" young offender and a "distinctive" young offender—a distinction that is fundamental to intervening with young offenders (Le Blanc 1983). To do so, one must take into consideration the young offender's conduct and personality, and undertake a psychosocial evaluation. Such an assessment aims to identify the right measure at the right time for the right person.

The right measure at the right time is based on the offence for which the adolescent must assume responsibility according to his capacity to do so. The measure must be determined within the limits of the gravity of the offence. Within these limits, the aim is to protect and reaffirm reprobation for the offence while favouring education and rehabilitation measures; it also targets the needs and rights of victims. This measure takes into consideration the adolescent's entire situation to be influenced through tailor made decisions and measures that take into account specific needs.

. . . This measure is the result of an equilibrium that is difficult to reach among the following concerns: taking proper, fair, moderated and personalized decisions and measures; the need to take into consideration the gravity of the offence and the reprobation of society; and the importance of intervening at the right moment. The choice and application of such measures are clearly challenging.[2]

alternative justice agencies
Quebec-based agencies that are responsible for the application of the extrajudicial programs for youth, who are referred either by the police or by the provincial director, in accordance with the YCJA. Measures can include information and awareness programs on shoplifting, drugs, and law reinforcement as well as mediation or damage repair for the victim or, if that is not possible, damage repair through community service.

extrajudicial programs
Measures that are designed to hold youth responsible for their actions without the creation of a criminal record. They are generally applied to youth who are not engaged in a serious delinquent trajectory.

In accordance with the YCJA, prosecution in youth court and the imposition of specific sentences should be limited to adolescents in situations (1) where the criminal conduct is an indication of a "distinctive delinquency" (Le Blanc and Fréchette 1989), (2) where there are risks for public security, or (3) where the offences are serious. Serious interventions ordered by the court are designed for juveniles with important developmental deficiencies. These measures take into account both the young person's actions and the meaning these actions have for the young offender. This approach depends on the differential evaluation of each situation, taking into account the young offender's specific needs, especially in terms of rehabilitation and social reintegration. The intervention model in Quebec for young offenders is based on a differential evaluation before any intervention measures are taken. This approach was the result of extensive dialogue among judges, prosecutors, lawyers, and psychosocial professionals, following the YOA's implementation. This was evident in Judge Jasmin's 1995 report and has been supported since the 1970s by experts from both the judicial and social systems who have agreed to value prevention and rehabilitation.

As a consequence of this judicial evolution, there have been profound and dynamic transformations in the way interventions are designed, whether the youth offenders are in open custody, in secure custody, or in the community, or whether alternative measures are being used.

The Evolution of Interventions

Transformation of Open-Custody Interventions

Beginning in the 1950s, during the creation of the court for "social welfare," uprisings against youth imprisonment and large repressive institutions intensified. At the same time, groups of professionals began setting up pilot experiments in rehabilitation, like that of **Boscoville** (Rumilly 1978), which will be discussed below (see Box 15.1). Educators and other professionals took young offenders out of prisons and integrated them into newly designed rehabilitation programs, considered as alternatives to adult prisons and reform schools.

Boscoville became the new rehabilitative project for young delinquents in Montreal and had an important influence on the evolution of rehabilitation throughout the rest of Quebec. In the larger institutions at the time, there were 200 to 300 young people along with only a few staff who were members of the church and had no specific training (Ménard 2003). On the other hand, at Boscoville, there were only about 50 teens. They were divided into small groups of 12 to 15, and they lived in cottages similar to family homes. There were no guardians, only educators who lived with the youth and led this innovative program, which included academics, sports, art, and social activities. The intention of the program was to contribute to the youths' re-education. This approach was inspired by innovations from European specialized educators (see Capul and Lemay 1996) after the Second World War and by the Americans Redl and Wineman (1951). Boscoville was structured as systematic action research that led to a theoretical concept of rehabilitation (Guindon 1970) as well as to a method of intervention (Gendreau 1978).

Boscoville
A unique program introduced in the 1950s in Quebec that was based on a social welfare and psycho-educative model and that introduced elements in its program designed to teach delinquent youth the necessary skills, values, and attitudes that would allow them to develop a sense of social responsibility.

Box 15.1   Youth Justice in Action

Elements of the Boscoville Program

- Rehabilitation centre for delinquent teens ages 14 to 18 years
- Initiated as a summer camp toward the end of the 1940s
- Six groups of 15 adolescents in duplex-style apartments
- Staffed by trained educators who specialized in psycho-education (undergraduate- or master's-level education)
- Known as the birthplace of the psycho-educational treatment model and of psycho-education as a profession
- Program composed of activities addressing adolescent development, including academics, arts and crafts (theatre, ceramics, etc.), sports, group meetings; democratic means of engaging youths in collective arrangements, decisions, and individualized treatment; all activities aimed at achieving rehabilitation

Results of an evaluation conducted by Le Blanc (1983) showed that compared to similar programs, Boscoville resulted in lower recidivism rates than most other programs reviewed. For example, one year after attending the program, the adolescents who participated in the program had a 65 per cent rate of non-recidivism and showed significant improvement in their social functioning.

Critical Thinking Questions

What key elements of young offender programs can be identified in the Boscoville experience? How can/might these elements be linked to actual evidence-based practices?

The program at Boscoville contributed to psycho-education, one of its areas of specialty being the rehabilitation of troubled youth. The **psycho-education model** was unique to Quebec. This profession was created on the basis of several assumptions. The first assumption was that "love" was not sufficient for working with youth. Contrary to what is believed in some religious environments, this model proposed that the worker must be relatively competent in certain areas. Therefore, educators working with young offenders in the program had to develop specific competencies in order to intervene effectively (e.g., everyday life skills, the capacity to plan and direct rehabilitative activities, knowledge of normal and abnormal adolescent development, the ability to perform educational clinical evaluations and to conduct educational monitoring interviews). The second assumption was that re-education of young offenders must be integrated into every activity throughout the day and shared with the psycho-educator so that these youths would have a chance to change and take responsibility for their development. Intense interactions between the young offenders and the educator were seen as crucial for effective rehabilitation. This concept was new at the time, and there was resistance from both those who defended a more conservative concept—by limiting worker competencies and incorporating a dose of religious idealism and physical force—and those who were passionate about new therapeutic approaches. For the latter, it was important to offer competent workers who were capable of using psychotherapy with young people. Unfortunately, psychotherapy failed with these young persons (Trieschman, Brendtro, and Whittaker 1969).

Training for special educators working with young offenders and other troubled youth began to take shape with a program first developed at the University of Montreal.

psycho-educative model
Developed in Quebec, this model followed the Boscoville experience and is now recognized as a profession specializing in the intervention of troubled youth.

Today, five Quebec universities offer a bachelor's and master's degree in this area, and two of them dispense a doctorate in psycho-education (i.e., Université de Montréal and Université du Québec à Trois-Rivières).

Since 2000, psycho-education has been recognized and structured by a professional organization. The model used for the psycho-educative intervention has been the subject of both qualitative and quantitative research (see Szabo and Le Blanc 1994). This research was conducted over a 10-year period and evaluated the effects of programs used in open custody. Le Blanc (1983) showed that the Boscoville process, in using the psycho-educative intervention model, was able to create a positive social atmosphere. In other words, the social situation is a countervailing force on the negative effects of the delinquent subculture, and it is often created in environments where young offenders are housed. The results of the study also showed that 68 per cent of the youths who participated in the program were not involved in any recidivist activity for up to one year. These results are among the most significant reported in the literature on intervention programs for young offenders. The research also showed how effective rehabilitation programs can be in comparison to the absence of specific interventions and to strict detention. In fact, only 10 per cent of young offenders who appeared before a youth court and were placed in detention centres without rehabilitation programs did not recidivate within the year following the end of their sentence compared to the 68 per cent from the program who did not.

Another important contributor to the differential perspective for treating youth is the Philippe-Pinel Institute (see Box 15.2), which is a psychiatric penitentiary hospital with a special unit for teens with mental health problems associated with their delinquency. In the 1960s, some judges and political authorities made it possible for young offenders who had committed homicide to be integrated into the rehabilitation program. This practice made it clear that it was possible to re-educate even these young offenders in open custody with intervention programs adapted to their needs and societal expectations. Approximately 10 young offenders participated in this experiment throughout the 1960s. Most youths convicted of murder took part in Boscoville's internal program for three to five years, followed by two to three years of support in the community while they were being reintegrated into society. Both social adaptation and non-recidivism proved to be a success (Boisvert, Bisaillon, and Adam 1988; Ducharme 1999).

Research at the Philippe-Pinel Institute showed how important the differential intervention concept is when attempts were made to rehabilitate young offenders. Clearly, the intervention model used at Boscoville had many positive effects for some teen delinquents. According to Le Blanc (1983), the program was more effective with youth offenders presenting neurotic disorders (e.g., anxiety) than with highly criminalized teens presenting psychopathic disorders. However, it was not effective enough for certain types of offenders. This convinced researchers of the need to create a new generation of intervention programming whereby the type of program would match the type of young offender. This differential perspective has prevailed in many innovative attempts since the early 1990s (see Le Blanc, Dionne, Grégoire, Proulx, and Trudeau-Le Blanc 1998; Cournoyer and Dionne 2007). The results of the various studies on the psycho-educative model

Box 15.2   Youth Justice in Action

The Philippe-Pinel Institute

Established in 1970, the Philippe-Pinel Institute is
1. A forensic psychiatric hospital.
2. A leading-edge evaluation and treatment facility for forensic psychiatry. Multidisciplinary teams treat patients suffering from severe mental health disorders who pose threats to society. These teams apply treatment programs designed to address specific mental health disorders among adults. The facility also houses a special unit for adolescents that is dedicated to offering forensic evaluation and rehabilitation beyond the capacity of youth centres.
3. A research centre studying mental health disorders with the purpose of enhancing evaluation and treatment methods. For instance, since the

1970s, the Philippe-Pinel Institute's team and its associated researchers have produced numerous studies and reports on prisoners and mental health problems, as well as on the characteristics, treatment, and personalities of sexual abusers, murderers, and other types of aggressors.

Critical Thinking Questions

What are the main motives for referring youth offenders to a forensic psychiatric hospital? Why is it important to be able to evaluate and assess young persons suspected of needing such services?

applied at Boscoville convinced many authorities that rehabilitation with rigorous and well-implemented programs is necessary. Like Boscoville, institutions were interested in applying the best practices developed elsewhere. For example, inspired by Boscoville, many tried using the Interpersonal Maturity Levels Theory for young offenders for the first time as a model of differential intervention. This typology, developed in the United States (Sullivan, Grant, and Grant 1957) was used to assess different levels of maturity that are associated with modes of reaction and for which a specific intervention can be put in place. This was the groundwork for the first attempts at differential intervention (see Warren 1966). Early in the 1970s, researchers became involved with intervention centres and contributed to their development and implementation in Quebec. Other factors and events, including the evolution of secure-custody interventions, were also partly responsible for improving the service delivery system for young offenders in Quebec.

The Transformation of Secure-Custody Intervention

By the mid-1970s, Montreal had a detention centre with a structure similar to that of a prison, called le Centre Berthelet. In 1975, a riot broke out and many young offenders were injured and the buildings were ransacked and set on fire. The riot attracted considerable media attention and prompted an important reorganization of the centre. This reorganization had an enormous influence on how other secure-custody centres in the province operated. Although change and reform were gradual, the process leading up to change provided new knowledge about the conditions necessary to support rehabilitative efforts within a secure-custody centre.

Even though Martinson (1974) and some of his supporters believed that "nothing works" with offenders, Boscoville and other programs contradicted that view and confirmed that rehabilitation was possible in open custody. For high-recidivism-risk teens requiring secure custody, however, rehabilitation was still thought to be impossible. Besides initiatives such as that by Agee (1979) in the United States, few attempts at rehabilitation have been recorded in such environments. After the Berthelet riot, a new team of directors took over the centre. They changed its name to Cité des Prairies and concentrated restructuring efforts on putting in place a rehabilitation program that could satisfy the needs of youth offenders as well as the need for public protection. The main guidelines were as follows:

1. *To take the necessary means to find competent and well-trained employees.* The hiring process for the management, educators, and security staff was rigorous. The selection was completed through a continuous training mechanism for all the staff. This exhaustive process of changing the organizational culture favoured rehabilitation over physical control and confinement.

2. *To implement programs with activities intent on socializing the clientele and inspired by intervention methods proven to be effective.* This second principle led to the implementation of a program with academic, sport, and art activities that emphasized rehabilitation. The program included an individual clinical support process for each young offender that consisted of a thorough psychosocial assessment, an individualized intervention plan, regular educative sessions, as well as meetings with the family/guardians. In addition, a series of activities supported a harmonious social reinsertion for each youth.

3. *To establish an adequate equilibrium between dynamic and static security.* Secure-custody institutions are preoccupied with static security—that is, the physical control of the incarcerated person—comprising different dimensions such as the height of the walls, locks on doors, the use of surveillance cameras, and the presence of security guards. **Dynamic security** is ensured by the relational dimension within the institution. In a secure-custody rehabilitation centre, dynamic security is achieved by the constant presence of educators and the bonds built between the youths and the educators. As a result, the quality of the social climate is improved among peers, which in turn contributes to the security of the institution. While the new centre was being reorganized, tensions ran high for several months between the security staff and the educators, who were securing their relationships with the youths to ensure the dynamic security. This tension demanded efforts and dialogue to resolve conflicts between the two parties and to find a new equilibrium between rehabilitation practices and the necessity of a certain level of physical control (Le Blanc 1991).

dynamic security
Security that is ensured by the relational dimension. It is achieved by the constant presence of educators and the bonds built between the youths and them. As a result, the quality of the social climate is improved among peers, who in turn contribute to the security of the institution.

After a few years of difficult teamwork, the concept materialized and transformed the centre, which had a major influence on new centres that were being implemented or on existing ones that were being reorganized in the province. The Cité des Prairies was transformed into a secure-custody centre for young offenders. It was the first demonstration of the feasibility of modifying the marginalized and delinquent subculture known to prevail in prisons and detention centres and transforming it into a pro-social subculture that valued rehabilitation and was able to counter the iatrogenic effects felt in secure-custody establishments.

Unfortunately, it was not possible to evaluate the results on a large scale as was done at Boscoville (Borgo 1987). However, researchers have observed positive effects of this reorganization on the organizational culture as well as a change in behaviour among the clientele (Le Blanc et al. 1998).

The Evolution of Community Intervention

Since the early 1960s in Quebec, there has been enormous progress in community follow-up methods, whether the offender is on probation or under an extrajudicial measure. In the past, the justice department took care of the intervention while the youth offenders were on probation, and there was no difference between services for adults or for young offenders. Probation officers were responsible for a great number of cases (approximately 100 per caseworker), which did not encourage meaningful intervention. Interventions were more or less intermittent in their effectiveness. The transfer of juvenile probation services to the Ministry of Health and Social Services (Ministère de la Santé et des Services sociaux du Québec) in 1976 marked a turning point in the philosophy and means of intervention. From then on, juveniles on probation received intensive services based on supervision, monitoring, and guidance as well as help and counselling. The YOA brought about an important expansion in the development of clinical interventions during probation, and there was an awareness of the "right measures at the right time." Youth centres invested in training for their staff, notably on evaluation tools (e.g., the Jesness Inventory, which is a short 55-question survey that measures a number of different asocial tendencies); on intervention models, such as reality therapy (Glasser 1990); on the rational emotive approach (Ellis and Dryden 1997); or on the implementation of the Interpersonal Maturity Theory (Sullivan, Grant, and Grant 1957; Warren 1966, 1969).

The 1990s began with different intensive probation experiments in Quebec. Results from research projects carried out in the United States (Armstrong and Altshuler 1991) and Great Britain made this possible. The first documented experiment for which there was a formal evaluation was done by Quebec's Youth Centre (Piché and Fréchette 1995). Others in Montérégie, Estrie, and Montreal followed.

Research conducted in Ontario and elsewhere in Canada on the risk-need-responsivity model for offender assessment and rehabilitation (Andrews and Bonta 1998), as well as some experiments on intensive supervision in probation and parole (Armstrong and Altshuler 1991; Gendreau, Coggin, and Fulton 2000), inspired studies of intensive probation follow-ups with treatment for offenders presenting moderate to high risks of recidivism (Cournoyer and Dionne 2007). The research showed that the program significantly lowered the risks of criminal recidivism of the youths. In fact, 76 per cent of those who participated in the program had not recidivated one year after they completed the program. This study led to the implementation in 2009 of a new pilot program of intensive differential follow-up (sid or "suivi intensif différencié") for youths associated with gangs in Montreal, which has been under evaluation since 2011 (see http://www.securitepublique.gc.ca/cnt/rsrcs/pblctns/prgrm-sv-ntsf/index-fra.aspx, accessed 12 December 2014).

In addition to the efforts made to improve rehabilitation methods in institutions and to the rigorous community follow-up for moderate to high-risk offenders, there was also an opportunity to create community interventions with lower-risk offenders. These represented the first steps in creating alternative justice agencies.

The alternative justice measures were significantly influenced by one of the first projects called Projet Intervention Jeunesse de Montréal (Montreal's Youth Intervention Project), which was carried out from 1977 to 1979. The project's aim was to help young offenders avoid the judiciary process by offering alternative solutions: community work, direct reconciliation with the victim, paying for damages, or participation in measures that would improve social aptitudes. These options were proposed as alternative measures to prosecution, particularly as a consequence of the implementation of Chapter 40 of the Act of Youth Protection from 1979 to 1984 in Quebec. In some ways, as described earlier in the chapter, it is possible to say that the Alternative Measures Program, elaborated in 1984 within the framework of the YOA, has its roots in these projects.

The Evolution of Criminological Research

Another important factor in keeping young offenders out of Quebec prisons was the dynamics of the research in criminology, psychology, psycho-education, social work, and, at times, psychiatry (see Szabo and Le Blanc 2004). These studies shed light on youth characteristics, their evolution, and the characteristics of institutions for minors and the effects of their intervention programs (Le Blanc et al. 1998).

As mentioned earlier, open-custody research, conducted by Le Blanc (1983), and the study of the trajectories of 400 criminalized delinquents done by Le Blanc and Fréchette (1989) helped distinguish between "common" delinquency and "distinctive" delinquency. These notions are the basis for the differential intervention model used in many Quebec youth centres. According to these authors, common delinquency is committed by a large number of teens and represents an epiphenomenon that is part of the developmental process in teens. The results of the studies show that most youth commit an infraction in the process of exploring their social environment without their actions being due to important personal, family, or social deficits (also see Chapters 9 and 10 in this textbook). Even though common delinquency is not usually a serious or repetitive commission of delinquent gestures, some acts are serious or repetitive. Intervention involving education, awareness, and the repairing of damages can provoke feelings of responsibility if one is dealing with "conventional" teens who have the necessary acquired knowledge and experience for adequate social development. Taking into account the potential the majority of teens have for social adaptation, even without intervention, this type of delinquency usually disappears by itself (Le Blanc and Fréchette 1989). Using youth court with this type of delinquency appears unnecessary and even abusive.

The second category of delinquency deals with crimes that are more repetitive and that become a lifestyle that continues to more advanced stages. This includes about 5 per cent of youth. Making the distinction between the transition of young offenders exhibiting a typical personality development process and real criminal activities that appear at the same age is essential for intervention. Therefore, adolescent young offenders demand a particular approach that is focused on their needs during their personal and social development phase. This type of delinquency, described in studies done by Fréchette and Le Blanc (1987), is qualified as "distinctive" delinquency. It is distinctive because of the important personality deficits identified in these young offenders and is characterized by a behavioural state in which the offensive gestures appear early, persist, are abundant, and are serious. Even though this type of offending is present in only a limited number of teens, it still represents an important part of offences committed by young persons. The behaviour associated with this type of delinquency is diverse and includes serious offences.

Differential intervention is based on identifying the type of young offender by the behavioural, social, and psychological course that the young person takes. Making a distinction between common and distinctive delinquency is fundamental to the intervention measures taken with young offenders. One does this by taking into account the delinquent conduct and the teen's personality and by confirming one's conclusion on the basis of a psychosocial assessment. As previously mentioned, this evaluation aims to match the right intervention, at the right moment, with the right person.

Today's Services for Young Offenders

Over the past 40-odd years in Quebec, services for young offenders have been under the responsibility of Health and Social Services. Youth rehabilitation centres, social service centres, and youth protection centres joined forces in 1993. At the same time, 16 youth centres were created throughout the province of Quebec. These centres, under the YPA, the YCJA, the Act Respecting Health Services and Social Services (Loi sur le système de santé et les services sociaux), and the Civil Code of Quebec, offer juveniles and their parents psychosocial services and rehabilitation. In each of the youth centres, a director of youth protection (DYP), named according to the Youth Protection Act Quebec, is responsible for receiving reports concerning a child who may have his or her security or development compromised as a result of physical or sexual abuse, neglect, psychological cruelty, abandonment, or serious behavioural problems. The DYP is also responsible for evaluating the reports and proposing either voluntary measures or court measures to address and ameliorate the situation, as indicated previously in this chapter. When the YOA came into effect in Quebec in 1984, the duties accorded to the provincial director (PD) under the Act were devolved to the DYPs of the province. This disposition was maintained under the YCJA. Therefore, the PD is responsible for applying many aspects of the YCJA. To do so, she or he delegates authority to a number of people. These delegated individuals work, for the most part, in one of the 16 youth centres in the province.

In addition to the youth centres, Quebec provides a network of community centres. These centres are under the authority of the Ministry of Health and Social Services of Quebec and are mainly concerned with how teens become reconciled with their victims or the community for their wrongdoings. Known as alternative justice agencies, they are united in a provincial organization and are the first to collaborate with the youth centres in applying the YCJA. Centres can be found throughout Quebec, and they all offer the same types of services. Services offered for extrajudicial sanctions are determined by an agreement between the alternative justice agencies and the youth centres that standardizes the underlying philosophy for intervention and how the roles are assigned.

Quebec is a vast province composed of different regions, each with its own characteristics. No matter where the adolescent lives, however, he or she will receive roughly the same service with the same rehabilitation perspective. The PD, under the Quebec's Youth Centres Association and after enforcement of the YCJA, reaffirmed a number of statements of principles that guide staff working with youth throughout the province. The following section will briefly describe the steps for applying the Act by specifying each clinical position supported by the PDs and Quebec's YCJA working group. This group produced a reference manual guiding the application of the YCJA in youth centres (Hamel and Paradis 2004) that is based on the scientific literature and on the values derived from the evolving services.

Extrajudicial Measures

Police Measures

The YCJA introduced a preliminary step that was referred to as "exchange measures." Under the Act, it was considered that a certain number of youth who committed offences could benefit from measures applied directly by the police. Besides the possibility of laying charges, the police could decide to not apply any measure, to give a warning, or to direct the adolescent to a community centre where measures would be taken. The inter-ministerial committee of the YCJA in Quebec prepared a framework for these measures before implementing the law. The framework anticipates the type of offence and the measures that are necessary according to the severity of the offence, to traces of the offences left in the youth's police file (Centre Renseignement Policier Québec), and to the role each partner plays in applying measures (i.e., police officers, prosecutors, alternative justice agencies, and provincial director). The framework also includes allowances for regional committees under the authority of the PD who follows its progress. The alternative justice agencies take care of some of the measures for teens referred by the police. Most of these measures are information and awareness programs on shoplifting, drugs, law reinforcement, and so on. Though non-participation has no consequences, since 2003 young offenders in Quebec have participated in significant numbers.

Extrajudicial Sanctions

As mentioned in the previous section, extrajudicial measures define some offences for which the young offender can be held liable for criminal and penal prosecution. All other offences are referred to the PD for evaluation and implementation of the possible extrajudicial sanctions. Every youth centre has staff dedicated to this task. Staff members meet the adolescent and the parents for a brief evaluation of the circumstances surrounding the offence, the adolescent's situation, and his or her personal and social functioning. If possible, the provincial director's delegate proposes a measure to the youth. The outline of the agreement in alternative justice agencies–youth centres anticipates that before the delegate carries out the evaluation, the alternative justice agency contacts the victim. That way, when meeting with the adolescent, the delegate has the victim's point of view regarding the damage and can consider measures to address the damage that are suitable for the youth. The agreement in question also provides for a hierarchy of measures: the first measure allows some damage repair for the victim, but if that is not possible, repairing the damage in terms of the community would be considered. While the responsibility for evaluation and orientation resides with the professionals at the youth centres, the alternative justice agency sets the conditions so that the adolescent can carry out the measures.

During the evaluation process, the youth delegate must determine whether the youth is considered normal in terms of social and psychological development (i.e., determine if the youth is manifesting common delinquency) (Fréchette and Le Blanc 1987) and whether applying an extrajudicial measure appears sufficient to assist the young person. If the evaluation of the situation surrounding the minor (e.g., prior offences, behaviour, and social and psychological difficulties) leads the delegate to believe that she or he is getting into distinctive delinquency (ibid.), the delegate can choose to return the case to the prosecutor and legal action may then be taken with measures geared toward establishing a structure and path that will discourage delinquency.

This program has been in place since 1984, and recent annual statistics collected by the PD between 2003 and 2014 indicate that approximately 93 per cent of young offenders with extrajudicial sanctions have successfully carried out the measures imposed. Although these results are encouraging, further studies on young offenders returning to the justice system are needed to get a better sense of what these numbers mean. However, since the YCJA came into effect, the program has been used much less. The number of evaluations/orientations done by the PD dropped from 10,383 in 2002 to 7525 in 2007 (Ministry of Health and Social Services 2008). In the annual PD report of 2013–14, it is reported that 5156 evaluations/orientations were done. This drop might be a result of the fact that many prospective cases included provisions dictated by the police. This introduces at least two problems: first, the decisions taken by police are not based on psychosocial assessments or on the risk of recidivism; and second, the decisions generally do not consider the victim's opinion or measures aimed at repairing damages.

The Role of Social Proceedings in Provisional Detention: The Liaison Services in Place and Supervision before Sentencing

Youth Centres in many parts of Quebec have implemented liaison mechanisms with the judicial services. In most regions, a youth delegate must liaise with the prosecutor and with youth centre services. The delegate handles the evaluations requested by the prosecutor, the reports demanded by the court, and the rulings involving the PD. These services allow the exchanges to run more efficiently and effectively. The judicial system is thus ensured that requests sent to the PD arrive quickly and that rulings are applied the day they come into effect.

As well as conducting the liaison service, most youth centres, under Health and Social Services, implement voluntary services for adolescents and their parents before the adolescents go to court. For example, when a young person is released, support and concrete help are offered to both the parents and the adolescent. In particular, in cases of family violence, where the family is in crisis and requires immediate help, youth centres provide educative support or temporarily lodge the adolescent in another environment. Whether the program is referred to as "rapid intervention for delinquency" (*intervention rapide en délinquance*) or "follow-up programs before sentencing" (*programme de suivi avant peine*), it allows for rapid intervention and often prevents further deterioration of a potentially explosive family situation (Duret 2004).

The Pre-sentence Reports

The Youth Tribunal can request a pre-sentence report if more clarification of the case is required before making a ruling. If necessary, the court asks the PD to file the pre-sentence report. As well as answering the judge's questions to assist in the ruling, the report will trace the young person's differential profile and suggest measures according to his or her needs and the perceived risk of recidivism. To further the goals of the differential intervention perspective, youth centres train their staff to use clinical tools that allow them to establish the youth's profile and situation so that they can suggest the measures most likely to positively affect recidivism and rehabilitation. The pre-sentence report deals with the elements related to the present and past history of the adolescent's delinquency, including early manifestations of delinquent episodes, aggravation, polymorphism, and persistence. The report will also determine whether the offence(s) are premeditated and organized, whether the youth is alone or involved in some type of organized group, and so forth. In addition to mentioning the behavioural variables, the report will also provide information about the youth's social history, including family history, school records, working experiences, leisure activities, friends, and present and past social life, to assess the youth's social capacities as a basis for intervention. Finally, the psychological profile will be informed by observations made during interviews, through information given by the parents, or through psychometric testing. The tools most often used in Quebec are the Jesness Personality Inventory, a research version of the Youth Level of Service-Case Management Inventory (Hoge and Andrews 1994), and the Crimino-Metric Grid (Piché and Fréchette 1995). These tools allow a better assessment of the youth's risk level and criminal capacity, as well as help to identify potential protective factors (i.e., his or her social capacity).

In Quebec, a pre-sentence report is always accompanied by a series of recommendations made by the youth delegate. The recommendations typically include measures thought to have a real impact on recidivism and on the youth's ability to reintegrate back into society.

Sentence Follow-Ups

Whether the pre-sentence measures involve follow-up in the community or in custody, clinical intervention undertaken by the PD is systematic. Before examining specific aspects of each measure, the PD will examine the general characteristics of the clinical intervention for the young offender in youth centres.

A Planned Intervention

The Quebec legislation on Health and Social Services mandates participation in developing an intervention plan for anyone who receives services from any Health and Social Services organization. No client subject to the YCJA is exempt from this intervention plan. The plan must be signed by the young person and his or her parent(s) or guardian and is subject to review every six months.

Community intervention necessarily requires the young offender to respect various conditions. There is a need for clinical and legal conditions. The youth must participate in the clinical structure, which includes pro-social activities as well as activities that help him or her learn new skills. The youth offender's family is also integrated into the intervention. The aim is to help parents and guardians take control over the family structure and learn to resolve conflict. Intervention plans are also prepared if the young offender is in custody. In such cases, the intervention plan clarifies the work that the youth must undertake while in custody as well as the responsibilities of the youth delegate in contact with the parent(s) or guardian(s). Intervention of this kind is re-adaptive, not repressive, and continues to protect society.

An Individualized Intervention: The Differential Approach

A well-judged intervention is based on an extensive assessment that measures the criminal risks as well as the adolescent's personal and social strengths and weaknesses. Such an intervention will be modulated to fit the adolescent's specific characteristics, and the intensity of the support, supervision, and control will vary depending on the type of offender.

A Specialized Intervention

Whether follow-up is in the community or in custody, intervention with young offenders is completed by a psychosocial or rehabilitation professional. Criminologists, social workers, psycho-educators, and special educators may work with the young offender in youth centres. Throughout their career, qualified staff members receive training on evaluation tools and intervention approaches or models. The intervention is, therefore, very specialized and structured according to rigorous practice standards.

Follow-up in the Community

A number of provisions in the YCJA (Chapters 102 to 109) allow for follow-up in the community through a court order. The most commonly used provision is probation. According to the Quebec guide on juvenile probation (Piché 2006, p. 26), probation is defined as "a judicial measure of re-socialization which at the same time guarantees public protection and endeavours to establish personal social functionality of the youth offender . . . while ensuring structure and assistance . . . so he can learn to adjust to the requirements of life in society." Probation, therefore, unites control and support to facilitate the development of the skills the young offender needs to enhance his or her social capacity while controlling the temptation to engage in criminal activity.

Probation follow-up normally consists of interventions that impose conditions in order to control the adolescent and of clinical measures such as addressing social obligations—going to school, working, and participating in structured leisure activities or clinical group activities. Intervention will also offer support and assistance, since it aims to help the teen's efforts toward social integration. Probation can consist of regular group and individual meetings at a local probation office. The nature of the follow-up depends on the young offender's identified needs and criminal risk. For example, in Montreal, a tool is available that helps make decisions about the intensity of the services needed; services can go from one meeting every two weeks for regular probation to at least three direct interventions a week for those following an intensive differential program (Laporte 2005).

In addition to providing support for the youth, the delegate also offers support to the parents or guardians. This "wraparound" service is designed to defuse conflicts between the parents and their child.

When appropriate, the surrounding community will also be involved in the intervention. Whether it is at school, at work, or during leisure activities, the delegate will mobilize surrounding resources to collaborate in restructuring and supporting the adolescent. Indeed, some measures embedded in the YCJA (e.g., Chapter 42) imply follow-up in the community. Examples include the obligation to participate in an intensive program offering support and supervision; deferred custody and supervision; and post-custody supervision. The intervention method and the objectives of these measures are the same as in probation but are intensified because those adolescents subjected to these measures generally have a higher criminal risk.

Only a few regions in Quebec (e.g., Quebec City and Montérégie) have developed support and supervision programs approved by the PD. Although there is a lack of approval for these programs in other regions, all youth centres are able to offer intense follow-up in the community. The organization and resources of these services, however, vary from one region to another. In Montreal, for example, intervention cells consisting of several members who work together allow them to do a more intensive intervention in a community follow-up program.

Placements under Custody

Every youth centre has a number of units reserved for youths held in provisional detention or in secure custody. Adolescents placed in open custody are placed in resources that are, in many regions, dedicated to teens who present serious behavioural problems, such as those under the Youth Protection Act.

The young offenders placed in secure custody are confined to a physical space that they cannot leave without permission. Youths placed in secure custody are subject to having to participate in a rehabilitation program that aims to increase their awareness and to make changes to their modes of thinking and behaving. Often based on a psycho-educative model, the program consists of a variety of elements that create equilibrium between different mediums and, therefore, allows the adolescent to develop skills in many different areas. Schooling is mandatory, whether it is an academic program or is in preparation for integration into the labour force. Participating in activities in order to complete social and personal development is also mandatory: sports, artistic expression, and activities to develop social competencies. Every moment of the day is employed to facilitate rehabilitation.

In addition, there are also group clinical activities aimed at teaching social skills, anger management, problem-solving, moral reasoning, and empathy development. The program also touches on the issue of drug consumption through group or individual activities.

Quebec's Guidelines for Youth Offenders' Rehabilitation

In Quebec, the PDs recommend differential intervention at each level of intervention. The introduction of Bill C-7 in penal law for adolescents provoked an uproar in the province. Quebec was for the most part opposed to the federal government's wish to modify the foundations of the YOA. An important coalition of professionals from the justice department, social and community services, universities, and professional associations like the Quebec Bar manifested their opposition to the bill. Particularly, representatives from both the justice department and the social networks who work daily with young offenders were concerned about the impact this new bill could have. Principles like "sentencing" were introduced, inspired by rules that had usually been applied only to adults, thus facilitating the subjection of teens to adult sentencing. Specifically, introducing the idea that the sentence should be proportionate to the gravity of the offence as a guiding principle in determining the sentence was in total opposition to the approach used in Quebec (Trépanier 2004). As was indicated earlier, Quebec's approach encouraged an assessment of the situation that the adolescent was living in, including the offence, its gravity, and the circumstances of its perpetration, but also the psychosocial and developmental aspects of the adolescent.

In Quebec, it was agreed that the YOA was excellent and the foundations of its principles should be maintained. If there were problems, they were most likely related to its enforcement. A few amendments would have been sufficient to correct it. In reaction to Bill C-7, the Quebec government requested that the Quebec Court of Appeal pronounce on the legality of certain aspects of the bill. Thus, on 5 September 2001, the Quebec government adopted Decree 1021-2001 concerning an amendment to the Court of Appeal relating to Bill C-7 and its penal justice for adolescents. This decree asked the court to examine questions related to the bill's conformity to the United Nations agreement on children's rights, to the international pact of civil and political rights, and to rights guaranteed by clause 7 and paragraph 15(1) of the Canadian Charter of Rights and Freedoms.

On 31 March 2003, the Quebec Court of Appeal pronounced its verdict. To answer the questions of the decree, it ruled that the clauses on sentencing proposed with articles 38 to 82 did indeed infringe on the rights guaranteed by clause 7 and paragraph 15(1) of the Canadian Charter of Rights and Freedoms. This ruling was based on the rules of presumption, which would send juveniles to the penal justice system as adults at the age of 14. This was also true for the presumption of exceptions to confidential information when an adolescent is subjected to adult sentencing or to presumption related to this type of sentencing. The Supreme Court also declared that presuming an adult sentence in the ruling of *R. v. D.B.*, 2008 C.S.C. 25 was unconstitutional.

Even though these rulings declared certain dispositions on subjecting adolescents to adult sentencing unconstitutional in Quebec, those involved in intervention remained concerned. The dispositions targeted a minority of the youth involved with the penal justice system, but for the majority, the dispositions of the YCJA applied completely. For example, the priority given by the YCJA to the principle of sentence proportionality and the criteria limiting the recourse for custody go against the principle of the right measure at the right moment at the right time, which, in turn, imposes a series of measures based only on the nature of the offence and its gravity and accords little importance to the adolescent's needs or criminal risk (see Chapters 3 and 4 of this text for further discussion). The effect of this approach delays the social service and judicial systems' ability to apply the right measure at the right time. The right measures applied too late in the lives of teens are less likely to result in positive change.

As mentioned previously, when the YCJA came into effect, the values and the principles at the base of the Quebec intervention model were confirmed and guided interventions with young offenders during the application of legal proceedings. The PDs recommended a clinical approach based on the differential assessment of each adolescent. The implementation of the YCJA in Quebec was based on two premises:

- The established Quebec young offender intervention model should be preserved.

- Advantage should be taken of all possibilities offered by the YCJA to preserve the psychosocial and rehabilitation interventions.

The PDs recommended that interventions with young offenders rely on the values and the clinical vision of the following principles:

- The young person is a developing individual who has not reached full maturity and thus has different needs from adults. The intervention must correspond to this state of development.

- The particular characteristics of each young person's situation have to be taken into account to provide the right service at the right time. For this, it is important that professionals working with the youth have the required skills. Young offenders need interventions with diversified approaches, methods, and resources. This principle highlights the need to adapt intervention to the nature and amplitude of the problem without a predetermined schedule.

- Rapid intervention is necessary, since the notion of time for an adolescent is significantly different from the adult's, particularly because changes happen rapidly during this phase of development. In the case of distinctive delinquency, pinpointing it early can be a turning point. It is necessary to intervene before the delinquent behaviour becomes entrenched.

- Parental involvement in intervention is essential. It must be sought out, valued, and supported throughout the intervention.

- The victims must be considered and the impact of the offence on them must be kept in mind. The young offender must be made aware of his or her actions and the damage caused. If appropriate, a process to repair damages must be proposed.

- Success of social intervention requires partners with the specific resources needed to confront the needs of the adolescent.

PDs consider the differential assessment of the young offender to determine services and to promote a differential approach during all phases of the intervention process. The assessment relies on the adolescent's delinquent trajectory and on his or her evolution in different areas of life. The assessment situates the risk of recidivism and identifies factors responsible for delinquency and its persistence. The differential assessment also helps determine the intensity and objective of the needed intervention in order both to protect the public and to resolve the adolescent's problems related to recidivism risk factors. Throughout the intervention, assessment must be continuous so that the intervention can be adjusted to the adolescent's evolution. This individualized approach allows the adolescent's needs to be prioritized during the intervention. To help reach targeted objectives, a choice of resources is established. As described earlier, Quebec has a network of community organizations with specialized staff who can offer young offenders a variety of quality services.

The differential assessment of young offenders is the foundation of all phases of intervention in delinquency: extrajudicial sanction programs, pre-sentence reports, community follow-up, custody and supervision in the community, reviews, and so on. As well, PDs support the use of a variety of clinical tools that contribute to systemizing data collection according to validated instruments and evaluating certain personality dimensions less accessible during interviews. Objectives of differential assessment include the following:

- to determine the adolescent's level of involvement in delinquency;

- to identify the factors contributing to delinquency;

- to determine the risk of recidivism;

- to assess the adolescent's resources and his/her capacity to benefit from available resources and services, as well as from those of his/her family;

- to identify the most appropriate services to prevent recidivism using supervision, monitoring, guidance, help, and counselling; and

- to establish intervention objectives.

Efforts to elaborate on principles that guide intervention for young offenders and to implement the necessary resources were spread out over the past 20-odd years and provided Quebec with a justice system and a system of intervention and rehabilitation that is recognized for its flexibility and efficiency.

The intervention model for young offenders and their families that is applied in Quebec youth centres can be summarized as follows:

- It is a differentiated intervention.

- It is based on a differential assessment of the young offender's situation.

- It is supported by known theories and validated clinical tools.

- It favours alternatives to judicial measures and prioritizes mediation with victims for adolescents presenting "common" delinquency.

- It uses the most appropriate measures within the judicial system of the YCJA to satisfy specific needs of adolescents with "distinctive" delinquency.

- It involves parents as well as the collaboration of community resources.

- It takes into account the victims' interests.

Summary

In 2011/12, next to Manitoba, Quebec had the second lowest custody rate (9 per cent versus 10 per cent respectively) of young offenders in Canada (Dauvergne 2013; also see Chapter 2). As a result, there have been a number of inquiries as to how and why Quebec has maintained one of the lowest custody rates and what (if any) the implications have been. Without comparing the evolution of the youth offender systems in other provinces to that of Quebec, it appears that many answers to these questions can be found in Quebec's unique cultural, social, and political history related to the evolution of approaches to young offenders. Most of what is presented in this chapter is intended to help provide insight into the opposition in Quebec to the YCJA when it was submitted, as well as to the amendment proposed in Bill C-4. There was also opposition to the YCJA elsewhere in Canada, especially from the Canadian Criminal Justice Association (1998).

From a historical standpoint, one of the first elements presented in this chapter was the implementation of modalities to take charge of youth offenders that were distinct from those for adults, in recognition of their different needs. In terms of Quebec, the JDA was another important moment regarding the history of the youth offender system (Dubois and Trépanier 1999). In the 1950s, a series of initiatives in Quebec demonstrated that it is possible to implement effective rehabilitation programs for youth offenders being held in open custody (Le Blanc 1983). The opening of the Philippe-Pinel Institute enabled the creation of specialized assessment and treatment programs for young offenders who presented with severe mental disorders. Throughout the 1970s, four events had a major impact on improving rehabilitation services for youth offenders in Quebec: (1) initiatives that tested alternative measures for young offenders; (2) the major reorganization of all social services; (3) the creation of social service centres; and (4) the Youth Protection Act of Quebec. Under the YPA, youth protection directors were appointed, and later, in the 1980s, they were mandated under the YOA. All of these events were significant in the development of today's services and today's philosophy behind the care of young offenders in Quebec.

Following the experiment in Boscoville, it became clear that one unique method of rehabilitation was not sufficient for all youth offenders. Research demonstrated the need to develop a differential perspective. As noted in the Jasmin II Report (1995), a consensus of all actors of the judicial and social service systems stated that it is possible to implement effective interventions that respect youth rights and offer the right measure at the right time. Assessments were recognized as fundamental in determining the best measures for young offenders. In addition to the provision of assistance to less serious types of young offenders, it became evident that there was a need to develop specialized programs for high-risk offenders. Programs involving intensive probation with treatment were then tested for youth offenders (offenders who would have normally been placed in custody) who were receptive to the intervention and who had families to support them and participate in the rehabilitation process.

Because of the YCJA's emphasis on the gravity of the offence and because the Act does not take into account the youth's needs, recourse to such a differential approach became almost impossible. For example, for professionals, it appeared it was no longer possible to direct young offenders who had committed serious offences to intensive follow-up programs in the community. The overall rigidity of the YCJA was one of the main reasons for Quebec's opposition to the Act. Specifically, it has been recognized for some time now that the offence for which a young person is arrested is rarely a realistic reflection of his or her criminal capacity or of his or her prior offences (Le Blanc 1986).

The development of psycho-education and criminology as professions also contributed to the improvement of practices and influenced the move toward the rehabilitation of young offenders in Quebec. The training given to the personnel working with youth offenders during the 1960s and 1970s was particularly important; indeed, most youth workers today have a university education in their field.

The principles associated with the rehabilitation of young offenders in Quebec have been supported by a meta-analysis (see Lipsey 2009). The "Quebec model" has also been supported by the research work of Canadian experts in the field. For example, Andrews and Bonta (2003) have documented the necessity of choosing the best measure when considering offenders' risk of recidivism, their criminogenic needs, and the most effective approach for treatment given their characteristics. Supported by research and reinforced by the historical evolution of measures for youth offenders in the province of Quebec, provincial directors, clinicians, researchers, politicians, and a large part of the Quebec population have opposed, and still firmly oppose, the YCJA, which, for them, gives too much importance to the gravity of the offence to the detriment of the adolescents' needs and capacity.

But is the position of Quebec really different from that of the rest of Canada? As cited by Trépanier (2004), the Federal-Provincial-Territorial Task Force on Youth Justice (1996) already exposed that important differences do exist between Quebec and the rest of Canada:

Quebec's approach to youth justice appears to be more in keeping with what is found in western European countries: the over-arching goal is the rehabilitation of young offenders within a framework that respects the rights of young persons. . . . Quebec's approach to youth justice cannot be simply transplanted to the rest of the country. Quebec's approach serves as an important reminder, however, that the apparent "need" to reform the Act is as much or more a function of values, attitudes and perceptions as it is of real (or objectifiable) needs.[3]

Is this still true? . . . History will speak for itself.

Key Terms

alternative justice agencies

Boscoville

differential intervention

dynamic security

extrajudicial programs

psycho-educative model

Review Questions

1. Explain why the expression "the right measure at the right time for the right person" is particular to Quebec.

2. Identify five measures applied in Quebec under the YCJA that exemplify the principle "the right measure at the right time for the right person."

3. How do you understand Quebec's opposition to the YCJA?

4. How does psycho-education apply to young offenders' rehabilitation?

5. Name seven characteristics of the intervention model used by Quebec's youth centres.

Critical Thinking Questions

1. After comparing this chapter to others in the book, do you have any information that demonstrates that Quebec's rehabilitation model is really different from that of other provinces?

2. How do you explain the difference in custody rate between Quebec and the rest of Canada?

3. After reading this chapter, do you consider that the precedence of social intervention over court intervention is justified?

4. Explain how the meta-analyses of the past decades on offenders' rehabilitation can justify Quebec's position toward the rehabilitation of youth offenders.

Endnotes

1. All custody measures in Quebec consist of a rehabilitation program that allows a series of systematic and intensive interventions and uses the most appropriate techniques to redirect the juvenile delinquent. In every rehabilitation centre, only trained professionals intervene, not the keepers or guardians.
2. Unofficial translation from excerpts of Ministère de la Justice et ministère de la Santé et des Services sociaux du Québec (1995): Les jeunes contrevenants: Au nom . . . et au-delà de la loi, rapport du groupe de travail chargé d'étudier l'application de la Lois sur les jeunes contrevenant au Québec (Rapport Jasmin II), pp. 36–7.
3. Fuller accounts can be found in McGuire 1997.

References

Agee, V.L. (1979). *Treatment of the violent incorrigible adolescent.* Lexington, MA: Lexington Books.

Andrews, D.A., and Bonta, J. (1998). *The psychology of criminal conduct* (2nd ed.). Cincinnati, OH: Anderson Publishing Co.

Andrews, D.A., and Bonta, J. (2003). *The psychology of criminal conduct* (3rd ed.). Cincinnati, OH: Anderson Publishing Co.

Armstrong, T.L., and Altshuler, P.M. (1991). *Intensive interventions with high-risks youths: Promising approaches in juvenile probation and parole.* Monsey, NY: Criminal Justice Press.

Association des centres jeunesse du Québec. (2014). *Bilan des directeurs de la protection de la jeunesse/directeurs provinciaux* (Results from directors of youth protection/provincial directors, Association of Youth Protectors of Quebec). Retrieved from http://www.acjq.qc.ca/public/a14178bc-45b5-4a12-b27e-38017be2da39/mes_documents/bilans/acj1402_bilan_2014_rev2.pdf

Boisvert, Y., Bisaillon, C., and Adam, J. (1988). *Les jeunes auteurs d'homicide: Rétrospective et prospective: L'expérience de Boscoville.* Montreal: Les Cahiers de Boscoville.

Borgo, J. (1987). Treating the violent offender. In J.M. MacLatchie (Ed.), *Insights into violence in contemporary Canadian society* (pp. 298–304). Ottawa: John Howard Society of Canada.

Canadian Criminal Justice Association. (1998). *Comments of the Canadian Criminal Justice Association on strategy for the renewal of youth justice.* Ottawa: Canadian Criminal Justice Association.

Capul, M., and Lemay, M. (1996). *De l'éducation spécialisée.* Paris: Érès.

Cournoyer, L.G., and Dionne, J. (2007). Efficacité du programme de probation intensive du centre jeunesse de Montréal-Institut Universitaire: La récidive officielle. *Criminologie, 40*(1): 155–83.

Dauvergne, M. (2013). Youth court statistics in Canada, 2011/12. Statistics Canada. Retrieved from http://www.statcan.gc.ca/pub/85-002-x/2013001/article/11803-eng.htm?fpv=2693

Dubois, P., and Trépanier, J. (1999). L'adoption de la loi sur les jeunes délinquants de 1908. Étude comparée des quotidiens Montréalais et Torontois. *Revue d'histoire de l'Amérique française, 52*(3): 345–81.

Ducharme, J. (1999). *Saute d'abord! Un parcours de trente-cinq ans en psychoéducation.* Montreal: Sciences et Culture.

Duret, A. (2004). LSJPA: La mobilisation du jeune et de ses parents dans le continuum de services aux jeunes contrevenants: Deuxième partie: Le projet intervention rapide en délinquance (Mobilization of the youth and the parents in the continuum of services to youth offenders: The rapid intervention project for delinquency). *Défi jeunesse, 10*(2): 8–13.

Ellis, A., and Dryden, W. (1997). *The practice of rational emotive behavior therapy.* New York: Springer.

Foucault, P. (1984). *Aider . . . malgré tout: Essai sur l'historique des centres de réadaptation au Québec.* Montreal: Les Éditions des centres d'accueil du Québec.

Fréchette, M., and Le Blanc, M. (1987). *Délinquances et délinquants.* Chicoutimi, QC: Gaëtan Morin.

Gendreau, G. (1978). *L'intervention psychoéducative: Solution ou défi?* Paris: Éditions Fleurus.

Gendreau, P., Coggin, C., and Fulton, B. (2000). Intensive supervision in probation and parole. In C.R. Hollin (Ed.), *Handbook of offender assessment and treatment* (pp. 195–204). Chichester, UK: John Wiley.

Glasser, W. (1990). *Reality therapy: A new approach to psychiatry.* New York: Harper Row.

Guindon, J. (1970). *Les étapes de la rééducation des jeunes délinquants et des autres.* . . .Paris: Fleurus.

Hamel, P., and Paradis, R. (2004). *L'application de la loi sur le système de justice pénale pour les adolescents dans les centres jeunesse: Manuel de référence* (Reference manual guiding the application of the Youth Criminal Justice Act in youth centres). Ministère de la santé et des services sociaux du Québec. Quebec: Gouvernement du Québec.

Hoge, R.D., and Andrews, D.A. (1994). *The youth level of service/Case management inventory and manual.* Ottawa: Department of Psychology, Carleton University.

Joyal, R. (2000). *L'évolution de la protection de l'enfance au Québec: Des origines à nos jours.* Sainte-Foy, QC: Presses de l'Université du Québec.

Laporte, C. (2005). *Suivi intensif différencié dans la communauté* (Differentiated intensive follow-up in the community) (unpublished manuscript). Montreal: Centre d'expertise sur la délinquance des jeunes et les difficultés du comportement, Centre jeunesse de Montréal–Institut universitaire.

Le Blanc, M. (1983). *Boscoville: La rééducation évaluée.* Montreal: HMH.

Le Blanc, M. (1986). Pour une approche intégrative de la conduite délinquante des adolescents. *Criminologie, 19*(2): 73–96.

LeBlanc, M. (1991). Juvenile justice in Quebec: The anatomy of legislative and administrative changes and their impact on dispositions. In J. Junger-Tas, L. Boendermaker, and P.H. van der Laan (Eds), *The future of the juvenile justice systems.* Leuven, Belgium: Acco.

Le Blanc, M., Dionne, J., Grégoire, J., Proulx, J., and Trudeau-Le Blanc, P. (1998). *Intervenir autrement: Un modèle différentiel pour les adolescents en difficulté.* Montreal: Les Presses de l'Université de Montréal.

Le Blanc, M., and Fréchette, M. (1989). *Male criminal activity from childhood through youth: Multilevel and developmental perspectives.* New York: Springer-Verlag.

Lipsey, M.W. (2009). The primary factors that characterize effective interventions with juvenile offenders: A meta-analytic overview. *Victims & Offenders, 4*(2): 124–47.

McGuire, M. (1997). C-19—An act to amend the Young Offenders Act and the Criminal Code: "Getting tougher?" *Canadian Journal of Criminology, 39:* 185–214.

Martinson, R. (1974). What works? Questions and answers about prison reform. *Public Interest, 35:* 22–54.

Ménard, S. (2003). Des enfants sous surveillance: La rééducation des jeunes délinquants au Québec (1840–1950). Montreal: VLB Éditeur.

Ministère de la Justice et Ministère de la Santé et des Services Sociaux du Québec. (1995). Les jeunes contrevenants: *Au nom . . . et au-delà de la loi* (In the name of the law and beyond it): *Rapport du groupe chargé d'étudier l'application de la loi sur les jeunes contrevenants au Québec (Rapport Jasmin II).* Quebec: Gouvernement du Québec.

Ministry of Health and Social Services. (2008). *Statistical annual report of youth centers* (AS-480 forms) (unpublished manuscript). Quebec: Ministère de la Santé et des Services sociaux.

Parizeau, A. (1976). Le droit des mineurs et l'emprisonnement des jeunes au Québec. *Criminologie, 9*(1–2): 118–47.

Piché, J.-P. (2006). *L'encadrement des jeunes contrevenants dans la communauté: Guide d'intervention en matière de probation juvénile.* Ministère de la Santé et des Services Sociaux (The follow-up of youth offenders in the community: Intervention guide in juvenile probation). Quebec: Gouvernement du Québec.

Piché, J-P., and Fréchette, M. (1995). *Mesure probatoire intensive pour adolescents contrevenants: Application et efficacité.* Quebec: Les Centres jeunesse de Québec.

Platt, A.M. (1997). *The child savers: The invention of delinquency.* Chicago: University of Chicago Press.

Redl, F., and Wineman, D. (1951). *Children who hate.* New York: Free Press.

Rumilly, R. (1978). *Boscoville.* Montreal: Éditions Fides.

Sullivan, C., Grant, M.Q., and Grant, J.D. (1957). The development of interpersonal maturity: Applications to delinquency. *Psychiatry, 20*(4): 373–95.

Szabo, D., and Le Blanc, M. (1994). *Traité de criminologie empirique.* Montreal: Les Presses de l'Université de Montréal.

Szabo, D., and Le Blanc, M. (2004). *Traité de criminologie empirique* (2nd ed.). Montreal: Les Presses de l'Université de Montréal.

Trépanier, J. (2004). What did Quebec not want? Opposition to the adoption of the Youth Criminal Justice Act in Quebec. *Canadian Journal of Criminology and Criminal Justice, 46*(3): 276–300.

Trieschman, A.E., Brendtro, L.K., and Whittaker, J.K. (1969). *The other 23 hours: Child-care work with emotionally disturbed children in a therapeutic milieu*. Piscataway, NJ: Transaction Publishers.

Warren, M.Q. (1966). *Interpersonal maturity level classification: Juvenile diagnosis and treatment for low, middle and high maturity delinquents*. Sacramento, CA: Youth Authority.

Warren, M.Q. (1969). The case for differential treatment of delinquents. *Annals of the American Academy of Political and Social Science, 381*: 47–59.

Juvenile Justice and Restorative Justice: Reflecting on Developments in British Columbia

Brenda Morrison and Colleen Pawlychka

Overview

This chapter focuses on the development of restorative justice in British Columbia (BC) within a wider theoretical and institutional analysis of justice reforms in BC and Canada. The chapter begins with broad reflections on juvenile justice practice and outcomes, suggesting that despite various legislative reforms the juvenile justice system remains focused on the juvenile as the bad apple within a system of social control. The theory and practice of restorative justice widens the humanistic lens of justice, moving from a mechanism of social control to one of social engagement. The chapter also reflects on legislation as well as diversionary restorative practices that have influenced developments in BC, particularly victim–offender reconciliation programs, circle sentencing, conferencing, and community accountability programs. The chapter then reflects on recent reforms in the United Kingdom and BC, and on Roca, an innovative youth-at-risk program based in Chelsea, Massachusetts. These reflections indicate that holistic reform within the Canadian juvenile justice system has yet to come because the justice system has yet to adequately embrace theoretical and practical research developments that have emerged internationally regarding potentially effective restorative justice programs, nested within responsive regulatory frameworks.

Key Objectives

After reading this chapter, you should be able to:

- Describe specific legislative changes to juvenile justice related to restorative justice.
- Describe the development of restorative justice in BC.
- Contextualize these developments in the context of state- and community-driven policy.
- Discuss Roca, a case study of effective community engagement.
- Provide a comparative case of why Canada, once at the forefront of restorative justice, now falls behind other countries.

Introduction

Over 25 years have passed since *Taking Responsibility*, a 1988 report authored by a House of Commons Justice Committee chaired by David Daubney (QC, MP), recommended the use and evaluation of restorative justice in Canada. The report stated that the "[c]ommittee found the evidence it heard across the country about the principles of restorative justice [RJ] compelling," and it recommended (No. 19) that governments, at all levels, support the expansion and evaluation of RJ programs at all stages of the criminal justice process (Daubney 2010). In particular, **victim–offender reconciliation programs (VORP)** were found to (a) provide substantial support to victims through effective victim services, and (b) encourage a high degree of community participation. In 1990, the *United Nations Minimum Standard Rules for Non-Custodial Measures* (i.e., the "Tokyo Rules") essentially echoed this recommendation through Rule 2.4, which called for greater use of alternatives (i.e., community-based measures) and complemented Rule 5 of the 1985 United Nations Standard Minimum Rules for the Administration of Juvenile Justice (i.e., the "Beijing Rules") (Winterdyk 2015).

In 1996, through the provision of reparations to victims and communities, Canada became the first country in the world to include restorative justice as a legitimate option within the Criminal Code (CC; see s. 718.2 (e)). Canada has a proud range of contributions to the development and expansion of **restorative justice (RJ)** programs and practices; however, programs and practices currently remain at the margins of the Canadian justice system, particularly when compared to developments in other countries. This chapter explores the history of the development of RJ as it relates to juvenile justice, using developments in BC as a case study.

victim–offender reconciliation programs (VORP)
A process through which a trained mediator, often a volunteer, brings offenders and victims in a criminal event together to achieve a resolution that is satisfactory to both parties (Community Justice Initiatives Association 2011; see also Stutzman Amstutz 2009).

restorative justice (RJ)
A process whereby all the parties with a stake in a particular offence resolve collectively how to deal with the aftermath of the offence and its implications for the future (Marshall 2003, p. 28).

Reconceptualizing "Crime"

In order to discuss practices of restorative justice in connection with legislative direction, we should first note that restorative justice practices differ from conventional practices primarily because crime itself is viewed from a fundamentally different perspective. In the conventional criminal (juvenile) justice literature, a crime is legally defined as a breach of a state-created criminal law (i.e., a breach of the CC), which can involve a person (or persons) or property. From a sociological perspective, crime is a breakdown/violation of formalized norms and/or values and a state's CC proscribes the appropriate punishment. Conversely, an RJ perspective views crime as a violation of people and relationships that creates obligations to repair harm to victims and communities (Zehr 1990); it thus focuses on responsibility and healing rather than on punishment. Accordingly, RJ advocates commonly use a less conflictual lexicon, including such terms as *harm*, *conflict*, *disputes*, and *broken social liaisons* to more accurately reflect the nature and tone of wrongdoing and a RJ conception of justice (see McLauglin, Fergusson, Hughes, and Westmerland 2003; Gavrielides and Artinopoulou 2013, pp. 344–8).

Juvenile Justice Legislation: Social Control to "Off Ramps"

Canada has come a long way since the Juvenile Delinquents Act (JDA) of 1908, under which youth were convicted of juvenile delinquency rather than of criminal behaviour and were considered to be misguided products of an improper upbringing by their family (Tustin and Lutes 2010; see also Chapter 1). Because youth were not considered responsible for their actions, the focus of conviction was on rehabilitation, re-education, and guidance, with the state taking over the parental role and decision-making of the youth.

Replacing the JDA in 1984, the Young Offenders Act (YOA) reflected then dominant societal views—specifically, that youth were responsible and should therefore be held accountable for their behaviours and crimes. While protecting youth by guaranteeing due process, this Act extended much the same treatment to youth as was extended to adults. Youth were referred to as offenders rather than as delinquents and were represented by counsel in court proceedings; moreover, similar to courts of adults, the courts dealing with young offenders were open to the public (Winterdyk 2015). Young offenders, like adult offenders, came to be viewed as the "bad apples" of society, and punishment, mainly in the form of custody—an institutional mechanism—was believed necessary to change their behaviours.

While the YOA increased the use of custody for young offenders, various societal factors contributed to the wide criticism that the justice system was not tough enough on them, overprotecting repeat offenders while allowing the increasing victimization of innocent, law-abiding citizens. Inaccurate or incomplete media reports of individual cases combined with misconceptions, even within the justice sector, eroded public confidence in the YOA, fuelling a public demand for a still more punitive response to youth crime (Tustin and Lutes 2010). By the 1990s, with youth crime decreasing and a public belief that levels were significantly increasing, there was "clearly . . . a gap between fact and public perception of youth crime levels" (Green and Healy 2003, p. 32). Accordingly, the use of custody increased until 1999, when Anne McLellan, then Canada's justice minister, declared that we "incarcerate youth at a rate of four times that of adults and twice that of many US states" (ibid., p. 32). In fact, Canada's youth incarceration rate was the highest in the Western world (see Winterdyk 2015).

Earlier chapters of this textbook (see in particular Chapter 3) outline specific provisions of the Youth Criminal Justice Act (YCJA 2003). We, therefore, highlight here only specific sections of the Act that are relevant to promoting the use of restorative justice measures and programs and providing legislative direction; in particular, the recognition that a range of factors—limited developmental capacity, education, mental health, family, and community—affect the behaviour of youth during a pivotal time of development and growth.

Specific restorative justice values that may be seen to underlie this legislation include the following:

- It is a societal responsibility to address the developmental challenges and needs of young persons in order to guide them into adulthood.

- Communities and families should work in partnership, through multidisciplinary approaches, to address crime prevention by addressing its underlying causes, providing guidance and support to young persons, particularly those at risk.

- Information regarding youth justice, crime, and measures taken to address youth crime should be publicly available.

- Young persons have rights and freedoms, including those set out in the United Nations Convention on the Rights of the Child, the Canadian Charter of Rights and Freedoms, and the Canadian Bill of Rights.

- The youth criminal justice system should command respect and take into account the interests of victims.

- The youth justice system should foster responsibility and ensure accountability through meaningful consequences and effective rehabilitation and reintegration.

- The youth justice system should reserve its most serious interventions for the most serious crimes and reduce over-reliance on incarceration. (Department of Justice 2002)

These general principles are outlined in the preamble of the Act; in essence, they reflect the acceptance of an approach that is consistent with restorative justice. For instance, the YCJA seeks to prevent crime by addressing the underlying circumstances of offending behaviours and by emphasizing rehabilitation and reintegration of young persons into society, with specific consideration given to the reduced level of maturity of young persons and their greater level of dependency on adults. Meaningful consequence for the young person(s) is the legislative directive that upholds accountability while being fair and proportionate to the crime.

The YCJA also makes specific provisions for young persons to be heard and involved in the processes that lead to decision-making. Finally, section 3(1) of the Act emphasizes that measures taken against young persons should

(c) (i) Reinforce respect for societal values;
(ii) Encourage the repair of harm done to victims and the community;

    (iii) Be meaningful for the individual young person given his or her needs and level of development and, where appropriate, involve the parents, the extended family, the community and social or other agencies in the young person's rehabilitation and reintegration; and

    (iv) Respect gender, ethnic, cultural and linguistic differences and respond to the needs of aboriginal young persons and of young persons with special requirements. (Department of Justice 2002)

Thus, although the YCJA makes no direct reference to restorative justice, there is general agreement that the Act "does seem to open the door to the development of initiatives generally associated with restorative justice" (Charbonneau 2005, p. 75). For example, numerous extrajudicial measures form an essential first response to youth crime rather than a possible alternative to court, as was the case under the YOA. That is, the Act requires that police and Crown attorneys consider extrajudicial measures, including informal warnings, police or Crown cautions, police referrals to community programs or agencies, referrals to pre-charge screening programs or youth justice committees, or conferences (Tustin and Lutes 2010; see also Chapters 3 and 4).

Two primary methods of allowing for restorative justice initiatives are the inclusion of victims in the process and the authorization of restorative justice conferences. Under section 5, the YCJA directs (in part) that extrajudicial measures must:

- encourage acknowledgement and reparation of harm to the victim and community;

- encourage families, including extended families, of young persons and the community to become involved in the design and implementation of those measures; and

- provide an opportunity for victims to participate in decisions related to the measures selected and to receive reparation.

The YCJA authorizes the use of conferences by a youth justice court judge, the provincial director, a police officer, a justice of the peace, a prosecutor or youth worker, or a youth justice committee. Defined in the YCJA, section 2(1), as "a group of persons who are convened to give advice in accordance with section 19," conferences refer to various types of processes in which affected or interested parties come together to formulate plans to "address the circumstances and needs involved" (Department of Justice Canada 2002, p. 6) and may take the form of "**family group conferencing**, youth justice committees, community accountability panels, **sentencing circles** and inter-agency case conferences" (Department of Justice Canada 2002, p. 6). The inclusion of conferences in the YCJA and the broad nature of their mandate allow for some restorative justice initiatives through the inclusion of victims in the process of reparation of harm and through the healing of young persons and communities.

With the requirement that extrajudicial measures, including RJ initiatives, be considered, there has been a decline in the number of young persons charged by police, "with a 30 per cent rate of youths cleared otherwise" since implementation of the YCJA (Tustin and Lutes 2010, p. 27). This indicates some measure of success in the YCJA

family group conferencing
". . . a process of collaborative planning in situations where decisions need to be made for children or youth. It is a formal meeting where members of a child or youth's immediate family come together with extended kin and members."
(Source: Ministry of Children and Family Development 2005, p. 2)

sentencing circles
"Sentencing circles . . . invite . . . members of the community to join the judge, prosecutor, defence counsel, police, social service providers, community elders, along with the offender, the victim and their families and supporters, [to] meet in a circle to discuss the offence, factors that may have contributed to it, sentencing options, and ways of reintegrating the offender into the community."
(Source: Department of Justice Canada 2002)

(see also Chapter 3 in this textbook for additional data in support of this argument). However, use of these extrajudicial measures is not mandatory; rather, police and Crown attorneys need only *consider* such measures in order to satisfy legislative requirements. Therefore, it is important to examine not only the reduction in charges but also the primary factors that play a role in police and Crown attorney decision-making regarding whether to divert these youth and where they should be diverted to. That is, given that the police and prosecutors play a key role in ensuring that youth are diverted out of the formal system (as noted in Chapter 4), there must be adequate "off ramps" toward which we can divert youth. These off ramps (referring to diversionary or extrajudicial measures) might include existing community programs, school mediation programs, or programs operated by local agencies. It is equally important that police and Crown attorneys support these initiatives and consider them to be the best possible avenue to hold the youth accountable. To this end, the reality is that despite the availability of numerous initiatives within communities, programs tend to be widely used and recognized only if they are endorsed by the attorney general, to whom Crown attorneys are accountable (Tustin and Lutes 2010, p. 30).

Despite legislative changes that have influenced RJ initiatives, particularly within BC, the evidence suggests that these legislative changes alone are not enough (Representative for Children and Youth [RCY] 2014a; Representative for Children and Youth 2014b). In fact, recent reports find that "it is still not possible to say with certainty whether things are getting better for BC's vulnerable children and youth" (RCY 2014a, p. 5).

The Development of Restorative Justice in BC: The Intersection of Three Practices

Victim–Offender Reconciliation Programs

The evolution of youth and adult restorative justice initiatives in BC are intertwined, and therefore the following discussion includes both adult and youth developments. The RJ movement in Canada traces its inception in part to a landmark 1974 juvenile justice case in Elmira, Ontario, which launched the Kitchener Experiment (see Peachey 1989), where two young men destroyed the property of 22 victims. The courageous and insightful decisions and actions of Mark Yantzi, a Mennonite probation officer, and Judge Gordon McConnell set a precedent for a new response to juvenile delinquency in Canada. Officer Yantzi, with the support of Dave Worth of the Mennonite Central Committee, recommended in his pre-sentence report that the offending juveniles be ordered to knock on the doors of their victims, apologize for their crimes, listen to what the victims had to say, determine from the victims the amount of restitution, and ask for forgiveness. Judge McConnell saw no legal precedence for ordering these actions by the juveniles. Officer Yantzi, weighing the benefits offered by the court with those of a face-to-face meeting with the victims, spoke with the juveniles, convincing them that volunteering to perform these acts of restoration would allow the judge to include them as part of a probation order. The youth volunteered. Russ Kelly (2010) was one of those two young offenders:

> On that day, my life changed forever as I managed to overcome the challenges of a punitive society and turn my life around. Meeting my victims taught me a valuable lesson in humanity and I never damaged anyone's property after that.

This landmark case marked the beginning of Kitchener's victim–offender reconciliation program (VORP), which became a foundational program for community justice initiatives in Kitchener-Waterloo, Ontario. As interest grew within Mennonite communities, the program's influence spread across Canada to Langley, BC.

David Gustafson received BC's first VORP referral in 1982, with funding support from the Langley Mennonite Fellowship. Fraser Valley Community Justice Initiatives (FVCJI) was formed in 1985 after being awarded an alternative measures contract with BC's Ministry of the Attorney General to operate VORP and other related programming for both juveniles and adults (Gustafson 2004). VORP then expanded into the adjacent cities of Surrey, White Rock, and Delta. In 2002, provincial funding was cut for adult cases, limiting the program to juveniles. Despite these cutbacks and as reported in FVCJI's annual reports, the evidence of VORP's effectiveness with respect to youth accountability to the community is remarkable. FVCJI's funding for juvenile programs from the Ministry of Children and Family Development ended 31 July 2004, and with this came the end of VORP in BC. Despite this loss of funding and recognition, FVCJI remained committed to serving young people in its community. Building local partnerships, FVCJI developed a new annual fund-raising structure and developed Restorative Youth Services to replace VORP.

VORP research and development has been more fully realized in the United States than in Canada. In 1978, following the Kitchener experiment, VORP was initiated in Elkhart, Indiana, under the direction of Howard Zehr (1990)—generally acknowledged as the "grandfather" of restorative justice in North America—and spread across the country (Claasen and Zehr 1989). For example, Central Valley, California, began using VORP in 1982, and since 2002 the Center for Peacemaking and Conflict Studies at Fresno Pacific University has also administered the program. The centre's data shows that, between 1983 and 2012, 11,052 cases have been managed (an average of 409/year) by the Central Valley Program, with the largest number of VORP cases (over 1000) occurring in 2006. In an evaluation of the VORP programs across six counties in California, Evje and Cushman (2000, p. 1) found "that generally, as compared with juveniles not participating in the program, juveniles in VORPs paid more restitution and were less likely to reoffend, and that VORP participants (both victims and offenders) were satisfied with the program." This early work in California set the stage for the National Council on Crime and Delinquency (NCCD) to conduct a feasibility study on restorative community conferencing (RCC) to better understand its potential to be used in a Pay for Success (PFS) project. The study concluded that RCC has a promising preventive focus and favourable outcomes for youth. For example, based on available data gathered since 2012, youth who completed the program had a lower re-arrest rate—26.5 per cent compared to 45.0 per cent of the matched sample. Significant cost savings for RCC ($4500 USD per case), when compared to youth probation ($23,000 USD per year), were also noted (NCCD 2015).

In 1998, a survey administered by the Center for Restorative Justice and Peacemaking at the University of Minnesota estimated that about 300 programs existed in the United States and about 700 in Europe, with Germany having the most programs at 348 (Umbreit and Greenwood 1998). No national survey has been conducted in Canada. Other than the meta-analysis carried out by the Department of Justice (Latimer, Dowden, and Muise 2001), there has been little effort to collect systematic data, from mapping existing programs to process- and outcome-based evaluations, across this country. VORP is widely considered to be the foundational program within the rise of the RJ movement, particularly in North America (see Zehr 1990). Its influence has also spread beyond North America, particularly to European countries such as Germany, Finland, and the United Kingdom. Given this influence, the rise and fall of VORP in BC, a community-based program with solid evaluation data, raises deeper questions of policy and praxis.

Sentencing/Peacemaking Circles

The harsh realities of the justice system for Canada's Aboriginal people began to be more fully recognized in the late 1980s and early 1990s, specifically disproportional representation and high recidivism and crime rates (see Dickson-Gilmore and La Prairie 2005). This was particularly true in the northern territories and Prairie provinces. Adjourning the case of R. v. Moses (1992)—in which the defendant pled guilty to carrying a baseball bat with the intention of assaulting a police officer—former Yukon territorial court judge Barry Stuart convened the first sentencing circle, drawing on traditional Aboriginal practice in the Yukon Territory (see Stuart 1996).

Since then, sentencing circles have been used in many Aboriginal communities in an attempt to incorporate what are identified as Aboriginal traditions and values. The sentencing circle itself, however, is not a traditional practice of Aboriginal peoples in Canada that is now being reinstituted. Rather, it is a creation of the existing system, introduced within Aboriginal communities primarily by the judiciary serving these communities (Crnkovich 1995, p. 2).

Traditional practice is based on three guiding premises: (1) a criminal offence represents a breach of the relationship between the offender and the victim/community; (2) the well-being of the community is dependent on healing these breaches; and (3) the community is the best resource to address these breaches. A sentencing circle, as it was originally conceived, is a community-directed process that partners with the criminal justice system in an effort to build consensus on a sentencing plan (Boyce-Watson 2008; Pranis 2005). Sentencing circles include a wide range of community members in the process: victims, victim supporters, offenders, offender supporters, judge, prosecutor, defence counsel, police, and court workers. Initially, judges were the primary facilitators of circle hearings, and this evolved to community members co-facilitating the circles (Crnkovich 1995).

The Supreme Court of Canada supported the use of sentencing circles in 1999 in the case of R. v. Gladue

as an approach to remedying crime in which it is understood that all things are interrelated and that crime disrupts the harmony which existed prior to its occurrence, or at least which it is felt should exist . . . [and in which the] appropriateness of a particular sanction is largely determined by the needs of the victim, and the community, as well as the offender.

The Gladue case encouraged the use of alternatives to incarceration and, in endeavouring to remedy the adverse background cultural impact factors and overrepresentation of Aboriginals in Canadian prisons, recognized that restorative approaches resonated with traditional Aboriginal ways of dealing with conflict. Consequently, the Gladue decision was legislated in a Criminal Code amendment (s. 718.2(e)), the sentencing principle of which states that "all available sanctions other than imprisonment that are reasonable in the circumstances should be considered for all offenders, with particular attention to the circumstances of aboriginal offenders" (Elliott and Gordon 2005, p. 135).

peacemaking circles
Peacemaking circles draw directly from the tradition of the talking circle, common among Indigenous people of North America. The physical format of the circle symbolizes shared leadership, equality, connection, and inclusion. Using very intentional structural elements—ceremony, a talking piece, a facilitator or keeper, guidelines, and consensus decision-making—circles aim to create a safe space for authentic dialogue (Pranis, Stuart, and Wedge 2003).

The use of sentencing circles facilitated or co-facilitated by judges never took hold in BC. However, the use of **peacemaking circles**, facilitated by elders and community members, rests on the three same guiding principles and has been widely adopted in BC as an important aspect of the Aboriginal Justice Strategy (AJS). This program is cost-shared federally, supporting approximately 31 programs. The program supports the use of traditional justice in Aboriginal communities, which may or may not include the use of peacekeeping circles. For example, the Vancouver Aboriginal Transformative Justice Services Society provides prevention, diversion, and alternative measures to Aboriginal people in the city of Vancouver. This program's main objectives are to offer a community-based process that focuses on repairing relationships among those affected by crime—that is, the victim, the offender, their families, and the community—and to empower individuals to formulate appropriate responses and strategies to deal with the crime and participate directly in processes that affect the community's overall well-being. To accomplish these objectives, the society utilizes a community council forum, including volunteers, an elder, the victim, offender, and their support people, to discuss the offence, its effects, and the causes of the behaviour that led to the offence. At the forum's conclusion, a healing plan is developed with the goal of making amends and reintegrating the offender into the community. This requires a longer commitment than other restorative justice programs:

> For some clients who have multiple or more chronic problems, the healing journey may be quite long, and VATJS sees their role as one of merely beginning a healing path and being available on an ongoing basis whenever they are needed. It's that ongoing relationship and time commitment—making clients feel they are part of, responsible to, and supported by, a community—that VATJS sees as an important element that distinguishes what they do. (Palys, Isaak, and Nuszdorfer 2015, p. 15)

As Palys and his colleagues concluded, the time is ripe to take Aboriginal justice seriously through fostering coexistence of mutually respectful systems:

> There will be systems of Aboriginal justice in place in the future that maintain a respectful and communicative relationship with the Canadian system. As

exemplars of their respective systems of justice, the DCC [Downtown Community Court] and VATJS have the opportunity to show BC, Canada and the rest of the world how to manage that relationship in a way that is beneficial to their respective peoples and, in so doing, contributes to the greater social good. (Palys, Isaak, and Nuszdorfer 2015, p. 28)

Goldbach (2011) cautions that distinct world views between Euro-Canadian and Aboriginal justice systems often clash and that without further evaluation sentencing circles, and other alternative dispute resolution process, can become a mechanism of recolonization.

Again, as of 2015, there are no systematic data regarding sentencing or peacekeeping circles that details the extent of use or outcomes achieved in BC. Rather, the most rigorous evaluations of sentencing circles to date have been conducted in New South Wales (NSW), Australia, where a pilot program in Nowra began in February 2002. In the first 12 months of the program's operation, 13 offender participants and 8 cases were examined. Surveys were completed by defence solicitors, police, prosecutors, the magistrate, defendants, and victims. The evaluation supported the effectiveness of sentencing circles, noting that this alternative justice process was effective in reducing barriers between the courts and Aboriginal people, raising the level of support for Aboriginal people, incorporating victim support, empowering the Aboriginal community, offering relevant sentencing options with community support, and reducing recidivism. The only deficit noted was the significant time commitment required to process an offender through a sentencing circle. Based on the recommendation contained in the evaluation's final report—that sentencing circles be expanded to other regions of the state where Aboriginal people reside—other programs began operating throughout NSW.

A rigorous evaluation of sentencing circles was also commissioned in 2006 (see NSW Department of Justice and Attorney General 2008), examining three aspects of recidivism (within a 15-month period), including (1) reduction in frequency, (2) time to reoffend, and (3) reduction in seriousness of offending. This study suggested that, compared to the court processes, circle sentencing has no effect on any of these recidivism outcomes. As such, this more rigorous study did not replicate the findings of the pilot study, which did report a reduction in recidivism. However, the findings should not be generalized to conclude that circle sentencing has no value simply because they showed a lack of short-term impact on reoffending, since this study did not examine the impact of any of the other objectives of sentencing circles. For example, if the process strengthens informal social controls in the communities it serves, it may have a crime prevention value that cannot be quantified in studies of reoffending. It also may be the case that other objectives, such as increasing the confidence of Aboriginal communities in the sentencing process, must be realized before the reoffending objective is realized. Beyond the justice system, other systemic influences (e.g., family, peer groups, alcohol and drug programs) may also need to be addressed through integrated community support mechanisms. In fact, the review of sentencing circles commissioned by the NSW Department of Justice and Attorney General concluded that

[o]ne of the most important unintended benefits of Circle Sentencing is the positive impact that participation has had for many of the Elders involved. Many of
the Elders included in the research had a strong sense of achievement as a result
of their participation, with discussions about the impact on their levels of pride,
confidence and community status. (NSW Department of Justice and Attorney
General 2008, p. 7)

Another unintended benefit includes perceptions that community members' responsibility for actions of other members increases through their involvement in circle sentencing. It was also suggested in one location that circle sentencing has reduced the impact
of factional issues. Finally, several stakeholders highlighted its benefits as a community-
based approach to addressing domestic violence in Aboriginal communities, although
more research and development is required on this issue. To this end, the department
recommended increasing numbers of referrals, ensuring greater consistency in type of
referrals, improving follow-up post-sentencing, ensuring greater consistency of program
operations, and ensuring better support of elders.

Family Group Conferencing

Family group conferencing (FGC) is likely the most internationally recognized model of
restorative justice. Developed in New Zealand and legislated through the Children, Young
Persons and Their Families Act in 1989 as a youth justice mechanism, this model includes
police warnings, police youth diversion, and FGC (MacRae and Zehr 2004). Rather than
being diverted from court to restorative justice (as is the case in BC), young offenders in
New Zealand are directed from RJ to court when FGC, alone, is not deemed appropriate.
In New Zealand, youth court is typically reserved for very serious offences. Like VORP,
FGC involves a facilitator; however, the range of participants is much broader and brings
together the family and friends of the offender and victim. The mandate of FGC is to
(a) build understanding of the consequence of the crime, allowing young offenders to hear
the full impact of the crime; and (b) develop a reparative plan. An important step in New
Zealand's FGC is private family time between these two stages. This process is widely held
to be derived from traditional Maori practice. For example, the *Handbook of Restorative
Justice Programs* (United Nations 2006, p. 20) describes FGC as:

> based on the centuries old sanctioning and dispute resolution traditions of the
> Maori, the New Zealand aboriginal group. The model is now also widely used in
> modified form as a police-initiated diversion approach in South Australia, South
> Africa, Ireland, Lesotho, as well as cities in [the American states of] Minnesota,
> Pennsylvania, and Montana.

Interestingly, neither Canada nor BC is mentioned here, even though the *Handbook* was
written by two Canadian researchers from BC. Nevertheless, what appears most important is the Maori influence in the change of legislation, as Shannon Pakura (2005, p. 2)
states:

Regarding the origins of this development, let me emphasize that the law changed primarily because Maori were dissatisfied with the way professionals made decisions about them. Maori were distressed about the impact on them of these decisions and were no longer prepared to tolerate legal or professional systems that gave little weight to Maori customs, values and beliefs.

While there are historical connections with the Maori people in New Zealand, the connection between the indigenous peoples of New Zealand and family group conferencing has been deeply criticized (Cunneen 1997; Snyder 2001; Hakiaha 2004). In particular, the inclusion of family group decision-making within a Western system of common law falls out of step with the larger cultural context of traditional Maori life and, as such, has not served to create more just responses for the indigenous people of New Zealand. Indeed, it has been argued that extracting certain elements of Maori traditional justice out of a broader system of Maori justice leads to "selective and ahistorical claims . . . about indigenous social control conforming with the principles of restorative justice, while conveniently ignoring others" (Cunneen 2007, p. 43). Despite these criticisms, adaptations of New Zealand's FGC are widely used internationally. For example, in 2009 the Canadian Child Welfare Research Portal organization produced a handbook for FGC for child welfare cases (see http://cwrp.ca/node/1004). Similarly, the Alberta McMan Youth Family and Community Services Association also includes FGC in its program services (see https://www.mcman.ca/HOME.aspx).

FGC jumped the Tasman Sea from New Zealand to Australia in the early 1990s. In some Australian states, private family group time remained part of the FGC process, while in others it was omitted. For example, the well-known scripted Wagga Wagga model of FGC does not include private family time; instead, all participants (victims, offenders, and their respective communities of care) remain together throughout the process, as the emphasis is on the *encounter* between the parties affected by the harm (see McDonald, Thorsborne, Moore, Hyndman, and O'Connell 1995). This adapted model was brought to BC in the late 1990s and was adopted by the Royal Canadian Mounted Police (RCMP) as a diversion from the court process (see Chatterjee and Elliott 2003). While sometimes known as FGC, this scripted model has also been called a **community justice forum** and a community conference. For example, in 1998, Corporal James Cooley of the RCMP "E" Division was trained and began facilitating community justice forums and mentoring other individuals interested in restorative justice. In 2003, he became RCMP "E" Division's restorative justice program director. Despite a diverse range of communities and schools being served, no systematic data are readily available.

The BC Ministry of Child and Family Development (MCFD) (2010), which has the provincial government mandate for youth justice, started to use FGC shortly after the implementation of the YCJA. The MCFD has six conference specialists who work on both youth justice and child protection cases. Probation officers also facilitate FGC. Referrals for restorative conferencing are based on voluntary participation and on a judge's order and can be requested by a probation officer, Crown counsel, or defence counsel. There are no readily available data on the extent of use or on the outcomes achieved by this program at the provincial level.

community justice forum
A safe, controlled environment in which the offender, the victim, and their families or supporters are brought together under the guidance of a trained facilitator. Together, using a scripted-dialogue process, they discuss the offence and how they have all been affected, and jointly develop a plan to correct what has occurred.

The most rigorous testing of FGC (the scripted version, with no private family time) was conducted in Australia and England through the ongoing reintegrative shaming experiments (RISE), using randomized control trials (Strang, Sherman, Mayo-Wilson, Woods, and Ariel 2013). On repeat offending, Sherman and Strang (2007, p. 8) conclude that

> [i]n general, RJ seems to reduce crime more effectively with more, rather than less, serious crimes . . . works better with crimes involving personal victims . . . works with violent crimes more consistently than with property crimes. . . . These findings run counter to conventional wisdom, and could become the basis for substantial inroads in demarcating when it is "in the public interest" to seek RJ rather than CJ [criminal justice].
>
> Victims also benefit through increased satisfaction in the outcome and feelings of safety, and decreased likelihood of revenge. They are more likely to receive an apology and reduce their post-traumatic stress symptoms.

This level of research and development has yet to be carried out in Canada.

British Columbia's Justice Reforms

An understanding of how different models of restorative justice have worked in BC must be framed within the context of strategic justice reforms that have been initiated. A news release on 13 November 1996 from the Attorney General's Office expressed the initial intention of the ministry to adopt an RJ approach to criminal justice. This was followed by the release of a number of documents, including *Strategic Reforms of British Columbia's Justice System* (April 1997), *Restorative Justice Framework* (January 1998), and *Community Accountability Programs Information Package* (1998, 2004).

The overall policy shift reflected in these reforms and framework was stated by the attorney general at that time, Ujjal Dosanjh, as a belief "in a restorative justice system that gives communities a primary role in developing policies and programs." At that time, the RJ portfolio was located within the Community Programs Division of the Attorney General's Office. In 2001/2, the Ministry of the Attorney General was split into the Ministry of Public Safety and Solicitor General (Community Safety and Crime Prevention) and the Ministry of the Attorney General. The RJ portfolio moved to the office of the Ministry of Public Safety and Solicitor General, and the 2004 version of Community Accountability Programs Information Package was produced. This information package specified the scope of community accountability programs (CAP): they must be volunteer based; adhere to the ministry's Framework for Restorative Justice; demonstrate community and criminal justice support, including victims' organizations; and accept referrals for category 3 and 4 offences only (i.e., for less serious offending such as mischief and property crime).

The Directory of Restorative Justice Programs (2010) listed 49 community-based RJ groups, many of which are in Metro Vancouver and Vancouver Island, as well as in the Central Interior, east to the Rockies, and as far north as Fort Nelson. Most of these programs take police diversion cases for first-time offenders; a few take referrals from Crown counsel; and others take referrals from schools and the community at large. These community-based groups could use any one of the models of RJ described above, as well as other models (e.g., other forms of circles and community panels/boards/ conferencing).

While little is written on these community-based programs in BC, Dhami and Joy (2007) offer a rare overview of the challenges in establishing volunteer-run, community-based restorative justice programs. They use a community-based program in Victoria as a case study, and their paper reaches this conclusion:

> As RJ programs are associated with the criminal justice system and its programs and processes, there is danger that rather than altering the state's way of do-ing business, these programs will themselves be co-opted and diluted by the pull of retributive and punitive practices. One of the greatest challenges will be to ensure that volunteer-run, community-based RJ programs, with their per-sonal and humanizing appeal for participants at all levels, do not become so routine and formal that they lose their flexibility, their vitality, and eventually their effectiveness.

It is difficult to know whether or not this concern has efficacy, as there is little time for reflective practice and development within small community-based programs. Indeed, only a handful of CAP programs have been evaluated, including Abbotsford (Squires 2009), Communities Embracing Restorative Action in Coquitlam (Roberts and Couch 2009), and North Shore Restorative Justice (Roberts 2010).

Over this past decade of reforms and development in BC, there has been a notable amount of growth. But what marks the substance of that growth? For example, one of the most promising community-based programs—VORP—has been lost. This pro-gram enjoyed a much more substantial and sustainable community-based juvenile justice role in the province than the current community accountability programs, particularly in relation to funding and referrals. Despite the challenges, a few of these community programs have been creative in carrying out evaluations through part-nering with their local universities. In contrast, provincial government programs are much better funded but have yet to be evaluated. Thus, in terms of fulfilling at least one recommendation (19) of the House of Commons Standing Committee on Justice, BC has failed in that VORP is no longer supported in the province and there is a very poor evidence base across existing programs that have replaced VORP. In other words, BC lacks the research and development that was recommended over 25 years ago. Hence, both in practice and in evaluation, RJ remains a marginal practice on the fringes of the justice system in BC. The larger question that needs to be addressed is whether the marginal experience of RJ programs in BC is being replicated in other jurisdictions across Canada and elsewhere.

Chris Cunneen and Carolyn Hoyle (2010) point out that even in Australia, where they do have some level of evaluation, RJ lacks praxis. According to these authors, despite "clearly articulated legislative and administrative procedures for the use of conferences" as well as the development of RJ practices for youth, RJ remains a "peripheral add-on to the main workings of the criminal justice system," with minimal police or court referrals (p. 184). In fact, they point out that police prefer traditional forms of intervention, referring only 2 to 4 per cent of youths to conferences, and that for every one young person appearing in a restorative justice conference, about 15 appear in court" (p. 185).

Cunneen and Hoyle (2010) conclude that the RJ movement does not actively engage in research and development relating to current RJ practices within the context of the broader justice system, and that to move beyond the margins of the justice system, there needs to be a constantly reflexive, dialectical relationship between RJ theory and practice. They argue that RJ "lacks an analysis of its own significant shortcomings; it lacks an analysis of political power and social power; it lacks a transformative politics" (p. 186). In particular, Cunneen and Hoyle argue that RJ, reduced to a marginal normative theory, has failed indigenous youth in Australia.

Based on the evidence to date, these claims also ring true for BC and for Canada in general. There has been no consistent support to engage in praxis, particularly praxis that engages community- and state-based policy, programs, and practice. There is no good reason, other than political will, that RJ practice should remain relegated to a marginal normative theory when its theoretical roots span both normative and explanatory theory (see Braithwaite 2002a, 2002b; Gavrielides and Artinopoulou 2013, in general for an overview) and when there are community groups willing to engage in research and development—that is, engage in praxis.

Roca: The Praxis of Engagement

While the development of peacekeeping circles in BC has lacked praxis, this is certainly not the case in Chelsea, Maine, where the use of peacekeeping circles as an organizational strategy has made a significant impact on a community-based organization called Roca. This outcome-driven organization has a clearly defined mission: to help disengaged and disenfranchised young people, ages 14 to 24, move out of violence and poverty. Their vision is clear:

> Young people will leave the streets and gangs to take responsibility for their actions and have jobs. Young immigrant mothers will raise their children in safety and will be recognized for their contributions to society. Our communities will have the ability to keep young people out of harm's way and in turn, thrive through their participation and leadership. (Roca 2010)

Roca describes its peacemaking circle strategy as a method that

> teaches young people and families an alternative communication method that allows them to deal with extremely painful and difficult issues, how to manage their own healing process, and how to make agreements that promote safety so they can live in a healthy way. Circles are effective for identifying real issues and seeking appropriate solutions when there are conflict situations, when there is a need for healing or understanding, or a desire to reach consensus.

Mentored by the Tagish Tlingit people in the Yukon, along with Barry Stuart and Kay Pranis, Roca finds that "circles bring people together in a way that creates trust, respect, intimacy, good will, belonging, generosity, mutuality and reciprocity. The process is never about changing others but, rather, is an invitation to change oneself and one's relationship with the community." Roca uses circle processes in a variety of ways with and without young people, internally and externally, often partnering with other agencies, groups, and community members.

Building on its peacemaking circle strategy is Roca's **engaged institutions (EI) strategy**. This strategy recognizes that a range of institutions are important and influential to the economic, social, and emotional well-being of a young person, including schools, local government, agencies, and organizations. As such, Roca creates a strong community base of partnerships with these institutions and organizations. Wheeler (2006) articulates the purpose and outcomes of the engaged institutions strategy as being to "ensure that the systems and institutions contribute to young people's self-sufficiency and help them to be out of harm's way" (p. 44). As a community-based organization, Roca seeks to (1) increase institutions' ability to understand and be more responsive to youths' needs; (2) be accountable for services they provide; and (3) understand the impact they have on young people's lives. The processes of engaging institutions mirror those used to engage young people.

The evidence to date is promising. In the 2014 financial year (FY), Roca actively served 494 high-risk young males through its intervention model. While most programs struggle with serving and retaining this population, 80 per cent of Roca's target population were retained, indicating that Roca does not lose these young people. Of the young men retained for 24 months or longer by the end of the FY, 92 per cent had no new arrests, 98 per cent had no new technical violations, and 89 per cent retained employment for at least 90 days (Roca 2014).

In January 2014, Roca and the Commonwealth of Massachusetts launched the ground-breaking Juvenile Justice Pay for Success Project, and Roca was chosen as the primary service provider for the five-year pilot phase of the program, which includes rigorous evaluation. Through its commitment to youth, Roca is building the foundation of a rich evidence base of innovation and change at the individual, community, and institutional level.

When Roca was founded in 1988, many thought that, like other non-profits that serve vulnerable communities, the program was destined to fail. Yet, more than two decades later, over 15,000 teens and young adults have been served by Roca's high-risk youth intervention model. Roca has grown into a solid community-based organization, while others have failed. Its mission is clear: to disrupt the cycle of incarceration and poverty by helping young people transform their lives (Roca 2014):

> Roca's job is to help young men and women get off the streets, stay out of jail, get good jobs, and create a better future for themselves. We believe that when we ask high-risk young people to make difficult changes in their own lives—to put down guns, to stop selling drugs, to show up at work on time, and become responsible adults—we too must have the courage to do things differently. We have learned that the only way forward is to focus on what works, to let

engaged institutions (EI) strategy (Innovation Centre for Community and Youth Development 2006) The EI strategy recognizes that positive collaboration between institutions, through the use of peacemaking circles, can originate from core organizational values regardless of financial or practical incentives. For example, Roca realized that its core values of belonging, generosity, competence, and independence needed to be lived not only among staff members and participants of the organization, but in its relationships with other public and private agencies in its locality.

go of what doesn't, and to hold ourselves accountable to the highest standards possible.

This strategic model is based on a philosophy of advancing the social engagement of young people at risk. This is a significant shift in praxis, moving from a paradigm of social control to one of social engagement (Morrison 2010). The city of Chelsea's city manager adds that "the real story is larger than that. Roca's work, their success with individuals, their bringing together community partners to work together for common goals all make Chelsea a much stronger community" (Lesley University 2011). As Molly Baldwin, the founder of Roca concludes:

> We know of no other community-based, non-mandated authority driving to outcomes and tracking efforts at this level. . . . In turn, we hope this will aid in others learning from what we have learned in the field. . . . Our penal system—the primary provider of "services" to the young people we work most with—isn't effective and it's dangerous and expensive. We've gone a long way to showing there are better ways—and we want to bring it further. (ibid.)

Roca is a prime example of a thriving and sustainable community-based "off ramp" from the justice system. At the level of the state, the mantra of justice is "order and control"; at the level of community-based NGOs, the mantra can be, as exemplified by Roca, engagement and transformation. This resonates with Van Ness's (1990) suggestion that the government can bring order, but only the community can bring peace.

Off Ramps: The Importance of NGOs

Over two decades ago at a conference in Nova Scotia, John Braithwaite (1996, p. 9) put forward a strong argument for the importance of NGOs to engage in deliberative problem-solving, RJ, community, and democracy:

> The lived experience of modern democracy is alienation. The feeling is that elites run things, that we do not have a say in any meaningful sense. . . . Once citizens learn to be actively responsible as opposed to learning to rely totally on protection by a state that enforces passive responsibility, they will become active in social movement politics. NGOs offer the second great avenue for revitalizing meaningful forms of citizen participation in a democracy. . . . NGO influence can feed back into restorative justice conferences as advocacy of making the personal political, by invoking the possibility of agitating for structural change. The most important way this happens is when the justice of the people puts pressure on the justice of the law to change.

The importance of NGOs to driving active responsibility through participatory deliberation has continued to be an emergent factor of Braithwaite's (2006) current work on comparative peace building in the South Pacific. This resonates with Christie's (1977, p. 8) seminal paper on "Conflict as Property" in which he argues the need to address a range of problems inherent in state-based justice:

> This loss is first and foremost a loss in *opportunities for norm-clarification*. It is a loss of pedagogical possibilities. It is a loss of opportunities for a continuous discussion of what represents the law of the land. How wrong was the thief, how right was the victim? Lawyers are, as we say, trained into agreement on what is relevant in a case. But that means a trained incapacity in letting the parties decide what they think is relevant.

Interestingly, what BC gained in terms of the emergence of restorative justice in the early 1990s through community justice initiatives and VORP has been lost again to the state. Community-based NGOs have a greater capacity to evoke the experience of civil society and meaningful deliberation when the core of RJ for juveniles is community based rather than state based. Given the experience of NGOs in BC, Christie's point is even more salient in that the state has now stolen the conflict—and the deliberative process—back from the community. In seeking state-based social control of RJ, the state has failed to deliver justice to communities and an evidence base to support its practice. Roca, as a community-based NGO, has delivered on this front by being true to its mission statement of delivering hope for a sustainable future to young people and for those young people to live out of harm's way. Roca has captured the essence of Braithwaite's (2002b) work in coupling RJ with responsive regulation through two levers of change that work hand in hand: programmatic and organizational. The fundamental premise is that individual change is best leveraged through responsive regulation at a community level.

The practice of RJ, coupled with responsive regulation, enables communities to tap into the rich ecologies of individual lives by creating safe spaces to dialogue through storytelling and listening. Communities cut across institutional domains of social control and order and can respond in ways that broaden the scope for achieving safe and productive communities (see Morrison 2010).

Developing community-based civic capacity is good for the state too, as communities have a capacity for problem-solving that is often thwarted by leaders at a state level, resulting in process paralysis (Briggs 2008). The role of mediating institutions at the level of community has long been argued in public policy. For example, Berger and Neuhaus (1977) argue that community-based institutions serve as alternative mechanisms to provide for social welfare, allowing the public to continue to respond to major social problems without creating the sense of alienation characteristic of the state. Fundamental questions arise, then, in implementing RJ for juveniles, such as: What is the proper role of government in RJ? How can the government empower community-based NGOs and maintain its need for order? These are bold questions that require bold governance and policy direction. England is now engaging with these very questions.

Justice Reform: Responding and Engaging with Communities in Criminal Justice

Twenty years following Canada's development of *Taking Responsibility* in response to concerns raised in the House of Commons, England's Justice Committee (2009/10) was asked to respond to similar concerns and produced *Cutting Crime: Case for Justice Reinvestment*. As with Canada, a number of recommendations were put forward, including:

* community-based services to prevent potential offenders from entering the criminal justice system and to divert them from the offending behaviour, which can lead to custody; and

* the creation of a well-resourced, credible, nationally available but locally responsive system of community sentences that our evidence shows would be more effective than custody in reducing reoffending.

Unlike Canada, however, England quickly turned the recommendations put forward by the Justice Committee into a 2010 Green Paper called *Breaking the Cycle*, for wider public consultation and feedback. Chapter 5 of that Green Paper covers youth justice and puts forward the following policy recommendation:

To increase the use of Restorative Justice we will build on the role currently performed by volunteer youth offender panel members and ensure that referral orders have a strengthened restorative approach. We will support panel members to increase their skills and confidence in using Restorative Justice in referral orders. (Ministry of Justice 2010)

In addition, Chapter 6 of the Green Paper recognizes the importance of community engagement through neighbourhoods. Public feedback has been enormous, with the Restorative Justice Council of the UK (2011) drawing the following conclusion:

Overall, the focus from the national level should be on putting in place measures to engage communities in a meaningful way which has real impact, while expanding the use of restorative justice, which has proven positive effects, and carrying out a broader examination of the potential benefits of justice reinvestment. This follows considerable recent interest in the latter issue, including from the House of Commons Justice Committee, the All Party Parliamentary Local Government Group and the Commission on English Prisons Today. (Ministry of Justice 2010)

This speaks to the questions raised about the role of the relationship between the state and the community. Many other individuals, communities, NGOs, and government committees continue to respond, and only history can reveal how these bold recommendations will unfold. What is clear, at this point, is that England, through engagement with a range of stakeholders, has turned the page that Canada failed to turn 25-odd years ago.

Box 16.1   Youth Justice in Action

Blue Ribbon Panel

In BC, there is still some hope that the page will turn. In February 2012, the BC government launched a Justice Reform Initiative, beginning with the Ministries of the Attorney General and Solicitor General re-merging within the Ministry of Justice and the launch of a Green Paper: *Modernizing British Columbia's Justice System*. Following extensive consultation, *A Criminal Justice System for the 21st Century* (Cowper 2012), recommended a broad suite of changes including the development of a province-wide crime-reduction plan. In June 2013, a parliamentary secretary for crime reduction, MLA Dr Darrel Plecas, was appointed and convened a **Blue Ribbon Panel** of experts to study crime reduction. Following extensive consultation with all levels of government, NGOs, community foundations, and universities, *Getting Serious about Crime Reduction* was released in December 2014, making six major recommendations, including increasing BC's capacity to deliver restorative justice (i.e., see Recommendation #3 and Appendix F in the report). Following Cowper's (2012) recommendation, the Blue Ribbon Panel reiterated that the government should develop a province-wide plan for diversion, including restorative justice, along with education, quality assurance and control, performance measures,

reporting, and evaluation. The panel heard strong support for effective diversion mechanisms and recommended that the government work in collaboration with the Union of British Columbia Municipalities to develop province-wide standards to govern the implementation and management of diversion and RJ programs. The hope is that the government will have the courage and conviction to take these recommendations seriously, that it will engage with the community and measure what works to develop a responsive evidence-based system of accountability and support at all levels: individual, community, and government. Commenting on the Blue Ribbon Panel report, the BC parliamentary secretary for crime reduction said:

> In recent years, no jurisdiction in the western world has done a better job reducing crime than B.C. The panel's recommendations focus on prolific offender management, treatment, *restorative justice*, "designing-out" environments that encourage opportunistic criminals, and other, proven approaches to build on this success and further our efforts to make B.C. Canada's safest province. (News Release 2014, emphasis added)

Summary

This chapter calls for a shift from social control to social engagement as a practical approach to dealing with problems surrounding youth crime. The evidence that has emerged from this analysis suggests that Barry Stuart's reflections on his experience of RJ in Canada still ring true: "Canada's role in the development of RJ is as an exporter. We invent it, and others develop it in a fuller capacity" (Balanced and Restorative Justice Conference 2007). One of the common adages in the field of RJ is to create opportunities to learn from our mistakes. Canada has the opportunity, and the capacity, to learn from this international experiment in RJ to which it has so proudly contributed. Moreover, Canada has the capacity to renew the promise of RJ as a domestic import. The lesson learned is that we must engage in praxis locally, provincially, nationally, and internationally—such as is being done by the European Forum for Restorative Justice. We must import as much as we export and develop the sustainable capacity of "off ramps" to community. For government and community, this will take the same courage and compassion of those early pioneers—from Judge Gordon McConnell, to probation officer Mark Yantzi, to members of communities and NGOs, like Dave Worth, and indeed to the young people themselves, such as Russ Kelly. It is in these people's hands that the promise of RJ resides. As stated by Eleanor Roosevelt many years ago,

Blue Ribbon Panel
In 2013, the British Columbia government established a five-person Blue Ribbon Panel charged with the responsibility of conducting an inquiry into identifying and developing a province-wide crime-reduction plan and opportunities.

Where, after all, do universal human rights begin? In small places, close to home—so close and so small that they cannot be seen on any map of the world. Yet they *are* the world of the individual person: the neighborhood he lives in; the school or college he attends; the factory, farm or office where he works. Such are the places where every man, woman, and child seeks equal justice, equal opportunity, equal dignity without discrimination. Unless these rights have meaning there, they have little meaning anywhere. Without concerted citizen action to uphold them close to home, we shall look in vain for progress in the larger world. (Eleanor Roosevelt, "In Your Hands," 1958)

Key Terms

Blue Ribbon Panel
community justice forum
engaged institutions (EI) strategy
family group conferencing

peacemaking circles
restorative justice (RJ)
sentencing circles
victim–offender reconciliation programs

Review Questions

1. What is a diversionary process, and what are possible avenues (or points of referral) for entry of youth into diversion? What other "off ramps" do youth need?

2. Discuss Christie's (1977) argument that state-based justice results in a "trained incapacity" (p. 8) for decision-making and norm clarification.

3. What is VORP, and how has it contributed to the history of restorative justice in Canada?

4. What is Roca? What is Roca's primary vision, and how are peacekeeping circles important to Roca in achieving its vision?

5. What is *Taking Responsibility*? When was it developed, and what, in particular, did Recommendation 19 contribute to youth justice in Canada?

Critical Thinking Questions

1. Consider the impact of data collection on the development and implementation of restorative justice programs for youth.

2. Discuss the potential to meet the provisions of the YCJA that require addressing youth's developmental challenges and needs as they grow into adulthood, through RJ processes as opposed to traditional criminal justice processes.

3. Do you think it is more effective for justice officials (police, Crown prosecutors, etc.) to make decisions as to diversion on a case-by-case basis, or do you think

a system-wide directive such as that in New Zealand where *all* youth experience restorative justice as a first approach is more effective? Why or why not?

4. What are the future directions and possibilities for RJ in Canada?

5. RJ tends to use the terms *harm, conflict,* and *dispute* instead of *crime* in its discourse. How and why might such terminology affect our conceptualization of crime/conflict?

References

Balanced and Restorative Justice Conference. (2007). *Sustaining restorative justice: The challenge of systemic and community transformation in juvenile justice reform*. Boca Raton, FL, 21–3 March.

Berger, P., and Neuhaus, R. (1977). *To empower people: The role of mediating structures in public policy*. Washington, DC: American Enterprise Institute.

Boyce-Watson, C. (2008). *Peacemaking circles and urban youth: Bringing justice home*. St Paul, MN: Living Justice Press.

Braithwaite, J. (1996). Restorative justice and a better future. *Dalhousie Review, 76*(1): 9–32. Reprinted in E. McLaughlin, R. Fergusson, G. Hughes, and L. Westmorland (Eds), (2003), *Restorative justice: Critical issues*. London: Sage.

Braithwaite, J. (2002a). *Restorative justice and responsive regulation*. New York: Oxford University Press.

Braithwaite, J. (2002b). Setting standards for restorative justice. *British Journal of Criminology, 42*(3): 563–77.

Braithwaite, J. (2006). Accountability and responsibility through restorative justice. In M.D. Dowdle (Ed.), *Public accountability, designs, dilemmas and experiences* (pp. 33–51). Cambridge, UK: Cambridge University Press.

Briggs, X.S. (2008). *Democracy as problem solving: Civic capacity in communities across the globe*. Cambridge, MA: MIT Press.

Charbonneau, S. (2005). The Canadian Youth Criminal Justice Act 2003: A step forward for advocates of restorative justice. In E. Elliott and R.M. Gordon (Eds), *New directions in restorative justice: Issues, practice, evaluation* (pp. 75–86). Cullompton, UK: Willan Publishing.

Chatterjee, J., and Elliott, L. (2003). Restorative policing in Canada: The Royal Canadian Mounted Police, community justice forums, and the Youth Criminal Justice Act. *Police Practice and Research, 4*(4): 1.

Christie, N. (1977). Conflict as property. *British Journal of Criminology, 17*(1): 1–14.

Claasen, R., and Zehr, H. (1989). *VORP: Organizing a foundation in the church* (Mennonite Central Committee US). Elkhart, IN: Office of Criminal Justice.

Community Justice Initiatives Association. (2011). Victim offender reconciliation. Retrieved from http:// www.cjibc.org/victim_reconciliation

Cowper, D.G. (2012). *A criminal justice system for the 21st century: Final report to the Minister of Justice and Attorney General Honourable Shirley Bond*. Victoria, BC.

Crnkovich, M. (1995). Report on sentencing circles in Nunavik. In Pautuutit Women's Association, *Inuit women and justice: Progress report no. 1*.

Cunneen, C. (1997). Community conferencing and the fiction of indigenous control. *Australian and New Zealand Journal of Criminology, 30*(3): 292–311.

Cunneen, C. (2007). Reviving restorative justice traditions. In J. Johnstone and D. Van Ness (Eds), *The handbook of restorative justice*. Cullompton, UK: Willan Publishing.

Cunneen, C., and Hoyle, C. (2010). *Debating restorative justice*. Oxford: Hart Publishing.

Daubney, D. (2010, November). *The role the 1987–88 Justice Committee of the House of Commons played in encouraging the use of restorative justice in Canada*. Paper presented at Restorative Justice Week 2010, Ottawa.

Department of Justice Canada. (2002). *The Youth Criminal Justice Act: Summary and background*. Retrieved from http//www.justice.gc.ca/en/ps/yj/ycja/explan.html

Dhami, M.K., and Joy, P. (2007). Challenges to establishing volunteer-run, community-based restorative justice programs. *Contemporary Justice Review, 10*(1): 9–22.

Dickson-Gilmore, J., and La Prairie, C. (2005). *Will the circle be unbroken: Aboriginal communities, restorative justice and the challenges of conflict and change.* Toronto: University of Toronto Press.

Elliott, E., and Gordon, R. (Eds). (2005). *New directions in restorative justice: Issues, practices and evaluations.* Cullompton, UK: Willan Publishing.

Evje, A., and Cushman, R. (2000). *A summary of the evaluations of six California victim offender rehabilitation programs.* San Francisco: Judicial Council of California, Administrative Office of the Courts.

Gavrielides, T., and Artinopoulou, V. (2013). *Reconstructing restorative justice philosophy.* Farnham, UK: Ashgate.

Goldbach, T.S. (2011). Culture and conflict obscured: Sentencing circles, worldviews, and the case of Christopher Pauchay. *Journal of the Centre for Studies in Religion and Society Graduate Students Association, 10*(1): 53–76.

Green, R., and Healy, K.F. (2003). *Tough on kids: Rethinking approaches to youth justice.* Saskatoon: Purich Publishing.

Gustafson, D. (2004). Is restorative justice taking too few, or too many risks? In H. Zehr and B. Toews (Eds), *Critical issues in restorative justice* (pp. 299–309). Monsey, NY, and Cullompton, UK: Criminal Justice Press and Willan Publishing.

Hakiaha, M. (2004). What is the state's role in Indigenous justice processes? In H. Zehr and B. Toews (Eds), *Critical issues in restorative justice* (pp. 351–9). Monsey, NY, and Cullompton, UK: Criminal Justice Press and Willan Publishing.

House of Commons Justice Committee. (1988). *Taking responsibility: Report of standing committee on justice and Solicitor General on its review of sentencing, conditional release and related aspects of corrections.* Ottawa, Canada: Standing Committee on Justice and Solicitor General.

House of Commons Justice Committee. (2010). *Cutting crime: The case for justice reinvestment* (HC 94-1). London: Stationery Office Limited.

Johnstone, G., and Van Ness, D. (Eds). (2007). *The handbook of restorative justice.* Cullompton, UK: Willan Publishing.

Kelly, R. (2010, November). *The Elmira case . . . and beyond!* Paper presented at Restorative Justice Week 2010, Canada. Retrieved from http:// www.csc-scc.gc.ca/text/rj/rj2010/kit/3-eng.shtml

Latimer, J., Dowden, C., and Muise, D. (2001). *The effectiveness of restorative justice practices: A meta-analysis.* Ottawa: Department of Justice, Research and Statistics Division.

Lesley University. (2011). *Roca, driving positive outcomes for the most at-risk youth.* Retrieved 15 April 2011 from http://news.lesley.edu/2011/01/roca-driving-positive-outcomes-for-the-most-at-risk-youth.shtml

McDonald, J., Thorsborne, M., Moore, D., Hyndman, M., and O'Connell, T. (1995). *Real justice training manual: Coordinating family group conferences.* Pipersville, PA: Piper's Press.

McLauglin, E., Fergusson, R., Hughes, G., and Westmerland, L. (2003). *Restorative justice: Critical issues.* London: Sage.

MacRae, A., and Zehr, H. (2004). *The little book of family group conferences: A hopeful approach when youth cause harm.* Intercourse, PA: Good Books.

Marshall, Tony F. (2003). Restorative justice: An overview. In G. Johnstone (Ed.), *A restorative justice reader: Texts, sources, context.* Portland, OR: Willan Publishing.

Ministry of Children and Family Development. (2004). *Best practice approaches: Child protection and violence against women.* Victoria, BC.

Ministry of Children and Family Development. (2005, August). *Family group conference reference guide.* Victoria, BC: Child and Family Development Division. Retrieved from http:// www.mcf.gov .bc.ca/child_protection/pdf/fgc_guide_internet.pdf

Ministry of Justice. (2010). *Breaking the cycle: Effective punishment, rehabilitation and sentencing of offenders.* (Cm 7972). UK: Stationery Office Limited.

Ministry of Justice. (2012). *Modernizing British Columbia's justice system.* Victoria, BC.

Ministry of Justice. (2014). *Getting serious about reducing crime: Report of the Blue Ribbon Panel.* British Columbia.

Ministry of Public Safety and Solicitor General. (1998). *Community accountability programs* (information package). British Columbia.

Ministry of Public Safety and Solicitor General. (2004). *Community accountability programs* (information package). British Columbia.

Morrison, B.E. (2010). From social control to social engagement: Finding the time and place to talk. In N.A. Frost, J.D. Freilich, and T.R. Clear (Eds), *Contemporary issues in criminal justice policy*. Policy Proposals from the American Society of Criminology Conference. San Francisco, November 2009.

NCCD (National Council on Crime and Delinquency). (2015). *Scaling restorative community conferencing through a pay for success model: A feasibility assessment report*. Oakland, CA.

New South Wales Department of Justice and Attorney General. (2008). *Evaluation of circle sentencing program report*. Leichhardt, NSW: Cultural and Indigenous Research Centre Australia.

News Release: Crime reduction and corrections safety reports released. (2014, 18 December). Retrieved from http://www2.news.gov.bc.ca/news_releases_2013-2017/2014JAG0348-001911.htm

Pakura, S. (2005, March). *The family group conference 14-year journey: Celebrating the successes, learning the lessons, embracing the challenges*. Symposium conducted at the American Humane Association's Family Group Decision Making Conference and Skills-Building Institute, Harrisburg, PA.

Palys, T., Isaak, R., and Nuszdorfer, J. (2015). *Taking Indigenous justice seriously: Fostering a mutually respectful coexistence of Aboriginal and Canadian justice*. Research report prepared for Vancouver's Downtown Community Court and Vancouver Aboriginal Transformative Justice Services.

Peachey, D.E. (1989). The Kitchener experiment. In M. Wright and B. Galaway (Eds), *Mediation and criminal justice: Victims, offenders and community* (pp. 14–26). London: Sage.

Pranis, K. (2005). *The little book of circle processes*. Intercourse, PA: Good Books.

Pranis, K., Stuart, B., and Wedge, M. (2003). *From crime to community*. St Paul, MN: Living Justice Press.

Representative for Children and Youth. (2014a). *Not fully invested: A follow-up report on the Representative's past recommendations to help vulnerable children in B.C.* Victoria.

Representative for Children and Youth. (2014b). *Who cares? B.C. children with complex medical, psychological and developmental needs and their families deserve better*. Victoria.

Restorative Justice Council. (2011). *A new way of doing justice—Restorative Justice Council response to Breaking the Cycle Green Paper*. Retrieved 15 April 2011 from http://www.restorativejustice.org.uk/resource/a_new_way_of_doing_justice__restorative_justice_council_response_to_breaking_the_cycle_green_paper_5hybc/

Roberts, M., and Couch, L. (2009). *CERA program evaluation report*. Coquitlam, BC: CERA.

Roberts, M.L. (2010). *Evaluating evaluation: An investigation into the purpose and practice of evaluation in restorative justice based programs*. Paper presented as thesis defence at Simon Fraser University, School of Criminology.

Roca. (2010). *In the streets and in their lives* (annual report). Chelsea, MA.

Roca. (2014). *Less jail, more future* (annual report). Chelsea, MA.

Sherman, L.W., and Strang, H. (2007). *Restorative justice: The evidence*. London: Smith Institute.

Snyder, T.R. (2001). *The Protestant ethic and the spirit of punishment*. Grand Rapids, MI: William B. Eerdmans.

Squires, C. (2009). *Evaluation of Abbotsford Restorative Justice Program*. Abbotsford, BC.

Strang, H., Sherman, L., Mayo-Wilson, E., Woods, D., and Ariel, B. (2013). *Restorative justice conferencing (RJC) using face-to-face meetings of offenders and victims: Effects on offender recidivism and victim satisfaction. A systematic review*. Oslo, Norway: Campbell Collaboration.

Stuart, B. (1996). Circle sentencing in Yukon Territory, Canada: A partnership of the community and the criminal justice system. *International Journal of Comparative and Applied Criminal Justice, 20*(1–2): 291–309.

Stutzman Amstutz, L. (2009). *The little book of victim offender conferencing: Bringing victims and offenders together in dialogue*. Intercourse, PA: Good Books.

Tustin, L., and Lutes, R.E. (2010). *A guide to the Youth Criminal Justice Act*. Toronto: Butterworths.

Umbreit, M.S., and Greenwood, J. (1998). *National survey of victim offender mediation programs in the United States*. US: Department of Justice.

United Nations. (2006). *Handbook on restorative justice programs*. Criminal Justice Handbook Series. United Nations Office on Drugs and Crime.

Van Ness, D.W. (1990). Restorative justice. In B. Galaway and J. Hudson (Eds), *Criminal justice, restitution, and reconciliation*. New York: Willow Tree Press.

Victim offender mediation: A national perspective. (2000). Washington, DC: Office for Victims of Crime. Retrieved from https://www.ncjrs.gov/ovc_archives/reports/96517-gdlines_victims-sens/guide4.html

Victim Services and Crime Prevention. (2010). *Directory of restorative justice programs, agencies, and contacts*. Abbotsford, BC.

Wheeler, W. (2006, 7 February). *Encircling institutions: Surrounding youth in crisis with mutual engagement and trust*. Takoma Park, MD: Innovation Center for Community and Youth Development.

Winterdyk, J. (Ed.). (2015). *Juvenile justice: International perspectives, model and trends*. Boca Raton, FL: CRC Press.

Zehr, H. (1990). *Changing lenses: A new focus for crime and justice*. Scottsdale, PA: Herald Press.

Statutes Cited

Criminal Code, R.S., c. C-46 (1985). Retrieved from http://laws.justice.gc.ca/en/C-46/index.html

Juvenile Delinquents Act, S.C. c. 40. (1908). Retrieved from http://www.justice.gc.ca/eng/pi/icg-gci/jj2-jm2/sec02.html

R. v. Gladue, 1 S.C.R. 688 (1999). Retrieved from http://www.indigenousbar.ca/cases/gladue.htm

R. v. Moses, 71 C.C.C. 347 (1992). Retrieved from http://www.usask.ca/nativelaw/factums/view.php?id=124

Young Offenders Act, S.C. c. Y-1 (1985). Retrieved from http://laws-lois.justice.gc.ca/P DF/Y-1.pdf

Youth Criminal Justice Act, S.C. c. 1 (2002). Retrieved from http://www.justice.gc.ca/en g/pi/yj-jj/ycja-lsjpa/ycja-lsjpa.html

Glossary

Aboriginal   Includes individuals who identify as First Nations, Métis, or Inuit.

abuse   Characterized by a pattern of recurrent use of a substance where at least one of the following occurs: failure to fulfill roles in major life areas, use in physically dangerous situations, recurrent alcohol- or drug-related problems, and continued use despite this use contributing to social or interpersonal problems.

access period   The designated time frame during which a young person's youth record is active or disclosable and can be shared among relevant individuals attached to the young person as outlined in the YCJA (e.g., the youth, his/her parents, defence counsel, Crown counsel, detention centre, or correctional facility director).

administrative offences   Offences against the administration of justice—that is, violations of court-ordered behavioural requirements, such as complying with a curfew, attending mandated programs, and following through on all manner of bail conditions and probation orders. Under section 4 of the YCJA, there are provisions under the extrajudicial measures that allow for charges to be laid if the young person fails to comply with his or her disposition or fails to appear before the court. The charge can be initiated by either the police or the Crown.

adolescence   A term popularized by child development expert G. Stanley Hall to refer to the stage of life during which a person progresses, both biologically and emotionally, from being a child to being an adult.

adulteration   The dismantling of a distinct system of criminal justice for youth and the re-merging with systems of justice for adults.

alternative justice agencies   Quebec-based agencies responsible for the application of the extrajudicial programs for youth to which youth are referred either by the police or by the provincial director under the YCJA. Measures can include information and awareness programs on shoplifting, drugs, and law reinforcement as well as mediation or damage repair for the victim or, if that is not possible, damage repair through community service.

anomie   The sense of normlessness and frustration that is a product of the way society is organized. Anomie can be a source of deviance. The organization or disorganization of society causes anomie, which leaves people confused about what norms should regulate their behaviour.

bail   Also referred to as *judicial interim release*. Occurs when a young person has been formally charged by the police but has been determined by the courts to be eligible for release from custody while the youth awaits his/her next court appearance. During this release, the young person will be held by a specific set of conditions.

bail surety   A promise made by someone connected to the youth to pay the court money if the young person who was released on bail fails to return to court on the subsequent court date.

best interests of the child   When the interests of a young person are paramount in decision-making regarding his or her experience in the criminal justice system.

bifurcated youth justice system   Literally, a two-pronged justice system, meaning that it provides avenues for diverting first-time and less serious young offenders out of the system while at the same time making possible more punitive forms of punishment for more serious offenders.

binge drinking   Heavy alcohol consumption over a short period of time for the purpose of becoming intoxicated. Generally, the concept is operationalized as the consumption of five or more drinks on one occasion (four or more for females).

biopsychosocial model   An approach that addresses biological, psychological, and social risk factors related to criminality that have been applied to the study of youth female criminality and youth gang involvement.

Blue Ribbon Panel   In 2013, the British Columbia government established a five-person Blue Ribbon Panel charged with the responsibility of conducting an inquiry into identifying and developing a province-wide crime-reduction plan and opportunities.

Boscoville   A unique program introduced in the 1950s in Quebec that was based on a social welfare and psycho-educative model and that introduced elements in its program designed to teach delinquent youth the necessary skills, values, and attitudes that would allow them to develop a sense of social responsibility.

chargeable young person   A young person who has been identified by police as an offender and against whom a charge could be laid.

child welfare   In Canada, this term is used to describe a set of government and private services intended to protect children and encourage family stability. The main purpose of these services is to safeguard children from abuse and neglect. Hence, one of the primary activities of the child welfare agencies is the investigation of allegations of abuse and neglect.

coercion   A personal or an impersonal force that compels or frightens individuals to behave in a certain way.

colonization   Refers to historical and ongoing processes that began with the arrival of Europeans to the country and that include attempts to dominate and assimilate Indigenous peoples.

community-based sentence   A sentence that is served in the community (and, therefore, not in a custodial facility); also known as a *non-custodial sentence*.

community justice forum   A safe, controlled environment in which the offender, the victim, and their families or supporters are brought together under the guidance of a trained facilitator. Together, using a scripted-dialogue process, they discuss the offence and how they have all been affected, and jointly develop a plan to correct what has occurred.

co-morbidity   Two or more independent and coexisting medical conditions.

conferencing   A collaborative and non-conventional approach to decision-making in youth court.

context analysis   Analyzing media content for themes such as sensationalism or distortion.

control balance   The degree of control that individuals perceive they have over their environment relative to the degree of control they perceive their environment has over them.

convergence   When a current issue is framed in terms of its relation to a previous one.

Crime Severity Index (CSI)   Developed and introduced by Statistics Canada, the csi uses a weighting system to measure (youth) offences according to their seriousness. Although introduced in 2009, csi data are available back to 1998.

criminalization   The process whereby individuals are assigned the label of "criminal."

criminogenic   Producing or tending to produce crime or criminals.

critical criminology   Scholarship on crime and justice that seeks to examine and alter inequalities, marginalization, and social exclusion.

critical discourse analysis   An approach in sociolinguistics that links discourse with political structure.

cultivation hypothesis   The hypothesis that the media inundate the public with ideas about crime.

cumulative continuity   A developmental model that outlines how crime in adolescence has negative consequences for future life chances in areas such as education, relationships, and employment, and increases the likelihood that criminal behaviour will continue into adulthood. These in turn undermine further life chances, escalating the probability of continued, persistent criminal behaviour.

custodial sanctions   Under the Youth Criminal Justice Act, the sentencing of a young person to custody.

custodial sentence   A sentence that is served in a custodial facility; under the YCJA, this may be an open or a closed facility.

customer   An individual who is a consumer and pursues the opportunity to purchase activity from a sex-trade worker.

dark figure of crime   Refers to incidents of crime or delinquency that go undetected or unreported by the police.

deconstruction   Involves opening up words to their hidden or closed-off possibilities in an attempt to reveal what is going on behind language.

deferred custody and supervision order (DCSO)   In the YCJA, a community-based alternative to a custodial sentence under which the young person will serve his or her sentence in the community under a set of strict conditions. If these conditions are not followed, the young person may be sent to custody to serve the balance of that sentence.

dependence   When an individual feels that use of a substance is necessary for normal daily functioning or when substance use leads to tolerance. Abruptly stopping use may lead to symptoms of withdrawal.

differential intervention   Based on the identification of the type of delinquency associated with the behaviours of young offenders, the interventions must then be tailored to meet young offenders' treatment needs and the level of risk they pose to society (risk of

recidivism). Takes into account that people do not come in one-size-fits-all packages and therefore refrains from applying the same approach to each person involved in a class, program, or other form of group-based change process.

diminished criminal responsibility   The general view that individuals who are not adults should not be held fully responsible for their criminal behaviour.

discretion   The autonomy/freedom/latitude assigned to police officers and other professionals in the Canadian youth criminal justice system to decide how best to respond to a young person's delinquent or criminal behaviour before laying a formal charge.

disposition   For young offenders, this is the equivalent of sentencing for adults. Under the YCJA, a disposition should in theory be more rehabilitative and/or restorative than retributive.

disrupted social control   Events or life circumstances that weaken or destroy the relationships, attachments, and activities that provide barriers to engaging in criminal activities.

doli incapax   A legal doctrine that literally translated means "incapable of doing harm" and refers to the English common-law presumption that children between 7 and 14 years of age could not be prosecuted for committing criminal offences, unless this presumption was contested by the Crown.

drug recognition expert (DRE) evaluation   A standardized procedure performed by a trained drug recognition expert—involving visual cues, vital signs, questioning, and the provision of bodily fluids by the potentially impaired driver—that is used for determining impairment by drugs or by a drug in combination with alcohol.

dynamic risk factors   Risk factors that are changeable; they are factors that may also contribute to criminal behaviour but can be modified through targeted interventions and/or treatment.

dynamic security   Security that is ensured by the relational dimension. It is achieved by the constant presence of educators and the bonds built between the youths and them. As a result, the quality of the social climate is improved among peers, who in turn contribute to the security of the institution.

engaged institutions (EI) strategy (Innovation Centre for Community and Youth Development 2006)   The engaged institutions (EI) strategy recognizes that positive collaboration between institutions, through the use of peacemaking circles, can originate from core organizational values regardless of any financial or practical incentives. For example, Roca realized that its core values of belonging, generosity, competence, and independence needed to be lived not only among staff members and participants of the organization, but in its relationships with other public and private agencies in its locality.

ethnography   A form of participatory research that involves immersion in the field of study. Because it allows for rich and descriptive findings on areas that are often hidden from view, ethnographic research is fundamental to cultural criminology.

evidence-based principles   Principles based on a foundation of reliable research.

experiential   Refers to an individual who has worked and lived the lifestyle of a sex-trade worker.

extrajudicial measures Under the YCJA, measures other than judicial proceedings (i.e., youth court) that are used to deal with a young person alleged to have committed an offence (including extrajudicial sanctions).

extrajudicial programs Measures that are designed to hold youths responsible for their actions without the creation of a criminal record. They are generally applied to youths who are not engaged in a serious delinquent trajectory.

extrajudicial sanctions Under the YCJA, relatively formal diversion programs that have been authorized by the provincial authorities.

family group conferencing "…a process of collaborative planning in situations where decisions need to be made for children or youth. It is a formal meeting where members of a child or youth's immediate family come together with extended kin and members" (*Source*: BC Ministry of Children and Family Development, *Family Group Conference Reference Guige,* August 2005, www.mcf.gov.bc.ca/child_protection/pdf/fgc_guide_internet.pdf).

fear-based communication Messages used to frighten youth away from experimentation with substances by emphasizing the potential negative effects of use.

fetal alcohol spectrum disorder (FASD) The umbrella term used to describe the entire continuum of disabilities, from most severe to least severe, of prenatal exposure to alcohol. It includes the related conditions of fetal alcohol syndrome (FAS), fetal alcohol effects (FAE), alcohol-related birth effects (ARBE), and alcohol-related neurodevelopmental disorder (ARND).

folk devils Any group that is perceived to pose a threat to the traditional values and institutions of society.

frame analysis Analyzing media content to see how crime and criminals are depicted.

gay bashing The humiliation and violence that sex-trade workers are at risk of from customers and the community.

gay for pay A person who is heterosexual but who, in order to survive, will work in the sex trade as a homosexual.

gender gap Acknowledges the difference in the rates at which males and females do things. In the field of criminology, there exists a persistent and well-documented difference in the arrest rates for males and females, with males consistently committing significantly more crime than females.

gender role theories Those explanations of delinquent and criminal behaviour that focus on the role that gender plays in the lives and behaviours of both females and males.

gender-sensitive responses Responses that recognize that the pathways to criminal involvement and the needs of female offenders are different from those of male offenders. Such approaches include risk assessments, treatments, and supervision.

harm-reduction strategies Any policies or programs that are designed to reduce the level of harm associated with substance use and abuse without requiring the cessation of use.

homeless youth Youths who have either left or have been urged to leave home with the full knowledge or approval of legal guardians. They have no alternative home in which to live.

hospitality An unrestrained welcome to a stranger. It calls for open spaces that welcome the other as he or she arrives.

ideological flexibility Where the portrayal of persons is ambiguous—for example, a young offender is portrayed as both villain and victim.

indeterminate sentences Sentences of incarceration that have no fixed expiration date, which means that a person can be held in custody until he or she is deemed by correctional officials either to be rehabilitated or to no longer pose a threat to society.

informal social control The control over people's behaviour that develops as a result of relationships and attachments to significant others and investments in conventional activities that could be damaged by engagement in illegal activities.

intensive support and supervision program (ISSP) In the YCJA, a community-based sentence that provides more supervision than a probation order and, in provinces where such programs exist, can provide young offenders with access to programs that are appropriate to their specific needs (e.g., mental health needs).

intersectionality Refers to a movement away from thinking categorically and toward thinking about the connections and crossroads between social facets. Intersectional thinking and theorizing recognizes the multiple, changing, and often overlapping dimensions, demographics, roles, and identities of criminals, victims, other individuals, and collectives.

intervention Approaches that address the needs of youth once they are involved in gangs.

justice (Derrida) For Derrida, justice is a messianic promise of a more just future "to come."

juvenile courts Specialized courts first created in the late nineteenth century to apply juvenile justice laws in the care of dependent and delinquent children.

juvenile delinquency The legal term that came into popular use in the nineteenth century to describe violations of the law by persons who had not reached the legal age of adulthood.

Juvenile Delinquents Act (JDA) Canada's first juvenile delinquency legislation enacted in 1908 and in force until 1984.

labelling The stigmatization of a young person as deviant.

life-course turning points Events such as marriage/divorce or employment/unemployment that serve to direct an individual's developmental criminal career path toward either desistance or onset.

life-cycle model This model proposes a series of stages that youth encounter on the street and includes an initial engagement in street life, a stage where youth become more comfortable with street life, and, finally, periods of crisis during which some youth may transition off the street. A cyclical pattern is noted, however, in that many youths who exit the street may become re-involved.

low self-control A trait made up of impulsivity, short-sightedness, risk-taking, physicality, insensitivity, and low frustration tolerance, which leaves individuals less able to refrain from activities that provide short-term pleasure or gain.

marginalization The partial exclusion of certain groups from mainstream society who routinely suffer as the result of gross inequalities.

method of administration   The path by which a drug or other substance is brought into contact with the body. Common methods include smoking, ingestion, injection, and intranasal inhalation.

mitigating factors   Information presented to the courts in relation to the facts of the case and the accused that may result in a lesser charge or sentence if he or she is found guilty. Conversely, aggravating factors are facts presented to the court surrounding the offence or offender's circumstances that may aggravate or increase the severity of the offence.

moral actions   Actions steered by moral rules that outline what behaviours are allowed or disallowed in particular circumstances.

moral panic   Exaggerated fears about social problems, including youth deviance, partly generated by the media.

net narrowing   A phenomenon that occurs when youth who have been diverted from the criminal justice system struggle to access adequate resources.

net widening   A process whereby, in the attempt to divert individuals away from the criminal justice system, certain policies result instead in a greater number of individuals being formally processed.

not criminally responsible on account of mental disorder (NCRMD)   Based on the Criminal Code's definition, a mental disorder is viewed as a "disease of the mind." For an individual to be found NCRMD, there must be a mental abnormality (not caused by voluntary intoxication, temporary mental conditions, or uncontrollable urges) causing significant impairment to preclude the individual's understanding of their behaviour.

official data   The Canadian Centre for Justice Statistics, a branch of Statistics Canada, collects offender and offence data from the police, courts, and corrections for administrative purposes. The centre produces regular reports that are readily available to the public.

parens patriae   The legal doctrine that the state has a duty to assume the role of a substitute parent in the case of delinquent or dependent children who do not have parents who are able to adequately control or care for them.

parent   Includes any person who is under a legal duty to provide for a young person or any person who has the custody or control of a young person.

peacemaking circles   Peacemaking circles draw directly from the tradition of the talking circle, common among Indigenous people of North America. The physical format of the circle symbolizes shared leadership, equality, connection, and inclusion. Using very intentional structural elements—ceremony, a talking piece, a facilitator or keeper, guidelines, and consensus decision-making—circles aim to create a safe space for authentic dialogue.

power (Foucault)   Rather than as a quantity held or possessed by the state, Foucault understood power to be relational, positive, and exercised.

power-control theory   Refers to John Hagan and colleagues' 1989 integrated (conflict and social control theories) and feminist-informed explanation of the role of gender socialization in crime distributions.

pre-charge diversion   The diverting of young offenders from the formal youth criminal justice system before they are charged with an offence by the police under the Criminal Code.

preliminary inquiry   Occurs before the case proceeds to trial and is a hearing in which the judge can determine if there is sufficient evidence to proceed to trial.

pre-sentence report   Report prepared by a probation officer or youth centre councillor in Quebec; these written documents present the youth court with detailed information on the young person.

presumption   A rule of law that permits a court to assume something is true until such time as there is evidence that disproves (rebuts) the presumption.

pre-trial detention   The practice of holding a person in a custodial facility before or during his or her court appearance(s); also known as *remand custody*.

prevention   Approaches that prevent young people from joining gangs.

proactive police work   Enforcement activities that are police initiated rather than in response to a call for service.

protective factors   Circumstances and experiences that buffer young people's involvement in behaviours that would be damaging to themselves and to others.

psycho-educative model   Developed in Quebec, this model followed the Boscoville experience and is now recognized as a profession specializing in the intervention of troubled youths.

psychosis   A symptom of mental illness involving a substantial alteration to an individual's personality and a loss of contact with objective reality.

punishable young offender   A term coined by Bryan Hogeveen (2005) to describe the discursive construction of some young offenders as "troublesome" and therefore requiring punishment in order to make them accountable for their criminal acts.

punitive turn thesis   The argument that in recent decades the criminal justice systems of many Western countries have become more punishment oriented, with longer prison sentences and higher rates of incarceration.

racial profiling   The increased surveillance of certain racial groups or culturally distinct neighbourhoods by the police that cannot be explained by such groups' actual increased involvement in criminal activities.

recidivism   Repetition of criminal and/or delinquent behaviour. Recidivism can be measured through official sources or through self-report surveys.

reformable young offender   A term coined by Bryan Hogeveen (2005) to describe the discursive construction of some young offenders as "troubled" and therefore needing intervention in the hope they can be rehabilitated.

rehabilitation   A fundamental concept of the Youth Criminal Justice Act that holds that a young person can be reformed or changed as a result of appropriate treatment programs. Also, a penological theory that an offender can be returned by appropriate programs to a state of non-offending; also, practices and programs based on that theory.

reintegration   The introduction of the young person back into the community as a productive member of society.

remand custody   The practice of holding a person in a custodial facility before or during his or her court appearance(s); also known as *pre-trial detention*.

resiliency   The ability of children and youth to develop positive self-esteem and self-efficacy despite facing crisis, challenges, or adversity.

restorative justice (RJ)   While conceptualized in many different ways—*encounter*, *reparative*, and *transformative*—RJ is a theory of justice that emphasizes repairing the harm caused or revealed by unjust behaviour. Restoration is best accomplished through inclusive and co-operative processes (Johnstone and Van Ness 2007).

risk   The calculated probability of an event or a circumstance. Risks are calculated and managed through class, gender, age, and race categories.

risk assessment tools   Instruments used to assess the multitude of risk and protective factors that have been and/or are present in young people's lives that can influence the likelihood of recidivism. Youths are rated as low, medium, or high risk, and individualized interventions are developed based on these risk assessment outcomes.

risk factors   Factors that may cause a young person to be more likely to offend. These factors can be individual, environmental, etc.

risk society   This refers to a break with modernity into an emerging societal form characterized by the production of risks and of tools for their management. In contrast to the view that social problems are to be solved, issues in the risk society (i.e., crime) are risks to be managed.

runaways   Youths who run away from their family or child welfare placement, at least overnight, without parental or caretaker permission. They often leave as a result of family conflict or maltreatment.

screening tools   Instruments used to identify at-risk youth and assist in their referrals to appropriate programs and services.

Sebastien's Law   In 2010, the federal government introduced Bill C-4 as a measure to get tough on repeat young offenders. The bill was subsequently amended to become part of the Omnibus Crime Bill, passed in 2012. Section 3(1)(a) of the YCJA was subsequently slightly amended to read "protect the public," which encompasses the spirit of Sebastien's Law. The namesake of the law is 19-year-old Sebastien Lacasse, who was beaten and stabbed to death at a 2004 house party in Quebec by a 17-year-old. The incident prompted the courts to consider adult sentences for youth 14 or older found guilty of serious crimes like murder and aggravated assault.

secure custody   A form of custody under the Youth Criminal Justice Act whereby youth are removed from a community and confined to an institution.

self-report (SR) survey   A social-science questionnaire survey designed to ask respondents to report on their involvement in criminal or delinquent activities.

sentenced custody   Being held in a custodial facility as a result of a court sentence (as opposed to *remand custody*).

sentencing circles   "Sentencing circles . . . invite . . . members of the community to join the judge, prosecutor, defence counsel, police, social service providers, community elders, along with the offender, the victim and their families and supporters, [to] meet in a circle to discuss the offence, factors that may have contributed to it, sentencing options, and ways of reintegrating the offender into the community" (*Source*: Department of Justice Canada 2002).

sexual exploitation   The abuse of children and youth through the exchange of sexual activity for money, drugs, and/or basic needs.

sitters   Individuals who are paid to tend to and protect the plants in a marijuana growing operation. Sitters may also appear to legitimately occupy a residence to avoid drawing suspicion.

situated choice   The choices individuals make to become involved in certain relationships, be they work or personal, that are situated under certain structural and historical conditions and that can influence future behaviour.

social bonds   The degree to which individuals, through socialization, have connections to people and institutions in a society and believe in the rules of the society. These connections serve as restraints against criminal opportunities and behaviour.

social constructionism   An approach that sees social problems as constructed in the media; see *moral panic*.

social desirability effects   Biases in research caused by respondents' desire to provide what they feel is the socially acceptable response or "what the researcher wants to hear."

squeegee kids   A group of street-involved youths who are resourceful in attempting to develop and maintain a livelihood and means of survival by offering to clean windshields at major intersections.

static risk factors   Risk factors that are unchangeable; they include those traits that may contribute to an offender's offending and recidivism and cannot be altered through rehabilitation programming.

status offences   Behaviours that are considered delinquent or criminal only because the person who engages in the behaviour is not yet an adult. Examples include truancy (skipping school), underage drinking, and promiscuous sexual behaviour.

stigma   A behaviour or an attribute that causes an individual to be discredited, rejected socially, or negatively stereotyped.

straight for pay   A person who is homosexual but who, in order to survive, will work in the sexual exploitation trade as a heterosexual.

strains   Experiences or situations that individuals perceive as being negative, creating a negative emotional reaction that provides the possible incentive for using crime as a coping mechanism.

street-involved youth   Youths 25 years of age or younger who do not have a safe home or are underhoused; who have been forced to leave their family of origin; who have run away from their home without the consent of their parents or guardian or who left foster- or group-care placements; or who are not living on the street but who experiment and engage in street-involved activities and identify with street culture and street peer groupings.

substance abuse   Excessive, unhealthy use of a substance such as alcohol, tobacco, or illicit drugs.

suppression   Policing approach to dealing with gangs.

surveillance   The direct or indirect observation of conduct, which is intended to produce a desired outcome (i.e., conformity).

throwaways   Youths who are asked, or encouraged, to leave home by their parents/guardians, with the purpose of ending parental responsibility for the well-being of the youths.

trace   The silent elements that provide words with their essential meaning (Spivak 1976) and that underlie all language.

trajectories   Paths or avenues of development throughout the lifespan. These are long-term patterns of behaviour that often consist of marriage, parenthood, employment, and involvement in criminal activities.

transgender   A person who crosses gender roles in one way or another, including as a transsexual, drag queen, or transvestite.

trauma   Experience that is psychologically painful, distressful, or shocking (such as suffering sexual abuse or witnessing serious violence) and that often results in long-term mental or physical problems (such as depression, anxiety, or insomnia). Also, the community-level and individual-level damage, pain, and suffering of Indigenous peoples—physically, spiritually, emotionally, and psychically—as a result of the historical and current processes of colonization.

triangulation   A research methods technique that involves using more than one source of criminological data to access the validity of what is being observed. For example, this technique can include combining official crime data with self-report data to obtain a clearer picture of crime or delinquency facts.

underhoused   Youths who are underhoused live in housing that is temporary in nature, inadequate for space, does not meet safety or health thresholds, or has high risk for eviction.

unfit to stand trial (UFT)   When an individual is not fully capable of instructing counsel or understanding the nature and consequences of their trial.

unofficial data   Refers to data that are collected and usually published by private or independent researchers or research facilities. The primary data-collection techniques are self-report surveys and victimization surveys. Unofficial data are often used to enrich official data.

values   A collective conception of what is considered proper, desirable, and good—or improper, undesirable, and bad—in a culture.

victimization   The experience of being a victim, which can be linked to future criminalization.

victimization survey   A social-science questionnaire survey designed to measure the experiences of respondents as victims of crime(s).

victim–offender reconciliation programs (VORP)   A process through which a trained mediator, often a volunteer, brings offenders and victims in a criminal event together to achieve a resolution that is satisfactory to both parties (Community Justice Initiatives Association 2011; see also Stutzman Amstutz 2009).

Young Offenders Act (YOA)   The federal legislation that replaced the Juvenile Delinquents Act from 1984 to 2003.

young person   A youth age 12 to 17 years charged under the YCJA with having committed an offence.

youth at risk   Refers to young people who are "at risk" of offending or being victimized because of various social, family, and/or personal factors.

youth-centric programming model   Youth play a significant role in developing and evaluating programs, and agencies continue to be flexible in adapting to the changing needs of street-involved youth.

Youth Criminal Justice Act (YCJA)   The federal legislation enacted in 2002 to replace the Young Offenders Act and which came into effect on 1 April 2003.

youth criminal justice systems   A term often used today as a substitute for juvenile courts. Critical criminologists argue that it signifies a shift toward treating young offenders more like adult offenders.

youth engagement   "The meaningful participation and sustained involvement of a young person in an activity, which has a focus outside of him or herself" (Centres of Excellence for Children's Well-Being, www.tgmag.ca/centresnew/files/Whatis_WEB_e.pdf). Full engagement consists of a behavioural component, an affective component, and a cognitive component.

youth in care   Refers to children and youth involved with Canada's child welfare system.

youth justice   A separate and distinct criminal justice system that explicitly meets the unique needs of young people.

youth justice court   The court in which young people charged with an offence created by Parliament, usually under the Criminal Code or the Controlled Drugs and Substances Act, appear in order to enter a plea and then to have their trial or be sentenced.

Index